Frommer's®

San Francisco

D0595726

Here's what the critics say about Frommer's:

"Amazingly easy to use. Very portable, very complete."
—*Booklist*

◆

"The only mainstream guide to list specific prices. The Walter Cronkite of guidebooks—with all that implies."
—*Travel & Leisure*

◆

"Complete, concise, and filled with useful information."
—*New York Daily News*

◆

"Hotel information is close to encyclopedic."
—*Des Moines Sunday Register*

Other Great Guides for Your Trip:

Frommer's San Francisco from $60 a Day

Frommer's Portable San Francisco

Frommer's Memorable Walks in San Francisco

Frommer's Portable California Wine Country

The Complete Idiot's Travel Guide to San Francisco

The Unofficial Guide to San Francisco

Frommer's California

Frommer's Driving Tours in California

Frommer's® 99

San Francisco

by Erika Lenkert
and
Matthew R. Poole

MACMILLAN • USA

ABOUT THE AUTHORS

A native San Franciscan, **Erika Lenkert** spends half her time in Los Angeles and the other half traveling to San Francisco and throughout the state. She's currently a contributing writer for *Los Angeles* magazine, co-author of dozens of guides to California, the restaurant editor for *California Homes* magazine, and has contributed to *Brides, Cosmopolitan,* and *Time Out.* Erika is pleased she actually gets paid to force her opinions onto others—something she'd done pro bono for years. Her next challenge? To convince San Franciscans that LA's actually kind of cool.

Matthew R. Poole, a native Californian, has authored 17 travel guides to California and Hawaii. A graduate of the University of California, Santa Barbara, Poole has managed to combine three of his stronger passions—writing, photography, and traveling—to his advantage. Before becoming a full-time travel writer, Matthew worked as an English tutor in Prague, ski instructor in the Swiss Alps, scuba instructor in Maui, and bartender in Santa Barbara. Addicted to a life of chronic freedom, he spends most of his time on the road doing research and avoiding commitments. He currently lives in San Francisco and can be reached at mrpoole@sirius.com.

MACMILLAN TRAVEL

A Simon & Schuster Macmillan Company
1633 Broadway
New York, NY 10019

Find us online at **www.frommers.com**

ISBN 0-02-862359-2
ISSN 0899-3254

Editor: Bob O'Sullivan
Production Editor: Carol Sheehan
Photo Editor: Richard Fox
Design by Michele Laseau
Digital Cartography by Ortelius Design
Page Creation by Troy Barnes, Trudy Coler, Toi Davis, Heather Pope, and Angel Perez

SPECIAL SALES

Bulk purchases (10+ copies) of Frommer's and selected Macmillan travel guides are available to corporations, organizations, mail-order catalogs, institutions, and charities at special discounts, and can be customized to suit individual needs. For more information write to Special Sales, Macmillan General Reference, 1633 Broadway, New York, NY 10019.

Manufactured in the United States of America

Contents

6 Dining 98

7 What to See & Do in San Francisco 154

8 City Strolls 192

9 Shopping 203

List of Maps

Acknowledgments

Matthew and Erika would like to thank Emily Goldman, Donalyn Mason, Tom Walton, and Cyndi Holcombe for their contributions.

An Invitation to the Reader

When we first started writing for Frommer's, we'd call our editors after each of our books was published and excitedly ask, "Any reader mail?" We were just dying to learn whether folks were enjoying our books—or actually reading them for that matter. When we were disappointed that we'd received almost no mail, our editors assured us it was a compliment; most people write only to complain, so we must be doing something right. But the fact is, we want to hear what you think. What did you love? What did you hate? What was over- or underrated? Did you find a hotel, restaurant, bar, attraction—whatever—that we should have included? Tell us your opinion, so we can share the information with your fellow travelers in upcoming editions. That way, perhaps we'll stop accosting and questioning poor, innocent tourists when we see them carrying our guides through the streets of our favorite city. C'mon, drop us a note. Write to:

Frommer's San Francisco '99
Macmillan Travel
1633 Broadway
New York, NY 10019

An Additional Note

Please be advised that travel information is subject to change at any time—and this is especially true of prices. We therefore suggest that you write or call ahead for confirmation when making your travel plans. The authors, editors, and publisher cannot be held responsible for the experiences of readers while traveling. Your safety is important to us, however, so we encourage you to stay alert and be aware of your surroundings. Keep a close eye on cameras, purses, and wallets—all favorite targets of thieves and pickpockets.

What the Symbols Mean

✪ Frommer's Favorites

Our favorite places and experiences—outstanding for quality, value, or both.

The following abbreviations are used for credit cards:

AE	American Express	EURO	Eurocard
CB	Carte Blanche	JCB	Japan Credit Bank
DC	Diners Club	MC	MasterCard
DISC	Discover	V	Visa

Find Frommer's Online

Arthur Frommer's Outspoken Encyclopedia of Travel (www.frommers.com) offers more than 6,000 pages of up-to-the-minute travel information—including the latest bargains and candid, personal articles updated daily by Arthur Frommer himself. No other Web site offers such comprehensive and timely coverage of the world of travel.

The San Francisco Experience

You are standing on the corner of Powell and Geary streets at San Francisco's famed Union Square, pausing a moment to catch your breath. Bags in hand bear the rewards of a memorable day of shopping. It's about four in the afternoon on a summer Sunday; a stiff, cool breeze from the west mocks the cloudless skies. Above the din and traffic you hear the clang of a bell, and moments later a cable car—precariously overloaded with wide-eyed tourists—approaches from behind, groaning its way up yet another steep hill. A steady stream of chattering pedestrians passes by, few of whom seem to speak English as a first language. Across the way a bellman hails a taxi for an older couple, both men dressed in black. Though the sun is out, glimmering skyscrapers block any hope of a warm ray. "Should've dressed warmer," you reply to a shiver as you head back to your hotel to get ready for dinner. As you round the corner, an old man selling flowers on the street corner smiles and hands you a rose—a fitting end to a thoroughly enjoyable day.

Welcome to San Francisco.

Consistently rated one of the top tourist destinations in the world, San Francisco is awash with multiple dimensions: Its famous, thrilling streets go up, and they go down; its multifarious citizens—along with their native culture, architecture, and cuisine—hail from San Antonio to Singapore; and its politics range from hyper-liberalism to an ever-encroaching wave of conservatism. Even something as mundane as fog takes on a new dimension as it creeps from the ocean and slowly envelops San Francisco in a resplendent blanket of mist.

The result is a wee bit o' heaven for everyone: In a city so multifaceted, so enamored with itself, it's truly hard not to find what you're looking for. Feel the cool blast of salt air as you stroll across the Golden Gate. Stuff yourself on a Chinatown dim sum. Browse the Haight for incense and crystals. Walk along the beach, pierce your nose, see a play, rent a Harley—the list is endless. Like an eternal world's fair, it's all happening in San Francisco, and everyone's invited.

1 Frommer's Favorite San Francisco Experiences

- **Cafe-Hopping in North Beach.** One of the most pleasurable smells of San Francisco is the aroma of roasted coffee beans wafting down Columbus Avenue. Start the day with a cup of Viennese at Caffè Trieste (a haven for true San Francisco characters), followed by a walk in and around Washington Square, lunch at Mario's Bohemian Cigar Store (à la focaccia sandwiches), book browsing at City Lights, more coffee at Caffè Greco, and dinner at L'Osteria del Forno or Moose's. Finish off the day with a little flamenco dancing at La Bodega or a nightcap with Enrico Caruso on the jukebox at Tosca.

- **A Walk Along the Coastal Trail.** Walk the forested coastal trail from the Cliff House to the Golden Gate Bridge, and you'll see why San Franciscans put up with living on a fault line. Start at the parking lot just above Cliff House and head north. On a clear day you'll have incredible views of the Marin Headlands, but even on foggy days it's worth the trek to scamper over old bunkers and relish the crisp, cool air. Dress warmly.

- **A Drive to Muir Woods, Stinson Beach, and Point Reyes.** If you have wheels, reserve a day for a trip across the Golden Gate. Take the Stinson Beach exit off Highway 101, spend a few hours gawking at the monolithic redwoods at Muir Woods (people, I'm telling you, this place is amazing), continue on to Stinson Beach for lunch at the Parkside Café, then head up the coast to the spectacular Point Reyes National Seashore. Rain or shine, it's a day trip you'll never forget.

- **An Adventure to Alcatraz.** Even if you loathe tourist attractions, you'll like Alcatraz. The rangers have done a fantastic job of preserving The Rock—enough to give you the heebie-jeebies just looking at it—and they give excellent guided tours (highly recommended). Heck, even the boat ride across the bay is worth the price, so don't miss this one.

- **A Stroll Through Chinatown.** Chinatown is a trip. We've been through it at least 100 times, and it's never failed to entertain us. Skip the crummy camera and luggage stores and head straight for the outdoor markets, where a cornucopia of the bizarre, unbelievable, and just plain weird sits in boxes for you to scrutinize (one day we saw an armadillo for sale, and it wasn't meant to be a pet). Better yet, take one of Shirley Fong Torres's Wok Wiz tours of Chinatown for the full effect.

- **A Date in the Haight.** Though the flowers of power have wilted, the Haight is still, more or less, the Haight: a sort of resting home for aging hippies, dazed Dead-heads, skate punks, and an assortment of rather pathetic young panhandlers. Think of it as visiting a "people" zoo as you walk down the rows of used clothing stores and leather shops, trying hard not to stare at that girl (at least we *think* it's a girl) with the pierced eyebrows and shaved head. End the mystery tour with a plate of mussels at Cha Cha Cha, one of San Francisco's top restaurants.

- **An Afternoon at the Marin Headlands.** San Francisco's backyard of sorts, the Marin Headlands are located just across the Golden Gate Bridge to the west and offer not only the best views of the city, but also a wealth of outdoor activities. Bird watching, hiking, mountain biking, horseback riding—the list goes on—are all fair game at this glorious national park. Don't miss the Marine Mammal Center, a ward for injured or abandoned seals (cute little buggers) and sea lions.

- **A Walk Across the Golden Gate Bridge.** Don your windbreaker and walking shoes and prepare for a wind-blasted, exhilarating walk across San Francisco's most famous landmark. It's simply one of those things you have to do at least once in your life.

- **A Cruise Through the Castro.** The most populated and festive street in the city is not just for gays and lesbians (though the best cruising in town is right here). While there are some great shops and cafes—particularly Café Flore for lunch—

Impressions

Of all cities in the United States I have seen, San Francisco is the most beautiful.

—Nikita S. Khrushchev

it's the people-watching that makes the trip a must. And if you have the time, catch a flick at the beautiful 1930s Spanish colonial movie palace, the Castro Theatre.

- **A Day in Golden Gate Park.** A day at Golden Gate Park is a day well spent. Its arboreal paths stretch from the Haight all the way to Ocean Beach, offering dozens of fun things to do along the way. Top sites are the Conservatory of Flowers, Japanese Tea Garden, Asian Art Museum, and the Steinhart Aquarium. The best time to go is Sunday, when portions of the park are closed to traffic (rent skates or a bike for the full effect). Toward the end of the day, head west to the beach and watch the sunset.
- **A Soul-Stirring Sunday Morning Service at Glide.** Preacher Cecil Williams turns church-going into a spiritual party that leaves you feeling elated, hopeful, and unified with the world. All walks of life attend the service, which focuses not on any particular religion, but on what we have in common as people. It's great fun, with plenty of singing and hand clapping.
- **An Early Morning Cable Car Ride.** Skip the boring California line and take the Powell-Hyde cable car down to Fisherman's Wharf—the ride is worth the wait. When you reach the top of Nob Hill, grab the rail in one hand and hold the camera with the other, because you're about to see a view of the bay that'll make you a believer. Oh, and don't call it a trolley.
- **A Visit to MOMA.** Ever since the new MOMA opened in 1995, its been the best place to go for a quick dose of culture. Start by touring the museum, then head straight for the gift shop (oftentimes more entertaining than the rotating exhibits). Have a light lunch at Caffè Museo, where the food is a vast improvement from most museums' mush, then finish the trip with a stroll through the Yerba Buena Gardens across from the museum.

2 The City Today

Shaken but not stirred by the Loma Prieta earthquake in 1989, San Francisco has witnessed a spectacular rebound in recent years. The seaside Embarcadero, once plagued by a horrendously ugly freeway overpass, has been revitalized by a multi-million-dollar face-lift, complete with palm trees, a new trolley line, and wide cobblestone walkways. SoMa, the once shady neighborhood south of Market Street, has exploded with new development, including the world-class Museum of Modern Art, the beautiful Yerba Buena Gardens, and a slew of hip new clubs and cafes. Even the city's dress code has improved: Hit the clubs wearing jeans, sneakers, and a T-shirt and you may just be asked to leave (even dress-down Fridays have changed to dress-up Fridays). In short, it's hot to be hip these days in San Francisco: Black is back, cigars are in, the blues rule, pool is cool again, and the 1950s are back with a vengeance.

And though it seems hard to believe that one man could turn a city around, since the day Willie Brown was voted into office as mayor of San Francisco, things have been looking up for the city's state of affairs. After giving just about every member of former-mayor Frank Jordan's administration the boot, the legendary ex-speaker of the house for California's State Assembly has been administering steady doses of shock therapy to this proud but oft-troubled city. Public transportation, always a thorny issue with the people, has improved (one bus driver, with the help of family, went so far as to clean his entire bus overnight to honor the new mayor); homelessness is no longer a crime and shelters and work programs are on the rise; the city's beleaguered 911 system is back on track; and San Franciscans in general are starting to take a renewed pride in their city since "da Mayor" started running the show.

All that glitters is not the Golden Gate, however. At the end of World War II, San Francisco was the largest and wealthiest city on the West Coast. Since then, it has been demoted to the fourth-largest city in California, home to only 750,000 people, less than 5% of the state's total. The industrial heart of the city has been knocked out and shipped off to less costly locations such as Oakland and Los Angeles, and increasingly San Francisco has had to fall back on tourism as a major source of revenue. If the process continues unabated, the city may someday become another Venice or (egad!) Las Vegas, whose only raison d'être will be pleasing its visitors like one vast Fisherman's Wharf—a frightening premonition. Then, of course, there are the typical big-city problems. Crime is up along with drug use, homelessness and panhandling have gotten way out of hand, and a nationwide resurgence in racism hasn't left San Francisco—once a bastion of freethinkers—untouched. (One odd predicament is the increase in drivers who run red lights, which has plagued the city and created fearful, angry pedestrians and nasty fender benders.)

But as a whole, San Francisco is doing just fine these days. Its symphony is in the black, its convention halls are fully booked, levels in city coffers are on the rise, the mayor's fired up—even AIDS is on the decline. It's hard to think of a whole city as having its ups and downs, but after nearly a decade of getting thumped by the recession and poor management (among other things), San Francisco is on a definite upswing. Though it may never relive its heady days as the king of the West Coast, San Francisco will undoubtedly retain the title as most everyone's favorite California city. As one resident put it, "Anything but LA."

3 A Look at the Past

Dateline

- 1542 Juan Rodriguez Cabrillo sails up the California coast.
- 1579 Sir Francis Drake lands near San Francisco, missing the entrance to the bay.
- 1769 Members of the Spanish expedition led by Gaspar de Portolá become the first Europeans to see San Francisco Bay.
- 1775 The *San Carlos* is the first European ship to sail into San Francisco Bay.
- 1776 Captain Juan Bautista de Anza establishes a

continues

Born as an out-of-the-way backwater of colonial Spain and blessed with a harbor that would have been the envy of any of the great cities of Europe, San Francisco boasts a story that is as varied as the millions of people who have passed through its Golden Gate.

THE AGE OF DISCOVERY   After the "discovery" of the New World by Columbus in 1492, legends of the fertile land of California were discussed in the universities and taverns of Europe, even though no one really understood where the mythical land was. (Some evidence of arrivals in California by Chinese merchants hundreds of years before Columbus's landing has been unearthed, although few scholars are willing to draw definite conclusions.) The first documented visit by a European to northern California, however, was by the

Portuguese explorer Juan Rodriguez Cabrillo , who circumnavigated the southern tip of South America as far north as the Russian River in 1542. Nearly 40 years later, in 1579, Sir Francis Drake landed on the northern California coast, stopping for a time to repair his ships and to claim the territory for Queen Elizabeth I of England. He was followed several years later by another Portuguese, Sebastian Cermeño, "discoverer" of Punta de los Reyes (King's Point) in the mid-1590s. Ironically, all three adventurers completely missed the narrow entrance to San Francisco Bay, either because it was enshrouded in fog or, more likely, because they simply weren't looking for it. Believe it or not, the bay's entrance is nearly impossible to see from the open ocean.

It would be another 2 centuries before a European actually saw the bay that would later extend Spain's influence over much of the American West. Gaspar de Portolá, a soldier sent from Spain to meddle in a rather ugly conflict between the Jesuits and the Franciscans, accidentally stumbled upon the bay in 1769, en route to somewhere else, but then stoically plodded on to his original destination, Monterey Bay, more than 100 miles to the south. Six years later, Juan Ayala, while on a mapping expedition for the Spanish, actually sailed into San Francisco Bay, and immediately realized the enormous strategic importance of his find.

Colonization quickly followed. Juan Bautista de Anza and around 30 Spanish-speaking families marched through the deserts from Sonora, Mexico, arriving after many hardships at the northern tip of modern-day San Francisco in June 1776. They immediately claimed the peninsula for Spain. (Ironically, their claim of allegiance to Spain occurred only about a week before the 13 English-speaking colonies of North America's Eastern seaboard, a continent away, declared their independence from Britain.) Their headquarters was an adobe fortress, the Presidio, built on the site of today's park with the same name. The settlers' church, built a mile to the south, was the first of five Spanish missions later developed around the edges of San Francisco Bay. Although the name of the church was officially *Nuestra Señora de Dolores,* it was dedicated to St. Francis of Assisi and nicknamed San Francisco by the Franciscan priests. Later, the name was applied to the entire bay.

In 1821, Mexico broke away from Spain, secularized the Spanish missions, and abandoned all

presidio (military fort); San Francisco de Asis Mission opens.

- **1821** Mexico wins independence from Spain and annexes California.

- **1835** The town of Yerba Buena develops around the port; the United States tries unsuccessfully to purchase San Francisco Bay from Mexico.

- **1846** Mexican-American War.

- **1847** Americans annex Yerba Buena and rename it San Francisco.

- **1848** Gold is discovered in Coloma, near Sacramento.

- **1849** In the year of the gold rush, San Francisco's population swells from about 800 to 25,000.

- **1851** Lawlessness becomes acute before attempts are made to curb it.

- **1869** The transcontinental railroad reaches San Francisco.

- **1873** Andrew S. Hallidie invents the cable car.

- **1906** The Great Earthquake strikes, and the resulting fire levels the city.

- **1915** The Panama Pacific International Exposition celebrates San Francisco's restoration and the completion of the Panama Canal.

- **1936** The Bay Bridge is built.

- **1937** The Golden Gate Bridge is completed.

- **1945** The United Nations Charter is drafted and adopted by the representatives of 50 countries meeting in San Francisco.

- **1950** The beat generation moves into the bars and cafes of North Beach.

- **1967** A free concert in Golden Gate Park attracts 20,000 people, ushering in

continues

the Summer of Love and the hippie era.

- **1974** BART's high-speed transit system opens the tunnel linking San Francisco with the East Bay.
- **1978** Harvey Milk, a city supervisor and America's first openly gay politician, is assassinated, along with Mayor George Moscone, by political rival Dan White.
- **1989** An earthquake registering 7.1 on the Richter scale hits San Francisco during a World Series baseball game, as 100 million watch on TV; the city quickly rebuilds.
- **1991** Fire rages through the Berkeley/Oakland hills, destroying 2,800 homes.
- **1993** Yerba Buena Center for the Arts opens.
- **1995** New San Francisco Museum of Modern Art opens.
- **1996** Former Assembly Speaker Willie Brown elected mayor of San Francisco.
- **1998** El Niño deluges San Francisco with its second-highest rainfall in history.

interest in the Indian natives. Freed of Spanish restrictions, California's ports were suddenly opened to trade. The region around San Francisco Bay supplied large numbers of hides and tallow for transport around Cape Horn to the tanneries and factories of New England and New York. The prospects for prosperity persuaded an English-born sailor, William Richardson, to jump ship in 1822 and settle on the site of what is now San Francisco. To impress the commandant of the Presidio, whose daughter he loved, Richardson converted to Catholicism and established the beginnings of what would soon became a thriving trading post and colony. Richard named his trading post *Yerba Buena* (or "good herb") because of a species of wild mint that grew there, near the site of today's Montgomery Street. (The city's original name was recalled with endless mirth 120 years later during San Francisco's hippie era.) He conducted a profitable hide-trading business and eventually became harbormaster and the city's first merchant prince. By 1839, the place was a veritable town, with a mostly English-speaking populace and a saloon of dubious virtue.

Throughout the 19th century, armed hostilities between English-speaking settlers from the Eastern seaboard and the Spanish-speaking colonies of Spain and Mexico erupted in places as widely scattered as Texas, Puerto Rico, and along the frequently shifting U.S.-Mexico border. In 1846, a group of U.S. Marines from the warship *Portsmouth* seized the sleepy main plaza of Yerba Buena, ran the U.S. flag up a pole, and declared California an American territory. The Presidio (occupied by about a dozen unmotivated Mexican soldiers) surrendered without a fuss. The first move the new, mostly Yankee citizenry made was to officially adopt the name of the bay as the name of their town.

THE GOLD RUSH   The year 1848 was one of the most pivotal years in European history, with unrest sweeping through Europe, horrendous poverty in Ireland, and widespread disillusionment about the hopes for prosperity throughout Europe and the eastern coast of the United States. Stories about the golden port of San Francisco and the agrarian wealth of the American West filtered slowly east, attracting slow-moving groups of settlers. Ex-sailor Richard Henry Dana extolled the virtues of California in his best-selling novel *Two Years Before the Mast*, and helped fire the public's imagination about the territory's bounty, particularly that of the Bay Area.

The first overland party crossed the Sierra and arrived in California in 1841. San Francisco grew steadily, reaching a population of approximately 900 by April 1848, but nothing hinted at the population explosion that was to follow. Historian Barry Parr has referred to the California gold rush as the most extraordinary event to ever befall an American city in peacetime. In time, San Francisco's winning combination of raw materials, healthful climate, and freedom would have attracted thousands of settlers even without the lure of gold. But the gleam of the soft metal is said to have compressed 50 years of normal growth into less than 6 months. In 1848, the year gold was first discovered, the population of San Francisco jumped from under 1,000 to 26,000 in less than 6 months. As many as 100,000 more passed through San Francisco in the space of less than a year on their way to the rocky hinterlands where the gold was rumored to be.

If not for the discovery of some small particles of gold at a sawmill that he owned, Swiss-born John Augustus Sutter's legacy would have been far less flamboyant. Despite Sutter's wish to keep the discovery quiet, his employee, John Marshall, leaked word of the discovery to friends. It eventually appeared in local papers, and smart investors on the East Coast took immediate heed. The rush did not start, however, until Sam Brannan, a Mormon preacher and famous charlatan, ran through the streets of San Francisco shouting, "Gold! Gold in the American River!" (Brannan, incidentally, bought up all of the harbor-front real estate he could get, and cornered the market on shovels, pickaxes, and canned food, just before making the announcement that was heard around the world.)

A world on the brink of change responded almost frantically. The gold rush was on. Shop owners hung GONE TO THE DIGGINGS signs in their windows. Flotillas of ships set sail from ports throughout Europe, South America, Australia, and the East Coast, sometimes nearly sinking with the weight of mining equipment. Townspeople from the Midwest headed overland, tent cities sprang up, and the sociology of a nation was transformed almost overnight. Not since the Crusades of the Middle Ages had so many people been mobilized in so short a period of time. Daily business stopped; ships arrived in San Francisco and were almost immediately deserted by their crews. News of the gold strike spread like a plague through every discontented hamlet in the known world. Although other settlements were closer to the gold strike, San Francisco was the famous name, and, therefore, where the gold-diggers disembarked. Tent cities sprung up, demand for virtually everything skyrocketed, and although some miners actually found gold, smart merchants quickly discovered that more enduring hopes lay in servicing the needs of the thousands of miners who arrived ill-equipped and ignorant of the lay of the land. Prices soared. Miners, faced with staggeringly inflated prices for goods and services, barely scraped a profit after expenses. Most prospectors failed, many died of hardship, others committed suicide at the alarming rate of 1,000 a year. Yet despite the tragedies, graft, and vice associated with the gold rush, within mere months San Francisco was forever transformed from a tranquil Spanish settlement into a roaring, boisterous boomtown.

BOOMTOWN FEVER   By 1855, most of California's surface gold had already been panned out, leaving only the richer but deeper veins of ore, which individual miners couldn't retrieve without massive capital investments. Despite that, San Francisco had evolved into a vast commercial magnet, sucking into its warehouses and banks the staggering riches that overworked newcomers had dragged, ripped, and distilled from the rocks, fields, and forests of western North America.

Investment funds were being lavished on more than mining, however. Speculation on the newly established San Francisco stock exchange could make or destroy an investor in a single day, and several noteworthy writers (including Mark Twain) were among the young men forever influenced by the boomtown spirit. The American Civil War left California firmly in the Union camp, ready, willing, and able to receive hordes of disillusioned soldiers fed up with the internecine war-mongering of the Eastern seaboard. In 1869, the transcontinental railway linked the Eastern and Western seaboards of the United States, ensuring the fortunes of the barons who controlled it. The railways, however, also shifted economic power bases as cheap manufactured goods from the East undercut the high prices hitherto charged for goods that sailed or steamed their way around the tip of South America. Ownership of the newly formed Central Pacific and Southern Pacific railroads was almost completely controlled by the "Big Four," all iron-willed capitalists—Leland Stanford, Mark Hopkins, Collis P. Huntington, and Charles Crocker—whose ruthlessness was legendary. (Much of the bone-crushing labor for their railway was executed by low-paid Chinese newcomers, most of whom arrived in overcrowded ships at San Francisco ports.) As the 19th century came to a close, civil unrest became more frequent as the monopolistic grip of the railways and robber barons became more obvious. Adding to the discontent were the uncounted thousands of Chinese immigrants who fled starvation and unrest in Asia at rates rivaling those of the Italians, Poles, Irish, and British.

During the 1870s, the flood of profits from the Comstock Lode in western Nevada diminished to a trickle, a cycle of droughts wiped out part of California's agricultural bounty, and local industry struggled to survive against the flood of manufactured goods imported via railway from the well-established factories of the East Coast and Midwest. Often, discontented workers blamed their woes on the now-unwanted hordes of Chinese workers, who by preference and for mutual protection had congregated into teeming all-Asian communities.

Despite these downward cycles, the city enjoyed other bouts of prosperity around the turn of the century thanks to the Klondike gold rush in Alaska and the Spanish-American War. Long accustomed to making a buck off gold fever, San Francisco managed to position itself as a point of embarkation for supplies bound for Alaska. Also during this time emerged the Bank of America, which eventually evolved into the largest bank in the world. Founded in North Beach in 1904, Bank of America was the brainchild of Italian-born A. P. Giannini, who later funded part of the construction for a bridge that many critics said was preposterous: the Golden Gate.

THE GREAT FIRE   On the morning of April 18, 1906, San Francisco changed for all time. The city has never experienced an earthquake as destructive as the one that hit at 5:13am (scientists estimate its strength at 8.1 on the Richter scale). All but a handful of the city's 400,000 inhabitants lay fast asleep when the ground beneath the city went into a series of convulsions. As one eyewitness put it, "The earth was shaking . . . it was undulating, rolling like an ocean breaker." The quake ruptured every water main in the city, and simultaneously started a chain of fires that rapidly fused into one gigantic conflagration. The fire brigades were helpless, and for 3 days San Francisco burned.

Militia troops finally stopped the flames from advancing by dynamiting entire city blocks, but not before more than 28,000 buildings lay in ruins. Minor tremors lasted another 3 days. The final damage stretched across a path of destruction 450 miles long and 50 miles wide. In all, 497 city blocks were razed, or about one-third of the city. As Jack London wrote in a heartrending newspaper dispatch, "The city of San Francisco is no more." The earthquake and subsequent fire so decisively changed the city that post-1906 San Francisco bears little resemblance to the town before the quake. Out of the ashes rose a bigger, healthier, and more beautiful town, though latter-day urbanologists regret that the rebuilding that followed the San Francisco earthquake did not follow a more enlightened plan. So eager was the city to rebuild that the old, somewhat unimaginative gridiron plan was reinstated, despite the opportunities for more daring visions that the aftermath of the quake afforded.

In 1915, in celebration of the opening of the Panama Canal and to prove to the world that San Francisco was restored to it full glory, the city hosted the Panama Pacific International Exhibition, a world's fair that exposed hundreds of thousands of visitors to the city's unique charms. The general frenzy of civic boosterism, however, reached its peak during the years just before World War I, when investments and civic pride might have reached an all-time high. Despite Prohibition, speakeasies did a thriving business in and around the city, and building sprees were as high-blown and lavish as the profits on the San Francisco stock exchange.

WORLD WAR II The Japanese attack on Pearl Harbor on December 7, 1941, mobilized the United States into a massive war machine, with many shipyards strategically positioned along the Pacific Coast, including San Francisco. Within less than a year, several shipyards were producing up to one new warship per day, employing hundreds of thousands of people working in 24-hour shifts (the largest, Kaiser Shipyards in Richmond, employed more than 100,000 workers alone). In search of work and the excitement of life away from their villages and cornfields, workers flooded into the city from virtually everywhere, forcing an enormous boom in housing. Hundreds found themselves separated from their small towns for the first time in their lives and reveled in their newfound freedom.

After the hostilities ended, many soldiers remembered San Francisco as the site of their finest hours and returned to live there permanently. The economic prosperity of the postwar years enabled massive enlargements of the city, including freeways, housing developments, a booming financial district, and pockets of counterculture enthusiasts such as the beatniks, gays, and hippies.

THE 1950s: THE BEATS San Francisco's reputation as a rollicking place where anything goes dates from the Barbary Coast days when gang warfare, prostitution, gambling, and drinking were major city pursuits, and citizens took law and order into their own hands. Its more modern role as a catalyst for social change and the avant-garde began in the 1950s when a group of young writers, philosophers, and poets challenged the materialism and conformity of American society by embracing anarchy and Eastern philosophy, expressing their notions in poetry. They adopted a uniform of jeans, sweater, sandals, and beret, called themselves beats, and hung out in North Beach where rents were low and cheap wine was plentiful. *San Francisco Chronicle* columnist Herb Caen, to whom they were totally alien, dubbed them *beatniks* in his column.

Allen Ginsberg, Gregory Corso, and Jack Kerouac had begun writing at Columbia University in New York, but it wasn't until they came west and hooked up with Lawrence Ferlinghetti, Kenneth Rexroth, Gary Snyder, and others that the movement gained national attention. The bible of the beats was Ginsberg's *Howl,* which he first read at the Six Gallery on October 13, 1955. By the time he finished reading, Ginsberg was crying, the audience was chanting, and his fellow poets were announcing the arrival of an epic bard. Ferlinghetti published *Howl,* which was deemed obscene, in 1956. A trial followed, but the court found that the book had redeeming social value, thereby reaffirming the right of free expression. The other major work, Jack Kerouac's *On the Road,* was published in 1957, instantly becoming a best-seller (he had written it as one long paragraph in 20 days in 1951). The freedom and sense of possibility that this book conveyed became the bellwether for a generation.

While the beats gave poetry readings and generated controversy, two clubs in North Beach were making waves, notably the "hungry i" and the Purple Onion, where everyone who was anyone or became anyone on the entertainment scene appeared—Mort Sahl, Dick Gregory, Lenny Bruce, Barbra Streisand, and Woody Allen all worked here. Maya Angelou appeared as a singer and dancer at the Purple Onion. The cafes of North Beach were the center of bohemian life in the fifties: the Black Cat, Vesuvio's, Caffè Trieste and Caffè Tosca, and Enrico's Sidewalk Cafe. When the tour buses started rolling in, rents went up, and Broadway was turned into a sex-club strip in the early 1960s. Thus ended an era, and the beats moved on. The alternative scene shifted to Berkeley and the Haight.

THE 1960s: THE HAIGHT　The torch of freedom had been passed from the beats and North Beach to Haight-Ashbury and the hippies, but it was a radically different torch. The hippies replaced the beats' angst, anarchy, negativism, nihilism, alcohol, and poetry with love, communalism, openness, drugs, rock music, and a back-to-nature philosophy. Although the scent of marijuana wafted everywhere— on the streets, in the cafes, in Golden Gate Park—the real drugs of choice were LSD (a tab of good acid cost $5) and other hallucinogenics. Timothy Leary experimented with its effects and exhorted youth to "turn on, tune in, and drop out." Instead of hanging out in coffeehouses, the hippies went to concerts at the Fillmore or the Avalon Ballroom to dance. The first Family Dog Rock 'n' Roll Dance and Concert, "A Tribute to Dr. Strange," was given at the Longshoreman's Hall in fall 1965, featuring the Jefferson Airplane, the Marbles, the Great Society, and the Charlatans. At this event, the first major happening of the 1960s, Ginsberg led a snake dance through the crowd. In January 1966, the 3-day Trips Festival, organized by rock promoter Bill Graham, was also held at the Longshoreman's Hall. The climax came with Ken Kesey and the Merry Pranksters Acid Test show, which used five movie screens, psychedelic visions, and the sounds of the Grateful Dead and Big Brother and the Holding Company. The "be-in" followed in the summer of 1966 at the polo grounds in Golden Gate Park, when an estimated 20,000 heard the Jefferson Airplane perform and Ginsberg chant, while the Hell's Angels acted as unofficial police. It was followed by the Summer of Love in 1967 as thousands of young people streamed into the city in search of drugs and sex.

The sixties Haight scene was very different from the fifties beat scene. The hippies were much younger than the beats had been, constituting the first youth movement to take over the nation. Ironically, they also became the first generation of young, independent, and moneyed consumers to be courted by corporations. Ultimately, the Haight and the hippie movement deteriorated from love and flowers into drugs and crime, drawing a fringe of crazies like Charles Manson and leaving only a legacy of sex, drugs, violence, and consumerism. As early as October 1967, the "Diggers," who had opened a free shop and soup kitchen in the Haight, symbolically buried the dream in a clay casket in Buena Vista Park.

The end of the Vietnam War and the resignation of President Nixon took the edge off politics. The last fling of the mentality that had driven the 1960s occurred in 1974 when Patty Hearst was kidnapped from her Berkeley apartment by the Symbionese Liberation Army and taken on a bank-robbing spree before surrendering in San Francisco.

THE 1970s: GAY RIGHTS　The homosexual community in San Francisco developed at the end of World War II, when thousands of military personnel were discharged back to the United States via San Francisco. A substantial number of those men were homosexual and decided to stay on in San Francisco. A gay community grew up along Polk Street between Sutter and California. Later, the larger community moved into the Castro, where it remains today.

The gay political-protest movement is usually dated from the 1969 Stonewall raid that occurred in Greenwich Village. Although the political movement started in New York, California had already given birth to two major organizations for gay rights: the Mattachine Society, founded in 1951 by Henry Hay in Los Angeles, and the Daughters of Bilitis, a lesbian organization founded in 1955 in San Francisco.

After Stonewall, the Committee for Homosexual Freedom was created in spring 1969 in San Francisco; a Gay Liberation Front chapter was organized at Berkeley. In fall 1969, Robert Patterson, a columnist for the *San Francisco Examiner*, referred to homosexuals as "semi males," "drag darlings," and "women who aren't exactly women." On October 31 at noon, a group began a peaceful picket of the *Examiner*. Peace reigned until someone threw a bag of printer's ink from an *Examiner* window. Someone wrote "Fuck the Examiner" on the wall, and the police moved in to clear the crowd, clubbing them as they went. The remaining pickets retreated to Glide Methodist Church and then marched on city hall. Unfortunately, the mayor was away. Unable to air their grievances, they started a sit-in that lasted until 5pm, when they were ordered to leave. Most did, but three remained and were arrested.

Later that year, an anti-Thanksgiving rally was staged at which gays protested against several national and local businesses: Western and Delta airlines, the former for firing lesbian stewardesses, the latter for refusing to sell a ticket to a young man wearing a Gay Power button; KFOG, for its antihomosexual broadcasting; and also some local gay bars for exploitation. On May 14, 1970, a group of gay and women's liberationists invaded the convention of the American Psychiatric Association in San Francisco to protest the reading of a paper on aversion therapy for homosexuals, forcing the meeting to adjourn.

The rage against intolerance was appearing on all fronts. At the National Gay Liberation conference held in August 1970 in the city, Charles Thorp, chairman of the San Francisco State Liberation Front, called for militancy and issued a challenge to come out with a rallying cry of "Blatant is beautiful." He also argued for the use of what he felt was the more positive, celebratory term "gay" instead of "homosexual," and decried the fact that homosexuals were kept in their place at the three B's: the bars, the beaches, and the baths. As the movement grew in size and power, debates on strategy and tactics occurred, most dramatically between those who wanted to withdraw into separate ghettos and those who wanted to enter mainstream society. The most extreme proposal was made in California by Don Jackson, who proposed establishing a gay territory in California's Alpine County, about 10 miles south of Lake Tahoe. It would have had a totally gay administration, civil service, university, museum—everything. The residents of Alpine County were not pleased with the proposal. But before the situation turned really ugly, Jackson's idea was abandoned because of lack of support in the gay community. In the end, the movement would concentrate on integration and civil rights, not separatism. They would elect politicians who were sympathetic to their cause and celebrate their new identity by establishing National Gay Celebration Day and Gay Pride Week, the first of which was celebrated in June 1970, when 1,000 to 2,000 marched in New York, 1,000 in Los Angeles, and a few hundred in San Francisco.

By the mid-1970s, the gay community craved a more central role in San Francisco politics. Harvey Milk, owner of a camera store in the Castro, decided to run as an openly gay man for the board of supervisors. He won, becoming the first openly gay person to hold a major public office. He and liberal Mayor George Moscone developed a gay rights agenda, but in 1978 both were killed by former

Supervisor Dan White, who shot them after Moscone refused his request for rein-statement. White, a Catholic and former police officer, had consistently opposed Milk's and Moscone's more liberal policies. At his trial, White successfully pleaded temporary insanity caused by additives in his fast-food diet. The media dubbed it a "Twinkie defense," but the murder charges against White were reduced to manslaughter. On that day, angry and grieving, the gay community rioted, over-turning and burning police cars in a night of rage. To this day a candlelight memorial parade is held on November 27. Milk's martyrdom was both a political and a practical inspiration to gay candidates across the country.

The emphasis in the gay movement shifted abruptly in the 1980s when the AIDS epidemic struck the community. AIDS has had a dramatic impact on the Castro. While it's still a thriving and lively community, it's no longer the constant party that it once was. The hedonistic lifestyle that had played out in the discos, bars, baths, and streets changed as the seriousness of the epidemic sunk in and the number of deaths increased. Political efforts have shifted away from enfranchisement and toward demanding money for social services and research money to deal with the AIDS crisis. The gay community has developed its own organizations, such as Project Inform and Gay Men's Health Crisis, to publicize information about the disease, treatments available, and safe sex. Though new cases of AIDS within the gay community are on the decline in San Francisco, it still remains a serious problem.

THE 1980s: THE BIG ONE, PART TWO   The eighties may have arrived in San Francisco with a whimper (compared to previous generations), but they went out with quite a bang. At 5:04pm on Tuesday, October 17, 1989, as more than 62,000 fans filled Candlestick Park for the third game of the World Series—and the San Francisco Bay Area commute moved into its heaviest flow—an earthquake of magnitude 7.1 struck. Within the next 20 seconds, 63 lives would be lost, $10 billion in damage would occur, and the entire Bay Area community would be reminded of their humble insignificance. Centered about 60 miles south of San Francisco within the Forest of Nisene Marks, the deadly temblor was felt as far away as San Diego and Nevada.

Though scientists had predicted an earthquake would hit on this section of the San Andreas Fault, certain structures that were built to withstand such an earth-quake failed miserably. The most catastrophic event was the collapse of the elevated Cypress Street section of Interstate 880 in Oakland, where the upper level of the freeway literally pancaked the lower level, crushing everything with such force that cars were reduced to inches. Other structures heavily damaged included the San Francisco–Oakland Bay Bridge, shut down for months when a section of the roadbed collapsed; San Francisco's Marina District, where several multimillion-dollar homes collapsed on their weak, shifting bases of landfill and sand; and the Pacific Garden Mall in Santa Cruz, which was completely devastated.

President Bush declared the seven hardest-hit counties a disaster area, where at least 3,700 people were reported injured and more than 12,000 were displaced. More than 18,000 homes were damaged and 963 others destroyed. Although fire raged within the city and water supply systems were damaged, the major fires sparked within the Marina District were brought under control within 3 hours, due mostly to the heroic efforts of San Francisco's firefighters.

After the rubble had finally settled, it was unanimously agreed that San Francisco and the Bay Area had pulled through miraculously well—particularly when compared to the more recent earthquake in Kobe, Japan, which killed thousands and displaced an entire city. After the quake, a feeling of esprit de corps swept the city as neighbors helped each other rebuild and donations poured in from all over the world. Though its been nearly a decade since, San Francisco is still feeling the effects of the quake, most noticeably during rush hour as commuters take a variety of detours to circumvent freeways that were damaged or destroyed and are still under construction. That another "big one" will strike is inevitable: It's the price you pay for living on a fault line. But if there is ever a city that is prepared for a major shakedown, it's San Francisco.

4 Famous San Franciscans

Ansel Adams (1902–84)   Photographer. Born in San Francisco, Adams is famous for his photographs of Yosemite and the Sierra. He organized the first college-of-art photography department at the California School of Fine Arts in 1946.

Willie Brown (b. 1934)   Current mayor of San Francisco. Formerly California Assembly speaker of the house, Brown's flamboyant style, lavish tastes, and masterful politicking led to his rapid rise as California's most powerful and outspoken democrat.

Dave Brubeck (b. 1920)   Pianist and jazz composer. Born in Concord, California, Brubeck led experimental jazz groups in San Francisco in the 1940s. In 1951, he organized a quartet with alto saxophonist Paul Desmond and went on to international fame in the 1950s and 1960s. Gerry Mulligan was also a member of the group. Brubeck's signature composition is *Take Five.*

Herb Caen (1916–97)   Author, Pulitzer Prize–winning newspaper columnist. Caen, born in Sacramento, moved to San Francisco in 1936 to eventually become "Mr. San Francisco," having written his column for the *San Francisco Chronicle* for more than half a century. His recent death was mourned not just by San Franciscans, but by a whole nation.

Francis Ford Coppola (b. 1939)   One of America's most successful contemporary filmmakers. Coppola is best known for *The Godfather* and *Apocalypse Now.* He continues to live in San Francisco, working from his office within the Columbus Tower in North Beach.

Joe DiMaggio (b. 1914)   One of the greatest baseball players of all time. He began his career with the San Francisco Seals before becoming the New York Yankees' star center fielder. During the 1950s, he married Marilyn Monroe in San Francisco.

Dianne Feinstein (b. 1933)   Politician. Born in San Francisco and educated at nearby Stanford, Feinstein served as the city's mayor and is now a U.S. senator. A political "centrist," Feinstein is supportive of alternative lifestyles and reproductive rights.

Jerry Garcia (1942–95)   Rock and bluegrass musician. Garcia was best known as the lead guitarist and vocalist of the psychedelic rock band the Grateful Dead. Soon after his death, the Grateful Dead disbanded and an era ended.

Danny Glover (b. 1947)   Actor. Graduate of San Francisco State University and Black Actors' Workshop of the American Conservatory Theatre, Glover's roles include the domineering husband in *The Color Purple* (1985) and Mel Gibson's partner in the *Lethal Weapon* movies. Continues to live in San Francisco.

Bill Graham (1931–92)   Music promoter. Before his death in a helicopter accident in 1992, Graham was one of the leading concert promoters in the country. Many of his first concerts were staged at the Fillmore Auditorium.

Dashiell Hammett (1894–1961)   Author. Drawing on his experience with the Pinkerton Detective Agency, Hammett penned hard-boiled detective novels, including *The Maltese Falcon* and *The Thin Man*. He was imprisoned for refusing to testify during the House Un-American Activities Committee "witch-hunts" in the 1950s.

William Randolph Hearst (1863–1951)   Media mogul. Famous for his opulent lifestyle and grand castle at San Simeon, Hearst was a publishing magnate, who as a young man worked for the *San Francisco Examiner*. He later acquired a string of successful radio stations, motion-picture companies, and daily newspapers.

Chris Isaak (b. 1956)   Singer. San Francisco's swooning, surfing heartthrob, Isaak got his start playing in small clubs around the city. Hits include "Somebody's Crying," "Wicked Game," and "San Francisco Days." Currently lives in the Sunset District.

Janis Joplin (1943–70)   Rock star. One of the 1960s' most charismatic rock 'n' roll voices, Joplin moved from Texas at the age of 18 and began her career in San Francisco with Big Brother and the Holding Company. She died from an overdose of heroin in 1970.

Jack Kerouac (1922–69)   Author. The leader of the "beat generation," Kerouac was born in Lowell, Massachusetts, and came to San Francisco in the 1950s to write the beats' bible, *On the Road*.

Jack London (1876–1916)   Author. Born in the SoMa District (an area south of Market Street), London later moved to Oakland where he grew up, helping support his family by working on the waterfront. As a teenager he became an oyster pirate. A legendary figure, London was a hobo, factory worker, sailor, and prospector. Among the more than 40 books he wrote in his abbreviated life were *Call of the Wild* and *The Sea Wolf*.

Harvey Milk (1931–78)   Activist. Originally from Brooklyn, Milk owned a camera store at 575 Castro St. He ran for the board of supervisors in 1977, becoming the first openly gay person to hold a major public office. He was assassinated in 1978 in city hall, along with Mayor George Moscone, by Dan White. Milk is memorialized in Harvey Milk Plaza, and a candlelight parade is held every year in November to mark his death.

Joe Montana (b. 1956)   Retired 49ers quarterback. Considered one of the greatest quarterbacks of all time. Led the 49ers to four Super Bowl championships; voted most valuable player (MVP) in three.

Amy Tan (b. 1952)   Author. Born in Oakland to parents who emigrated from China. Her first book, *The Joy Luck Club*, became a best-seller and provides a moving portrait of life in San Francisco's Chinatown. Other books include *The Kitchen God's Wife*.

Hunter S. Thompson (b. 1939)   Gonzo journalist. A longtime political columnist for the *San Francisco Examiner*, Thompson is also the national-affairs editor at *Rolling Stone* and author of several best-selling books including *Fear and Loathing in Las Vegas* and *Fear and Loathing on the Campaign Trail*.

Robin Williams (b. 1952)   Actor, comedian. A San Francisco local, Williams nurtured his career in comedy clubs along the West Coast. National exposure as the extraterrestrial Mork from Ork led to a series of starring roles in such films as *Mrs. Doubtfire*, *Dead Poets Society*, and *The Birdcage*. Frequently seen dining at Stars.

Planning a Trip to San Francisco 2

Regardless of whether you chart your vacation months in advance or travel on a whim, you'll need to do a little advance planning to make the most of your stay. This chapter will help you with all the logistics.

1 Visitor Information & Money

Visitors from outside the United States should also see chapter 3, "For Foreign Visitors," for entry requirements and other pertinent information.

VISITOR INFORMATION

The San Francisco Convention and Visitors Bureau, 900 Market St. (at Powell Street), Hallidie Plaza, Lower Level, San Francisco, CA 94102 (☎ 415/391-2000; www.sfvisitor.org), is the best source for any kind of specialized information about the city. Even if you don't have a specific question, you may want to send them $2 for their 100-page magazine, *The San Francisco Book*, which includes a 3-month calendar of events, city history, shopping and dining information, and several good, clear maps, as well as an additional 50-page lodging guide. The bureau only highlights members' establishments, so if they don't have what you're looking for, it doesn't mean it's nonexistent.

You can also get the latest on San Francisco at the following on-line addresses:

- *Bay Guardian,* free weekly's city page: **www.sfbayguardian.com**
- Hotel accommodations, reserve on-line: **www.hotelres.com/**
- *Q San Francisco,* for gays and lesbians: **www.qsanfrancisco. com/**
- *SF Gate,* the city's combined *Chronicle* and *Examiner* newspapers: **www.sfgate.com**
- Channel 7, ABC, and KGO's city guide: **www.citysearch7. com**

MONEY

In addition to the details below, foreign visitors should see chapter 3, "For Foreign Visitors," for further information about money.

U.S.-dollar traveler's checks are the safest, most negotiable way to carry currency. They are accepted by most restaurants, hotels, and

What Things Cost in San Francisco	U.S. $
Taxi from airport to city center (tip included)	36.00
Bus fare to any destination within the city (adult)	1.00
Bus fare to any destination within the city (children and seniors)	.35
Double room at Campton Place Hotel (expensive)	285.00
Double room at Savoy Hotel (moderate)	140.00
Double room at the Commodore International Hotel (inexpensive)	99.00
Lunch for one at Betelnut (moderate)	20.00
Lunch for one at Mario's Bohemian Cigar Store (inexpensive)	8.00
Dinner for one, without wine, at Fleur de Lys (expensive)	85.00
Dinner for one, without wine, at Fringale (moderate)	34.00
Dinner for one, without wine, at Cha Cha Cha (inexpensive)	20.00
Glass of beer	2.75
Coca-Cola	1.50
Cup of coffee	1.30
Admission to the top of Coit Tower	3.00
Movie ticket	8.00
Theater ticket	8.00–50.00

shops, and can be exchanged for cash at banks and check-issuing offices. American Express offices are open Monday to Friday from 8:30am to 5:30pm and on Saturday from 9am until 2pm. See "Fast Facts: San Francisco," in chapter 4, for office locations.

Most banks have automated teller machines (ATMs), which accept cards connected to networks like Cirrus and PLUS. You'll find them on almost every commercial street, or for specific locations call ☎ 800/424-7787 for the Cirrus network, ☎ 800/843-7587 for the PLUS system.

Of course, credit cards are almost as good as cash and are accepted in most establishments. Also, ATMs will make cash advances against MasterCard and Visa cards. American Express cardholders can write a personal check, guaranteed against their card, for up to $1,000 in cash at an American Express office. See "Fast Facts: San Francisco" in chapter 4 for office addresses.

2 When to Go

If you're dreaming of convertibles, Frisbee on the beach, and tank-topped evenings, change your reservations and head to Los Angeles. Contrary to California's sunshine-and-bikini image, San Francisco weather is mild and can often be downright fickle—it's nothing like that of neighboring southern California. While summer is the most popular time to visit, it's also often characterized by damp, foggy days, cold, windy nights, and crowded tourist destinations. A good bet is to visit in spring, or better yet, autumn. Every September, right about the time San Franciscans mourn being gypped (or fogged) out of another summer, something wonderful happens: The thermostat rises, the skies clear, and the locals call in sick to work and head for the beach. It's what residents call "Indian summer." The city is also delightful during winter, when the opera and ballet seasons are in full swing, there

---

Travel Tip

Even if it's sunny out, don't forget to bring a jacket; the weather can change almost instantly from sunny and warm to windy and cold.

---

are fewer tourists, many hotel prices are lower, and downtown bustles with holiday cheer.

CLIMATE

Northern California weather has been extraordinary recently. In the past 2 years, the Bay Area has experienced one sizzling and one nonexistent summer, one winter that ended in late June (and kept Tahoe's ski lifts open until Aug), a series of floods in the surrounding 'burbs (thanks to the infamous El Niño), and a storm whose 80-mile-per-hour winds blew century-old trees right out of the ground. However, San Francisco's temperate, marine climate usually means relatively mild weather year-round. In summer, temperatures rarely top 70°F, and the city's chilling fog rolls in most mornings and evenings. Even when autumn's heat occasionally stretches into the 80s and 90s, you should still dress in layers, or by early evening you'll learn first-hand why sweatshirt sales are a great business at Fisherman's Wharf. In winter, the mercury seldom falls below freezing, and snow is almost unheard of, but that doesn't mean you won't be whimpering if you forget a coat. Still, compared to most of the States' varied weather conditions, San Francisco is consistently pleasant.

It's that beautifully fluffy, chilly, wet, heavy, and sweeping fog that makes the city's weather so precarious. Northern California's summer fog bank is produced by a rare combination of water, wind, and topography. It lies off the coast and is pulled in by rising air currents when the land heats up. Held back by coastal mountains along a 600-mile front, the low clouds seek out any passage they can find. And the access most readily available is the slot where the Pacific Ocean penetrates the continental wall—the Golden Gate.

San Francisco's Average Temperatures (°F) & Rainfall (in.)

	Jan	Feb	Mar	Apr	May	June	July	Aug	Sept	Oct	Nov	Dec
High	56	59	60	61	63	64	64	65	69	68	63	57
Low	46	48	49	49	51	53	53	54	56	55	52	47
Rain	4.5	2.8	2.6	1.5	0.4	0.2	0.1	0.1	0.2	1.1	2.5	3.5

SAN FRANCISCO CALENDAR OF EVENTS

January

- **San Francisco Sports and Boat Show,** Cow Palace. Draws thousands of boat enthusiasts over a 9-day period. Call **Cow Palace Box Office** (☎ **415/ 469-6065**) for details. Mid-January.

February

○ **Chinese New Year,** Chinatown. In 1999, the year of the rabbit, public celebrations will again spill onto every street in Chinatown. Festivities begin with the crowning of "Miss Chinatown USA" pageant parade, and climax a week later with a celebratory parade of marching bands, rolling floats, barrages of fireworks, and a block-long dragon writhing in and out of the crowds. New Year is February 16 and the parade is scheduled for February 27; festivities go for several weeks and wrap up with a memorable parade through Chinatown. Arrive early for a good viewing spot on Grant Avenue. Make your hotel reservations early. For information call ☎ 415/982-3000.

March

- **St. Patrick's Day Parade.** Almost everyone's honorarily Irish at this festive affair starting at 12:30pm at Market and Fifth streets and continuing toward the Ferry Building. But the party doesn't stop there. Head down to the Embarcadero's Harrington's bar after work hours and celebrate with hundreds of the Irish-for-a-day as they gallivant amidst the closed-off streets and numerous pubs. Call ☎ 415/391-2000 for details. The Sunday before March 17.

April

- **Cherry Blossom Festival,** Japantown. Meander through the arts-and-crafts and food booths aligning the blocked-off streets; watch traditional drumming, sumo wrestling, flower arranging, origami, or a parade celebrating the cherry blossom and Japanese culture. Call ☎ 415/563-2313 for information. Mid- to late April.

- ✪ **San Francisco International Film Festival,** the AMC Kabuki 8 Cinemas, at Fillmore and Post streets and many other locations. Started 40 years ago, this is one of America's oldest film festivals, featuring more than 100 films and videos from more than 30 countries. Tickets are relatively inexpensive, and screenings are very accessible to the general public. Entries include new films by beginning and established directors. For a schedule or information call ☎ 415/931-FILM. Mid-April to early May.

May

- **Cinco de Mayo Celebration,** Mission District. This is the day the Latino community celebrates the victory of the Mexicans over the French at Puebla in 1862. Mariachi bands, dancers, food, and a parade fill the streets of the Mission. Parade starts at 10am at 24th and Bryant streets and ends at Civic Center. Sunday before May 5.

- ✪ **Bay to Breakers Foot Race,** Golden Gate Park. Even if you don't participate, you can't avoid this run from downtown to Ocean Beach that stops morning traffic throughout the city. Around 80,000 entrants gather—many dressed in wacky, innovative, and sometimes X-rated costumes—for the approximately 7½-mile run. If you're feeling lazy, join the throng of spectators who line the route in the form of sidewalk parties, bands, and cheerleaders of all ages to get a good dose of true San Francisco fun. The event is sponsored by the *San Francisco Examiner* (☎ 415/777-7770). Third Sunday of May.

- ✪ **Carnival,** Mission Street between 14th and 24th streets, and Harrison Street between 15th and 21st streets. The San Francisco Mission District's largest annual event, Carnival, is a 2-day series of festivities that culminates with a parade on Mission Street over Memorial Day weekend. One of San Franciscans' favorite events, more than half a million spectators line the route, and the samba musicians and dancers continue to play on 14th Street, near Harrison, at the end of the march. Just show up, or call the **Mission Economic and Cultural Association** (☎ 415/826-1401) for complete information.

June

- **Union Street Fair,** along Union Street from Fillmore to Gough streets. Stalls sell arts, crafts, food, and drink. You'll also find a lot of great-looking, young, yuppie cocktailers packing every bar and spilling out into the street. Music and entertainment are on a number of stages. Call ☎ 415/346-4446 for more information. First weekend of June.

- **Haight Street Fair.** Featuring alternative crafts, ethnic foods, rock bands, and a healthy number of hippies and young street kids whooping it up and slamming beers in front of the blaring rock 'n' roll stage. The fair usually extends along

Haight between Stanyan and Ashbury streets. For details call ☎ 415/661-8025. In June; call for date.

○ **North Beach Festival,** Grant Street in North Beach. Nineteen ninety-nine marks the 45th year this party has taken place, and organizers claim its the oldest urban street fair in the country. Close to 80,000 city folk meander Grant Avenue, between Vallejo and Union streets, to eat, drink, and browse the arts-and-crafts booths. But the most enjoyable part of the event is listening to music and people-watching. Call ☎ 415/989-6426 for details. Usually Father's Day weekend.

• **Lesbian and Gay Freedom Day Parade,** Market Street. A prideful event drawing up to half a million participants. The parade's start and finish have been moved around in recent years to accommodate road construction. Regardless of its path, it ends with hundreds of food, art, and information booths and sound-stages. Call ☎ 415/864-3733 for information and location. Usually the third or last weekend of June.

○ **Stern Grove Midsummer Music Festival.** Pack a picnic and head out early to join thousands who come here to lie in the grass and enjoy classical, jazz, and ethnic music and dance in the Grove at 19th Avenue and Sloat Boulevard. These free concerts are held every Sunday at 2pm. Either show up with a lawn chair or blanket. There are food booths if you forget snacks, but you'll be dying to leave if you don't bring warm clothes—the Sunset District can be one of the coldest parts of the city. Call ☎ 415/252-6252 for listings. Mid-June through August.

July

• **Jazz and All That Art on Fillmore.** The first weekend in July starts off with a bang when the upscale portion of Fillmore (between Post and Jackson streets) closes off traffic and fills the street with several blocks of arts and crafts, gourmet food, and live jazz. The festivities will be held on July 4 and 5 from 10am to 6pm. Call ☎ 415/346-4446 for further information.

• **Fourth of July Celebration and Fireworks.** This event can be somewhat of a joke, since more often than not, like everyone else, fog comes into the city on this day to join in the festivities. Sometimes it's almost impossible to view the million-dollar fireworks from Pier 39 on the northern waterfront. Still, it's a party and if the skies are clear, it's a damn good show.

• **San Francisco Marathon.** One of the largest marathons in the world. For entry information contact IMG, the event organizer, at ☎ 415/296-7111 or 415/648-9410. Usually the second weekend in July.

August

• **Renaissance Pleasure Faire.** An expensive but enjoyable festival takes place north of San Francisco and takes you back to Renaissance times—with games, plays, and arts-and-crafts and food booths. The fair is located in Black Point Forest, just east of Novato, opens the weekend before Labor Day, and runs six to eight weekends and on Labor Day (☎ 800/52-FAIRE or 415/892-0937).

○ **A La Carte, A La Park,** usually at Sharon Meadow, Golden Gate Park. You probably won't get to go to all the restaurants you'd like while you're visiting the city, but you can get a good sampling if you attend this annual event. Over 40 of the town's favorite chefs, accompanied by 20 microbreweries and 20 wineries, offer tastings in the midst of San Francisco's favorite park. There's entertainment as well, and proceeds benefit the San Francisco Shakespeare Festival. Admission was $8.50 adults, $7 seniors, and free for children under 12 in 1998. Prices were not determined for 1999 when this book went to press. Call ☎ 415/383-9378 for details. Always Labor Day weekend.

September
- **Opera in the Park.** Each year the San Francisco Opera launches its season with a free concert featuring a selection of arias. Usually in Sharon Meadow, Golden Gate Park, on the first Saturday after Labor Day, but call ☎ 415/861-4008 to confirm the date.
- ✪ **San Francisco Blues Festival,** on the grounds of Fort Mason. The largest outdoor blues music event on the West Coast will be 27 years old in 1999 and will again feature both local and national musicians performing back-to-back during the 3-day extravaganza. You can charge tickets by phone through **BASS Ticketmaster** (☎ 510/762-2277). For **schedule** information call ☎ 415/826-6837. Usually in late September.
- **Castro Street Fair.** Celebrates life in the city's most famous gay neighborhood. Call ☎ 415/467-3354 for information. Usually end of September or beginning of October.
- ✪ **Sausalito Art Festival,** Sausalito. A juried exhibit of more than 180 artists. It is accompanied by music—provided by Bay Area jazz, rock, and blues performers—and international cuisine, enhanced by wines from some 50 different Napa and Sonoma producers. Parking is impossible; take the **Blue & Gold Fleet ferry** (☎ 415/705-5555) from Fisherman's Wharf to the festival site. For more information call ☎ 415/332-3555. Labor Day weekend, early September.

October
- **Columbus Day Festivities.** The city's Italian community leads the festivities around Fisherman's Wharf celebrating Columbus's landing in America. The festival includes a parade along Columbus Avenue and sporting events, but for the most part, it's just a great excuse to hang out in North Beach and people-watch. For information call ☎ 415/434-1492. Sunday before Columbus Day.
- **Reggae in the Park,** usually in Sharon Meadow in Golden Gate Park. Going into its 10th year, this event draws thousands to Golden Gate Park to dance and celebrate the soulful sounds. Big-name reggae and world-beat bands play all weekend long, and ethnic arts-and-crafts and food booths are set up along the stage's periphery. Tickets are around $12 in advance, and a few dollars more on-site. Two-day passes are available at a discounted rate. Free for children under 12. Call ☎ 415/383-9378 for further details. Always the second weekend in October.
- **Exotic Erotic Halloween Ball.** Friday or Saturday night before Halloween, thousands come dressed in costume, lingerie, and sometimes even less than that. It's a wild fantasy affair with bands, dancing, and costume contests. Beware: It can be somewhat cheesy. Tickets cost approximately $35 per person. For information call ☎ 415/567-BALL. For tickets call ☎ 510/762-BASS.
- **Halloween.** A huge night in San Francisco. A fantastical parade is organized at Market and Castro, and a mixed gay/straight crowd revels in costumes of extraordinary imagination. While the past few years they've been trying to divert festivities to the Civic Center, the action's still best in the Castro. October 31.
- **San Francisco Jazz Festival.** This festival presents eclectic programming in an array of fabulous jazz venues throughout the city. With close to 2 weeks of nightly entertainment and dozens of performers, the jazz festival is a hot ticket. Past events have featured Herbie Hancock, Dave Brubeck, the Modern Jazz Quartet, Wayne Shorter, and Bill Frisell. For information call ☎ 800/627-5277 or 415/398-5655. End of October, beginning of November.

December
- **The Nutcracker,** War Memorial Opera House. Performed annually by the **San Francisco Ballet** (☎ 415/776-1999). Tickets to this Tchaikovsky tradition should be purchased well in advance.

3 Safety

San Francisco, like any large city, has its fair share of crime, but unlike New York and Los Angeles, most folks here don't have firsthand horror stories. There are some areas where you need to exercise extra caution, particularly at night—notably the Tenderloin, the Western Addition, the Mission District, and around the Civic Center. In addition, there are a substantial number of homeless people throughout the city with concentrations in and around Union Square, the Theater District, the Tenderloin, and Haight Street, so don't be alarmed if you're approached for spare change. Basically, just use common sense.

See "Fast Facts: San Francisco," in chapter 4, for city-specific safety tips. For additional crime-prevention information, phone **San Francisco SAFE** (☎ 415/553-1984).

4 Tips for Travelers with Special Needs

FOR PEOPLE WITH DISABILITIES

Most of San Francisco's major museums and tourist attractions are fitted with wheelchair ramps. In addition, many hotels offer special accommodations and services for wheelchair-bound and other visitors with disabilities. These include extra-large bathrooms and ramps for the wheelchair-bound and telecommunication devices for deaf people. The San Francisco Convention and Visitors Bureau (see section 1, "Visitor Information & Money," above) has the most up-to-date information.

Travelers in wheelchairs can secure special ramped taxis by calling **Yellow Cab** (☎ 415/626-2345), which charges regular rates for the service. Travelers with disabilities may also obtain a free copy of the *Muni Access Guide,* published by the San Francisco Municipal Railway, Accessible Services Program, Municipal Railway, 949 Presidio Ave., San Francisco, CA 94115 (☎ 415/923-6142). Call this number Monday to Friday from 8am to 5pm.

FOR GAY MEN & LESBIANS

If you head down to the Castro—an area surrounding Castro Street near Market Street that's predominantly a gay and lesbian community—you'll understand why the city is a mecca for gay and lesbian travelers. Since the 1970s, this unique part of town has remained the colorfully festive gay neighborhood teeming with "outed" city folk who meander the streets shopping, eating, partying, or cruising. If anyone feels like an outsider in this part of town, it's heterosexuals, who, although warmly welcomed in the community, may feel uncomfortable or downright threatened if they harbor any homophobia or aversion to being "cruised." For many San Franciscans, it's just a fun area (especially on Halloween) with some wonderful shops.

It is estimated that gays and lesbians form one-fourth to one-third of the population of San Francisco, so it's no surprise that in recent years clubs and bars catering to them have popped up all around town. Although lesbian interests are concentrated primarily in the East Bay (especially Oakland), a significant community resides in the Mission District, around 16th Street and Valencia.

Several local publications are dedicated to in-depth coverage of news, information, and listings of goings-on around town for gay men and lesbians. The *Bay Area Reporter* has the most comprehensive listings, including a weekly calendar of events, and is distributed free on Thursdays. It can be found stacked at the corner of 18th and Castro streets and at Ninth and Harrison streets, as well as in bars, bookshops, and various stores around town. It may also be available in gay and lesbian bookstores elsewhere in the country.

GUIDES & PUBLICATIONS   Gay men and lesbians might like to get either of the guides specifically for San Francisco, *Betty and Pansy's Severe Queer Review of San Francisco* ($10.95) and *The Official San Francisco Gay Guide* ($10.95). For accommodations, check with two international guides: *Odysseus* ($29) and *Inn Places* ($16). These books and others are available by mail from **Giovanni's Room,** 1145 Pine St., Philadelphia, PA 19107 (☎ **215/923-2960;** E-mail: giophilp@netaxs.com) and **A Different Light bookstore,** 489 Castro St., San Francisco, CA 94114 (☎ **415/431-0891;** Web site: www.adlbooks.com). Other locations are in New York City (☎ **212/989-4850**) and Los Angeles (☎ **310/854-6601**).

Our World, 1104 N. Nova Rd., Suite 251, Daytona Beach, FL 32117 (☎ **904/441-5367**), is a magazine devoted to gay and lesbian travel worldwide. It costs $35 for 10 issues. *Out and About,* 8 W. 19th St., Suite 401, New York, NY 10011 (☎ **800/929-2268;** Web site: www.outandabout.com), has been hailed for its "straight" reporting about gay travel. It profiles the best gay or gay-friendly hotels, restaurants, clubs, and other places, with coverage of destinations throughout the world. It costs $49 a year for 10 information-packed issues. *Out and About* aims for the more upscale gay or lesbian traveler and has been praised by everybody from *Travel and Leisure* to the *New York Times.* Both these publications are also available at most gay and lesbian bookstores.

ORGANIZATIONS   The **International Gay Travel Association (IGTA),** P.O. Box 4974, Key West, FL 33041 (☎ **800/448-8550** for a voice mailbox, or 305/292-0217), encourages gay and lesbian travel worldwide. With around 1,200 member agencies, it offers quarterly newsletters, marketing mailings, and a membership directory that is updated four times a year. Travel agents who are IGTA members will be tied into this organization's vast information resources, or you can E-mail them at IGTA@aol.com or visit their Web site at www.rainbow-mall.com./igta.

TRAVEL AGENCIES   In California a few leading gay-friendly options for travel arrangements are **Now Voyager,** 4406 18th St., San Francisco, CA 94114 (☎ **800/255-6951** or 415/626-1169), and **Gunderson Travel Inc.,** 8543 Santa Monica Blvd., Suite 8, West Los Angeles, CA 90069 (☎ **800/899-1944** or 800/872-8457 in the U.S., or 310/657-3944); E-mail them at **gunderson-travel@compuserve.com**.

Also in California, **Skylink Women's Travel,** 3577 Moorland Ave., Santa Rosa, CA 95407 (☎ **800/225-5759** or 310/452-0506), and **Thanks Babs!** (☎ **888/WOW-BABS**), can help custom-design your visit to the area.

FOR WOMEN

Women's services are often lumped together in the lesbian category, but there are resources geared toward women without regard to sexuality. The **Bay Area Women's and Children's Center,** 318 Leavenworth St. (☎ **415/474-2400**), offers specialized services and city information to women. The **Women's Building,** 3543 18th St. (☎ **415/431-1180**), is a Mission-area space housing feminist art shows and political events and offering classes in yoga, aerobics, movement, and tai chi chuan. The **Rape Crisis Hotline** (☎ 415/647-7273) is staffed 24 hours daily.

FOR SENIORS

Seniors regularly receive discounts at museums and attractions and on public transportation; such discounts, when available, are listed in this guide, under their appropriate headings. Ask for discounts everywhere—at hotels, movie theaters, museums, restaurants, and attractions. You may be surprised how often you'll be offered reduced rates. When making airline reservations, ask about a seniors' discount, but find out if there is a cheaper promotional fare before committing yourself.

The **Senior Citizen Information Line** (☎ 415/626-1033) offers advice, referrals, and information on city services. The **Friendship Line for the Elderly** (☎ 415/752-3778) is a support, referral, and crisis-intervention service.

FOR FAMILIES

San Francisco is full of sightseeing opportunities and special activities geared toward children. See "Especially for Kids," in chapter 7, "What to See & Do in San Francisco," for information and ideas for families. *Frommer's San Francisco with Kids* is a comprehensive guide geared specifically toward families; it is available at bookstores.

5 Getting There

BY PLANE

THE MAJOR AIRLINES   San Francisco is serviced by the following major domestic airlines: **American Airlines,** 433 California St. (☎ **800/433-7300**); **Delta Airlines,** 433 California St. and 124 Geary St. (☎ **800/221-1212**); **Northwest Airlines,** 124 Geary St. and 433 California St. (☎ **800/225-2525**); **Southwest Airlines,** at the airport (☎ **800/I-FLY-SWA**); **TWA,** 595 Market St., Suite 2240, at the corner of Second Street (☎ **800/221-2000**); **United Airlines,** 433 California St., 124 Geary, and Embarcadero One (☎ **800/241-6522**); and **US Airways,** 433 California St. (☎ **800/428-4322**).

FINDING THE BEST AIRFARE   Check your newspaper and call the airlines, asking for the lowest promotional or special fare available. Note, though, that the lowest-priced fares will often be nonrefundable, require advance purchase of 1 to 3 weeks and a certain length of stay, and carry penalties for changing dates of travel.

If you can be flexible, ask if you can secure a cheaper fare by staying an extra day or by flying midweek. Many airlines won't volunteer this information. At the time of this writing, the lowest round-trip fare on one airline from New York was $315, but you had to purchase 14 days in advance, stay at least 1 Saturday night in San Francisco, and travel during certain hours. Otherwise the price was $465. From Chicago, the trip cost $318. From Los Angeles, fares ranged from $96 round-trip (21 days advance purchase) to $400 (7 days advance purchase). Of course, fares change radically depending on the time of year and whether there's a sale going on. In business class, expect to pay about $1,355 one way from New York and $1,226 from Chicago. First class costs about $1,465 one way from New York and $1,322 from Chicago.

Don't overlook a **consolidator,** or "bucket shop," when hunting for low domestic fares. By negotiating directly with the airlines, the "buckets" can sell discounted tickets but they will also carry restrictions and penalties for changes or cancellation.

The lowest-priced bucket shops are usually local operations with low profiles and overheads. Look for their advertisements in the travel section or the classifieds of your local newspaper. Nationally advertised businesses are usually not as competitive as the smaller operations, but they have toll-free telephone numbers and are easily accessible.

Discounted fares have pared the number of charters, but they are still available. Most charter operators advertise and sell their seats through travel agents, thus making these local professionals your best source of information for available flights. Before deciding to take a charter flight, check the restrictions on the ticket: You may be asked to purchase a tour package, to pay in advance, to be amenable if the day of departure is changed, to pay a service charge, to fly on an airline you're not familiar with (this usually is not the case), and to pay harsh penalties if you cancel but be understanding if the charter doesn't fill up and is canceled up to 10 days before departure. Summer charters fill up more quickly than others and are almost sure to fly, but if you decide on a charter flight, seriously consider cancellation and baggage insurance.

Courier flights are primarily long-haul jobs and are usually not available on domestic flights. Companies that hire couriers use your luggage allowance for their business baggage; in return, you get a deeply discounted ticket. Flights are often offered at the last minute, and you may have to arrange a pretrip interview to make sure you're right for the job. **Now Voyager,** open Monday to Friday from 10am to 5:30pm and Saturday from noon to 4:30pm (☎ **212/431-1616**), flies from New York and sometimes has flights to San Francisco for as little as $199 round-trip. Now Voyager also offers noncourier discounted fares, so call the company even if you don't want to fly as a courier.

THE MAJOR AIRPORTS   Two major airports serve the Bay Area: San Francisco International and Oakland International.

San Francisco International Airport   San Francisco International Airport, located 14 miles south of downtown directly on U.S. 101, is served by almost four dozen major scheduled carriers. Travel time to downtown during commuter rush hours is about 40 minutes; at other times it's about 20 to 25 minutes.

The airport offers a toll-free **hot line** available weekdays from 7:30am to 5pm (PST) for information on ground transportation (☎ **800/736-2008**). During operating hours the line is answered weekdays by a real person who will provide you with a rundown of all your options for getting into the city from the airport. Each of the three main terminals also has a desk where you can get the same information.

A cab from the airport to downtown will cost $28 to $32, plus tip.

SFO Airporter buses (☎ **415/495-8404**) depart from outside the lower-level baggage-claim area to downtown San Francisco every 15 to 30 minutes from 6:15am to midnight (picking up at hotels as early as 5am). They stop at several Union Square–area hotels, including the Grand Hyatt, San Francisco Hilton, San Francisco Marriott, Westin St. Francis, Parc Fifty-Five, Hyatt Regency, and Sheraton Palace. No reservations are needed. The cost is $10 each way, and children under 2 ride for free.

Other private shuttle companies offer door-to-door airport service, in which you share a van with a few other passengers. **SuperShuttle** (☎ **415/558-8500**) will take you anywhere in the city, charging $10 per person to a hotel; $12 to a residence or business, plus $8 for each additional person; and $40 to charter an entire van for up to seven passengers. **Yellow Airport Shuttle** (☎ **415/282-7433**) charges $10 per person. Each shuttle stops every 20 minutes or so and picks up passengers from the marked areas outside the terminals' upper level. Reservations are required for the return trip to the airport only and should be made 1 day before departure. Keep in mind that these shuttles demand they pick you up 2 hours before your flight, 3 hours during holidays.

The San Mateo County Transit system, **SamTrans** (☎ **800/660-4287** within northern California, or 650/508-6200) runs two buses between the airport and the Transbay Terminal at First and Mission streets. The 7B bus costs $1 and makes the trip in about 55 minutes. The 7F bus costs $2 and takes only 35 minutes but permits only one carry-on bag. Both buses run daily, every half hour from about 5:30am to 7pm, then hourly until about midnight.

Oakland International Airport   Located about 5 miles south of downtown Oakland, at the Hagenberger Road exit of Calif. 17 (U.S. 880), **Oakland International Airport** (☎ **510/577-4000**) is used primarily by passengers with East Bay destinations. Some San Franciscans, however, prefer this less-crowded, accessible airport when flying during busy periods.

Again, taxis from the airport to downtown San Francisco are expensive, costing approximately $45, plus tip.

Bayporter Express (☎ **415/467-1800**) is a shuttle service that charges $20 for the first person, $10 each additional to downtown San Francisco (it costs more to outer areas of town). **Easy Way Out** (☎ **510/430-9090**) is another option, which charges $20 per person, $10 each additional rider. Both accept advance reservations. To the right of the airport exit there are usually shuttles that will take you to the city for around $20 per person. Keep in mind that they are independently owned and prices vary.

The cheapest way to downtown San Francisco is to take the shuttle bus from the airport to **BART** (Bay Area Rapid Transit; ☎ **510/464-6000**). The AirBART shuttle bus runs about every 15 minutes Monday to Saturday from 6am to 11:30pm and Sunday from 8:30am to 11:30pm, stopping in front of Terminals 1 and 2 near the ground transportation signs. The cost is $2 for the 10-minute ride to BART's Coliseum terminal. BART fares vary, depending on your destination; the trip to downtown San Francisco costs $2.45 and takes 20 minutes once onboard. The entire excursion should take around 45 minutes.

RENTING A CAR   All the major companies operate in the city and have desks at the airports. Call their toll-free numbers before leaving home, and shop around for the best price. When we last checked, a compact car could be secured for a week for about $190, including all taxes and other charges, but prices change dramatically on a daily basis, as well as depending on which company you rent from.

Most rental firms pad their profits by selling an additional loss/damage waiver (LDW), which can cost an extra $19 or more per day. Before agreeing to this, check with your insurance carrier and credit-card company. Many people don't realize that they are already covered by either one or both. If you're not, the LDW is a wise investment.

A minimum-age requirement—usually 25—is set by most car-rental agencies. Some also have a maximum-age limit. If you're concerned that these limits may affect you, ask about rental requirements at the time of booking to avoid problems later.

Some of the national car-rental companies operating in San Francisco include: **Alamo** (☎ 800/327-9633), **Avis** (☎ 800/331-1212), **Budget** (☎ 800/527-0700), **Dollar** (☎ 800/800-4000), **Hertz** (☎ 800/654-3131), **National** (☎ 800/227-7368), and **Thrifty** (☎ 800/367-2277).

In addition to the big chains, there are dozens of regional rental places in San Francisco, many of which offer lower rates. These include **A-One Rent-A-Car,** 434 O'Farrell St. (☎ 415/771-3977) and **Bay Area Rentals,** 229 Seventh St. (☎ 415/621-8989).

BY TRAIN

Traveling by train takes a long time and usually costs as much as, or more than, flying, but if you want to take a leisurely ride across America, rail may be a good option.

San Francisco–bound **Amtrak** (☎ 800/872-7245 or 800/USA-RAIL) trains leave from New York and cross the country via Chicago. The journey takes about 3½ days, and seats sell quickly. At this writing, the lowest round-trip fare would cost anywhere from $318 to $570 from New York and from $246 to $446 from Chicago. These heavily restricted tickets are good for 45 to 180 days and allow up to three stops along the way, depending on your ticket.

Round-trip tickets from Los Angeles can be purchased for as little as $92 or as much as $154. Trains actually arrive in Emeryville, just north of Oakland, and connect with regularly scheduled buses to San Francisco's Ferry Building and CalTrain station in downtown San Francisco.

CalTrain (☎ 800/660-4287 or 415/546-4461) operates train services between San Francisco and the towns of the peninsula. The city depot is at 700 Fourth St., at Townsend Street.

BY BUS

Bus travel is an inexpensive and often flexible option. **Greyhound/Trailways** (☎ 800/231-2222) operates to San Francisco from anywhere and offers several money-saving multiday bus passes. Round-trip fares vary, depending on your point of origin, but few, if any, ever exceed $300. The main San Francisco bus station is the **Transbay Terminal,** 425 Mission St. at First Street. For information call ☎ 800/231-2222.

BY CAR

San Francisco is easily accessed by major highways: Interstate 5, from the north, and U.S. 101, which cuts south-north through the peninsula from San Jose and across the Golden Gate Bridge to points north. If you drive from Los Angeles, you can either take the longer coastal route (437 miles and 11 hr.) or the inland route (389 miles and 8 hr.). From Mendocino, it's 156 miles and 4 hours; from Sacramento it's 88 miles and 1½ hours; and from Yosemite it's 210 miles and 4 hours.

If you are driving and aren't already a member, then it's worth joining the **American Automobile Association (AAA)** (☎ 800/922-8228), which charges $40 to $60 per year (with an additional one-time joining fee), depending on where you join, and provides roadside and other services to motorists. **Amoco Motor Club** (☎ 800/334-3300) is another recommended choice.

PACKAGES & TOURS

Tours and packages combining transportation, hotel accommodations, meals, and sightseeing are sometimes available to San Francisco. Sometimes it's worth signing onto a tour package just to secure the savings that operators can achieve by buying travel services in bulk. Often you'll pay much less than if you had organized the same trip independently, and you can always opt out of the preplanned activities. To find out what tours and packages are available to you, check the ads in the travel section of your newspaper or visit your travel agent.

For Foreign Visitors   3

The pervasiveness of American culture around the world may make you feel that you know the USA pretty well, but leaving your own country for the States still requires an additional degree of planning. This chapter will help prepare you for the more common problems (expected and unexpected) that you may encounter during your trip to San Francisco.

1 Preparing for Your Trip

ENTRY REQUIREMENTS

Immigration laws are a hot political issue in the United States these days, and the following requirements may have changed somewhat by the time you plan your trip. Check at any U.S. embassy or consulate for current information and requirements.

DOCUMENT REGULATIONS

The U.S. State Department has a **Visa Waiver Pilot Program** allowing citizens of certain countries to enter the United States without a visa for stays of up to 90 days. At press time these included Andorra, Austria, Belgium, Brunei, Denmark, Finland, France, Germany, Iceland, Ireland, Italy, Japan, Liechtenstein, Luxembourg, Monaco, the Netherlands, New Zealand, Norway, San Marino, Spain, Sweden, Switzerland, and the United Kingdom. Citizens of these countries need only a valid passport and a round-trip air or cruise ticket in their possession upon arrival. If they first enter the United States, they may then visit Mexico, Canada, Bermuda, and/or the Caribbean islands and return to the United States without needing a visa. Further information is available from any U.S. embassy or consulate. Canadian citizens may enter the United States without visas; they need only proof of residence.

Citizens of all other countries, including Australia, must have (1) a valid **passport** with an expiration date at least 6 months later than the scheduled end of their visit to the United States; and (2) a **tourist visa,** which may be obtained without charge from the nearest U.S. consulate.

To obtain a visa, the traveler must submit a completed application form (either in person or by mail) with a 1½ -inch-square photo, and must demonstrate binding ties to a residence abroad. Usually you can obtain a visa at once or within 24 hours, but it may

---

Travel Tip ————————————————————————————————

Any questions you have about U.S. immigration policies or laws can be answered by calling the **Immigration Office** at the San Francisco International Airport (☎ 650/876-2876). Otherwise, call San Francisco's **INS Ask Immigration System** (☎ 415/705-4411).

---

take longer during the summer rush from June through August. If you cannot go in person, contact the nearest U.S. embassy or consulate for directions on applying by mail. Your travel agent or airline office may also be able to provide you with visa applications and instructions. The U.S. consulate or embassy that issues your visa will determine whether you will be issued a multiple- or single-entry visa and any restrictions regarding the length of your stay.

British subjects can obtain up-to-date passport and visa information by calling the **U.S. Embassy Visa Information Line** (☎ 0891/200-290) or the **London Passport Office** (☎ 0990/210-410 for recorded information).

Foreign driver's licenses are recognized in San Francisco, although you may want to get an international driver's license if your home license is not written in English.

MEDICAL REQUIREMENTS

Unless you're arriving from an area known to be suffering from an epidemic (particularly cholera or yellow fever), no inoculations or vaccinations are required to enter the United States. If you have a disease requiring treatment with medications containing narcotics or drugs requiring a syringe, carry a valid signed prescription from your physician to allay any suspicions that you may be smuggling drugs.

For HIV-positive visitors, requirements for entering the United States are somewhat vague and change frequently. According to the latest publication of *HIV and Immigrants: A Manual for AIDS Service Providers,* "although INS doesn't require a medical exam for every one trying to come into the United States, INS officials may keep out people who they suspect are HIV positive. INS may stop people because they look sick or because they are carrying AIDS/HIV medicine. For this reason, visitors (non-immigrants) should try not to carry their HIV medicine or literature about AIDS in their luggage when they come into the United States.

If an HIV-positive noncitizen applying for a non-immigrant visa knows that HIV is a communicable disease of public health significance but checks 'no' on the question about communicable diseases, INS may deny the visa because it thinks the applicant committed fraud. If a non-immigrant visa applicant checks 'yes,' or if INS suspects the person is HIV positive, it will deny the visa unless the applicant asks for a special waiver for visitors. This waiver is for people visiting the United States for a short time, such as to attend a conference, to visit close relatives, or to receive medical treatment." For more information concerning HIV-positive travelers, contact an AIDS center in your area, or call the Bar Association of San Francisco **Immigration Project** at ☎ 415/477-2390.

CUSTOMS REQUIREMENTS

Every visitor over 21 years of age may bring in, free of duty, the following: (1) 1 liter of wine or hard liquor; (2) 200 cigarettes, 100 cigars (but not from Cuba), or 3 pounds of smoking tobacco; and (3) $100 worth of gifts. These exemptions are offered to travelers who spend at least 72 hours in the United States and who have not claimed them within the preceding 6 months. It is altogether forbidden to bring into the country foodstuffs (particularly fruit, cooked meats, and canned goods) and plants (vegetables, seeds, tropical plants, and the like). Foreign tourists may bring in or take out up to $10,000 in U.S. or foreign currency with no formalities; larger sums must be declared to U.S. Customs on entering or leaving, which includes filing form CM 4790. For more specific information regarding U.S. Customs, call your nearest U.S. embassy or consulate, or the U.S. Customs office at the San Francisco **International Airport** at ☎ **650/876-2816.**

INSURANCE

Although it's not required of travelers, health insurance is highly recommended. Unlike many European countries, the United States does not usually offer free or low-cost medical care to its citizens or visitors. Doctors and hospitals are expensive, and in most cases will require advance payment or proof of coverage before they render their services. Policies can cover everything from the loss or theft of your baggage and trip cancellation to the guarantee of bail in case you're arrested. Good policies will also cover costs of an accident, repatriation, or death. Such packages are sold by automobile clubs, as well as by insurance companies and travel agents.

Though lack of health insurance may prevent you from being admitted to a hospital in nonemergencies, don't worry about being left on a street corner to die: The American way is to fix you now and bill the living daylights out of you later.

FOR BRITISH TRAVELERS   Most big travel agents offer their own insurance, and will probably try to sell you their package when you book a holiday. Think before you sign. Britain's Consumers' Association recommends that you insist on seeing the policy and reading the fine print before buying travel insurance. **The Association of British Insurers** (☎ **0171/600-3333**) gives advice by phone and publishes the free *Holiday Insurance,* a guide to policy provisions and prices. You might also shop around for better deals: Try **Columbus Travel Insurance Ltd.** (☎ **0171/375-0011**) or, for students, **Campus Travel** (☎ **0171/730-2101**).

MONEY
CURRENCY

The U.S. monetary system is painfully simple: The most common bills (all ugly, all green) are the $1 (colloquially, a "buck"), $5, $10, and $20 denominations. There are also $2 bills (seldom encountered), $50 bills, and $100 bills (the last two are usually not welcome when paying for small purchases). Note that a newly redesigned $100 bill was introduced in mid-1996. Despite rumors to the contrary, the old-style bill is still legal tender.

There are six denominations of coins: 1¢ (1 cent, or a penny); 5¢ (5 cents, or a nickel); 10¢ (10 cents, or a dime); 25¢ (25 cents, or a quarter); 50¢ (50 cents, or a half dollar); and, prized by collectors, the rare $1 piece (the older, large silver dollar and the newer, small Susan B. Anthony coin).

Note: The "foreign-exchange bureaus" so common in Europe are rare even at airports in the United States, and nonexistent outside major cities. It's best not to change foreign money (or traveler's checks denominated in a currency other than U.S. dollars) at a small-town bank, or even a branch in a big city; in fact, leave any currency other than U.S. dollars at home—it may prove a greater nuisance to you than it's worth.

TRAVELER'S CHECKS

Though traveler's checks are widely accepted, make sure that they're denominated in U.S. dollars, as foreign-currency checks are often difficult to exchange. The three most widely recognized traveler's checks—and least likely to be denied—are Visa, American Express, and Thomas Cook. Be sure to record the numbers of the checks, and keep that information separately should they get lost or stolen. San Francisco businesses are pretty good about taking traveler's checks, but you're better off cashing them in at a bank (in small amounts, of course) and paying in cash. *Remember:* You'll need identification, such as a driver's license or passport, to change a traveler's check.

CREDIT CARDS & ATMS

Most major credit cards are accepted at San Francisco's larger hotels, and Visa and MasterCard are accepted just about everywhere else. There are, however, a handful of stores and restaurants that do not take credit cards, so be sure to ask in advance. Most businesses display a sticker near their entrance to let you know which cards they accept. (*Note:* Often businesses require a minimum purchase price, usually around $10, to use a credit card.)

It is strongly recommended that you bring at least one major credit card. Hotels, car-rental companies, and airlines usually require a credit-card imprint as a deposit against expenses, and in an emergency a credit card can be priceless.

In downtown San Francisco there's an automated teller machine (ATM) on just about every block. Most accept Visa, MasterCard, and American Express, as well as ATM cards from other U.S. banks. Expect to be charged up to $3 per transaction if you're not using your own bank's ATM. *Tip:* The way around this is to ask for cash back at stores (e.g., Safeway) that accept ATM cards and don't charge usage fees. Of course, you'll have to purchase something first.

SAFETY
GENERAL SAFETY TIPS

While most San Francisco tourist areas are generally safe, there are a few neighborhoods you should leave out of your itinerary, such as the Tenderloin and Hunter's Point areas.

Avoid deserted areas, especially at night, and don't go into any of the parks at night unless there's a concert or similar occasion that attracts crowds.

Avoid carrying valuables with you on the street, and don't display expensive cameras or electronic equipment. Hold onto your pocketbook, and place your billfold in an inside pocket. In theaters, restaurants, and other public places, keep your possessions in sight.

Remember also that hotels are open to the public, and in a large hotel, security may not be able to screen everyone entering. Always lock your room door—don't assume that once inside your hotel you are automatically safe and no longer need to be aware of your surroundings.

See "Fast Facts: San Francisco" in chapter 4 for more city-specific safety tips.

DRIVING SAFETY

Driving safety is important too, especially given the highly publicized carjackings of foreign tourists in Florida. Question your rental agency about personal safety and ask for a traveler-safety-tips brochure when you pick up your car. Obtain written directions—or a map with the route clearly marked—from the agency showing how to get to your destination. And, if possible, arrive and depart during daylight hours.

Recently, more and more crime has involved cars and drivers. If you drive off a highway into a doubtful neighborhood, leave the area as quickly as possible. If you have an accident, even on the highway, stay in your car with the doors locked until

Travel Tip

Be sure to keep a copy of all your travel papers separate from your wallet or purse, and leave a copy with someone at home should you need it faxed in an emergency.

you assess the situation or until the police arrive. If you're bumped from behind on the street or are involved in a minor accident with no injuries and the situation appears to be suspicious, motion to the other driver to follow you. *Never* get out of your car in such situations. You can also keep a premade sign in your car that reads: PLEASE FOLLOW THIS VEHICLE TO REPORT THE ACCIDENT. Show the sign to the other driver and go directly to the nearest police precinct, well-lit service station, or 24-hour store.

Always try to park in well-lit and well-traveled areas if possible. If you leave your rental car unlocked and empty of your valuables, you're probably safer than locking your car with valuables in plain view. Never leave any packages or valuables in sight. If someone attempts to rob you or steal your car, don't try to resist the thief/carjacker—report the incident to the police department immediately.

2 Getting to the U.S.

Traveling overseas on a budget is something of an oxymoron, but there are ways to knock down the price of a plane ticket by several hundred dollars if you take the time to shop around. For example, travelers from overseas can take advantage of the APEX (Advance Purchase Excursion) reduced fares offered by all major U.S. and European carriers. For more money-saving airline advice, see "Getting There," in chapter 2.

In addition to the domestic American airlines listed under "Getting There" in chapter 2, several international carriers also service the Bay Area airports, including (with their domestic toll-free phone numbers): **Aer Lingus** (☎ 800/223-6537), **Air Canada** (☎ 800/776-3000), **British Airways** (☎ 800/247-9297), **Japan Airlines** (☎ 800/525-3663), **Qantas** (☎ 800/227-4500), **Scandinavian Airline System (SAS)** (☎ 800/221-2350), and **Virgin Atlantic** (☎ 800/862-8621). For the best rates, compare fares and be flexible with the dates and times of travel.

Visitors arriving by air, no matter what the port of entry, should cultivate patience and resignation before setting foot on U.S. soil. Getting through immigration control may take as long as 2 hours on some days, especially on summer weekends, so be sure to have this guidebook or something else to read. Add the time it takes to clear Customs, and you'll see that you should make a very generous allowance for delay in planning connections between international and domestic flights—figure on 2 to 3 hours at least.

In contrast, for the traveler arriving by car or rail from Canada, the border-crossing formalities have been streamlined to the vanishing point. And for the traveler by air from Canada, Bermuda, and some places in the Caribbean, you can sometimes go through Customs and Immigration at the point of departure, which is much quicker.

FROM THE UNITED KINGDOM & IRELAND　Many airlines offer service from the United Kingdom or Ireland to the United States. If they do not have direct flights from London to San Francisco, they can book you straight through on a connecting flight. You can make reservations by calling the following numbers in London: **American Airlines** (☎ 0181/572-5555), **British Airways** (☎ 0345/222-111), **Continental Airlines** (☎ 0293/776-464), **Delta Airlines** (☎ 0800/414-767), **United Airlines** (☎ 0181/990-9900), and **Virgin Atlantic** (☎ 01293/747-747).

Residents of Ireland can call **Aer Lingus** (☎ **01/844-4747** in Dublin, or 061/415-556 in Shannon).

If possible, try to book a direct flight. Airlines that offer direct flights from London include British Airways, United, and Virgin. See also "Getting There," in chapter 2, for information on alternative low-cost air travel.

FROM AUSTRALIA & NEW ZEALAND   Qantas (☎ **008/177-767** in Australia) has direct flights from Sydney to San Francisco. You can also take **United** (☎ **02/237-8888** in Sydney, 008/230-322 in the rest of Australia) from Australia to San Francisco.

Air New Zealand (☎ **0800/737-000** in Auckland or 643/379-5200 in Christchurch) offers service to Los Angeles International Airport.

FROM CANADA   Canadian readers might also consider **Air Canada** (☎ **800/268-7240** or 800/361-8620 in Canada), which offers direct service from Toronto, Montréal, Calgary, and Vancouver to San Francisco. Many American carriers also serve similar routes.

3 Getting Around the U.S.

BY PLANE   Some large airlines (for example, Northwest and Delta) offer travelers on their transatlantic or transpacific flights special discount tickets under the name Visit USA, allowing travel between any U.S. destinations at minimum rates. These discount tickets are not on sale in the United States and must be purchased abroad in conjunction with your international ticket. This system is the best, easiest, and fastest way to see the United States at low cost. You should obtain information well in advance from your travel agent or the office of the airline concerned, since the conditions attached to these discount tickets can be changed without advance notice.

BY TRAIN   International visitors can also buy a **USA Railpass,** good for 15 or 30 days of unlimited travel on Amtrak (☎ **800/USA-RAIL**). The pass is available through many foreign travel agents. Prices in 1998 for a 15-day pass were $300 off-peak, $400 peak; a 30-day pass costs $450 off-peak, $645 peak. (With a foreign passport, you can also buy passes at some Amtrak offices in the United States, including locations in San Francisco, Los Angeles, Chicago, New York, Miami, Boston, and Washington, D.C.) Reservations are generally required and should be made for each part of your trip as early as possible.

BY BUS   Although ticket prices for short hops between cities are often the most economical form of public transit, bus travel in the United States can be both slow and uncomfortable, so this option isn't for everyone (particularly when Amtrak, which is far more luxurious, offers similar rates). **Greyhound/Trailways** (☎ **800/231-2222**), the sole nationwide bus line, offers an **Ameripass** for unlimited travel for 7 days at $179, 15 days at $289, 30 days at $399, and 60 days at $599. Passes must be purchased at a Greyhound terminal.

BY CAR   The most cost-effective, convenient, and comfortable way to travel around the United States—especially California—is by car. The Interstate highway system connects cities and towns all over the country; in addition to these high-speed, limited-access roadways, there's an extensive network of federal, state, and local highways and roads. Some of the national car-rental companies that have offices in San Francisco include **Alamo** (☎ 800/327-9633), **Avis** (☎ 800/331-1212), **Budget** (☎ 800/527-0700), **Dollar** (☎ 800/800-4000), **Hertz** (☎ 800/654-3131), **National** (☎ 800/227-7368), and **Thrifty** (☎ 800/367-2277).

If you plan on renting a car in the United States, you probably won't need the services of an additional automobile organization. If you're planning to buy or borrow a car, automobile-association membership is recommended. The **American Automobile Association (AAA),** 150 Van Ness Ave., San Francisco, CA 94102 (☎ **800/922-8228**), is the country's largest auto club and supplies its members with maps, insurance, and, most important, emergency road service. The cost of joining runs from $63 for singles to $87 for families, but if you're a member of a foreign auto club with reciprocal arrangements, you can enjoy free AAA service in America. See "Getting There" in chapter 2 for more information.

FAST FACTS: For the Foreign Traveler

Business Hours   See "Fast Facts: San Francisco," in chapter 4.

Climate   See "When to Go," in chapter 2.

Currency & Exchange   Foreign-exchange bureaus are rare in the United States, and most banks are not equipped to handle currency exchange. San Francisco's money-changing offices include the following: **Bank of America**, 345 Montgomery St. (☎ **415/622-2451**), open Monday to Friday from 9am to 6pm; and **Thomas Cook,** 75 Geary St. (☎ **415/362-3452**), open Monday to Friday from 9am to 5pm and on Saturday from 10am to 4pm.

Drinking Laws   The legal age for purchase and consumption of alcoholic beverages is 21; proof of age is required and often requested at bars, nightclubs, and restaurants, so it's always a good idea to bring ID when you go out. In San Francisco, liquor is sold in supermarkets and grocery and liquor stores daily from 6am to 2am. Licensed restaurants are permitted to sell alcohol during the same hours. Note that many eateries are licensed only for beer and wine.

A big no-no is having an open container of alcohol in your car or any public area that isn't zoned for alcohol consumption. The police can, and probably will, fine you on the spot. And nothing will ruin your trip faster than getting a citation for DUI ("driving under the influence"), so don't even think about driving while intoxicated.

Electricity   U.S. wall outlets give power at 110 to 115 volts, 60 cycles, compared with 220 volts, 50 cycles in most of Europe. In addition to a 100-volt transformer, small foreign appliances, such as hair dryers and shavers, will require a plug adapter (available at most hardware stores) with two flat, parallel pins.

Embassies & Consulates   All embassies are located in the nation's capital, Washington, D.C. In addition, several of the major English-speaking countries also have consulates in San Francisco or in Los Angeles.

The embassy of **Australia** is at 1601 Massachusetts Ave. NW, Washington, DC 20036 (☎ **202/797-3000**); a consulate-general is at 1 Bush St., Suite 700, San Francisco, CA 94104 (☎ **415/362-6160**). The embassy of **Canada** is at 501 Pennsylvania Ave. NW, Washington, DC 20001 (☎ **202/682-1740**); the nearest consulate is at 300 S. Grand Ave., 10th Floor, California Plaza, Los

Angeles, CA 90071 (☎ 213/346-2700). The embassy of the **Republic of Ireland** is at 2234 Massachusetts Ave. NW, Washington, DC 20008 (☎ **202/ 462-3939**); a consulate is at 44 Montgomery St., Suite 3830, San Francisco, CA 94104 (☎ **415/392-4214**). The embassy of **New Zealand** is at 37 Observatory Circle NW, Washington, DC 20008 (☎ **202/328-4800**); the nearest consulate is at 12400 Wilshire Blvd., Suite 1150, Los Angeles, CA 90025 (☎ **310/ 207-1605**). The embassy of the **United Kingdom** is at 3100 Massachusetts Ave. NW, Washington, DC 20008 (☎ **202/462-1340**); the nearest consulate is at 1 Sansome St., Suite 850, San Francisco, CA 94104 (☎ **415/981-3030**). The embassy of **Japan** is at 2520 Massachusetts Ave. NW, Washington, DC 20008 (☎ **202/939-6700**); the consulate-general of Japan is located at 50 Fremont St., San Francisco, CA 94105 (☎ **415/777-3533**).

If you are from another country, you can get the telephone number of your embassy by calling "Information" (directory assistance) in Washington, D.C. (☎ **202/555-1212**).

Emergencies You can call the police, an ambulance, or the fire department through the single emergency telephone number ☎ **911** from any phone or pay phone (no coins needed). If that doesn't work, another useful way of reporting an emergency is to call the telephone company operator by dialing 0 (zero, not the letter O).

Gasoline (Petrol) Prices vary, but expect to pay anywhere between $1.35 and $1.65 for 1 U.S. gallon (about 3.8 liters) of "regular" unleaded gasoline (petrol). Higher-octane fuels are also available at most gas stations for slightly higher prices. Taxes are already included in the printed price.

Holidays On the following legal national holidays, banks, government offices, post offices, and many stores, restaurants, and museums are closed: New Year's Day (Jan 1), Martin Luther King Jr. Day (third Mon in Jan), Presidents' Day (third Mon in Feb), Memorial Day (last Mon in May), Independence Day (July 4), Labor Day (first Mon in Sept), Columbus Day (second Mon in Oct), Veterans Day (Nov 11), Thanksgiving Day (last Thurs in Nov), and Christmas Day (Dec 25). Election Day, for national elections, falls on the Tuesday following the first Monday in November. It's a legal national holiday during a presidential election, which occurs every fourth year (next in 2000).

Mail If you want to receive mail, but aren't exactly sure where you'll be, have it sent to you, in your name, **[c/o] General Delivery (Poste Restante)** at the main post office of the city or region you're visiting (call ☎ **800/275-8777** for information on the nearest post office). The addressee must pick it up in person and produce proof of identity (driver's license, credit card, passport). Most post offices will hold your mail up to 1 month, and are open Monday to Saturday from 8am to 6pm.

Generally found at street intersections, mailboxes are blue and carry the inscription U.S. MAIL. If your mail is addressed to a U.S. destination, don't forget to add the five-digit zip code after the two-letter abbreviation of the state to which the mail is addressed (CA for California).

For overseas mail, **postal rates** are as follows: A first-class letter of up to one-half ounce costs 60¢ (46¢ to Canada and 40¢ to Mexico); a first-class postcard costs 50¢ (40¢ to Canada and 35¢ Mexico); and a preprinted postal aerogramme costs 50¢.

Medical Emergencies   To call an ambulance, dial ☎ **911** from any phone—no coins are needed. For hospitals and other emergency information, see "Fast Facts: San Francisco" in chapter 4.

Newspapers & Magazines   Many of San Francisco's newsstands offer a selection of foreign periodicals and newspapers, such as The Economist, Le Monde, and Der Spiegel. For information on local literature and specific newsstand locations, see "Fast Facts: San Francisco," in chapter 4.

Post Office   See "Mail," above.

Radio & Television   There are five national television networks that are broadcast over the air: ABC (Channel 7), CBS (Channel 5), NBC (Channel 4), PBS (Channel 9), and Fox (Channel 2). Cable television includes the national networks as well as 50 or so other cable stations, including the Cable News Network (CNN), ESPN (sports channel), and MTV. Most hotels offer a dozen cable stations to choose from, as well as pay-per-view movies. You'll also find a wide choice of local radio stations, each broadcasting particular kinds of talk shows and/or music—classical, country, jazz, rock, pop, gospel—punctuated by news broadcasts and frequent commercials.

Smoking   Heavy smokers are in for a tough time in San Francisco. There is no smoking allowed in public buildings, sports arenas, elevators, theaters, banks, lobbies, restaurants, offices, stores, bed-and-breakfasts, most small hotels, and bars. Yes, that's right, as of January 1, 1998, you can't even smoke in a bar in California, the only exception being a bar where drinks are served solely by the owner.

Taxes   In the United States there is no value-added tax (VAT) or other direct tax at a national level. Every state, as well as every city, is allowed to levy its own local sales tax on all purchases, including hotel and restaurant checks and airline tickets. Taxes are already included in the price of certain services, such as public transportation, cab fares, phone calls, and gasoline. The amount of sales tax varies from 4% to 10%, depending on the state and city, so when you are making major purchases, such as photographic equipment, clothing, or high-fidelity components, it can be a significant part of the cost.

In addition, many cities charge a separate "bed" or room tax on accommodations, above and beyond any sales tax.

For information on sales and room taxes in San Francisco, see "Fast Facts: San Francisco," in chapter 4.

Telephone & Fax   Pay phones can be found almost everywhere—at street corners, in bars and restaurants, and in hotels. Outside the metropolitan area, however, public telephones are more difficult to find; stores and gas stations are your best bet.

Phones do not accept pennies and few will take anything larger than a quarter. Some public phones, especially those in airports and large hotels, accept credit cards, such as MasterCard, Visa, and American Express. Credit cards are especially handy for international calls; instructions are printed on the phone.

In San Francisco, **local calls** cost 35¢. To make local calls, dial the seven-digit local number. For domestic long-distance calls or international calls, stock up with a supply of quarters; first dial the number, then a recorded voice will instruct you when and in what quantity you should put the coins into the slot. For **domestic long-distance calls,** first dial 1 (the long-distance access code), the area code, and the seven-digit local number. For **direct overseas calls,** dial 011 first (the international access code), then the country code (Australia, 61; Republic of Ireland, 353; New Zealand, 64; United Kingdom, 44), followed by the city code, and then the local number you wish to call. To place a call to Canada or the Caribbean, just dial 1, the area code, and the local number.

Before calling from a hotel room, always ask the hotel phone operator if there are any telephone surcharges. These can sometimes be reduced by calling collect or by using a telephone charge card. Hotel charges, which can be exorbitant, may be avoided altogether by using a pay phone in the lobby.

Note that almost all calls to phone numbers in area codes 800 and 888 are toll-free.

For **local directory assistance** ("information"), dial ☎ **411;** for **long-distance information** in the United States and Canada, dial 1, then the appropriate area code and **555-1212.**

For "collect" (reversed-charge) calls and for "person-to-person" calls, dial 0 (zero, not the letter O) followed by the area code and the number you want; an operator or recording will then come on the line, and you should specify that you are calling collect or person-to-person, or both. If your operator-assisted call is international, just dial 0 and wait for the operator.

Like the telephone system, **telegraph and telex** services are provided by private corporations, such as ITT, MCI, and above all, **Western Union.** You can bring your telegram to a Western Union office or dictate it over the phone (☎ **800/325-6000**). You can also telegraph money, or have it telegraphed to you, very quickly. In San Francisco, a Western Union office, located near the Civic Center, is at 61 Gough St., at Market Street (☎ **415/621-2031**). There are several other locations around town, too; call ☎ **800/325-6000** for the one nearest you.

You'll find **fax facilities** widely available. They can be found in most hotels and many other establishments. Try Mailboxes Etc. or any photocopying shop.

Telephone Directory There are two kinds of telephone directories in the United States. The general directory is the so-called White Pages, in which private and business subscribers are listed in alphabetical order. The inside front cover lists the emergency number for police, fire, and ambulance, and other vital numbers (like the Coast Guard, poison-control center, crime-victims hot line, and so on). The first few pages are devoted to community-service numbers, including a guide to long-distance and international calling, complete with country codes and area codes.

The second directory, printed on yellow paper (hence its name, **Yellow Pages**), lists all local services, businesses, and industries by type of activity, with an index at the back. The listings cover not only such obvious items as automobile repairs by make of car, or drugstores (pharmacies), often by geographical location, but also restaurants by type of cuisine and geographical location, bookstores by special subject and/or language, places of worship by religious denomination, and other information that the tourist might otherwise not readily find. The Yellow Pages also include city plans or detailed maps, often showing postal zip codes and public-transportation routes.

Time The United States is divided into four time zones (six, if Alaska and Hawaii are included). From east to west, these are eastern standard time (EST), central standard time (CST), mountain standard time (MST), and Pacific standard time (PST). There are also Alaska standard time (AST) and Hawaii standard time (HST). San Francisco is on Pacific standard time, which is 8 hours behind Greenwich mean time. Noon in New York City (EST) is 11am in Chicago (CST), 10am in Denver (MST), 9am in San Francisco (PST), 8am in Anchorage (AST), and 7am in Honolulu (HST).

Daylight-saving time is in effect from the first Sunday in April until 2am on the last Sunday in October, except in Arizona, Hawaii, part of Indiana, and Puerto Rico. Daylight saving time moves the clock 1 hour ahead of standard time.

Tipping   Service in America is some of the best in the world, and is rarely included in the price of anything. In fact, it's part of the American way of life to tip, on the principle that you must expect to pay for any service you get. Many personnel receive little direct salary and must depend on tips for their income. In fact, the U.S. federal government imposes income taxes on service personnel based on an estimate of how much they should have earned in tips relative to their employer's total receipts. In other words, they may have to pay taxes on a tip you didn't give them!

Here are some rules of thumb:

In **hotels,** tip bellhops at least $1 per piece of luggage ($2 to $3 if you have a lot of luggage) and tip the chamber staff $1 per day. Tip the doorman or concierge only if he or she has provided you with some specific service (for example, calling a cab for you or obtaining difficult-to-get theater tickets). Tip the valet parking attendant $1 every time you get your car.

In **restaurants, bars, and nightclubs,** tip service staff 15% to 20% of the check, tip bartenders 10% to 15%, tip checkroom attendants $1 per garment, and tip valet-parking attendants $1 per vehicle. Tip the doorman only if he has provided you with some specific service (such as calling a cab for you). Tipping is not expected in cafeterias and fast-food restaurants.

Tip **cab drivers 15%** of the fare.

As for **other service personnel,** tip skycaps at airports at least $1 per piece ($2 to $3 if you have a lot of luggage) and tip hairdressers and barbers 15% to 20%.

Tipping ushers at movies and theaters, and gas-station attendants, is not expected.

Toilets   Public toilets can be hard to find in San Francisco. There are only a handful of fancy new French stalls strategically placed on high-volume streets, and few small stores will allow you access to their facilities. You can almost always find a toilet in restaurants and bars; note, however, a growing practice in some restaurants and bars of displaying a notice that toilets are for the use of patrons only. You can ignore this sign, or better yet, avoid arguments by paying for a cup of coffee or soft drink, which will qualify you as a patron. Large hotels and fast-food restaurants are probably the best bet for good, clean facilities. Museums, department stores, shopping malls, and, in a pinch, gas stations, all have public toilets. If possible, avoid the toilets at parks and beaches, which are a real crap shoot (pun intended) when it comes to cleanliness.

4 Getting to Know San Francisco

Half the fun in becoming familiar with San Francisco is wandering around and haphazardly stumbling upon great shops, restaurants, and viewpoints that even locals may not know exist. But you'll find that although metropolitan, San Francisco is a small town, and you won't feel like a stranger for long. If you get disoriented, just remember that downtown is east, Golden Gate Bridge is north, and even if you do get lost, you probably won't go too far since three sides of the city are surrounded by water. The most difficult challenge you'll have, if traveling by car, is mastering the maze of one-way streets. This chapter offers useful information on how to become better acquainted with the city.

1 Orientation

VISITOR INFORMATION

Once in the city, visit the **San Francisco Visitor Information Center,** on the lower level of Hallidie Plaza, 900 Market St., at Powell Street (☎ **415/391-2000;** fax 415/362-7323), for information, brochures, discount coupons, and advice on restaurants, sights, and events in the city. They can provide answers in German, Japanese, French, Italian, and Spanish, as well as English, of course. To find the office, descend the escalator at the cable-car turn-around.

Dial ☎ **415/391-2001** anytime, day or night, for a recorded message about current cultural, theater, music, sports, and other special events. This information is also available in German, French, Japanese, and Spanish.

Keep in mind that this service supports only members of the Convention and Visitors Bureau and is very tourist-oriented. While there's tons of information here, it's not representative of all the city has to offer. The office is open Monday to Friday from 9am to 5:30pm, on Saturday from 9am to 3pm, and on Sunday from 10am to 2pm. It's closed on Thanksgiving Day, Christmas Day, and New Year's Day.

Pick up a copy of the *Bay Guardian.* The city's free alternative paper lists all city happenings—their kiosks are located throughout the city and in most coffee shops.

For specialized information on Chinatown's shops and services, and on the city's Chinese community in general, contact the

Chinese Chamber of Commerce, 730 Sacramento St., San Francisco, CA 94108 (☎ 415/982-3000), open daily from 9am to 5pm.

The **Visitors Information Center of the Redwood Empire Association,** in The Cannery, 2801 Leavenworth, 2nd Floor, San Francisco, CA 94133 (☎ 800/ 200-8334 or 415/543-8334; www.redwoodempire.com), offers informative brochures and a very knowledgeable desk staff who are able to plan tours both in San Francisco and north of the city. Their annual 48-page *Redwood Empire Visitors' Guide* ($3 by mail—check, cash, or money order—in the U.S.; $5 by mail internationally; free in person) offers information on everything from San Francisco hotels, walking tours, and museums to visit in northern California. The office is open Tuesday through Saturday from 10am to 6pm.

CITY LAYOUT

San Francisco occupies the tip of a 32-mile-long peninsula between San Francisco Bay and the Pacific Ocean. Its land area measures about 46 square miles. Twin Peaks, in the geographic center of the city, is more than 900 feet high.

San Francisco may seem confusing at first, but it quickly becomes easy to negotiate. The city's downtown streets are arranged in a simple grid pattern, with the exception of Market Street and Columbus Avenue, which cut across the grid at right angles to each other. Hills appear to distort this pattern, however, and can be disorienting. But as you learn your way around, these same hills will become your landmarks and reference points.

MAIN ARTERIES & STREETS   Market Street is San Francisco's main thoroughfare. Most of the city's buses travel this route on their way to the Financial District from the outer neighborhoods to the west and south. The tall office buildings clustered downtown are at the northeast end of Market; 1 block beyond lie the Embarcadero and the bay.

The **Embarcadero** curves along San Francisco Bay from south of the Bay Bridge to the northeast perimeter of the city and terminates at Fisherman's Wharf, the famous tourist-oriented pier. Aquatic Park, Fort Mason, and the Golden Gate National Recreation area are located farther on around the bay, occupying the northernmost point of the peninsula.

From the eastern perimeter of Fort Mason, **Van Ness Avenue** runs due south, back to Market Street. The area we have just described forms a rough triangle, with Market Street as its southeastern boundary, the waterfront as its northern boundary, and Van Ness Avenue as its western boundary. Within this triangle lie most of the city's main tourist sights.

FINDING AN ADDRESS   Since most of the city's streets are laid out in a grid pattern, finding an address is easy when you know the nearest cross street. When asking for directions, find out the nearest cross street and the neighborhood in which your destination is located, but be careful not to confuse numerical avenues with numerical streets. Numerical avenues (Third Avenue, etc.) are found in the Richmond and Sunset districts in the western part of the city. Numerical streets (Third Street, etc.) are south of Market in the east and south parts of town.

NEIGHBORHOODS & DISTRICTS IN BRIEF

Union Square   Union Square is the commercial hub of the city. Most major hotels and department stores are crammed into the area surrounding the actual square (named for a series of violent pro-union mass demonstrations staged here

San Francisco at a Glance

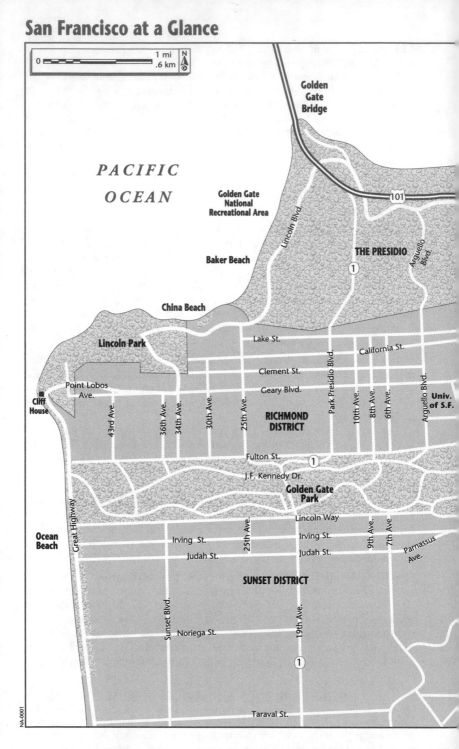

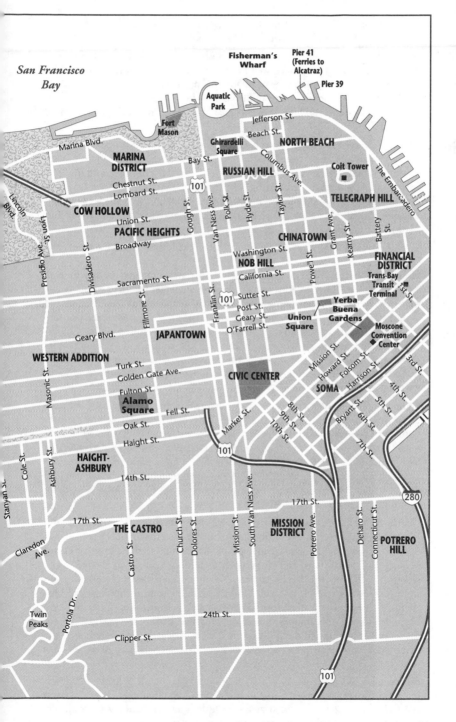

San Francisco
Bay

Fisherman's
Wharf

Pier 41
(Ferries to
Alcatraz)

Pier 39

Aquatic
Park

Fort
Mason

Marina Blvd.

Jefferson St.

Beach St.

Ghirardelli
Square

NORTH BEACH

MARINA
DISTRICT

Bay St.

RUSSIAN HILL

Columbus Ave.

Coit Tower

Chestnut St.

Lombard St.

101

Cough St.

Van Ness Ave.

Polk St.

Hyde St.

Taylor St.

TELEGRAPH HILL

The Embarcadero

COW HOLLOW

Union St.

PACIFIC HEIGHTS

Broadway

Presidio Ave.

Lyon St.

Divisadero St.

Fillmore St.

Washington St.

CHINATOWN

Grant Ave.

Kearny St.

Battery St.

Sacramento St.

NOB HILL

California St.

Powell St.

FINANCIAL
DISTRICT

Trans-Bay
Transit
Terminal

Franklin St.

101

Sutter St.

Post St.

Geary St.

O'Farrell St.

Union
Square

Yerba
Buena
Gardens

1st St.

Geary Blvd.

JAPANTOWN

Moscone
Convention
Center

Masonic St.

WESTERN ADDITION

Turk St.

Golden Gate Ave.

Fulton St.

Alamo
Square

Fell St.

CIVIC CENTER

Mission St.

Howard St.

Folsom St.

Harrison St.

SOMA

3rd St.

4th St.

5th St.

Oak St.

Haight St.

8th St.

9th St.

10th St.

Bryant St.

6th St.

7th St.

Stanyan St.

Cole St.

Ashbury St.

HAIGHT-
ASHBURY

14th St.

Market St.

101

280

Claredon
Ave.

17th St.

THE CASTRO

Castro St.

Church St.

Dolores St.

Mission St.

South Van Ness Ave.

17th St.

MISSION
DISTRICT

Potrero Ave.

Deharo St.

Connecticut St.

POTRERO
HILL

Twin
Peaks

Portola Dr.

24th St.

Clipper St.

101

on the eve of the Civil War), and there is a plethora of upscale boutiques, restaurants, and galleries tucked between the larger buildings.

Nob Hill/Russian Hill Bounded by Bush, Larkin, Pacific, and Stockton streets, Nob Hill is the genteel, well-heeled district of the city, still occupied by the major power brokers and the neighborhood businesses they frequent. Russian Hill extends from Pacific to Bay and from Polk to Mason. It is marked by steep streets, lush gardens, and high-rises occupied by both the moneyed and the more bohemian.

SoMa In recent years, high rents have forced residents and businesses into once desolate South of Market (dubbed "SoMa"). The area is still predominantly warehouses and industrial spaces, but now many of them are brimming with life. The area is officially demarcated by the Embarcadero, Highway 101, and Market Street, with the greatest concentrations of interest around Yerba Buena Center, along Folsom and Harrison streets between Steuart and Sixth, and Brannan and Market. Along the waterfront are an array of restaurants. Farther west, around Folsom between 7th and 11th streets, is where much of the city's nightclubbing occurs.

Financial District East of Union Square, this area bordered by the Embarcadero, Market, Third, Kearny, and Washington streets is the city's business district, and the stomping grounds for many major corporations. The pointy TransAmerica Pyramid, at Montgomery and Clay streets, is one of the district's most conspicuous architectural features. To its east stands the sprawling Embarcadero Center, an 8½-acre complex housing offices, shops, and restaurants. Farther east still is the World Trade Center, standing adjacent to the old Ferry Building, the city's pre-bridge transportation hub. Ferries to Sausalito and Larkspur still leave from this point.

Chinatown The official entrance to Chinatown is marked by a large red-and-green gate on Grant Avenue at Bush Street. Beyond lies a 24-block labyrinth, bordered by Broadway, Bush, Kearny, and Stockton streets, filled with restaurants, markets, temples, and shops—and, of course, a substantial percentage of San Francisco's Chinese residents. Chinatown is a great place for urban exploration all along Stockton, Grant, and Portsmouth Square, and the alleys that lead off them like Ross and Waverly. This area is jam-packed, so don't even *think* about driving here.

North Beach The Italian quarter, which stretches from Montgomery and Jackson to Bay Street, is one of the best places in the city to grab a coffee, pull up a cafe chair, and do some serious people-watching. Nightlife is equally happening; restaurants, bars, and clubs along Columbus and Grant avenues bring folks from all over the Bay Area here to fight for a parking place and romp through the festive neighborhood. Down Columbus toward the Financial District are the remains of the city's beat-generation landmarks, including Ferlinghetti's City Lights Bookstore and Vesuvio's Bar. Broadway—a short strip of sex joints—cuts through the heart of the district. Telegraph Hill looms over the east side of North Beach, topped by Coit Tower, one of San Francisco's best vantage points.

Fisherman's Wharf North Beach runs into Fisherman's Wharf, which was once the busy heart of the city's great harbor and waterfront industries. Today, it is a tacky-but-interesting tourist area with little if any authentic waterfront life, except for recreational boating and some friendly sea lions.

Marina District   Created on landfill for the Pan Pacific Exposition of 1915, the Marina boasts some of the best views of the Golden Gate, as well as plenty of grassy fields alongside the San Francisco Bay. Streets are lined with elegant Mediterranean-style homes and apartments, which are inhabited by the city's well-to-do singles and wealthy families. Here, too, are the Palace of Fine Arts, the Exploratorium, and Fort Mason Center. The main street is Chestnut between Franklin and Lyon, which is lined with shops, cafes, and boutiques. Because of its landfill foundation, the Marina was one of the city's hardest-hit districts in the 1989 quake.

Cow Hollow   Located west of Van Ness Avenue, between Russian Hill and the Presidio, this flat, grazable area supported 30 dairy farms in 1861. Today, Cow Hollow is largely residential and occupied by the city's Young and Yuppie. Its two primary commercial thoroughfares are Lombard Street, known for its many relatively inexpensive motels and Union Street, a flourishing shopping sector filled with restaurants, pubs, cafes, and shops.

Pacific Heights   The ultra-elite, such as the Gettys and Danielle Steele—and those lucky enough to buy before the real-estate boom—reside in the mansions and homes that make up Pacific Heights. When the rich meander out of their fortresses, they wander down to Union Street, a long stretch of boutiques, restaurants, cafes, and bars.

Japantown   Bounded by Octavia, Fillmore, California, and Geary, Japantown shelters only about 4% of the city's Japanese population, but it's still a cultural experience to explore these few square blocks and the shops and restaurants within them.

Civic Center   Although millions of dollars have been expended on brick sidewalks, ornate lampposts, and elaborate street plantings, the southwestern section of Market Street remains downright dilapidated. The Civic Center, at the "bottom" of Market Street, is an exception. This large complex of buildings includes the domed City Hall, the Opera House, Davies Symphony Hall, and the city's main library. The landscaped plaza connecting the buildings is the staging area for San Francisco's frequent demonstrations for or against just about everything.

Haight-Ashbury   Part trendy, part nostalgic, part funky, the Haight, as it's most commonly known, was the soul of the psychedelic and free-loving 1960s and the center of the counterculture movement. Today, the neighborhood straddling upper Haight Street on the eastern border of Golden Gate Park is more gentrified, but the commercial area still harbors all walks of life. Leftover aged hippies mingle with grungy, begging street kids outside Ben and Jerry's ice-cream shop (where they may still be talking about Jerry Garcia), nondescript marijuana dealers whisper "Buds" as shoppers pass, and many people walking down the street have Day-Glo hair. But you don't need to be a freak or wear tie-dye to enjoy the Haight—the food, shops, and bars cover all tastes. From Haight, walk south on Cole Street, for a more peaceful and quaint neighborhood experience.

The Castro   One of the liveliest streets in town, Castro is practically synonymous with San Francisco's gay community, even though technically it is only a street in the Noe Valley district. Located at the very end of Market Street, between 17th and 18th streets, Castro supports dozens of shops, restaurants, and bars catering to the gay community. Open-minded straight people are welcome, too.

Mission District The Mexican and Latin American populations, along with their cuisine, traditions, and art, make the Mission District a vibrant area to visit. Because some parts of the neighborhood are poor and sprinkled with the homeless, gangs, and drug addicts, many tourists duck into Mission Dolores, cruise by a few of the 200-plus amazing murals, and head back downtown. But there's plenty more to see in the Mission District. There's a substantial community of lesbians around Valencia Street, several alternative arts organizations, and most recently the ultimate in young hipster nightlife. New bars, clubs, and restaurants are popping up on Mission between 18th and 24th streets and Valencia at 16th Street. Don't be afraid to visit this area, but do use caution at night.

2 Getting Around

BY PUBLIC TRANSPORTATION

The **San Francisco Municipal Railway**, 949 Presidio Ave., better known as **Muni** (☎ 415/673-6864), operates the city's cable cars, buses, and Metro streetcars. Together, these three public transportation services crisscross the entire city, making San Francisco fully accessible to everyone. Buses and Metro streetcars cost $1 for adults, 35¢ for ages 5 to 17, and 35¢ for seniors over 65. Cable cars cost a whopping $2 for all people over 5 ($1 for seniors from 9pm to midnight and from 6 to 7am). Needless to say, they're packed primarily with tourists. Exact change is required on all vehicles except cable cars. Fares quoted here are subject to change.

For detailed route information, phone Muni or consult the bus map at the front of the Yellow Pages. If you plan on making extensive use of public transportation, you may want to invest in a comprehensive route map ($2), sold at the San Francisco Visitor Information Center (see "Visitor Information" in "Orientation," above) and in many downtown retail outlets.

Muni **discount passes,** called "Passports," entitle holders to unlimited rides on buses, Metro streetcars, and cable cars. A Passport costs $6 for 1 day, and $10 or $15 for 3 or 7 consecutive days. As a bonus, your Passport also entitles you to admission discounts at 24 of the city's major attractions, including the M. H. De Young Memorial Museum, the Asian Art Museum, the California Academy of Sciences, and the Japanese Tea Garden (all in Golden Gate Park); the Museum of Modern Art; Coit Tower; the Exploratorium; the zoo; and the National Maritime Museum and Historic Ships (where you may visit the USS *Pampanito* and the SS *Jeremiah O'Brien*). Among the places where you can purchase a Passport are the San Francisco Visitor Information Center, the Holiday Inn Civic Center, and the TIX Bay Area booth at Union Square.

BY CABLE CAR San Francisco's cable cars may not be the most practical means of transport, but these rolling historic landmarks sure are a fun ride. There are only three lines in the city, and they're all condensed in the downtown area. The most scenic, and exciting, is the **Powell-Hyde line,** which follows a zigzag route from the corner of Powell and Market streets, over both Nob Hill and Russian Hill, to a turntable at gas-lit Victorian Square in front of Aquatic Park. The **Powell-Mason line** starts at the same intersection and climbs over Nob Hill before descending to Bay Street, just 3 blocks from Fisherman's Wharf. The least scenic is the **California Street line,** which begins at the foot of Market Street and runs a straight course through Chinatown and over Nob Hill to Van Ness Avenue. All riders must exit at the last stop and wait in line for the return trip. The cable-car system operates from approximately 6:30am to 12:30am.

BY BUS Buses reach almost every corner of San Francisco, and beyond—they travel over the bridges to Marin County and Oakland. Some buses are powered by overhead electric cables; others use conventional gas engines; and all are numbered and display their destinations on the front. Stops are designated by signs, curb markings, and yellow bands on adjacent utility poles, and most bus shelters exhibit Muni's transportation map and schedule. Many buses travel along Market Street or pass near Union Square and run from about 6am to midnight, after which there is infrequent all-night "Owl" service. If you can help it, for safety purposes, avoid taking buses late at night.

Popular tourist routes are traveled by bus nos. 5, 7, and 71, all of which run to Golden Gate Park; 41 and 45, which travel along Union Street; and 30, which runs between Union Square and Ghirardelli Square.

BY METRO STREETCAR Five of Muni's six Metro streetcar lines, designated J, K, L, M, and N, run underground downtown and on the street in the outer neighborhoods. The sleek railcars make the same stops as BART (see below) along Market Street, including Embarcadero Station (in the Financial District), Montgomery and Powell streets (both near Union Square), and the Civic Center (near City Hall). Past the Civic Center, the routes branch off in different directions: The J line will take you to Mission Dolores; the K, L, and M lines to Castro Street; and the N line parallels Golden Gate Park. Metros run about every 15 minutes—more frequently during rush hours. Service is offered Monday to Friday from 5am to 12:30am, on Saturday from 6am to 12:20am, and on Sunday from 8am to 12:20am.

The most recent streetcar addition is not a newcomer at all, but is, in fact, San Francisco's beloved rejuvenated 1930s streetcars. The beautiful green-and-cream–colored F-Market line runs from downtown Market Street to the Castro and back. It's a quick and charming way to get up- and downtown without any hassle.

BY BART BART, an acronym for **Bay Area Rapid Transit (☎ 650/992-2278)**, is a futuristic-looking, high-speed rail network that connects San Francisco with the East Bay—Oakland, Richmond, Concord, and Fremont. Four stations are located along Market Street (see "By Metro Streetcar," above). Fares range from $1 to $3.55, depending on how far you go. Tickets are dispensed from machines in the stations and are magnetically encoded with a dollar amount. Computerized exits automatically deduct the correct fare. Children 4 and under ride free. Trains run every 15 to 20 minutes, Monday to Friday from 4am to midnight, on Saturday from 6am to midnight, and on Sunday from 8am to midnight.

A $2.5-billion, 33-mile BART extension, currently under construction, includes a southern line that is planned to extend all the way to San Francisco International Airport. It will open, presumably, around the year 2000.

BY TAXI

This isn't New York, so don't expect a taxi to appear whenever you need one. If you're downtown during rush hour or leaving a major hotel, it won't be hard to hail a cab—just look for the lighted sign on the roof that indicates if one is free. Otherwise, it's a good idea to call one of the following companies to arrange a ride: **Veteran's Cab (☎ 415/552-1300)**, **Desoto Cab Co. (☎ 415/673-1414)**, **Luxor Cabs (☎ 415/282-4141)**, **Yellow Cab (☎ 415/626-2345)**, or **Pacific (☎ 415/986-7220)**. Rates are approximately $2 for the first mile and $1.80 for each mile thereafter.

San Francisco Mass Transit

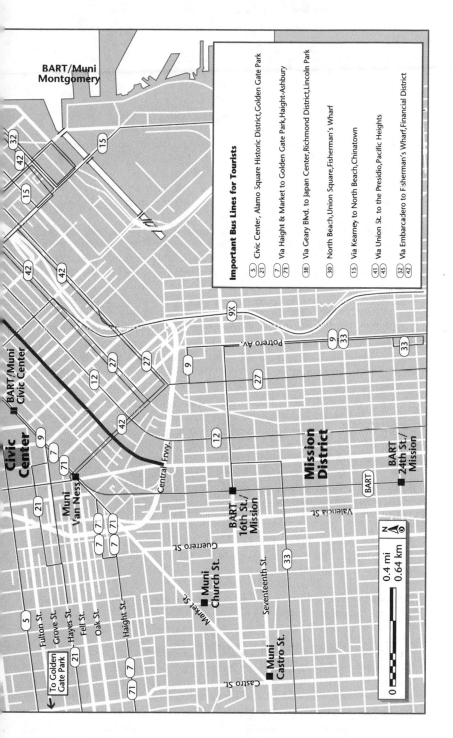

BART/Muni Montgomery

Important Bus Lines for Tourists

5 Civic Center, Alamo Square Historic District, Golden Gate Park
21

7 Via Haight & Market to Golden Gate Park, Haight-Ashbury
71

38 Via Geary Blvd. to Japan Center, Richmond District, Lincoln Park

30 North Beach, Union Square, Fisherman's Wharf

15 Via Kearney to North Beach, Chinatown

41 Via Union St. to the Presidio, Pacific Heights
45

32 Via Embarcadero to Fisherman's Wharf, Financial District
42

Civic Center

BART/Muni Civic Center

Muni Van Ness

Central Frwy.

Potrero Av.

BART 16th St./ Mission

Mission District

BART

BART 24th St./ Mission

Valencia St.

Guerrero St.

Muni Church St.

Seventeenth St.

Market St.

Muni Castro St.

Castro St.

Fulton St.
Grove St.
Hayes St.
Fell St.
Oak St.
Haight St.

To Golden Gate Park

N

0 | 0.4 mi
0 | 0.64 km

BY CAR

You don't need a car to explore downtown San Francisco, and in fact, in central areas, such as Chinatown, Union Square, and the Financial District, a car can be your worst nightmare. But if you want to venture outside of the city, driving is the best way to go. If you need to rent a car, see the car-rental information in chapter 2. Before heading outside the city, especially in winter, call for California **road conditions** (☎ 415/557-3755).

PARKING   If you want to have a relaxing vacation here, don't even attempt to find street parking in Nob Hill, North Beach, Chinatown, by Fisherman's Wharf, or on Telegraph Hill. Park in a garage or take a cab or a bus. If you do find street parking, pay attention to street signs that will explain when you can park and for how long. Be especially careful not to park in zones that are tow areas during rush hours.

Curb colors also indicate parking regulations. *Red* means no stopping or parking; *blue* is reserved for drivers with disabilities who have a California-issued disabled plate or a placard; *white* means there's a 5-minute limit; *green* indicates a 10-minute limit; and *yellow* and *yellow-black* curbs are for commercial vehicles only. Also, don't park at a bus stop or in front of a fire hydrant, and watch out for street-cleaning signs. If you violate the law, you may get a hefty ticket or your car may be towed. To get your car back, you must obtain a release from the nearest district police department, then go to the towing company to pick up the vehicle.

When parking on a hill, apply the hand brake, put the car in gear, and *curb your wheels*—toward the curb when facing downhill, away from the curb when facing uphill. Curbing your wheels will not only prevent a possible "runaway," but will also keep you from getting a ticket—an expensive fine that is aggressively enforced.

DRIVING RULES   California law requires that both drivers and passengers wear seat belts. You may turn right at a red light (unless otherwise indicated), after yielding to traffic and pedestrians, and after making a complete stop. Cable cars always have the right-of-way, as do pedestrians at intersections and crosswalks. Pay attention to signs and arrows on the streets and roadways or you may find yourself suddenly in a lane that requires exiting or turning when you really want to go straight ahead. What's more, San Francisco's many one-way streets can drive you in circles, but most road maps of the city indicate which way traffic flows.

BY FERRY

TO/FROM SAUSALITO   The **Golden Gate Ferry Service** fleet (☎ 415/923-2000) shuttles passengers daily between the San Francisco Ferry Building, located at the foot of Market Street, and downtown Sausalito. Service is frequent, departing at reasonable intervals every day of the year except New Year's Day, Thanksgiving Day, and Christmas Day. Phone for exact schedule. The ride takes a half hour, and one-way fares are $4.25 for adults and $3.20 for kids 6 to 12. Senior and disabled passengers ride for $2.10; children 5 and under ride free. Family rates are also available.

Ferries of the **Blue & Gold Fleet** (recorded info: ☎ 415/773-1188; tickets: ☎ 415/705-5555) also provide round-trip service to downtown Sausalito, leaving from Fisherman's Wharf at Pier 41. The cost is $11 round-trip, half price for kids 5 to 11. Boats run on a seasonal schedule; phone for departure information.

TO/FROM LARKSPUR   The **Golden Gate Ferry Service** fleet (☎ 415/923-2000) also shuttles passengers daily between the San Francisco Ferry Building, located at the foot of Market Street, and downtown Larkspur. The Larkspur ferry is primarily a commuter service during the week, with frequent departures around the rush hours and limited service on weekends. Boats make the 13-mile trip in about 45 minutes and cost $2.50 for adults, $1.90 for kids ages 6 to 12, and $1.25 for seniors and passengers with disabilities; on weekends, prices rise to $4.25 for adults, $3.40 for young riders, and $2.10 for seniors and passengers with disabilities; children 5 and under ride free.

TO/FROM ANGEL ISLAND & TIBURON   Ferries of the **Blue & Gold Fleet** (recorded info: ☎ **415/773-1188;** tickets: ☎ **415/705-5555)** leave from Pier 43½ (Fisherman's Wharf) and travel to both Angel Island and Tiburon. Boats run on a seasonal schedule; phone for departure information. The round-trip fare is $10 to Angel Island, $11 to Tiburon; half price for kids 5 to 11.

FAST FACTS: San Francisco

Airport   See "Getting There," in chapter 2.

American Express   For travel arrangements, traveler's checks, currency exchange, and other member services, American Express has an office at 295 California St., at Battery Street (☎ **415/536-2686),** and at 455 Market St., at First Street (☎ **415/536-2600),** in the Financial District, open Monday to Friday from 8:30am to 5:30pm and Saturday from 9am to 2pm. To report lost or stolen traveler's checks, call ☎ **800/221-7282.** For American Express Global Assist call ☎ **800/554-2639.**

Area Code   The area code for San Francisco is **415;** Oakland, Berkeley, and much of the East Bay use the 510 area code, and the peninsula is generally 650. Most phone numbers in this book are in San Francisco's 415 area code, but there's no need to dial it if you're within city limits.

Baby-sitters   Hotels can often recommend a baby-sitter or child-care service. If yours can't, try **Temporary Tot Tending** (☎ **650/355-7377,** or 650/871-5790 after 6pm), which offers child care by licensed teachers by the hour for children from 3 weeks to 12 years of age. It's open Monday to Friday from 6am to 7pm (weekend service is available only during convention times).

Business Hours   Most banks are open Monday to Friday from 9am to 3pm. Several stay open until about 5pm at least 1 day a week. Many banks also feature ATMs for 24-hour banking (see "Visitor Information & Money," in chapter 2).

Most stores are open Monday to Saturday from 10am or 11am to at least 6pm, with restricted hours on Sunday. But there are exceptions: Stores in Chinatown, Ghirardelli Square, and Pier 39 stay open much later during the tourist season; and large department stores, including Macy's and Nordstrom, keep late hours.

Most restaurants serve lunch from about 11:30am to 2:30pm and dinner from 5:30 to 10pm. You can sometimes get served later on weekends. Nightclubs and bars are usually open daily until 2am, when they are legally bound to stop serving alcohol.

Car Rentals   For car-rental information, see chapter 2.

Climate   See "When to Go," in chapter 2.

Convention Center   The **Moscone Convention Center,** 774 Howard St. (☎ **415/974-4000),** between Third and Fourth streets, was completed in 1981 and named for slain San Francisco mayor George Moscone. Part of a large revitalization project in the SoMa District, the center contains one of the world's largest column-free exhibition halls.

Dentist   In the event of a dental emergency, see your hotel concierge or contact the **San Francisco Dental Society** (☎ 415/421-1435) for 24-hour referral to a specialist. The **San Francisco Dental Office,** 132 The Embarcadero (☎ 415/777-5115), between Mission and Howard streets, offers emergency service and comprehensive dental care Monday, Tuesday, and Friday from 8am to 4:30pm, Wednesday and Thursday from 10:30am to 6:30pm.

Doctor   Saint Francis Memorial Hospital, 900 Hyde St., between Bush and Pine streets on Nob Hill (☎ 415/353-6000), provides emergency-care service 24 hours; no appointment is necessary. The hospital also operates a **physician-referral** service (☎ 415/353-6566).

Driving Rules   See "Getting Around," earlier in this chapter.

Drugstores   There are **Walgreens** pharmacies all over town, including one at 135 Powell St. (☎ 415/391-4433). The store is open Monday to Saturday from 8am to midnight and on Sunday from 9am to 9pm, but the pharmacy has more limited hours: Monday to Friday they're open from 8am to 8pm, Saturday from 9am to 5pm, and Sunday from 10am to 6pm. The branch on Divisadero Street at Lombard (☎ 415/931-6415) has a 24-hour pharmacy. **Merrill's** pharmacy, 805 Market St. (☎ 415/431-5466), is open Monday to Saturday from 9am to 6pm, while the rest of the drugstore is open Monday to Friday from 7am to 8pm, Saturday from 9am to 7pm, and Sunday from 9:30am to 6pm. Both chains accept MasterCard and Visa.

Earthquakes   There will always be earthquakes in California, most of which you'll never notice. However, in case of a significant shaker, there are a few basic precautionary measures you should know. When you are inside a building, seek cover; do not run outside. Stand under a doorway or against a wall and stay away from windows. If you exit a building after a substantial quake, use stairwells, not elevators. If you are in your car, pull over to the side of the road and stop—but not until you are away from bridges, overpasses, telephone poles, and power lines. Stay in your car. If you're out walking, stay outside and away from trees, power lines, and the sides of buildings. If you're in an area with tall buildings, find a doorway in which to stand.

Emergencies   Dial ☎ 911 for police, an ambulance, or the fire department; no coins are needed from a public phone. Emergency hot lines include the **Poison Control Center** (☎ 800/523-2222) and **Rape Crisis** (☎ 415/647-7273).

Information   See "Visitor Information," earlier in this chapter.

Liquor Laws   Liquor and grocery stores, as well as some drugstores, can sell packaged alcoholic beverages between 6am and 2am. Most restaurants, nightclubs, and bars are licensed to serve alcoholic beverages during the same hours. The legal age for purchase and consumption is 21; proof of age is required.

Maps   See "City Layout," earlier in this chapter.

Newspapers & Magazines   The city's two main dailies are the *San Francisco Chronicle* and the *San Francisco Examiner;* both are distributed throughout the city. The two papers combine for a massive Sunday edition that includes a pink "Datebook" section—an excellent preview of the week's upcoming events. The free weekly *San Francisco Bay Guardian,* a tabloid of news and listings, is indispensable for nightlife information; it's widely distributed through street-corner dispensers and at city cafes and restaurants.

Of the many free tourist-oriented publications, the most widely read are *Key* and *San Francisco Guide*. Both of these handbook-size weeklies contain maps and information on current events. They can be found in most hotels, shops, and restaurants in the major tourist areas.

Pharmacies   See "Drugstores," above.

Police   For emergencies dial ☎ **911** from any phone; no coins are needed. For other matters, call ☎ **415/553-0123.**

Post Office   There are dozens of post offices located all around the city. The closest office to Union Square is inside Macy's department store, 170 O'Farrell St. (☎ **800/275-8777**). You can pick up mail addressed to you and marked "General Delivery" (Poste Restante), at the **Civic Center Post Office Box Unit,** P.O. Box 429991, San Francisco, CA 94142-9991 (☎ **800/275-8777**).

Safety   Few locals would recommend that you walk alone late at night in certain areas, particularly the Tenderloin, between Union Square and the Civic Center. Compared with similar areas in other cities, however, even this section of San Francisco is relatively tranquil. Other areas where you should be particularly alert are the Mission District, around 16th and Mission streets; the lower Fillmore area, around lower Haight Street; and the SoMa area south of Market Street. See "Safety," in chapter 2, for additional safety tips.

Smoking   If San Francisco is the state's most European city, the comparison stops here. Each year smoking laws are becoming more and more strict. As of January 1, 1998, smoking is prohibited from restaurants and bars. Although there's been argument against it, so far the new law's been enforced in most establishments. Hotels are also offering more nonsmoking rooms, which is often leaving those who like to puff out in the cold—literally.

Taxes   An 8.5% sales tax is added at the register for all goods and services purchased in San Francisco. The city hotel tax is a whopping 12%. There is no airport tax.

Taxis   See "Getting Around," earlier in this chapter.

Television   In addition to cable stations, available in most hotels, all the major networks and several independent stations are represented. They include: Channel 2, KTVU (FOX); Channel 4, KRON (NBC); Channel 5, KPIX (CBS); Channel 7, KGO (ABC); and Channel 9, KQED (PBS).

Time Zone   San Francisco is in the Pacific standard time zone, which is 8 hours behind Greenwich mean time and 3 hours behind eastern standard time. To find out what time it is, call ☎ **415/767-8900.**

Transit Information   The San Francisco Municipal Railway, better known as Muni, operates the city's cable cars, buses, and Metro streetcars. For customer service call **Muni** at ☎ **415/673-6864** during the week between 7am and 5pm and on the weekends between 9am and 5pm. At other times, recorded information is available.

Useful Telephone Numbers   Tourist information (☎ **415/391-2001**); highway conditions (☎ **415/557-3755**); KFOG Entertainment Line (☎ **415/777-1045**); Movie Phone Line (☎ **415/777-FILM**); Grateful Dead Hot Line (☎ **415/457-6388**).

Weather   Call ☎ **415/936-1212** to find out when the next fog bank is rolling in.

5 Accommodations

Whether you want a room with a view or just a room, San Francisco is more than accommodating for its 11 million annual guests. Most of the city's 180 hotels are concentrated around Union Square, but there are also some smaller independent gems scattered around town. When reading over your options, keep in mind that prices listed are hotel rack rates (the published rates) and you should always ask for special discounts or, even better, vacation packages. It's possible that you could get the room you want for $100 less than what's quoted here, except in summer when the hotels are packed and bargaining is close to impossible.

Hunting for hotels in San Francisco can be a tricky business, particularly if you're not a seasoned traveler. What you don't know—and the reservation agent may not tell you—may very well ruin your vacation, so keep the following pointers in mind when it comes time to book a room:

- Prices listed below do not include state and city taxes, which total 14%. Other hidden extras include parking fees and hefty surcharges—up to $1 per local call—for telephone use.
- San Francisco is Convention City, so if you wish to secure rooms at a particular hotel during high season, book well in advance.
- Be sure to have a credit card in hand when making a reservation, and don't be surprised if you're asked to pay for a least 1 night in advance (this doesn't happen often, though).
- Reservations are usually held until 6pm. If you don't tell the hotel you'll be arriving late, you may lose your room.
- Almost every hotel in San Francisco requires a credit card imprint for "incidentals" (and to prevent walkouts). If you don't have a credit card, then be sure to make special arrangements with the management before you hang up the phone, and take down names.

The hotels listed below are classified first by area and then by price, using the following categories: **Very Expensive,** more than $180 per night; **Expensive,** $135 to $180 per night; **Moderate,** $90 to $135 per night; and **Inexpensive,** less than $90 per night. These categories reflect the price of an average double room during the high season, which runs approximately from April through September. Read each of the entries carefully: Many hotels also offer rooms at rates above and below the price category that they have been assigned in this guidebook. Also note that we do not list single rates. However, some hotels, particularly more budget-oriented establishments, do offer lower rates for singles, so inquire about these if you are traveling alone.

In general, hotel rates in San Francisco are rather inelastic; they don't vary much during the year because the city is so popular year-round. You should always ask about weekend discounts, corporate rates, and family plans; most larger hotels, and many smaller ones, offer them, but many establishments do not mention these discounts unless you make a specific inquiry. You will find nonsmoking rooms available in all of the larger hotels and many of the smaller hotels; establishments that are entirely nonsmoking are listed as such. Nowadays, the best advice for smokers is to confirm a smoking-permitted room in advance.

Most larger hotels will also be able to accommodate guests confined to wheelchairs or those who have other special needs. Ask when you make a reservation to ensure that your hotel of choice will be able to accommodate your needs, especially if you are interested in a bed-and-breakfast.

1 Best Bets

- **Best for Families:** Kids like the **Westin St. Francis,** 335 Powell St. (☎ **800/228-3000** or 415/397-7000), because all children under 12 are given a Kids Club hat on arrival and special sports bottles and complimentary refills in the restaurants, while those ages 3 to 7 are given dinosaur soaps and sponges and coloring books.
- **Best Romantic Rendezvous:** Secure a garden suite at the **Sherman House,** 2160 Green St. (☎ **800/424-5777** or 415/563-3600), with French doors leading out onto a sunken garden terrace with gazebo and pond, or the Paderewski suite with a fireplace in the bathroom. Honorable mentions include the Archbishop's Mansion, Hotel Bohème, and Hotel Majestic.
- **Best Historic Hotel:** The **Sheraton Palace Hotel,** 2 New Montgomery St. (☎ **800/325-3535** or 415/392-8600), the extravagant creation of banker Bonanza King Will Ralston in 1875, has one of the grandest rooms in the city: the Garden Court. Running a close second is the magnificent lobby at the Fairmont Hotel on Nob Hill.
- **Best Old-World Hotel:** Those who appreciate comfort, beautiful surroundings, absolute privacy, and unobtrusive service should choose the **Huntington Hotel,** 1075 California St. (☎ **800/227-4683,** 800/652-1539 in Calif., or 415/474-5400).
- **Best for the Culture Vulture:** The **Inn at the Opera,** 333 Fulton St. (☎ **800/325-2708** or 415/863-8400), an intimate hotel frequented by musicians and other performing artists, is perfect for its location close to all the city's cultural icons, including the opera and Davies Symphony Hall. And the lounge and Ovation at the Opera are intimate places for an after-show supper in the warm glow of firelight.
- **Best for Your Budget:** Sure, the rooms are small at **San Remo,** 2237 Mason St. (☎ **800/352-REMO** or 415/776-8688), but the North Beach location, friendly staff, and low prices can't be beat. Besides, you're here to see the city, not your hotel room. In the Union Square area, you won't find a hotel with more budget-blessing amenities than those at the friendly and comfortable Brady Acres. And for overall extra amenities, we vote for the adorable and supercheap Marina Inn.
- **Best Moderately Priced Hotel: Petite Auberge,** 863 Bush St. (☎ **415/928 6000**), is a delightful rendering of a French country inn. The 26 rooms

---

Reservation Services

Having reservations about your reservations? Then leave it up to the pros:

Bed-and-Breakfast California, P.O. Box 282910, San Francisco, CA 94128 (☎ **800/677-1500** or 415/696-1690; fax 415/696-1699; Web site: www.bbintl.com; E-mail info@bbintl.com), offers a selection of B&Bs ranging from $60 to $140 per night (2-night minimum). Accommodations range from simple rooms in private homes to luxurious, full-service carriage houses, houseboats, and Victorian homes.

San Francisco Reservations, 22 Second St., San Francisco, CA 94105 (☎ **800/677-1500** or 415/227-1500), arranges reservations for more than 300 of San Francisco's hotels and often offers discounted rates. Ask about their Events and Hotel Packages that include VIP or discount admissions to various San Francisco museums. This service also has a nifty World Wide Web site that allows Internet users to make their reservations on-line. Plug in at www.hotelres.com.

---

have attractive furnishings and lace curtains; the tiled breakfast room opens onto a small garden where guests enjoy afternoon tea and wine. If the Auberge is full, try the equally quaint White Swan Inn down the street.

- **Best Bed-and-Breakfast:** It's a tie between the **Union Street Inn,** 2229 Union St. (☎ **415/346-0424**), and **Bed & Breakfast Inn,** 4 Charlton Court (☎ **415/921-9784**). Both inns live up to the expectations of B&B enthusiasts.
- **Best Funky Hotel:** The **Phoenix Hotel,** 601 Eddy St. (☎ **800/248-9466** or 415/776-1380), wouldn't look out of place at Palm Springs. It's a favorite with the rock and movie set, including Sinead O'Connor, k.d. lang, and the Red Hot Chili Peppers, and has one of the bluest and most bizarre restaurant/bars in town.
- **Best Views:** From the rooms in the **Mandarin Oriental,** 222 Sansome St. (☎ **800/622-0404** or 415/276-9888), all of which are on the 38th to the 48th floors, you have a great view of the city and the entire Bay Area. Pricey, though.
- **Best Service:** The small, luxurious **Campton Place Hotel,** 340 Stockton St. (☎ **800/235-4300** or 415/781-5555); the historic, eager-to-please **Ritz-Carlton,** 600 Stockton St. (☎ **800/241-3333** or 415/296-7465); the large, elegant **Clift,** 495 Geary St. (☎ **800/437-8243** in the U.S., or 415/775-4700); and the modern, pampering **Mandarin Oriental** (see above) all rate at the very top for service. Any one of these will deliver on this promise.
- **Best Dining Room:** Never a hotel to do anything second best, the **Ritz-Carlton** (see above) is renowned for pampering its guests as if they were royalty, and the Dining Room is no exception.

2 Union Square

VERY EXPENSIVE

✪ **Campton Place Hotel.** 340 Stockton St. (between Post and Sutter sts.), San Francisco, CA 94108. ☎ **800/235-4300** or 415/781-5555. Fax 415/955-5536. 127 units. A/C MINIBAR TV TEL. $230–$345 double; from $450 suite. Continental breakfast $12.50 extra. AE, CB, DC, MC, V. Parking $25. Cable car: Powell-Hyde and Powell-Mason lines (1 block west). Bus: 2, 3, 4, 30, or 45.

They don't miss a trick at this small, elegant luxury hotel. From the beautifully appointed guest rooms with extra-large beds and exquisite marble bathrooms to the bathrobes and top-notch toiletries, every necessity and whim is covered at Campton Place. The only downside: The rooms and hotel itself are cramped enough to make you wonder what you're forking over the big bucks for, but the superlative service almost makes up for it.

Dining: The Campton Place Restaurant, which serves three meals a day, is highly revered. The menu is contemporary American, with such dishes as tuna tartare with American caviar, and Chilean sea bass, priced from $22 to $38.

Amenities: Concierge, 24-hour room service, laundry, valet, complimentary overnight shoe-shine, morning newspaper, evening turndown, in-room massage, twice-daily maid service, baby-sitting, express checkout, video rentals, access to nearby health club, conference rooms. Business services such as typing, translating, and faxing available by request at the front desk.

✪ **The Clift Hotel.** 495 Geary St. (at Taylor St., 2 blocks west of Union Square), San Francisco, CA 94102. ☎ **800/437-8243** in the U.S., or 415/775-4700. Fax 415/441-4621. 357 units. A/C MINIBAR TV TEL. $255–$400 double; from $405 suite. Continental breakfast $12.50 extra. AE, CB, DC, MC, V. Parking $25. Cable car: Powell-Hyde and Powell-Mason lines (2 blocks east). Bus: 2, 3, 4, 30, 38, or 45.

Since Ian Schrager, king of such ultrahip hotels as New York's Royalton and Paramount, Los Angeles's Mondrian, and Miami's Delano, picked up this property almost 2 years ago, we've been waiting to see him put his Midas spin on it. But it wasn't until March 1998 that room renovations began (scheduled to continue through the end of 1998), and while furniture and textiles will be replaced, the hotel's classic style will remain. The Clift is still one of San Francisco's top luxury hotels and won Five-Star and Five-Diamond awards 10 years in a row just before the Schrager takeover. Located in the city's Theater District, 2 blocks from Union Square, the Clift has been known for its staff, who excel at pampering their guests and even manage to be cordial to the droves of tourists who wander slack-jawed through the palatial lobby. Rooms are old-fashioned, with high ceilings, elaborate moldings and woodwork, Georgian reproductions, and marble bathrooms with everything from hair dryers to plush terry-cloth robes. Thoughtful extras include padded hangers, individual climate controls, two-line telephones, and a scale in your dressing room. The windows also open—a nice touch for those guests who appreciate fresh air.

The Clift's "Young Travelers Program" provides traveling families with toys and games, diapers, bottles, children's books, and other amenities to help children and their parents feel at home. The hotel also accepts and pampers pets.

Dining/Diversions: Unless Schrager's team finally creates a new venue, The French Room remains open for breakfast, lunch, and dinner, specializing in seasonally appropriate California-French cuisine. The hotel's dramatic Redwood Room, which opened in 1933 and remains one of San Francisco's most opulent piano bars, has beautiful 22-foot-tall fluted redwood columns and is also famous for its Gustav Klimt murals. The lobby lounge serves cocktails daily and a traditional English tea Monday to Saturday.

Amenities: Concierge, 24-hour room service, overnight laundry and shoe polishing, 1-hour pressing, evening turndown, twice-daily maid service, complimentary in-room fax and computers, extensive fitness facility, 24-hour business center, gift shop.

Accommodations Near Union Square & Nob Hill

Polk St.

Larkin St.

Hyde St.

Golden Ct.

Leroy St.

Jones St.

Taylor St.

California St.

15

Pine St.

F. Norris St.

Eureka Pl.

Bush St.

14

Fern St.

13

Taylor St.

Sutter St.

1

Hemlock St.

Cosmo Pl.

12 **11**

Post St.

2 **3**

Cedar St.

4

10

5 **6**

Geary St.

7 **8**

Polk St.

Larkin St.

Hyde St.

Leavenworth St.

Jones St.

Myrtle St.

O'Farrell St.

Olive St.

Ellis St.

Willow St.

Eddy St.

NA-0003

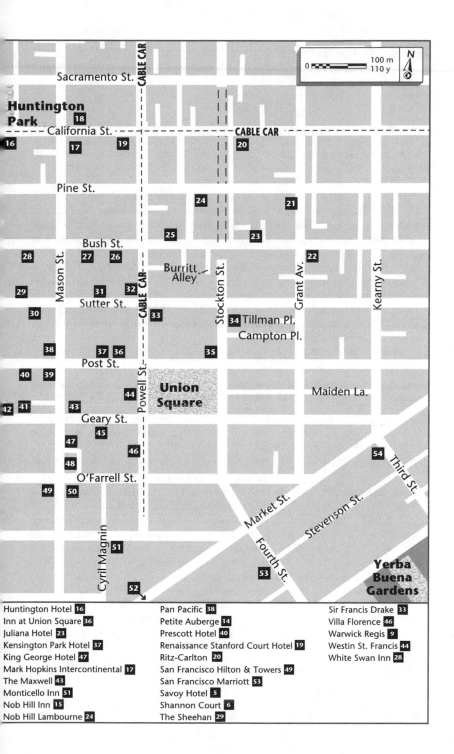

Sacramento St.

CABLE CAR

Huntington
Park **18**

California St. **16** **17** **19** CABLE CAR **20**

Pine St.

24 **21**

25 **23**

Bush St.

28 **27** **26** **22**

Mason St.

Burritt
Alley

29 **31** **32** CABLE CAR

30 **33** Sutter St.

Stockton St.

34 Tillman Pl.
Campton Pl.

38 **37** **36** **35**

Post St.

40 **39**

44

42 **41** **43**

Union
Square

Maiden La.

Geary St.

45

47

46

48

O'Farrell St.

49 **50**

Grant Av.

Kearny St.

Powell St.

Cyril Magnin

51

52

Market St.

Fourth St.

Stevenson St.

53

Third St.

54

Yerba
Buena
Gardens

57

Hotel Trivia

The Clift Hotel charged a mere $2 per night when it first opened in 1915. The price for a room now? More than $200.

Donatello. 501 Post St. (at Mason St.), San Francisco, CA 94102. ☎ **800/227-3184** or 415/441-7100. Fax 415/885-8842. 93 units. A/C TV TEL. $180–$239 double; from $350 suite. Additional person $25. Children under 12 stay free in parents' room. Continental breakfast $11 extra. AE, CB, DC, DISC, MC, V. Valet parking $25. Cable car: Powell-Hyde and Powell-Mason lines (2 blocks west). Bus: 2, 3, 4, 30, or 45.

If you're not looking for trendy or common corporate accommodations, but rather old-world class, book a room here. The Donatello is, in a word, dignified. The lobby is classy, with Italian marble and a serious staff. The rooms, which are some of the largest in the city (an average of 425 square ft.!), are airy and decorated with traditional dark-wood antiques, tapestries, and original art. Unfortunately, most of the extra-large windows lack great views, and some of the furnishings need to be updated, but each room comes with a dish of hard candies and bottled Italian water as well as guaranteed service from an attentive (though sometimes stuffy) staff. In-room amenities include extra-long beds, voice-mail phones, data ports, and terry-cloth bathrobes. Another plus is the roof-terrace lounge; too bad much of the view is blocked by surrounding buildings.

Dining/Diversions: Zingari serves Italian cuisine at lunch and dinner; cocktails are available in the lounge.

Grand Hyatt San Francisco on Union Square. 345 Stockton St. (between Post and Sutter sts.), San Francisco, CA 94108. ☎ **800/233-1234** or 415/398-1234. Fax 415/391-1780. 693 units. A/C MINIBAR TV TEL. $189–$290 double (doesn't include breakfast); $224–$325 Regency Club rm (including continental breakfast); from $450 suite. Continental breakfast $14.50 extra. AE, CB, DC, JCB, MC, V. Parking $24. Cable car: Powell-Hyde and Powell-Mason lines (2 blocks west). Bus: 2, 3, 4, 30, 38, or 45.

If the thought of a 10-second walk to Saks Fifth Avenue makes you drool and your credit cards start to sweat, this hotel is the place for you. Not only is the Grand Hyatt surrounded by all the downtown shopping, but it also boasts some of the best views in the area. The lobby is indeed grand, with Chinese artifacts and enormous ceramic vases, but sadly the well-kept rooms are little more than upscale basic with a corporate flare. They do have some elbow room and a small table and chairs, and the views from most of the 36 floors are truly spectacular. Accommodations include such amenities as TVs in the bathroom, first-run movies, and a telephone with computer-connection capability. Regency rooms are larger, and prices include continental breakfast and evening hors d'oeuvres. Three floors are also dedicated to Business Plan rooms, which contain private fax, telephone with computer hookup, enhanced lighting, coffeemaker, iron and board, and hair dryer. They also include special services—24-hour access to compatible printer, photocopier, and office supplies, free local calls and credit-card phone access, and daily newspaper. All for an additional $15.

Dining/Diversions: The brand new 36th floor's Grandviews Restaurant opened in spring of 1998 and serves three meals a day with live jazz on selected evenings.

Amenities: Concierge, room service, free weekday-morning town-car service to the Financial District, fitness center, fully equipped business center, car-rental desk, tour desk.

◯ Hotel Monaco. 501 Geary St. (at Taylor St.), San Francisco, CA 94102. ☎ **800/ 214-4220** or 415/292-0100. Fax 415/292-0111. 210 units. A/C MINIBAR TV TEL. From $175 double; from $295 suite. Call for discounted rates. AE, DC, DISC, JCB, MC, V. Valet parking $24. Bus: 2, 3, 4, 27, or 38.

This remodeled 1910 beaux arts building debuted in June 1995 and is the new diva of Union Square luxury hotels. For $24 million, the Kimpton Group did this place right—from the cozy main lobby with a two-story French inglenook fireplace to the guest rooms with canopy beds, Chinese-inspired armoires, bamboo writing desks, bold stripes, and vibrant color. Everything is fresh, in the best of taste, and as playful as it is serious. The decor, combined with the breathtaking neighboring restaurant, make this our favorite luxury hotel in the city. The only downside is that many rooms are too small.

Dining/Diversions: The hotel's restaurant, the Grand Cafe, is the best room downtown (competing only with Kuleto's new Farallon). It is grand, in the true sense of the word, with sky-high ceilings, elaborate 1920s and 1930s style, and an amazing collection of local art. In the past year, chef Denis Soriano has really settled into his kitchen, making the Grand Cafe one seriously hot dining spot (see chapter 6, "Dining," for complete information).

Amenities: Computer; concierge; room service; laundry/dry cleaning; overnight shoe-shine; newspaper delivery; in-room massage; twice-daily maid service; baby-sitting; two-line phones; secretarial services; express checkout; valet parking; courtesy car; complimentary wine-hour nightly; health club with steam, sauna, and massage; meeting, business, and banquet facilities.

Hotel Nikko. 222 Mason St. (at O'Farrell St.), San Francisco, CA 94102. ☎ **800/645-5687** or 415/394-1111. Fax 415/421-0455. 522 units. A/C MINIBAR TV TEL. $280–$350 double; $525–$2,000 suite. AE, CB, DISC, JCB, MC, V. Parking $25. Cable car: Powell-Hyde and Powell-Mason lines. Bus: 2, 3, 4, 30, 38, or 45.

Part of Japan Airlines's international fleet of superluxury hotels, the 25-story Hotel Nikko combines the luxuries of both Eastern and Western cultures with heavenly results. Work out in the fitness center, take a few laps in the glass-enclosed indoor swimming pool, rest in the Jacuzzi, Japanese sauna, or soaking tub, then top off the morning with a shiatsu massage before starting your day—what more could you ask for?

Ideally located near Union Square and the Theater District, the Nikko's penchant for pampering also carries on to the guest rooms, which feature top-of-the-line amenities such as two-line speaker phones with modem ports, blackout curtains, large windows with views of the city, and huge, marble bathrooms with separate tubs and showers. Suites include separate sitting areas, stereos with CD players, and entry halls (a Japanese tradition). Though the hotel's decor might be a bit too staid for Western tastes—simple furnishings and beige tones predominate—the element of luxury ultimately prevails.

Dining/Diversions: The bistro-style Cafe 222 serves both California and Japanese cuisine for breakfast, lunch, and dinner. On the lobby level is a small sushi bar offering made-to-order sushi, as well as afternoon hors d'oeuvres and live music.

Amenities: Concierge, 24-hour room service, laundry/valet, twice-daily maid service, swimming pool, fitness center, sauna, hot tub, shiatsu massage, tanning booth, business center, gift and other shops.

Pan Pacific. 500 Post St. (at Mason St.), San Francisco, CA 94102. ☎ **800/533-6465** or 415/771-8600. Fax 415/398-0267. 329 units. A/C MINIBAR TV TEL. $280–$370 double; from

$410 suite. Continental breakfast $12 extra; American breakfast $14.25 extra. AE, DC, DISC, JCB, MC, V. Valet parking $25. Cable car: Powell Hyde and Powell Mason lines. Bus: 2, 3, 4, 30, 38, or 45.

The Pan Pacific is 21st century with *Star Wars*–like lighted corridors, artistically glitzy, enormous, and somehow romantic, all at the same time. If this were a Hollywood set, James Bond might hoodwink a villain here, magically drop down the skyrise's atrium, and disappear into the night. But all is quiet and intimate in the third-floor lobby, even though the skylight ceiling is another 18 floors up. The lobby's marble fountain with four dancing figures and its player piano set the mood for guests relaxing in front of the fireplace. The rooms are rather corporate, but in very good taste, large, and immaculately clean and well stocked with all the luxurious extras, including lavish marble bathrooms with mini-TVs at the sink. In the past year all soft-goods were replaced—from bedspreads to upholstery, drapes, and carpet—with more colorful designs. Other amenities offered are in-room safes, three touch-tone phones, fax machines, voice mail, and bathrobes. The hotel is also conveniently located close to Union Square.

Dining: The Pacific dining room serves breakfast, lunch, and dinner featuring excellent California cuisine with Asian and French accents. See chapter 6, "Dining," for details.

Amenities: Concierge, 24-hour room service, laundry/valet, newspaper delivery, in-room massage, twice-daily maid service, baby-sitting, secretarial services, complimentary Rolls Royce transportation in the city, health club, business center, conference rooms.

✪ Prescott Hotel. 545 Post St. (between Mason and Taylor sts.), San Francisco, CA 94102. ☎ **800/283-7322** or 415/563-0303. Fax 415/563-6831. 199 units. A/C MINIBAR TV TEL. $205 double; $255 concierge-level double (including breakfast and evening cocktail reception); from $295 suite. AE, CB, DC, MC, V. Valet parking $25. Cable car: Powell-Hyde and Powell-Mason lines (1 block east). Bus: 2, 3, 4, 30, 38, or 45.

The Prescott has always been one of our favorite hotels in San Francisco. The staff treats you like royalty, the rooms are beautiful and immaculate, the location— 1 block from Union Square—is perfect, and room service is provided by one of the best restaurants in the city: Postrio. (In fact, it's not unheard of for visitors to check into the Prescott just to get preferred seating.)

Dark tones of green, plum, and burgundy blend well with the cherry-wood furnishings within each of the soundproofed rooms; the view, alas, isn't so pleasant. All bathrooms are supplied with terry-cloth robes and hair dryers, though only the suites have whirlpool bathtubs. "Concierge-level" guests are pampered with free continental breakfast, evening cocktails, and exercise bicycles or rowing machines brought up to your room on request (all for only $20 extra per night).

Dining: The hotel provides preferred seating for guests at Postrio Restaurant. Be sure to make reservations when you book your room (see chapter 6, "Dining," for complete information).

Amenities: Concierge; room service from the Postrio; same-day valet/laundry service; overnight shoe-shine; newspaper delivery; nightly turndown; twice-daily maid service; valet parking; limousine service weekday mornings to the Financial District; complimentary coffee and tea each morning; wine and hors d'oeuvres every evening in the living room; access to off-premises health club ($10), including swimming pool, free weights, and sauna; conference rooms.

San Francisco Hilton & Towers. 333 O'Farrell St. (between Mason and Taylor sts.), San Francisco, CA 94102. ☎ **800/445-8667** or 415/771-1400. Fax 415/771-6807. 1,794 units.

A/C MINIBAR TV TEL. $205–$285 double; from $350 suite. Children stay free in parents' rm. AE, CB, DC, DISC, MC, V. Parking $27. Cable car: Powell-Hyde and Powell-Mason lines (1 block east). Bus: 2, 3, 4, 30, 38, or 45.

Complete with bustling conventioneers, anxious smokers, and a line to register that resembles airport check-in, the Hilton's lobby is so enormous and busy it feels more like a convention hall than a hotel. It's the Hilton's three connecting buildings (the original 19-story main building, a 46-story tower topped by a panoramic restaurant, and a 23-story landmark with an additional 386 luxurious rooms and suites) that bring the swarms of visitors clamoring for a room. But even during quieter times, the sheer enormity of the place makes the Hilton somewhat overwhelming and its contents mysterious.

After you get past the sweeping grand lobby, jump on an elevator, and wind through endless corridors to your room, you'll find the mystique ends with common, corporate accommodations. Some of the main tower's rooms' floor-to-ceiling views may be memorable, but the decor definitely is not. Room size is simply standard. Unless you're staying in one of the more luxurious abodes, the feel and decor here are impersonal and plain—perfect for the conventioneers, but not for a romantic weekend. One bonus: The Hilton is always upgrading somewhere on the property, and over 400 rooms were renovated in the past year.

Dining: Cityscape, on the 46th floor, serves classic California cuisine with a breathtaking 360° view; the retractable skylight exposes the night sky in all its grandeur. Kiku of Tokyo offers Japanese cuisine. The Mason Street Deli serves breakfast and lunch, and Intermezzo offers Italian-style food to eat in or to go. An elegant sidewalk cafe, The Café on the Square, provides a spot for watching the passing parade.

Amenities: Concierge, room service (6am to midnight), laundry, shoe-shine, swimming pool, health club ($6 fee), business center, tour desk, shopping arcade. Towers-level accommodations offer upgraded services, including separate registration lounge with complimentary breakfast and hors d'oeuvres and daily newspaper.

San Francisco Marriott. 55 Fourth St. (between Market and Mission sts.), San Francisco, CA 94103. ☎ **800/228-9290** or 415/896-1600. Fax 415/777-2799. 1,500 units. A/C MINIBAR TV TEL. $179–$249 double; $350–$2,500 suite. AE, CB, DC, JCB, MC, V. Parking $25. Cable car: Powell-Hyde and Powell-Mason lines (3 blocks west). Muni Metro: All Market St. trams. Bus: All Market St. buses.

Some call it a masterpiece, others liken it to the world's biggest parking meter. Regardless, the Marriott is one of the largest buildings in the city, making it a popular stopover for convention-goers and those looking for a room with a view. Fortunately, the controversy does not extend to the newly renovated rooms, so expect pleasant accommodations, floral patterns, large bathrooms and beds, and exceptional city vistas. Upon arrival, enter from Fourth Street, between Market and Mission, to avoid a long trek to the registration area.

Dining/Diversions: Kinoko is a Japanese teppanyaki restaurant and sushi bar. The Garden Terrace, facing the hotel's central fountain, has a breakfast bar and two buffets that prepare made-to-order omelets; there is also a varied lunch-and-dinner menu. You can choose between the Atrium Lounge and the View Lounge, which has a truly panoramic view of the bay and Golden Gate Bridge (assuming there's no fog) as well as live entertainment.

Amenities: Indoor pool and health club, business center, tour desk, car-rental, and gift shop.

Hotel Trivia

For nearly a century, the most popular place for visitors to rendezvous in San Francisco has been under the magnificent hand-carved grandfather clock in the lobby of the Westin St. Francis Hotel.

✪ **Westin St. Francis.** 335 Powell St. (between Geary and Post sts.), San Francisco, CA 94102. ☎ **800/228-3000** or 415/397-7000. Fax 415/774-0124. 1,275 units. A/C MINIBAR TV TEL. Main building: $229–$405 double; from $395 suite. Tower: $360–$405 double; from $425 suite. Extra person $30. Continental breakfast $12.50 extra. AE, DC, DISC, JCB, MC, V. Valet parking $26. Cable car: Powell-Hyde and Powell-Mason lines (direct stop). Bus: 2, 3, 4, 30, 45, or 76.

At the turn of the century, Charles T. Crocker and a few of his wealthy buddies decided that San Francisco needed a world-class hotel, and up went the St. Francis. Since then, hordes of VIPs have hung their hats and hosiery here, including Emperor Hirohito, Queen Elizabeth II, Mother Teresa, King Juan Carlos of Spain, the Shah of Iran, and all the U.S. presidents since Taft. In 1972 the 32-story Tower was added, doubling the capacity and adding the requisite banquet and conference centers. The older rooms of the main building vary in size and have more old-world charm than the newer tower rooms, but the Tower is remarkable for its great views of the city once you rise above the 18th floor.

Though too massive to offer the personal service you get at the smaller deluxe hotels on Nob Hill, few other hotels in San Francisco can match the majestic aura of the St. Francis. We know it sounds corny, but the St. Francis is so intertwined with the city's past that it truly is San Francisco: Stroll through the vast, ornate lobby and you can feel 100 years of history oozing from its hand-carved redwood paneling. The hotel did a massive $50-million renovation in 1996, replacing the carpeting, furniture, and bedding in every guest room, gussying up the lobby, and restoring the facade, which makes it all the more surprising that pets are welcome here. But even if you stay elsewhere, it's worth a visit if only to partake in high tea at the Compass Rose, one of San Francisco's most enduring and enjoyable traditions.

Dining/Diversions: The lobby-level Dewey's, a sports bar, offers a do-it-yourself luncheon buffet, and burgers and pizzas at night. The St. Francis Cafe, also on the lower level, offers a basic breakfast and dinner menu. The Compass Rose is open daily for lunch and afternoon tea (3 to 5pm), with live music, dancing, champagne, cocktails, and caviar tasting in the evening.

Amenities: Concierge, 24-hour room service, laundry, newspaper delivery, in-room massage, twice-daily maid service, baby-sitting referral, Westin Kids Club (great for families), secretarial services, fitness center, business center, tour and car-rental desks, barber/beauty salon, gift shop.

EXPENSIVE

Handlery Union Square Hotel. 351 Geary St. (between Mason and Powell sts.), San Francisco, CA 94102. ☎ **800/843-4343** or 415/781-7800. Fax 415/781-0269. 397 units. A/C TV TEL. $150–$185 double. Club section: from $185 double; from $225 suite. Extra person $10. AE, CB, DC, MC, V. Parking $19. Cable car: Powell-Hyde and Powell-Mason lines (direct stop). Bus: 2, 3, 4, 30, 38, or 45.

Think of the Handlery as a place where Matlock would love to stay. A mere half a block from Union Square, the Handlery covers all bets by offering every amenity you could possibly need combined with completely nonoffensive (read: dull as

Hotel Trivia

The Westin St. Francis operates the world's only legal money-laundering operation. Back in 1938 the hotel's manager ordered that all coinage be sorted, scrubbed, polished, and dried to keep ladies' white gloves from getting dirty, and today the tradition continues.

Grandma's house) rooms. All the large, newly redecorated guest rooms come with the basic accoutrements, including cable TVs, clock radios, hair dryers, coffeemakers, phones with voice mail, and Nintendo systems. An extra $10 per night buys you a membership to "The Club," which provides its members with a complimentary morning newspaper and turndown service, an extra dressing room, bathroom scale, robes, two phones, refrigerator, and—here's the clincher—an electric shoe polisher. Hip-hoppers can skip this one; it's the nuclear families and older folks that the Handlery caters to.

Amenities: Multilingual concierge staff, room service (limited hours), same-day laundry, baby-sitting, express checkout, valet parking, Spectravision movie channels (fee), heated outdoor swimming pool and sauna, access to nearby health club, conference rooms, barber shop, tour desk, gift shop.

✪ **Hotel Diva.** 440 Geary St. (between Mason and Taylor sts.), San Francisco, CA 94102. ☎ **800/553-1900** or 415/885-0200. Fax 415/346-6613. 110 units. A/C TV TEL. $169 double; $195 junior suite; $500 villa suite. Rates include continental breakfast. AE, DC, DISC, JCB, MC, V. Parking $17. Cable car: Powell-Mason. Bus: 38 or 38L.

Appropriately named, the Diva is the prima donna of San Francisco's modern hotels and one of our favorites. A showbiz darling when it opened in 1985, the Diva won "Best Hotel Design" by *Interiors* magazine for its sleek, ultramodern interiors. A stunning profusion of curvaceous glass, marble, and steel mark the Euro-tech lobby, while the rooms, each spotless and neat, are softened with utterly fashionable "Italian Modern" furnishings. Nary a beat is missed with the toys and services either: VCRs (with discreet video vending machine), Nintendo, pay-per-view movies, valet parking, room service, complimentary room-delivered breakfast, and on-site fitness and business centers complete the package. *Insider tip:* Reserve one of the rooms ending in "09," which come with extra-large bathrooms with vanity mirrors and makeup tables.

Hotel Milano. 55 Fifth St. (between Market and Mission sts.), San Francisco, CA 94103. ☎ **800/398-7555** in the U.S., or 415/543-8555. Fax 415/543-5885. 108 units. A/C MINIBAR TV TEL. $149–$189 double. Extra person $20. AE, DC, JCB, MC, V. Valet parking $19. Bus: All Market St. buses.

Contemporary Italian design, simple and elegantly streamlined rooms, and its central location make Hotel Milano a popular choice for tourists and businesspeople alike. The hotel also has a film-production facility and private screening room to entice the entertainment lot. But corporate travelers also resonate to the spacious guest rooms, which feature everything a business executive could want, from fax/computer modem hookups to a Nintendo game system. Other features include in-room safes and soundproof windows. Some have a spa tub, bidet, double lavatories, and television with VCR.

Dining: M Point, which opened in early 1997, serves breakfast, lunch, and dinner with an American/Asian flair.

Amenities: Concierge, room service, laundry/valet, fitness center and spa with steam and sauna, business center.

Hotel Rex. 562 Sutter St. (between Powell and Mason sts.), San Francisco, CA 94102. ☎ **800/433-4434** or 415/433-4434. Fax 415/433-3695. 94 units. MINIBAR TV TEL. $155–$275 double; $575 suite. AE, CB, DC, MC, V. Parking $19. Cable car: Powell-Hyde and Powell-Mason lines (1 block east). Bus: 2, 3, 4, 30, 38, or 45.

Joie de Vivre, the most creative hotel group in the city, recently acquired this historic building (formerly the Orchard Hotel), which is situated near several fine galleries, theaters, and restaurants. They've kept some of the hotel's imported furnishings, and it will remain a European boutique hotel, but they have given the lobby and rooms a half-million-dollar face-lift, adding a decorative flair that makes their hotels among the most popular in town. The clublike lobby lounge is modeled after a 1920s library and is, like all their properties, cleverly stylish. Joie de Vivre is positioning the Rex as a hotel for the arts and literary community (not unlike the Algonquin Hotel in New York City), and in that spirit an antiquarian bookstore adjoins the lobby.

The renovated rooms, which are all above average in size, feature telephones with voice mail and data port and a new electronic key-card system. If you have one of the rooms in the back, you'll look out over a shady, peaceful courtyard (that's something you won't get in New York City). Attention to the details makes Hotel Rex one of the better choices in this price range downtown.

Amenities: Concierge, room service (for deluxe continental breakfast only), same-day laundry/dry cleaning, complimentary newspaper, complimentary evening wine hour, access to an off-premises health club across the street for $10 per day.

○ Hotel Triton. 342 Grant Ave. (at Bush St.), San Francisco, CA 94108. ☎ **800/433-6611** or 415/394-0500. Fax 415/394-0555. 147 units. A/C MINIBAR TV TEL. $159–$199 double; $299–$315 suite. AE, DC, DISC, MC, V. Parking $22. Cable car: Powell-Hyde and Powell-Mason lines (2 blocks west).

Executing a bold idea that was long overdue, hotelier magnate Bill Kimpton requisitioned a cadre of local artists and designers to "do their thing" to his latest acquisition, the Hotel Triton. The result was San Francisco's first three-star hotel to finally break the boring barrier. Described as vogue, chic, retro-futuristic, and even neo-Baroque, the Triton begs attention from the Daliesque lobby to the sumptuous designer suites à la Jerry Garcia, Wyland (the ocean artist), and Joe Boxer. Two dozen environmentally sensitive "EcoRooms"—biodegradable soaps, filtered water and air, all-natural linens—were also installed to please the tree-hugger in all of us. A mild caveat: Don't expect perfection; many of the rooms could use a little touching up here and there (stained curtains, chipped furniture), and service isn't as snappy as it could be. If you can live with this, and want to inject a little fun and style into your stay, then come join Dorothy and Toto for a trip far from Kansas.

Dining/Diversions: Café de la Presse, a European-style newsstand and outdoor cafe, serves breakfast, lunch, and dinner. In the hotel lobby, complimentary coffee is served each morning and wine each evening.

Amenities: Room service, same-day laundry, exercise room, business center.

Hotel Vintage Court. 650 Bush St. (between Powell and Stockton sts.), San Francisco, CA 94108. ☎ **800/654-1100** or 415/392-4666. Fax 415/433-4065. 107 units. A/C MINIBAR TV TEL. $129–$169 double; $300 penthouse suite. AE, CB, DC, DISC, MC, V. Parking $21. Cable car: Powell-Hyde and Powell-Mason lines (direct stop). Bus: 2, 3, 4, 30, 45, or 76.

Consistent personal service has prompted a loyal clientele at this European-style hotel located 2 blocks north of Union Square. The lobby, accented with dark wood, deep green, and rose, is welcoming enough to actually spend a little time in, especially when the nightly complimentary California wines are being poured.

But the varietals don't stop at ground level. Each tidy room, renovated in 1995, is named after a winery and mimics a wine-country excursion with its floral bed-spreads, matching drapes, and trellised wall-to-wall loop carpeting. Opus One, the deluxe, two-room penthouse suite, includes an original 1912 stained-glass skylight, a wood-burning fireplace, a whirlpool tub, a complete entertainment center, and panoramic views of the city.

Dining/Diversions: The hotel's dining room, Masa's, serving traditional French fare, is one of the top restaurants in San Francisco (see chapter 6, "Dining," for complete information). Breakfast is available in the dining room, and the comple-mentary evening wine service from 5:30 to 7p.m. features fine California reds and whites.

Amenities: Free morning transportation to the Financial District, tour desk, and car-rental service, access to an off-premises health club at a fee of $10 per day.

Inn at Union Square. 440 Post St. (between Mason and Powell sts.), San Francisco, CA 94102. ☎ **800/288-4346** or 415/397-3510. Fax 415/989-0529. 30 units. TV TEL. $165–$350 double. Rates include continental breakfast. AE, CB, DC, DISC, JCB, MC, V. Valet parking $22. Cable car: Powell-Hyde and Powell-Mason lines. Bus: 2, 3, 4, 30, 38, or 45.

As narrow as an Amsterdam abode, the Inn at Union Square is a veritable antithesis to the big, impersonal hotels that surround Union Square. If you need plenty of elbow room, skip this one. But if you're looking for the type of inn whose staff knows the names of each guest and afternoon tea comes with crisp cucumber sand-wiches, then read on. A half block west of the square, the seven-story inn makes up for its small stature by spoiling its guests with a pile of perks. Mornings start with breakfast served at your door along with the *New York Times,* followed by afternoon tea and evening hors d'oeuvres served in adorable little fireplace lounges at the end of each hall. The rooms, each handsomely and individually decorated with Geor-gian reproductions and floral fabrics, are smaller than average but infinitely more appreciable than the cookie-cutter rooms of most larger hotels.

Amenities: Complete business services available, use of a health club.

Juliana Hotel. 590 Bush St. (at Stockton St.), San Francisco, CA 94108. ☎ **800/328-3880** or 415/392-2540. Fax 415/391-8447. 106 units. A/C MINIBAR TV TEL. $145–$195 double; $179–$225 junior suite; $185–$235 executive suite; $300–$500 2-bedroom suite. Special winter packages available. Continental breakfast $7.95 extra. AE, CB, DC, MC, V. Parking $21. Cable car: Powell-Hyde and Powell-Mason lines (1 block west). Bus: 2, 3, 4, 30, 38, or 45.

We love the lobby at this small, European-style hotel. With its rich, homey sur-roundings, English prints, and comfy couches facing a blazing fire, which is ensconced in brass and marble, it feels more like a rich friend's study than the entrance to a hotel. With the addition of daily papers hanging on a wooden rack, the Juliana has created a place that makes us want to kick up our feet and stay awhile. And with the complimentary coffee here by day and wine by night, there's no real reason to leave.

The rooms were renovated in 1997, and are a substantial departure from their previous decor. Now surroundings are trendy-bright, with yellow-and-pale-blue–striped wallpaper, candy-striped yellow and red upholstered chairs, floral pat-terned bedspreads with matching curtains, and blue carpeting. It's vibrant and cheery, for sure, but not the kind of place in which you'd want to nurse a wicked hangover. Extra bonuses are aplenty: irons and ironing boards, in-room faxes, and coffeemakers. The bathrooms were renovated, too, and have lovely golden diamond-patterned wallpaper, a large, well-lit mirror, hair dryer, and a basket of soap and other toiletries. Rooms can be on the small side, but the junior suites have plenty of elbow room and adorable homey touches.

Amenities: Room service, laundry/valet, morning transport to the Financial District, access to an off-premises health club.

Kensington Park Hotel. 450 Post St. (between Powell and Mason sts.), San Francisco, CA 94102. ☎ **800/553-1900** or 415/788-6400. Fax 415/399-9484. 86 units. TV TEL. $170 double; $550 suite. Rates include continental breakfast. Extra person $10. AE, CB, DC, MC, V. Parking $17. Cable car: Powell-Hyde and Powell-Mason lines (2 blocks east).

The Kensington caught us by surprise. We were expecting another boutique hotel with bland decor and wrinkles from age. What we found was a cheery, eager-to-please staff, tasteful accommodations, and extra efforts that showed the hotel really cared about its guests. Rooms, located on the 5th through 12th floors and recently upgraded, are reminiscent of old England, with traditional ornate mahogany furnishings, beautiful damask fabrics, and enormous armoires—far more attractive than most hotel furnishings. Bathrooms may be small, but they're sweetly appointed in brass and marble. As for the views, ask for an upper corner room and you'll be getting far beyond your money's worth. Additional services include complimentary coffee and croissants, available on each floor every morning from 7 to 10am; complimentary tea, sherry, and cookies every afternoon; and a complimentary piano-accompanied wine hour on Thursdays. If you really want the full treatment, book the Royal Suite, which contains a canopy bed, fireplace, and Jacuzzi. Guests have access to an off-premises health club.

Dining: Farallon, the hottest new restaurant in town, adjoins the hotel (see chapter 6, "Dining," for complete details).

Amenities: Concierge, room service, same-day laundry, morning newspaper, complimentary morning limo to the Financial District, and fax and secretarial services are also available.

❂ The Maxwell. 386 Geary St. (at Mason St.), San Francisco, CA 94102. ☎ **888/734-6299** or 415/986-2000. Fax 415/397-2447. 153 units. A/C TV TEL. $135–$185 double; $475–$670 suite. Extra person $10. Corporate discounts available. AE, CB, DC, DISC, MC, V. Parking $17. Cable car: Powell-Hyde and Powell-Mason lines (1 block east). Bus: 2, 3, 4, 30, 38, or 45.

What a pleasant surprise to see what Joie de Vivre (owners of the Commodore, the Phoenix, and Archbishop's Mansion) did when they acquired this hotel and reopened it in 1997. What was once an old, somewhat rundown hotel in an excellent location (1 block from Union Square) is now an incredibly chic-boutique experience. Rooms blend velvets, brocades, stripes, plaids, rich color, and handcrafted artistic accents into what the management calls Theatre deco fused with Victoriana decor (a sort of smoking club/study atmosphere). Ambers, reds, greens, and browns dominate the color scheme, and rooms come with upholstered chairs, hand-painted bedside lamps, luxurious pillows, boldly tiled sinks, and respectable prints hanging on the walls. Other plusses are writing desks, hair dryers, and two phones. The suites, which are more like rich personal penthouse apartments, are some of the most stunning in town; unfortunately, from their location you can hear the old elevator kick into gear every time it's beckoned.

Dining/Diversions: Adjoining Gracie's Restaurant looks great but its fare and service are nothing to write home about. It does, however, do the trick if you're looking for a decent bite, a couple of oysters, or a little live jazz (Mon to Sat).

Sir Francis Drake. 450 Powell St. (at Sutter St.), San Francisco, CA 94102. ☎ **800/227-5480** or 415/392-7755. Fax 415/391-8719. 417 units. A/C MINIBAR TV TEL. $165–$245 double; $350–$650 suite. AE, CB, DC, DISC, MC, V. Parking $24. Cable car: Powell-Hyde and Powell-Mason lines (direct stop). Bus: 2, 3, 4, 45, or 76.

Hotel Trivia

Tom Sweeny, the head doorman at the Sir Francis Drake Hotel, is San Francisco's living historical monument. Dressed in traditional Beefeater attire (you can't miss those $1,400 duds), he's been the subject of countless snapshots for the past 19 years—an average 200 per day—and has shaken hands with every president since Jerry Ford.

It took a change of ownership and a multimillion-dollar restoration to save the Sir Francis Drake from becoming a Starbucks, but now this stately old queen is once again housing guests in grand fashion. Granted, this venerable septuagenarian is still showing signs of age (the owners admit there's more work to be done), but the price of imperfection is certainly reflected in the room rate: a good $100 less per night than its Nob Hill cousins. The new Sir Francis Drake is a hotel for people who are willing to trade a chipped bathroom tile or oddly matched furniture for the opportunity to vacation in pseudo-grand fashion. Allow Tom Sweeny, the ever-ebullient (and legendary) Beefeater doorman, to handle your bags as you make your entrance into the elegant, captivating lobby. Sip cocktails at the superchic Starlight Lounge overlooking the city. Dine at Scala's Bistro, one of the hottest restaurants downtown. In short, live like the king or queen of Union Square without all the pomp, circumstance, and credit-card bills.

Dining/Diversions: Scala's Bistro at the lobby level serves excellent Italian cuisine in a stylish setting (see chapter 6, "Dining," for complete information); Café Expresso, a small Parisian-style corner cafe, does an equally commendable job serving coffees, pastries, and sandwiches daily. The Starlight Room on the 21st floor offers cocktails, entertainment, and dancing nightly with a panoramic view of the city.

Amenities: Concierge, room service, business services, laundry, valet, exercise room, extensive meeting facilities.

Villa Florence. 225 Powell St. (between Geary and O'Farrell sts.), San Francisco, CA 94102. ☎ **800/553-4411** or 415/397-7700. Fax 415/397-1006. 181 units. A/C MINIBAR TV TEL. $145–$185 double; $179–$199 studio king. Continental breakfast $8.50 extra. AE, CB, DC, DISC, MC, V. Valet parking $23. Cable car: Powell-Hyde and Powell-Mason lines (direct stop). Bus: 2, 3, 4, 30, 38, or 45.

Located half a block south of Union Square and fronting the Powell Street cable car line, the seven-story Villa Florence is parked in one of the liveliest sections of the city (no need to drive, 'cause you're already here). A recent—and sorely needed–renovation has brightened up the rooms considerably. Essentially it's a lower-end replica of the spectacular rooms at the Hotel Monaco (which is owned by the same company), with lots of bold stripes and vibrant colors. You'll like the large, comfortable bed and the bathroom equipped with hand-milled soap and hair dryers. But never mind the rooms: It's the hotel's restaurant that makes it a worthy contender among Union Square's medium-priced inns. As if the location alone weren't reason enough to book a room.

Dining/Diversions: Adjoining the hotel is Kuleto's, one of San Francisco's most popular and stylish Italian restaurants (trust us, you'll want to make a reservation for dinner along with your room). See chapter 6, "Dining," for complete information.

✪ **White Swan Inn.** 845 Bush St. (between Taylor and Mason sts.), San Francisco, CA 94108. ☎ **415/775-1755.** Fax 415/775-5717. 26 units. MINIBAR TV TEL. $150–$165 double; $195 romance suite; $250 2-room suite. Extra person $15. Rates include full breakfast. AE, MC, V. Parking $19. Cable car: California St. line (1 block north). Bus: 1, 2, 3, 4, 27, or 45.

From the moment you are buzzed in to this well-secured inn, you'll know you're not in a generic bed-and-breakfast. More than 50 teddy bears grace the lobby, and if that doesn't cure homesickness, complimentary homemade cookies, tea, and coffee will. The romantically homey rooms are warm and cozy—the perfect place to snuggle up with a good book. They're also quite big, with hardwood entryways, rich, dark-wood furniture, working fireplaces, and an assortment of books tucked in nooks (in case you forgot one). The decor is English elegance at its best, if not to excess, with floral prints almost everywhere. Wine and hors d'oeuvres are served every evening. The Romance suites are not much better than regular rooms, just a little bigger with the addition of chocolates, champagne, and a VCR. Its location—2½ blocks from Union Square—makes this 1900s building a charming and serene choice with service and style to satisfy the most discriminating traveler.

Dining/Diversions: Each morning a generous breakfast is served in a common room just off a tiny garden. Afternoon tea is also served, with hors d'oeuvres, sherry, wine, and home-baked pastries. You can have your sherry in front of the fireplace while you browse through the books in the library. Note that there's no smoking.

Amenities: Concierge, laundry, overnight shoe-shine, morning newspaper, evening turndown. Guests have access to an off-premises health club for an extra $15 per day.

MODERATE

Andrews Hotel. 624 Post St. (between Jones and Taylor sts.), San Francisco, CA 94109. ☎ **800/926-3739** or 415/563-6877. Fax 415/928-6919. 48 units. MINIBAR TV TEL. $89–$119 double; $129 petite suite. Rates include continental breakfast and evening wine. AE, DC, JCB, MC, V. Self-parking $15. Cable car: Powell-Hyde and Powell-Mason lines (3 blocks east). Bus: 2, 3, 4, 30, 38, or 45.

Two blocks west of Union Square, the Andrews was formerly a Turkish bath before its conversion in 1981. As is fitting with Euro-style hotels, the rooms are small but well maintained and comfortable; white lace curtains and fresh flowers in each room add a light touch. Some rooms have shower only, and bathrooms in general tend to be tiny, but for the location—a few blocks from Union Square—and price, the Andrews is a safe bet for an enjoyable stay in the city. An added bonus is the adjoining Fino Bar and Ristorante, which offers complimentary wine to its hotel guests in the evening.

Beresford Arms. 701 Post St. (at Jones St.), San Francisco, CA 94109. ☎ **800/533-6533** or 415/673-2600. Fax 415/929-1535. 144 units. MINIBAR TV TEL. $119 double; $140 Jacuzzi suite; $175 parlor suite. Rates include continental breakfast. Extra person $10. Children under 12 stay free in parents' rm. Senior-citizen discount available. AE, CB, DC, DISC, MC, V. Parking $15. Cable car: Powell-Hyde line (3 blocks east). Bus: 2, 3, 4, 27, or 38.

Every time we visit the Beresford Arms, its lobby always seems filled with happy, chatty Europeans. Maybe it's the Jacuzzi whirlpool bathtubs and bidets that keep them smiling, or the "Manager's Social Hour" with free wine and snacks. The price is fair, too: $140 for a large, reasonably attractive (though a bit old-fashioned) suite with a choice of wet bar or fully equipped kitchen—a key for families. Modest business services are available, as is valet or self-parking. The hotel's location, sandwiched between the Theater District and Union Square in a quieter section of San Francisco, is ideal for car-free visitors.

Cartwright Hotel. 524 Sutter St. (at Powell St.), San Francisco, CA 94102. ☎ **800/227-3844** or 415/421-2865. Fax 415/983-6244. 114 units. TV TEL. $119–$149 double or twin; $199–$259 family suite sleeping 4. Rates include continental breakfast and evening wine. AE, CB, DC, DISC, MC, V. Parking $21. Cable car: Powell-Hyde and Powell-Mason lines (direct stop). Bus: 2, 3, 4, 30, or 45.

Diametrically opposed to the hip-hop, happenin' Hotel Triton down the street, the Cartwright Hotel is geared toward the "older, mature traveler" (as hotel marketers like to put it). The hotel management takes pride in its reputation for offering clean, comfortable rooms at fair prices, which explains why most of its guests have been repeat customers for a long time. Remarkably quiet despite its convenient location near one of the busiest downtown corners, the eight-story hotel looks not unlike it did some 80 years ago when it first opened. High-quality antiques collected during its decades of faithful service furnish the lobby, as well as each of the individually decorated rooms. A nice perk usually reserved for fancier hotels is the fully equipped bathrooms, all of which have tubs, shower massages, thick fluffy towels, and terry-cloth robes. *Tip:* Request a room with a view of the backyard; they're the quietest. Guests have access to a nearby health club; complimentary wine, tea, and cookies are served in the small library adjacent to the lobby from 5 to 6pm.

Clarion Bedford Hotel. 761 Post St. (between Leavenworth and Jones sts.), San Francisco, CA 94109. ☎ **800/227-5642** or 415/673-6040. Fax 415/563-6739. 144 units. MINIBAR TV TEL. $119–$169 double; from $175 suite. Continental breakfast $8.50 extra. AE, CB, DC, JCB, MC, V. Parking $18. Cable car: Powell-Hyde and Powell-Mason lines (4 blocks east). Bus: 2, 3, 4, or 27.

For the price and location (3 blocks from Union Square) the 17-story Bedford offers a darn good deal. Your hard-earned dollars will get you a large, spotless, recently renovated room with flowery decor that's not exactly en vogue but definitely in fine taste, as well as service from an incredibly enthusiastic, attentive, and professional staff. Each accommodation is well furnished with king, queen, or two double beds, writing desk, armchair, and well-stocked honor bar with plenty of munchies. Big closets are a trade for the small bathrooms. Most rooms are sunny and bright and have priceless views of the city (the higher the floor, the better the view).

The hotel's bistro, Crushed Tomato's, has a small, beautiful mahogany bar opposite the registration desk. Canvas Café, an enormous eatery located behind the lobby, is under separate management. There's also room service (for breakfast only), dry cleaning, laundry, secretarial services, valet parking, free morning limousine service to the Financial District, and complimentary wine in the lobby each evening from 5 to 6pm.

✪ **Commodore International.** 825 Sutter St. (at Jones St.), San Francisco, CA 94109. ☎ **800/338-6848** or 415/923-6800. Fax 415/923-6804. 113 units. TV TEL. $99–$119 double or twin. AE, DC, MC, V. Parking $15. Bus: 2, 3, 4, 27, or 76.

If you're looking to pump a little fun and fantasy into your vacation, this is the place. Before its new owners revamped the aging Commodore from top to bottom, it . . . well, okay, it sucked. Then along came San Francisco hotelier Chip Conley who, amped on his success in transforming the Phoenix Hotel into a rocker's retreat, instantly recognized this dilapidated eyesore's potential, added it to his collection, then let his hip-hop decor designers do their magic. The result? One groovy hotel. Stealing the show is the Red Room, a Big Apple–style bar and lounge that reflects no other color of the spectrum but ruby red (you gotta see this one). The stylish lobby comes in a close second, followed by the adjoining Titanic Café, a cute little diner serving buckwheat griddlecakes, Vietnamese tofu sandwiches, and dragon-fire salads. Appealing to the masses, Chip left the first four floors as standard no-frills—though quite clean and comfortable—rooms, while decking out the top two floors in neo-deco overtones (well worth the extra $10 per night).

Cornell Hotel. 715 Bush St. (between Powell and Mason sts.), San Francisco, CA 94108. ☎ **800/232-9698** or 415/421-3154. Fax 415/399-1442. 60 units. TV TEL. $95–$115 double. Rates include full breakfast. Weekly rm package including 7 breakfasts and 5 dinners, $525–$795 double per week. AE, CB, DC, MC, V. Parking $15. Cable car: Powell-Hyde and Powell-Mason lines. Bus: 2, 3, 4, 30, or 45.

It's the quirks that make this hotel more charming than many in its price range. You'll be greeted by Rameau, the house golden retriever, when you enter this small French-style hotel. Pass the office, where a few faces will glance up in your direction and smile, and embark on a ride in the old-fashioned elevator to get to your room. Each floor is dedicated to a French painter and is decorated with reproductions. Rooms are all plain and comfortable, with a desk and chairs, and individually decorated in a simple, modern style. No smoking is allowed in any of them. A full breakfast is included in the cavernlike provincial basement dining room, Jeanne d'Arc, and Union Square is a few blocks away.

The Fitzgerald. 620 Post St. (between Jones and Taylor sts.), San Francisco, CA 94109. ☎ **800/334-6835** or 415/775-8100. Fax 415/775-1278. 47 units. TV TEL. $79–$175 double. Rates include continental breakfast. Extra person $10. Lower rates in winter. AE, DC, DISC, JCB, MC, V. Self-parking $15. Bus: 2, 3, 4, or 27.

If you think the guy at the front desk looks cramped in his nook of a lobby, wait till you get to your room. The Fitzgerald's 47 guest accommodations may be outfitted with newish furniture that's accented with bright bedspreads and patterned carpet, but some of the rooms are really small (one that we saw had a dresser less than a foot from the bed). Ask for a larger room. If you can live without a sizable closet (read: tiny), the price, breakfast, and newness of this hotel make it a good value. Families will especially appreciate the two-bedroom suites, which offer one queen- and one full-size bed. Take heed: The view of the Golden Gate that's printed on the brochure is not actually visible from the hotel.

Breakfasts include home-baked breads, scones, muffins, juice, tea, and coffee.

Amenities include a concierge, dry cleaning, laundry service, in-room massage, complimentary coffee in the lobby, and free access to a nearby off-premises indoor pool and health club.

Hotel Beresford. 635 Sutter St. (near Mason St.), San Francisco, CA 94102. ☎ **800/ 533-6533** or 415/673-9900. Fax 415/474-0449. 114 units. MINIBAR TV TEL. $109–$119 double. Rates include continental breakfast. Extra person $10. Children under 12 stay free in parents' rm. Senior citizen discounts available. Ask for special rates. AE, CB, DC, DISC, MC, V. Parking $15. Cable car: Powell-Hyde line (1 block east). Bus: 2, 3, 4, 30, 38, or 45.

Small and friendly, the seven-floor Hotel Beresford is a decent, moderately priced choice near Union Square. Rooms have a mish-mash of furniture and stocked fridges, and to block out the street noise, they've recently installed soundproof windows. Everything's well kept, but don't expect much more than a clean place to rest.

The White Horse Tavern, an attractive replica of an old English pub, serves a complimentary continental breakfast, as well as lunch and dinner.

Hotel David Bed & Breakfast. 480 Geary St. (between Taylor and Mason sts.), San Francisco, CA 94102. ☎ **800/524-1888** or 415/771-1600. Fax 415/931-5442. 56 units. TV TEL. $119 double. AE, DISC, MC, V. Rates include full breakfast. Valet parking $15.

No hotel in the area offers so many amenities for so little money as Hotel David. So what if entering this small, pensionelike hotel via the adjoining large, kosher deli is a little odd. That's the beauty of this place; it's so well hidden that no one knows it's there (not to mention there's easy access to a decent matzo-ball soup and hot pas-trami on rye). But even beyond that, Hotel David's full of surprises. Whether you come in through the street-side entrance or the restaurant, step off the elevator and you'll find immaculate, smallish rooms, with chic-moderne decor, streamlined maple furnishings, and colorful accents. Expect often-overlooked extras like an AM/FM radio, hot towel racks, voice mail, and soundproofed walls. And there's more: free transportation from the S.F. airport (for guests staying 2 or more nights), valet parking (currently $15 per night); and a free full and hearty breakfast—served at David's Deli, of course. *Note:* Those whose hotel experience is heightened by entering and lingering in a grand, proper lobby should seek a room elsewhere.

King George Hotel. 334 Mason St. (between Geary and O'Farrell sts.), San Francisco, CA 94102. ☎ **800/288-6005** or 415/781-5050. Fax 415/391-6976. 141 units. TV TEL. $75–$150 double; $225 suite. Special-value packages available seasonally. Continental breakfast $5.75 extra. AE, CB, DC, DISC, JCB, MC, V. Self-parking $16.50. Cable car: Powell-Hyde and Powell-Mason lines (1 block west). Bus: 2, 3, 4, 30, 38, or 45.

Built in 1914 for the Panama-Pacific Exhibition when rooms went for $1 per night, the King George has fared well over the years, continuing to draw a mostly Euro-pean clientele. The location—surrounded by cable-car lines, the Theater District, Union Square, and dozens of restaurants—is superb, and the rooms are surprisingly quiet for such a busy location. Though the decor is a bit old-fashioned, a recent ren-ovation has upgraded the rooms to new old-fashioned—each one is meticulously neat and clean with full private bathrooms and large beds. A big hit since it started a few years back is the hotel's English afternoon tea, served above the lobby Monday to Saturday from 3 to 6pm.

Services include 24-hour room service, concierge, laundry/valet, baby-sitting, business center, and free access to the nearby 24-hour Nautilus center.

Monticello Inn. 127 Ellis St. (between Mason and Powell sts.), San Francisco, CA 94102. ☎ **800/669-7777** or 415/392-8800. Fax 415/398-2650. 123 units. A/C MINIBAR TV TEL. From $115 double; from $165 suite. Rates include continental breakfast, afternoon tea, and evening wine. Extra person $15. AE, CB, DC, DISC, MC, V. Valet parking $18. Cable car: Powell-Hyde and Powell-Mason lines (direct stop). Muni Metro: All Market St. metros. Bus: All Market St. buses.

Okay, we'll admit it: We didn't know Monticello was the estate of Thomas Jefferson, and we also didn't know that the Monticello mansion is on the tail side of the nickel (Tom's noggin is on the front.) Why the history lesson? In addition to the moniker, "Monticello" is also the hotel's theme. Federal-style decor, Chippendale furnishings, grandfather clocks, Revolutionary War paintings, a toasty, brass-mantled fireplace, and various other old stuff scattered around the lobby attempt to create a colonial milieu. Though it makes for a pleasant entrance, unfortunately the period effect doesn't quite follow through to the rooms. Though the rooms are comfortable, spa-cious, and reasonably attractive, the stark blue carpets and floral upholstery don't have the same faux-Federal theme (certainly the homely air conditioners recessed into the walls don't help). If you can live with this, however, you'll be quite content here. The service is wonderful, the downtown location is primo, parking comes with in-out privileges, and there's even access to a great fitness club around the block (for a $10 fee).

The hotel's restaurant, Puccini & Pinetti, features modern Italian cuisine; it's located next door, at the corner of Ellis and Cyril Magnin streets.

✪ Petite Auberge. 863 Bush St. (between Taylor and Mason sts.), San Francisco, CA 94108. ☎ **415/928-6000.** Fax 415/775-5717. 26 units. TV TEL. $110–$160 double; $225 petite suite. Rates include full breakfast. AE, DC, MC, V. Parking $19. Cable car: Powell-Hyde and Powell-Mason lines. Bus: 2, 3, 4, 30, 38, or 45.

The Petite Auberge is so pathetically cute we can't stand it. We want to say it's overdone, that any hotel filled with teddy bears is absurd, but we can't. Bribed each year with fresh-baked cookies from their never-empty platter, we make our rounds through the rooms and ruefully admit to ourselves that we're just going to have to use that word we loath to hear: adorable.

Nobody does French country like the Petite Auberge. Handcrafted armoires, delicate lace curtains, cozy little fireplaces, adorable (there's that word again) little antiques and knickknacks—no hotel in Provence ever had it this good. Honeymooners should splurge on the Petite suite, which has its own private entrance, deck, spa tub, refrigerator, and coffeemaker. The breakfast room, with its mural of a country market scene, terra-cotta tile floors, French-country decor, and goldyellow tablecloths, opens onto a small garden. There are complimentary California wines, tea, and hors d'oeuvres served each afternoon.

Savoy Hotel. 580 Geary St. (between Taylor and Jones sts.), San Francisco, CA 94102. ☎ **800/227-4223** or 415/441-2700. Fax 415/441-2700. 83 units. MINIBAR TV TEL. $115–$145 double; from $205 suite. Ask about package, government, senior, and corporate rates. AE, CB, DC, DISC, MC, V. Parking $18. Bus: 2, 3, 4, 27, or 38.

When the Savoy opened it was deemed by travelers and *Travel & Leisure* as one of the sweetest affordable options off Union Square. While that's still the case, unfortunately the hotel hasn't kept up with the wear and tear associated with brisk business. However, rooms, which can be small, are still cozy French provincial, with 18th-century period furnishings, featherbeds, and goose-down pillows—plus modern conveniences such as remote-control color TVs and hair dryers. Not all rooms are alike, but each has beautiful patterned draperies, triple sheets, turndown service, full-length mirrors, and two-line telephones. Guests also enjoy concierge service and overnight shoe-shine free of charge. Rates include late-afternoon sherry and tea, served in the Brasserie Savoy, a seafood restaurant (see chapter 6, "Dining," for complete details).

The Shannon Court. 550 Geary St. (between Jones and Taylor sts.), San Francisco, CA 94102. ☎ **800/821-0493** or 415/775-5000. Fax 415/928-6813. 173 units. TV TEL. $129–$149 double or twin; from $350 suite. Extra person $15. Senior, government, AAA, group, and promotional rates available. AE, CB, DC, MC, V. Parking $17. Cable car: Powell-Hyde and Powell-Mason lines (3 blocks east). Bus: 2, 3, 4, 30, 38, or 45.

Spacious rooms rarely come as cheaply as they do here, but you'll be trading a little ambiance for the few dollars you save. The Shannon Court's 1929 landmark building maintains some of its original Spanish flavor, with gracefully curved arches, white stucco walls, and brass fixtures in the lobby. When you head off for your room, however, the cheery atmosphere disappears in the dark, cold hallways. But don't turn and head for the nearest motel yet. You'll be pleasantly surprised at how large, quiet (especially in the back portion of the building), and sunny the rooms are. Because all the rooms' carpeting, bedspreads, and drapes were replaced in 1997, rooms are looking especially dapper, and most have either a sitting area or an extended bathroom. Extras include a small, unstocked fridge, and many rooms have couches and writing desks. The hotel's five suites are on the 16th floor; two have rooftop terraces. Regardless of the upkeep, the building is almost 70 years old, so expect to see some age.

Complimentary morning coffee and afternoon tea are available in the lobby. The City of Paris restaurant, which is popular with the theater crowd, adjoins the hotel and is open daily for breakfast, lunch, and dinner; aside from decent fare at affordable prices, there's also an oyster bar, a good wine list, and a full bar that remains open until 2am.

Warwick Regis. 490 Geary St. (between Mason and Taylor sts.), San Francisco, CA 94102. ☎ **800/827-3447** or 415/928-7900. Fax 415/441-8788. 80 units. MINIBAR TV TEL. $125–$225 double. Rates include continental breakfast. AE, CB, DC, DISC, MC, V. Parking $23. Cable car: Powell-Hyde and Powell Mason lines. Bus: 2, 3, 4, 27, or 38.

Louis XVI may have been a rotten monarch, but he certainly had taste. Fashioned in the style of pre-Revolutionary France (ca. 18th century), the Warwick is awash with pristine French and English antiques, Italian marble, chandeliers, four-poster beds, hand-carved headboards, and the like. The result is an expensive-looking hotel that, for all its pleasantries and perks, is surprisingly affordable when compared to its Union Square contemporaries (singles are as low as $125). Honeymooners should splurge on the Fireplace rooms with canopy beds—ooh la la! Amenities include 24-hour room and concierge service, dry cleaning, laundry, twice-daily maid service, complimentary shoe-shine and newspaper, and valet parking. Adjoining the lobby is fashionable La Scene Café, the perfect place to start your day with a latte and end it with a nightcap.

There's access to a nearby health club, a business center, and conference rooms on the premises.

INEXPENSIVE

✪ **Adelaide Inn.** 5 Isadora Duncan Court (formerly Adelaide Place, off Taylor St., between Post and Geary sts.), San Francisco, CA 94102. ☎ **415/441-2261.** Fax 415/441-0161. 18 units, all with shared bathroom. TV. $52–$58 double with shared bathroom. AE, DC, MC, V. Rates include continental breakfast. Bus: 2, 3, 4, 27, 38, 76.

They say San Francisco is America's most European city, and if you're into the facade, the Adelaide will definitely complete the illusion. The last of the true old-style pensiones, this three-level building tucked in a surprisingly quiet cul-de-sac is bright, cheery, and decorated in long-forgotten ornamentation (remember textured wallpaper?). Colors and furniture hark back to the 1960s not because the owner's gone retro, but probably because he hasn't changed the furnishings since then. But in an inexplicably quaint way, the atmosphere works. Perhaps its the sunny and funky rooms; the small, bright breakfast room; the stairway skylight; or the shared fridge in the kitchen (it certainly isn't the spongy mattresses or tiny bathrooms and old, wet-smelling showers). Whatever it is, this place does feel a lot like home. Services include morning complimentary coffee and rolls, and on-the-premises pay phones. *Note:* This place may not appeal to older travelers—it has steep stairs and no elevators.

Amsterdam Hotel. 749 Taylor St. (between Sutter and Bush sts.), San Francisco, CA 94108 ☎ **800/637-3444** or 415/673-3277. Fax 415/673-0453. 34 units. TV TEL. $79–$89 double (including continental breakfast). AE, MC, V. Parking $12. Bus: 2, 3, 4, or 76.

The lobby feels like that of a cheap motel, and the rooms, though some are decorated with oak furnishings, are a mixture of old and new, tasteful and cheesy. The owners continue to remodel with Jacuzzi tubs, new drapes and carpet, and marble or black-lacquer bathrooms, but it's clear there's no interior designer leading the way. The value is great, though, considering all the perks. On sunny days folks head to the small dining patio out back to enjoy their continental breakfasts.

AYH Hostel at Union Square. 312 Mason St. (between Geary and O'Farrell sts.), San Francisco, CA 94102. ☎ **415/788-5604.** Fax 415/788-3023. 230 beds. Mar–Nov $18 per person for Hostelling International members; $21 for nonmembers. Dec–Feb $16 for members; $19 for nonmembers. Half price for children under 12 when accompanied by a parent. Maximum stay 14 nights per year. MC, V. No parking on premises. A public parking lot on Mission between 4th and 5th sts. charges $12 per 24-hr. period. Cable car: Powell-Mason line. Bus: 7B or 38.

For less than $20 per night you can relive college-dorm life in an old San Francisco–style building right in the heart of Union Square. Occupying five sparsely decorated floors, rooms here are simple and clean, each with two or three bunk beds, its own sink, and a closet; best of all, you can lock your door and take the key with you. Although most rooms share hallway bathrooms, a few have private facilities. Suite rooms are reserved for families. Freshly painted hallways are adorned with laminated posters, and there are several common rooms, including a reading room, a smoking room, and a large kitchen with lots of tables, chairs, and refrigerator space. There are laundry facilities nearby, and a helpful information desk offering tour reservations and sightseeing trips. The hostel is open 24 hours, and reservations are essential during the summer. Persons under 18 may not stay without a parent unless they have a notarized letter, and then they must pay the adult rate.

○ **Brady Acres.** 649 Jones St. (between Geary and Post sts.), San Francisco, CA 94102. ☎ **800/627-2396** or 415/929-8033. Fax 415/441-8033. www.bradyacres.com. 25 units. TV TEL. $75–$95 double per day May–Sept with special weekly rates. Available only by the week Oct–Apr; special weekly rates. MC, V. Parking garage nearby for $15 per day. Bus: 2, 3, 4, 27, or 38.

Inside this small, four-story brick building is a penny-pincher's dream come true. Enter through a black-and-gold door, and you'll find everything you need to keep costs to a minimum. The small but very clean rooms have microwave ovens, small refrigerators, toasters, and coffeemakers; hair dryers and alarm clocks; direct-dial phones (with free local calls) and answering machines; color TVs and radio/cassette players. Bathrooms are newly renovated, and a coin-operated washer and dryer are located in the basement, along with free laundry soap and irons. Owner Deborah Liane Brady and her staff are usually on hand to offer friendly, personal service, making this option all in all an unbeatable deal. Keep in mind that during the low season you can only rent by the week.

Golden Gate Hotel. 775 Bush St. (between Powell and Mason sts.), San Francisco, CA 94108. ☎ **800/835-1118** or 415/392-3702. Fax 415/392-6202. 23 units, 14 with bathroom. TV. $65–$75 double without bathroom; $99–$115 double with bathroom. Rates include continental breakfast. AE, CB, DC, MC, V. Parking $14. Cable car: Powell-Hyde and Powell-Mason lines (1 block east). Bus: 2, 3, 4, 30, 38, or 45.

Among San Francisco's small hotels occupying historic turn-of-the-century buildings are some real gems, and the Golden Gate Hotel is one of them. It's 2 blocks north of Union Square and 2 blocks down (literally) from the crest of Nob Hill, with cable-car stops at the corner for easy access to Fisherman's Wharf and Chinatown (the city's theaters and best restaurants are also within walking distance). But the best thing about the Golden Gate Hotel is that this is a family-run establishment: John and Renate Kenaston are hospitable innkeepers who take obvious pleasure in making their guests comfortable. Each individually decorated room has handsome antique furnishings (plenty of wicker) from the early 1900s, quilted bedspreads, and fresh flowers (request a room with a claw-foot tub if you enjoy a good, hot soak). All rooms have phones, and complimentary afternoon tea is served daily from 4 to 7pm.

Grant Plaza Hotel. 465 Grant Ave. (at the corner of Pine St.), San Francisco, CA 94108. ☎ **800/472-6899** or 415/434-3883. Fax 415/434-3886. 72 units. TV TEL. $59–$75 double. AE, CB, MC, V. Nearby parking $11.50. Cable car: Powell-Hyde and Powell-Mason lines (2 blocks west).

You won't find any free little bottles of shampoo here. What you will find are cheap accommodations and basic—and we mean basic—rooms right in the middle of Union Square/Chinatown action. Many of the small, well-kept rooms in this six-story building overlook Chinatown's main street, and all of them had new bedspreads, draperies, and hair dryers added in 1997. The downside is the minuscule bathrooms and small shower (most don't have tubs). Corner rooms on higher floors are both larger and brighter. Ask for a room on the top floor—they're the newest and are substantially nicer than the older rooms.

The Sheehan. 620 Sutter St. (near Mason St.), San Francisco, CA 94102. ☎ **800/848-1529** or 415/775-6500. Fax 415/775-3271. www.citysearch.com/sfo/sheehanhotel. 65 units. TV TEL. $89–$139 double with bathroom. Rates include continental breakfast. AE, DC, MC, V. Parking $16. Cable car: Powell-Hyde and Powell-Mason lines (2 blocks east). Bus: 2, 3, 4, 30, 38, or 45.

Formerly a YWCA hotel, the Sheehan is dirt-cheap considering its location is 2 blocks from Union Square. Of course, this isn't the Ritz—some walls could use a little paint and there are plenty of areas that would benefit from a little TLC, but ask for one of the remodeled rooms and you'll do just fine. Rooms are clean and simply furnished and come with cable color TV, and the bathrooms are brand new. The hotel has a clean, pleasant lobby; a comfortable tearoom open for light lunches and afternoon tea; and an indoor, heated lap pool and workout area.

3 Nob Hill

VERY EXPENSIVE

Fairmont Hotel & Tower. 950 Mason St. (at California St.), San Francisco, CA 94108. ☎ **800/527-4727** or 415/772-5000. Fax 415/772-5013. 600 units. A/C MINIBAR TV TEL. Main building: $229–$279 double; from $530 suite. Tower: $269–$359 double; from $800 suite. Extra person $30. Continental breakfast $13.50 extra. AE, CB, DC, DISC, MC, V. Parking $27. Cable car: California St. line (direct stop).

The granddaddy of Nob Hill's elite cadre of ritzy hotels, the Fairmont wins top honors for the most awe-inspiring lobby in San Francisco. Even if you're not staying at the Fairmont, it's worth a side trip to gape at its massive, marble Corinthian columns, vaulted ceilings, velvet chairs, gilded mirrors, and spectacular wraparound staircase. Unfortunately, such ostentation doesn't carry over to the guest rooms, which are surprisingly ordinary (aside from the spectacular views from the top floors). In addition to the expected luxuries, guests will appreciate such details as goose-down pillows, electric shoe buffers, bathroom scales, large walk-in closets, and multiline phones with private voice mail.

Dining/Diversions: Masons serves contemporary California cuisine, with live music Tuesday to Sunday. Bella Voce Ristorante features Italian American for breakfast and lunch, while the Crown Room offers deli lunches, dinner buffets, and Sunday brunch, with a panoramic view of the Bay Area. The Tonga Room offers Chinese and Polynesian specialties in a tropical ambiance, as well as dancing and a generous happy hour. Afternoon tea is served daily in the hotel's lobby.

Amenities: 24-hour concierge, 24-hour room service, laundry/valet, complimentary shoe-shine, evening turndown, twice-daily maid service, baby sitting services, doctor on-call, complimentary morning limousine to the Financial District, health club, business center, barbershop, beauty salon, pharmacy, shopping arcade.

✪ **Huntington Hotel.** 1075 California St. (between Mason and Taylor sts.), San Francisco, CA 94108. ☎ **800/227-4683,** 800/652-1539 in CA, or 415/474-5400. Fax 415/474-6227. 140 units. A/C MINIBAR TV TEL. $235–$345 double; from $400–$935 suite. Special packages available. Continental breakfast $11. AE, CB, DC, DISC, MC, V. Valet parking $19.50. Cable car: California St. line (direct stop). Bus: 1.

One of the kings of Nob Hill, the stately Huntington Hotel has long been a favorite retreat for Hollywood stars and political VIPs who desire privacy and security. Family-owned since 1924—an extreme rarity among large hotels—the Huntington eschews pomp and circumstance; absolute privacy and unobtrusive service are its mainstay. Though the lobby, decorated in a grand 19th-century style, is rather petite, the guest rooms are quite large and feature Brunschwig and Fils fabrics and bed coverings, antique French furnishings, and views of the city. The lavish suites, so opulent as to be featured in *Architectural Digest,* are individually decorated with custom-made and antique furnishings. Prices are steep, as you would expect, but special offers such as the Romance Package ($240 per couple, including free champagne, sherry, and limousine service) make the Huntington worth considering for a special occasion.

Dining/Diversions: The Big Four restaurant offers expensive seasonal continental cuisine in one of the city's most handsome dining rooms (see chapter 6, "Dining," for a full description). Live piano music plays nightly in the lounge.

Amenities: Concierge, room service, laundry, overnight shoe-shine, evening turndown, complimentary morning newspaper, twice-daily maid service, complimentary limousine to the Financial District and Union Square, complimentary formal tea or sherry upon arrival, access to off-premises health club and spa ($15).

Mark Hopkins Intercontinental. 1 Nob Hill (at California and Mason sts.), San Francisco, CA 94108. ☎ **800/327-0200** or 415/392-3434. Fax 415/421-3302. 418 units. A/C MINIBAR TV TEL. $220–$320 double; from $450 suite. Breakfast buffet $18 extra. AE, CB, DC, DISC, MC, V. Valet parking $25. Cable car: California St. line (direct stop). Bus: 1.

Built in 1926 on the spot where railroad millionaire Mark Hopkins's turreted mansion once stood, the 19-story Mark Hopkins gained global fame during World War II when it was considered de rigueur for Pacific-bound servicemen to toast their good-bye to the States in the Top of the Mark cocktail lounge. Nowadays, the hotel caters mostly to convention-bound corporate executives who can afford the high rates. Each neoclassical room comes with all the fancy amenities you would expect from a world-class hotel, including custom furniture, plush fabrics, sumptuous bathrooms, and extraordinary views of the city. A minor caveat with the hotel is that it has only three guest elevators, making a quick trip up to your room difficult during busy periods.

Dining/Diversions: The plush and decidedly formal Nob Hill Restaurant offers international cuisine with a California flair nightly (as well as continental buffet breakfast each morning), while the Nob Hill Terrace, adjacent to the lobby, serves lunch, afternoon tea, cocktails, and dinner daily. The world-renowned Top of the Mark lounge serves cocktails from 4pm to 1:30pm daily, Sunday brunch from 10am to 2pm, and dancing to live music every night.

Amenities: Concierge, room service, laundry, overnight shoe-shine, newspaper delivery, evening turndown on request, in-room massage, twice-daily maid service, baby-sitting, valet parking, courtesy limousine weekday mornings, multilingual guest relations, health club, business center, Executive Club floor, car-rental desk.

Hotel Trivia

The Ritz-Carlton's bar holds claim to the country's largest collection of single-malt scotches. Prices range from $7.25 to $66 per glass.

Renaissance Stanford Court Hotel. 905 California St. (at Powell St.), San Francisco, CA 94108. ☎ **800/227-4736,** 800/622-0957 in CA, or 415/989-3500. Fax 415/391-0513. 385 units. A/C TV TEL. $240–$335 double; from $675 suite. Continental breakfast $12.50 extra; American breakfast $22.50 extra. AE, DC, DISC, MC, V. Valet parking $24. Cable car: Powell-Hyde and Powell-Mason lines (direct stop). Bus: 1.

The Stanford Court has maintained a long and discreet reputation as one of San Francisco's most exclusive—and expensive—hotels. Holding company with the Ritz, Fairmont, Mark Hopkins, and Huntington hotels atop Nob Hill, it was originally the mansion of Leland Stanford, whose legacy lives on in the many portraits and biographies that adorn the rooms. Frequented mostly by corporate executives, at first the rooms come across as austere and antiquated compared to most other top-dollar business hotels, but the quality and comfort of the furnishings are so superior that you're forced to admit there's simply no room for improvement. The Stanford Court also prides itself on its impeccable service; a nice touch is the complimentary tray of tea or coffee placed outside your door upon your request. The lobby, furnished in a 19th-century theme with Baccarat chandeliers, French antiques, and a gorgeous stained-glass dome, makes for a grand entrance.

Many of the guest rooms have partially canopied beds, and all have writing desks, extremely comfortable beds, and oak armoires that conceal aging-but-adequate television sets. Bathrooms include mini-TV, telephone, heated towel racks, overhead heat lamps, and makeup mirrors.

Dining: Fournou's Ovens, the hotel's award-winning restaurant, features contemporary American cuisine in a romantic multilevel setting.

Amenities: Concierge, 24-hour room service, 24-hour laundry/valet, complimentary overnight shoe-shine, complimentary morning newspaper and coffee or tea, evening turndown service, baby-sitter on call, complimentary chauffeured car service to downtown destinations. Spectravision movie channels (fee), fitness center, state-of-the-art business center, conference rooms, car-rental desk.

✪ **Ritz-Carlton.** 600 Stockton St. (between Pine and California sts.), San Francisco, CA 94108. ☎ **800/241-3333** or 415/296-7465. Fax 415/291-0288. 336 units. A/C MINIBAR TV TEL. $350 double; $450 club-level double; from $550 suite. Weekend discounts and packages available. Continental breakfast $15.25 extra; breakfast buffet $14 extra; Sun brunch $42. AE, CB, DC, DISC, MC, V. Parking $29. Cable car: Powell-Hyde and Powell-Mason lines (direct stop).

Ranked among the top hotels in the world by readers of *Conde Nast Traveler* (as well as the top hotel in the city), the Ritz-Carlton has been the benchmark of San Francisco's luxury hotels since it opened in 1991. A Nob Hill landmark, this former Metropolitan Insurance headquarters stood vacant for years until the Ritz-Carlton company acquired it and embarked on a massive 4-year renovation. The interior was completely gutted and restored with fine furnishings, fabrics, and artwork, including a pair of Louis XVI French, blue marble-covered urns with gilt mounts, and 19th-century Waterford candelabras. The rooms offer every possible amenity and service: Italian-marble bathrooms with double sinks, telephone, and name-brand toiletries, plush terry bathrobes, and an in-room safe. The more expensive rooms take advantage of the hotel's location—the south slope of Nob Hill—and have good views of the city. Club rooms, located on the eighth and ninth floors, have a dedicated concierge, separate elevator-key access, and complimentary meals throughout the day.

Dining/Diversions: The Ritz-Carlton Dining Room, voted among the nation's top restaurants by several magazines, serves dinner Monday to Saturday (see chapter 6, "Dining," for complete information). The Terrace Restaurant, less formal than the dining room, offers contemporary French cuisine and outdoor dining in the courtyard. The lobby lounge offers afternoon tea and cocktails and sushi daily with low-key live entertainment from 3pm to 1am. Sunday brunch is easily one of the best in town.

Amenities: Concierge, 24-hour room service, same-day laundry/dry cleaning, valet, shoe-shine, complimentary morning newspaper, child care, business center, gift boutique, an outstanding fitness center with pool.

EXPENSIVE

Nob Hill Lambourne. 725 Pine St. (between Powell and Stockton sts.), San Francisco, CA 94108. ☎ **800/274-8466** or 415/433-2287. 20 units. MINIBAR TV TEL. $180 double; $200 executive; $280 suite. Rates include continental breakfast. AE, CB, DC, DISC, MC, V. Valet parking $22. Cable car: California St. line (1 block north).

One of San Francisco's top "business-boutique" hotels, the Nob Hill Lambourne bills itself as an urban health spa, offering on-site massages, facials, body scrubs, aromatherapy, waxing, and yoga lessons to ease corporate-level stress. Even without this "hook," the Lambourne deserves a top-of-the-class rating. Sporting one of San Francisco's most stylish interiors, the hotel flaunts the comfort and quality of its contemporary French design. Top-quality, hand-sewn mattresses and goose-down comforters are complemented by a host of in-room accoutrements that include laptop computers with Internet access, fax machines, irons and ironing boards, VCRs, stereos, kitchenettes, and coffeemakers. Bathrooms contain oversized tubs and hair dryers. Suites include an additional sitting room, plus a choice of treadmill, Lifecycle, or rowing machine. Guests are invited to enjoy a complimentary wine hour starting at 6pm. Smokers should seek a room elsewhere: this place prohibits puffing.

Amenities: Evening turndown, business services, spa treatment room.

MODERATE

✪ **Nob Hill Inn.** 1000 Pine St. (at Taylor St.), San Francisco, CA 94109. ☎ **415/673-6080.** Fax 415/673-6098. 21 units. TV TEL. $99–$169 double; $219–$249 suite. Rates include afternoon tea/sherry. AE, DC, MC, V. Cable car: California St. line. Bus: 1.

Though most of the rooms at the luxurious Nob Hill Inn are well out of budget range, their three "Gramercy" rooms are among the most opulent you will find in the city for under $100. Built in 1907 as a private home, the four-story inn has been masterfully refurbished with Louis XV antiques, expensive fabrics, museum-quality artwork, and a magnificent etched-glass European-style lift. Yet even their lowest priced rooms are given equal attention: large bathrooms with marble sinks and claw-foot tubs, antique furnishings, faux-antique phones and discreetly placed televisions, a comfortable full-size bed, and pin-drop silence. Granted, the Gramercy rooms *are* small, but so utterly charming that it's difficult to complain, especially when you consider that it comes with complimentary afternoon tea and sherry, nightly turndown service, and the distinction of being among the city's most prestigious hotels.

Free Parking: Pass GO, Do Not Pay $200

With parking fees averaging $20 a night at most hotels (talk about a monopoly), you might want to consider staying at one of the establishments listed below if you're crazy enough to drive the sinister streets of San Francisco (As one seasoned driver put it, "We separate pedestrians between the quick and the dead.") All offer free parking—some even offer free covered parking—and are moderate- to low-priced:

- **Dolores Park Inn,** 3641 17th St.; ☎ 415/621-0482. See page 95.
- **Phoenix Hotel,** 601 Eddy St. (at Larkin St.); ☎ 800/248-9466 or 415/776-1380. See page 93.
- **Holiday Lodge & Garden Hotel,** 1901 Van Ness Ave. (between Clay and Washington sts.); ☎ 415/776-4469. See page 89.
- **Cow Hollow Motor Inn & Suites,** 2190 Lombard St. (between Steiner and Fillmore sts.); ☎ 415/921-5800. See page 89.
- **Fort Mason Youth Hostel,** Building 240, Fort Mason; ☎ 415/771-7277. See page 89.

4 SoMa

VERY EXPENSIVE

Harbor Court. 165 Steuart St. (between Mission and Howard sts.), San Francisco, CA 94105. ☎ 800/346-0555 in the U.S., or 415/882-1300. Fax 415/882-1313. 131 units. A/C MINIBAR TV TEL. $195–$245 double. Continental breakfast $6.95 extra. AE, CB, DC, MC, V. Parking $19. Muni Metro: Embarcadero. Bus: 14, 32, or 80x.

When the Embarcadero Freeway was torn down after the Big One in 1989, one of the major benefactors was the Harbor Court hotel: Its backyard view went from a wall of cement to a dazzling view of the Bay Bridge (be sure to request a bay-view room, which is $50 extra). Located just off the Embarcadero at the edge of the Financial District, this former YMCA books a lot of corporate travelers, but anyone who prefers stylish, high-quality accommodations—half-canopy beds, large armoires, writing desks, soundproof windows—with a superb view and lively scene will be perfectly content here. A major bonus for health nuts is the free use of the adjoining top-quality fitness club with indoor, Olympic-size swimming pool.

Dining/Diversions: In the evening the hotel's dark, velvety restaurant, Harry Denton's, transforms into the Financial District's hot spot for hungry singles.

Amenities: Concierge, limited room service, dry cleaning, laundry, secretarial services, excellent fitness club, valet, courtesy car, free refreshments in lobby.

Hotel Griffon. 155 Steuart St. (between Mission and Howard sts.), San Francisco, CA 94105. ☎ 800/321-2201 or 415/495-2100. Fax 415/495-3522. 65 units. A/C MINIBAR TV TEL. $215–$260 double; $315 penthouse suite. Rates include continental breakfast and newspaper. AE, CB, DC, DISC, MC, V. Parking $15. All Market St. buses, BART, and ferries.

After dumping a cool $10 million on a complete rehab in 1989, the Hotel Griffon emerged as a top contender among San Francisco's small hotels. Ideally situated on San Francisco's historic waterfront and only steps from the heart of the Financial District, the Griffon is impeccably outfitted with contemporary features such as whitewashed brick walls, lofty ceilings, marble vanities, window seats, cherry-wood

Accommodations Around Town

Abigail Hotel **23**
Archbishop's Mansion **13**
Beck's Motor Lodge **18**
Bed & Breakfast Inn **7**
Castillo Inn **15**
Cow Hollow Motor Inn & Suites **3**
Dolores Park Inn **20**
Edward II Inn & Pub **4**
Fort Mason Youth Hostel **1**
Harbor Court **36**
Herb 'n Inn **21**
Holiday Lodge & Garden Hotel **26**
Hotel Bohème **32**
Hotel Griffon **36**
Hotel Majestic **10**
Hotel Richelieu **25**
Hyatt Regency San Francisco **35**
The Inn at the Opera **14**
Inn on Castro **19**
Jackson Court **8**
Mandarin Oriental **34**
The Mansions **9**
Marina Inn **2**
Park Hyatt **33**
The Parker House **17**
Phoenix Hotel **24**
Queen Anne Hotel **10**
Radisson Miyako Hotel **11**
San Remo Hotel **27**
Seal Rock Inn **12**
Sheraton at Fisherman's Wharf **30**
Sheraton Palace Hotel **37**
The Sherman House **6**
Stanyan Park Hotel **22**
Tuscan Inn **28**
24 Henry **16**
Union Street Inn **5**
Washington Square Inn **31**
The Wharf Inn **29**
Willows Bed & Breakfast Inn **6**

Haight-Ashbury

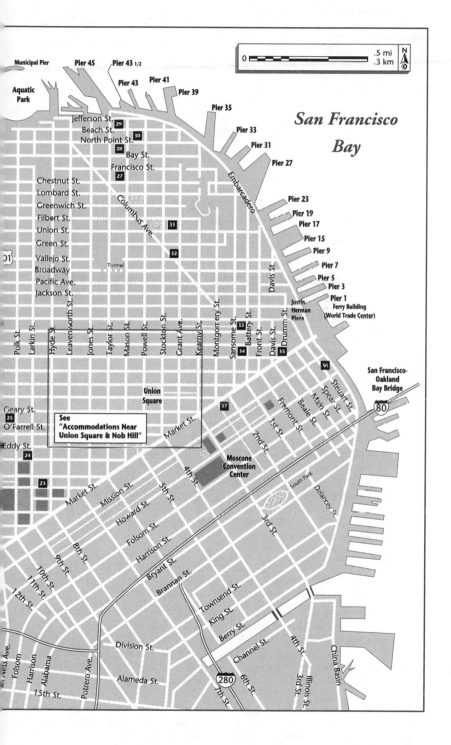

Municipal Pier
Pier 45
Pier 43 1/2
Pier 43
Pier 41
Pier 39
Aquatic Park
Pier 35
Pier 33
Pier 31
Pier 27

San Francisco Bay

Jefferson St.
Beach St.
North Point St.
Bay St.
Francisco St.

Embarcadero

Pier 23
Pier 19
Pier 17
Pier 15
Pier 9
Pier 7
Pier 5
Pier 3
Pier 1
Ferry Building
(World Trade Center)

Chestnut St.
Lombard St.
Greenwich St.
Filbert St.
Union St.
Green St.
Vallejo St.
Broadway
Pacific Ave.
Jackson St.

Columbus Ave.

Tunnel

Davis St.

Justin Herman Plaza

Polk St.
Larkin St.
Hyde St.
Leavenworth St.
Jones St.
Taylor St.
Mason St.
Powell St.
Stockton St.
Grant Ave.
Kearny St.
Montgomery St.
Sansome St.
Battery St.
Front St.
Davis St.
Drumm St.

San Francisco–Oakland Bay Bridge

80

Union Square

Stewart St.
Spear St.
Main St.
Beale St.
Fremont St.
1st St.

Geary St.
O'Farrell St.
Eddy St.

See "Accommodations Near Union Square & Nob Hill"

Market St.

2nd St.

Moscone Convention Center

South Park

4th St.

3rd St.

Delancey St.

Market St.
Mission St.
Howard St.
Folsom St.
Harrison St.
Bryant St.
Brannan St.

5th St.

8th St.
9th St.
10th St.
11th St.
12th St.

Townsend St.
King St.
Berry St.
Channel St.

4th St.
3rd St.

China Basin

Division St.

280

Van Ness Ave.
Folsom
Harrison
Alabama
Potrero Ave.
15th St.

Alameda St.

6th St.
7th St.

Illinois St.

0   .5 mi
     .3 km

N

81

Hotel Trivia

Fitness magazine recently named the Embarcadero YMCA as one of the top-10 hotel health clubs in the United States.

furniture, and art-deco–style lamps (really, this place is smooth). Be sure to request a Bay View room overlooking the Bay Bridge—the added perks and view make it well worth the extra $40—and inquire about the excellent weekend packages the hotel occasionally offers.

Dining/Diversions: Rôti, which has evolved into a prime lunch spot for the nearby Financial District, occupies one side of the lobby, offering California-style food prepared on spit roasts and wood-burning ovens, and served from an open kitchen. The dining room and mezzanine contain rich wood accents and a view of the San Francisco Bay and Bay Bridge.

Amenities: Concierge, limited room service, laundry/valet, in-room massage, baby-sitting, secretarial services, free access to nearby deluxe health center.

5 Financial District

VERY EXPENSIVE

ANA Hotel San Francisco. 50 Third St. (between Market and Mission sts.), San Francisco, CA 94103. ☎ **800/262-4683** or 415/974-6400. Fax 415/495-6152. 667 units. A/C MINIBAR TV TEL. $245–$265 double; from $420 suite. AE, DC, DISC, JCB, MC, V. Parking $25. Muni Metro: All Market St. trams. Bus: All Market St. buses.

The hotel's large number of rooms and fine location—just 1 block south of Market Street, and 1 block from the Moscone Convention Center—makes the ANA attractive to both groups and business travelers.

Rooms have floor-to-ceiling windows and are well outfitted with three telephones (with voice mail and data port for computer modem connection). Corner suites look across the Bay Bridge and to Candlestick ("3Com") Park, and Executive Level rooms include continental breakfast and evening hors d'oeuvres.

Dining/Diversions: Café Fifty-Three serves three meals daily, plus a special Sunday brunch, and offers garden terrace seating. The adjacent lobby bar serves cocktails, wine, beer, and appetizers.

Amenities: Concierge, room service, laundry/valet, twice-daily maid service, fitness center, business center.

Hyatt Regency San Francisco. 5 Embarcadero Center, San Francisco, CA 94111. ☎ **800/233-1234** or 415/788-1234. Fax 415/398-2567. 850 units. A/C TV TEL. $199–$300 double; $349–$450 suite. Continental breakfast $7.95 extra. AE, CB, DC, DISC, MC, V. Valet parking $25. Muni Metro: All Market St. trams. Bus: All Market St. buses.

The Hyatt Regency, a convention favorite, rises from the edge of the Embarcadero Center at the foot of Market Street. The structure, with a 1970s, gray-concrete, bunkerlike facade, is shaped like a vertical triangle, serrated with long rows of jutting balconies. The 17-story atrium lobby, illuminated by museum-quality theater lighting, features flowing water and a simulated environment of California grasslands and wildflowers. The hotel was totally renovated in 1993.

Rooms are comfortably furnished. Each also has a hair dryer, voice mail, telephone and VCR; computer ports for modems are available upon request. Rooms for "Gold Passport" members have tea- and coffee-making facilities, and private fax machines are available free upon request. Rooms with two double beds also include a sofa or easy chair. The hotel's 16th and 17th floors house the Regency Club, with 102 larger guest rooms, complimentary continental breakfast, and after-dinner cordials.

Dining/Diversions: The Eclipse Café serves three meals daily; the Thirteen-Views Bar seats about 200 and is open for morning coffee and evening cocktails. The Equinox, which underwent a $500,000 renovation in 1997, is a revolving rooftop restaurant and bar offering 360° city views.

Amenities: Concierge, 24-hour room service, laundry, overnight shoe-shine, newspaper delivery, twice-daily maid service, express checkout, valet parking. Access to off-premises health club, swimming pool, tennis courts, business center, conference room, Avis car-rental desk.

✪ **Mandarin Oriental.** 222 Sansome St. (between Pine and California sts.), San Francisco, CA 94104. ☎ **800/622-0404** or 415/276-9888. Fax 415/433-0289. 158 units. A/C MINIBAR TV TEL. $325–$415 double; from $475–$520 junior suite. Continental breakfast $18 extra. AE, DC, JCB, MC, V. Parking $25. Muni Metro: Montgomery. Bus: All Market St. buses.

If we were seeking respite from researching this guide, we'd probably head straight here, jump into a Jacuzzi, and, from 48 floors up, relax and admire the city we love most. We'd choose this hotel because all the rooms are located between the 38th and 48th floors of a downtown high-rise, which allows each of the large accommodations extraordinary panoramic views of the bay and city. Not all rooms have tub-side views, but they do have luxurious marble bathrooms, each stocked with a natural loofah, a large selection of English toiletries, terry- and cotton cloth robes, hair dryer, makeup mirror, and silk slippers. The rooms are less opulent, with a kind of reserved-contemporary decor of light colors, Asian accents, and handsome furnishings, which include a spacious desk and sitting area. Since high rates make this mostly a business hotel, additional amenities include three two-line phones with fax hookups, as well as TVs with on-command video access to more than 80 movies.

Dining/Diversions: Silks is a serene dining room that has won rave reviews melding California and Asian ingredients. See chapter 6, "Dining," for complete details.

Amenities: Concierge; 24-hour room service; laundry/valet; complimentary newspaper and shoe-shine; brand-new fitness center with cardio, Nautilus, and free weights; business center.

Park Hyatt San Francisco. 333 Battery St. (at Clay St.), San Francisco, CA 94111. ☎ **800/HYATT-CA** or 415/392-1234. Fax 415/421-2433. 360 units. A/C TV TEL. $320–$370 double; $395–$3,350 suite. AE, CB, DC, JCB, MC, V. Parking $24. Cable car: California line. Bus: 41, 15, 12, 42, 83.

If you're looking for a small luxury business hotel in the heart of San Francisco's Financial District, we strongly recommend a stay at the Park Hyatt San Francisco. About half the size of Hyatt's typical mega-hotels, the 27-story Park Hyatt has a rather plain exterior, but is a pleasure to behold from within. The lobby, for example, is lavishly appointed with Australian lacewood paneling, polished Italian granite, handmade custom carpets from China, and opalescent Spanish alabaster chandeliers. A magnificent spiral staircase, encircling a rather phallic bronze sculpture by Italian sculptor Arnaldo Pomodoro, leads to the upper-level restaurant. The 360 rooms are a bit more understated, with Italian wood furnishings, large bathrooms, exceedingly comfortable beds, and extraordinary views of the city, particularly from the corner suites on the upper floors, which also come with outdoor balconies or a Jacuzzi tub (a tough choice). Ten executive suites have a separate office complete with fax machine and data-port hookups. Though the hotel lacks

---

Sleeping Seaside

You would think that a city surrounded on three sides by water would have a slew of seaside hotels. Oddly enough, it only has one: the **Seal Rock Inn.** It's about as far from Union Square and Fisherman's Wharf as you can place a hotel in San Francisco, but that just makes it all the more unique. The hotel fronts Sutro Heights park, which in turn fronts Ocean Beach. Most rooms in the four-story structure have at least partial views of the ocean; at night, guests are lulled to sleep by the sound of the surf and distant foghorns. The rooms, though large and spotless, obviously haven't been redecorated since the Nixon administration; a monotone hue of beige, brown, and gray make you feel as if you're colorblind. Amenity options range from kitchenettes to two-room suites with wood-burning fireplaces; phones, TVs, covered parking, and free use of the enclosed patio and pool area are standard. Adjacent to the inn is a small cafe serving breakfast and lunch. Golden Gate Park and the Presidio are both nearby, and the Geary bus—which snails its way to Union Square and Market Street—stops right out front.

The Seal Rock Inn (☎ **415/752-8000;** fax 415/752-6034) is located at 545 Point Lobos Ave. (at 48th Avenue), in San Francisco. Double rooms range from $86 to $122.

---

an exercise room, complimentary rowing machines and exercise cycles can be delivered to your room. Another nice perk is the complimentary Mercedes-Benz house car service to anywhere within the downtown area.

Dining/Diversions: The hotel's Park Grill, open for breakfast, lunch, and dinner, offers upscale American cuisine in an elegant setting (the wine list is excellent). More casual alfresco dining is available at the Outdoor Terrace, where lighter fare is served in a garden setting. There's also a full bar on the lobby level.

Amenities: 24-hour room and concierge service, free chauffeur service to the downtown area, laundry, massage, currency exchange, secretarial and business services, valet parking, extensive business services, boardroom, library with international newspapers, meeting facilities at the adjacent Federal Reserve Building.

✪ **Sheraton Palace Hotel.** 2 New Montgomery St. (at Market St.), San Francisco, CA 94105. ☎ **800/325-3535** or 415/392-8600. Fax 415/543-0671. 550 units. A/C MINIBAR TV TEL. $300–$390 double; from $550 suite. Additional person $20. Children under 18 sharing existing bedding stay free in parents' rm. Weekend rates and packages available. Continental breakfast $13.50 extra; deluxe continental $15.75 extra. AE, DC, DISC, JCB, MC, V. Parking $22. Muni Metro: Bus: All Market St. trams. All Market St. buses.

The original 1875 Palace was one of the world's largest and most luxurious hotels, and every time you walk through the doors, you'll be reminded how incredibly majestic old luxury really is. The hotel was rebuilt after the 1906 quake and renovated in 1991, but the most spectacular attribute here is still the old regal lobby and the Garden Court, a San Francisco landmark that has been restored to its original 1909 grandeur. The court is flanked by a double row of massive Italian-marble Ionic columns, and dangles 10 huge chandeliers. The real heart-stopper, however, is the 80,000-pane stained-glass ceiling. Regrettably, the rooms have that standardized, chain-hotel appearance. The on-site, fourth-floor health club features a skylight-covered lap pool, whirlpool, sauna, and exercise room.

Dining/Diversions: On special holidays the Garden Court serves a $55 brunch worth indulging in, while a scaled-down version takes place on other weekends.

Maxfields's Restaurant, a traditional San Francisco grill, has turn-of-the-century charm and is open daily for lunch and dinner. Kyo-ya is an authentic Japanese restaurant with a separate street entrance. The Pied Piper Bar is named after the $2.5-million Maxfield Parrish mural that dominates the room.

Amenities: Concierge, 24-hour room service, laundry/valet, evening turndown, health club, business service center, lobby-level shops.

6 North Beach/Fisherman's Wharf

EXPENSIVE

The Sheraton at Fisherman's Wharf. 2500 Mason St. (between Beach and North Point sts.), San Francisco, CA 94133. ☎ **800/325-3535** or 415/362-5500. Fax 415/956-5275. 524 units. A/C TV TEL. $150–$280 double; from $400 suite. Extra person $20. Continental breakfast $7.95 extra. AE, CB, DC, DISC, MC, V. Parking $14. Cable car: Powell-Mason line (1 block east, 2 blocks south). Bus: 15, 32, or 42.

Built in the mid-1970s, this modern, three-story hotel isn't the most visually appealing of hotels (even their brochure doesn't show it from the outside), but it offers the reliable comforts of a Sheraton within San Francisco's most popular tourist area. In 1995, the hotel spent $4 million renovating the rooms and adding a Corporate Floor catering exclusively to business travelers

Dining/Diversions: Chanen's is a Victorian-style cafe serving breakfast, lunch, and dinner. Live jazz is played several nights a week along with cocktails and assorted appetizers.

Amenities: Concierge, room service, evening turndown, outdoor heated swimming pool, access to nearby health club, business center, hair salon, car-rental desk, travel desk.

Tuscan Inn. 425 North Point St. (at Mason St.), San Francisco, CA 94133. ☎ **800/648-4626** or 415/561-1100. Fax 415/561-1199. 221 units. A/C MINIBAR TV TEL. $135–$188 double; $198–$258 suite. Rates include coffee, tea, and evening fireside wine reception. AE, DC, DISC, MC, V. Parking $17. Cable car: Powell-Mason line. Bus: 42, 15, 32.

The Tuscan Inn is, in our opinion, the best hotel at Fisherman's Wharf. Like an island of respectability in a sea of touristy schlock, the Tuscan exudes a level of style and comfort far beyond its neighboring competitors. Splurge on parking—cheaper than the wharf's outrageously priced garages—then saunter your way toward the plush lobby warmed by a grand fireplace. Even the rooms, each equipped with writing desks and armchairs, are a definite cut above competing Fisherman's Wharf hotels. The only caveat is the lack of scenic views; a small price to pay for a good hotel in a great location.

Dining/Diversions: The adjoining Cafe Pescatore, open for breakfast, lunch, and dinner, serves standard Italian fare in an airy, partial alfresco setting. (See chapter 6, "Dining," for complete information).

Amenities: Concierge, room service, laundry service

MODERATE

✪ **Hotel Bohème.** 444 Columbus St., (between Vallejo and Green sts.), San Francisco, CA 94133. ☎ **415/433-9111.** Fax 415/362-6292. 15 units. TV TEL. $125 double. AE, CB, DISC, DC, JCB, MC, V. Parking $23 at nearby public garage. Cable car: Powell-Mason line. Bus: 12, 15, 30, 41, 45, or 83.

North Beach romance awaits you at the Bohème. Although located on the busiest strip in North Beach, this recently renovated hotel's style and demeanor are more reminiscent of a prestigious home in upscale Nob Hill. The decor reminisces the beat generation, which flourished here in the 1950s; rooms are small but hopelessly romantic, with gauze-draped canopies and walls artistically accented with lavender, sage green, black, and pumpkin. The staff is ultrahospitable, and bonuses include hair dryers and complimentary sherry in the lobby each afternoon. Outside the front door, it's a few steps to some of the greatest cafes, restaurants, bars, and shops in the city, and Chinatown and Union Square are within walking distance. *Take note:* While the bathrooms are sweet, they're also absolutely tiny. *Tip:* Request a room off the street side; they're quieter.

Washington Square Inn. 1660 Stockton St. (between Filbert and Union sts.), San Francisco, CA 94133. ☎ **800/388-0220** or 415/981-4220. Fax 415/397-7242. 15 units, 2 with bathroom across from the rm. TV TEL. $125–$195 double. Rates include continental breakfast. AE, DISC, MC, V. Valet parking $20. Bus: 15, 30, 41, or 45.

Reminiscent of a traditional English inn right down to the cucumber sandwiches served during afternoon tea, this small, comely bed-and-breakfast is ideal for older couples who prefer a more quiet, subdued environment than the commotion of downtown San Francisco. It's located across from Washington Square in the North Beach District—a coffee-craver's haven—and within walking distance of Fisherman's Wharf and Chinatown. Each room is decorated in English floral fabrics with quality European antique furnishings and plenty of fresh flowers; all have private bathrooms. A continental breakfast is included, as are afternoon tea, wine, and hors d'oeuvres. Fax and VCRs are available upon request.

The Wharf Inn. 2601 Mason St. (at Beach St.), San Francisco, CA 94133. ☎ **800/ 548-9918** or 415/673-7411. Fax 415/776-2181. 51 units. TV TEL. $98–$158 double; penthouse $250–$350. AE, CB, DC, DISC, MC, V. Free parking. Cable car: Powell-Mason. Bus: 15, 32, or 42.

Our top choice for budget lodging at Fisherman's Wharf, The Wharf Inn offers above-average accommodations amidst one of the most popular tourist attractions in the world. The newly refurbished rooms, done in handsome tones of forest green, burgundy, and pale yellow, come with all the standard amenities, including complimentary coffee and tea. Its main attribute, however, is its location—right smack dab in the middle of the wharf, 2 blocks away from Pier 39 and the cable-car turnaround, and within walking distance of the Embarcadero and North Beach. The inn is ideal for car-bound families because parking is free (there's $25-a-day saved) and there's no charge for packing along an extra person.

INEXPENSIVE

○ **San Remo Hotel.** 2237 Mason St. (at Chestnut St.) San Francisco, CA 94133. ☎ **800/352-REMO** or 415/776-8688. Fax 415/776-2811. E-mail: info@sanremohotel.com. 63 units, 1 with bathroom. $60–$70 double; $125 suite. AE, DC, JCB, MC, V. Parking $8–$12. Cable car: Powell-Mason line. Bus: 15, 22, 30 or 42.

This small, European-style pensione is one of the best budget hotels in San Francisco. Located in a quiet North Beach neighborhood and within walking distance of Fisherman's Wharf, the San Remo originally served as a boardinghouse for dockworkers displaced by the great fire of 1906. As a result, the rooms are small and bathrooms are shared, but all is forgiven when it comes time to pay the bill. Rooms are decorated in a cozy country style with brass and iron beds, oak, maple, or pine armoires, and wicker furnishings; most have ceiling fans. The shared bathrooms, each one immaculately clean, feature claw-foot tubs and brass pull-chain toilets with oak tanks and brass fixtures. If the penthouse is available, book it: you won't find a more romantic place to stay in San Francisco for so little money.

7 Pacific Heights / Cow Hollow

VERY EXPENSIVE

✪ **El Drisco.** 2901 Pacific Ave (at Broderick St.), San Francisco, CA 94115. ☎ **800/ 634-7277** or 415/346-2880. Fax 415/567-5537. 43 units. A/C TV TEL. $210–$310 double; $280–$550 suite. Rates include continental breakfast. AE, DC, DISC, MC, V. Bus: 3 or 24.

Perched on one of the most coveted blocks of residential property in all of San Francisco, the El Drisco Hotel is one of the finest small hotels in the city. The stately six-story structure was originally built in 1903 as a boarding house for the servants of Pacific Heights's well-to-do, but after some major refinements by interior designer Glenn Texeira (who also did the Ritz-Carlton in Manila), it now caters to a far more affluent clientele. All 24 rooms and 19 suites—swathed in soothing shades of alabaster, celadon, and buttercup yellow—are graced with superior fabrics, quality antiques, and exceedingly comfortable mattresses. Standard amenities include two-line phones with modem hookup, CD players, discreetly hidden VCR/TVs, and minibars; suites include a couch that unfolds into a bed (though you would never guess from the looks of it), an additional phone and TV, and superior views. The marble-laden bathrooms are quite spacious, and are equipped with hair dryers, plush robes, and bathtubs (in most rooms). Our favorite room is 304A, a corner suite with an extraordinary view of the Pacific Heights mansions and surrounding bay. An extended continental breakfast is served in one of the hotel's three quiet, comfortable common rooms, as is 24-hour coffee/tea service. The only things that prevents a four-star ranking, unfortunately, are the service, which is nowhere near the level of the Ritz-Carlton, and the lack of valet parking.

✪ **Sherman House.** 2160 Green St. (between Webster and Fillmore sts.), San Francisco, CA 94123. ☎ **800/424-5777** or 415/563-3600. Fax 415/563-1882. 14 units. TV TEL. $310–$395 double; from $650 suite. Continental breakfast $15 extra. AE, CB, DC, MC, V. Valet parking $16. Cable car: Powell-Hyde line. Bus: 22, 41, or 45.

How expensive is a night at the Sherman House? Put it this way: If you have to ask, you can't afford it. Built in 1876 by philanthropist/music publisher Leander Sherman, this magnificent Pacific Heights Victorian doubled as his home and playhouse for such guest stars as Enrico Caruso, Lillian Russell, and Victor Herbert. After years of neglect, it took 4 years and a small fortune to restore the estate to its original splendor. Today the Sherman House sets the standard in San Francisco for privacy, personal service, and sumptuous furnishings. All rooms are individually decorated with authentic antiques in French Second Empire, Biedermeier, or English Jacobean style and contain queen-size canopy featherbeds along with ultrarich tapestry fabrics and down comforters; all except one have fireplaces. Rooms also feature TVs, VCRs, and stereos, and black granite bathrooms complete with bathrobes and whirlpool bathtubs. The English-style Hyde Park room offers a fine bay view from its cushioned window seat. The Jacobean-style Paderewski suite was formerly the Billiards room, and it retains the dark wainscoting and beamed ceiling. The least expensive room (no. 203) is a twin furnished with English antiques, but it lacks a fireplace. The most expensive suite is the Thomas Church Garden suite, which consists of two rooms with 1½ bathrooms, with an adjoining sunken garden terrace with gazebo and pond.

   Dining/Diversions: The dining room has a very fine reputation, but because of a zoning dispute, it has lost its license to serve food to nonguests and is now open only to residents; this change may affect the standards. Currently, a fixed-price menu, without wine, is available for $75; main courses from the à la carte items run from about $29 to $35. Although prices are steep, the meal is quite elaborate.

Amenities: Concierge, room service, butler (who will discreetly unpack luggage), dry cleaning/laundry, complimentary newspaper delivery, massage, twice-daily maid service, baby-sitting, secretarial services, personalized shopping, chauffeuring.

EXPENSIVE

Jackson Court. 2198 Jackson St. (at Buchanan St.) San Francisco, CA 94115. ☎ **415/929-7670.** Fax 415/929-1405. 10 units. TV TEL. $139–$195 double. Rates include continental breakfast. AE, MC, V. Parking on street only.

The Jackson Court, a stately three-story brownstone Victorian mansion, is located in one of San Francisco's most exclusive neighborhoods, Pacific Heights. Its only fault—that it's far from the action—is also its blessing: If you crave a blissfully quiet vacation while swathed in elegant surroundings, this is the place. Each newly renovated room is individually furnished with superior-quality antique furnishings; two have wood-burning fireplaces (de rigueur in the winter). The Blue Room, for example, features a brass-and-porcelain bed and inviting window seat, while the Garden Suite has handcrafted wood paneling and a large picture window looking out at the private garden patio. After breakfast, spend the day browsing the shops along nearby Union and Fillmore streets, then return in time for afternoon tea.

✪ Union Street Inn. 2229 Union St. (between Fillmore and Steiner sts.), San Francisco, CA 94123. ☎ **415/346-0424.** Fax 415/922-8046. www.unionstreetinn.com. 5 units, 1 cottage. TV TEL. $135–$195 standard double; $245 cottage. Rates include breakfast, hors d'oeuvres, and evening beverages. AE, MC, V. Parking $15. Bus: 22, 41, 45, or 47.

Who would have guessed that one of the most delightful B&Bs in California would be in San Francisco? This two-story Edwardian may front the perpetually busy (and trendy) Union Street, but it's quiet as a church on the inside. All individually decorated rooms are comfortably furnished, and most come with canopied or brass beds with down comforters, fresh flowers, bay windows (beg for one with a view of the garden), and private bathrooms (a few even have Jacuzzi tubs). An extended continental breakfast is served either in the parlor, in your room, or on an outdoor terrace overlooking a lovely English garden. The ultimate honeymoon retreat is the private carriage house behind the inn, but any room at this warm, friendly inn is guaranteed to please.

MODERATE

✪ Bed & Breakfast Inn. 4 Charlton Court (off Union St., between Buchanan and Laguna sts.), San Francisco, CA 94123. ☎ **415/921-9784.** Fax 415/921-0544. 13 units, 4 with shared bathroom. $70–$90 double without bathroom; $115–$140 double with bathroom; $190–$275 suite. Rates include continental breakfast. No credit cards. Parking $10 a day at nearby garage. Bus: 41 or 45.

San Francisco's first bed-and-breakfast is composed of a trio of Victorian houses all gussied up in English-country style, hidden in a cul-de-sac just off Union Street. While it doesn't have quite the casual ambiance of neighboring Union Street Inn, the Bed & Breakfast Inn is loaded with charm. Each room is uniquely decorated with family antiques, original art, and a profusion of fresh flowers. The Garden Suite—highly recommended for families or groups of four—comes with a fully stocked kitchen, a living room with fireplace, two bedrooms, two bathrooms (one with a Jacuzzi tub), a study, and French doors leading out into the garden. Breakfast (freshly baked croissants; fresh fruit; orange juice; and coffee, tea, or cocoa) is either brought to your room on a tray with flowers and a morning newspaper, or served in a sunny Victorian breakfast room with antique china.

Holiday Lodge & Garden Hotel. 1901 Van Ness Ave. (between Clay and Washington sts.), San Francisco, CA 94109. ☎ **415/776-4469.** Fax 415/474-7046. 77 units (12 with kitchenettes). TV TEL. $99–$109 double; $119 double with kitchenette; $145–$165 suite. AE, DC, DISC, MC, V. Free parking. Cable car: Powell-Hyde line. Bus: 42, 47, or 49.

Decorated in what could be called tropical contemporary style, the focal point of the property is the outdoor heated pool and courtyard. The modern rooms were recarpeted in 1996 and contain a TV with HBO. Kids are welcomed with crayons and board games. No breakfast is offered, but there's complimentary coffee in the lobby. Services offered include room service (from a local restaurant delivery service), concierge, laundry/valet, and massage.

INEXPENSIVE

Cow Hollow Motor Inn & Suites. 2190 Lombard St. (between Steiner and Fillmore sts.), San Francisco, CA 94123. ☎ **415/921-5800.** Fax 415/922-8515. 130 units. A/C TV TEL. $82 double, $8 extra per person; from $185 suite, $10 extra person. AE, DC, MC, V. Free parking. Bus: 28, 43, or 76.

If you're less interested in being downtown and more into playing in and around the beautiful bay-front Marina, check out this modest brick hotel smack in the middle of busy Lombard Street. There's no fancy theme here, but each room comes loaded with such amenities as cable TV, free local phone calls, free covered parking, and in-room coffeemakers. All the rooms were renovated in 1996, so you'll be sure to sleep on a nice firm mattress surrounded by clean, new carpeting and drapes. Families will appreciate the one- and two-bedroom suites, which have full kitchens and dining areas.

◗ **Edward II Inn & Pub.** 3155 Scott St. (at Lombard St.), San Francisco, CA 94123. ☎ **800/473-2846** or 415/922-3000. Fax 415/931-5784. 32 units, 11 with shared bath. TV TEL. $76 double with shared bathroom; $96 double with private bathroom; $165–$225 suite/cottage. Rates include continental breakfast and evening sherry. AE, DC, MC, V. Self-parking $9 across the street. Bus: 28, 43, or 76.

This self-styled three-story "English country" inn has a room for almost anyone's budget, ranging from pensione rooms with shared bathrooms to luxuriously appointed suites and cottages with living rooms, kitchens, and whirlpool bathtubs. Originally built to house guests who attended the 1915 Pan-Pacific Exposition, it's now run by innkeepers Denise and Bob Holland, who have done a fantastic job maintaining its worldly charm. Regardless of their rate, all rooms are spotlessly clean and comfortably appointed with cozy antique furnishings and plenty of fresh flowers. The only caveat is that its Lombard Street location is usually congested with traffic, although nearby Chestnut and Union Streets offer some of the best shopping and dining in the city. Complimentary breakfast and evening drinks are served in the adjoining pub.

Fort Mason Youth Hostel. Fort Mason, Building 240, San Francisco, CA 94123. ☎ **415/771-7277.** Fax 415/771-1468. 155 beds. $17 per night. MC, V. Reservations needed well in advance. Breakfast included in the rate.

Unbelievable but true, you can get front-row bay views for a mere $17 nightly. The hostel is on national-park property, provides dorm-style accommodations for 155 guests, and offers easy access to the Marina's shops and restaurants. Rooms sleep 4 to 12 persons, and communal space includes a fireplace, pool table, kitchen, dining room, coffee bar, complimentary movies, laundry facilities, and free parking. The complimentary breakfast alone practically makes it worth the price.

⚙ Marina Inn. 3110 Octavia St. (at Lombard St.), San Francisco, CA 94123. ☎ **800/ 274-1420** or 415/928-1000. Fax 415/928-5909. 40 units. TV TEL. Nov 1–Feb 29 $55–$95 double; Mar 1–May 31 $65–$105 double; June 1–Oct 31 $75–$115 double. Rates include continental breakfast, afternoon sherry, and turndown service. AE, MC, V. Bus: 28, 43, or 76.

The Marina Inn is, without question, the best low-priced hotel in San Francisco. How they offer so much for so little is mystifying. Each guest room within this 1924 four-story Victorian looks as if it has been culled from a Country Furnishings catalog, complete with rustic pine-wood furnishings, a four-poster bed with silk-soft comforter, pretty wallpaper, and soothing tones of rose, hunter green, and pale yellow. There's even high-class touches that many of the city's expensive hotels don't include, such as new remote-control televisions discreetly hidden in pine cabinetry, full bathtubs with showers, and nightly turndown service with chocolates on your pillow—all for as little as *$65 a night* (*$55* in the winter). Combine that with complimentary continental breakfast, afternoon sherry, friendly service, and an armada of shops and restaurants within easy walking distance, and there you have it: Our no. 1 choice for Best Overall Value.

8 Japantown & Environs

EXPENSIVE

The Archbishop's Mansion. 1000 Fulton St. (at Steiner St.), San Francisco, CA 94117. ☎ **800/543-5820** or 415/563-7872. Fax 415/885-3193. 15 units. TEL TV. $149–$385 double. Rates include continental breakfast. AE, CB, DC, MC, V. Limited free parking. Bus: 5 or 22.

One thing is for certain: The archbishop who built this 1904 belle-epoque beauty was no Puritan. Drippingly romantic, the Archbishop's Mansion is one of the most opulent and fabulously adorned B&Bs you could possibly hope to stay in. The Don Giovanni suite—larger than most San Francisco houses—comes with a huge, cherub-encrusted four-poster bed imported from a French castle, a palatial fireplace, elaborately embroidered linens, and a seven-head shower that you'll never want to leave. Slightly closer to earth is the Carmen suite, which has a deadly romantic combination of a claw-foot bathtub fronting a toasty, wood-burning fireplace. In the morning, breakfast is delivered to the guest rooms, and in the evening, complimentary wine is served in the elegant parlor.

Amenities: Concierge, limited room service, laundry/valet, complimentary morning newspaper, limousine service.

⚙ Hotel Majestic. 1500 Sutter St. (between Octavia and Gough sts.), San Francisco, CA 94109. ☎ **800/869-8966** or 415/441-1100. Fax 415/673-7331. 60 units. TV TEL. $135–$195 double; from $315 suite. Group, government, corporate, and relocation rates available. Continental breakfast $8.50 extra. AE, CB, DC, DISC, MC, V. Valet parking $18.

Both tourists and business travelers adore the Majestic because it covers every professional need while retaining the ambiance of a luxurious old-world hotel. It was built in 1902 and thankfully retains its original integrity—the lobby alone will sweep guests into another era with an overabundance of tapestries, tasseled brocades, Corinthian columns, and intricate, lavish detail.

Rooms are furnished with French and English antiques, the centerpiece of each being a large four-poster canopy bed; you'll also find custom-made, mirrored armoires and antique reproductions. All drapes, fabrics, carpet, and bedspreads were replaced in 1997, which ensures you'll rest not only in style, but in freshness as well. Conveniences include a full-size, well-lit desk and clock-radio; extra bathroom amenities include bathrobes. Some rooms also have fireplaces.

Dining/Diversions: Café Majestic and Bar serves California/Asian fare in a romantic setting and continues to intrigue a local clientele. Cocktails are offered in the adjacent bar complete with French mahogany marble-topped bar and a collection of African butterflies.

Amenities: Concierge, room service, valet, dry cleaning, laundry service, complimentary newspaper, in-room massage, baby-sitting, secretarial service, courtesy car on weekdays, and afternoon sherry and fresh-baked cookies from 6 to 8pm nightly.

Radisson Miyako Hotel. 1625 Post St. (at Laguna St.), San Francisco, CA 94115. ☎ **800/533-4567** or 415/922-3200. Fax 415/921-0417. 218 units. A/C MINIBAR TV TEL. $199–$209 double or twin; from $299 suite. Children 12 and under stay free in parents' rm. Continental breakfast $7.50 extra; breakfast buffet $12.50 extra. AE, CB, DC, DISC, MC, V. Valet parking $15; self-parking $10. Bus: 2, 3, 4, or 38.

Japantown's Miyako is a tranquil alternative to staying downtown (and it's only about a mile away). The 15-story tower and five-story Garden Wing overlook the Japan Center, which is home to the city's largest complex of Japanese shops, restaurants, and a huge movie complex, but the hotel manages to maintain a feeling of peace and quiet you'd expect somewhere much more remote. Rooms are Zen-like with East-meets-West decor plus such amenities as an iron and ironing board and hair dryer; the Western-style (don't think cowboy) rooms are fine, but romantics and adventurers should opt for the traditional-style Japanese rooms with tatami mats and futons, *yukatas* (cotton robes), a *tokonoma* (alcove for displaying art), and Shoji screens that slide away to frame views of the city. Two futon luxury suites have Japanese rock gardens and deep-tub Japanese bathrooms. Added bonus: Fillmore Street's upscale boutiques are a few blocks away.

Dining/Diversions: YOYO Bistro, the hotel's restaurant, offers fantastic food, including "Tsumami," Japanese-style cocktail food, in an intimate dining area. See chapter 6, "Dining," for complete details.

Amenities: Limited concierge and room service, dry cleaning, newspaper delivery, evening turndown, in-room shiatsu massage, on-call baby-sitting, express checkout, valet parking, limited exercise room and access to nearby health club, business center, conference rooms, gift shop, car-rental desk.

MODERATE

The Mansions. 2220 Sacramento St. (between Laguna and Buchanan sts.), San Francisco, CA 94115. ☎ **415/929-9444.** 26 units. TV TEL. $129 double; from $225 suite. Rates include full breakfast. AE, DC, DISC, MC, V. Parking $15. Bus: 1, 3, or 83.

Bob Pritikin's inn is one of San Francisco's most unusual and eclectic hideaways, attracting the likes of Robin Williams and Barbra Streisand. Set in a terraced garden adorned with sculptures, The Mansions is actually two historic buildings connected by an interior corridor. Their total and often theatrical originality is reflected in Pritikin's philosophy that "The Mansions is only as good as its last performance."

Each room is different, but most units look out on a rose or sculpture garden, and all are furnished with well-chosen Victorian antiques. All have fresh flowers and TVs (delivered on request). Each unit is named for a famous San Franciscan and includes a wall mural depicting that person's story. The ultimate indulgence is the opulent Empress Josephine Room. There's even an all-glass Garden Room, partly done in spectacular stained glass. Breakfast includes scrambled eggs with hash and toast, fruit, freshly-squeezed orange juice, and coffee.

A fixed-price dinner is served nightly, with prices ranging from $37 on week-nights to $47 on weekends. The Victorian Cabaret Theater stages nightly perfor-mances by virtuoso pianist Claudia the Ghost, playing requests with invisible fingers. Some nights, she performs extraordinary feats of magic, and Pritikin, "America's foremost saw player," also entertains. There's also a game room with bil-liard tables.

Queen Anne Hotel. 1590 Sutter St. (between Gough and Octavia sts.), San Francisco, CA 94109. ☎ **800/227-3970** or 415/441-2828. Fax 415/775-5212. 44 units. TV TEL. $130–$180 double; $185–$295 suite. Extra person $10. Rates include continental breakfast. AE, CB, DC, DISC, MC, V. Parking $12. Bus: 2, 3, or 4.

The majestic 1890 Victorian, which was once a grooming school for upper-class young women, is today a stunning hotel. Restored in 1981 and renovated in 1995, the four-story building remains true to its heritage and emulates San Francisco's golden days. Walk under rich, red drapery to the immaculate and lavish "grand salon" lobby complete with English oak-paneling and period antiques. Rooms follow suit with antiques—armoires, marble-top dressers, and other Victorian pieces. Some have corner turret bay windows that look out on tree-lined streets, as well as separate parlor areas and wet bars; others have cozy reading nooks and fire-places. All rooms have a telephone in the bathroom, a computer hookup, and refrig-erator. Guests can relax in the parlor, with fluted columns and an impressive floor-to-ceiling fireplace, or in the hotel library. There's a complimentary conti-nental breakfast. Services include room service, concierge, morning newspaper, and complimentary afternoon tea and sherry. There's also access to an off-premises health club with a lap pool. If you're not partial to Union Square, this hotel comes highly recommended.

9 Civic Center

EXPENSIVE

✪ **The Inn at the Opera.** 333 Fulton St. (at Franklin St.), San Francisco, CA 94102. ☎ **800/325-2708** or 415/863-8400. Fax 415/861-0821. 48 units. MINIBAR TV TEL. $165–$190 double; from $235 suite. Extra person $15. Rates include European buffet break-fast. AE, DC, MC, V. Parking $19. Bus: 5, 21, 47, or 49.

Judging from its mild-mannered facade and offbeat location behind the Opera House, few would ever guess that The Inn at the Opera is one of San Francisco's, if not California's, finest small hotels. From the minute you walk in through the mul-lioned front door to a lobby decorated with silk and damask, upholstered antique chairs, hand-painted French screen, and loads of marble, you know you're about to be spoiled with sumptuousness. But don't take our word for it; Luciano Pavarotti, Placido Domingo, Mikhail Baryshnikov, and dozens of other stars of the stage throw their slumber parties here regularly, requisitioning the inn's luxurious restau-rant and lounge, Ovation at the Opera, along with a floor or two of rooms. Queen-size beds with huge stuffed pillows are standard in each pastel-hued guest room, along with elegant furnishings, minibars, microwave ovens, refrigerators, and bou-quets of fresh flowers. Suite bathrooms include hair dryers, scales, terry-cloth robes, and French milled soaps. The larger rooms and suites are especially recommended for those who need elbow room; typical of small hotels, the least expensive "stan-dard" rooms are short on space.

Dining/Diversions: Ovation at the Opera, the hotel's fine dining room, pro-vides an intimate setting for dinner, while the adjacent lounge with its leather chairs, glowing fire, and soft piano music is a favorite city meeting place.

Amenities: Concierge, 24-hour room service, laundry/valet, complimentary light pressing and overnight shoe-shine, morning newspaper, evening turndown, staff physician, complimentary limousine service to the Financial District, business center.

MODERATE

Hotel Richelieu. 1050 Van Ness (at Geary Blvd.), San Francisco, CA 94109. ☎ **800/ 295-RICH** or 415/673-4711. Fax 415/673-9362. 168 units. MINIBAR (nonalcoholic) TV TEL. Nov–Mar $109–$119 double; Apr–Oct $129 double. Suites $139–$189. AE, DC, DISC, MC, V. AAA and other discounts available. Parking $13. Bus: 2, 3, 4, 38, 42, 47, 49, or 76.

Considering all the extras, this place offers one heck of a bargain. At one time, the Richelieu must have been a high-end contender: the 1908 building has a grand, welcoming lobby and was built with enough rooms to house a small army. But in modern times its location on Van Ness, the city's street-level Highway 101 thoroughfare, has made it a less desirable spot. Nonetheless, The Richelieu has all kinds of things going for it. For starters, with all the discounts they offer, most guests pay far below $100 per night. Further, the rooms—which are all different—can be quite large and have decent dark wood furnishings; colorful, newish textiles; in-room safes; iron and ironing board (in most rooms); spotless bathrooms; and hair dryers. An added bonus is the new adjoining restaurant—one of our favorite late-night burger joints, wonderfully greasy Mel's Diner. Renovations of the already suitable rooms were completed in spring '98, which means the rooms are even more spiffy and the new lobby, where complimentary coffee and afternoon cookies are served, is looking especially dapper. It's location, 2 blocks from the California Street cable car and near the Opera House, is safer. One bummer: local calls are 60¢ even if your party doesn't answer the phone. *Tip:* Noisier rooms are facing Van Ness. Request something facing the courtyard for a quieter room.

○ **Phoenix Hotel.** 601 Eddy St. (at Larkin St.), San Francisco, CA 94109. ☎ **800/ 248-9466** or 415/776-1380. Fax 415/885-3109. 44 units. TV TEL. $99–$119 double; $149 suite. Rates include continental breakfast. AE, DC, MC, V. Free parking. Bus: 19, 31, or 38.

If you'd like to tell your friends back home that you've stayed in the same hotel as Linda Ronstadt, Arlo Guthrie, and the Red Hot Chili Peppers, this is the place. Situated on the fringes of San Francisco's less-than-pleasant Tenderloin District, this retro 1950s-style hotel has been described by *People* as the hippest hotel in town, a gathering place for visiting rock musicians, writers, and filmmakers who crave a dose of southern California—hence the palm trees and pastel colors—on their trips to San Francisco. The focal point of the Palm Springs–style hotel is a small, heated outdoor pool adorned with a paisley mural by artist Francis Forlenza and ensconced by a modern-sculpture garden.

The rooms, while far from plush, were upgraded in 1998 are comfortably equipped with bamboo furnishings, potted plants, and original local art. In addition to the usual amenities, the inn offers VCRs and movies upon request. Services include an on-site massage therapist, concierge, laundry/valet, and—whoo hoo!—free parking. Adjoining the hotel is Backflip (formerly Miss Pearl's Jam House), a superhip and oh-so-blue cocktail lounge serving tapas and Caribbean-style appetizers and a heck of a lot of San Francisco attitude.

INEXPENSIVE

Abigail Hotel. 246 McAllister St. (between Hyde and Larkin sts.), San Francisco, CA 94102. ☎ **800/243-6510** or 415/861-9728. Fax 415/861-5848. 60 units. TV TEL. $79 double standard; $89 deluxe; $149 suite. Extra person $10. Rates include continental breakfast. AE, CB, DC, MC, V. Parking $12.50. Muni Metro: All Market St. trams. Bus: All Market St. buses.

The Abigail is one of San Francisco's rare sleeper hotels: Though it doesn't get much press, this is one of the better medium-priced hotels in the city. Built in 1925 to house celebrities performing at the world-renowned Fox Theater, what the Abigail lacks in luxury is more than made up in charm. The rooms, while on the small side, are clean, cute, and comfortably furnished with cozy antiques and down comforters. Morning coffee, pastries, and complimentary newspapers greet you in the beautiful faux-marble lobby designed by Shawn Hall, while dinner is served downstairs in the "organic" restaurant, Millennium (see chapter 6, "Dining," for complete information). Access to a nearby health club ($10) and laundry and massage services are available upon request.

10 Haight-Ashbury

MODERATE

Stanyan Park Hotel. 750 Stanyan St. (at Waller St.), San Francisco, CA 94117. ☎ **415/751-1000.** Fax 415/668-5454. www.stanyanpark.com. 36 units. TV TEL. $115–$160 double; from $195 suite. Rates include continental breakfast. Rollaway bed $20; free cribs. AE, CB, DC, DISC, MC, V. Off-site parking $5. Muni Metro: N line. Bus: 7, 33, 71, or 73.

Considering this small inn is the only real hotel on the east end of Golden Gate Park, it's your only real option if you want the stay in the Haight-Ashbury (unless you go for the far-out-and-funky Red Vic). The Victorian has operated as a hotel under a variety of names since 1904, is on the National Register of Historic Places, and is a charming, three-story establishment decorated with antique furnishings, Victorian wallpaper, and pastel quilts, curtains, and carpets. Tub/shower bathrooms come complete with massaging shower head, shampoos, and fancy soaps.

There are one- and two-bedroom suites. Each has a full kitchen and formal dining and living rooms, and can sleep up to six comfortably; they're ideal for families. There's a complimentary tea service each afternoon and evening. Continental breakfast is served in a pleasant room off the lobby.

INEXPENSIVE

The Herb 'n Inn. 525 Ashbury St. (between Page and Haight sts.), San Francisco, CA 94117. ☎ **415/553-8542.** Fax 415/553-8541. 4 units. TV (upon request). $70–$85 double. 2-night minimum. MC, V. Parking with advance notice. Bus: 6, 7, 33, 43, 66, or 71.

For those of you who want to immerse yourself in the sights and sounds of San Francisco's legendary Haight-Ashbury District without compromising on high-quality (and low-cost) accommodations, there's The Herb 'n Inn. Run by sister/brother duo Pam and Bruce Brennan—who know the history and highlights of the Haight better than anyone—this modernized Victorian inn consists of four attractive guest rooms, a huge country-style kitchen, a sunny back garden, and the beginnings of Bruce's Psychedelic History Museum (a.k.a. the dining room). Top choice among the guest rooms is the Cilantro Room, which, besides being the largest, has the only private bathroom and a view of the garden—all for only $10 extra per night. The Tarragon Room has two small beds and a private deck (optimal for smokers, who aren't allowed to fire up inside the house), while the large Coriander Room faces the near-mythical intersection of Haight and Ashbury streets, where there's always something going on. A hearty full breakfast—such as waffles, crepes, popovers, or potato pancakes—is included, as well as office services (including forwarded E-mail), personal city tours à la Bruce, and plenty of free advice on how to spend your day in the city. Kids and gay couples are welcome.

11 The Castro

Though everyone is welcome, most hotels in the Castro cater to a gay and lesbian clientele. Unfortunately, there are few choices, and their amenities don't really compare to most of the better hotels in the city. However, if you'd like to stay in the heart of the Castro, the following are a few options.

MODERATE

Dolores Park Inn. ℅ Bernie H. Vielwerth, 3641 17th St., San Francisco, CA 94114. ☎ 415/621-0482. Fax is the same; please call before faxing. 3 units, none with bathroom; 1 suite (with kitchenette). TV. $109 double; $179 suite; $295 carriage house. Rates include full breakfast. MC, V. Free parking. Muni Metro: F, J, K, L, or M. Bus: 22 or 24.

Conveniently located in the Castro, this inn is within easy walking distance to many shops and clubs and a quick jaunt to downtown. Each bedroom is individually decorated with beautiful antiques and a queen-size bed. Rumor has it celebrities (Tom Cruise, members of the *Sister Act* cast, Robert Downey, Jr., and others) have stayed here to avoid hype. The owner takes special care in providing a warm, hospitable, and romantic environment with helpful service and such bonuses as coffeemakers and hair dryers. The suite has a 20-foot sundeck looking up at Twin Peaks, and a four-poster bed, while the Carriage House offers a heated marble floor, kitchen, washer/dryer, fireplace, Jacuzzi, and VCR. A 2-night minimum stay is required, and there is no smoking allowed.

✪ **The Parker House.** 520 Church St., (between 17th and 18th sts.), San Francisco, CA 94114. ☎ 888/520-PARK or 415/621-3222. Fax 415/621-4139. Members.aol.com/parkerhse/sf.html or parkerhse@aol.com. 5 units. $99–$199 double. Rates include complimentary breakfast. AE, MC, V. Self-parking $15.

This is the best B&B option in the Castro. The neighborhood's "newest and grandest guest house" is a 5,000-square-foot, 1909 Edwardian located in a cheery neighborhood a few blocks from the heart of the action and half a block from grassy Dolores Park. It also happens to be the best choice in the area. Along with a well-decorated common library with fireplace and piano, breakfast room, formal dining room, and garden with patio, lawn, "fern den," and fountains. Each room features a private bathroom, voice mail, cable TV, and modem hookups.

24 Henry. 24 Henry St. (at Noe St.), San Francisco, CA 94114. ☎ 800/900-5686 or 415/864-5686. Fax 415/864-0406. E-mail: WalteRian@aol.com. 9 units, 5 with bathroom. $75–$90 double; $95 suite. $25 extra person. Rates include continental breakfast. AE, MC, V. Muni Metro: J, F, K, L, M, or N. Bus: 8, 22 or 37.

Its Castro location is not the only thing that makes 24 Henry a good choice for gay travelers. The building, a 123-year-old Victorian on a serene side street, is quite charming. The five guest rooms have high ceilings, are adorned with period furniture, and have private phone lines with voice mail. Guests tired of tromping around the neighborhood can watch TV or read in the double parlor (where breakfast is also served). The apartment suites sleep three comfortably and include parlors, separate entrances, phones, and TVs; two have full kitchens. All rooms are nonsmoking.

INEXPENSIVE

Beck's Motor Lodge. 2222 Market St. (at 15th St.), San Francisco, CA 94114. ☎ 800/227-4360 in the U.S., except CA; 415/621-8212 (if in CA, call collect to make reservations). Fax 415/241-0435. 57 units. TV TEL. $75–$125. Rates include parking. AE, CB, DC, DISC, MC, V. Metro: F. Bus: 8 or 37.

In a town where D.I.N.K. (double income, no kids) tourists happily spend fistfuls of money, you'd think someone would create a gay luxury hotel—or even a moderate hotel for that matter. But absurdly, the most commercial and modern accommodation in the ever-touristy Castro District is this run-of-the-mill motel. Standard, but contemporary, the ultratidy rooms include coffeemakers, refrigerators, free HBO, and access to coin-operated washing machines, a sundeck overlooking upper-Market Street, and free parking. Unless you're into the homey B&Bs, this is really your only choice in the area—fortunately, it's very well maintained.

Castillo Inn. 48 Henry St., San Francisco, CA 94114. ☎ **800/865-5112** or 415/864-5111. Fax 415/641-1321. 4 units, none with bathroom. $75 double; $160 suite. Suite rate negotiable depending on season and number of guests. Rates include a deluxe American breakfast. MC, V. Muni Metro: F, K, L, or M. Bus: 8, 22, 24, or 37.

Just 2 minutes from the heart of the Castro District, this charming little house provides a safe, quiet, and clean environment for its clientele. Catering mostly to gay men (though anyone is welcome), the Castillo makes its clientele feel at home while away. Hardwood floors decorated with throw rugs aid in the warmth. Bedrooms are small yet cozy, and phone messages via phone mail are collected at the front desk. The Castillo also provides the shared usage of a large refrigerator and microwave oven in the kitchen. One enormous, two-bedroom suite that sleeps four comfortably has a full kitchen, two TVs, VCR, parking, and a deck.

Inn on Castro. 321 Castro St. (at Market St.), San Francisco, CA 94114. ☎ **415/861-0321.** 8 units. TEL. $85–$140 double; $140–$165 suite. Rates include full breakfast and evening brandy. AE, MC, V. Muni Metro: Castro.

One of the better choices in the Castro, half a block away from all the action, is this Edwardian-style inn decorated with contemporary furnishings, original modern art, and fresh flowers throughout. Almost all rooms have private bathrooms and direct-dial phones; color TVs are available upon request. Most rooms share a small back patio, and the suite has its own private outdoor sitting area. There's also a two-bedroom apartment available for $140 to $200.

The Willows Bed & Breakfast Inn. 710 14th St. (between Church and Market sts.), San Francisco, CA 94114. ☎ **415/431-4770.** Fax 415/431-5295. www.WillowsSF.com. 13 units, 1 with bathroom. TEL. $86–$104 double; $110–$130 suite. Rates include continental breakfast. AE, DISC, MC, V. Limited on-street parking. Muni Metro: Church St. Station (across the street) or F. Bus: 22 or 37.

Right in the heart of the gay Castro District, The Willows Inn employs a staff eager to greet and attend to visitors to San Francisco. The inn's willow furnishings, antiques, and Laura Ashley prints add a touch of romantic elegance. After a long and eventful day of sightseeing and shopping, followed by a night of dancing and cruising, you will be tucked in with a "sherry-and-chocolate turndown." The staff will appear the next morning with your personalized breakfast delivered with a freshly cut flower and the morning newspaper. The place has simple elegance and quality and is eagerly sought out by discriminating gay visitors to San Francisco. Extra amenities include direct-dial phones, alarm-clock radios, and kimono bathrobes.

12 Near the Airport

Comfort Suites. 121 E. Grand Ave., South San Francisco, CA 94080. ☎ **800/228-5150** or 650/589-7100. Fax 650/589-7796. 169 units. A/C TV TEL. $129 double. AE, DC, DISC, MC, V.

Two miles north of the airport, but still well outside of the heart of the city, Comfort Suites is a well-appointed option for travelers on their way in or out of town. Each studio-suite has a king bed, queen sleeper sofa (great for the kids), fridge, microwave, coffeemaker, iron and board, hair dryer, and enough pay-cable channels to keep you glued to your TV set for an entire day, although you'll have to fight the kids over whether it's the HBO special or another round of Nintendo, which is also en suite. Rooms are fine, but it's the freebies here that are most attractive: continental breakfast, evening soup-and-bread bar, airport shuttle, and use of the outdoor hot tub.

Embassy Suites. 250 Gateway Blvd., South San Francisco, CA 94080. ☎ **800/362-2779** or 650/589-3400. Fax 650/876-0305. www.embassy-suites.com. 312 units. A/C MINIBAR TV TEL. $119–$209 double. AE, DC, MC, V.

Your best pick—and most expensive—of the airport chain hotels is Embassy Suites, which does its darnedest to make you forget you're in the middle of drab south San Francisco. The property's got an indoor pool, whirlpool, sauna, and fitness center, a courtyard with a fountain, palm plants, and bar/restaurant and the tastefully decorated two-room suites have wet bar, fridge, microwave, coffeemaker, hair dryer, iron et al., two TVs, and two phones. A cooked-to-order breakfast comes with the cost of the room, which you can have delivered to your door before you're whisked to the airport via their free shuttle.

Holiday Inn. San Francisco International Airport North, 275 S. Airport Blvd. (off Hwy. 101), South San Francisco, CA 04080. ☎ **800/HOLIDAY** or 650/873-3550. Fax 650/873-4524. 224 units. A/C MINIBAR TV TEL. $85–$169 double. AE, CB, DC, DISC, MC, V.

Considering all the free amenities—health spa, movie channels, 24-hour airport shuttle, guest parking—a room at this Holiday Inn is surprisingly reasonable, starting at $85 per night. Granted, there's nary a thing to see or do within a 10-mile radius, but as a layover for next morning's flight out of San Francisco, the Holiday Inn is always a safe bet because the airport is a mere 5 minutes away via the hotel's complimentary shuttle. The rooms are classic Holiday Inn: large, clean, and inoffensively dull, with the usual amenities such as coffeemakers, hairdryers, and minibars. To keep you occupied before your flight departs, the hotel has a gym, sauna, Jacuzzi, and tanning bed, as well as full business services, a gift shop, and Rookie's Sports Bar & Grill, which does a brisk bar business most evenings (the smaller City Café serves American-style breakfast, lunch, and dinner as well).

San Francisco Airport North Travelodge. 326 S. Airport Blvd. (off Hwy. 101), South San Francisco, CA 04080. ☎ **800/578-7878** or 650/583-9600. Fax 650/873-9392. 200 units. A/C TV TEL. $90–$99 double. AE, CB, DC, DISC, MC, V.

The Travelodge is a good choice for families, mainly due to the hotel's large heated pool, which allows the kids to let off some steam while the parents bask in South San Francisco's typically balmy weather. Yes, the rooms are as ordinary as you'd expect from a Travelodge, but they're quite clean and comfortable, and each comes with complimentary HBO, in-room coffee and tea, voice mail, a complimentary copy of *USA Today,* and free local, toll-free, and credit-card calls. The clincher, however, is the 24-hour complimentary shuttle, which makes the 2-mile trip to SFO in a mere 5 minutes. A 24-hour restaurant serving standard American grub is nearby, as is Rookie's Sports Bar & Grill, at the Holiday Inn down the street.

6 Dining

Restaurants are to San Franciscans as bagels are to New Yorkers: indispensable. At last count, city residents had more than 3,300 reasons to avoid cooking at home, and actually spent more money on dining out than those of any other city in the nation.

As one of the world's cultural crossroads, San Francisco is blessed with a cornucopia of cuisines. Afghan, Cajun, Burmese, Jewish, Moroccan, Persian, Cambodian, Vegan—whatever you're in the mood for tonight, this town has got it covered. All you need is money, reservations, and an adventurous palate, because half the fun of visiting San Francisco is the rare opportunity to sample the flavors of the world in one fell swoop.

While dining in San Francisco is almost always a hassle-free experience, there are a few things you should keep in mind your next time out:

- If you want a table at the expensive restaurants with the best reputations, you will probably need to book 6 to 8 weeks ahead for weekends and several weeks ahead for a table during the week.
- If there's a long wait for a free table, ask if you can order at the bar, which is often faster and more fun.
- Don't leave *anything* valuable in your car while dining (particularly in or near high-crime areas), and only give the valet the key to your car, *not* your hotel room or house key.
- *Remember:* It is against the law to smoke in any restaurant in San Francisco, even if it has a separate bar or lounge area. You're welcome to smoke outside, however.

The restaurants below are divided first by area, then by price, using the following guide: **expensive,** more than $45 per person; **moderate,** $25 to $45 per person; **inexpensive,** less than $25 per person. These categories reflect the price of the majority of dinner menu items and include an appetizer, main course, coffee, dessert, tax, and tip.

1 Best Bets

- **Best for Cutting a Deal:** Nob Hill elite and local politicians pitch their proposals at **Moose's,** 1652 Stockton St. (☎ 415/989-7800), where well-prepared food and the high-profile atmosphere put everyone in the mood to negotiate.

- **Best Romantic Spot:** Anyone could be seduced at **Fleur de Lys,** 777 Sutter St. (☎ 415/673-7779), under the rich burgundy-tented canopy that swathes the elegant room in romance. Lots of question-popping here, too.
- **Best for a Celebration:** Great food, a full bar, and a lively atmosphere are the three key ingredients that make **Boulevard,** 1 Mission St. (☎ 415/543-6084), the place to celebrate.
- **Best Decor:** Celeb restaurant-designer Pat Kuleto spent a week sketching sea life at the Monterey Bay Aquarium before laying his Midas touch to **Farallon,** 450 Post St. (☎ 415/956-6969). The result is an orgy of oceanic artwork, from jellyfish lamps to sea urchin chandeliers. It's truly a spectacular achievement in restaurant design.
- **Best Wine List:** Owners of the small **PlumpJack Café,** 3127 Fillmore St. (☎ 415/563-4755), also operate one of the city's best wine stores of the same name. The list, which consists of California wines, is expertly picked and offers more than 80 bottles and 33 selections by the glass. And it's reasonably priced.
- **Best Pizza:** Has **Pauline's,** 260 Valencia St. (☎ 415/552-2050), perfected the pizza? Quite possibly. At least it's the best we've ever had. Pauline's only does two things—pizzas and salads—but does them both better than any other restaurant in the city.
- **Best Desserts:** If nothing else, make sure to stop by **Rumpus,** 1 Tillman Place (☎ 415/421-2300), for one of the best desserts we've ever had: the puddinglike chocolate brioche cake. We've introduced it to out-of-town guests, and they've cursed us ever since because they now know it exists and can't get it at home.
- **Best Value:** Nowhere else in town will you find such heaping plates of fresh pasta at penny-pinching prices than **Pasta Pomodoro,** 655 Union St. (☎ 415/399-0300), 2027 Chestnut St. (☎ 415/474-3400); 2304 Market St. (☎415/558-8123); 3611 California St. (☎ 415/831-0900); and 816 Irving St. (☎415/566-0900).
- **Best Brunch:** On Sunday, the brunch at the **Ritz-Carlton,** 600 Stockton St. (☎ 415/296-7465), will set your eyes popping and your feet tapping. Strut around to the lavish buffets featuring sushi, caviar, freshly made blinis, and more traditional egg dishes. A jazz trio brings joy to it all.
- **Best Newcomers:** The two hot new restaurants for 1998 were **Farallon** (see above), which also wins the Best Decor category, and **Jardinière,** 300 Grove St. (☎ 415/861-5555), the sleek new politico hangout near City Hall. If you want to hobnob with San Francisco's best and brightest, this is where they are.
- **Best Bistro:** Casual and comfortable, **Fringale,** 570 Fourth St. (☎ 415/543-0573), offers some of the best moderately priced French food in the city. Start with a scrumptious galette and finish with the crème brûlée with vanilla bean. The middle's all yours.
- **Best Dim Sum:** Downtown and Chinatown dim-sum restaurants may be more centrally located, but that's all they've got on the **Hong Kong Flower Lounge,** 5322 Geary Blvd. (☎ 415/668-8998), which serves up the best shark-fin soup, seafood dumplings, and salt-fried shrimp this side of China. **Ton Kiang,** located down the street at 5821 Geary Blvd. (☎ 415/387-8273), is also one of our favorites.
- **Best Vegetarian:** For the food, the view of the Golden Gate, and the redwood booths, go to **Greens,** Building A, Fort Mason Center (☎ 415/771-6222). If you want to experience how rich and varied vegetables can taste, then this is the place to sample an extraordinary five-course tasting menu.

- **Best Party Scene:** Throw back a few glasses of sangria with your tapas at **Cha Cha Cha,** 1801 Haight St. (☎ 415/386-5758), and you'll quickly be swinging with the rest of the crowd.
- **Best Coffee Shop or Cafe:** With all the wonderfully unique coffee shops throughout this cafe town, there can be no one winner. We do, however, love the authentic atmosphere at **Mario's Bohemian Cigar Store,** 566 Columbus Ave. (☎ 415/362-0536), and **Caffé Trieste,** 601 Vallejo Ave. (☎ 415/392-6739) (see page 232). Our advice is this: If you see one you like, pull up a chair. Just do yourself one favor: Stay away from the ever-trendy Starbucks.
- **Funkiest Atmosphere:** San Francisco's most . . . *alternative* burger joint is **Hamburger Mary's,** 1582 Folsom St. (☎ 415/626-5767), a popular hangout for gays, lesbians, and just about everyone else eschewing society's norms (and you don't even need leather undies to join the party).

2 Restaurants by Cuisine

AMERICAN
Balboa Café (Pacific Heights/Cow Hollow, *M*)
Bix (North Beach, *E*)
Boulevard (SoMa, *E*)
Cypress Club (North Beach, *E*)
Doidge's (Pacific Heights/Cow Hollow, *I*)
Dottie's True Blue Café (Union Square, *I*)
Fog City Diner (North Beach/Telegraph Hill, *M*)
Hamburger Mary's (SoMa, *I*)
Hard Rock Cafe (Nob Hill/Russian Hill *M*)
Harris' (Pacific Heights/Cow Hollow, *E*)
John's Grill (Union Square, *M*)
Mel's Diner (Pacific Heights/Cow Hollow, *I*)
Patio Café (Castro, *I*)
Planet Hollywood (Union Square, *I*)
Postrio (Union Square, *E*)
Salmagundi (Union Square, *I*)
Sears Fine Foods (Union Square, *I*)
Silks (Financial District, *E*)
Tommy's Joynt (Civic Center, *I*)
Woodward's Garden (Around Town, *M*)

AMERICAN/FRENCH
Universal Café (Mission District, *M*)

AMERICAN/PROVENÇAL
Socca (Richmond/Sunset Districts, *M*)

ASIAN/FRENCH
YOYO Bistro (Japan Center & Environs, *M*)

ASIAN/ITALIAN
Oritalia (Pacific Heights/Cow Hollow, *M*)

CALIFORNIA
Bix (North Beach, *E*)
Café Flore (Castro, *I*)
Cliff House (Richmond/Sunset Districts, *M*)
Gordon Biersch Brewery (SoMa, *M*)
Hawthorne Lane (SoMa, *E*)
Moose's (North Beach, *E*)
One Market (Financial District, *E*)
Rumpus (Union Square, *M*)
Stars (Civic Center, *E*)
2223 (Castro, *M*)
Val 21 (Mission District, *M*)

CALIFORNIA/EAST-WEST
Cafe Kati (Pacific Heights/Cow Hollow, *M*)

CALIFORNIA/FRENCH
The Big Four (Nob Hill, *E*)
Brasserie Savoy (Union Square, *M*)

Key to abbreviations: *E* = Expensive, *M* = Moderate, *I* = Inexpensive.

Grand Cafe (Union Square, *M*)
Ritz-Carlton Dining Room (Nob Hill, *E*)

CALIFORNIA/FUSION
Pacific (Union Square, *E*)

CAJUN/CREOLE
The Elite Café (Pacific Heights/Cow Hollow, *M*)

CALIFORNIA/FRENCH/MEDITERRANEAN
PlumpJack Café (Pacific Heights/Cow Hollow, *M*)

CARIBBEAN
Cha Cha Cha (Haight-Ashbury, *M*)

CHINESE
Brandy Ho's Hunan Food (Chinatown, *M*)
Harbor Village (Financial District, *E*)
House of Nanking (Chinatown, *I*)
The Mandarin (Fisherman's Wharf, *E*)
Sam Woh (Chinatown, *I*)
Tommy Toy's (Financial District, *E*)

CHINESE/DIM SUM
Hong Kong Flower Lounge (Richmond/Sunset Districts, *M*)
Yank Sing (Financial District, *M*)

CONTINENTAL
Carnelian Room (Financial District, *E*)
Lulu (SoMa, *M*)

EAST-WEST FUSION
Eos (Haight-Ashbury, *M*)

FRENCH
Café Claude (Union Square, *M*)
Charles Nob Hill (Nob Hill, *E*)
Fleur de Lys (Union Square, *E*)
Flying Saucer (Mission District, *E*)
Fringale Restaurant (SoMa, *M*)
La Folie (Pacific Heights/Cow Hollow, *E*)
Masa's (Union Square, *E*)
Rubicon (Financial District, *E*)
South Park Café (SoMa, *I*)

FRENCH/ITALIAN
Bizou (SoMa, *M*)
Scala's Bistro (Union Square, *M*)

INDIAN
North India Restaurant (Pacific Heights/Cow Hollow, *M*)

INTERNATIONAL
World Wrapps (Pacific Heights/Cow Hollow, *I*)

ITALIAN
A. Sabella's (Fisherman's Wharf, *E*)
Cafe Pescatore (Fisherman's Wharf, *M*)
Caffè Freddy's (North Beach, *I*)
Caffè Luna Piena (Castro, *M*)
Caffè Sport (North Beach, *E*)
Gira Polli (North Beach, *I*)
Il Fornaio (North Beach/Telegraph Hill, *M*)
Kuleto's (Union Square, *M*)
L'Osteria del Forno (North Beach, *I*)
Mario's Bohemian Cigar Store (North Beach, *I*)
Pane e Vino (Pacific Heights/Cow Hollow, *M*)
Pasta Pomodoro (North Beach, *I*)
Prego (Pacific Heights/Cow Hollow, *M*)
Rose Pistola (North Beach, *M*)
Splendido (Financial District, *M*)
Stinking Rose (North Beach, *M*)
Tommaso's (North Beach, *M*)
Zinzino (Pacific Heights/Cow Hollow, *M*)

ITALIAN/ARGENTINEAN
Il Pollaio (North Beach, *I*)

JAPANESE
Ace Wasabi's (Pacific Heights/Cow Hollow, *M*)
Kabuto Sushi (Richmond/Sunset Districts, *M*)
Kyo-Ya (Financial District, *E*)
Osome (Pacific Heights/Cow Hollow, *M*)
Sanppo (Japan Center & Environs, *I*)

MEDITERRANEAN

Bruno's (Mission District, *M*)
Enrico's (North Beach, *M*)
42 Degrees (Around Town, *M*)
Mecca (Castro, *M*)
Moose's (North Beach, *E*)
Zuni Café (Civic Center, *M*)

MEXICAN

Café Marimba (Pacific Heights/Cow Hollow, *M*)
La Canasta (Pacific Heights/Cow Hollow, *I*)
Sweet Heat (Pacific Heights/Cow Hollow, *I*)
Zona Rosa (Haight-Ashbury, *I*)

PERSIAN/MIDDLE EASTERN

Maykadeh (North Beach, *M*)

PIZZA

Marcello's Pizza (Castro, *I*)

SEAFOOD

A. Sabella's (Fisherman's Wharf, *E*)
Alioto's (Fisherman's Wharf, *E*)
Aqua (Financial District, *E*)
Cliff House (Richmond/Sunset Districts, *M*)
Hayes Street Grill (Civic Center, *M*)
Sam's Grill & Seafood Restaurant (Financial District, *M*)
Swan Oyster Depot (Nob Hill/Russian Hill, *I*)
Tadich Grill (Financial District, *M*)

SINGAPOREAN

Straits Café (Richmond/Sunset Districts, *M*)

SOUPS/SALADS/SANDWICHES

Tassajara (Haight-Ashbury *I*)

SOUTHEAST ASIAN

Betelnut (Pacific Heights/Cow Hollow, *M*)

SPANISH

Thirsty Bear Brewing Company (SoMa, *M*)

SUSHI

Ace Wasabi's (Pacific Heights/Cow Hollow, *M*)
Kabuto Sushi (Richmond/Sunset Districts, *M*)
Kyo-Ya (Financial District, *E*)

THAI

Khan Toke Thai House (Richmond/Sunset Districts, *M*)
Manora's (SoMa, *I*)

VEGAN

Millennium (Civic Center, *M*)

VEGETARIAN

Greens Restaurant, Fort Mason (Pacific Heights/Cow Hollow, *M*)

VIETNAMESE

The Slanted Door (Mission District, *M*)
Tú Lan (SoMa, *I*)

---

3 Union Square

EXPENSIVE

✪ **Farallon.** 450 Post St. (between Mason and Powell sts.). ☎ **415/956-6969.** Reservations recommended. Main courses $18.75–$26. AE, DC, DISC, MC, V. Daily noon–midnight. Bus: 2, 3, 4, 38. Valet parking $7. COASTAL CUISINE/SEAFOOD.

If there is one hot new restaurant that's a must-visit, this is it. Here the multimillion-dollar attraction is seafood, from the outrageous decor to the stellar "coastal" cuisine. Handblown Jellyfish lamps, kelp-bed–like back-lit columns, glass clam shells, sea-urchin light fixtures, a sea-life mosaic floor, and a tentacle-encircled bar sets the scene. Thankfully, during designer Pat Kuleto's impressive renovation of this 1924 building, the original gothic arches were left intact, making the main dining room one of the most impressive in the entire city. (Though the bright and busy front room and intimate and incognito balcony aren't exactly shabby either.) If you think the atmosphere is undeniably appealing and lavish, wait till you try the food. Chef Mark Franz, who opened Stars with Jeremiah Tower, is at the helm of the $5-million kitchen, offering starters ranging from the expected (oysters) to the more ambitious—iced Atlantic and Pacific shellfish indulgence, a cornucopia of oysters, clams, crayfish, prawns, mussels, and scallops with a horseradish mignonette ($16.75 per person); spot prawn, sea scallop, and lobster pyramid (the only mildly disappointing dish of the evening); and knockout main lobster and prawns with potato gnocchi. While most main courses, such as the ginger-steamed wild salmon and striped bass "pillows" with prawn mousse, napa cabbage, and foie-gras coulis, stick with the seaside theme, meat and game eaters are also honored with grilled squab breast stuffed with mushrooms and served with braised Swiss chard and grilled filet of beef with truffled potatoes, caramelized torpedo onions and wild-mushroom sauce. While the whimsy-meets-sophistication does extend to the food, the service and wine list (over 300 by the bottle; 24 by the glass) are seriously professional. This place has been quite the scene since it opened in mid-1997, so reserve well in advance. And if it's available, don't miss the huckleberry bombolini, a refreshingly different dessert.

✪ **Fleur de Lys.** 777 Sutter St. (at Jones St.). ☎ **415/673-7779.** Reservations recommended. Main courses $29–$35; 5-course tasting menu $68; 4-course vegetarian menu $55. AE, DC, MC, V. Mon–Thurs 6–9:30pm; Fri–Sat 5:30–10:30pm. Bus: 2, 3, 4, 27, or 38. FRENCH.

Imagine a large version of Jeannie's (as in "I Dream of Jeannie") live-in bottle: dark, cozy, with 700 yards of rich red floor-to-ceiling hand-painted fabric enclosing the room in lavish intimacy. Throw in dimly lit French candelabras, an extraordinary sculptural floral centerpiece, and about 20 tables filled with well-dressed diners. Welcome to one of the most renowned dining rooms in San Francisco. Fleur de Lys does everything seriously, from its foie-gras starter to its petit fours after dinner. And with Chef Hubert Keller (who was President Clinton's first guest chef at the White House) in the kitchen, it's impossible to go wrong. You can order à la carte, from the five-course tasting menu, or from the four-course vegetarian menu. Start with the knockout blue potato chips with cauliflower purée and caviar. Try any of the "symphony" of appetizers, which include crispy sweetbreads with rock-shrimp mousseline, citrus-and-peppercorn vinaigrette, and Beluga caviar with celery-root blinis. Venture on to a main course, which might include herb-crusted salmon with mushrooms and spinach noodle pie or lamb loin with black truffles. Desserts are artistic creations and may feature chocolate-mousse mice or swans with meringue wings and raspberry coulis. A selection of 300 French and California wines makes this an all-around dining fantasy.

✪ **Masa's.** In the Hotel Vintage Court, 648 Bush St. (at Stockton St.). ☎ **415/989-7154.** Reservations required; accepted up to 21 days in advance. Fixed-price dinner $72–$77. AE, CB, DC, DISC, MC, V. Tues–Sat 6–9:30pm. Closed 1st 2 weeks in Jan and 1st week in July. Cable car: Powell-Mason and Powell-Hyde lines. Bus: 2, 3, 4, 30, or 45. FRENCH.

After the death of founder Masataha Kobayashi in 1984, local gourmets questioned the future of Masa's—but no more. Chef Julian Serrano's brilliant cuisine matched with a flawless wine list and exemplary (even unpretentious) service has solidified Masa's reputation as one of the country's great French outposts.

Either fixed-price or à la carte, dinner is a memorable expense-be-damned experience from start to finish. If you wish, you can simply leave the decisions up to the kitchen. Serrano's passion for using only the highest-quality ingredients accounts for the restaurant's four-star ranking—and budget-busting prices. A typical dinner

Union Square & Financial District Dining

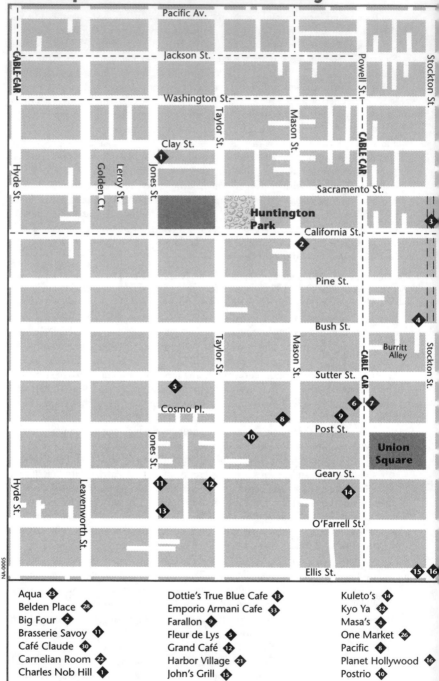

Aqua 23
Belden Place 28
Big Four 2
Brasserie Savoy 11
Café Claude 30
Carnelian Room 22
Charles Nob Hill 1

Dottie's True Blue Cafe 13
Emporio Armani Cafe 33
Farallon 9
Fleur de Lys 5
Grand Café 12
Harbor Village 21
John's Grill 15

Kuleto's 14
Kyo Ya 32
Masa's 4
One Market 26
Pacific 8
Planet Hollywood 16
Postrio 10

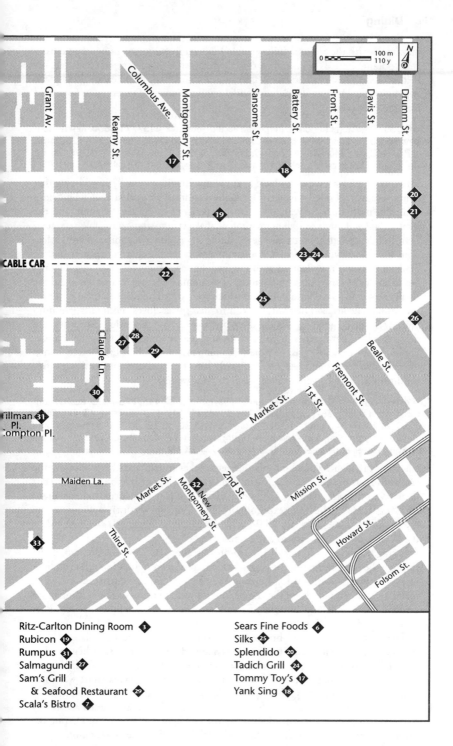

Ritz-Carlton Dining Room 3
Rubicon 19
Rumpus 31
Salmagundi 27
Sam's Grill
   & Seafood Restaurant 29
Scala's Bistro 7

Sears Fine Foods 6
Silks 25
Splendido 20
Tadich Grill 24
Tommy Toy's 17
Yank Sing 18

may begin with the Sonoma foie gras in a Madeira truffle sauce, or poached lobster with potatoes, fried leek, and a truffle vinaigrette. Main entrees may include medaillons of New Zealand fallow deer with zinfandel sauce and caramelized green apples, or the Atlantic black bass with a saffron sauce. Dessert, as you would imagine, is heavenly.

Pacific. 500 Post St. (at Mason St. in the Pan Pacific Hotel). ☎ **415/771-8600.** Reservations recommended for dinner. Main courses $3.50–$13 breakfast, $8–$16 lunch, $17–$26 dinner. AE, DC, MC, V. Mon–Fri 6:30am–9:30pm; Sat–Sun 7am–10pm; Sat–Sun brunch 10am–2:30pm. Cable car: Powell-Mason line. Bus: 2, 3, 4, or 76. CALIFORNIA/FUSION.

It's surprising how few people have heard about Pacific, especially considering that it has recently acquired Michael Otsuka, a wondrously talented chef who brings with him more than 14 years of culinary experience in France, Belgium, and the United States. Combine this with professional yet unpretentious table service, a beautiful, marble-rich, mezzanine-level dining room, and a phenomenal wine selection, and what you end up with is a truly memorable dining experience.

On our last visit, we started with the fresh Sonoma foie-gras sauté with Granny Smith apples prepared three different ways—caramelized, raw, and frozen—and the Dungeness crab "Tart Tatin," both of which were outstanding (you have *got* to try the Tatin). The grilled rare ahi tuna with roasted garlic cloves and mushroom miso sauce was equally good, as was the duck breast layered with a wild-berry sauce and delectable little corn crepes. If you really want to have some fun, allow the sommelier to choose a suitable glass of wine to accompany each dish. A little secret: Lunch offers similar service and selections at nearly half the price, and valet parking is free for diners (though be sure to mention it to your waiter).

✪ Postrio. 545 Post St. (between Mason and Taylor sts.). ☎ **415/776-7825.** Reservations required. Main courses $6–$15 breakfast, $14–$15 lunch, $19–$30 dinner. AE, CB, DC, DISC, MC, V. Mon–Fri 7–10am, 11:30am–2pm, and 5:30–10:30pm; Sat 9am–2pm and 5:30–10:30pm; Sun 9am–2pm and 5:30–10pm; bar daily 11:30am–2am. Cable car: Powell-Mason and Powell-Hyde lines. Bus: 2, 3, 4, or 38. AMERICAN.

They say the higher you climb, the longer it takes to fall, and that's certainly the case with Postrio. Ever since chefs Anne and David Gingrass left the kitchen to start their own enterprise, rumors have been flying that San Francisco's top restaurant isn't what it used to be (poor execution from the line tops the list). If its owners are crying, however, they're crying all the way to the bank, because it's a rare night when the kitchen doesn't perform to a full house.

Eating, however, is only half the reason one comes to Postrio. After squeezing through the perpetually swinging bar—which, in its own right, dishes out excellent tapas and pizzas from a wood-burning oven in the corner—guests are forced to make a grand entrance down the antebellum staircase to the cavernous dining room below (it's everyone's 15 seconds of fame, so make sure your fly is zipped). Pure Hollywood, for sure, but fun.

The menu, prepared by brothers Mitchell and Steven Rosenthal, combines Italian, Asian, French, and California styles with mixed results. When we last visited Postrio, the sautéed salmon, for example, was a bit overcooked, but the accompanying plum glaze, wasabi mashed potatoes, and miso vinaigrette were outstanding. Again with the grilled squab: It lacked flavor, but the accompaniment—a sweet potato foie-gras spring roll—was pure genius. The desserts, each artistically sculpted by pastry chef Janet Rikala, were the highlight of the evening. Despite the prime-time rush, service was friendly and infallible, as was the presentation.

MODERATE

Brasserie Savoy. In the Savoy Hotel, 580 Geary St. (at Jones St.). ☎ **415/441-2700.** Reservations recommended. Main courses $16–$19. AE, CB, DC, DISC, MC, V. Daily 6:30–11am; Sun–Thurs 5–10:30pm; Fri–Sat 5–11pm. Bus: 2, 3, 4, 27, or 38. CALIFORNIA/FRENCH.

If you're headed to the theater or are just looking for a good meal downtown, Brasserie Savoy is an excellent option. The atmosphere is French bistro, with a bright, busy dining room, black-and-white marble floors, and tables with beige and black leather and woven chairs. The food is consistent, affordable, and delicious. Choices may include beef tenderloin with port sauce and green peppercorn butter, or duck breast with mille-feuille of potato and mushrooms served with a date purée and coffee sauce. On the lighter side, the crawfish risotto with red and green peppers, scallions, celery, and chive lemongrass butter is a perfect dish. Among the appetizers, the napoleon of braised rabbit with red onions, mushrooms, kalamata olives, and *anise tuiles* (a thin, crisp anise-flavored cookie shaped like a roof tile) is a preferred choice, or any one of several freshly made salads. To finish, try the innovative crème brûlée.

Café Claude. 7 Claude Lane. ☎ **415/392-3505.** Reservations recommended. Main courses $7–$13. AE, DC, MC, V. Lunch Mon–Sat 11:30am–5:30pm; dinner Mon–Sat 5:30–11:30pm; Sun brunch 11am–4pm. Cable car: Powell-Mason and Powell-Hyde lines. FRENCH.

Euro-transplants love Café Claude, a crowded and lively restaurant tucked in a narrow lane near Union Square. Seemingly everything—every table, every spoon, every saltshaker, and every waiter—is imported from France. There is usually live jazz Tuesday to Thursday and Saturday after 7pm; Friday after 8pm. Outdoor seating is available when weather permits. With prices topping out at about $11 for main courses such as *cassoulet* (white beans with duck confit and sausage), *poussin rôti* (roast Cornish hen with potatoes and aioli), French shepherd's pie, or the *poisson du jour* (fish of the day), Café Claude is a good value.

✪ **Grand Cafe.** 501 Geary St. (at Taylor St., adjacent to the Hotel Monaco). ☎ **415/292-0101.** Reservations accepted. Main courses $13–$24. AE, CB, DC, DISC, MC, V. Daily 7am–2:30pm; Sun–Thurs 5:30–10pm (cafe menu until 11pm); Fri–Sat 5:30–11pm (cafe menu until midnight). Valet parking $7 for 3 hr. Bus: 2, 3, 4, 27, or 38. CALIFORNIA/FRENCH.

With the exception of Farallon restaurant, the Grand Cafe has the most stunningly beautiful dining room in San Francisco. The cocktail area alone is impressive, but the *pièce de résistance* is the enormous turn-of-the-century grand ballroom, a magnificent combination of old Europe and art nouveau. From every angle you'll see playful sculptures, original murals, and a cadre of dazzling deco chandeliers. Until recently, the fare had never quite lived up to the view, but chef Denis Soriano and his crew have finally worked out the kinks and are now enjoying that most coveted of clientele: the repeat customer. On a recent visit, seated in a plush booth with deep brown velvet and framed in walnut, we feasted on poached mussels in a savory celery-and-saffron sauce, a tender, pan-seared duck leg confit with cabbage-walnut dressing, and a tender baby-spinach salad with sliced pears, feta, walnuts, and fresh raspberry vinaigrette. Recommended entrees are the roasted duck breast with mission figs and huckleberry sauce, and the grilled filet mignon in a mushroom-shallot sauce—the most tender cut of meat we've ever encountered. Service was both friendly and prompt, making the entire dining experience a pleasure. *Note:* The bar area has it's own exhibition kitchen and menu, offering similar dishes for about half the price. The pizzas from the wood-burning oven are excellent, as is the grilled marinated skirt steak with whipped potatoes and red-wine sauce.

[San Francisco is] the city that knows how.

—Pres. William Howard Taft

[San Francisco is] the city that knows chow.

—Trader Vic, Restaurateur

John's Grill. 63 Ellis St. (at Stockton St.). ☎ **415/986-DASH.** Reservations accepted. Main courses $12–$25. AE, DC, DISC, MC, V. Mon–Sat 11am–10pm; Sun 5–10pm. Cable car: Powell-Mason and Powell-Hyde lines. Muni Metro: All Market St. trams. Bus: 38 or any Market St. bus. AMERICAN.

John's Grill was one of Dashiell Hammett's regular hangouts in the 1920s, and the restaurant has been cashing in on that connection ever since. You may recall that in *The Maltese Falcon*, Sam Spade stops here for chops, a baked potato, and sliced tomatoes, before setting out on a wild-goose chase after the mysterious Brigid O'Shaughnessy. The real mystery, however, is why people still come here. We've eaten here three times, and on each occasion the food was ill-prepared and over-sauced (as well as overpriced), and the service was atrociously unprofessional. Sam Spade buffs are better off just stopping in for a drink at the memorabilia-filled bar and lounge, which looks much the same as it did in Hammett's day, and offers live jazz nightly.

Kuleto's. 221 Powell St. (between Geary and O'Farrell sts., in the Villa Florence Hotel). ☎ **415/397-7720.** Reservations recommended. Breakfast $5–$10; main courses $8–$18. AE, CB, DC, DISC, MC, V. Mon–Fri 7–10:30am; Sat and Sun 8–10:30am; daily 11:30am–11pm. Cable car: Powell-Mason and Powell-Hyde lines. Muni Metro: Powell. Bus: 2, 3, 4, or 38. ITALIAN.

Story has it the owners of this popular downtown bistro were so delighted with the design of their new restaurant that they named it after the architect, Pat Kuleto. Whatever the reason, Kuleto's is a beautiful place filled with beautiful people who are here to see and be seen (don't come underdressed). The best plan of action is to skip the wait for a table, muscle a seat at the antipasto bar, and fill up on appetizers (which are often better than the entrees). For a main course, try the penne pasta drenched in a tangy lamb-sausage marinara sauce, the clam linguini (generously overloaded with fresh clams), or any of the fresh-fish specials grilled over hardwoods. If you don't arrive by 6pm, expect to wait—this place fills up fast.

Rumpus. 1 Tillman Place (off Grant Ave., between Sutter and Post sts.). ☎ **415/421-2300.** Reservations recommended. Main courses $11.95–$19.95. AE, DC, MC, V. Mon–Sat 11:30am–2:30pm; Sun–Thurs 5:30–10pm; Fri–Sat 5:30–11pm. Bus: 2, 3, 4, 30, 45, 76. Cable car: Powell-Hyde and Powell-Mason lines. CALIFORNIA.

Tucked into a small cul-de-sac off Grant Avenue you'll find Rumpus, a fantastic restaurant serving well-prepared California fare at reasonable prices. The perfect place for a business lunch, shopping break, or dinner with friends, Rumpus is architecturally playful, colorful, and buzzing with conversation. The menu is affordable, offering a delight of flavorful options, such as the pan-roasted chicken whose crispy and flavorful crust is almost as delightful as the perfectly cooked chicken and mashed potatoes beneath it; and the quality cut of New York steak comes with savory mashed potatoes. If nothing else, make sure to stop in here for one of the best desserts we've ever had: the puddinglike chocolate brioche cake. (We've introduced it to out-of-town guests, and they've cursed us ever since because they now know it exists and can't get it at home.)

Scala's Bistro. 432 Powell St. (at Sutter St.). ☎ **415/395-8555.** Reservations recommended. Breakfast $7–$10; lunch and dinner main courses $9–$18. AE, CB, DC, DISC, MC, V. Mon–Fri 7am–midnight; Sat–Sun 8am–midnight. Cable car: Powell-Hyde line. Bus: 2, 3, 4, 30, 45, or 76. FRENCH/ITALIAN.

We had heard so much hype about Scala's Bistro when it first opened that we were sure it wouldn't live up to our expectations. Let's just say we were happily mistaken. Firmly entrenched at the base of the refurbished Sir Francis Drake Hotel, this latest venture by husband-and-wife team Giovanni (the host) and Donna (the chef) is one of the better restaurants in the city. The Parisian-bistro/old-world atmosphere blends just the right balance of elegance and informality, which means it's perfectly okay to have some fun here (and apparently most people do).

Drawing from her success at Bistro Don Giovanni in Napa, Donna has put together a fantastic array of Italian and French dishes that are priced surprisingly low. Start with the Earth and Surf calamari appetizer (better than anything we've sampled along the Mediterranean) or the grilled portobello mushrooms. The Golden Beet salad and Anchor Steam mussels are also good bets. Generous portions of the moist, rich duck-leg confit will satisfy hungry appetites, but if you can only order one thing, make it Scala's signature dish: the seared salmon. Resting on a bed of creamy buttermilk mashed potatoes and ensconced with a tomato, chive, and white-wine sauce, it's one of the best salmon dishes we've ever tasted. Finish with the creamy Bostini cream pie, a dreamy combo of vanilla custard and orange chiffon cake with a warm chocolate glaze.

INEXPENSIVE

Dottie's True Blue Café. 522 Jones St. (at O'Farrell St.). ☎ **415/885-2767.** Reservations not accepted. Breakfast $4.25–$8; main courses $4–$8. DISC, MC, V. Wed–Mon 7:30am–2pm. Cable car: Powell-Mason line. Bus: 2, 3, 4, 27, or 38. AMERICAN.

This family-owned breakfast restaurant within the Pacific Bay Inn is our favorite downtown diner. It's the kind of place you'd expect to see off Route 66, where most customers are on a first-name basis with the staff and everyone is welcomed with a hearty hello and steaming mug of coffee. Dottie's serves above-average American morning fare (big portions of French toast, pancakes, bacon and eggs, omelets, and the like) delivered to blue-and-white checkerboard tablecloths on rugged, diner-quality plates. Whatever you order arrives with delicious homemade bread, muffins, or scones. There are also daily specials and vegetarian dishes.

Emporio Armani Cafe. 1 Grant Ave. (at O'Farrell St., off Market St.). ☎ **415/677-9010.** Main courses $6–$13. AE, DC, DISC, MC, V. Mon–Sat 11:30am–4:30pm, Sun noon–4:30pm. Bus: All Union Square buses. ITALIAN.

All the hobnobbing of an elite dining club comes cheaply at the counter of the Armani Cafe. It's nothing more than a circular counter located in the middle of Armani's ever-fashionable (and expensive) clothing store. But the fare and upscale/casual atmosphere are enough to lure folks who only have lunch, not a new designer suit, on their minds. Local favorites include a homemade antipasto misto, artichoke-heart salad with baby greens and shaved Parmesan, and penne with smoked salmon, tomato, vodka, mascarpone cheese, and chives. There's also a nice variety of sandwiches and, as always, a large dose of attitude. Although there are a few dishes that cost more than $10, you can easily get by on a 10-spot here. Outside seating is available when weather permits.

Planet Hollywood. 2 Stockton St. (at Market St.). ☎ **415/421-7827.** Reservations not accepted except for parties of 20 or more. $8.50–$18.95. AE, DC, DISC, MC, V. Daily 11am–1am. Bus: 38 or any Market St. bus. Muni Metro: any line. AMERICAN.

You won't find any locals here (or movie stars, for that matter), but for some reason tourists can't help but flock to Planet Hollywood. Similar to the Hard Rock, this is a theme-restaurant chain that, instead of music, exhibits movie memorabilia. Expect long lines to get in, plenty of fellow tourists, and a menu featuring salads, sandwiches, pastas, burgers, pizzas, fajitas, and a few grilled-meat items.

Salmagundi. 308 Kearny St. (at Bush St.). ☎ **415/981-SOUP.** Soups and salads $3.50–$8.50. AE, MC, V. Mon–Sat 8am–6pm. Bus: 15. AMERICAN.

If you're pinching pennies on this trip, there's no better deal on a meal near Union Square than at Salmagundi. Bright, pleasant, and sparkling clean, this cafeteria-style restaurant offers a variety of soups, salads, sandwiches, and the occasional special. Among the more unusual soup choices are English country cheddar, Hungarian goulash, North Beach minestrone, and their most popular—sopa de tortilla.

Sears Fine Foods. 439 Powell St. (between Post and Sutter sts.). ☎ **415/986-1160.** Reservations for parties of 6 or more. Breakfast $3–$8; salads and soups $3–$18; main courses $5–$10. No credit cards. Daily 6:30am–2:30pm. Cable car: Powell-Mason and Powell-Hyde lines. Bus: 2, 3, 4, or 38. AMERICAN.

Sears would be the perfect place for breakfast on the way to work, but you can't always guarantee you'll get in the door before 9am. It's not just another pink-tabled diner run by motherly matrons—it's an institution, famous for its crispy, dark-brown waffles, light sourdough French toast, and Swedish, silver-dollar–sized pancakes. As the story goes, Sears was founded in 1938 by Ben Sears, a retired clown. It was his Swedish wife Hilbur, however, who was responsible for the legendary pancakes, which are still whipped up according to her family's secret recipe. Keeping up with the nineties trend, the menu also offers a "healthy-heart menu."

4 Financial District

EXPENSIVE

✪ **Aqua.** 252 California St. (between Battery and Front sts.). ☎ **415/956-9662.** Reservations recommended. Main courses $26–$35; 6-course tasting menu $65; vegetarian tasting menu $45. AE, DC, MC, V. Mon–Fri 11:30am–2:15pm; Mon–Sat 5:30–10:30pm. All Market St. buses. SEAFOOD.

Without question, Aqua is San Francisco's finest seafood restaurant, light years beyond the genre of shrimp cocktails and lemon-butter sauce. Heralded Chef Michael Mina dazzles his customers with a bewildering juxtaposition of earth and sea in his seasonally changing menus. The poached steelhead salmon, for example, rests in a bed of potato and leek purée infused with Dungeness crab, beurre blanc, and oxtre caviar. The miso glazed black cod steak in vegetable jus is another work of art, perfectly paired with rock shrimp and vegetable strudel. Mina's passion for exotic mushrooms pervades most dishes, for taste as well as for show (Mina is, to a fault, amazingly adept at the art of presentation). Desserts are equally impressive, particularly the Aqua soufflé-of-the-day. Steep prices prevent most people from making a regular appearance, but for special occasions or billable lunches, Aqua is highly recommended.

Carnelian Room. 555 California St. (at Montgomery St.). ☎ **415/433-7500.** Reservations recommended. Main courses $22–$39; Sun brunch $27 adults, $13 children. AE, CB, DC,

DISC, MC, V. Daily 6pm–9:30pm; Sun brunch 10am–1:30pm. Cable car: California. Self-parking $7. Bus: 1, 15, 9, or 42. CONTINENTAL.

By day, the Carnelian Room is the exclusive Banker's Club, accessible only to members or by invitation, but at night anyone with a big-enough bankroll can dine among the clouds. Soaring 52 stories above San Francisco's Financial District on the top floor of the Bank of America building, the Carnelian Room is a definite contender for "Best View." Dark oak paneling, brass railings, and huge picture windows reek with romanticism, particularly if you're fortunate enough to get a window table. The upscale menu used to cater to old-style banker's tastes—expensive meat dishes with rich, thick sauces—but the recent trend toward healthier eating has rounded out the menu considerably, and now you can find numerous fish, fowl, and pasta dishes along with such Carnelian classics as prime rib and thick-cut New York steak. A recommend dish is the smoked sturgeon with caviar-whipped potatocs, though it's hard to pass up the rack of lamb with port wine and rosemary sauce. A wine cellar of some 36,000 bottles and the restaurant's accomplished sommelier all but guarantee the proper vintage to accompany your meal.

Harbor Village. 4 Embarcadero Center, lobby level (at Drumm St. between Sacramento and Clay sts.). ☎ **415/781-8833.** Reservations recommended. Main courses $9–$32. AE, DC, MC, V. Mon–Fri 11am–2:30pm; Sat 10:30am–2:30pm; Sun 10am–2:30pm; daily 5:30–9:30pm. Bus: 15, 45, or 76. CHINESE.

Voted best Chinese restaurant in town by *San Francisco* magazine, this is one of the city's most upscale Chinese restaurants, serving primarily Cantonese dishes along with spicy Szechuan specials.

The courteous staff will guide you through the extensive menu, which includes some 30 seafood dishes alone, such as striped bass steamed with ginger and scallions. If you've never had shark-fin soup, this is the place to try it. Unique appetizers include shredded spicy chicken and minced squab in lettuce cups. Stir-fried garlic prawns, beggar's chicken cooked in a clay pot, and sizzling beef in black-pepper sauce are excellent main-course choices. Dim-sum lunch is served daily (from 11am weekdays, 10:30am on Sat, and 10am on Sun) and is definitely worth trying (although the Hong Kong Flower Lounge is better if you don't mind venturing to the Richmond District). The wait staff brings trays full of steaming hot appetizers (they will happily explain what they are) from which you can choose what you like. Try the Shanghai-style steamed pork dumplings flavored with ginger and scallions, the rice-paper dumplings filled with sweet shrimp, taro cake, or the curried beef wonton.

The restaurant offers validated parking at all the Embarcadero Center garages (located at the foot of Clay Street). It'll cost you a few dollars during weekdays, but it's free after 5pm Monday to Friday and all day on weekends and holidays.

Kyo-Ya. In the Sheraton Palace Hotel, 2 New Montgomery St. (at Market St.). ☎ **415/546-5090.** Reservations recommended. Sushi $4–$8; main courses $25–$35; fixed-price menus $45–$65. AE, CB, DC, DISC, JCB, MC, V. Tues–Fri 11:30am–2pm; Tues–Sat 6–10pm. All Market St. trams. All Market St. buses. JAPANESE/SUSHI.

It's anything but cheap, but this restaurant offers an authentic Japanese experience, from the decor down to the service and most assuredly the stellar food. Specialties feature the freshest sushi and sashimi, as well as grilled and *nabemono* dishes (kettle dishes cooked at the table). To start, try any of the appetizers, and move on to the grilled butter fish with miso sauce. Complete dinners include kobachi, soup, rice, pickles, and dessert. Most consider this—along with Kabuto—the best sushi in the city.

One Market. 1 Market St. (at Steuart across from Justin Herman Plaza). ☎ **415/777-5577.** Reservations recommended. Main courses $18–$30. AE, DC, MC, V. Mon–Thurs 11:30am–2pm and 5:30–9pm; Fri 11:30am–2pm and 5:30–10pm; Sat 5–10pm. All Market St. buses. Valet parking $7. CALIFORNIA.

The enormous restaurant's decor, which is both cosmopolitan and folk-artsy, has been recently fine-tuned to complement executive-chef George Morrone's (previously at Aqua) farm-fresh menu. Amidst tapestry, banquettes, mahogany, and slate floors, there's seating for 170 in the main dining area. The bar, which features gold walls and sponge-painted mustard columns, displays a prominent colorful mural of a market scene. The menu changes frequently to reflect the freshest local ingredients. Start with a dozen of the Skookum and Fanny Bay oysters with homemade cocktail sauce and chili malt vinegar dressing, followed by the maple-glazed day-boat scallops with pumpkin ravioli. Main courses range from wild steelhead with foie-gras mashed potatoes and green-apple jus to herb-poached baby chicken with white-pepper dumplings, bouillon, and turnip greens. Whatever you choose, you're bound to find a perfectly accompanying wine from the "cellar," which has over 500 selections of American vintages. A corporate crowd convenes from 5 to 7pm weeknights for $1 beers. The room picks up with live jazz nightly.

Rubicon. 558 Sacramento St. (between Sansome and Montgomery sts.). ☎ **415/434-4100.** Reservations recommended. Main courses $19–$29. AE, MC, V. Mon–Fri 11:30am–2:30pm; Mon–Sat 5:30–10:30pm. Bus: 15 or 41. FRENCH CONTEMPORARY.

Opened in 1994, Rubicon won instant publicity because of the fame of its owners, film director Francis Ford Coppola and actor Robert DeNiro. Named for Coppola's Napa Valley wine, Rubicon features a contemporary and somewhat stiff dining room frequented by big-business power-lunchers and an upscale, middle-aged crowd.

Until 1997, renowned chef Traci Des Jardins reigned in the kitchen, but she was recently replaced by Scott Newman. While the menu changes frequently, favorites among the 10 or so appetizers include the ahi-tuna tartare with ponzu mignonette, foie gras with brandied cherries, and carpaccio of salmon with cucumber mint vinaigrette. About eight main courses are available daily, and may include a sautéed salmon with savoy cabbage, pearl onions, smoked bacon, and red-wine sauce; loin of lamb with potato and celery-root galette and chervil sauce; or Muscovy duck breast with braised turnips and tat-soi honey coriander sauce.

Silks. In the Mandarin Oriental Hotel, 222 Sansome St. (between Pine and California sts.). ☎ **415/885-0999.** Reservations recommended. Main courses at dinner $23–$30; 5-course tasting menu $60, $85 with wine. AE, DC, MC, V. Mon–Fri 6:30–10:30am, 11:30am–2pm, and 6–9:30pm; Sat–Sun 7–11am and 6–9:30pm. CONTEMPORARY AMERICAN.

In mid-1997, Silks shirked its reputation for serving some of the best in California cuisine to follow a hotter trend: contemporary American. Now Charlie Palmer, of New York's reputed Aureole restaurant, acts as "consulting chef," which means he's presiding over the menu, but not the kitchen. On hand, however, is protégé chef Dante Boccuzzi, who ensures that the ever-evolving cuisine meets Palmer's high standards. Expect to indulge in eclectic, seasonal fare with influences from Asia and beyond, such as the exciting tamarind barbecue quail with foie-gras shu mai and star anise juice starter, or such exotic main courses as the crab-stuffed brook trout in a rice-flour crepe with carrot-curry pan jus, or prosciutto-crusted rabbit saddle with crisp sage. Those into the full experience should opt for the five-course tasting menu, which can be accompanied by complementing wines.

The Sun on Your Face at Belden Place

As cosmopolitan as San Francisco claims to be, it's woefully lacking in the alfresco dining department compared to most European cities. One exception, however, is Belden Place, an adorable little brick alley in the heart of the Financial District that is closed to everything but foot traffic. When the weather is agreeable, the restaurants that line the alley break out the big umbrellas, tables, and chairs à la *Boulevard Saint-Michel* and voilà—a bit of Paris just off of Pine Street.

The four cafes that line Belden Place offer a wide variety of cuisine. From south to north they are **Cafe Bastille,** 22 Belden Place (☎ 415/986-5673), your classic French bistro serving excellent crepes, mussels, and French onion soup along with live jazz on weekends; **Cafe Tiramisu,** 28 Belden Place (☎ 415/421-7044), a superb—and stylish—Italian hot spot serving additive risottos and gnocchi; **Plouf,** 40 Belden Place (☎ 415/986-6491), which specializes in big bowls of mussels slathered in a choice of seven sauces as well as fresh seafood; and **Fizz Supper Club,** 471 Pine St. (☎ 415/421-3499), a chic American-Mediterranean bistro serving such entrees as Andouille-stuffed quail with saffron risotto cake and braised rabbit with jalapeno peach chutney. There's also live jazz nightly at Fizz, but it's a cloudless San Francisco day that draws the city's sun-starved culinary cognoscenti to all four of these *très chic* cafes.

Tommy Toy's. 655 Montgomery St. (at Columbus Ave. and Washington St.) ☎ 415/397-4888. Main courses $14.95–$28. Fixed-price dinner $39.50. AE, DC, DISC, JCB, MC, V. Mon–Fri 11:30am–2:30pm; daily 6–9:30pm. Closed Thanksgiving and Christmas. Valet parking $3.50 (dinner only). CHINESE.

Chinese food is to San Franciscans what pizza is to college students: fast, delicious, and cheap. But Tommy Toy's turned Chinese from a take-out affair to a dress-up affair when he created an opulent, dark, and unmistakably Asian fine-dining environment that cost a cool $1.5 million. The dining room, created after the 19th-century empress dowager's reading room, is accented with dimly lit candelabras and ancient paintings. Most evenings, the restaurant is crowded with tourists and some locals who come for the five-course fixed-price meal, which usually includes minced squab in lettuce leaves, lobster bisque soup served in a coconut and topped with puffed pastry, a whole lobster sautéed with peanuts and mushrooms, duck served with plum sauce, medaillons of beef, and finally a light dessert of peach mousse. The à la carte menu flaunts vanilla prawns and other such delicacies. On the two occasions we've been here, once the food was very good, the next time it was just okay, and both times the portions were substantial. Our only issue with Tommy Toy's is that if we were to throw down around $50 for a feast, we would do it at La Folie or Fleur de Lys, where the food is remarkably special. But if you want romantic Chinese, this is as good as it gets in the US of A.

MODERATE

Sam's Grill & Seafood Restaurant. 374 Bush St. (between Montgomery and Kearny sts.). ☎ 415/421-0594. Reservations accepted for dinner and for 5 or more at lunch. Main courses $9–$23.50. AE, CB, DC, MC, V. Mon–Fri 11am–9pm. Bus: 15, 45, or 76. SEAFOOD.

Power-lunching at Sam's is a San Francisco tradition, and they've been doing a brisk business with Financial District types for what seems like forever (they opened in

Dining Around Town

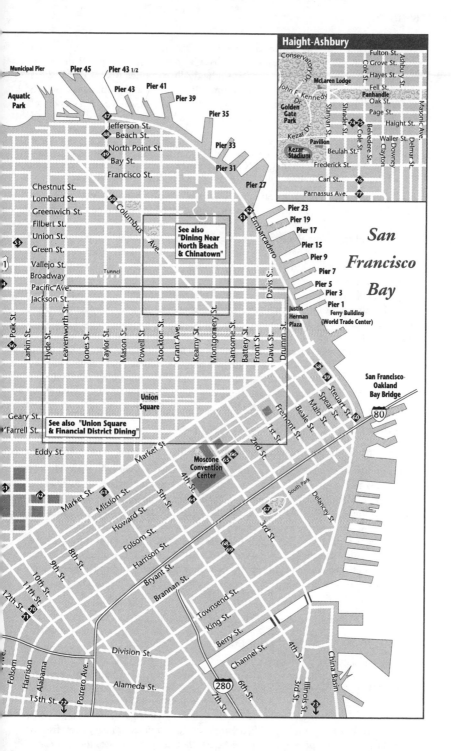

Municipal Pier
Pier 45
Pier 43 1/2
Pier 43
Pier 41
Pier 39
Pier 35
Pier 33
Pier 31
Pier 27
Pier 23
Pier 19
Pier 17
Pier 15
Pier 9
Pier 7
Pier 5
Pier 3
Pier 1

Aquatic Park

Haight-Ashbury

Conservatory Dr.
Fulton St.
Grove St.
Hayes St.
Fell St.
Oak St.
Page St.
Haight St.
Waller St.
Frederick St.
Carl St..
Parnassus Ave.

McLaren Lodge
John F. Kennedy Dr
Golden Gate Park
Kezar Dr
Pavilion
Kezar Stadium
Beulah St.

Ashbury St.
Cole St.
Panhandle
Stanyan St.
Shrader St.
Belvedere St.
Cole St.
Clayton
Downey
Masonic Ave.
Delmar St.

Jefferson St.
Beach St.
North Point St.
Bay St.
Francisco St.

Chestnut St.
Lombard St.
Greenwich St.
Filbert St.
Union St.
Green St.
Vallejo St.
Broadway
Pacific Ave.
Jackson St.

Columbus Ave.

See also "Dining Near North Beach & Chinatown"

Tunnel

Embarcadero

San Francisco Bay

Polk St
Larkin St
Hyde St.
Leavenworth St.
Jones St.
Taylor St.
Mason St.
Powell St.
Stockton St.
Grant Ave.
Kearny St.
Montgomery St.
Sansome St.
Battery St.
Front St.
Davis St.
Drumm St.

Davis St.

Justin Herman Plaza

Ferry Building (World Trade Center)

Union Square

See also "Union Square & Financial District Dining"

Geary St.
"Farrell St.
Eddy St.

Steuart St.
Spear St.
Main St.
Beale St.
Fremont St.
2nd St.
1st St.

San Francisco-Oakland Bay Bridge

80

Market St.
Mission St.
Howard St.
Folsom St.
Harrison St.
Bryant St.
Brannan St.

4th St.
5th St.
8th St.
9th St.
10th St.
11th St.
12th St.

Moscone Convention Center

South Park

3rd St.

Delancey St.

Townsend St.
King St.
Berry St.
Channel St.

Division St.
Alameda St.
15th St.

Harrison
Alabama
Potrero Ave.

280

6th St.
7th St.
4th St.
3rd St.
Illinois St.
China Basin

Folsom

1967). The entrance, which holds a polished, small mahogany bar, opens onto a main dining room with high-backed booths. It's noisy at midday, but if privacy is your primary concern, choose one of the individually curtained booths that line the corridor to the left of the main dining room. Once you've settled in, consider such favorites as the clam chowder, a charcoal-broiled fillet of fish, and a dessert of French pancakes anisette. Shellfish, steak, and veal dishes round out the dinner menu.

Splendido. 4 Embarcadero Center (at Clay and Drumm sts.). ☎ **415/986-3222.** Main courses $11–$26. AE, DC, DISC, MC, V. Mon–Fri 11:30am–2:30pm; bar menu 2:30pm–5:30pm; daily 5:30–10pm. Bus: 15, 45, or 76. CONTEMPORARY ITALIAN.

Warm olive wood, flickering candles, rustic stone walls, hand-painted tiles, and hand-hewn beams create the illusion of an old Mediterranean getaway in the middle of metropolitan Embarcadero Four.

But it's not the decor alone that procures kudos from *Gourmet* and other culinary magazines. The food is beautifully presented, lovingly prepared, and consistently tasty. Starters might include a light and flavorful Mediterranean seafood soup and crab cakes, which are large but too bready for our tastes. Main courses, which are served on colorful, individually decorated plates, might include a wonderful grilled salmon with pearl-onion carrot confit, which is cooked to perfection and accompanied by a crisp, subtle broth; or oven-roasted pork loin with braised cabbage, onions, and a lentil salad. Dessert is a decadent affair, with such belt-busters as an amaretto-and-espresso tiramisu and ever-popular house-made profiteroles with warm chocolate sauce. When the weather is pleasant, you can eat under a canopy on the outdoor patio, or choose the seating in front of the open kitchen. Be sure to glance in the exhibition bakery near the entrance, where you might see chefs rolling fresh pasta.

✪ Tadich Grill. 240 California St. (between Battery and Front sts.). ☎ **415/391-1849.** Reservations not accepted. Main courses $12–$18. MC, V. Mon–Fri 11am–9:30pm; Sat 11:30am–9:30pm. Muni Metro: All Market St. trams, BART. All Market St. buses. SEAFOOD.

This famous, venerated California institution arrived with the gold rush in 1849 and claims to be the very first to broil seafood over mesquite charcoal, back in the early 1920s. The original mahogany bar extends the entire length of the restaurant while no-nonsense white-linen–draped tables are topped with big plates of sourdough bread. Power-lunchers get one of the seven enclosed, private booths.

For a light meal, try one of the delicious seafood salads, such as shrimp or prawn Louis. Hot dishes include baked avocado with shrimp diablo, baked casserole of stuffed turbot with crab and shrimp à la Newburg, and charcoal-broiled petrale sole with butter sauce, a local favorite. Almost everyone gets a side order of big, tasty french fries.

Yank Sing. 427 Battery St. (between Clay and Washington sts.). ☎ **415/781-1111.** Dim sum $2.30–$5 for 3 to 4 pieces. AE, DC, MC, V. Mon–Fri 11am–3pm; Sat–Sun 10am–4pm. Cable car: California St. line. Bus: 1 or 42. CHINESE/DIM SUM.

Loosely translated as "a delight of the heart," Yank Sing does dim sum like no other Chinese restaurant we've visited. Poor quality of ingredients has always been the shortcoming of all but the most expensive Chinese restaurants, but Yank Sing manages to be both affordable and excellent. Confident, experienced servers take the nervousness out of novices—they're good at guessing your gastric threshold. Most dim-sum dishes are dumplings, filled with tasty concoctions of pork, beef, fish, or vegetables. *Congees* (porridges), spareribs, stuffed crab claws, scallion pancakes, shrimp balls, pork buns, and other palate-pleasers complete the menu. Like most good dim-sum meals, at Yank Sing you get to choose the small dishes from a cart that's continually wheeled around the dining room. While the food is delicious, the location makes this the most popular tourist spot. A second location is at 49 Stevenson St., off First Street (☎ 415/541-4949). Ideally, we still prefer the Richmond's Hong Kong Flower Lounge. *Tip:* Sit by the kitchen and you're guaranteed to get it while it's hot.

5 Nob Hill/Russian Hill

EXPENSIVE

The Big Four. In the Huntington Hotel, 1075 California St. (between Mason and Taylor sts.). ☎ **415/474-5400.** Reservations recommended. Breakfast from $10.95; main courses $15–$27. AE, CB, DC, DISC, MC, V. Mon–Fri 7–10am and 11:30am–3pm; Sat–Sun 7–11am; daily 5:30–11pm. Cable car: California St. line. (direct stop). Bus: 1. Valet parking $6. CALIFORNIA/FRENCH.

Shining brass, historic California photographs, forest-green leather banquettes, and ram's-horn sconces establish the clubby atmosphere at this Nob Hill restaurant that's known for its seasonal wild-game specialties. At dinner, you might find venison chili with black beans, cheddar, and onion crisps to start, as well as a rib eye of buffalo in a zinfandel-laced rosemary sauce to follow. Even Australian ostrich saddle and Louisiana alligator medaillons have been rumored to be on the menu. If game doesn't interest you, there are plenty of other down-to-earth dishes, including grilled halibut over vine-ripened tomatoes and spinach with black-olive vinaigrette, or the angel-hair pasta with Monterey prawns, eggplant, garlic, basil, and shaved Romano. If you can't do dinner here, at least drop by for a nightcap to see what the Big Four railroad tycoons considered high fashion back then.

✪ **Charles Nob Hill.** 1250 Jones St. (at Clay St.). ☎ **415/771-5400.** Main courses $25–$35. AE, MC, V. Tues–Sun 5:30–10pm. Valet parking $7. Cable car: California St. and Powell-Hyde lines. Bus: 1, 12, 27, or 83. FRENCH.

We never knew beef could actually melt in your mouth until Aqua owner Charles Condy bought historic restaurant "Le Club" and introduced us to Chef Ron Seagal's culinary magic (it really did melt!). The "classically inspired light French fare," as he prefers to call it, is served in two dining rooms with velvet banquettes, fresh floral arrangements, and the loud buzz of the older socialite crowd. Start with a bowl of the soup of the day, which, when we dined here, was a spinach-and-roasted-garlic soup with cumin-scented rock shrimp and crumbled bacon that was surprisingly beautiful, electric green, and overflowing with flavor. Scallop-and-black-truffle pot pie is another must-try. And for the main course, you might choose the Poele of beef tenderloin with wild-mushroom and potato torte, balsamic glazed onions, and foie gras, or a flavorful squab with veal sweetbread, lentils, and mushroom fricassee. Better yet, opt for the $65 six-course tasting menu and let the chef's preference lead you through the meal. Although the room itself is romantic, the atmosphere and noise level are too convivial for real intimacy. Wrap up the evening with the outstanding pear-and-Roquefort tart. *Tip:* No matter what, don't drive here unless you can pay the valet; you may spend over an hour looking for parking.

✪ **Ritz-Carlton Dining Room.** 600 Stockton St. (at California St.). ☎ **415/296-7465.** Reservations recommended. Fixed-price menus $55–$69. AE, CB, DC, DISC, MC, V. Mon–Sat 6–9:30pm. Valet parking $9. Cable car: Powell-Hyde and Powell-Mason lines (direct stop). Bus: 1. CALIFORNIA/FRENCH.

Never a hotel to do anything second best, the Ritz-Carlton Hotel is renowned for pampering its guests as if they were royalty, and the Dining Room is no exception. On our last visit, no less then five tuxedoed wait staff were surreptitiously attending to our needs (no half-empty water glasses in this joint) as we fussed over the wine list and debated the proper pronunciation of "tatin." The setting, as you would imagine, is quite regal and sumptuous: crystal chandeliers, rich brocade, elegant table settings, cushy high-backed chairs, and live harp music reek of formality. Unfortunately, celebrity chef Gary Danko—winner of the 1995 James Beard Award, the Academy Award of the food world—is no longer with the Ritz; his replacement, chef Sylvain Portay, now runs the kitchen with similar aplomb, but the loss is noticeable—dishes such as the roast Maine lobster and striped-bass fillet were quite good, but certainly not of the four-star caliber Danko's fans are accustomed to. A few dishes, however, were outstanding, particularly crayfish bisque (one of the best dishes we have ever tasted) and the risotto with butternut squash and roasted squab. Dessert, alas, was also deigned for mere mortals, though the warm port-poached pear in vanilla sauce was superb. The menu, which changes monthly, offers a choice of three-, four-, or five-course dinners ranging from $55 to $69, the latter of which includes wine pairing per course by master-sommelier Emmanuel Kemiji for an additional $43. The Dining Room also features the country's only "rolling" cheese cart, laden with at least two dozen individually ripened cheeses.

MODERATE

Hard Rock Cafe. 1699 Van Ness Ave. (at Sacramento St.). ☎ **415/885-1699.** Reservations accepted for groups of 15 or more. Main courses $6–$16. AE, DC, MC, V. Sun–Thurs 11:30am–11pm; Fri–Sat 11:30am–midnight. Valet $4.25 for 2 hr. Cable car: California St. line. Bus: 1. AMERICAN.

Like its affiliated restaurants around the world, this loud, nostalgia-laden place offers big portions of decent food at moderate prices and plenty of blaring music to an almost exclusively tourist clientele. The real draw, of course, is the merchandise shop, which often has as long a line as the restaurant.

The cafe is decorated with a profusion of framed gold records, musical instruments, signed rock-star photos, historic front pages, and the usual "Save the Planet" montage. The menu offers burgers, fajitas, baby-back ribs, grilled fish, chicken, salads, and sandwiches; we usually go for the chicken sandwich with a side of onion rings, both of which are pretty darn good. Although it's nothing unique to San Francisco, the Hard Rock is a fine place to bring the kids and grab a bite.

✪ **Swan Oyster Depot.** 1517 Polk St. (between California and Sacramento sts.). ☎ **415/673-1101.** Reservations not accepted. Seafood cocktails $5–$8; clams and oysters on the half shell $6–$7.50 per half dozen. No credit cards. Mon–Sat 8am–5:30pm. Bus: 27. SEAFOOD.

Pushing 90 years of faithful service to Bay Area chowder-heads, the Swan Oyster Depot is classic San Francisco; a unique dining experience you shouldn't miss. Opened in 1912, this tiny hole in the wall run by the city's friendliest and vivacious servers is little more than a narrow fish market that decided to slap down some bar stools. There are only 20 or so seats jammed cheek by jowl along a long marble bar. Most patrons come for a quick cup of chowder or a plate of half-shelled oysters that arrive chilling on crushed ice. The menu is limited to fresh crab, shrimp, oyster, and clam cocktails, Maine lobster, and Boston-style clam chowder, all of which are exceedingly fresh. *Note:* Don't let the lunchtime line dissuade you—it moves fast.

In case you want
to see the world.

At American Express, we're here to make your journey a smooth one. So we have over 1,700 travel service locations in over 120 countries ready to help. What else would you expect from the world's largest travel agency?

do more

AMERICAN
EXPRESS

Travel

http://www.americanexpress.com/travel

And just in case.

We're here with American Express® Travelers Cheques and Cheques *for Two*® They're the safest way to carry money on your vacation and the surest way to get a refund, practically anywhere, anytime.

Another way we help you...

do more

AMERICAN EXPRESS

Travelers Cheques

6 South of Market (SoMa)

EXPENSIVE

✪ **Boulevard.** 1 Mission St. (at Embarcadero and Steuart St.). ☎ **415/543-6084.** Reservations recommended. Main courses $19–$27. AE, CB, DC, DISC, MC, V. Mon–Fri 11:30am–2pm; bistro 2:30–5:15pm; dinner Mon–Wed and Sun 5:30–10pm, Thurs–Sat 5:30–10:30pm. Bus: 15, 30, 32, 42, or 45. Valet parking $6. AMERICAN.

Master restaurant designer Pat Kuleto and chef Nancy Oaks teamed up to create one of San Francisco's most exciting restaurants, and though it's been over 5 years since its debut, it's still as popular as ever. What's the winning combination? The dramatically artistic belle-epoch interior with vaulted brick ceilings, floral-design banquettes, a mosaic floor, and fluid, tulip-shaped lamps combined with Oaks's equally impressive sculptural and mouth-watering dishes. Start with the delicate crab and mascarpone ravioli with truffle beurre blanc and tomato cream, then embark on such wonderful concoctions as grilled wild king salmon with leek and sweet corn mashed potatoes, French beans, and herb salad (she makes a mean honey-cured pork loin, too). Vegetarian items, such as wild-mushroom risotto with fresh chanterelles and Parmesan, are also offered. Three levels of formality—bar, open kitchen, and main dining room—keep things from getting too snobby. Though steep prices prevent most from making Boulevard a regular gig, you'd be hard-pressed to find a better place for a special, fun-filled occasion.

✪ **Hawthorne Lane.** 22 Hawthorne Lane (at Howard St. between Second and Third sts.). ☎ **415/777-9779.** Reservations recommended. Jacket appropriate but not required. Main courses $9.50–$13 lunch, $18–$25 dinner. CB, DC, DISC, JCB, MC, V. Mon–Fri 11:30am–2pm; Sun–Thurs 5:30–10pm; Fri–Sat 5:30–10:30pm. BART: Montgomery Station. Muni Metro: F, J, K, L, M, or N. Bus: 12, 30, 45, or 76. CALIFORNIA.

Anne and David Gingrass, who hailed from Postrio, preside over the kitchen at Hawthorne Lane, their SoMa restaurant strategically located a block away from the Museum of Modern Art. Anne and David are a culinary team who prepare their menu based on the best and freshest ingredients available. Menus change with the seasons and reflect the Asian and European influences that made them famous under Wolfgang Puck.

Step through the doors and you'll immediately notice this restaurant was planned by seasoned professionals. The bar area is comfortable and inviting, with both cocktail tables and bar seating; continue on to the dining room, where earthquake reinforcement beams divide the room in a way that is not only functional, but is also decorative and creates the illusion that each section is a more intimate environment. Even the decor is just right: not too fancy or pretentious, but well-lit and decorated with bright artwork, fresh floral arrangements, and a leaf motif throughout.

But where the Gingrass's expertise really shines is in the food. The bread basket that arrives at your table is overflowing with fresh-baked goods of all tastes and types. Each dish arrives beautifully presented without being too contrived, but usually with a whimsical accent, such as a leaf-shaped pastry or a bird made of a carrot sliver. Dishes are remarkably well balanced, and accompaniments are often more exciting than the main course itself. If it's on the menu, don't pass up the black-cod appetizer served with a miso glaze and spinach rolls. The light, flaky lobster tempura with a vegetable salad is another show-stopper, as is the main course of quail glazed with maple and perched on the most delightful potato gratin. Desserts are as good to look at as they are to eat.

MODERATE

Bizou. 598 Fourth St. (at Brannan St.). ☎ **415/543-2222.** Reservations recommended. Main courses $12.50–$21. AE, MC, V. Mon–Fri 11:30am–2:30pm; Mon–Thurs 5:30–10pm; Fri–Sat 5:30–10:30pm. Bus: 15, 30, 32, 42, or 45. FRENCH/ITALIAN.

Around town, almost everyone sings Bizou's praises and with good reason: The restaurant's golden-yellow walls and terra-cotta ceiling are warmly lit by antique light fixtures and art-deco wall sconces, and provide an atmosphere perfect for a first date or an evening out with Mom. The wait staff is friendly and professional, and all the ingredients are fresh and in creative combinations. Our only complaint is that literally every dish is so rich and powerfully flavorful (including the salads), it's a bit of a sensory overload. The menu's starters include an Italian flat bread with caramelized onions, fresh herbs, and Parmesan cheese, Sonoma duck-liver terrine, and baked shrimp with white beans, tomato, and feta. The main courses may include a grilled veal chop with broccoli-rabe potato gratin or stuffed chicken with celeriac, apple, and goat cheese. All main-course portions are substantial here, so don't overindulge on appetizers. And save a little room for dessert—the meringue covered in chocolate and topped with coffee ice cream and candied almonds is quite a treat. Too bad there are no cots in a back room here—after your meal, you'll need a nap.

✪ Fringale Restaurant. 570 Fourth St. (between Brannan and Bryant sts.). ☎ **415/543-0573.** Reservations recommended. Main courses $4–$12 at lunch, $11–$19 at dinner. AE, MC, V. Mon–Fri 11:30am–3pm; Mon–Sat 5:30–10:30pm. Bus: 30 or 45. FRENCH.

One of San Francisco's best restaurants for the money, Fringale—French colloquial for "sudden urge to eat"—has enjoyed a weeklong waiting list since the day chef/co-owner Gerald Hirigoyen first opened this small SoMa bistro. Sponged, eggshell-blue walls and other muted sand and earth tones provide a serene dining environment, which is all but shattered when the 18-table room inevitably fills with Hirigoyen's fans. For starters, try the steamed mussels with roasted red pepper, basil, and vinaigrette, or the sheep's-milk cheese and prosciutto tureen with figs and greens. Among the dozen or so main courses on the seasonally changing menu you might find rack of lamb with potato gratin or pork tenderloin confit with onion and apple marmalade. Desserts are worth savoring, too, particularly the hazelnut-and-roasted-almond mousse cake or the signature crème brûlée with vanilla bean. The mostly French waiters provide uncharacteristically charming service, and prices are surprisingly reasonable for such high-quality cuisine. It's one of our favorites.

Gordon Biersch Brewery Restaurant. 2 Harrison St. (on the Embarcadero). ☎ **415/243-8246.** Reservations recommended. Main courses $7.50–$17. AE, DC, DISC, MC, V. Lunch Mon–Fri 11:30am–3pm; Sat–Sun 11:30am–4pm. Dinner Sun–Mon 5–9pm; Tues–Thurs 5–10pm; Fri–Sat 5–10:30pm (bar stays open later). Bus: 32. CALIFORNIA.

Popular with the young Republican crowd (loose ties and tight skirts predominate), this modern, two-tiered brewery and restaurant eschews the traditional brew-pub fare—no spicy chicken wings on this menu—in an attempt to attract a more upscale clientele. And it works: It's been months since our last visit, and we still can't get over how wonderful the beer-braised lamb shank tasted. The baby-back ribs with garlic fries is their best-seller, followed by the lemon roasted half chicken with garlic mashed potatoes. Start with the delicate and crunchy calamari fritti appetizer or, if you're garlic hounds like us, the tangy Caesar salad. Most dishes can be paired with one of the brewery's lagers. *Note:* Couples bent on a quiet, romantic dinner can skip this one; when the lower-level bar fills up, you practically have to shout to be heard. But food- and beer-lovers will be quite content.

Lulu. 816 Folsom St. (at Fourth St.). ☎ **415/495-5775.** Reservations recommended. Main courses $7–$13 lunch, $9–$17 dinner. AE, MC, V. Sun–Thurs 11:30am–10:30pm; Fri–Sat 11:30am–11pm. Bus: 15, 30, 32, 42, or 45. CONTINENTAL.

After reigning for 4 years as one of San Francisco's top restaurants, the celebrity staff left to open Rose Pistola, taking a good chunk of its status along with it. The energy within the enormous dining room, however, still radiates as the cadre of cooks, communicating via headsets, slide bubbling plates of pizza and shellfish in and out of the open kitchen's wood-fired ovens. Watching the carefully orchestrated chaos makes dining here something of an event. The main room seats 170, but even as you sit amidst a sea of stylish diners, the room somehow feels warm and convivial. And then there's the food, which is consistently delicious. Locals return again and again for the roasted mussels piled high on an iron skillet; the chopped salad with lemon, anchovies, and tomatoes; the pork loin with fennel, garlic, and olive oil; and any of the other wonderful dishes. Everything is served family-style and is meant to be shared. Save room for dessert; opt for the gooey chocolate cake, which oozes with chocolate to be scooped up with the side of melting ice cream. The adjoining cafe serves the same menu, with the addition of gourmet sandwiches, on a first-come, first-served basis.

✪ **Thirsty Bear Brewing Company.** 661 Howard St. (1 block east of the Moscone Center). ☎ **415/974-0905.** Reservations recommended. Main courses $10–$17. AE, DC, MC, V. Mon–Sun 11:30am–1am. Bus: 12, 15, 30, 45, or 76. SPANISH.

Despite the dumb name, the Thirsty Bear Brewing Company has quickly become a favorite of the Financial District/SoMa crowd, who come as much for the excellent house-made brews as they do for chef Daniel Olivella's outstanding Spanish food. A native of Catalunia, Spain, Olivella is a master of paella. His Paella Valenciana—a sizzling combo of chicken, shrimp, sausage, shellfish, and saffron-laden rice served in a cast-iron skillet—is the best we've had outside of Barcelona. Upscale pub grub includes a variety of hot and cold tapas, a few of our favorites being the Escalivada (Olivella's mother's version of roasted vegetables—spicy caramelized onions are wild—served at room temperature) and the Espinacas à la Catalana (spinach sautéed with garlic, pine nuts, and raisins). Ask the waiter which brews best accompany the dishes. Olivella's signature dessert is his La Sagrada Familia—twin towers of sugar cones (fans of Gaudí will recognize them immediately) filled with chocolate mousse that rest upon a bed of Chantilly cream and fresh berries. Almost as impressive as the food is the costly conversion from a high-ceilinged brick warehouse to a two-level industrial-chic brew pub complete with pool tables, dart boards, and live music (including jazz, flamenco, blues, alternative, and classical).

INEXPENSIVE

Hamburger Mary's. 1582 Folsom St. (at 12th St.). ☎ **415/626-5767.** Reservations recommended. Breakfast $5–$9; main courses $6–$10. AE, DC, DISC, MC, V. Mon–Thurs 11:30am–1am; Fri 11:30am–2am; Sat 10am–2am; Sun 10am–1am. Bus: 9, 12, 42, or 47. AMERICAN.

San Francisco's most . . . alternative burger joint, Hamburger Mary's is a popular hangout for gays, lesbians, and just about everyone else eschewing society's norms. The restaurant's kitsch decor includes thrift-shop floral wallpaper, family photos, garage-sale prints, stained glass, religious drawings, and Oriental screens. You'll get to know the bar well—it's where you'll stand with the tattooed masses while you wait for a table. Don't despair: They mix a good drink, and people-watching is what you're here for anyway. Sandwiches, salads, and vegetarian dishes provide an alternative to their famous greasy burgers, served on healthful nine-grain bread (like it makes a difference). *Tip:* Go with the home fries over the french fries. In the morning, Hamburger Mary's doubles as a breakfast joint, a good stop for a three-egg omelet or French toast.

Long Life Noodle Company & Jook Joint. 139 Steuart St. (near Mission St.). ☎ **415/281-3818.** Main courses $5.50–$8.50. MC, V. Mon–Thurs 11:30am–10pm; Fri 11:30am–11pm; Sat 5pm–11am; Sun 5–10pm. Bus: 15, 30, 32, 42, or 45. NOODLES.

Asian noodles are all the rage these days, so it comes as no surprise that big-time restaurateurs such as George Chen of Betelnut are willing to invest big bucks in what has traditionally been a small-change business. The concept at Long Life is to offer a wide range of unfamiliar noodle dishes gleaned from China, Korea, Japan, and other Asian lands and serve them in a familiar Westernized setting (in this case, a sleek, supermodern interior with lots of neon and Plexiglas). The problem is choosing from the 30 or so noodle dishes, all of which are wildly different. Do you go with Buddha's Bliss (ramen noodles in miso broth with smoked trout, tofu, and endoki mushrooms) or the Enchanted Heat (a "Chinese hangover cure" comprised of whole-wheat noodles, lily pods, tree ears, and secret healing ginseng herbs)? We recommend you try the Ghengis' Buns, crisp sesame biscuits filled with Chinese roast beef, cucumber, cilantro, and hoisin sauce, and wash it all down with either the Cool Cucumber Juice or Ginseng Ginger Ale.

✪ Manora's. 1600 Folsom St. (at 12th St.). ☎ **415/861-6224.** Main courses $5.95–$11. MC, V. Mon–Fri 11:30am–2:30pm and 5–10:30pm; Sat 5:30–10:30pm; Sun 5:30–10pm. Bus: 9, 12, or 47. THAI.

Manora's cranks out some of the best Thai in town and is well worth a jaunt to its SoMa location. But this is no relaxed dining affair. It's perpetually packed (unless you come early), and you'll be seated sardinelike at one of the cramped but well-appointed tables. During the dinner rush, the noise level can make conversation almost impossible among larger parties, but the food is so darn good, you'll probably prefer to turn your head toward your plate and stuff your face. Start with a Thai iced tea or coffee and one of the tangy soups or the chicken satay, which comes with a decadent peanut sauce. Follow up with any of the wonderful dinner dishes—which should be shared—and a side of rice. There are endless options, including a vast array of vegetarian plates. Every remarkably flavorful dish arrives seemingly seconds after you order it, which is great if you're hungry, a bummer if you were planning a long, leisurely dinner. Come before seven or after nine if you don't want a loud, rushed meal.

South Park Café. 108 S. Park Ave. (between Brannan and Bryant sts.). ☎ **415/495-7275.** Reservations recommended. Main courses $11.50–$17. AE, MC, V. Mon–Fri 7:30am–10pm; Sat 6–10pm. Bus: 15, 30, 32, 42, 45, or 76. FRENCH.

Whenever we get the urge to dump everything and fly to Paris (which is about every day), we drive across town to the South Park Café—it's not quite the same thing as a bistro on Boulevard Montparnasse, but it's close. Usually we're content with an espresso and pastry; a splurge involves the saffron mussels or blood sausage served with sautéed apples. For the ultimate romantic intention, bring a blanket and dine *sur l'herbe* at the adorable park across the street. Beware of the midweek lunch rush, though.

Tú Lan. 8 Sixth St. (at Market St.). ☎ **415/626-0927.** Main courses $3.50–$7. No credit cards. Mon–Sat 11am–9pm. Bus: 6, 7, 27, 31, 66, or 71. Cable car: Powell-Mason and Powell-Hyde lines. Muni Metro: F, J, K, L, M, N. VIETNAMESE.

If you can handle walking down Sixth Street past the winos, weirdos, and street stench, you won't find better (or cheaper) Vietnamese food than at this honest-to-goodness dive. Even Julia Child (whose face graces the greasy old menus) has been known to pull up a chair at this shack of a restaurant to feast on such goodies as imperial rolls on a bed of rice noodles, lettuce, peanuts, and mint (under $5). Take pity on the poor waiter who never seems to bring water no matter how many times you ask; he's been working here forever, he's the only server, and the place is always packed. For the price, this has been one of our all-time favorite restaurants for more than a decade. *Take note:* Some finicky folks can't handle the down-and-dirty atmosphere.

7 Chinatown

MODERATE

Brandy Ho's Hunan Food. 217 Columbus Ave. (at Pacific Ave.). ☎ **415/788-7527.** Reservations accepted. Main courses $8–$13. AE, DC, DISC, MC, V. Sun–Thurs 11:30am–11pm; Fri–Sat 11:30am–midnight. Bus: 15 or 41. CHINESE.

Fancy black-and-white granite tabletops and a large, open kitchen give you the first clue that the food here is a cut above the usual Hunanese fare. Take our advice and start immediately with the fried dumplings (in the sweet-and-sour sauce) or cold chicken salad. Next, move on to the fish-ball soup with spinach, bamboo shoots, noodles, and other goodies. The best main course is Three Delicacies, a combination of scallops, shrimp, and chicken with onion, bell pepper, and bamboo shoots, seasoned with ginger, garlic, and wine, and served with black-bean sauce. Most dishes here are quite hot and spicy, but the kitchen will adjust the level to meet your specifications. There is a small selection of wines and beers, including plum wine and sake.

INEXPENSIVE

House of Nanking. 919 Kearny St. (at Columbus Ave.). ☎ **415/421-1429.** Reservations accepted for 6 or more. Main courses $4.95–$8.95. No credit cards. Mon–Fri 11am–10pm; Sat noon–10pm; Sun 4–10pm. Bus: 9, 12, 15, or 30. CHINESE.

To the unknowing passerby, the House of Nanking has "greasy dive" written all over it. To its legion of fans, however, the wait—sometimes up to an hour—is worth what's on the plate. Located on the edge of Chinatown just off Columbus Avenue, this inconspicuous little diner is one of San Francisco's worst-kept secrets. When the line is reasonable, we drop by for a plate of pot stickers (still the best we've ever tasted) and chef/owner Peter Fang's signature shrimp-and-green-onion pancake served with peanut sauce. Trust the waiter when he recommends a special, or simply point to what looks good on someone else's table. Even with a new expansion that's doubled the elbow room, seating is tight, so prepare to be bumped around a bit, and don't expect good service—it's all part of the Nanking experience.

Sam Woh. 813 Washington St. (by Grant Ave.). ☎ **415/982-0596.** Reservations not accepted. Main courses $3.50–$6. No credit cards. Mon–Sat 11am–3am. Bus: 15, 30, 41, or 45. CHINESE.

Very handy for late-nighters, Sam's is a total dive that's well known and often packed. The restaurant's two pocket-size dining rooms are located on top of each other, on the second and third floors—take the stairs past the first-floor kitchen. You'll have to share a table, but this place is for mingling almost as much as for eating. The house specialty is *jook* (known as congee in its native Hong Kong)—a thick rice gruel flavored with fish, shrimp, chicken, beef, or pork; the best is

---

⑪ Family-Friendly Restaurants

Caffè Freddy's *(see p. 129)*   This longtime family favorite will please not only the kids but their parents as well, especially with its low prices. But the food is good, too: an array of gourmet pizzas, pastas, sandwiches, and unusual salads along with main-dish specialties.

Planet Hollywood *(see p. 110)*   Okay, so it's another schlocky theme-restaurant chain, but kids still love the place (and kid-friendly restaurants are far and few between in this town), it's in the thick of the city action, and it actually makes a pretty darn good burger.

Hard Rock Cafe *(see p. 118)*   Like its affiliates around the world, this loud, nostalgia-laden place offers big portions of decent food at moderate prices, and plenty of blaring music to an almost exclusively tourist clientele. Although it's nothing unique to San Francisco, the Hard Rock is a fine place to bring the kids and grab a bite.

Mel's Diner *(see p. 139)*   This retro-style burger-slinging joint is not only neat to look at (it was the diner that starred in the movie *American Graffiti*), it also caters to kids. Youngsters get their own color-in menu (crayons are already on the table), and some meals are served in boxes shaped like classic American cars. Jukeboxes at each table will keep the whole family busy figuring out which oldie to select.

Sampan, made with rice and seafood. Try sweet-and-sour pork rice, wonton soup with duck, or a roast-pork/rice-noodle roll. More traditional fried noodles and rice plates are available, too, our favorites being the tomato beef with noodles and the house special chow mien. Chinese doughnuts sell for 50¢ each.

8 North Beach / Telegraph Hill

EXPENSIVE

Bix. 56 Gold St. (between Sansome and Montgomery sts.). ☎ **415/433-6300.** Reservations recommended. Main courses $7–$14 lunch, $15–$25 dinner. AE, CB, DC, DISC, MC, V. Mon–Thurs 11:30am–11pm; Fri 11:30am–midnight; Sat 5:30pm–midnight; Sun 6–10pm. Bus: 15, 30, 41, or 45. CLASSIC AMERICAN/CALIFORNIA.

If you feel like dressing up and hittin' the town, this suave little back-alley bar and restaurant is a good place to start. Fashioned after a 1920s supper club, Bix is better known for its martinis than for its menu. Curving Honduran mahogany, massive silver columns, and art-deco–style lighting set the stage for dancing to live music, though most locals settle for chatting with the friendly bartenders and noshing on appetizers. While the ultrastylish setting tends to overshadow the food, Bix actually serves some pretty good grub. The fresh fettuccine with seared day-boat scallops, wild mushrooms, butternut squash, and tomato fondue is the undisputed favorite, followed by the grilled filet mignon with mushrooms and chicken hash à la Bix. And for that special occasion, how can you say no to a round of $118 Beluga caviar on toast?

Caffè Sport. 574 Green St. (between Grant and Columbus aves.). ☎ **415/981-1251.** Reservations accepted only for parties of 4 or more. Main courses $15–$24. No credit cards. Tues–Thurs noon–2pm; Fri–Sat noon–2:30pm; Tues–Thurs seatings at 5, 6:30, 8:30, and 10pm; Fri–Sat at 6:30, 8:30, and 10pm. Bus: 15, 30, 41, or 45. ITALIAN.

Dining Near North Beach & Chinatown

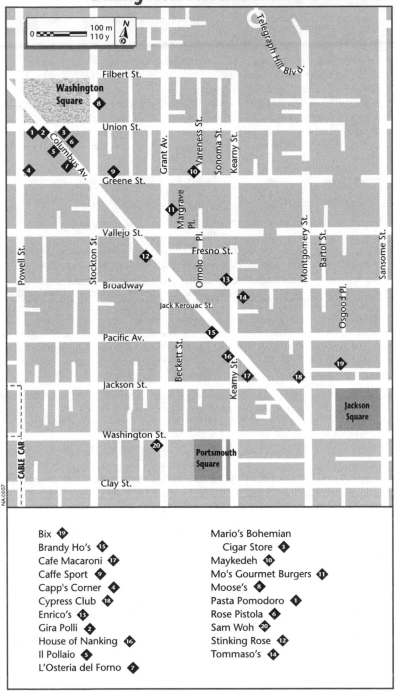

Bix **19**
Brandy Ho's **15**
Cafe Macaroni **17**
Caffe Sport **9**
Capp's Corner **4**
Cypress Club **18**
Enrico's **13**
Gira Polli **2**
House of Nanking **16**
Il Pollaio **5**
L'Osteria del Forno **7**

Mario's Bohemian
   Cigar Store **3**
Maykedeh **10**
Mo's Gourmet Burgers **11**
Moose's **8**
Pasta Pomodoro **1**
Rose Pistola **6**
Sam Woh **20**
Stinking Rose **12**
Tommaso's **14**

People either love or hate this stodgy Sicilian eatery. Cluttered with hanging hams, fishnets, decorative plates, dolls, mirrors, and 2 decades worth of dust, Caffè Sport is better known for its surly staff and eclectic ambiance than for its food. Owner/chef/artiste Antonio Latona serves up healthy portions of attitude along with garlic-laden pasta dishes and is happy to report that this is Senator Dianne Feinstein's favorite North Beach hangout. Lunch is tame in comparison to dinner, when the Sport is mobbed and lively. Disregard the framed menu that sits on each table and accept the waiter's "suggestions." Whatever arrives—whether it be a dish of calamari, mussels, and shrimp in tomato-garlic sauce, or pasta in pesto sauce—it's bound to be *bene*. Bring a huge appetite, but above all, don't be late if you have a reservation.

Cypress Club. 500 Jackson St. (between Montgomery St. and Columbus Ave.). ☎ **415/296-8555.** Reservations recommended. Main courses $23–$28. AE, CB, DC, MC, V. Sun–Thurs 5:30–10pm; Fri–Sat 5:30–11pm. Bus: 15 or 41. AMERICAN.

Combine Aladdin's bedchamber, a handful of "Far Side" cartoons, and few hits of acid, and you still won't match the Daliesque decor of this pseudo supper club. It's not hard to find; just look for the tourists peering in the windows. Gilt banquettes, bulbous gilt columns, and udder-shaped light fixtures covered in billowing fabric create a lavish neo-Arabian atmosphere that, if you're in the neighborhood, is definitely worth a gander. Most of the regular clientele, dressed to blend, saunters around the bar. Those who wish to dine might start with foie gras, Dungeness crab rillettes, or the sea scallops with curry, lemongrass, mango, and chervil. Main courses are equally extravagant, including the lobster with lemon emulsion and shaved black truffle; the maple-cured pork chop with pecan pancakes, collard greens, and grilled apple; or the wood-roasted chicken with wild mushrooms and rosemary soubise. Desserts are as creative as the decor.

Moose's. 1652 Stockton St. (between Filbert and Union sts.). ☎ **415/989-7800.** www.mooses.com. Reservations recommended. Main courses $13–$26. AE, CB, DC, JCB, MC, V. Mon–Thurs 11:30am–11pm; Fri–Sat 11:30am–midnight; Sun 10:30am–11pm. Valet parking $9 for 3 hr. Bus: 15, 30, 41, or 45. MEDITERRANEAN/CALIFORNIA.

Within the last 2 years, Moose's has brought on chef Brian Whitmer of Montrio in Carmel, pastry chef Ellen Doren, and sommelier William Sherer—perhaps the only one who could improve the wine list that's already received an award of excellence from the *Wine Spectator.* You'll see the big blue neon Moose out front long before you pass through the doors, and once inside you'll notice you're in the largest dining room in North Beach. This is where Nob Hill socialites and local politicians come to dine and be seen, but Moose's is not just an image—in fact, the dining room itself is rather sparse and unintimate. The food, however, well *that's* a different story. Everything that comes out of Moose's kitchen is way above par. The appetizers are innovative, fresh, and well balanced (try the Mediterranean fish soup with rouille and croutons that's cooked in the wood-fired oven), and the main courses (especially the meats) are perfectly prepared. The menu changes every few months and might include a grilled veal chop with potato galette and a variety of pasta, chicken, and fish dishes.

The bar, separated from the main dining room by a low, frosted-glass partition, remains busy long after the kitchen closes. Jazz featuring piano and bass is played there nightly, as well as during Sunday brunch.

MODERATE

Enrico's. 504 Broadway (at Kearny St.). ☎ **415/982-6223.** Reservations recommended. Main courses $8–$13 lunch, $13–$19 dinner. AE, DC, DISC, MC, V. Mon–Sun

11:30–11pm; Fri–Sat 11:30–midnight; bar daily noon–2am. Bus: 12, 15, 30, or 83. MEDI-
TERRANEAN.

Though it's taking its sweet time, North Beach's bawdy stretch of Broadway is on
the road to rehabilitation. Helping things along is the newly refurbished version of
Enrico's, a glitzy sidewalk restaurant and supper club that was once the place to
hang out before Broadway took its seedy downward spiral. Families may want to
skip this one, but anyone with an appreciation for live jazz (played nightly), late-
night noshing, and weirdo-watching from the outdoor patio would be quite content spending an alfresco evening under the heat lamps. Chewy brick-oven pizza,
zesty tapas, and thick steaks are hot items on the monthly changing menu. The best
part? No cover charge, killer burgers served until midnight on weekends, and valet
parking.

Fog City Diner. 1300 Battery St. (at Lombard St.). ☎ **415/982-2000.** Reservations
accepted. Main courses $12–$18. CB, DC, DISC, MC, V. Sun–Thurs 11:30am–11pm; Fri–Sat
11:30am–midnight. Bus: 42. AMERICAN.

Now more popular because of its Visa commercial than its food, Fog City has
become a tourist destination, with a few locals straggling in for business lunches.
The restaurant looks like a genuine American metallic diner—but only from the
outside. Inside, dark polished woods, inspired lighting, and a well-stocked raw bar
tell you this is no hash-slinger.

Dressed-up dinner dishes include gourmet chili dogs, salads, sandwiches,
burgers, pork chops, and pot roast. Fancier fish and meat meals include grilled
catches of the day and thick-cut steaks. Lighter eaters can make a meal out of the
long list of "small plates" that include crab cakes or quesadilla with chili peppers and
almonds. The place is cute and the food is fine, but if your heart is set on coming
here, do so at lunch—you'll be better off elsewhere if you want a special dinner.

Il Fornaio. Levi Plaza, 1265 Battery St. (bounded by Sansome, Battery, Union, and Greenwich
sts.). ☎ **415/986-0100.** Main courses $9–$18. AE, DC, MC, V. Mon–Fri 7am–11pm;
Sat–Sun 9am–11pm. Bus: 12, 32, or 42. Valet parking $5. ITALIAN.

While we can't say Il Fornaio would be our choice if we could only eat at one spot
for the rest of our lives, it's one of our favorite standbys, producing consistently
good Italian fare at decent prices. Located in Levi Plaza a few minutes away from
Pier 39, this trattoria has great atmosphere: It bustles, it's big, and though a little
cramped, the decor is not overwhelming but smart Italian. By day it is buzzing with
Financial District types and socialites, by night, with couples and gathering friends.

Stacks of fresh-baked Italian cookies behind glass greet you when you first walk
through the door. If you don't have a reservation and can't wait to eat, pull up a stool
at the marble-topped bar, where the view of the open kitchen and dining room is
unobstructed. Better yet, on a sunny day, grab a patio table that looks onto Levi
Plaza's fountain. The divided dining room, with high ceilings and enormous,
Italian-style paintings, is also warm and convivial. The first of many delights is the
basket of fresh-baked breads and breadsticks that arrive at your table accompanied
by a dipping dish of olive oil. Complement them with any of the delicious salads or
the daily soup (especially if it's carrot), then venture onward to any of the pastas,
pizzas, or main courses. Our favorite is the rotisserie duck in balsamic vinegar,
which Il Fornaio somehow serves without all the fat you'd expect from duck and all
the crispy skin you wish for. Parents especially appreciate the "bambini" menu,
which features pint-size fare for under $6. Desserts are decadent and wonderful. Try
the tiramisu and a glass of rose grappa—a perfect way to end the meal. Breakfasts
here are a treat as well.

Maykadeh. 470 Green St. (between Kearny St. and Grant Ave.). ☎ **415/362-8286.** Reservations recommended. Main courses $10–$16. MC, V. Daily 11:45am–10:30pm. Bus: 15 or 41. PERSIAN/MIDDLE EASTERN.

If you're looking to add a little adventure to your evening dinner plans, this is the place. Surrounded by a sea of Italian bistros, Maykadeh is one of San Francisco's best and most elegant Persian restaurants. The Middle East may no longer be the culinary capital of the world, but at Maykadeh you can still sample the exotic flavors that characterize Persian cuisine. Of the dozen or so appetizers offered on the menu, some of the best are the eggplant with mint garlic sauce, the stuffed grape leaves, and the lamb tongue with lime juice, sour cream, and saffron (c'mon, live a little). About eight mesquite-grilled items are offered, including fillet of lamb marinated in lime, homemade yogurt, saffron, and onions. House specialties include half a dozen vegetarian dishes, such as the eggplant braised with saffron, fresh tomato, and dried lime.

○ Rose Pistola. 532 Columbus Ave. (at Union and Green sts.). ☎ **415/399-0499.** Reservations highly recommended. Main courses $6.95–$18.50 lunch; most dishes $9–$21.50 dinner. AE, MC, V. Sun–Thurs 11:30am–10:30pm with late-night menu until midnight; Fri–Sat 11:30am–11:30pm with late-night menu until 1am. Valet parking $5 lunch, $8 dinner. Bus: 15, 30, 41, or 45. ITALIAN.

Undoubtedly the hottest new restaurant in 1997, Rose Pistola was created by the masterminds behind the ultrasuccessful SoMa restaurant Lulu. Like its North Beach neighborhood, the atmosphere is of a smart, bustling bistro. Although it's a larger dining room than most in the area, it's divided so it doesn't feel impersonal (though you'll want to avoid the tables next to the bar). Sidewalk seating is favored on sunny afternoons, but inside there's plenty to see as chefs crank out the eclectic food from the open kitchen. Fare here is meant to be shared, and aside from sandwiches, comes à la carte. The appetizer list features a barrage of hot and cold antipasti, which are reasonably priced between $2.75 and $7.50 but tend to be in small portions. We opted for fried chickpeas, an innovative and tasty new way to enjoy the seed; lemon, prosciutto, sweet pea, and mozzarella risotto fritters, which were wonderful but pricey for four golf-ball-size morsels ($4.75); and a boring—and again pricey—chopped salad ($5.50).

Along with meats and foul, you'll find a variety of fish choices on the menu. We tried mussels in a rich tomato broth, which was so flavorful we kept it around to soak up our bread long after the shellfish had been devoured. Our favorite dish, however, was the whole Arctic char, which came bathing in fennel and tapenade in a big iron skillet. The fish was crispy and perfectly seasoned on the outside, tender and juicy on the inside—definitely worth writing home about. The "flaming cream" dessert, three fried crème-brûlée–type diamonds that arrived afire with a Bacardi-and-apricot sauce, was creative and very tasty, but not worth the $7.50 asking price. Still, overall, we agree that Rose Pistola is hot for the right reasons: It's the place to be, the food is great, and the menu is varied enough for all tastes and budgets.

Stinking Rose. 325 Columbus Ave. (between Vallejo and Broadway). ☎ **415/781-7673.** Reservations accepted. Main courses $12–$18. AE, DC, JCB, MC, V. Sun–Thurs 11am–11pm; Fri–Sat 11am–midnight. Bus: 15, 30, 41, or 45. ITALIAN.

Garlic, of course, is the "flower" from which this restaurant gets its name. From soup to ice cream, the supposedly healthful herb is a star ingredient in most every dish. ("We season our garlic with food," exclaims the menu.) From a strictly gourmet point of view, the Stinking Rose is unremarkable. Pizzas, pastas, and meats smothered in simple, overpowering garlic sauces are tasty, but memorable only for their singular garlicky intensity. That said, this is a fun place; the restaurant's lively atmosphere and odoriferous aroma combine for good entertainment. Black-and-white floors, gray marble tables, and large windows overlooking the street help maintain the high energy. The best dishes here include garlic-steamed clams and mussels, garlic pizza, and 40-clove garlic chicken (served with garlic mashed potatoes, of course).

Tommaso's. 1042 Kearny St. (at Broadway). ☎ **415/398-9696.** Reservations not accepted. Pasta and pizza $8–$21; main courses $9–$15. AE, DC, MC, V. Tues–Sat 5–10:30pm; Sun 4–9:30pm. Closed Dec 15–Jan 15. Bus: 15 or 41. ITALIAN.

From the street, Tommaso's looks wholly unappealing; a drab, windowless brown facade sandwiched between sex shops. Then why are people always waiting in line to get in? Because everyone knows that Tommaso's bakes one of San Francisco's best traditional-style pizzas, and has for decades. The center of attention in the downstairs dining room is the chef, who continuously tosses huge hunks of garlic and mozzarella onto pizzas before sliding them into the oak-burning brick oven. Nineteen different toppings make pizza the dish of choice, even though Italian classics such as veal marsala, chicken cacciatore, and a superb lasagna are also available (they have wonderful calzones, too). Half bottles of house wines are sold, as are homemade cannoli and good Italian coffee. If you can overlook the seedy surroundings, this fun, boisterous restaurant is a great place to take the family.

INEXPENSIVE

Caffè Freddy's. 901 Columbus Ave. (corner of Lombard St.). ☎ **415/922-0151.** Reservations accepted. Main courses $2–$8 brunch, $4–$11.75 lunch, $5–$13.75 dinner. AE, MC, V. Tues 11:30am–9pm; Wed–Fri 11:30am–10pm; Sat 10am–10pm; Sun 10am–9pm. Bus: 15 or 41. ITALIAN.

Recognizable by the large, painted palms that frame the doorway, Caffè Freddy's attracts a young, hungry, and low-budgeted clientele that comes for the generous servings at generous prices. Pizzas, pastas, sandwiches, salads, and a large assortment of appetizers line the menu—try the antipasto plate of bruschetta, fresh melon, ham, sun-dried tomatoes, and pesto. Start with the warm cabbage salad with goat cheese, currants, walnuts, rosemary, and spinach, then move on to the restaurant's specialty: fresh seafood dishes such as mixed fish soup, steaming bowls of mussels, or thick cuts of Atlantic salmon for under $14. Granted, it's not the best Italian food you'll ever eat, but it's good, cheap, and plentiful.

Caffè Macaroni. 59 Columbus Ave. (at Jackson St.). ☎ **415/956-9737.** Reservations taken for lunch only. Main courses $6.95–$13.95. No credit cards. Mon–Fri 11:30am–2pm; Mon–Sat 5–10pm. Bus: 15 or 41. ITALIAN.

You wouldn't know it from the looks (or name) of it, but this tiny, funky restaurant on busy Columbus Avenue is one of the best southern Italian restaurants in the city. It looks as if it can only hold two customers at a time, and if you don't duck your head when entering the upstairs dining room you might as well ask for one lump or two. Fortunately, the kitchen also packs a wallop, dishing out a large variety of antipasti and excellent pastas. The spinach-and-cheese ravioli with wild-mushroom sauce is outstanding, and the gnocchi is probably the best you'll find outside Italy. The owners and staff are always vivacious and friendly, and young ladies in particular will enjoy the attentions of the charming Italian men manning the counter.

Capp's Corner. 1600 Powell St. (at Green St.). ☎ **415/989-2589.** Reservations recommended. Main courses $12–$14. AE, CB, DISC, MC, V. Mon–Thurs 4:30–10pm; Fri–Sat 4:30–11pm; Sun 4–10pm. Bus: 15 or 41. ITALIAN.

This funky old family-style Italian restaurant on the corner of Powell and Green streets is one of our favorite places to take a group of friends and pig out on hearty Italian fare. Capp's is a place of givens: It's a given that there's always some high-spirited regulars hunched over the bar; that Frank Sinatra's singing on the jukebox; and that you'll always be served huge portions at low prices in a raucous atmosphere that goes on until the wee hours. The waitresses, who have worked here since the Truman administration, are usually brusque and bossy, but always with a wink. Long tables are set up for family-style dining: bread, soup, salad, choice of main dish (herb-roasted leg of lamb, veal tortellini with sun-dried tomato sauce, osso buco with fresh polenta, fettuccine with rock shrimp), and dessert—all for only $12 or $14 per person, $9.50 for kids. You may have to wait an hour for a table, but you won't get bored if the old cronies at the bar take a liking to you. *Tip:* Discounted parking is available at the Green Street Mortuary across the street (hey, in San Francisco you park where you can park).

Gira Polli. 659 Union St. (at Columbus Ave.). ☎ **415/434-4472.** Reservations recommended. Main courses $7.50–$12.50. AE, MC, V. Daily 4:30–9:30pm. Bus: 15, 30, 39, 41, or 45. ITALIAN.

I (Matthew) used to live 3 blocks from Gira Polli, and man-oh-man do I miss it. Whenever I'd rent a video, I'd drop by here for the Gira Polli Special: a foil-lined bag filled with oh-so-tender wood-fired chicken, Palermo potatoes (the best in the city), a fresh garden salad, perfectly cooked vegetables, and a soft roll—all for under $10. Next, I'd nab a bottle of good, cheap wine from the liquor store next door, take my goodies home, disconnect the phone, and love life for a while. (*Tip:* On sunny days, there's no better place in North Beach for a picnic lunch than Washington Square, right across the street.)

Il Pollaio. 555 Columbus Ave. (between Green and Union sts.). ☎ **415/362-7727.** Main courses $6.75–$12.50. AE, MC, V. Mon–Sat 11:30am–9pm. Cable car: Powell-Mason line. Bus: 15, 30, 39, or 41. ITALIAN/ARGENTINEAN.

Simple, affordable, and consistently delicious is a winning combination at Il Pollaio. The dining room is casual, the menu simple, and the fresh-from-the-grill chicken is so moist it practically falls off the bone (you'll love the tangy lemon flavor). Each meal is served with a choice of salads, and if you're not in the mood for chicken, you can opt for rabbit, lamb, pork chop, or Italian sausage.

✪ L'Osteria del Forno. 519 Columbus Ave. (between Green and Union sts.). ☎ **415/ 982-1124.** Sandwiches $5–$6; pizzas $10–$13; main courses $6–$8.25. No credit cards. Mon–Wed 11:30am–10pm; Fri–Sat 11:30am–10:30pm; Sun 1–10pm. Bus: 15 or 41. ITALIAN.

L'Osteria del Forno may be only slightly larger than a walk-in closet, but it's one of the top-three Italian restaurants in North Beach. Peer in the window facing Columbus Avenue, and you'll probably see two Italian women with their hair up, sweating from the heat of their brick-lined oven that cranks out the best focaccia (and focaccia sandwiches) in the city. There's no pomp or circumstance involved: locals come here strictly to eat. The menu features a variety of superb pizzas and fresh pastas, plus a few daily specials (pray for the roast pork braised in milk). Small baskets of warm focaccia bread keep you going till the entrees arrive, which should always be accompanied by a glass of Italian red.

Mario's Bohemian Cigar Store. 566 Columbus Ave. ☎ **415/362-0536.** Sandwiches $5–$6.25. No credit cards. Daily 10am–midnight. Closed Dec 24–Jan 1. Bus: 15, 30, 41, or 45. ITALIAN.

Across the street from Washington Square is one of North Beach's most popular neighborhood hangouts: Mario's. The century-old bar—small, well worn, and perpetually busy—is best known for its focaccia sandwiches, including meatball or eggplant. Wash it all down with an excellent cappuccino or a house Campari as you watch the tourists stroll by. And yes, they do sell cigars.

Note: A new, larger location has opened at 2209 Polk St., between Green and Vallejo streets (☎ **415/776-8226**).

Mo's Gourmet Burgers. 1322 Grant Ave. (Vallejo and Green sts.). ☎ **415/788-3779.** Main courses $4.95–$7.75. MC, V. Mon–Thurs 11am–10:30pm; Fri 11am–11:30pm; Sat 9am–11:30pm; Sun 9am–10:30pm. Bus: 9X, 15, 30, 39, 41, or 45. AMERICAN/BURGERS.

Here you'll find the real deal: A burger so juicy that even with half a dozen napkins you're still likely to be wearing it when you leave. Mo's offers a simple but winning combination: big, thick grilled patties of fresh-ground, best-quality, center-cut chuck; fresh french fries; cabbage slaw, sautéed garlic mushrooms, or beans and rice—violà! You've got the city's burger of choice (Zuni's is an easy contender, but almost twice the price). The other food—spicy chicken sandwich; steak with veggies, garlic bread, and potatoes ($10.50); and token veggie dishes—is also up to snuff, but it's that messy and memorable burger that keeps the carnivores captivated (not to mention the sinisterly sweet shakes).

Pasta Pomodoro. 655 Union St. (at Columbus Ave.). ☎ **415/399-0300.** Main courses $4.60–$8.95. MC, V. Mon–Fri 11am–11pm; Sat noon–midnight; Sun noon–11pm. Cable car: Mason St. Bus: 15, 30, 41, or 45. ITALIAN.

If you're looking for a good, cheap meal in North Beach, this place across from Washington Square can't be beat. There's usually a 20-minute wait for a table, but after you're seated you'll be surprised at how promptly you're served. Every dish is fresh and sizable, and best of all, they cost a third of what you'll pay elsewhere. Winners include the spaghetti *frutti di mare* made with calamari, mussels, scallops, tomato, garlic and wine, or *cavatappi pollo* with roast chicken, sun-dried tomatoes, cream, mushrooms, and Parmesan—both are under $7. Avoid the cappellini Pomodoro or ask for extra sauce—it tends to be dry. Their other locations, at 2027 Chestnut St., at Fillmore (☎ **415/474-3400**); 2304 Market St., at 16th Street (☎ **415/558-8123**); 3611 California St. (☎ **415/831-0900**); and 816 Irving St., between 9th and 10th streets (☎ **415/566-0900**) are equally good.

9 Fisherman's Wharf

EXPENSIVE

Alioto's. Fisherman's Wharf (at Taylor St.). ☎ **415/673-0183.** Reservations recommended. Main courses $7–$14 at lunch; $18–$60 at dinner. AE, CB, DC, DISC, MC, V.   Daily 11am–11pm. Cable car: Powell-Hyde line. Bus: 30 or 42. SEAFOOD.

One of San Francisco's oldest restaurants, run by one of the city's most prominent families, the Aliotos, this Fisherman's Wharf landmark has a long-standing reputation for serving the Bay's best cioppino. The curbside crab stand, Oysteria Deli, and the new Steam Kettle Bar are great for a quick, inexpensive dose of San Francisco's finest; for more formal and fancy selections, continue up the carpeted stairs to the multilevel, harbor-view dining room. Don't mess around with the menu: It's the Dungeness crab you're after. Cracked, caked, stuffed, or stewed, its impossible to get your fill, so bring plenty of money—particularly if you intend to order from Alioto's prodigious (and pricey) wine list. If you happen to be insane and don't care for cracked crab, the griddle-fried sand dabs and rex sole served with tartar sauce are also quite good.

The Mandarin. At Ghirardelli Sq., 900 North Point St. ☎ **415/673-8812.** Reservations accepted. Main courses $23–$58; fixed-price dinners $23–$38. AE, CB, DC, MC, V. Daily 11:30am–11pm. Cable car: Hyde St. line. Bus: 19, 30, 42, 47, or 49. CHINESE.

Created by Madame Cecilia Chiang in 1968, The Mandarin is meant to feel like a cultured, northern Chinese home; fine furnishings, silk-covered walls, and good-quality Asian art create one of the most elegant Chinese restaurants in the city. Tables are spaced comfortably apart, and the better of two softly lit dining rooms offers matchless views of the bay.

True to its name, The Mandarin offers exceptional northern Chinese cuisine. Take our advice and start with the sesame shrimp or minced squab appetizer, then follow through with either the smoked tea duck (their version of Beijing duck, but smoked over burning tea leaves until crispy) or—if you have a party of two or more and call a day in advance—the Beggar's Chicken, which is encased in clay and cooked to slow perfection.

A. Sabella's. Fisherman's Wharf, 2766 Taylor St. (at Jefferson St.), 3rd floor. ☎ **415/771-6775.** Reservations accepted. Main courses $12–$47. AE, CB, DC, DISC, MC, V. Daily 11am–10:30pm. Cable car: Powell-Mason line. ITALIAN/SEAFOOD.

The Sabella family has been serving seafood in San Francisco since the turn of the century and has operated A. Sabella's restaurant on the wharf continuously since 1920. Catering heavily to the tourist trade, the menu offers something for everyone—steak, lamb, seafood, chicken, and pasta dishes, all made from scratch with fresh local ingredients. Where A. Sabella's really shines, however, is in the shellfish department. Its 1,000-gallon saltwater tank allows for fresh crab, abalone, and lobster year-round, which means no restaurant in the city can touch A. Sabella's when it comes to feasting on fresh Dungeness crab and abalone out of season. A nice touch is the live piano music played nightly in the spacious and rather chic dining room overlooking the wharf.

MODERATE

Cafe Pescatore. 2455 Mason St. (at North Point St.). ☎ **415/561-1111.** Reservations recommended. Main courses $3.95–$7.95 breakfast, $10–$16 lunch or dinner. AE, DC, DISC, MC, V. Mon–Thurs 11:30am–10pm; Fri 11:30am–11pm; Sat 5–11pm; Sun 5–10pm; Sat–Sun 7am–3pm brunch, 3–5pm cafe menu. Cable car: Powell-Mason line. Bus: 42, 15, or 39. ITALIAN.

Though San Francisco locals are a rarity at Cafe Pescatore, most agree that if they had to dine at Fisherman's Wharf, this cozy trattoria would be their first choice. Two walls of sliding glass doors offer pseudo-sidewalk seating when the weather's warm, although heavy vehicular traffic can detract from the alfresco experience. The general consensus is to order anything that's cooked in the open kitchen's wood-fired oven, such as the pizzas and roasts. A big hit with tourists is the *polenta al forno*—oak-roasted cheese polenta with marinara sauce and fresh pesto. The verde pizza (pesto-flavored prawns and spinach) and huge serving of roast chicken are also safe bets.

10 Pacific Heights/Cow Hollow

EXPENSIVE

Harris'. 2100 Van Ness Ave. (at Pacific Ave.). ☎ **415/673-1888.** Reservations recommended. Main courses $18–$34. AE, CB, DC, DISC, MC, V. Mon–Thurs 5:30–9:30pm; Fri 5:30–10:30pm; Sat 5–10:30pm; Sun 5–9:30pm. Bus: 38 or 45. STEAK HOUSE.

Every big city has a great steak restaurant, and in San Francisco it's Harris'—a comfortably elegant establishment sporting a handsome wood-paneled dining room with curving banquettes and stately waiters. Proprietor Ann Lee Harris knows steaks; she grew up on a cattle ranch and married the owner of the largest feedlot in California. In 1976, the couple opened the Harris Ranch Restaurant on Interstate 5 in central California, where they built a rock-solid reputation up and down the coast. The steaks, which can be seen hanging in a glass-windowed aging room off Pacific Avenue, are cut thick—either New York–style or T-bone—and are served with a baked potato and seasonal vegetables. Harris' also offers lamb chops, fresh fish, lobster, and roast duckling, as well as venison, buffalo, and other types of game when in season.

✪ **La Folie.** 2316 Polk St. (between Green and Union sts.). ☎ **415/776-5577.** Reservations recommended. Main courses $24–$32; 5-course tasting menu $65; vegetarian tasting menu $50. AE, CB, DC, DISC, MC, V. Mon–Sat 5:30–10:30pm. Bus: 19, 41, 45, 47, 49, or 76. FRENCH.

For fantastic French food without the highbrow attitude, La Folie is the place to feast. The minute you walk through the door you'll know why this is many locals' favorite restaurant. The country-French decor is tasteful but not too serious, with whimsical chandeliers and a cloudy sky painted overhead. The staff is friendly, knowledgeable, and very accommodating, and the food is truly outstanding. Unlike many renowned chefs, La Folie's Roland Passot is in the kitchen nightly, and it shows. Each of his California-influenced French creations is an architectural and culinary masterpiece. Best of all, they're served in a relaxed and comfortable environment. Start with an appetizer such as the roast quail and foie gras with salad, wild mushrooms, and roasted garlic—it's guaranteed to melt in your mouth. Main courses are not petite as in many French restaurants, and all are accompanied by flavorful and well-balanced sauces. Try the rôti of quail and squab stuffed with wild mushrooms and wrapped in crispy potato strings, or the roast venison with vegetables, quince, and huckleberry sauce. Finish off with any of the delectable desserts.

MODERATE

Ace Wasabi's. 3339 Steiner St. (at Chestnut St.). ☎ **415/567-4903.** Reservations not accepted. Main courses $4–$9. AE, MC, V. Mon–Thurs 5:30–10:30pm, Fri–Sat 5:30–11pm, Sun 5–10pm. Bus: 30. JAPANESE/SUSHI.

Yeah, more sushi, but this time with a twist. What differentiates this Marina hot spot (formerly known as Flying Kamikazes) from the usual sushi spots around town are the unique combinations, the varied menu, and the young, hip atmosphere. Ace Wasabi's innovative rolls are a nice welcome to those bored with the traditional styles, though they may be too much adventure for some (don't worry, there's plenty of nonsea and nonraw items on the menu). Don't miss the rainbow "Three Amigos" roll or the "Rock and Roll" with cooked eel, avocado, and cucumber. The buckwheat-noodle–and–julienne-vegetable salad is also a treat. The service could be improved—on busy nights you'll wait forever for your server to pour your Sapporo—but the staff is friendly and the atmosphere is fun, so nobody seems to mind.

Balboa Café. 3199 Fillmore St. (at Greenwich St.). ☎ **415/921-3944.** Reservations for 6 or more only. Main courses $7–$13 at lunch, $7–$19 at dinner, $7–$10 at weekend brunch. AE, MC, V. Mon–Sun 11am–10pm; bar daily 11am–2am. Bus: 22. AMERICAN.

Back in the 1980s the Balboa Café was San Francisco's main "meet market," filled each week with the young and the restless. Though things bottomed out in the early 1990s, the wheel is turning once again for this trendy, stylish Cow Hollow hangout since the crew at the wildly popular PlumpJack Café took over (in fact, patrons put on hold at PlumpJack are usually sent here for a predinner cocktail). Though Balboa isn't nearly on the caliber as its around-the-corner cousin, you'll probably be forced to mingle with the Marina "pretty people" crowd at the bar until a table frees up. The limited menu offers some upscale options, such as braised lamb shank with roasted tomatoes, white beans, and zucchini, but it's the Balboa Burgers and Caesar salads that get the most requests.

Betelnut. 2030 Union St. (at Buchanan St.). ☎ **415/929-8855.** Reservations recommended. Main courses $9–$16. CB, DC, DISC, MC, V. Sun–Thurs 11:30am–11pm; Fri–Sat 11:30am–midnight. Bus: 22, 41, or 45. SOUTHEAST ASIAN.

While San Francisco is teeming with Asian restaurants, few offer the posh, fashionable dining environment of this restaurant on upscale Union Street. As the menu explains, the restaurant is themed after "Pejui Wu," a traditional Asian beer house offering local brews and savory dishes. But with the bamboo paneling, red Formica countertops, and low-hanging lamps, the place feels less like an authentic harbor restaurant and more like a set out of Madonna's movie *Shanghai Surprise*. Still, the atmosphere is en vogue, with dimly lit booths, ringside seating overlooking the bustling stir-fry chefs, sidewalk tables (weather permitting), and body-to-body flirting at the cramped but festive bar. Starters include sashimi and tasty salt-and-pepper whole gulf prawns; main courses offer orange-glazed beef with asparagus, and oyster mushrooms and Singapore chili crab. While prices seem reasonable, it's the incidentals such as white rice ($1.50 per person) and tea ($3.50 per pot) that rack up the bill. Many locals and tourists absolutely adore this place, so we're hesitant to bash it. Unfortunately, when we've come here the food was merely fair and the wait staff so inattentive, the experience was ruined. In our minds, the main reason to choose this restaurant over others is the atmosphere and their heavenly signature dessert: a mouth-watering tapioca pudding with sweet red adzuki beans.

✪ **Cafe Kati.** 1963 Sutter St. (between Fillmore and Webster sts.). ☎ **415/775-7313.** Reservation recommended. Main courses $15–$20. MC, V. Tues–Sun 5:30–10pm. Bus: 2, 3, or 4. CALIFORNIA/EAST-WEST.

Chef Kirk Webber works small wonders in an even smaller kitchen at this diminutive yet distinctive restaurant just off Fillmore Street. The menu highlights California-style dishes spiced with a dash of the Orient and Italy, all of which are presented in high form, such as the signature Caesar salad sculpted into a towering monument of germane romaine. The seasonally changing menu offers such cross-cultural creations as pancetta-wrapped pork tenderloin bathed in a ragu of baby artichokes; miso-marinated Chilean sea bass saddled with tempura kabocha squash and chanterelle mushrooms; and crispy duck confit with sweet-potato gnocchi and wild mushrooms. When making a reservation, request a table in the front room—far more appealing—and don't make any plans afterwards as the kitchen takes its sweet time preparing your objet d'art.

Café Marimba. 2317 Chestnut St. (between Scott and Divisadero sts.). ☎ **415/776-1506.** Main courses $7–$14. AE, MC, V. Mon 5:30–10pm; Tues–Thurs and Sun 11:30am–10pm; Fri–Sat 11:30am–11pm. Bus: 30. MEXICAN.

As much as we hate to plug the yuppified Marina District, we have to admit that we're completely addicted to Café Marimba's grilled Yucatan-spiced snapper and grilled chicken tacos. Add just the right amount of guacamole and pineapple salsa, and *acheewahwah* that's good! The *shrimp mojo de ajo* (shrimp seared along with onions, garlic and jalapeño) is also a knockout (heck, even the chips and guac are the best in town). For parties of three or more, order the family-style platter of grilled meats and vegetables and prepare to do battle. We're obviously not the only ones who fancy this fun, festive cafe, so expect a long wait during peak hours (our M.O. is to sneak seats at the bar and order there). But *hasta mañana* the margaritas—*muy mál.*

The Elite Café. 2049 Fillmore St. (between Pine and California sts.). ☎ **415/346-8668.** Reservations not accepted. Main courses $10.95–$24. AE, DC, DISC, MC, V. Mon–Sat 5–11pm; Sun 10am–3pm and 5–10pm. Bus: 41 or 45. CAJUN/CREOLE.

If the shellfish in the window doesn't get you in the door, the festive atmosphere will. This place is always bustling with Pacific Heights's beautiful people who come for fresh oysters, blackened filet mignon with Cajun butter, jambalaya, redfish with crab and Creole cream sauce, or any of the other well-spiced Cajun dishes. The high-backed booths provide more intimate dining than the crowded tables and bar. Brunch is good, too, when all kinds of egg dishes—Benedict, sardou, Hangtown fry, and many more—are offered along with such goodies as bagels and lox and smoked chicken sausage.

Greens Restaurant, Fort Mason. Building A, Fort Mason Center (enter Fort Mason opposite the Safeway at Buchanan and Marina sts.). ☎ **415/771-6222.** Reservations recommended 2 weeks in advance. Main courses $11–$15; fixed-priced dinner $40; brunch $8–$11. DISC, MC, V. Mon 5:30–9:30pm; Tues–Fri 11:30am–2pm and 5:30–9:30pm; Sat 11:30am–2:30pm and 5:30–9pm; Sun brunch 10am–2pm. Bakery Mon–Sat 8am–4:30pm; Sun 9:30am–3:30pm. Bus: 28 or 30. VEGETARIAN.

Knowledgeable locals swear by Greens, where executive-chef Annie Somerville (author of *Fields of Greens*) cooks with the seasons, using produce from Green Gulch Farm and other local organic farms. Located in an old warehouse, with enormous windows overlooking the bridge and the bay, the restaurant is both a pioneer and a legend. A weeknight dinner might feature such appetizers as tomato, white-bean, and sorrel soup, or grilled asparagus with lemon, Parmesan cheese, and watercress, followed by such choices as spring-vegetable risotto with asparagus, peas, shiitake and crimini mushrooms, and Parmesan cheese, or Sri Lankan curry made of new potatoes, cauliflower, carrots, peppers, and snap peas stewed with tomatoes, coconut milk, ginger, and Sri Lankan spices.

A special five-course dinner is served on Saturday only. A recent example began with grilled asparagus, yellowfin potatoes, and peppers with blood-orange beurre blanc, followed by shiitake and crimini mushroom lasagna with leeks and mushroom port sauce. Desserts are equally adventuresome—try the chocolate pave with mint crème anglaise or the espresso ice cream with chocolate sauce (*Insider tip:* A "Late Evening Desert" is served Mon to Thurs from 9:30 to 11pm.). Lunch and brunch are somewhat simpler, but equally as inventive.

Like the restaurant, the adjacent bakery is also operated by the Zen Center. It sells homemade breads, sandwiches, soups, salads, and pastries to take home.

North India Restaurant. 3131 Webster St. (at Lombard St.). ☎ **415/931-1556.** Reservations recommended. Main courses $14.50–$19.95; fixed-price dinner $12.95. AE, DC, MC, V. Mon–Fri 11:30am–2:30pm; daily 5–10pm. Bus: 41 or 45. INDIAN.

While many Indian establishments lack atmosphere, chef Parvesh Sahi's full Indian menu is served in a plush, dimly lit dining room, providing the perfect ambiance for an intimate evening out with some ethnic flair. As you settle into a maroon velvet chair and browse the menu, soft Indian music reminds you what part of the world your taste buds will venture to. Start by ordering a cup of the sweet and spicy chai tea, and the oversized, moist samosas (spiced potatoes and green peas served in a crisp pocket), then venture onward with any of the tandoori specials, such as the mixed seafood dish with sea bass, jumbo prawns, and calamari. There are plenty of vegetarian dishes as well, ranging from *aloo gobi* (cauliflower and potatoes in curry sauce) to *baingan aloo masala* (eggplant, potatoes, tomatoes, ginger, garlic, green onions, and spices). All these tasty feasts are accompanied by bottomless pots of delicious mango chutney and cucumber-dill sauce. Anything you order here will be fresh, well prepared, and served by courteous waiters wearing vests adorned with Indian-style mirrors and gold embroidery. Although expensive for Indian food, it's worth the extra bucks if you want to be ensured good quality and atmosphere. Arrive between 5 and 7pm and you can opt for the very affordable fixed-price dinner for $12.95.

Oritalia. 1915 Fillmore St. (between Pine and Bush sts.). ☎ **415/346-1333.** Pasta $15.50–$17.75; main courses $18.50–$21.75. AE, MC, V. Mon–Sat 5–11pm; Sun 5–10pm. Bus: 41 or 45. ASIAN/ITALIAN.

If you can't decide between Italian and Asian food tonight, try both. Located on a busy section of Fillmore Street, Oritalia (the name is derived from Oriental and Italian) has made its niche by blending the flavors of Italy, China, Korea, and Southeast Asia to create some truly unique dishes that locals-in-the-know rave about. Seasonal menu items range from tuna tartare on sticky rice cakes with Asian pears to Nori-wrapped Dungeness crab cakes in lemongrass with ginger cream sauce. Though full entrees are available, an assortment of the "Small Plates" makes for a more adventurous, family-style dining experience. A charming, casual decor marked by papier-mâché paintings, hand-painted pendant lamps, painted gourds, and textured walls by Japanese artist Yoshi Hayashi are the perfect complement to the multicultural menu.

Osome. 1923 Fillmore St. (between Bush and Pine sts.). ☎ **415/346-2311.** Sushi $3–$7.50; main courses $8.95–$14.20. AE, MC, V. Mon–Sat 5:30–11pm; Sun 5–10:30pm. JAPANESE/SUSHI.

What this neighborhood restaurant lacks in decor (there are few adornments and, frankly, the place looks half-finished), it more than makes up for in fresh, well-presented Japanese cuisine. There are fewer than a dozen tables for large parties, but the best seats are definitely bar-side, where sushi chefs slice and roll *maguro* (tuna), *unagi* (eel), and close to 40 other savory rice-and-fish combinations. Many of our friends fill up before going out for sushi so they won't spend a fortune satisfying their hunger. There's no need to do that here because there's also a full, and reasonably priced, dinner menu with tempura, teriyaki, and sukiyaki. Start with the surprisingly sculptural spinach *goma ae,* a skyline of spinach towers bathing in a tangy sesame-seed sauce. From there, let your taste buds be your guide.

✪ **Pane e Vino.** 3011 Steiner St. (at Union St.). ☎ **415/346-2111.** Reservations recommended. Main courses $8.50–$19.95. MC, V. Mon–Thurs 11:30am–2:30pm and 5–10pm; Fri–Sat 11:30am–10:30pm; Sun 5–10pm. Bus: 41 or 45. ITALIAN.

Pane e Vino is one of San Francisco's top and most authentic Italian restaurants, as well as our personal favorite. The food is consistently excellent (careful not to fill up on the outstanding breads served upon seating), the prices reasonable, and the mostly Italian-accented staff always smooth and efficient under pressure (you'll see). The two small dining rooms, separated by an open kitchen that eminates heavenly aromas, offer only limited seating, so expect a wait even if you have a reservation. The menu offers a wide selection of appetizers, including a fine carpaccio, *vitello tonnato* (sliced roasted veal and capers in a lemony tuna sauce), and the hugely popular chilled artichoke stuffed with bread and tomatoes and served with a vinaigrette. Our favorite, the antipasti of mixed grilled vegetables, always spurs a fork fight. A similar broad selection of pastas is available, including a flavorful *pennette alla boscaiola* with porcini mushrooms and pancetta in a tomato cream sauce. Other specialties are grilled fish and meat dishes, including a chicken breast marinated in lime juice and herbs. Top dessert picks are any of the Italian ice creams, the crème caramel, and (but, of course) the creamy tiramisu.

PlumpJack Café. 3127 Fillmore St. (between Filbert and Greenwich sts.). ☎ **415/563-4755.** Reservations recommended. Main courses $15–$22. AE, MC, V. Mon–Fri 11:30am–2pm; Mon–Sat 5:30–10:30pm. Bus: 41 or 45. CALIFORNIA/FRENCH/MEDITERRANEAN.

Wildly popular among San Francisco's style-setters, this small Cow Hollow restaurant quickly became the "in" place to dine. This is partly due to the fact that it's run by one of the Getty clan (as in J. Paul), but mostly because Chef Maria Helm's food is just plain good and the whimsical decor is a veritable work of art.

Though the menu changes weekly, you might find such appetizers as smoked salmon with two kinds of caviar, or a salad of watercress and Belgian endive with kumquats, toasted pine nuts, shaved reggiano, and champagne vinaigrette. Main dishes range from risotto with spring onions, asparagus, pancetta, and chèvre to roasted duck-breast confit with potato rosti and thyme-roasted apples. Top it off with bittersweet chocolate soufflé or cinnamo-scented Alsatian apple cake. The extraordinarily extensive California wine list—gleaned from the PlumpJack wine shop down the street—is sold at next to retail, with many wines available by the glass.

Prego. 2000 Union St. (at Buchanan St.). ☎ **415/563-3305.** Reservations accepted. Pasta and pizza $9–$13; main courses $13–$20. AE, DC, MC, V. Mon–Sat 11:30am–midnight; Sun 10am–midnight. Bus: 22, 41, or 45. ITALIAN.

A light and airy trattoria, frequented by an upscale clientele, Prego is a place to be seen or people-watch as you dine beyond the windows facing Union Street. Specialties include thin-crust, oak-fired pizzas, pasta, and grilled fish and meats. Spit-roasted, free-range chicken is prepared on a rotisserie and served with potatoes and vegetables. A good selection of wine is also available by the glass or bottle. Prego also hosts a Sunday-morning brunch, but unless you're partial to the street-side view, breakfast can't be beat down the street at Doidge's (if you can get in, that is).

✪ **Zinzino.** 2355 Chestnut St. (at Divisadero St.). ☎ **415/346-6623.** Reservations accepted. Main courses $9–$16.50. AE, MC, V. Mon–Thurs 6–10pm; Fri–Sat 5:30–11pm; Sun 5:30–9:30pm. Bus: 22 or 30. ITALIAN.

Usually we're under the impression that San Francisco needs another cute Italian cafe like it needs a tsunami headed its way. Well, it may not happen often, but we were wrong. Owner Ken Zankel and Spago-sired chef Andrea Rappaport have combined forces to create one of the city's top Italian restaurants. Zinzino may look like a tiny trattoria from the outside, but you could fit a small nuclear sub in the space from the sun-drenched facade to the shaded back patio of this former Laundromat.

Italian movie posters, magazines, antiques, and furnishings evoke memories of past vacations, but we rarely recall the food in Italy being this good (and certainly not this cheap). Start off with the crispy calamari with a choice of herbed aioli or tomato sauces (second only to Scala's Earth and Surf), the roasted jumbo prawns wrapped in crisp pancetta and bathed in a tangy balsamic reduction sauce, or the peculiar-tasting shaved-fennel-and-mint salad—or try them all. Rappaport is giving Zuni Café a run for its money with her version of roasted half chicken, the most tender bird we've ever tasted ("It's all the wood-fired oven," she admits); the accompanying goat-cheese salad and potato frisee were also superb. New to the menu are Rappaport's weekly rotating specials, such as her roasted shellfish platter, oven-roasted half lobster, or baby lamb chops.

INEXPENSIVE

Andalé Taqueria. 2150 Chestnut St. (between Steiner and Pierce sts.). ☎ **415/749-0506.** Most dishes $5.25–$7. No credit cards. Mon–Thurs 11am–10pm; Fri–Sat 11am–11pm; Sun 11am–9pm. Bus: 22, 28, 30, 30X, 43, 76, or 82X. MEXICAN.

Andalé (Spanish for "hurry up") offers a high-end, fast-food resolution for the health-conscious eater. As the long menu explains, this small California chain prides itself on using all fresh ingredients and low-cal options: no lard or preservatives and no canned items; salad dressings made with cholesterol-free double virgin olive oil; whole vegetarian beans (not refried); skinless chicken; salsas and aguas frescas made from fresh fruits and veggies; and mesquite-grilled meats—heck, even the chips are fried in cholesterol-free Canola oil. Add the location (situated on the sunny shopping stretch of Chestnut), sophisticated decor, and check-me-out patio seating (complete with corner fireplace), and it's no wonder the good-looking, fitness-fanatic Marina District considers this place home. Prices are kept low by serving the fare cafeteria-style. *Bargain tips:* No one can complain about a quarter of a mesquite-roasted chicken with potatoes, salsa, and tortillas for $4.95. But if you want to go traditional, stick with the giant burritos or the $2.25 tacos—a nibbler's dream.

✪ **Doidge's.** 2217 Union St. (between Fillmore and Steiner sts.). ☎ **415/921-2149.** Reservations accepted and essential on weekends. Breakfast $4.50–$10; lunch $5–$8. MC, V. Mon–Fri 8am–1:45pm; Sat–Sun 8am–2:45pm. Bus: 41 or 45. AMERICAN.

Doidge's is sweet, small, and always packed, serving up one of the better breakfasts in San Francisco since 1971. Doidge's fame is based on eggs Benedict; eggs Florentine, prepared with thinly sliced Motherlode ham, runs a close second. Invariably, the menu includes a gourmet omelet packed with luscious combinations, and to delight the kid in you, hot chocolate comes in your very own teapot. The six seats at the original mahogany counter are still the most coveted by locals.

Home Plate. 2274 Lombard St. (at Pierce St.). ☎ **415/922-HOME.** Main courses $3.75–$6.50. MC, V. Daily 7am–4pm. Bus: 28, 30, 43, or 76. BREAKFAST.

Dollar for dollar, Home Plate just may be the best breakfast place in San Francisco. Many Marina residents kick off their hectic weekends by carbo-loading at Home Plate on big piles of buttermilk pancakes and waffles smothered with fresh fruit, or hefty omelets stuffed with everything from apple-wood–smoked ham to spinach.

Always the first dish to arrive is a coveted plate of freshly baked scones, best eaten with a bit of butter and a dab of jam. Be sure to look over the daily specials scrawled on the little green chalkboard before you order. And as every fan of this tiny cafe knows, it's best to call ahead and ask to have your name put on the waiting list before you slide into Home Plate.

La Canasta. 2219 Filbert St. (at Fillmore St.). ☎ **415/921-3003.** Main courses $2.80–$6.15. No credit cards. Mon–Sat 11am–10pm. Bus: 22, 41, or 45. MEXICAN.

Unless you forge to the Mission District, burritos don't get much better (or bigger) than those served here at this tiny take-out establishment where you can stuff yourself with a huge chicken burrito for around $5 (the meat's grilled fresh to order). There are no seats here, though, so you'll just have to find another place to devour your grub; fortunately, the Marina Green is a short walk away and offers a million-dollar view no other restaurant can boast. A second location is at 3006 Buchanan St., at Union Street (☎ **415/474-2627**).

Mel's Diner. 2165 Lombard St. (at Fillmore St.). ☎ **415/921-3039.** Reservations accepted. Main courses $4–$5.50 breakfast, $6–$8 lunch, $8–$12 dinner. No credit cards. Sun–Thurs 6am–3am; Fri–Sat 24 hr. (Lombard location only). Bus: 22, 43, or 30. AMERICAN.

Sure, it's contrived, touristy, and nowhere near healthy, but when you get that urge for a chocolate shake and banana cream pie at the stroke of midnight, no other place in the city comes through like Mel's Diner. Modeled after a classic 1950s diner right down to the nickel jukebox at each table, Mel's harks back to the halcyon days when cholesterol and fried foods didn't stroke your guilty conscience with every greasy, wonderful bite. Too bad the prices don't reflect the fifties; a burger with fries and a coke runs about $8, and they don't take credit. There's another Mel's at 3355 Geary at Stanyan Street (☎ **415/387-2244**).

Sweet Heat. 3324 Steiner St. (between Lombard and Chestnut sts.). ☎ **415/474-9191.** Reservations not accepted. All entrees under $8. MC, V. Daily 11am–11pm. MEXICAN.

If you're shopping on Chestnut Street and looking for a flavorful and light lunch, check out this casual place offering "healthy Mexican food to die for." Far from traditional Mexican food, Sweet Heat has capitalized on California's love affair with old-style food prepared in new ways—and the results are impressive. Prices are as low as $4.50 for a veggie burrito with grilled zucchini, red pepper, and roasted corn, or $5.95 for a tasty scallop burrito with green chili chutney. On a sunny day, the back patio is a great place to sun while you eat. Both locations have a tequila bar with 40 variations. Two other locations—at 1725 Haight St. (☎ **415/387-8845**) and 2141 Polk St. (☎ **415/387-8845**)—are equally popular and delicious.

World Wrapps. 2257 Chestnut St. (between Pierce and Scott sts.). ☎ **415/563-9727.** Burritos $3.53–$7.05. MC, V. Daily 8am–11pm. Bus: 22, 28, 30, 43, or 76. INTERNATIONAL.

You'll know you've found World Wrapps when you come upon the trendy, health-conscious crowd standing in line on yuppified Chestnut Street. There are hardly any tables here and plenty of other eateries nearby, so what's the big deal? It's yet another version of San Franciscans' beloved burrito—only this time it's not Mexican-influenced, but rather a tortilla filled with your choice of cuisine from around the world (hence the name). Fresh ingredients, cheap prices, and the love affair Marina residents have with hanging out on this street make World Wrapps the place to grab a bite. A second location is at 2227 Polk St., between Green and Vallejo streets (☎ **415/931-9727**).

11 Civic Center

EXPENSIVE

Jardinière. 300 Grove St. (at Franklin St.). ☎ 415/861-5555. Reservations recommended. Main courses $19–$29; 3-course dinner (before 7pm only) $35; 5-course tasting menu $65. AE, DC, DISC, MC, V. Daily 5:30–10:30pm regular menu; 10:30–midnight late menu. Bus: 19, 21. FRENCH/CALIFORNIA.

One of the hottest new restaurants in town, Jardinière is also the favored pre- and postsymphony alternative to Jeremiah Tower's Stars. The hoopla is a result of a culinary dream team: owner/chef Traci Des Jardins, who packed up her pots and pans at Rubicon to go solo; owner/designer Pat Kuleto, who created the swank ambiance; and general manager Doug Washington, who's good looks and unswerving charm won him local fame at Vertigo. Now the two-story brick structure is abuzz with the "in" crowd who sip cocktails at the centerpiece mahogany bar or watch the scene discreetly from the upstairs circular balcony. The restaurant's champagne theme is integrated via twinkling lights and fun ice buckets built into the balcony railing, making the atmosphere conducive to throwing back a few in the best of style—especially when there's live jazz. Actually, cocktailing is our recommended reason to visit here. While the daily changing menu is good, many locals argue that its way pricey, tiny in portion, and not exactly memorable. We're in partial agreement; when we dined here the food was good, but didn't pack the surprise punches necessary to impress us jaded San Francisco diners (although restaurant critic Michael Bauer would disagree). But anyone simply in search of a quality meal will not be disappointed. The sweet onion tart with cured salmon and herb salad, lobster, leek, and chanterelle strudel was tasty and the crisped chicken with chanterelles, ozette potatoes, and apple-wood–smoked bacon; striped bass with lobster saffron broth, fennel, and potatoes; and filet of beef with sunchoke gratin, mushrooms, and red-wine sauce are also recommended. A bonus for theatergoers is the "Staccato Menu," which is a three-courser that includes an appetizer, main course, and dessert and is available before 7pm. Late diners can also come here for a limited menu served from 10:30pm to midnight. We also have to give kudos to the great wine selection—many by the glass and over 300 bottles.

Stars. 150 Redwood Alley (between McAllister and Golden Gate off Van Ness). ☎ 415/861-7827. Reservations recommended. Main courses $18–$32. AE, MC, V. Daily 5:30–10pm. Bus: 19, 31, or 38. CALIFORNIA.

San Francisco's celebrity hot spot nonpareil, Stars was the brainchild of superstar chef Jeremiah Tower. The large, loud, and vibrant restaurant—swathed in glimmering hardwoods, brass, and mirrors—features the longest bar in the city, which does little to guarantee you'll find a free stool when the place is hopping. Critics complain the quality of the food is slipping (as prices increase) and the staff's attitude is borderline abusive, but it obviously doesn't deter local celebrities like Robin Williams and Mayor Willie Brown from making regular appearances.

Though the menu changes daily, among the half-dozen main courses you might find a braised veal ragout with egg noodles, cipollini onions, and wild mushrooms; medaillon of pork loin with cabbage, leeks, and sauce hachee; or sea scallops with braised Belgian endive, lobster cream sauce, and tarragon. First courses exhibit the same approach. Crisp duck-leg confit with white beans, mangos, and arugula; Belgian endive salad with white-truffle oil, pistachio vinaigrette, and a toasted cheese sandwich are just two examples, along with an innovative minestrone of fish and shellfish chez Prunier. If you want to treat yourself extra well, order the house-cured sturgeon with mushrooms and deviled eggs or the foie gras with hazelnut toasts and watercress salad. *Fair warning:* Prices are high for what little you receive, and the desserts—once considered extraordinary—have slipped far below San Francisco's top-10 list, but like they say, it's not what you get but who you know.

MODERATE

Hayes Street Grill. 320 Hayes St. (near Franklin St.). ☎ **415/863-5545.** Reservations recommended. Main courses $9.25–$18.75. AE, DC, DISC, MC, V. Mon–Fri 11:30am–2pm and 5–9:30pm; Sat 6–10:30pm; Sun 5–8:30pm. Bus: 19, 31, or 38. SEAFOOD.

This small, no-nonsense seafood restaurant has built a solid reputation among San Francisco's picky epicureans for its impeccably fresh fish. Choices ranging from Hawaiian swordfish to Puget Sound salmon—cooked to perfection, naturally—are matched with your sauce of choice (Szechuan peanut, tomatillo salsa, shallot butter) and a side of their signature french fries. Fancier seafood specials are available too, such as paella with clams, mussels, scallops, calamari, chorizo, and saffron rice, as well as an impressive selection of garden-fresh salads and local grilled meats. Finish with the outstanding crème brûlée.

Millennium. In the Abigail Hotel, 246 McAllister St. (at Hyde St.). ☎ **415/487-9800.** Reservations recommended. Main courses $11–$16. MC, V. Daily 5–9:30pm. Bus: 5, 9, or 71. VEGAN.

Banking on the trend toward lighter, healthier cooking, chef Eric Tucker and his band of merry waiters have set out to prove that a meatless menu doesn't mean you have to sacrifice taste. Set in a narrow, handsome Parisian-style dining room with checkered tile flooring, French windows, and sponge-painted walls, Millennium has had nothing but favorable reviews for its egg-, butter-, and dairy-free creations since the day it opened. Granted, it can be a hit-or-miss experience for nonvegans like ourselves, but we've also had some fantastic dishes (particularly the soups). Favorites include the root-vegetable–and–wild-mushroom terrine appetizer, as well as the sweet and spicy plantain torte served over a wonderful papaya and black-bean salsa. For the main course, try the filo purse filled with a ragout of wild mushrooms, leeks, and butternut squash, or the warm Yukon Gold potato salad with sautéed portobello mushrooms. Even the wine-and-beer list has a good selection of organic labels.

۞ Zuni Café. 1658 Market St. (at Franklin St.). ☎ **415/552-2522.** Reservations recommended. Main courses $15–$22.50. AE, MC, V. Tues–Sat 11:30am–midnight; Sun 11am–11pm. Valet parking $5. Muni Metro: All Market St. trams. Bus: 6, 7, 71, or 75. MEDITERRANEAN.

Even factoring in the sometimes snotty wait staff, Zuni Café is still one of our favorite places in the city to have lunch. Its expanse of windows and prime Market Street location guarantee good people-watching—a favorite San Francisco pastime—and chef Judy Rodgers's Mediterranean-influenced menu is wonderfully diverse and satisfying. For the full effect, sit at the bustling, copper-topped bar and peruse the foot-long oyster menu (a dozen or so varieties are on hand at all times); you can also sit in the stylish, exposed-brick dining room or on the outdoor patio. Though the changing menu always includes meat, such as New York steak with Belgian endive gratin, and fish—either grilled or braised in the kitchen's brick oven—the proven winners are Rodgers's brick-oven–roasted chicken for two with Tuscan-style bread salad, the polenta appetizer with mascarpone, and the hamburger on grilled rosemary focaccia bread (a strong contender for the city's best burger). Whatever you decide, be sure to order a side of the shoestring potatoes.

INEXPENSIVE

✪ **Eliza's.** 205 Oak St. (at Gough St.). ☎ **415/621-4819.** Main courses $4.50–$5.15 at lunch, $5.25–$9 at dinner. MC, V ($10 minimum). Mon–Fri 11am–3pm and 5–9pm; Sat 11am–9pm. Bus: 6, 7, 21, 66, or 71. CHINESE (HUNAN/MANDARIN).

Eliza's serves some of the freshest, best-tasting, cheap Chinese in town. But unlike most comparable options, here the atmosphere and presentation parallel the food. The fantastically fresh soups, salads, seafood, pork, chicken, duck, and such specials as spicy eggplant are outstanding and served on beautiful Italian plates. Large windows flank the front and allow natural light to warm the room, while the modern colorful decor and art keep the place attractive throughout the evening. We often come at midday and order the wonderful kung-pao–chicken lunch special: a mixture of tender chicken, peanuts, chili peppers, a subtly hot sauce, and perfectly crunchy vegetables. It's only 1 of 21 main-course choices that come with rice and soup for around $5. But the place is also jumping at night with the opera- and symphony-going crowd.

Tommy's Joynt. 1109 Geary St. (at Van Ness Ave.). ☎ **415/775-4216.** Reservations not accepted. Main courses $4–$7. No credit cards. Daily 10am–2am. Bus: 2, 3, 4, or 38. AMERICAN.

With its colorful mural exterior, it's hard to miss Tommy's Joynt, a late-night favorite for those in search of a cheap and hearty meal. The interior of Tommy's looks like a Buffalo Bill museum that imploded, a wild collage of stuffed birds, a mounted buffalo head, an ancient piano, rusty firearms, fading prints, a beer-guzzling lion, and Santa Claus masks. The Hofbrau-style buffet offers a cornucopia of rib-clinging à la carte dishes such as their signature buffalo stew, ham sandwiches, sloppy joes, oxtails, corned beef, meatballs, and mashed potatoes. There's also a slew of seating and almost 100 varieties of beer.

12 Japan Center & Environs

MODERATE

YOYO Bistro. In the Miyako Hotel, 1611 Post St. (at Laguna St.). ☎ **415/922-7788.** Reservations not necessary. Main courses $9–$14; continental breakfast buffet $7.50–$18. AE, CB, DC, JCB, MC, V. Daily 6:30am–11am, 11:30am–2:30pm, and 5:30–10pm. Parking in Japan Center garage; a fee is charged. Bus: 2, 3, 22, or 38. ASIAN/FRENCH.

You'd be wise to venture out of downtown for dinner in YOYO's dark, 50-person dining room, which is surrounded by authentic shoji screens. Previously Elka, the restaurant changed hands in 1996 and is now run by ex-Elka employees, who have put a great deal of care into creating a quality dining experience. The room and the food combine contemporary and ancient, Asian and French. One of the best times to come is between 5:30 and 10pm for *tsumami* (Japanese tapas) where you can order à la carte or choose four dishes for $14. These scrumptious little creations are anything from fresh oysters to pork ribs, and all come with outstanding sauces. Main courses from the dinner menu will include fresh fish, duck, and chicken—all very well prepared.

INEXPENSIVE

Sanppo. 1702 Post St. (at Laguna St.). ☎ **415/346-3486.** Reservations not accepted. Main courses $6–$15; combination dishes $10–$17. MC, V. Mon–Sat 11am–10pm; Sun 11:30am–10pm. Bus: 2, 3, 4, or 38. JAPANESE.

Simple and unpretentious though it is, Sanppo, across from the Japan Center, serves excellent, down-home Japanese food. You may be asked to share one of the few tables that surround a square counter in the small dining room. Lunches and dinners all include miso soup, rice, and pickled vegetables. At lunch you might have an order of fresh, thick-cut sashimi, teriyaki, tempura, beef donburi, or an order of *gyoza* (dumplings filled with savory meat and herbs) for $5 to $12. The same items are available at dinner for about $1 additional. Combination dishes, including tempura, sashimi, and gyoza, or tempura and teriyaki, are also available. Beer, wine, and sake are also served.

13 Haight-Ashbury

MODERATE

✪ **Cha Cha Cha.** 1801 Haight St. (at Shrader St.). ☎ **415/386-5758.** Reservations not accepted. Tapas $4.50–$7.75; main courses $9–$13. MC, V. Daily 11:30am–4pm; Sun–Thurs 5–11pm; Fri–Sat 5–11:30pm. Muni Metro: N. Bus: 6, 7, 66, 71, or 73. CARIBBEAN.

This is one of our all-time favorite places to come for dinner, but it's not for everybody. Cha Cha Cha is not a meal, it's an experience. Put your name on the mile-long list, crowd into the minuscule bar, and drink sangria while you wait (and try not to spill when you get bumped by all the young, attractive patrons who are also waiting). When you do finally get seated (it usually takes at least an hour), you'll dine in a loud—and we mean loud—dining room with Santeria altars, banana trees, and plastic tropical tablecloths. The best thing to do is order from the tapas menu and share the dishes family-style. The fried calamari, fried new potatoes, Cajun shrimp, and mussels in saffron broth are all bursting with flavor and are accompanied by rich, luscious sauces—but whatever you choose, you can't go wrong. This is the kind of place where you take friends in a partying mood, let your hair down, and make an evening of it. If you want all the flavor without the festivities, come during lunch.

✪ **Eos.** 901 Cole (at Carl St.). ☎ **415/566-3063.** Reservations recommended. Main courses $16–$26. AE, MC, V. Mon–Sat 5:30–11pm; Sun 5–11pm. Muni Metro: N. Bus: 6, 33, or 43. EAST-WEST FUSION.

Named after the Greek goddess of dawn, Eos is certainly basking in the spotlight thanks to chef/proprietor Arnold Wong, a master of texture and taste who perfected his craft while working at Masa's and Silks. It's not without a twinge of guilt that one mars the artistic presentation of each dish, such as the tender breast of Peking duck, smoked in ginger-peach tea leaves and served with a plum-kumquat chutney, or the blackened Asian catfish atop a bed of lemongrass risotto. For starters, try the almond-encrusted soft-shell crab dipped in spicy plum ponzu sauce. Unfortunately, the stark, industrial-deco decor does little to dampen the decibels, making a romantic outing nearly impossible unless you're into shouting. There is, however, a quiet, casual wine bar around the corner (same name) which stocks more than 400 vintages from around the globe.

✪ **Thep Phanom.** 400 Waller St. (at Fillmore St.). ☎ **415/431-2526.** Reservations recommended. Main courses $5.95–$10.95. AE, CB, DC, DISC, MC, V. Daily 5:30–10:30pm. Bus: 6, 7, 22, 66, or 71. THAI.

By successfully incorporating flavors from India, China, Burma, Malaysia, and more recently the West, Thep Phanom has risen the heady ranks to become one of the best Thai restaurants in San Francisco. Case in point: There's almost always a line out the front door. Start with the signature dish, ped swan—boneless duck in a light honey sauce served on a bed of spinach. The *larb ped* (minced duck salad), velvety basil-spiked seafood curry served on banana leaves, and spicy *yum plamuk* (calamari salad) are also recommended. Its Haight Street location attracts an eclectic crowd and informal atmosphere, though the decor is actually quite tasteful. Reservations are advised, and don't leave anything even remotely valuable in your car.

INEXPENSIVE

Tassajara. 1000 Cole St. (at Parnassus St.). ☎ **415/664-8947.** Pastries $1.30–$3.25; sandwiches $4.25. MC, V. Mon–Thurs 7am–9pm; Fri–Sat 7am–10pm; Sun 8am–9pm. Muni Metro: N. Bus: 6, 37, or 43. SOUPS/SALADS/SANDWICHES.

Once owned and operated by a Zen center of the same name, Tassajara may have been bought out by the local Just Desserts chain a few years back, but apparently the deal included the recipe for the best bear claws in town, and that's all we needed to know. Decor is not earthy, but rather bright and clean with vibrant original art and large windows. The vibe, however, is still mellow and vegetarian, though there's more sugar behind the glass to amp you up. Soups, sandwiches, breakfast pastries, and heavenly breads are interspersed with carrot, poppy-seed, and one helluva chocolate cake.

Ya Halla from Nadia. 494 Haight St. (at Fillmore St.). ☎ **415/522-1509.** Sandwiches and appetizers $4; dinner plates $6.25–$9. MC, V. Daily 11am–10:30pm. Bus: 6, 7, 22, 66, or 71. MEDITERRANEAN.

Great reviews and painless prices have brought a more expansive clientele to this Middle Eastern oasis in slum-chic lower Haight. Now mingling with the usual mellow alternative crowd and vegetarians (generally Gen-Xers) are an assemblage of adventurous diners who gather amid the cheerily decorated room brightened by white Christmas lights. Delicious falafels, hummus, baba ganoush, lamb kebabs, pitas, and thrifty combo plates are cranked out of the front-room ad-hoc exhibition kitchen—a remarkable feat considering that it's not much bigger than a closet—and served by a very hospitable service staff.

Zona Rosa. 1797 Haight St. (at Shrader St.). ☎ **415/668-7717.** Burritos $3.90–$4.90. No credit cards. Daily 11am–11pm. Muni Metro: N. Bus: 6, 7, 66, 71, or 73. MEXICAN.

This is a great place to stop and get a cheap (and healthful) bite. The most popular items here are the burritos, which are made to order and include your choice of beans (refried, whole pinto, or black), meats, or vegetarian ingredients. You can sit on a stool at the window and watch all the Haight Street freaks strolling by, relax at one of five colorful interior tables, or take it to go and head to Golden Gate Park (it's just 2 blocks away). Zona Rosa is one of the best burrito stores around.

14 Richmond / Sunset Districts

MODERATE

Beach Chalet Brewery & Restaurant. 1000 Great Hwy. (at the west end of Golden Gate Park near Fulton St.). ☎ **415/386-8439.** Reservations accepted. Lunch appetizers $5–$7.50; main courses $8–$12.50 at lunch, $12.50–$18 at dinner. MC, V. Mon–Thurs 11:30am–10pm (bistro menu 3–5:30pm); Fri–Sat 11:30am–11pm (bistro menu 3–5:30pm); Sun 10am–10pm. (Bar open until 2am nightly.) Bus: 18, 31, or 38. AMERICAN.

Since reopening on New Year's Eve 1996, the Beach Chalet has been one of the most popular reasons to make it out to the breakers. The restaurant occupies the upper floor of a historic public lounge that originally opened in 1900, was rebuilt in 1925, and, after being closed for more than 15 years, was recently renovated. Today, the main floor's wonderful restored WPA frescoes and historical displays on the area are enough to lure tourists and locals, but upstairs is something altogether different. The only thing harking back to yesteryear is the timeless view of the great Pacific Ocean. While the place is bright and cheery, we agree with the critics: The restaurant should have been more reminiscent of its heritage. Dinner is pricey and the view disappears with the sun, so come for lunch or bistro snacks, when you can eat your grilled pizzetta with peppers, artichokes, mozzarella, and basil, or smoked-ham–and–brie sandwich or herb-crusted rotisserie chicken with garlic mashed potatoes with one of the best vistas around. After dinner it's a more local thing, especially on Friday, Saturday, and Sunday when live blues accompany the cocktails and house-made brews. *Note:* Be careful getting into the parking lot (only accessible from the northbound side of the highway); it's a quick, sandy turn.

Cliff House. 1090 Point Lobos (at Merrie Way). ☎ **415/386-3330.** Two dining areas: upstairs and main room. Reservations recommended for upstairs and brunch only. Main courses $7–$11 upstairs breakfast; $7–$11 upstairs lunch, $7.50–$18 main lunch; $12–$19 main and upstairs dinner. AE, CB, DC, MC, V. Upstairs: Mon–Fri 9am–3:30pm and 5–10pm; Sat–Sun 8:30am–4pm and 5–10pm. Main room: Mon–Sat 11am–10:30pm; Sun 10am–3pm and 3:30–10:30pm. Bus: 38 or 18. SEAFOOD/CALIFORNIA.

Back in the old days (we're talking way back) the Cliff House was the place to go for a romantic night on the town. Nowadays, this aging San Francisco landmark caters mostly to tourists who arrive by the busloads to gander at the Sutro Bath remains next door.

Three restaurants in the main, two-story building give diners a choice of how much they wish to spend. Phineas T. Barnacle is the least expensive; sandwiches, salads, soups and such are served Hofbrau-style across from the elaborate saloon-style bar, after which you can seat yourself at the window-side tables overlooking the shore or beside the fireplace if you're chilled. A step up from the P.T.B. (literally) is Upstairs at the Cliff House, a slightly more formal setting that's best known for its breakfast omelets, and the main room, known as the Seafood and Beverage Co., the fanciest of the lot. Refurbished back to its glory days near the turn of the century, it offers superb ocean views, particularly at sunset, when the fog lets up; unfortunately, the food is a distant second to the scenery. The best M.O. is to arrive before dusk, request a window seat, order a few appetizers and cocktails, and enjoy the view, or opt for the elaborate Sunday brunch served from 10am to 3pm in the newly renovated Terrace Room.

✪ Hong Kong Flower Lounge. 5322 Geary Blvd. (between 17th and 18th aves.). ☎ **415/668-8998.** Most main dishes $7.95–$14.95; dim-sum dishes $1.80–$3.50. Mon–Fri 11am–2:30pm; Sat–Sun 10am–2:30pm; daily 5–9:30pm. Bus: 1, 2, or 38. CHINESE/DIM SUM.

You know you're at a good Chinese restaurant when most people waiting for a table are Chinese. And if you come for dim sum, be prepared to stand in line because you're not the only one who's heard this is the best in town. The Hong Kong Flower Lounge has been one of our very favorite restaurants for years now. It's not the pink and green decor or the live fish swimming in the tank, or even the beautiful marble bathrooms; it's simply that every little dish that comes our way is so darn good. Don't pass up taro cake, salt-fried shrimp, shark-fin soup, and shrimp or beef crepes.

✪ Kabuto Sushi. 5116 Geary Blvd. (at 15th Ave.). ☎ **415/752-5652.** Sushi $3–$8; main courses $11–$18. MC, V. Tues–Sat 5:30–11pm. Bus: 2, 28, or 38. JAPANESE/SUSHI.

For a town overflowing with seafood and pretentious taste buds, you'd think it'd be easier to find great sushi. But the truth is, finding an outstanding sushi restaurant in San Francisco is more challenging than spotting a parking space in Nob Hill. Still, chop-sticking these fish-and-rice delicacies is one of the most joyous and adventurous ways to dine, and Kabuto is one of the best (and most expensive) places to do it. Chef Sachio Kojima, who presides over the small, ever-crowded sushi bar, constructs each dish with smooth, lightning-fast movements known only to master

Hidden Treasures

Okay, so we couldn't find a neat category in which to place these two restaurants, but since they're among the city's best it would be a crime to leave them out. If you're not familiar with the streets of San Francisco, be sure to call first to get concise directions; otherwise, you'll spend more time driving than dining.

42 Degrees, 235 16th St., at Illinois Street, 1 block off Third Street (☎ 415/777-5558), tucked behind the Esprit Outlet in the industrial area, is an oh-so-chic jazz supper club. A three-piece jazz trio sets the mood in the warehouselike but velvet-soft, two-story dining room. Sleek cocktailers hang out at the dark bar area, which specializes in scotches, cognacs, and a selection of small vintners' wines. The dining mezzanine has a men's-smoking-club feel with a great view of the Bay Bridge, and the downstairs is all 1940s sophistication, from the red velvet curtains that frame 22-foot windows right down to the wait staff and clientele. There's also a dining patio that's a perfect spot for a sunny luncheon. Dishes are Mediterranean-influenced, and the menu changes weekly but usually includes house favorites such as hearts of romaine salad with Caesar dressing, marrow bones with toast, Atlantic salmon, and Niman-Schell meats. It's easier to book a table at lunch, but the time to come is for dinner when the chichi vibe is full-force; reservations are definitely recommended. Prices for main courses run from $16 to $22. Hours are Monday to Friday from 11:30am to 3pm and Wednesday to Saturday from 6:30pm to 11:30pm. The restaurant can be reached by Bus 22. MasterCard and Visa are accepted.

If you find yourself parking along a dank industrial street where no decent restaurant would dare to set up shop, you're in the right place:

Woodward's Garden, 1700 Mission St., at Duboce Avenue (☎ 415/621-7122), named after a turn-of-the-century amusement center in the same location, is the kind of gem many San Franciscans don't even know about. And good thing: There are only nine tables in the entire place. Local foodies will mention Woodward's as if everyone should know about it, but its location (under a freeway on-ramp in SoMa) and disguised exterior of simple curtains and an unobtrusive sign keep this upscale restaurant well under wraps. Still, its simple decor and intimate (okay, tiny) environment make for sincerely romantic dining. But it's not just the stealthy hype that keeps the place popular: The limited-but-ambitious menu makes this place an all-around winner. The five or so entrees might include a Chilean sea bass braised with wild mushrooms, white wine, lemon, and garlic on couscous with scallions and herbs, or a chicken breast stuffed with prosciutto and Gorgonzola with five-onion marmalade on grilled polenta with French green beans. To top it off, with so few tables and both the kitchen (formerly of Postrio and Greens) and the wait staff so attentive, you'll feel they opened their doors just for you. Don't traipse down here without reservations, or a car for that matter. Main courses are priced between $14 and $17. There are four dinner seatings each night from Wednesday to Sunday at 6, 6:30, 8, and 8:30pm. MasterCard and Visa are accepted.

chefs. Last time we were here, we were lucky enough to sit next to some businessmen visiting from Japan who were ordering things we'd never seen before. We followed their lead and had perhaps the best sushi dinner to date. If you're big on wasabi, ask for the stronger stuff Kojima serves on request.

Khan Toke Thai House. 5937 Geary Blvd. ☎ **415/668-6654.** Reservations recommended. Main courses $6–$11; fixed-price dinner $16.95. AE, MC, V. Daily 5–10pm. Bus: 38. THAI.

Khan Toke Thai is so traditional you're asked to remove your shoes before being seated. Popular for special occasions, this Richmond Distinct fixture is easily the prettiest Thai restaurant in the city; lavishly carved teak interiors evoke the ambiance of a Thai temple.

To start, order the *tom yam gong* lemongrass shrimp with mushroom, tomato, and cilantro soup. Follow with such well-flavored dishes as ground pork with fresh ginger, green onion, peanuts, and lemon juice; prawns with hot chilies, mint leaves, lime juice, lemongrass, and onions; or the chicken with cashew nuts, crispy chilies, and onions. For a real treat, have the deep-fried pompano topped with sautéed ginger, onions, peppers, pickled garlic, and yellow-bean sauce; or deep-fried red snapper with "three-flavors" sauce and hot basil leaves. A complete dinner including appetizer, soup, salad, two main courses, dessert, and coffee is a great value.

✪ **Socca.** 5800 Geary Blvd. (at 22nd Ave.). ☎ **415/379-6720.** Reservations accepted. Main courses $8.25–$16.95. AE, DC, DISC, MC, V. Sun Thurs 5:30 9:30pm; Fri–Sat 5:30–10pm. Valet parking $5–$6. Bus: 38 or 38L. AMERICAN/PROVENÇAL.

Host Cyrus Pahlavan and chef John Caputo (Campton Place, Le Reverebere) took a big chance by opening this trendy restaurant so far out in the Richmond District, but after 3 years of slow growth they're finally enjoying the kudos they deserve (as well as the attention of celebrities such as Nicolas Cage, who we spied dining with his wife, Patricia Arquette). Though most of the dishes on the menu are quite good, a few are outstanding, such as the succulent New Zealand grouper, perfectly cooked, resting on a bed of cauliflower purée encircled by red and black caviar and topped with a potato crust; the wild-mushroom risotto infused with moist fungi, Asiago cheese, and garlic confit (best ordered as an appetizer); and for the *coup de gras,* Socca's signature wicked warm chocolate cake with Chantilly cream. Service is flawless, but the beautifully appointed bar can really screw up their mixed drinks, so stick to the ample wine list. Take our word for it—this is one restaurant that's worth the drive.

Straits Café. 3300 Geary Blvd. (at Parker St.). ☎ **415/668-1783.** Reservations recommended. Main courses $6.95–$17.95. AE, DC, MC, V. Sun–Thurs 11:30am–10pm; Fri–Sat 11:30am–11pm. Bus: 2, 3, 4, or 38. SINGAPOREAN.

Straits Café is what we like to call "adventure dining," because you never know quite what you're going to get. Burlap palm trees, pastel-painted trompe l'oeil houses, faux balconies, and clotheslines strung across the walls evoke a surreal image of a Singaporean village at this Richmond District restaurant; the cuisine, however, is the real thing. Among chef Chris Yeo's spicy Malaysian/Indian/Chinese offerings there's *murtabak* (stuffed Indian bread), chili crab, basil chicken, *nonya daging rendang* (beef simmered in lime leaves), *ikan pangang* (fish stuffed with a chili paste), and hottest of all, *sambal udang* (prawns sautéed in a chili shallot sambal sauce). For dessert try the sago pudding or the *bo bo cha cha* (taro root and sweet potato in sweetened coconut milk). The best fun can be had at the banana-leaf lunches and brunch when you dine off banana-leaf platters with your fingers.

INEXPENSIVE

✪ **Ton Kiang.** 5821 Geary Blvd. (between 22nd and 23rd aves.) ☎ **415/387-8273.** Reservations not accepted. Dim sum $1.80–$4.50. Daily 10:30am–10pm. AE, MC. V. Bus: 38. DIM SUM.

We still love the Hong Kong Flower Lounge, but Ton Kiang is justifiably the number-one place in the city to do dim sum. Wait in the never-ending line (which is out the door anytime between 11am and 1:30pm), get a table on either the first or second floor, and get ready to party with your palate. From stuffed crab claws, roast Peking duck, and a gazillion dumpling selections (including scallop and vegetable, shrimp, and beef) to the delicious and hard-to-find "doa miu" (a.k.a. snow pea sprouts, which are flash sautéed with garlic and peanut oil), shark-fin soup, and a mesmerizing mango pudding, every tray of morsels coming from the kitchen is an absolute delight. This is definitely one of our favorite places to do lunch, and it happens to have an unusually friendly staff. Their second location (3148 Geary Blvd., at Spruce St., ☎415/752-4440), which is closer to downtown, does not serve dim sum but is known for its low prices, delicious Hakka cuisine, and claypot dishes.

15 The Castro

While you will see gay and lesbian singles and couples at almost any restaurant in San Francisco, the following spots cater particularly to the San Francisco gay community, though being gay is certainly not a requirement for enjoying them.

MODERATE

Caffè Luna Piena. 558 Castro St. (between 18th and 19th sts.). ☎ **415/621-2566.** Reservations recommended for brunch. Main courses $9–$16.50. AE, DISC, MC, V. Mon–Fri 11am–3pm; Sat–Sun 9am–3pm; Tues–Sun 5:30–10:30pm. Muni Metro: F, K, L, or M. Bus: 24, 35, or 37. ITALIAN.

Much to the relief of residents tired of the burger and pizza joints strewn throughout the Castro, this venue offers a more warm and sophisticated dining environment complete with rich yellow, brush-painted walls adorned with local artwork. The room stretches all the way back to the outdoor dining patio (yes, there are heat lamps) and a lush Japanese garden. The fare is contemporary American with Italian and Mediterranean influences. Lunch offers soups, salads, sandwiches (with a choice of garlic fries or a green salad), such as the grilled eggplant with roasted red pepper and smoked mozzarella on pane integrale; or main lunch courses that may include blanched vegetables, and a lemon caper vinaigrette. Dinner features such dishes as lamb shanks braised with rosemary and garlic and served with soft polenta or roasted vegetable lasagna with sweet-potato sauce. Desserts follow city folks' favorites: crème brûlée and a dose of chocolate with the chocolate budino. Counter diners can watch chefs at work in the partially open kitchen. If you come for Saturday or Sunday brunch, reserve in advance or be prepared to wait in line for a yeast-raised waffle with strawberries, poached eggs with soft polenta, smoked salmon and shrimp cream, or any of the other breakfast treats.

✪ **Mecca.** 2029 Market St. (between Duboce and Church sts.). ☎ **415/621-7000.** Reservations recommended. Main courses $12.75–$18. AE, DC, MC, V. Mon–Wed and Sun 6–11pm; Thurs–Sat 6pm–midnight. Muni Metro: F, K, L, or M. Bus: 8, 22, 24, or 37. MEDITERRANEAN.

In 1996, Mecca entered the scene in a decadent swirl of chocolate-brown velvet, stainless steel, cement, and brown Naugahyde, unveiling the kind of industrial-chic supper club that makes you want to order a martini just so you'll match the ambiance. And cocktail they do—that eclectic city clientele (with a heavy dash of same-sex couples) who mingle at the oval centerpiece bar. A night here promises a dose of live jazz, and a tasty, though sometimes unpredictable, California meal, which is served at tables tucked into several dining nooks. Menu options include such starters as pomegranate-glazed quail on endive and watercress, and herb-skewered prawns with romesco sauce and roasted potatoes. Main courses include the popular mustard-seed–crusted halibut, duck breast with roasted fig and huckleberry sauce and potatoes, and a veal chop with wild-mushroom potato cake. The food is very good, but it's that only-in-San-Francisco vibe that makes this place the smokin' hot spot to dine in the Castro.

2223. 2223 Market St. (between Sanchez and Noe sts.). ☎ **415/431-0692.** Reservations recommended. $12.95–$19.95. AE, MC, V. Sat–Sun 10am–2pm; Sun–Thurs 5:30–10pm; Fri–Sat 5:30–midnight. Muni Metro: F, L, K, or M. Bus: 8, 22, 24, or 37. CALIFORNIA.

Run by the owners of the renowned Cypress Club, the decor here is substantially less opulent than its counterpart, but the energy level is definitely more lively. Surrounded by hardwood floors, candles, streamlined modern light fixtures and loud music, festive gays and straights come here to cocktail on the heavy-handed specialty drinks and dine on grilled pork chops or the ever-popular roasted chicken with garlic mashed potatoes. Along with Mecca, this is currently the dining and schmoozing spot in the area.

INEXPENSIVE

Café Flore. 2298 Market St. (at Noe St.). ☎ **415/621-8579.** Reservations not accepted. American breakfast $5.95; main courses $4.50–$10. No credit cards. Sun–Thurs 7am–11:30pm; Fri–Sat 7am–midnight. Muni Metro: F. Bus: 8. CALIFORNIA.

Sheathed with glass on three sides, and overlooking Market Street, Noe Street, and a verdant patio in back, Café Flore attracts young, bright, and articulate members of the gay (mostly male) community. Local wits refer to it as a place where body piercing is encouraged but not mandatory, although this kind of exhibitionism tends to be more prevalent in the evening rather than during the daytime.

Many of the menu items are composed of mostly organic ingredients, and include a succulent version of roasted (sometimes free-range) chicken, soups, pastas, and steaks. Café latte costs $2 a cup. Plan on hearing a lot of noise and possibly seeing a handsome young man sending not particularly furtive glances your way. Those with late-night munchies take heed: while the place stays open later, the kitchen closes at 10:30pm.

Chow. 215 Church St. (near Market St.). ☎ **415/552-2469.** Main courses $4.95–$7.50. MC, V. Wed–Sat 11am–midnight; Sun–Tues 11am–10pm. Muni Metro: F, J, K, L, or M line. Bus: 8 or 37. AMERICAN.

Chow actually claims to serve American cuisine, but the management must be thinking of today's America, because the menu is not exactly baseball and apple pie. But that's just fine with us. If we can't decide between a burger, Italian, or Asian-influenced fare, we just come here. Mixed in with the expected cobb salad, fresh-fish dish, and grilled rosemary-lemon chicken are such exotic twists as noodles with peanut sauce; fuji apples and cucumber; an array of innovative pastas (starting at $4!); grilled meats, veggies, and fish; and wood-fired–oven pizzas. More traditional are the budget-efficient daily sandwich specials, which range from a scrambled egg, ham, Cheddar, and asparagus variety (Sun) to a chicken salad with bleu cheese, bacon, and apple selection (Thurs); both come with salad, soup, or fries for less than $7. While the food and prices alone would be a good argument for coming here, beer on tap, a great inexpensive wine selection, and a fun, tavernlike environment clinch the deal. However, if you're on the run, you can grab a pizza slice ($1.50) and other quick bits for a mere pittance.

✪ **Firewood Café.** 4248 18th St. (at Diamond St.). ☎ **415/252-0999.** Main courses $5.25–$7. MC, V. Sun–Thurs 11am–11pm; Fri–Sat 11am–midnight. Muni Metro: F, K, L, or M line. Bus: 8, 33, 35, or 37. MEDITERRANEAN.

It shouldn't take a genius to realize that aesthetics count even in cheap restaurants. But apparently it did, because until just recently, finding budget gourmet food and attractive decor together were about as likely as seeing Newt Gingrich dancing through the Castro wearing chaps. But times they are a-changin', and this restaurant is setting the standard. One of the sharpest rooms in the neighborhood, the colorful Firewood put its money in the essentials and eliminated extra overhead. There are no waiters or waitresses here; everyone orders at the counter, then relaxes at either the single, long family-style table or one of the small tables facing the huge street-side windows. Where they didn't skimp is with the cozy-chic atmosphere and inspired-but-limited Mediterranean menu: The fresh salads, which are all less than $5, come with a choice of three "fixin's" ranging from caramelized onions to spiced walnuts and three gourmet dressing options. Then there's the pastas—four tortellini selections, such as roasted chicken and mortadella—and gourmet pizzas: the calamari with lemon-garlic aioli is a winner. Or how about an herb-roasted half or whole chicken ($5.25 or $9.95, respectively) with roasted new potatoes? Wines cost $3.25 by the glass and a reasonable $16 to $18 by the bottle. Draft and bottled beers are also available, and desserts top off at $2.25. (Thank goodness *someone* realized that $6 for an after-dinner treat is bordering on ridiculous.)

Marcello's Pizza. 420 Castro St. (at Market St.). ☎ **415/863-3900.** Pizza slices $1.90–$2.80; pies $9.20–$21.50. No credit cards. Sun–Thurs 11am–1am; Fri–Sat 11am–2am. Muni Metro: L, M, or N to Castro St. Station. PIZZA.

Marcello's isn't a fancy place, just a traditional pizza joint with a couple of tables and tasty pizza by the slice and a few other basic dishes. Weekend nights there's a line out the door of drunk and/or stoned Castro Street partiers with the late-night munchies.

Patio Café. 531 Castro St. (at 18th St.). ☎ **415/621-4640.** Reservations not accepted. Main courses $4.75–$8.95 lunch, $6.95–$12.50 dinner. AE, MC, V. Daily 9am–10:30pm. Bus: 24 or 33. AMERICAN.

Since the early 1970s, this Castro Street bar and restaurant has served as the rendezvous point for uncounted numbers of trysts, peccadilloes, and love affairs of all kinds that have blossomed within the premises. Originally established as The Baker's Café, it retains the original ovens that contributed to its early reputation, which are today purely decorative. Ringed with trellises and verdant plants, and set in the back yard of a cluster of shops, the patio features a glass roof (whose entertainment value derives from the heft and brawn of the staff, who climb skyward to manually crank it open during clement weather). Menu items include virtually any drink you can think of and such dishes as Caesar salads, Chinese chicken salad (laced with fresh ginger), prime rib, and grilled salmon with Cajun hollandaise sauce. The most popular drinks include a Melon Margarita ($3.75) and a Patio Mai-Tai ($4.75).

16 Mission District

EXPENSIVE

Flying Saucer. 1000 Guerrero St. (at 22nd St.). ☎ **415/641-9955.** Reservations recommended. Main courses $15–$26. AE, MC, V. Tues–Sat 5:30–9:30pm. BART: 24th St. Station. Bus: 14 or 26. FRENCH.

Outrageously yet artfully presented food is the hallmark of this Mission District fixture. Peering into the glass-walled kitchen, diners can catch the kitchen staff leaning over plates, carefully standing a jumbo prawn on its head atop a baked column of potato polenta. Fish, beef, and fowl dishes are competently grilled, baked, or flamed before being surrounded by a flurry of sauces and garnishes. While the pricey food is certainly intense and flavorful, the overwhelming sensation at this bistro is visual. The party extends from the plate to the decor, where plastic flying saucers mingle with colorful murals and creative lighting. The menu changes frequently, and there are almost always specials. If you ask your waiter to bring you the chef's most flamboyant-looking offering, chances are you won't be disappointed. Reservations are essential, as is a blind eye to the sometimes infuriatingly snotty service.

MODERATE

Bruno's. 2389 Mission St. (between 19th and 20th sts.). ☎ **415/550-7455.** Reservations recommended. Main courses $14–$21. DC, MC, V. Tues–Thurs 6:30–11pm; Fri–Sat 6:30pm–midnight. Parking in back lot $5. ECLECTIC.

When the new owners scraped 60 years worth of grease and cigar smoke from the wood-paneled bar, added live music, and began serving flavorful fare in the fifties-style dining room, the hipsters came in droves. But even 3 years after its opening, crowds are still coming to this Mission District restaurant. The reason? Aside from people-watching, the food here actually competes with the ambiance. House specialties include apple salad, grilled boneless quail, and oxtail with mashed potatoes. After dinner, meander into the bar and beyond, where bands liven the crowd. *Note:* While the dining room is closed on Monday, you can still order appetizers and dessert at the bar.

✪ Pauline's. 260 Valencia St. (between 14th St. and Duboce Ave.). ☎ **415/552-2050.** Reservations recommended. Main courses $10.50–$21.50. MC, V. Tues–Sat 5–10pm. Bus: 14, 26, or 49. PIZZA.

The perfect pizza? Quite possibly. At least it's the best we've ever had. Housed in a cheery double-decker yellow building that stands out like a beacon in a somewhat seedy neighborhood, Pauline's only does two things—pizzas and salads—but does them better than any other restaurant in the city. It's worth running the gauntlet of panhandlers for a slice of Pauline's Italian sausage pizza on handmade thin-crust dough. The eclectic toppings range from house-spiced chicken to French goat cheese, roasted eggplant, Danish fontina cheese, and tasso (spiced pork shoulder). The salads are equally amazing: certified organic, hand-picked by California growers, and topped with fresh and dried herbs (including edible flowers) from Pauline's own gardens in Berkeley. The wine list offers a smart selection of low-priced wines, and service is excellent. Yes, prices are a bit steep (small pizzas start at $10.50), but what a paltry price to pay for perfection.

The Slanted Door. 584 Valencia St. (at 17th St.). ☎ **415/861-8032.** Reservations recommended. Lunch main courses $5.25–$16.50; most dinner dishes $5.75–$16.50. MC, V. Daily 11:30am–3:30pm; Sun–Thurs 5:30pm–10pm; Fri–Sat 5:30pm–10:30pm. Bus: 22, 26, 33, 49 or 53; BART: 16th St. station. VIETNAMESE.

We've tried, but the fact is, we just don't get why this place is all the rage. Sure, the food is fresh and well priced, and the room is certainly the most stylish one serving Vietnamese. But in our minds that doesn't make the spot a destination restaurant. It is, however, a great place to dine if you're in the neighborhood. Pull up a modern, color-washed chair in the industrial-but-colorful space and order anything from clay-pot catfish or green papaya salad to one of the inexpensive lunch rice dishes, which come in a large ceramic bowl and are topped with such options as grilled shrimp, curry chicken, or stir-fried eggplant. Dinner items, which change season-ally, may range from steamed chicken with black-bean sauce, long beans with shrimp to vegetarian noodles sautéed with mushrooms, lily buds, tofu, bamboo, and shiitake mushrooms. There's also an eclectic collection of teas, which come by the pot for $3 to $5. Perhaps one of the best elements to this restaurant is its eclectic clientele; since everyone thinks this is the place to be these days, it actually is.

○ **Universal Café.** 2814 19th St. (at Bryant St.). ☎ **415/821-4608.** Reservations recom-mended for dinner. Main courses $2–$8 at breakfast, $5–$10 at lunch, $8–$18 at dinner. AE, MC, V. Tues–Thur 7:30am–2:30pm and 6–10pm; Fri 9am–11:30pm; Sat 9am–2:30pm and 6–10pm; Sun 9am–2:30pm and 5:30–9:30pm. Bus: 27. AMERICAN/FRENCH.

We stumbled onto the Universal Café a few years ago completely by accident, coming home from a play in SoMa's semi-industrial sector. It was love at first sight (as well as bite). Not only does it look good—suave and stylish with thick floor-to-ceiling windows and a profusion of sculptured metal and marble—it also attracts a nightly gaggle of locals who come for the delicious focaccia sandwiches, inventive thin-crust pizzas, and gourmet salads for lunch, and superb dinner dishes such as braised duck leg on a bed of creamy polenta, sea bass served with risotto, spinach, and caramelized onions, or hearty pot roast with lumpy mashed potatoes and fresh veggies. Granted, it's on the way to nowhere, but if you're near the Mission and have a few minutes to spare, it's well worth the detour.

Val 21. 995 Valencia St. (at 21st St.). ☎ **415/821-6622.** Reservations recommended. Main courses $11.50–$19.50. AE, DC, MC, V. Brunch Sat–Sun 10am–2pm; Mon–Thurs 5:30–9:30pm; Fri–Sat 5:30–10:30pm; Sun 5:30–9:30pm. Muni Metro: J to 16th St. Station. CALIFORNIA.

Hip, eclectic decor, perpetually friendly service, and hefty portions of multiethnic fare have made Val 21 one of the Mission District's most popular restaurants. The menu changes frequently, although you might find such dishes as a tasty eggless Caesar salad, roasted marinated portobello mushroom (layered with zucchini, caramelized onions, chèvre, and bread crumbs), Southwestern blackened chicken, or grilled salmon in a coconut red-curry sauce (plenty of vegetarian plates, too). Sometimes the menu gets a little too creative, sending mixed messages to your mouth, but the overall dining experience is above-par and worth the trip.

INEXPENSIVE

○ **Taquerias La Cumbre.** 515 Valencia St. (between 16th and 17th sts.). ☎ **415/ 863-8205.** Tacos and burritos $2–$4.25; dinner plates $5–$7. No credit cards. Mon–Sat 11am–10pm; Sun noon–9pm. BART: Mission. Bus: 14, 22, 33, 49, or 53. MEXICAN.

If San Francisco commissioned a flag honoring its favorite food, we'd probably all be waving a banner of the Golden Gate Bridge bolstering a giant burrito—that's how much we love these mammoth tortilla-wrapped meals. And while most restau-rants gussy up their gastronomic goods with million-dollar decor and glamorous gimmicks, the burrito needs only to be craftily constructed of fresh pork, steak, chicken, or vegetables, plus cheese, beans, rice, salsa, and maybe a dash of gua-camole or sour cream, and practically the whole town will drive to the remotest cor-ners to taste it. In this case, the fact that it's served in a cafeterialike brick-lined room with overly shellacked tables and chairs is all the better: There's no mistaking the attraction here.

Ti Couz. 3108 16th St. (at Valencia St.). ☎ **415/252-7373.** Crepes $1.95–$8.25. MC, V. Mon–Fri 11am–11pm; Sat 10am–11pm; Sun 10am–10pm. BART: Mission. Bus: 14, 22, 33, 49, or 53. CREPES.

With fierce culinary competition around every corner, many restaurants try to invent new gourmet gimmicks to hook the hungry. Unfortunately, the results are often creative concoctions that verge on palate pandemonium. Not true for Ti Couz (say "Tee Cooz"), one of the most architecturally stylish and popular restaurants in the Mission. Here the headliner is simple: a delicate, paper-thin crepe. And while its fillings aren't exactly original, they're excellently executed and infinite in their combinations. The menu advises how to enjoy these wraps: Order a light crepe as an appetizer, a heftier one as a main course, and a drippingly sweet one for dessert. Recommended combinations are listed, but you can build your own from the 15 main-course selections (such as smoked salmon, mushrooms, sausage, ham, scallops, and onions) and 19 dessert options (caramel, fruit, chocolate, Nutella, and more). Soups and salads solicit the less adventurous palate but are equally stellar; the sensational seafood salad, for example, is a compilation shrimp, scallops, and ahi tuna with veggies and five kinds of lettuce. Ciders and beer complement the cuisine.

7

What to See & Do in San Francisco

San Francisco's parks, museums, tours, and landmarks are favorite haunts for travelers the world over and offer an array of activities to suit every visitor. But it's not any particular activity or place that makes the city the most popular tourist destination in the world. It's San Francisco itself—its charm, its atmosphere, its perfect blend of big metropolis with small-town hospitality. No matter what you do while you're here—whether you spend all your time in central areas like Union Square or North Beach or explore the intricacies of outer neighborhoods—you're bound to collect a treasure of vacation memories that can only be found in this culturally rich, strikingly beautiful City by the Bay.

1 Famous San Francisco Sights

✪ **Alcatraz Island.** Pier 41, near Fisherman's Wharf. ☎ **415/773-1188** (for info only; no ferry reservations accepted at this number). Admission (includes ferry trip and audio tour) $11 adults, $9.25 seniors 62 and older, $5.75 children 5–11. Winter daily 9:15am–2:30pm; summer daily 9:15am–4:15pm. Advance purchase advised. Ferries depart every half hour, at 15 and 45 min. after the hour on the weekends, and every 45 min. throughout the week. Arrive at least 20 min. before sailing time.

Visible from Fisherman's Wharf, Alcatraz Island (a.k.a. "The Rock") has seen a checkered history. It was discovered in 1775 by Juan Manuel Ayala, who named it after the many pelicans that nested on the island. From the 1850s to 1933, when the army vacated the island, it served as a military post protecting the bay shoreline. In 1934, the buildings of the military outpost were converted into a maximum-security prison. Given the sheer cliffs, treacherous tides and currents, and frigid temperatures of the waters, it was believed to be a totally escape-proof prison. Among the famous gangsters who were penned in cell blocks A through D were Al Capone; Robert Stroud, the so-called Birdman of Alcatraz (because he was an expert in ornithological diseases); Machine Gun Kelly; and Alvin Karpis. It cost a fortune to keep them imprisoned here because all supplies, including water, had to be shipped in. In 1963, after an apparent escape in which no bodies were recovered, the government closed the prison, and in 1972 it became part of the Golden Gate National Recreation Area. The wildlife that was driven away during the military and prison years has begun to return—the black-crested night heron and other seabirds are nesting here again—and a new trail has been built that passes through the island's nature areas. Tours, including an audio tour of the prison block and a slide show, are given by the park's rangers, who entertain their guests with interesting anecdotes.

It's a popular excursion and space is limited, so purchase tickets as far in advance as possible. The tour is operated by **Blue & Gold Fleet** (☎ **415/705-5555**) and can be charged to American Express, MasterCard, or Visa ($2 per ticket service charge on phone orders). Tickets may also be purchased in advance from the Blue & Gold ticket office on Pier 41.

Wear comfortable shoes and take a heavy sweater or windbreaker because even when the sun's out, it's cold. The National Parks Service also notes that there are a lot of steps to climb on the tour.

For those who want to get a closer look at Alcatraz without going ashore, two boat-tour operators offer short circumnavigations of the island (see "Self-Guided & Organized Tours," below, for complete information).

✪ **Cable Cars.** The Powell-Hyde and Powell-Mason lines begin at the base of Powell and Market sts.; the California St. line begins at the foot of Market St.

Although they may not be San Francisco's most practical means of transportation, cable cars are certainly the best loved. Designated official historic landmarks by the National Parks Service in 1964, they clank up and down the city's steep hills like mobile museum pieces, tirelessly hauling thousands of tourists each day to nowhere in particular.

San Francisco's cable cars were invented in 1869 by London-born engineer Andrew Hallidie, who got the idea by way of serendipity. As the story goes, Hallidie was watching a team of overworked horses haul a heavily laden carriage up a steep San Francisco slope. As he watched, one horse slipped and the car rolled back, dragging the other tired beasts with it. At that moment Hallidie resolved that he would invent a mechanical contraption to replace such horses, and just 4 years later, in 1873, the first cable car made its maiden run from the top of Clay Street. Promptly ridiculed as "Hallidie's Folly," the cars were slow to gain acceptance. One early onlooker voiced the general opinion by exclaiming, "I don't believe it—the damned thing works!"

Even today, many visitors have difficulty believing that these vehicles, which have no engines, actually work. The cars, each weighing about 6 tons, are hauled along by a steel cable, enclosed under the street in a center rail. You can't see the cable unless you peer straight down into the crack, but you'll hear its characteristic clickity-clanking sound whenever you're nearby. The cars move when the gripper (not the driver) pulls back a lever that closes a pincerlike "grip" on the cable. The speed of the car therefore is determined by the speed of the cable, which is a constant 9½ miles per hour—never more, never less.

The two types of cable cars in use hold, respectively, a maximum of 90 and 100 passengers, and the limits are rigidly enforced. The best views are had from the outer running boards, where you have to hold on tightly when taking curves. Everyone, it seems, prefers to ride on the running boards.

Often imitated but never duplicated, similar versions of Hallidie's cable cars have been used throughout the world, but all have been replaced by more efficient means of transportation. San Francisco planned to do so, too, but the proposal was met with so much opposition that the cable cars' perpetuation was actually written into the city charter in 1955. This mandate cannot be revoked without the approval of a majority of the city's voters—a distant and doubtful prospect.

Major San Francisco Sights

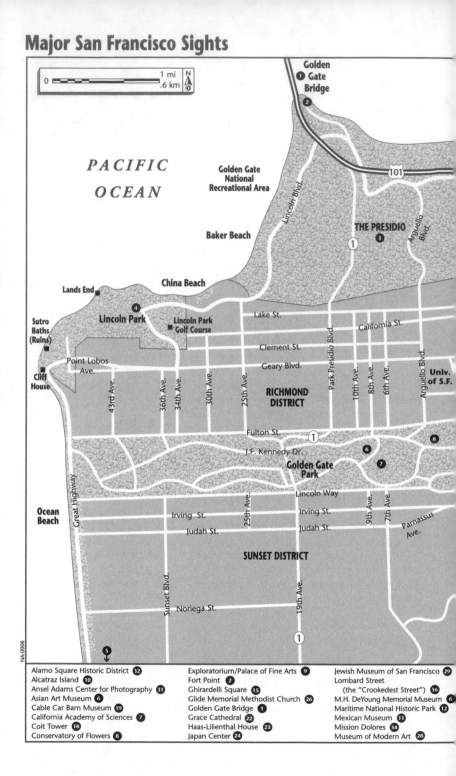

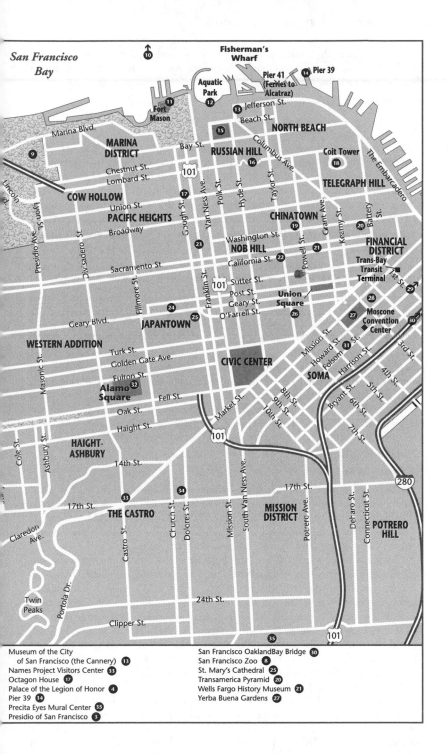

San Francisco Bay

San Francisco Bay

Fisherman's Wharf

Pier 41 (Ferries to Alcatraz)

Pier 39

Aquatic Park

Fort Mason

Jefferson St.

Beach St.

NORTH BEACH

Marina Blvd.

MARINA DISTRICT

Bay St.

Chestnut St.

Lombard St.

RUSSIAN HILL

Columbus Ave.

Coit Tower

101

TELEGRAPH HILL

COW HOLLOW

Union St.

PACIFIC HEIGHTS

Broadway

CHINATOWN

The Embarcadero

Sacramento St

NOB HILL

Washington St.

FINANCIAL DISTRICT

California St.

Trans-Bay Transit Terminal

Sutter St.

Post St.

Union Square

Geary St.

O'Farrell St.

Geary Blvd.

JAPANTOWN

Moscone Convention Center

WESTERN ADDITION

Turk St.

Golden Gate Ave.

Fulton St.

CIVIC CENTER

SOMA

Howard St.

Folsom St.

Harrison St.

Alamo Square

Fell St.

Oak St.

Market St.

Haight St.

280

HAIGHT-ASHBURY

14th St.

17th St.

17th St.

THE CASTRO

MISSION DISTRICT

POTRERO HILL

Twin Peaks

24th St.

Clipper St.

Museum of the City
  of San Francisco (the Cannery) 13
Names Project Visitors Center 33
Octagon House 17
Palace of the Legion of Honor 4
Pier 39 14
Precita Eyes Mural Center 35
Presidio of San Francisco 3

San Francisco OaklandBay Bridge 30
San Francisco Zoo 8
St. Mary's Cathedral 25
Transamerica Pyramid 20
Wells Fargo History Museum 21
Yerba Buena Gardens 27

San Francisco's three existing lines comprise the world's only surviving system of cable cars. For more information on riding them, see "Getting Around" in chapter 4, "Getting to Know San Francisco."

The Cannery. 2801 Leavenworth St. ☎ **415/771-3112.** www.thecannery.com.

The Cannery was built in 1894 as a fruit-canning plant and converted in the 1960s into a mall containing 50-plus shops, a paint-it-yourself ceramic studio, a comedy club, and several restaurants and galleries, including **Jack's Cannery Bar** (☎ **415/931-6400**), which features 110 beers on tap (the most anywhere in the country). Vendors' stalls and sidewalk cafes are set up in the courtyard amid a grove of century-old olive trees, and on summer weekends street performers are out in force entertaining tourists. **The Museum of the City of San Francisco** (☎ **415/928-0289**), which traces the city's development with displays and artifacts, is on the third floor. The museum is free and is open Wednesday to Sunday from 10am to 4pm.

Coit Tower. Atop Telegraph Hill. ☎ **415/362-0808.** Admission (to the top of the tower) $3 adults, $2 seniors, $1 children 6–12. Daily 10am–6pm. Bus: 39 ("Coit").

In a city known for its great views and vantage points, Coit Tower is tops. Located atop Telegraph Hill, just east of North Beach, the round, stone tower offers panoramic views of the city and the bay.

Completed in 1933, the tower is the legacy of Lillie Hitchcock Coit, a wealthy eccentric who left San Francisco a $125,000 bequest "for the purpose of adding beauty to the city I have always loved" and also as a memorial to its volunteer firemen. She had been saved from a fire as a child and thereafter held the city's firefighters in particularly high esteem.

Inside the base of the tower are the impressive murals titled *Life in California, 1934,* which were completed under the WPA during the New Deal. They were completed by more than 25 artists, many of whom had studied under Mexican muralist Diego Rivera.

Fisherman's Wharf & Pier 39

Few cities in America are as adept at wholesaling their historical sites as San Francisco, which has converted Fisherman's Wharf into one of the most popular tourist destinations in the world. Unless you come really early in the morning, you won't find any traces of the traditional waterfront life that once existed here; the only fishing going on around here is for tourists' dollars.

Originally called Meigg's Wharf, this bustling strip of waterfront got its present moniker from generations of fishers who used to base their boats here. Today, the bay has become so polluted with toxins that bright yellow placards warn against eating fish from these waters. A small fleet of fewer than 30 boats still operates from here, but basically Fisherman's Wharf has been converted into one long shopping mall stretching from Ghirardelli Square at the west end to Pier 39 at the east. Some people love it, others can't get far enough away from it, but most agree that Fisherman's Wharf, for better or for worse, has to be seen at least once in your life.

Ghirardelli Square, at 900 N. Point, between Polk and Larkin streets (☎ **415/775-5500**), dates from 1864 when it served as a factory making Civil War uniforms, but it's best known as the former chocolate-and-spice factory of Domingo Ghirardelli (say "Gear-a-deli"). The factory has been converted into a 10-level mall containing 50-plus stores and 20 dining establishments. Scheduled street performers play regularly in the West Plaza. The stores generally stay open from 10am to 9pm in the summer and until 6 or 7pm in the winter. Incidentally, the

Fisherman's Wharf & Vicinity

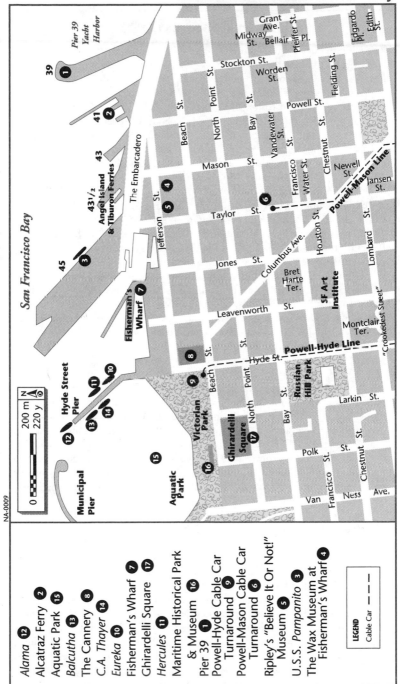

Legend
- - - Cable Car

Alama 12
Alcatraz Ferry 2
Aquatic Park 15
Balcutha 13
The Cannery 8
C.A. Thayer 14
Eureka 10
Fisherman's Wharf 7
Ghirardelli Square 17
Hercules 11
Maritime Historical Park & Museum 16
Pier 39 1
Powell-Hyde Cable Car Turnaround 9
Powell-Mason Cable Car Turnaround 6
Ripley's "Believe It Or Not!" Museum 5
U.S.S. Pampanito 3
The Wax Museum at Fisherman's Wharf 4

NA-0009

Favorites at Fisherman's Wharf

The following sights are all clustered on or near Fisherman's Wharf. To reach this area by cable car, take the Mason line to the last stop and walk to the wharf; by bus, take no. 30, 32, or 42. If you're arriving by car, park on adjacent streets or on the wharf between Taylor and Jones streets.

The Haunted Gold Mine, 113 Jefferson St. (☎ **415/202-0400**), under the same ownership as the Wax Museum, is a fun house complete with mazes, a hall of mirrors, spatial-disorientation tricks, wind tunnels, and animated ghouls. Even very young children will probably not find it too scary, and it's good old-fashioned carnival fun. Admission is $11.95 for adults, $9.95 for children ages 13 to 17, $8.95 for seniors, $5.95 for children ages 6 to 12, and free for children under 6. Summer hours are Sunday to Thursday from 9am to 11pm, and Friday and Saturday from 9am to midnight; winter hours are Sunday to Thursday from 9am to 10pm, and Friday and Saturday from 9am to 11pm.

The popular battle-scarred World War II fleet submarine **USS** *Pampanito,* Pier 45, Fisherman's Wharf (☎ **415/775-1943**), saw plenty of action in the Pacific. It has been completely restored, and visitors are free to crawl around inside. An audio tour is included with admission, which runs $5 for adults, $3 for children 13 to 17, and free for seniors and children under 12; there is also a family pass for $15 (two adults, up to four kids). The *Pampanito* is open daily May through October from 9am to 8pm; November through April it is open daily from 9am to 6pm (until 8pm Fri and Sat nights).

Ripley's Believe It or Not! Museum, 175 Jefferson St. (☎ **415/771-6188;** www.ripleysf.com), has been drawing curious spectators through its doors for 30 years. Inside, you'll experience the extraordinary world of improbabilities: a one-third scale match-stick cable car, a shrunken human torso once owned by Ernest Hemingway, a dinosaur made from car bumpers, a walk through a kaleidoscope tunnel, and video displays and illusions. Robert LeRoy Ripley's infamous arsenal may lead you to ponder whether truth is in fact stranger than fiction. Admission is $8.50 for adults, $7 for seniors over 60, $5.50 for children 5 to 12, and free for children under 5. From June 15 through Labor Day it is open Sunday to Thursday from 9am to 11pm, until midnight on Friday and Saturday; the rest of the year it is open Sunday to Thursday from 10am to 10pm, until midnight on Friday and Saturday. Call for special hours on major holidays.

Conceived and executed in the Madame Tussaud mold, San Francisco's **Wax Museum,** 145 Jefferson St. (☎ **415/202-0400**), features more than 250 lifelike figures of the rich and famous. The "museum" donates the lion's share of its space to images of modern superstars like singer Michael Jackson and political figures like former president George Bush. Tableaux include "Royalty," "Great Humanitarians," "Wickedest Ladies," "World Religions," and "Feared Leaders," the last including Fidel Castro, Nikita Kruschev, Benito Mussolini, and Adolf Hitler. The Chamber of Horrors, which features Dracula, Frankenstein, and a werewolf, along with bloody victims hanging from meat hooks, is the stuff tourist traps are made of. It may also scare younger children. Admission is $11.95 for adults, $9.95 for teens 13 to 17, $8.95 for seniors over 60, $5.95 for children 6 to 12, and free for children under 6. Summer hours are Sunday to Thursday from 9am to 11pm, until midnight on Friday and Saturday; the rest of the year the museum is open Sunday to Thursday from 9am to 10pm, until midnight on Friday and Saturday.

Ghirardelli Chocolate Company still makes chocolate, but it's located in a lower-rent district in the East Bay.

Pier 39, on the waterfront at Embarcadero and Beach Street (☎ 415/981-8030; shops are open daily from 10:30am to 8:30pm), is a 4½-acre, multilevel waterfront complex a few blocks east of Fisherman's Wharf. Constructed on an abandoned cargo pier, it is, ostensibly, a re-creation of a turn-of-the-century street scene, but don't expect a slice of old-time maritime life. This is the busiest mall of the lot and, according to the *London Observer,* the third most visited attraction in the world, behind Disney World and Disneyland—with more than 100 stores, 10 bay-view restaurants (including the Bubba Gump Shrimp Co., an over-buttered spin-off from the *Forrest Gump* movie), a two-tiered Venetian carousel, and a new big-screen Cinemax Theater showing the *Secret of San Francisco.*

The latest major addition to Fisherman's Wharf is **Underwater World,** a $38-million, 707,000-gallon marine attraction filled with sharks, stingrays, and more, all witnessed via a moving footpath that transports visitors through clear acrylic tunnels.

Accommodating a total of 350 boats, two marinas flank the pier and house the Blue & Gold bay-sightseeing fleet. In recent years, some 600 California sea lions have taken up residence on the adjacent floating docks. Until they abandon their new playground, which seems more and more unlikely, these playful, noisy creatures (some nights you can hear them all the way from Washington Square) create one of the best free attractions on the wharf. Ongoing docent-led programs are offered at Pier 39 on weekends from 11am to 5pm that teach visitors about the range, habitat, and adaptability of the California sea lion.

✪ Golden Gate Bridge

1996 marked the 60th birthday of what is possibly the most beautiful, and certainly the most photographed, bridge in the world. Often half-veiled by the city's trademark rolling fog, San Francisco's Golden Gate Bridge spans tidal currents, ocean waves, and battering winds to connect the City by the Bay with the Redwood Empire to the north.

With its gracefully swung single span, spidery bracing cables, and sky-zooming twin towers, the bridge looks more like a work of abstract art than the practical engineering feat that it is, among the greatest of this century. Construction began in May 1937 and was completed at the then-colossal cost of $35 million.

The mile-long steel link, which reaches a height of 746 feet above the water, is an awesome bridge to cross. Traffic usually moves quickly, so crossing by car won't give you too much time to see the sights. If you drive ($3 toll, payable southbound) from the city, park in the lot at the foot of the bridge on the city side and make the crossing by foot. Back in your car, continue to Marin's Vista Point, at the bridge's northern end. Look back and you'll be rewarded with one of the greatest views of San Francisco.

Millions of pedestrians walk or bike across the bridge each year, gazing up at the tall red towers, out at the vistas of San Francisco and Marin County, and down into the stacks of oceangoing liners. You can walk out onto the span from either end, but be prepared—it's usually windy and cold, and the bridge vibrates. Still, walking even a short way is one of the best ways to experience the immense scale of the structure.

Bridge-bound **Golden Gate Transit buses** (☎ 415/923-2000) depart every 30 to 60 minutes during the day for Marin County, starting from the Transbay Terminal at Mission and First streets and making convenient stops at Market and Seventh streets, at the Civic Center, and along Van Ness Avenue and Lombard Street.

A Room with a View

Few sights are more spectacular than gazing down upon a city from the top of a skyscraper. In San Francisco, the best place to go for an awesome aerial view is the **SkyDeck,** located on the 41st floor of the Embarcadero Center. Granted, it's no Empire State Building, but the view of the city and surrounding bay is far, far prettier than dirty ol' NYC. In addition to the sky-high scenery, the SkyDeck also features interactive kiosks that explore San Francisco's colorful history and neighborhoods (this is the home of Silicon Valley, after all).

The entrance and ticket booth to the SkyDeck are on the lobby level of One Embarcadero Center (those four slender, identical buildings with small rectangular windows), located between Battery and Front and Sacramento and Clay streets. It's open daily from noon to 9pm; last admission is at 8:30pm. Admission is $5 for adults, $3.50 for students and seniors 62 and older, $3 for children 5 to 12, and free for kids under 5. Complimentary docent tours are also available, starting at 12:30pm. Parking is available below all Embarcadero Center buildings, and is only $1 per hour on weekends and evenings. For more information call the SkyDeck at ☎ **888/737-5933** or 415/772-0555.

Lombard Street. Between Hyde and Leavenworth sts.

Known as the "crookedest street in the world," the whimsically winding block of Lombard Street draws thousands of visitors each year (much to the chagrin of neighborhood residents, most of whom would prefer to block off the street to tourists). The angle of the street is so steep that the road has to snake back and forth to make a descent possible. The brick-lined street zigzags around the residences' bright flower gardens that explode with color during warmer months. This short stretch of Lombard Street is one way, downhill, and fun to drive. Take the curves slowly and in low gear, and expect a wait during the weekend. Save your film for the bottom, where, if you're lucky, you can find a parking space and take a few snapshots of the silly spectacle. You can also walk the block, either up or down, via staircases (without curves) on either side of the street.

2 Museums

Ansel Adams Center for Photography. 250 Fourth St. ☎ **415/495-7000.** Admission $5 adults, $3 students, $2 seniors and children 13–17, free for children 12 and under. Tues–Sun 11am–5pm; until 8pm the 1st Thurs of each month. Muni Metro: Powell St. lines. Bus: 30, 45, or 9X.

This popular SoMa museum features five separate galleries for changing exhibitions of contemporary and historical photography. One area is dedicated solely to displaying the works and exploring the legacy of Ansel Adams.

Cable Car Barn Museum. Washington and Mason sts. ☎ **415/474-1887.** Free admission. Apr–Oct daily 10am–6pm; Nov–Mar daily 10am–5pm. Cable car: Both Powell St. lines stop by the museum.

If you've ever wondered how cable cars work, this nifty museum will explain (and demonstrate!) it all to you. Yes, this is a museum, but the Cable Car Barn is no stuffed shirt. It's the living powerhouse, repair shop, and storage place of the cable-car system and is in full operation. Built for the Ferries and Cliff House Railway in 1887, the building underwent an $18-million reconstruction to restore its original gaslight-era look, install an amazing spectators' gallery, and add a museum of San Francisco transit history.

The exposed machinery, which pulls the cables under San Francisco's streets, looks like a Rube Goldberg invention. Stand in the mezzanine gallery and become mesmerized by the massive groaning and vibrating winches as they thread the cable that hauls the cars through a huge figure eight and back into the system via slack-absorbing tension wheels. For a better view, move to the lower-level viewing room where you can see the massive pulleys and gears operating underground.

Also on display here is one of the first grip cars developed by Andrew S. Hallidie, operated for the first time on Clay Street on August 2, 1873. Other displays include an antique grip car and trailer that operated on Pacific Avenue until 1929, and dozens of exact-scale models of cars used on the various city lines. There's also a shop where you can buy a variety of cable-car gifts.

✪ California Palace of the Legion of Honor. In Lincoln Park (at 34th Ave. and Clement St.). ☎ **415/750-3600** or 415/863-3330 (for recorded information). Admission (including the Asian Art Museum and M. H. De Young Memorial Museum) $7 adults, $5 seniors 65 and over, $4 youths 12–17, free for children 11 and under (fees may be higher for special exhibitions); free the 1st Wed of each month when hours are 9:30am–8:45pm. Open Tues–Sun 9:30am–5pm; 1st Sat of the month until 8:45pm. Bus: 38 or 18.

Designed as a memorial to California's World War I casualties, the neoclassical structure is an exact replica of the Legion of Honor Palace in Paris, right down to the inscription "Honneur et Patrie" above the portal.

The Legion of Honor reopened in late 1995 after a 2-year, $34.6-million renovation and seismic upgrading that was stalled by the discovery of almost 300 turn-of-the-century coffins. The exterior's grassy expanses, cliff-side paths, and incredible view of the Golden Gate make this an absolute must-visit attraction before you even get in the door. But the inside is equally impressive. The museum's permanent collection covers 4,000 years of art and includes paintings, sculpture, and decorative arts from Europe, as well as international tapestries, prints, and drawings. The chronological display of more than 800 years of European art includes one of the world's finest collections of Rodin's sculptures.

Center for the Arts at Yerba Buena Gardens. 701 Mission St. ☎ **415/978-2700;** box office 415/978-ARTS. Admission $5 adults, $3 seniors and students; free every 1st Thurs of the month from 6–8pm. Tues–Sun 11am–6pm. Muni Metro: Powell or Montgomery. Bus: 30, 45, or 9X.

Cutting-edge computer art and multimedia shows are on view in the high-tech galleries. The initial exhibition, "The Art of *Star Wars,*" featured the special effects created by George Lucas for the film.

✪ The Exploratorium. 3601 Lyon St., in the Palace of Fine Arts (at Marina Blvd.). ☎ **415/563-7337** or 415/561-0360 (for recorded information). Admission $9 adults, $7 senior citizens and college students with ID, $5 children 6–17, $2.50 children 3–5, free for children under 3; free for everyone 1st Wed of each month. MC, V. Summer (Memorial Day–Labor Day) and holidays, Mon–Tues and Thurs–Sun 10am–6pm; Wed 10am–9:30pm. Rest of the year Tues and Thurs–Sun 10am–5pm; Wed 10am–9:30pm. Closed Thanksgiving Day, and Christmas Day. Free parking. Bus: 30 from Stockton St. to the Marina stop.

Scientific American magazine rates the Exploratorium as "the best science museum in the world"—pretty heady stuff for this exciting hands-on science fair that contains more than 650 permanent exhibits that explore everything from giant bubble blowing to Einstein's theory of relativity. It's like a mad scientist's penny arcade, an educational fun house, and an experimental laboratory all rolled into one. Touch a tornado, shape a glowing electrical current, finger-paint via computer, or take a sensory journey in total darkness in the Tactile Dome—you could spend all day here and still not see everything. Every exhibit at the Exploratorium is designed to be interactive, educational, safe, and most important, fun. And don't think this is just for kids; parents inevitably end up being the most reluctant to leave. On the way out, be sure to stop in the wonderful gift store, which is chock-full of afford-able brain candy.

The museum is located in San Francisco's Marina District at the beautiful Palace of Fine Arts, the only building left standing from the Panama-Pacific Exposition of 1915, which celebrated the opening of the Panama Canal. The adjoining park and lagoon—the perfect place for an afternoon picnic—is home to ducks, swans, sea-gulls, and grouchy geese, so bring bread.

Haas-Lilienthal House. 2007 Franklin St. (at Washington St.). ☎ **415/441-3004.** Admission $5 adults, $3 children 6–12 and seniors. Wed noon–3:15pm; Sun 11am–4:15pm (hours vary in July, call ahead). Cable car: California St. line.

Of the city's many gingerbread Victorians, this handsome Queen Anne house is one of the most flamboyant. The 1886 structure features all the architectural frills of the period, including dormer windows, flying cupolas, ornate trim, and wistful turrets. The elaborately styled house is now a museum, its rooms fully furnished with period pieces. The house is maintained by the Foundation for San Francisco's Archi-tectural Heritage, which offers tours 2 days a week. A new Costume Exhibit has been added, which features such themes as ragtime-era costumes, artifacts, and accessories.

The Jewish Museum San Francisco. 121 Steuart St. (between Mission and Howard sts.). ☎ **415/543-8880.** Admission $5 adults, $2.50 students and seniors; free the 1st Mon of each month. Sun–Wed 11am–5pm; Thurs 11am–8pm. Closed Fri–Sat. Bus: 14, 32.

The Jewish Museum San Francisco was inaugurated in 1984 to educate the com-munity about Jewish history, traditions, and values. The museum hosts a variety of shows that concentrate on the themes of immigration, assimilation, and identity of the Jewish community in the United States and around the world. They are illus-trated by paintings, sculptures, and photographs, as well as educational programs involving nonsectarian schools and summer camps.

Mexican Museum. Bldg. D, Fort Mason, Marina Blvd. (at Laguna St.). ☎ **415/202-9700.** Admission $3 adults, $2 children. Free 1st Wed of the month. Wed–Fri noon–5pm; Sat–Sun 11am–5pm. Bus: 76 or 28.

The first museum in the nation dedicated to the work of Mexican and other Latino artists, the Mexican Museum maintains an impressive collection of art covering pre-Hispanic, colonial, folk, Mexican fine art, and Chicano/Mexican-American art. Revolving art shows range from the art of New Mexican women to such subjects as Mexican surrealism. *Note:* The museum is expected to be relocated to the Yerba Buena Center at Third and Mission streets in 2000.

Octagon House. 2645 Gough St. (at Union St.). ☎ **415/441-7512.** Free admission (dona-tion suggested). Open only on the 2nd Sun and 2nd and 4th Thurs of each month, noon–3pm. Closed Jan and holidays. Bus: 41 or 45.

This unusual, eight-sided, cupola-topped house dates from 1861 and is maintained by the National Society of Colonial Dames of America. The architectural features are extraordinary, and from the second floor it is possible to look up into the cupola, which is illuminated at night. Now a small museum, you'll find furniture, silver-ware, and American pewter from the colonial and Federal periods. There are also some historic documents, including signatures of 54 of the 56 signers of the

Declaration of Independence. Even if you're not able to visit during opening hours, this strange structure is worth a look.

San Francisco Maritime National Historical Park. At the foot of Polk St. (near Fisherman's Wharf). ☎ **415/556-3002.** Museum free; ships $2 adults, $1 children 12–17, free for children 11 and under and seniors over 62. Museum daily 10am–5pm. Ships on Hyde St. Pier May 31–Sept 1 daily 10am–6pm; Sept 2–May 30 daily 9:30am–5pm. Closed Thanksgiving Day, Christmas Day, and New Year's Day. Cable car: Hyde St. line to the last stop. Bus: 19, 30, 32, 42, or 47.

Shaped like an art-deco ship, the Maritime Museum is filled with sailing, whaling, and fishing lore. Remarkably good exhibits include intricate model craft, scrimshaw, and a collection of shipwreck photographs and historic marine scenes, including an 1851 snapshot of hundreds of abandoned ships, deserted en masse by crews dashing off to participate in the gold rush. The museum's walls are lined with beautifully carved, brightly painted wooden figureheads from old windjammers.

Two blocks east, at the park's Hyde Street Pier, are several historic ships, now moored and open to the public.

The *Balclutha*, one of the last surviving square-riggers and the handsomest vessel in San Francisco Bay, was built in Glasgow, Scotland, in 1886 and used to carry grain from California at a near-record speed of 300 miles a day. The ship is now completely restored. Visitors are invited to spin the wheel, squint at the compass, and imagine they're weathering a mighty storm. Kids can climb into the bunking quarters, visit the "slop chest" (galley to you, matey), and read the sea chanteys (clean ones only) that decorate the walls.

The 1890 *Eureka* still carries a cargo of nostalgia for San Franciscans. It was the last of 50 paddle-wheel ferries that regularly plied the bay; it made its final trip in 1957. Restored to its original splendor at the height of the ferryboat era, the side-wheeler is loaded with deck cargo, including antique cars and trucks.

The black-hulled, three-masted *C. A. Thayer*, built in 1895, was crafted for the lumber trade and carried logs felled in the Pacific Northwest to the carpentry shops of California.

Other historic ships docked here include the tiny two-masted *Alma*, one of the last scow schooners to bring hay to the horses of San Francisco; the *Hercules*, a huge 1907 oceangoing steam tug; and the *Eppleton Hall*, a side-wheel tugboat built in England in 1914 to operate on London's River Thames.

At the pier's small-boat shop, visitors can follow the restoration progress of historic boats from the museum's collection. It's located behind the maritime bookstore on your right as you approach the ships.

San Francisco Museum of Modern Art (MOMA). 151 Third St. (2 blocks south of Market St., across from Yerba Buena Gardens). ☎ **415/357-4000.** Admission $8 adults, $5 senior citizens, $4 for students 14–with ID, free for children 12 and under; half price for everyone Thurs 6–9pm, and free for everyone the 1st Tues of each month. Labor Day–Memorial Day Thurs 11am–9pm; Fri–Tues 11am–6pm. Memorial Day–Labor Day Thurs 10am–9pm; Fri–Tues 10am–6pm. Closed Wed and major holidays. Muni Metro: J, K, L, or M to Montgomery Station. Bus: 15, 30, or 45.

Swiss architect Mario Botta, in association with Hellmuth, Obata, and Kassabaum, designed the $62-million museum, which opened in SoMa in January 1995. The building is the most welcomed new development in years and has made SoMa one of the more popular areas to visit for tourists and residents alike. The museum's collection consists of more than 15,000 works, including close to 5,000 paintings and sculptures by artists such as Henri Matisse, Jackson Pollock, and Willem de Kooning. Other artists represented include Diego Rivera, Georgia O'Keeffe,

Paul Klee, the Fauvists, and exceptional holdings of Richard Diebenkorn. MOMA was also one of the first to recognize photography as a major art form; its extensive collection includes more than 9,000 photographs by such notables as Ansel Adams, Alfred Stieglitz, Edward Weston, and Henri Cartier-Bresson. Docent-led tours are offered daily. Times are posted at the museum's admission desk. Phone for current details of upcoming special events.

The Caffè Museo, located to the right of the museum entrance sets a new precedent for museum food with flavorful and fresh soups, sandwiches, and salads that are as respectable as those served in many local restaurants.

No matter what, don't miss the MuseumStore, which carries a wonderful array of architectural gifts, books, and trinkets. It's one of the best stores in town.

Wells Fargo History Museum. 420 Montgomery St. (at California St.). ☎ **415/ 396-2619.** Free admission. Mon–Fri 9am–5pm. Closed bank holidays. Muni Metro: Montgomery St. Bus: any to Market St.

Wells Fargo, one of California's largest banks, got its start in the Wild West. Its history museum, at the bank's head office, houses hundreds of genuine relics from the company's whip-and-six-shooter days, including pistols, photographs, early banking articles, posters, and mining equipment.

3 Neighborhoods Worth a Visit

To really get to know San Francisco, break out of the downtown and Fisherman's Wharf areas to explore the ethnically and culturally diverse neighborhoods. Walk the streets, browse the shops, grab a bite at a local restaurant—you'll find that San Francisco's beauty and charm is around every corner, not just at the popular tourist destinations.

Note: For information on Fisherman's Wharf, see "Famous San Francisco Sights" above. (For information on other San Francisco neighborhoods and districts that aren't discussed here, see the "Neighborhoods & Districts in Brief" section in chapter 4.)

NOB HILL

When the cable car was invented in 1873, this hill became the exclusive residential area of the city. The "Big Four" and the "Comstock Bonanza kings" built their mansions here, but they were all destroyed by the earthquake and fire in 1906. The only two surviving buildings were the Flood Mansion, which serves today as the Pacific Union Club, and the Fairmont Hotel, which was under construction when the earthquake struck. Today the burned-out sites of former mansions are occupied by the city's luxury hotels—the Mark Hopkins, the Stanford Court, the Fairmont, and the Huntington—as well as spectacular Grace Cathedral, which stands on the Crocker mansion site. It's worth a visit to Nob Hill if only to stroll around Huntington Park, attend a Sunday service at the cathedral, or ooh and aah your way around the Fairmont's spectacular lobby.

SOUTH OF MARKET (SOMA)

From Market Street to Townsend and the Embarcadero to Division Street, SoMa has become the city's newest cultural and multimedia center. The process started when alternative clubs began opening in the old warehouses in the area nearly a decade ago, followed by a wave of entrepreneurs seeking to start new businesses in what was once an extremely low-rent district compared to the neighboring Financial District. Today, gentrification and high rents are well underway, spurned by a building boom that started with the Moscone Convention Center and continues today with the new Center for the Arts at Yerba Buena Gardens and the San Francisco Museum of Modern Art, all of which continue to be supplemented by other institutions, businesses, and museums that are moving into the area daily. A substantial portion of nightlife also takes place in warehouse spaces throughout the district.

NORTH BEACH

In the late 1800s, an enormous influx of Italian immigrants into North Beach firmly established this aromatic area as San Francisco's "Little Italy." Today, dozens of Italian restaurants and coffeehouses continue to flourish in what is still the center of the city's Italian community. Walk down Columbus Avenue any given morning and you're bound to be bombarded with the wonderful aromas of roasting coffee and savory pasta sauces. Though there are some interesting shops and bookstores in the area, it's the dozens of eclectic little cafes, delis, bakeries, and coffee shops that give North Beach its Italian-bohemian character.

For a proper perspective of North Beach, follow the detailed walking tour in chapter 8, "City Strolls," or sign up for a guided Javawalk with coffee-nut Elaine Sosa (see "Walking Tours" in this chapter).

✪ CHINATOWN

The first Chinese came to San Francisco in the early 1800s to work as servants. By 1851, there were 25,000 Chinese working in California, most of whom had settled in San Francisco's Chinatown. Fleeing famine and the Opium Wars, they had come seeking the promise of good fortune in the "Gold Mountain" of California, hoping to return with that prosperity to their families back in China. For the vast majority, the reality of life in California did not live up to the promise. First employed as workers in the gold mines during the gold rush, they were later used to build the railroads, working as little more than slaves and facing constant prejudice. Yet the community, segregated in the Chinatown ghetto, thrived. Growing prejudice led to the Chinese Exclusion Act of 1882, which halted all Chinese immigration for 10 years and limited it severely thereafter; the Chinese Exclusion Act was not repealed until 1943. The Chinese were also denied the opportunity to buy homes outside of the Chinatown ghetto until the 1950s.

Today San Francisco has the second largest community of Chinese in the United States (about 33% of the city's population is Chinese). More than 80,000 people live in Chinatown, but the majority of Chinese have moved out into newer areas like the Richmond and Sunset districts. Though frequented by tourists, the area continues to cater to the Chinese community who crowd the vegetable and herbal markets, restaurants, and shops. Tradition still runs deep here, too, and if you're lucky, through an open window you might hear women mixing mahjong tiles as they play the century-old game.

The gateway at Grant and Bush marks the entry to Chinatown. The **Chinese Historical Society of America,** at 650 Commercial St. (☎ **415/391-1188**), has a small but interesting collection relating to the Chinese in San Francisco, which can be viewed for free anytime Tuesday to Friday from 10am to 4pm. The heart of Chinatown is at Portsmouth Square where you'll find Chinese locals playing board games (often gambling) or just sitting quietly.

On Waverly Place, a street where the Chinese celebratory colors of red, yellow, and green are much in evidence, you'll find three temples, Jeng Sen at no. 146, Tien Hou at no. 125, and Norras at no. 109.

A block north of Grant, Stockton from 1000 to 1200 is the main shopping street of the community lined with grocers, fishmongers, tea sellers, herbalists, noodle parlors, and restaurants. Here, too, is the Kon Chow Temple at no. 855, above the Chinatown post office. Explore at your leisure.

JAPANTOWN

Today, more than 12,000 citizens of Japanese descent live in San Francisco, or *Soko,* as it is often called by the Japanese who first emigrated here. Initially, they settled in Chinatown and also South of Market along Stevenson and Jessie streets from Fourth to Seventh. After the earthquake in 1906, SoMa became a light industrial and warehouse area and the largest Japanese concentration took root in the Western Addition between Van Ness Avenue and Fillmore Street, the site of today's Japantown. By 1940 it covered 30 blocks.

In 1913 the Alien Land Law was passed, depriving Japanese Americans of the right to buy land. From 1924 to 1952 Japanese immigration was banned by the United States. During World War II, the U.S. government froze Japanese bank accounts, interned community leaders, and removed 112,000 Japanese Americans—two-thirds of them citizens—to camps in California, Utah, and Idaho. Japantown was emptied of Japanese, and their place was taken by war workers. Upon their release in 1945, the Japanese found their old neighborhood occupied. Most of them resettled in the Richmond and Sunset districts; some did return to Japantown but it had shrunk to a mere 6 or so blocks. Among the community's notable sights are the Buddhist Church of San Francisco at 1881 Pine St. at Octavia; the Konko Church of San Francisco at 1909 Bush at Laguna; the Sokoji-Soto Zen Buddhist Temple at 1691 Laguna St. at Sutter; and Nihonmachi Mall, 1700 block of Buchanan Street between Sutter and Post, which contains two steel fountains by Ruth Asawa; and the Japan Center.

Japan Center is an Asian-oriented shopping mall occupying 3 square blocks bounded by Post, Geary, Laguna, and Fillmore streets. At its center stands the five-tiered Peace Pagoda, designed by world-famous Japanese architect Yoshiro Taniguchi "to convey the friendship and goodwill of the Japanese to the people of the United States." Surrounding the pagoda, in a network of arcades, squares, and bridges, are dozens of shops and showrooms featuring everything from TVs and tansu chests to pearls, bonsai (dwarf trees), and kimonos. When it opened in 1968, the complex seemed as modern as a jumbo jet. Today, the concrete structure seems less impressive, but it still holds some interesting surprises. The **Kabuki Hot Spring,** at 1750 Geary Blvd. (☎ **415/922-6002**), is the center's most famous tenant, an authentic traditional Japanese bathhouse with deep ceramic communal tubs, as well as private baths. The Japan Center also houses numerous restaurants, teahouses, shops, and the luxurious 14-story Radisson Miyako Hotel (see chapter 5, "Accommodations," for complete information).

There is often live entertainment on summer weekends, including Japanese music and dance performances, tea ceremonies, flower-arranging demonstrations, martial-arts presentations, and other cultural events. The Japan Center is open Monday to Friday from 10am to 10pm, Saturday and Sunday from 9am to 10pm. It can be reached by the no. 2, 3, or 4 bus (exit on Buchanan and Sutter streets); or nos. 22 or 38 (exit on the northeast corner of Geary Boulevard and Fillmore Street).

HAIGHT-ASHBURY

Few of San Francisco's neighborhoods are as varied—or as famous—as the Haight-Ashbury. Walk along Haight Street and you'll encounter everything from

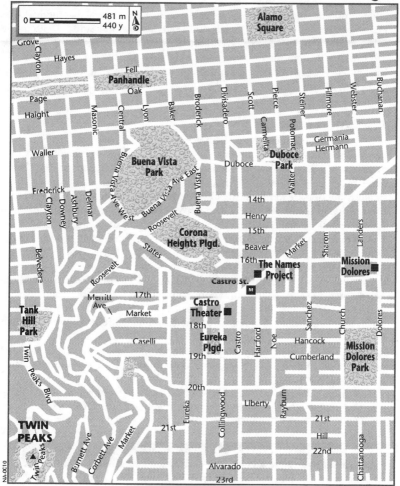

drug-dazed drifters begging for change to an armada of the city's most countercul-ture (read: cool) shops, clubs, and cafes. Yet turn anywhere off Haight, and instantly you're among the clean-cut, young urban professionals who are the only ones who can afford the steep rents in this hip 'hood. The result is an interesting mix of well-to-do and well-screw-you lifestyles rubbing shoulders with aging flower children, former Dead-heads, homeless people, and the throngs of tourists who try not to stare as they wander through this most human of zoos. Some find it depressing, others find it fascinating, but everyone agrees that it ain't what it was in the free-lovin' psychedelic Summer of Love. Is it still worth a visit? Absolutely, if only to enjoy a cone of Cherry Garcia at the now-famous Ben & Jerry's ice cream shop on the corner of Haight and Ashbury streets, then wander and gawk at the exotic people of the area.

THE CASTRO

Castro Street, between Market and 18th, is the center of the city's gay community, as well as a lovely strolling neighborhood teeming with shops, restaurants, bars, and other institutions that cater to the area's colorful clientele. Among the landmarks are Harvey Milk Plaza, the Names Project quilt, and the Castro Theatre, a 1930s movie palace with a Wurlitzer. The gay community began to move here in the late 1960s and early 1970s from the earlier gay neighborhood called Polk Gulch, which still has a number of gay-oriented bars and stores. Castro is one of the most lively streets in the city, and the perfect place to shop for gifts and revel in how free-spirited this town is.

THE MISSION DISTRICT

Once inhabited almost entirely by Irish immigrants, the Mission District is now the center of the city's Latino community, an oblong area stretching roughly from 14th to 30th streets between Potrero Avenue in the east and Dolores on the west. In the outer areas many of the city's finest Victorians still stand, though many seem strangely out of place in the mostly lower-income neighborhoods. The heart of the community lies along 24th Street between Van Ness and Potrero, where dozens of excellent ethnic restaurants, bakeries, bars, and specialty stores attract people from all over the city. The Mission District at night isn't exactly the safest place to be, and walking around the area should be done with caution, but it's usually quite safe during the day and highly recommended.

For an even better insight into the community, go to the **Precita Eyes Mural Arts Center,** 348 Precita Ave., at Folsom Street (☎ **415/285-2287**), and take one of the 1-hour-and-45-minute tours conducted on Saturday at 11am and 1:30pm, which cost $5 for adults, $4 for seniors, and $1 for under-18s. You'll see 85 murals in an 8-block walk. Every year they also hold a Mural Awareness Week (usually the 2nd week in May) when tours are given daily. Other signs of cultural life include a number of progressive theaters—Eureka, Theater Rhinoceros, and Theater Artaud, to name only a few.

At 16th and Dolores is the Mission San Francisco de Assisi (better known as Mission Dolores), which is the city's oldest surviving building (see the separate listing below) and the district's namesake.

4 Golden Gate Park

Everybody loves Golden Gate Park—people, dogs, birds, frogs, turtles, bison, trees, bushes, and flowers. Literally everything feels unified here in San Francisco's enormous arboreal front yard. But this great city landmark wasn't always a favorite place to convene. It was conceived in the 1860s and 1870s but took its current shape in the 1880s and 1890s thanks to the skill and effort of John McClaren, a Scot who arrived in 1887 and began the landscaping of the park. Totaling 1,017 acres, the park is a narrow strip that stretches from the Pacific coast inland. No one had thought about the challenge the sand dunes and wind would present to any landscape artist. McClaren developed a new strain of grass called "sea bent," which he had planted to hold the sandy soil along the Firth of Forth, and he used this to anchor the soil here too. He also built the two windmills that stand on the western edge of the park to pump water for irrigation. Every year the ocean eroded the western fringe of the park, and ultimately he solved this problem too. It took him 40 years to build a natural wall, putting out bundles of sticks which were then covered with sand by the tides. Under his brilliant eye, the park took shape.

Today's Golden Gate Park is a truly magical place. Spend one sunny day stretched out on the grass along JFK Drive, have a good read in Shakespeare

Golden Gate Park

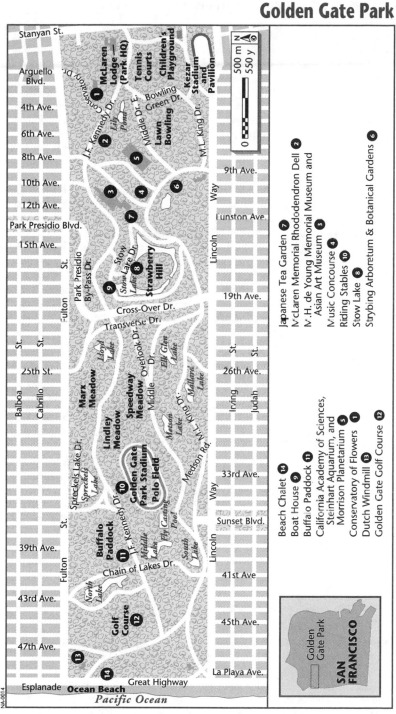

Japanese Tea Garden **7**
McLaren Memorial Rhododendron Dell **2**
M.H. de Young Memorial Museum and
Asian Art Museum **3**
Music Concourse **4**
Riding Stables **10**
Stow Lake **8**
Strybing Arboretum & Botanical Gardens **6**

Beach Chalet **14**
Boat House **9**
Buffalo Paddock **11**
California Academy of Sciences,
Steinhart Aquarium, and
Morrison Planetarium **5**
Conservatory of Flowers **1**
Dutch Windmill **13**
Golden Gate Golf Course **12**

Garden, or stroll around Stow Lake and you too will understand the allure. It's an interactive botanical symphony, and everyone is invited to play in the orchestra.

The park is made up of hundreds of gardens and attractions attached by wooded paths and paved roads. While many stop-worthy sites are clearly visible, there are infinite hidden treasures, so pick up information if you want to find the more obscure, quaint spots. For information on the park, head first to the **McClaren Lodge and Park Headquarters,** which is open Monday to Friday (☎ 415/ 831-2700). Of the dozens of special gardens in the park, most recognized are the Rhododendron Dell, the Rose Garden, the Strybing Arboretum, and at the western edge of the park a springtime array of thousands of tulips and daffodils around the Dutch windmill.

In addition to the highlights below, the park contains several recreational facilities: tennis courts, baseball, soccer and polo fields, golf course, riding stables, fly-casting pools, and boat rentals at the Strawberry Hill boathouse. It is also the home of three major museums: the M. H. De Young Memorial Museum, the Asian Art Museum, and the California Academy of Sciences (see their separate listings below). *Note:* There's talk of moving the De Young to an undetermined location, and the Asian Art Museum is moving to the old Main Library site in the Civic Center around 2001. If you plan to visit all the park's attractions, consider buying the **Culture Pass,** which enables you to visit the three museums and the Japanese Tea Garden for $12. Passes are available at each site and at the Visitor Information Center. For further information call ☎ 415/391-2000. Enter the park at Kezar Drive, an extension of Fell Street. Bus: 16AX, BX, 5, 6, 7, 66, or 71.

MUSEUMS INSIDE THE PARK

Asian Art Museum. In Golden Gate Park, near 10th Ave. and Fulton St. ☎ **415/379-8800;** 415/752-2635 for the hearing impaired. Admission (including the M. H. De Young Memorial Museum and California Palace of the Legion of Honor) $6 adults, $4 seniors 65 and over, $3 youths 12–17, free for children 11 and under (fees may be higher for special exhibitions); free admission for everyone the 1st Wed (all day) of each month. Wed–Sun 10am–4:45pm; 1st Wed each month 10am–8:45pm. Bus: 5, 44, or 71.

Adjacent to the M. H. De Young Museum and the Japanese Tea Garden, this exhibition space, opened in 1966, can only display about 1,800 pieces from the museum's vast collection of 12,000. About half of the works on exhibit are in the ground-floor Chinese and Korean galleries and include world-class sculptures, paintings, bronzes, ceramics, jades, and decorative objects spanning 6,000 years of history. There is also a wide range of exhibits from more than 40 Asian countries— Pakistan, India, Tibet, Japan, Southeast Asia—including the world's oldest-known "dated" Chinese Buddha. The museum's free daily guided tours are highly informative and sincerely recommended. Call for times.

California Academy of Sciences. On the Music Concourse of Golden Gate Park. ☎ 415/750-7145 for recorded information. Admission (aquarium and Natural History Museum) $8.50 adults, $5.50 students 12–17 and seniors 65 and over, $2 children 4–11, free for children under 4; free for everyone the 1st Wed of every month. Planetarium shows $2.50 adults, $1.25 children under 18 and seniors 65 and over. Labor Day–Memorial Day daily 10am–5pm; Memorial Day–Labor Day daily 9am–6pm; 1st Wed of every month 10am–9pm. Muni Metro: N to Golden Gate Park. Bus: 5, 71, or 44.

Clustered around the Music Concourse in Golden Gate Park are three outstanding world-class museums and exhibitions that are guaranteed to entertain every member of the family. The **Steinhart Aquarium,** for example, is the most diverse aquarium in the world, housing some 14,000 specimens, including amphibians, reptiles, marine mammals, penguins, and much more, in 189 displays. A huge hit with the youngsters is the California tide pool and a "hands-on" area where children can touch starfish and sea urchins. The living coral reef is the largest display of its kind in the country and the only one in the West. In the Fish Roundabout, visitors are surrounded by fast-swimming schools of fish kept in a 100,000-gallon tank. Seals and dolphins are fed every 2 hours, beginning at 10:30am; the penguins are fed at 11:30am and 4pm.

The **Morrison Planetarium** presents sky shows as well as laser-light shows. Its sky shows offer guided tours through the universe projected onto a 65-foot domed ceiling. Approximately four major exhibits, with titles such as "Star Death: The Birth of Black Holes" and "The Universe Unveiled," are presented each year. Related cosmos exhibits are located in the adjacent Earth and Space Hall. Sky shows are featured at 2pm on weekdays and hourly every weekend and holiday (☎ 415/750-7141 for more information). **Laserium laser-light shows** are also presented in the planetarium Thursday through Sunday nights (☎ 415/750-7138 for more information).

The **Natural History Museum** includes several halls displaying classic dioramas of fauna in their habitats. The Wattis Hall of Human Cultures traces the evolution of different human cultures and how they adapted to their natural environment; the "Wild California" exhibition in Meyer Hall includes a 14,000-gallon aquarium and seabird rookery, life-size battling elephant seals, and two larger-than-life views of microscopic life forms; in McBean-Peterson Hall visitors can walk through an exhibit tracing the course of 3½ billion years of evolution from the earliest life forms to the present day; in the Hohfeld Earth and Space Hall visitors can experience a simulation of two of San Francisco's biggest earthquakes, determine what their weight would be on other planets, see a real moon rock, and learn about the rotation of the planet at a replica of Foucault's Pendulum (the real one is in Paris).

M. H. De Young Memorial Museum. In Golden Gate Park (near 10th Ave. and Fulton St.). ☎ 415/750-3600 or 415/863-3330 (for recorded information). Admission (including the Asian Art Museum and California Palace of the Legion of Honor) $7 adults, $5 seniors over 65, $4 youths 12–17, free for children 11 and under (fees may be higher for special exhibitions); free the 1st Wed of each month. Wed–Sun 9:30am–5pm (1st Wed of the month until 8:45pm). Bus: 44.

One of the city's oldest museums, it's best known for its American art dating from colonial times to the 20th century, and includes paintings, sculptures, furniture, and decorative arts by Paul Revere, Winslow Homer, John Singer Sargent, and Georgia O'Keeffe. Special note should be taken of the American landscapes, as well as the fun trompe l'oeil and still-life works from the turn of the century.

Named after the late 19th-century publisher of the *San Francisco Chronicle,* the museum also possesses an important textile collection, with primary emphasis on rugs from central Asia and the Near East. Other collections on view include decorative art from Africa, Oceania, and the Americas. Major traveling exhibitions are equally eclectic, including everything from ancient rugs to great Dutch paintings. Call the museum to find out what's on. Tours are offered daily; call for times.

The museum's Café De Young is exceptional, serving daily specials that might include Peruvian stew, Chinese chicken salad, and Italian vegetables in tomato-basil sauce. In summer, visitors can dine in the garden, among bronze statuary. The cafe is open Wednesday through Sunday from 10am to 4pm.

OTHER HIGHLIGHTS

CONSERVATORY OF FLOWERS (1878) Built for the 1894 Midwinter Exposition, this striking assemblage of glass architecture usually exhibits a rotating display of plants and shrubs at all times of the year. Unfortunately, recent years' rough weather has damaged the already-delicate structure and renovations aren't scheduled to be complete until 2004. Still, the exterior, which is modeled on the famous glass house at Kew Gardens in London, is indeed grand.

JAPANESE TEA GARDEN (1894) McClaren hired the Hagiwara family to care for this garden developed for the 1894 Midwinter Exposition. It's a quiet place with cherry trees, shrubs, and bonsai crisscrossed by winding paths and high-arched bridges crossing over pools of water. Focal points and places for contemplation include the massive bronze Buddha that was cast in Japan in 1790 and donated by the Gump family, the Shinto wooden pagoda, and the Wishing Bridge, which reflected in the water looks as if it completes a circle. The garden is open daily October through February from 8:30am to 6pm (with the teahouse only open until 5:30pm), and March through September from 9am to 6:30pm. For **information** on admissions call ☎ **415/752-4227.** For the **teahouse** call ☎ **415/752-1171.**

STRYBING ARBORETUM & BOTANICAL GARDENS Six thousand plant species grow here; among them some very ancient plants in a special "primitive garden," rare species, and a grove of California redwoods. Docent tours are given at 1pm daily during operating hours, which are Monday to Friday from 8am to 4:30pm and Saturday and Sunday from 10am to 5pm. For more information call ☎ **415/753-7089.**

✪ STRAWBERRY HILL/STOW LAKE Rent a paddleboat, rowboat, or motorboat here and cruise around the circular lake as painters create still lifes and joggers pass along the grassy shoreline. Ducks waddle around waiting to be fed and turtles bathe on rocks and logs. Strawberry Hill, the 430-foot-high artificial island that lies at the center of Stow Lake, is a perfect picnic spot and boasts a bird's-eye view of San Francisco and the bay. It also has a waterfall and peace pagoda. To reach the **boathouse** call ☎ **415/752-0347.** Boat rentals are available daily from 9am to 4pm.

5 The Presidio & Golden Gate National Recreation Area

THE PRESIDIO

In October 1994, the Presidio was transferred from the U.S. Army to the National Park Service and became one of a handful of urban national parks that combines historical, architectural, and natural elements into one giant arboreal expanse. The 1,480-acre area incorporates a variety of terrain—coastal scrub, dunes, and prairie grasslands that shelter many rare plants and more than 150 species of birds, some of which nest here.

This military outpost has a 220-year history, stretching from its founding in September 1776 by the Spanish under José Joaquin Moraga to its closure in 1995. From 1822 to 1835 the property was in Mexican hands.

During the war with Mexico, American forces occupied the fort, and in 1848, when California became part of the Union, it was formally transferred to the United States. When San Francisco suddenly became an important urban area during the gold rush, the U.S. government installed battalions of soldiers, built Fort Point to protect the entry to the harbor, and expanded the post during the Civil

War and later during the Indian Wars of the 1870s and 1880s. By the 1890s, it was no longer a frontier post but a major base for American expansion into the Pacific. During the war with Spain in 1898, thousands of troops camped in tent cities awaiting shipment to the Philippines, and the sick and wounded were treated at the Army General Hospital. By 1905, 12 coastal defense batteries were built along the headlands. In 1914, troops under the command of Gen. John Pershing left here to pursue Pancho Villa and his men. The Presidio expanded during the 1920s when Crissy Army Airfield (the first airfield on the West Coast) was established, but the major action was seen during World War II after the attack on Pearl Harbor. Soldiers dug foxholes along nearby beaches, and the Presidio became the headquarters for the Western Defense Command. Some 1.6 million men shipped out from nearby Fort Mason to fight in the Pacific and many returned to the hospital, whose capacity peaked one year at 72,000 patients. In the 1950s, the Presidio served as the headquarters for the Sixth U.S. Army and a missile defense post, but its role has slowly been reduced. In 1972, it was included in new legislation establishing the Golden Gate National Recreation Area; in 1989, the Pentagon decided to close the post and transfer it to the National Park Service.

Today, the area features more than 510 historic buildings, a scenic golf course, a national cemetery, and a variety of terrain and natural habitats. The National Park Service offers a variety of walking and biking tours around the Presidio; reservations are suggested. The **Presidio Museum,** located at the corner of Lincoln Boulevard and Funston Avenue (open 10am to 4pm Wed to Sun), tells its story in dioramas, exhibitions, and photographs. For more information, call the **Visitor Information Center** at ☎ **415/561-4323.** Take the 82X, 28, or 76 bus.

San Francisco Zoo & Children's Zoo. Sloat Blvd. and 45th Ave. ☎ **415/753-7080.** Main zoo $7 adults, $3.50 seniors and youths 12–15, $1.50 for children 3–11, and free for children 2 and under if accompanied by an adult; children's zoo $1, free for children under 3 and free to everyone the 1st Wed of each month. Carousel $2. Main zoo daily 10am–5pm. Children's zoo Mon–Fri 11am–4pm; Sat–Sun 10:30am–4:30pm. Muni Metro: L from downtown Market St. to the end of the line.

Located between the Pacific Ocean and Lake Merced, in the southwest corner of the city, the San Francisco Zoo is among America's highest-rated animal parks. Begun in 1889 with a grizzly bear named Monarch donated by the *San Francisco Examiner,* the zoo now sprawls over 65 acres and is growing. It attracts up to a million visitors each year. Most of the 1,000-plus inhabitants are contained in landscaped enclosures guarded by concealed moats. The innovative Primate Discovery Center is particularly noteworthy for its many rare and endangered species. Expansive outdoor atriums, sprawling meadows, and a midnight world for exotic nocturnal primates house such species as the owl-faced macaque, ruffed-tailed lemur, black-and-white colobus monkeys, patas monkeys, and emperor tamarins— pint-size primates distinguished by their long, majestic mustaches.

Other highlights include Koala Crossing, which is linked to the Australian Walk-About exhibit that opened in 1995, housing kangaroos, emus, and wallaroos; Gorilla World, one of the world's largest exhibits of these gentle giants; and Penguin Island, home to a large breeding colony of Magellanic penguins. The new Feline Conservation Center is a wooded sanctuary and breeding facility for the zoo's endangered snow leopards, Persian leopards, and other jungle cats. Musk Ox Meadow is a 2½-acre habitat for a herd of rare white-fronted musk oxen brought from Alaska. The Otter River exhibit features waterfalls, logs, and boulders for the North American otters to climb on. And the Lion House is home to rare Sumatran

Golden Gate National Recreation Area

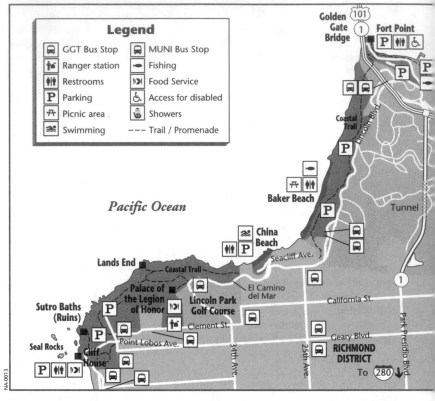

and Siberian tigers, Prince Charles (a rare white Bengal tiger), and the African lions (you can watch them being fed at 2pm Tues to Sun).

The Children's Zoo, adjacent to the main park, allows both kids and adults to get close to animals. The barnyard is alive with strokable domestic animals such as sheep, goats, ponies, and a llama. Also of interest is the Insect Zoo, which show-cases a multitude of insect species, including the hissing cockroach and walking sticks.

A free, informal walking tour of the zoo is available on weekends at 11am. The Zebra Zephyr train tour takes visitors on a 30-minute "safari" daily (only on week-ends in winter). The tour is $2.50 for adults, $1.50 for children 15 and under and seniors.

GOLDEN GATE NATIONAL RECREATIONAL AREA

The largest urban park in the world, the GGNRA makes New York's Central Park look like a putting green, covering three counties along 28 miles of stunning, condo-free shoreline. Run by the National Parks Service, the Recreation Area wraps around the northern and western edges of the city, and just about all of it is open to the public with no access fees. The Muni bus system provides transportation to the more popular sites, including Aquatic Park, the Cliff House, Fort Mason, and Ocean Beach. For more information, contact the **National Park Service** (☎ 415/556-0560). For more detailed information on particular sites, see the "Staying Active" section at the end of this chapter.

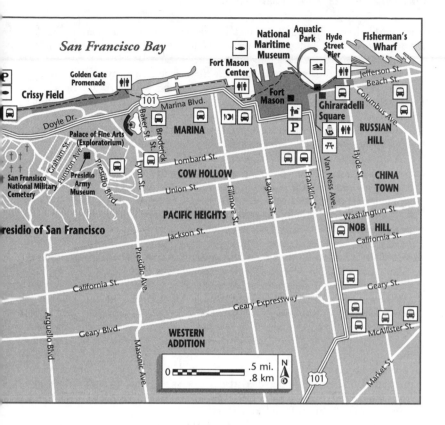

Here is a brief rundown of the salient features of the park's peninsula section, starting at the northern section and moving westward around the coastline:

Aquatic Park, adjacent to the Hyde Street Pier, has a small swimming beach, although it's not that appealing (and darn cold). Far more entertaining is a visit to the ship-shaped museum across the lawn that's part of the San Francisco Maritime National Historical Park (see above for more information).

Fort Mason Center occupies an area from Bay Street to the shoreline and consists of several buildings and piers that were used during World War II. Today they are occupied by a variety of museums, theaters, and organizations as well as by Greens vegetarian restaurant, which affords views of the Golden Gate Bridge (see chapter 6, "Dining," for more information). For information about Fort Mason events, call ☎ 415/441-5706. The park headquarters is also at Fort Mason.

Farther west along the bay at the northern end of Laguna Street is Marina Green, a favorite local spot for kite-flying, jogging, and walking along the Promenade. The St. Francis Yacht Club is also located here.

From here begins the 3½-mile paved Golden Gate Promenade, San Francisco's best and most scenic biking, jogging, and walking path, which runs along the shore past Crissy Field (be sure to stop and watch the gonzo windsurfers) and ends at Fort Point under the Golden Gate Bridge.

Fort Point (☎ 415/556-1693) was built in 1853 to protect the narrow entrance to the harbor. It was designed to house 500 soldiers manning 126 muzzle-loading cannons. By 1900, the fort's soldiers and obsolete guns had been removed, but the formidable brick edifice still remains. Fort Point is open Wednesday to Sunday from 10am to 5pm, and guided tours and cannon demonstrations are given at the site once or twice daily, depending on the time of year.

Lincoln Boulevard sweeps around the western edge of the bay to Baker Beach, where the waves roll ashore—a fine spot for sunbathing, walking, or fishing. Hikers can follow the Coastal Trail from Fort Point along this part of the coastline all the way to Lands End.

A short distance from Baker, China Beach is a small cove where swimming is permitted. Changing rooms, showers, a sundeck, and rest rooms are available.

A little farther around the coast appears Lands End looking out to Pyramid Rock. A lower and an upper trail provide a hiking opportunity amid windswept cypresses and pines on the cliffs above the Pacific.

Still farther along the coast lies Point Lobos, the Sutro Baths, and the Cliff House. The latter has been serving refreshments to visitors since 1863 and providing views of Seal Rocks, home to a colony of sea lions and many marine birds. There's an **information center** here (open daily from 10am to 5pm; ☎ 415/556-8642) as well as the incredible Musée Mecanique, an authentic old-fashioned arcade with 150 coin-operated amusement machines. Only traces of the Sutro Baths remain today to the northeast of the Cliff House. This swimming facility was a major summer attraction that could accommodate up to 24,000 people before it burned down in 1966.

A little farther inland at the western end of California Street is Lincoln Park, which contains a golf course and the spectacular Palace of the Legion of Honor museum.

At the southern end of Ocean Beach, 4 miles down the coast, is another area of the park around Fort Funston where there's an easy loop trail across the cliffs (**visitor center:** ☎ 415/239-2366). Here, too, you can watch the hang gliders taking advantage of the high cliffs and strong winds.

Farther south along route 280, Sweeney Ridge, which can only be reached by car, affords sweeping views of the coastline from the many trails that crisscross this 1,000 acres of land. It was from here that the expedition led by Don Gaspar de Portolá first saw San Francisco Bay in 1769. It's located in Pacifica and can be reached via Sneath Lane off Route 35 (Skyline Boulevard) in San Bruno.

The GGNRA also extends into Marin County, where it encompasses the Marin Headlands, Muir Woods National Monument, and the Olema Valley behind the Point Reyes National Seashore. See chapter 12 for information on these areas.

6 Churches & Religious Buildings

Some of San Francisco's churches and religious buildings are worth checking out.

✪ **Glide Memorial United Methodist Church.** 330 Ellis St. (west of Union Sq.). ☎ 415/771-6300. Services held Sun at 9 and 11am. Muni Metro: Powell. Bus: 37.

There would be nothing special about this Tenderloin-area church if it weren't for its exhilarating pastor, Cecil Williams. Reverend Williams's enthusiastic and uplifting preaching and singing with homeless and poor people of the neighborhood has attracted nationwide fame. In 1994, during the pastor's 30th-anniversary celebration, singers Angela Bofill and Bobby McFerrin joined with comedian Robin Williams, author Maya Angelou, and talk-show queen Oprah Winfrey to honor him publicly. Williams's nondogmatic, fun Sunday services attract a diverse audience that crosses all socioeconomic boundaries. Go for an uplifting experience.

Grace Cathedral. California St. (between Taylor and Jones sts.). ☎ **415/749-6300.**

Although this Nob Hill cathedral, designed by architect Lewis P. Hobart, looks like it is made of stone, it is in fact constructed of reinforced concrete, beaten to achieve a stonelike effect. Construction began for this cathedral on the site of the Crocker mansion in 1928, but it was not completed until 1964. Among the more interesting features of the building are its stained-glass windows, particularly those by the French Loire studios, depicting such modern figures as Thurgood Marshall, Robert Frost, and Albert Einstein; the replicas of Ghiberti's bronze *Doors of Paradise* at the east end; the series of religious frescoes completed in the 1940s by Polish artist John de Rosen; and the 44-bell carillon.

✪ Mission Dolores. 16th St. (at Dolores St.). ☎ **415/621-8203.** Admission $2 adults, $1 children 5–12. May–Oct daily 9am–4:30pm; Nov–Apr daily 9am–4pm; Good Friday 10am–noon. Closed Thanksgiving Day and Christmas Day. Muni Metro: J to the corner of Church and 16th sts. Bus: 22.

San Francisco's oldest standing structure, the Mission San Francisco de Assisi (a.k.a. Mission Dolores) has withstood the test of time, as well as two major earthquakes, relatively intact. In 1776, at the behest of Franciscan Missionary Junípero Serra, Father Francisco Palou came to the Bay Area to found the sixth in a series of missions that dotted the California coastline. From these humble beginnings grew what was to become the city of San Francisco. The mission's small, simple chapel, built solidly by Native Americans who were converted to Christianity, is a curious mixture of native construction methods and Spanish-colonial style. A statue of Father Serra stands in the mission garden, although the portrait looks somewhat more contemplative, and less energetic, than he must have been in real life. An audio tour is available, too, which lasts 45 minutes and costs $5 for adults, $4 for children, and is available during open hours.

7 Architectural Highlights

MUST-SEES FOR ARCHITECTURE BUFFS

ALAMO SQUARE HISTORIC DISTRICT   San Francisco's collection of Victorian houses, known as "Painted Ladies," is one of the city's most famous assets. Most of the 14,000 extant structures date from the second half of the 19th century and are private residences. Spread throughout the city, many have been beautifully restored and ornately painted. The small area bordered by Divisadero Street on the west, Golden Gate Avenue on the north, Webster Street on the east, and Fell Street on the south—about 10 blocks west of the Civic Center—has one of the city's greatest concentrations of these Painted Ladies. One of the most famous views of San Francisco—seen on postcards and posters all around the city—depicts sharp-edged Financial District skyscrapers behind a row of Victorians. This fantastic juxtaposition can be seen from Alamo Square, in the center of this historic district, at Fulton and Steiner streets.

CITY HALL & CIVIC CENTER   Built in 1881 to a design by Brown and Bakewell, it is part of this "City Beautiful" complex done in the beaux arts style. The dome rises to a height of 308 feet on the exterior and is ornamented with occuli and topped by a lantern. The interior rotunda soars 112 feet and is finished in oak, marble, and limestone with a monumental marble staircase leading to the second floor, but you won't be able to see it; City Hall is currently closed for a complete renovation and isn't expected to reopen for a few years.

The Civic Center

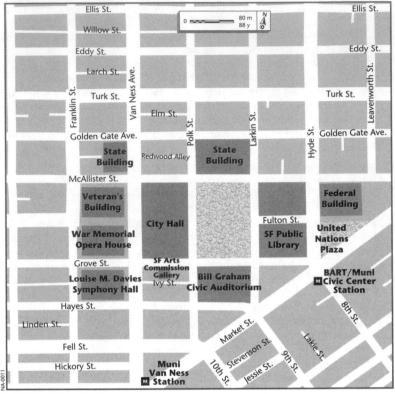

⭐ **YERBA BUENA GARDENS** Between Mission and Howard streets at Third Street, the Yerba Buena Center (☎ 415/978-2787), which opened in 1993 adjacent to the Moscone Convention Center, is the city's new cultural facility, similar to New York's Lincoln Center. It stands on top of the northern extension of the underground Moscone Convention Center. The Center for the Arts presents music, theater, dance, and visual arts. It consists of two buildings, a 755-seat theater designed by James Stewart Polshek, and the Galleries and Arts Forum designed by Fumihiko Maki, which features three galleries and a space designed specially for dance. The complex also includes a 5-acre garden featuring several artworks. The most dramatic outdoor art piece is an emotional mixed-media memorial to Martin Luther King, Jr. Created by sculptor Houston Conwill, poet Estella Majozo, and architect Joseph de Pace, it features 12 glass panels, each inscribed with quotations from King, sheltered behind a 50-foot-high waterfall. The new children's addition, called Zeum, (☎ 415/777-2800) includes a cafe, interactive cultural center, a 1906 historic carousel, interactive play and learning garden, and movie theaters. Also in the Yerba Buena Center is a bowling alley, child-care center, an ice-skating rink, and an IMAX theater. As part of the plan to develop this area as the city's cultural hub, the California Historical Society opened at 678 Mission in late 1995 and the Mexican Museum will relocate in the area in 2000. For recorded information and tickets, call ☎ 415/978-ARTS.

Take the Muni Metro to Powell or Montgomery, or the 30, 45, or 9X bus.

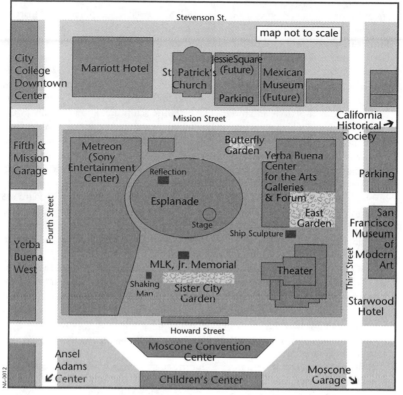

Yerba Buena Gardens

map not to scale

Stevenson St.

City College Downtown Center

Marriott Hotel

St. Patrick's Church

JessieSquare (Future)

Parking

Mexican Museum (Future)

California Historical → Society

Mission Street

Fifth & Mission Garage

Metreon (Sony Entertainment Center)

Reflection

Butterfly Garden

Yerba Buena Center for the Arts Galleries & Forum

Parking

Esplanade

Stage

East Garden

San Francisco Museum of Modern Art

Fourth Street

Ship Sculpture

Third Street

Yerba Buena West

MLK, Jr. Memorial

Shaking Man

Sister City Garden

Theater

Starwood Hotel

Howard Street

Ansel Adams ↙ Center

Moscone Convention Center

Children's Center

Moscone Garage ↘

NG-3012

OTHER ARCHITECTURAL HIGHLIGHTS

San Francisco is a center of many architecturally striking sights. This section concentrates on a few highlights.

Around Union Square and the Financial District is the now-closed **Circle Gallery** at 140 Maiden Lane. (Hopefully another business will have opened in the space by the time you get there so you can tour the interior.) It's the only building in the city designed by Frank Lloyd Wright (in 1948) and was the prototype for the seashell-shaped circular gallery space of the Guggenheim, even though it was meant to serve as a retail space for V. C. Morris, a purveyor of glass and crystal. Note the arresting exterior, a solid wall with a circular entryway to the left. Maiden Lane is just off Union Square between Geary and Post.

The **Hallidie Building,** at 130–150 Sutter St., which was designed by Willis Polk in 1917, is an ideal example of a glass-curtain building. The vast glass facade is miraculously suspended between the two cast-iron cornices. The fire escapes that course down each side of the building complete the prosceniumlike theatrical effect.

The **Medical Dental Building,** at 450 Sutter St., is a steel-frame structure beautifully clad in terra-cotta. It was designed by Miller and Pflueger in 1929. The entrance and the window frames are elaborately ornamented with Mayan relief work; the lobby ceiling is similarly decorated with additional gilding. Note the ornate elevators, too.

Two prominent pieces of San Francisco's skyline are in the Financial District. The **TransAmerica Pyramid,** at 600 Montgomery St. between Clay and Washington streets, is one of the tallest structures in San Francisco. This corporate headquarters was completed in 1972, stands 48 stories tall, and is capped by a 212-foot spire. The former **Bank of America World Headquarters,** at 555 California St., was designed by Wurster, Bernardi, and Emmons in conjunction with Skidmore, Owings, and Merrill. This carnelian-marble–covered building dates from 1969. Its 52 stories are topped by a panoramic restaurant and bar, the Carnelian Room (see chapter 10, "San Francisco After Dark," for complete information). The focal point of the building's formal plaza is an abstract black granite sculpture, known locally as the "Banker's Heart," which was designed by Japanese architect Masayuki Nagare.

At the foot of Market Street you will find the **Ferry Building.** Built between 1895 and 1903, it served as the city's major transportation hub before the Golden Gate and Bay bridges were built, and some 170 ferries docked here daily unloading Bay Area commuters until the 1930s. The tower that soars above the building was inspired by the Campanile of Venice and the Cathedral Tower in Seville. Plans are afoot to restore the building to its former glory, opening up the soaring galleries to the sky again. If you stop by the Ferry Building, you might also want to go to **Rincon Center,** at 99 Mission St. to see the WPA murals painted by the Russian artist Refregier in the post office that is located here.

Several important buildings can be found on or near Nob Hill. The **Flood Mansion,** at 1000 California St. at Mason Street, was built between 1885 and 1886 for James Clair Flood, who, thanks to the Comstock Lode, rose from being a bartender to being one of the city's wealthiest men. He established the Nevada bank that later merged with Wells Fargo. The house cost $1.5 million; the fence alone cost $30,000. It was designed by Augustus Laver and modified by Willis Polk after the earthquake to accommodate the Pacific Union Club.

Built by George Applegarth in 1913 for the sugar magnate Adolph Spreckels, the **Spreckels Mansion,** at 2080 Washington St., is currently home to romance novelist Danielle Steele (don't even try to get in to see her!). The extraordinary building has rounded-arch French doors on the first and second floors and curved balconies on the second floor. Inside, the original featured an indoor pool in the basement, Adamesque fireplaces, and a circular Pompeian room with fountain.

Finally, one of San Francisco's most ingenious architectural accomplishments is the **San Francisco–Oakland Bay Bridge.** Although it's visually less appealing than the nearby Golden Gate Bridge, the Bay Bridge is in many ways more spectacular. The silvery giant that links San Francisco with Oakland is 8¼ miles long and is one of the world's longest steel bridges. It opened in 1936, 6 months before the Golden Gate. Each of its two decks contains five automobile lanes. The Bay Bridge is not a single bridge at all but a superbly dovetailed series of spans joined in midbay, at Yerba Buena Island, by one of the world's largest (in diameter) tunnels. To the west of Yerba Buena, the bridge is really two separate suspension bridges, joined at a central anchorage. East of the island is a 1,400-foot cantilever span, followed by a succession of truss bridges. And it looks even more complex than it sounds. You can drive across the bridge (the toll is $2, paid westbound), or you can catch a bus at the Transbay Terminal (Mission at First Street) and ride to downtown Oakland.

8 Especially for Kids

The following San Francisco attractions have major appeal to kids of all ages:

- Alcatraz Island (see p. 154)
- Cable cars (see p. 155)
- Cable Car Barn Museum (see p. 162)

- California Academy of Sciences, including Steinhart Aquarium (see p. 171)
- The Exploratorium (see p. 163)
- Golden Gate Bridge (see p. 161)
- Golden Gate Park (including the Children's Playground, Bison Paddock, and Japanese Tea Garden) (see above and p. 170)
- National Maritime Museum and the historic ships anchored at Hyde Pier (see p. 165)
- The San Francisco Zoo (see p. 175)

In addition to the sights listed above, the following attractions are of particular interest to kids:

CHILDREN'S PLAYGROUNDS
One of the most enormous and fun playgrounds for kids is in Golden Gate Park. In addition, there are several others. The **Cow Hollow Playground,** on Baker Street between Greenwich and Filbert streets, is surrounded by apartment buildings on three of four sides. This landscaped playground features a bilevel play area fitted with well-conceived, colorful play structures including a tunnel, slides, swings, and a miniature cable car. **Huntington Park,** on Taylor Street, between Sacramento and California streets, sits atop Nob Hill. This tiny play area contains several small play structures that are particularly well suited to children under 5. **Julius Kahn Playground,** on West Pacific Avenue at Spruce Street, is a popular playground situated inside San Francisco's great Presidio park. Larger play structures and forested surroundings make this ground attractive to children and adults alike.

9 Self-Guided & Organized Tours

THE 49-MILE SCENIC DRIVE
The self-guided, 49-mile drive is one easy way to orient yourself and to grasp the beauty of San Francisco and its extraordinary location. Beginning in the city, it follows a rough circle around the bay and passes virtually all the best-known sights from Chinatown to the Golden Gate Bridge, Ocean Beach, Seal Rocks, Golden Gate Park, and Twin Peaks. Originally designed for the benefit of visitors to San Francisco's 1939 and 1940 Golden Gate International Exposition, the route is marked with blue-and-white seagull signs. Although it makes an excellent half-day tour, this miniexcursion can easily take longer if you decide, for example, to stop to walk across the Golden Gate Bridge or to have tea in Golden Gate Park's Japanese Tea Garden.

The San Francisco **Visitor Information Center,** at Powell and Market streets (see "Visitor Information" in chapter 4), distributes free route maps. Since a few of the Scenic Drive marker signs are missing, the map will come in handy. Try to avoid the downtown area during the weekday rush hours from 7 to 9am and 4 to 6pm.

A BART TOUR
One of the world's best commuter systems, **Bay Area Rapid Transit (BART)** runs along 71 miles of rail, linking eight San Francisco stations with Daly City to the south and 25 stations in the East Bay. Under the bay, BART runs through one of the longest underwater transit tubes in the world. This link opened in September 1974, 2 years behind schedule and 6 months after the general manager resigned under fire. The train cars are 70 feet long and are designed to represent the last word in public transport luxury. Twenty years later they no longer seem futuristic, but they're still attractively modern, with carpeted floors, tinted picture windows,

automatic air-conditioning, and recessed lighting. The trains can hit a top speed of 80 miles per hour; a computerized control system monitors and adjusts their speed.

The people who run BART think so highly of their trains and stations that they sell a $3.80 **"Excursion Ticket,"** which allows you, in effect, to "sightsee" the BART system. Tour the entire system as much as you like for up to 3 hours as long as you exit from the same station you entered (if you get out anywhere along the line, the fare gate will instantly compute the normal fare). For more information call ☎ **650/992-BART** (2278).

BOAT TOURS

One of the best ways to look at San Francisco is from a boat bobbing on the bay. There are several cruises to choose from, many of which start from Fisherman's Wharf. There is now only one major company.

Blue & Gold Fleet, at Pier 39, Fisherman's Wharf (☎ **415/773-1188**), tours the bay year-round in a sleek, 400-passenger sightseeing boat, complete with food and beverage facilities. The fully narrated, 1¼-hour cruise passes beneath the Golden Gate and Bay bridges, and comes within yards of Alcatraz Island. Frequent daily departures from Pier 39's West Marina begin at 10am during summer and 11am in winter. Tickets cost $16 for adults, $12 for juniors 5 to 17 and seniors over 62, $8 for children 5 to 11, and children under 5 sail free.

BUS TOURS

Gray Line, with offices in the Transbay Terminal, First and Mission streets, Pier 39, and Union Square (☎ **800/826-0202** or 415/558-9400), is San Francisco's largest bus-tour operator. They offer several itineraries on a daily basis. There is a free pickup and return service between centrally located hotels and departure locations. Reservations are required for most tours, which are available in several foreign languages including French, German, Spanish, Italian, Japanese, and Korean.

WALKING TOURS

Javawalk is a 2-hour walking tour by self-described "coffeehouse lizard" Elaine Sosa. As the name suggests, it's loosely a coffee walking tour through North Beach, but there's a lot more going on than drinking cups of brew. Javawalk also serves up a good share of historical and architectural trivia, offering something for everyone. The best part of the tour, however, may be the camaraderie that develops among the tour-goers. Sosa keeps the tour interactive and fun, and it's obvious that she knows a profusion of tales and trivia about the history of coffee and its North Beach roots. It's a guaranteed good time, particularly if you're addicted to caffeine. Javawalk is offered Tuesday to Saturday at 10am. The price is $20 per person, with kids 12 and under at half price. For information and reservations call ☎ **415/673-WALK** (9255).

Cruisin' the Castro (☎ **415/550-8110**) is an informative historical tour of San Francisco's most famous gay quarter and will give you a totally new insight into the contribution of the gay community to the political maturity, growth, and beauty of San Francisco. Tours are personally conducted by Trevor Hailey, who was involved in the development of the Castro in the 1970s. She knew Harvey Milk, the first openly gay politician elected to office in the United States. You'll learn about Milk's rise from shopkeeper to city supervisor and visit Harvey Milk Plaza, where most marches, rallies, and protests begin. In addition, you'll explore the Names Project visitors center, Castro Theatre, and side streets lined with beautifully restored Victorians, as well as the plethora of community-oriented stores on the Castro—gift

The Names Project AIDS Memorial Quilt

The Names Project began in 1987 as a memorial for people who have died from AIDS. The idea was to direct grief into positive action and help the world understand the devastating impact of AIDS. Sewing machines and fabric were acquired, and the public was invited to make coffin-sized panels for a giant memorial quilt. More than 40,000 individual panels now commemorate the lives of those who have died of complications related to AIDS. Each has been uniquely designed and sewn by the victims' friends, lovers, and family members.

The AIDS Memorial Quilt, which would cover 24 football fields if laid out end to end, was first displayed on the Capitol Mall in Washington, D.C., during a 1987 national march on Washington for lesbian and gay rights. Although sections of the quilt are often on tour throughout the world, portions of the largest community art project in the world are on display at **The Names Project AIDS Memorial Quilt Visitors Center & Panelmaking Workshop,** 2362-A Market St. (☎ **415/863-1966**). The center is open Thursday to Tuesday from noon to 7pm and Wednesday from noon to 10pm. To get there, take the Muni Metro K, L, or M line to the Castro Street station, or the F line to Church and Market streets; bus no. 24, 33, or 35 will also get you there. A sewing machine and fabrics, along with assistance from trained volunteers, are available for those interested in making a quilt panel for someone lost to AIDS.

shops, bookstores, restaurants, jewelers—whose owners Hailey knows personally. Tours are conducted Tuesday to Saturday from 10am to 1:45pm, and begin at Harvey Milk Plaza, atop the Castro Street Muni station. The cost includes lunch at Caffè Luna Piena (see page 000 in chapter 6, "Dining," for a complete review). Reservations are required. The tour, with lunch, costs $35 for adults, $30 for seniors 62 and over, and children's prices are negotiable.

The **Haight-Ashbury Flower Power Walking Tour** (☎ 415/863-1621) is for you if Woodstock 2 made you nostalgic for the 1960s or if you want to tour the hippie haunts with Pam and Bruce Brennan and revisit in 3 short hours the Grateful Dead's crash pad, Janis Joplin's house, and other reminders of the Summer of Love. Tours begin at 9:30am Tuesday and Saturday. The cost is $15 per person. Reservations are required.

San Francisco's Chinatown is always fascinating, but for many visitors with limited time it's hard to know where to search out the "nontouristy" shops, restaurants, and historical spots in this microcosm of Chinese culture. **Wok Wiz Chinatown Walking Tours & Cooking Center** (654 Commercial St. between Kearny and Montgomery streets; ☎ **800/281-9255** or 415/981-8989), founded 13 years ago by author, TV personality, cooking instructor, and restaurant critic Shirley Fong-Torres, is the answer. The Wok Wiz tours take you into nooks and crannies not usually seen by tourists. Most of her guides are Chinese, speak fluent Cantonese or Mandarin, and are intimately acquainted with all of Chinatown's alleys and small enterprises, as well as Chinatown's history, folklore, culture, and food.

Tours are conducted daily from 10am to 1:30pm and include dim sum (Chinese lunch). There's also a less expensive tour that does not include lunch. It's an easy walk, fun and fascinating, and you're bound to make new friends. Groups are generally held to a maximum of 12, and reservations are essential. Prices (including lunch) are $37 for adults, $35 for seniors 60 and older, and $30 for children under 12.

Shirley Fong-Torres also operates an **I Can't Believe I Ate My Way Through Chinatown** tour that starts with a Chinese breakfast in a noodle house, moves to a wok shop, and then makes further stops for nibbles at a vegetarian restaurant, rice-noodle factory, and a supermarket before taking a break for a sumptuous luncheon (most Saturdays; $65 per person), as well as a **Walk & Wok** tour that includes shopping for food in Chinatown, then cooking (and eating) it together at Shirley's Cooking Center (most Saturdays; $75 per person).

10 Staying Active

Half the fun in San Francisco takes place outdoors. If you're not in the mood to trek it, there are other things to do that will allow you to enjoy the surroundings.

BALLOONING

Though it'll take you a 1-hour drive to get there, more than a dozen hot-air ballooning companies will take you up for a silent flight over the Wine Country. These are two solid choices.

Adventures Aloft. P.O. Box 2500, Vintage 1870, Yountville, CA 94599. ☎ **800/944-4408** or 707/944-4408. Fee $185 per person. Flights daily 6–8am (weather permitting).

The Napa Valley's oldest hot-air balloon company is staffed with full-time professional pilots. Groups are small, and the flight will last about an hour. The cost of $185 per person includes a postadventure champagne brunch, and a framed "first-flight" certificate.

Calistoga Balloon Company. P.O. Box 795, Calistoga, CA 94515. ☎ **707/942-6546.** Fee $165 per person. Flights daily.

The 1-hour balloon flight costs $165 per person and includes a flight certificate and a champagne brunch afterward.

BEACHES

For beach information call ☎ 415/391-2000. Most days it's too chilly to hang out at the beach. But when the fog evaporates and the wind dies down, one of the best ways to spend the day is ocean-side in the city. On any truly hot day, thousands flock to worship the sun, build sand castles, and throw the ball around. Without a wet suit, swimming is a fiercely cold endeavor and there are only two beaches that are considered safe for swimming: **Aquatic Park** is adjacent to the Hyde Park Pier, and **China Beach** is a small cove on the western edge of the South Bay. But dip at your own risk—there are never lifeguards on duty.

Also on the South Bay, **Baker Beach** is ideal for picnicking, sunning, walking, or fishing against the backdrop of the Golden Gate.

Ocean Beach, at the end of Golden Gate Park, on the westernmost side of the city, is San Francisco's largest beach—4 miles long. Just offshore, at the northern end of the beach in front of Cliff House, are the jagged Seal Rocks inhabited by various shore birds and a large colony of barking sea lions (bring binoculars for a close-up view). To the left, Kelly's Cove is one of the more challenging surf spots in town. Ocean Beach is ideal for strolling or sunning, but don't swim here—tides are tricky, and each year bathers drown in the rough surf.

Stop by Ocean Beach bus terminal at the corner of Cabrillo and La Playa to learn about San Francisco's playful history in local artist Ray Beldner's whimsically historical sculpture garden. Then hike up the hill to explore the Cliff House and the ruins of Sutro Baths. These baths, able to accommodate 24,000 bathers, were lost to fire in 1966.

OTHER MUNICIPAL PARKS

In addition to **Golden Gate Park** and the **Golden Gate National Recreation Area** discussed above, San Francisco boasts more than 2,000 additional acres of parkland, most of which is perfect for picnicking or throwing around a Frisbee.

Smaller city parks include: **Buena Vista Park** (Haight Street between Baker and Central streets), which affords fine views of the Golden Gate and is also a favored lounging ground for gay lovers; **Ina Coolbrith Park** (Taylor Street between Vallejo and Green streets), offering views of the Bay Bridge and Alcatraz; and **Sigmund Stern Grove** (at 19th Avenue and Sloat Boulevard) in the Sunset District, which is the site of the famous free summer music festival.

One of our personal favorites is **Lincoln Park,** a 270-acre green on the northwestern side of the city at Clement Street and 34th Avenue. The California Palace of the Legion of Honor is here (see "Museums," above), as is a scenic 18-hole municipal golf course (see "Staying Active," below). But the best things about this park are the 200-foot cliffs that overlook the Golden Gate Bridge and San Francisco Bay. To get to the park, take bus no. 38 from Union Square to 33rd and Geary streets, then walk a few blocks to the park.

ACTIVITIES

BICYCLING   Two city-designated bike routes are maintained by the Parks and Recreations department. One winds 7½ miles through Golden Gate Park to Lake Merced; the other traverses the city, starting in the south, and follows a route over the Golden Gate Bridge. These routes are not dedicated to bicyclists, and caution must be exercised to avoid crashing into pedestrians. Helmets are recommended for adults, and required by law for kids under 18. A bike map is available from the San Francisco Visitor Information Center, at Powell and Mason streets (see "Visitor Information" in chapter 4), and from bicycle shops all around town.

Ocean Beach has a public walk- and bikeway that stretches along 5 waterfront blocks of the Great Highway between Noriega and Santiago streets. It's an easy ride from Cliff House or Golden Gate Park.

Park Cyclery, at 1749 Waller St. (☎ **415/751-7368**), is a shop in the Haight that rent bikes. Located next to Golden Gate Park, the cyclery rents mountain bikes exclusively, along with helmets. The charge is $5 per hour, $25 per day, and it's open Friday to Wednesday from 10am to 6pm.

BOATING   At the **Golden Gate Park Boat House** (☎ 415/752-0347) on Stow Lake, the park's largest body of water, you can rent a rowboat or pedal boat by the hour and steer over to Strawberry Hill, a large, round island in the middle of the lake, for lunch. There's usually a line on weekends. The boat house is open daily, June through September from 9am to 5pm, and the rest of the year daily from 9am to 4pm.

Cass Marina, 1702 Bridgeway, in Sausalito (☎ **800/472-4595** or 415/332-6789), rents sailboats measuring 22 to 101 feet. Sail under the Golden Gate Bridge on your own or with a licensed skipper. In addition, large sailing yachts leave from San Francisco and Sausalito on a regularly scheduled basis. Call for schedules, prices, and availability of sailboats or check them out on the Web at **cassmarina.com**. The marina is open daily from 9am to sunset.

CITY STAIR-CLIMBING   Many U.S. health clubs now have stair-climbing machines and step classes, but in San Francisco, you need only to go outside. The following city stair climbs will provide you not only with a good workout, but with great sightseeing too.

Filbert Street Steps, between Sansome Street and Telegraph Hill, are a particular challenge. Scaling the sheer eastern face of Telegraph Hill, this 377-step climb wends its way through verdant flower gardens and charming 19th-century cottages. Napier Lane, a narrow wooden plank walkway, leads to Montgomery Street. Turn right, and follow the path to the end of the cul-de-sac where another stairway continues to Telegraph's panoramic summit.

The **Lyon Street Steps,** between Green Street and Broadway, were built in 1916. This historic stairway street contains four steep sets of stairs totaling 288 steps in all. Begin at Green Street and climb all the way up, past manicured hedges and flower gardens, to an iron gate that opens into the Presidio. A block east, on Baker Street, another set of 369 steps descends to Green Street.

CROQUET   The San Francisco Croquet Club (☎ 415/776-4104) offers free public lessons from 10am to 1pm on the 1st Saturday of each month (or anytime by reservation for parties of four or more). The game is taught according to international six-wicket rules at the croquet lawns in Stern Grove, at 19th Avenue and Wawona Street.

FISHING   New Easy Rider Sport Fishing, at 225 University Ave. in Berkeley (☎ 415/285-2000), makes daily trips from Fisherman's Wharf for ling cod, rock fish, and many other types of game fish all year round, as well as salmon runs from June through October. Fishing equipment is available; the cost of $55 per person includes bait. Reservations are required, as are licenses for adults (1-day licenses can be purchased before departure). Departures are daily at 6am, returning at 4pm. Fish are cleaned, filleted, and bagged on the return trip for a small fee.

GOLF   San Francisco has a few beautiful golf courses. At press time, one of the most lavish, the **Presidio Golf Course (☎ 415/561-4664),** had just opened up to the public for the first time (greens fees $35 Mon to Thurs, $45 Fri, and $55 Sat–Sun.) There are also two decent municipal golf courses in town if you're itching to put on your golf shoes and swing some clubs.

Golden Gate Park Course. 47th Ave. and Fulton St. ☎ **415/751-8987.** Greens fees $10 per person Mon–Fri; $13 Sat–Sun. Daily 6am–dusk.

This small 9-hole course covers 1,357 yards and is par 27. All holes are par 3, tightly set, and well trapped with small greens. The course is a little weathered in spots, but it's a casual, fun, and inexpensive place to tee off local-style.

Lincoln Park Golf Course. 34th Ave. and Clement St. ☎ **415/221-9911.** Greens fees $23 per person Mon–Fri; $27 Sat–Sun. Daily 6:30am–dusk.

San Francisco's prettiest municipal course has terrific views and fairways lined with Monterey cypress trees. Its 18 holes encompass 5,081 yards, for a par 68, and the 17th hole has a glistening ocean view. This is the oldest course in the city and one of the oldest in the West.

Mission Bay Golf Center. Sixth St. at Channel St. (from downtown San Francisco, take Fourth St. south to Channel St. and turn right). ☎ **415/431-7888.** Bucket of balls $7. Mon 11:30am–11pm; Tues–Sun 7am–11pm. Last bucket sold at 10pm.

San Francisco's most popular driving range, the Mission Bay Golf Center is an impeccably maintained 7-acre facility that consists of a double-decker steel and concrete arc containing 66 covered practice bays. The grass landing area extends 300 yards, has nine target greens, and is lit for evening use. There's also a putting green, as well as a chipping and bunker practice area.

Work It Out

While San Francisco has plenty to offer in the way of outdoor exercise and activities, there are plenty of indoor places to relieve stress, work up a sweat, or treat your body to a little TLC.

The **San Francisco Bay Club,** located at 150 Greenwich St., at Battery Street (☎ 415/433-2200), is one of the most exclusive and extensive gym-turned-spas in the Bay Area. Celebrities such as Tom Cruise, Cindy Crawford, and Hugh Grant have flexed a few muscles here when on location, and regular members include the city's old and new elite. The club takes up almost a full block and offers three floors filled with health equipment, including two pools (one's heated); tennis, squash, racquetball, and basketball courts; aerobics and yoga; free weights, cardiovascular, and Nautilus equipment; a sundeck, sauna, steam room, and whirlpool; and a cafe. Although walk-in guests are not permitted, sign up for any of the luxurious spa treatments and you're extended full workout privileges for the day. Services include massage, facials, manicures, and pedicures.

A more spiritual workout can be found at **The Mindful Body,** a center for movement, body, and personal inner work. It is located at 2876 California St., between Broderick and Divisadero (☎ 415/931-2639 for class schedules). After an intense yoga or stretch class, guided meditation, or massage, you'll be a new person.

Adventurers can hone their skills at **Mission Cliffs Rock Climbing Center** at 2295 Harrison, at 19th Street (☎ 415/550-0515). For $16, or $8 if you come before 3pm (plus $6 if you need rental equipment), you can climb 14,000 feet of terrain and 2,000 square feet of boulders. Lessons, which cost extra and include children's and outdoor programs, can be arranged. Once you're worn out, relax in the sauna.

If getting your heart rate up seems like a chore, take a less painful approach at the **Metronome,** which offers ballroom, swing, Latin, nightclub, and salsa dance classes for individuals and groups. Call for information on class times, package deals, and weekend dance parties (☎ 415/252-9000).

HANDBALL   The city's best handball courts are in Golden Gate Park, opposite Seventh Avenue, south of Middle Drive East. Courts are available free, on a first-come, first-served basis.

RUNNING   The **Bay to Breakers Foot Race** is an annual 7½-mile run from downtown to Ocean Beach. About 80,000 entrants gather—many dressed in wacky, innovative, and sometimes X-rated costumes for what's considered one of San Francisco's favored trademark events. The event is sponsored by the *San Francisco Examiner* and is held the third Sunday of May. Call ☎ 415/777-7770 for details.

The San Francisco Marathon is held annually in the middle of July. For further information contact **USA Track and Field** (☎ 800/722-3466).

SKATING (Conventional & In-Line)   Although people skate in Golden Gate Park all week long, Sunday is best, when John F. Kennedy Drive between Kezar Drive and Transverse Road is closed to automobiles. A smooth "skate pad" is located on your right, just past the Conservatory. **Skates on Haight,** at 1818 Haight St.

(☎ 415/752-8376), is the best place to rent either in-line or conventional skates, and is located only 1 block from the park. Protective wrist guards and knee pads are included free. The cost is $8 per hour for in-line or "conventional" skates, $28 for all-day use. Major credit card and ID deposit are required. The shop is open Monday to Friday from 10am to 6:30pm, and Saturday and Sunday from 10am to 6pm.

TENNIS   More than 100 courts throughout the city are maintained by the **San Francisco Recreation and Parks Department** (☎ 415/753-7001). All are available free, on a first-come, first-served basis. The exceptions are the 21 courts in Golden Gate Park; a $4-to-$6 fee is charged for their use, and courts must be reserved in advance for weekend play. Call the number above on Wednesday between 7 and 9pm, or on Thursday and Friday from 9am to 5pm. For weekend reservations call ☎ 415/753-7101.

WALKING & HIKING   The **Golden Gate National Recreation Area** offers plenty of opportunities for walking and hiking. One pleasant walk, or bike ride for that matter, is along the Golden Gate Promenade, from Aquatic Park to the Golden Gate Bridge. The 3½-mile paved trail leads along the northern edge of the Presidio, out to Fort Point. You can also hike along the Coastal Trail all the way from near Fort Point to the Cliff House. The park service maintains several other trails in the city. For more information or to pick up a map of the Golden Gate National Recreation Area, stop by the park service headquarters at Fort Mason at the north end of Laguna Street (☎ 415/556-0560).

Though most drive to this spectacular vantage point, a more rejuvenating way to experience Twin Peaks is to walk up from the back roads of U.C. Medical Center (off Parnassus) or from either of the two roads that lead to the top (off Woodside or Clarendon avenues). Early morning is the best time to trek, when the city is quiet, the air is crisp, and the sightseers haven't crowded the parking lot. Keep an eye out for cars, since there's no real hiking trail, and be sure to walk beyond the lot and up to the highest vantage point.

11 Spectator Sports

The Bay Area's sports scene includes several major professional franchises, including football, baseball, and basketball. Check the local newspapers' sports sections for daily listings of local events.

Baseball is represented by the **San Francisco Giants,** who play at 3Com/ Candlestick Park, Giants Drive and Gilman Avenue (☎ 415/467-8000). From April through October, the National League Giants play their home games at Candlestick Park, off U.S. 101 about 8 miles south of downtown. Tickets are usually available up until game time, but seats can be dreadfully far from the action. You can get tickets through **BASS Ticketmaster** (☎ 510/762-2277). Special express bus service is available from Market Street on game days; call **Muni** (☎ 415/673-6864) for pickup points and schedule information. Bring a coat— this 60,000-seat stadium is known for its chilly winds.

The Bay Area's other team is the 1989 world-champion **Oakland Athletics,** who play across the bay at the Oakland Coliseum Complex, at the Hegenberger Road exit from I-880, in Oakland (☎ 510/430-8020). The stadium holds close to 50,000 spectators and is serviced by BART's Coliseum station. Tickets are available from the Coliseum Box Office or by phone through **BASS Ticketmaster** (☎ 510/762-2277).

Pro basketball is represented by the **Golden State Warriors,** who play at the Oakland Coliseum Complex, at the Hegenberger Road exit from I-880, in Oakland (☎ **510/986-2200**). The NBA Warriors play basketball in the 15,025-seat Oakland Coliseum Arena. The season runs from November through April, and most games are played at 7:30pm. Tickets are available at the arena, and by phone through BASS Ticketmaster (☎ **510/762-2277**).

As of 1995, the Bay Area once again plays home to two professional football teams. The **San Francisco 49ers** play at 3Com/Candlestick Park (Giants Drive and Gilman Avenue) (☎ **415/468-2249**). Games are played on Sundays from August through December; kickoff is usually at 1pm. Tickets sell out early in the season, but are available at higher prices through ticket agents beforehand and from scalpers at the gate. Ask your hotel concierge or visit **City Box Office,** 153 Kearny St., Suite 302 (☎ **415/392-4400**). Special express bus service is available from Market Street on game days; call **Muni** (☎ **415/673-6864**) for pickup points and schedule information.

Also back in the Bay Area are the 49ers' archenemy, the **Oakland Raiders.** Their home turf is the Oakland Alameda County Coliseum, off the 880 Freeway (Nimitz) (☎ **800/949-2626** for ticket information).

The **University of California Golden Bears** play in Memorial Stadium at 61 Harmon Gym, University of California, Berkeley (☎ **800/GO-BEARS** or 510/642-3277), on the university campus across the bay. Tickets are usually available at game time. Phone for schedules and information.

Fans can see horse racing at **Golden Gate Fields,** located on Gilman Street, off I-80, in Albany, 10 miles northeast of San Francisco (☎ **510/559-7300**). Scenic thoroughbred races are held here from January through March and from April to the end of June. The park is located on the seashore. Call for admission prices and post times.

The nearest autumn racing takes place at **Bay Meadows,** 2600 S. Delaware St., off U.S. 101, in San Mateo (☎ **650/574-7223**). This thoroughbred and quarter-horse track, on the peninsula about 20 miles south of downtown San Francisco, hosts races 4 or 5 days each week from September through January. Call for admission and post times.

8 City Strolls

Despite a handful of killer hills, San Francisco is a city best explored on foot. In this chapter, you'll find suggestions for introductory walks in two of the many great San Francisco neighborhoods. For more extensive city walks, check out *Frommer's Memorable Walks in San Francisco*.

WALKING TOUR 1
Chinatown: History, Culture, Dim Sum & Then Some

Start: Corner of Grant Avenue and Bush Street.
Public Transportation: 2, 3, 4, 9X, 15, 30, 38, 45 or 76 bus.
Finish: Commercial Street, between Montgomery and Kearny streets.
Time: 2 hours, not including museum or shopping stops.
Best Times: Daylight hours when there's the most action.
Worst Times: Too early or too late because shops will be closed and no one will be milling around.
Hills That Could Kill: None.

This tiny section of San Francisco, bounded loosely by Broadway, Stockton, Kearny, and Bush, is said to harbor one of the largest Chinese populations outside of Asia. Daily proof is the crowds of Chinese residents who shop the plethora of herbal stores, vegetable markets, and Chinese restaurants and businesses. Chinatown also marks the spot where the city began its development in the mid-1800s. Embark on this walk and you'll learn why Chinatown remains intriguing to all who wind its narrow and crowded streets and how its origins are responsible for the town as we know it.

To begin the tour, make your way to the corner of Bush Street and Grant Avenue where you can't miss the:

1. **Chinatown Gateway Arch.** It is traditional in China that villages have ceremonial gates like this one. This gate is a lot less formal than those in China, built here more for the benefit of the tourist industry than anything else.

Once you cross the threshold you'll be at the beginning of Chinatown's portion of:

2. **Grant Avenue,** a.k.a. the mecca for tourists who wander in and out of gift shops that offer a variety of unnecessary junk

Walking Tour—Chinatown

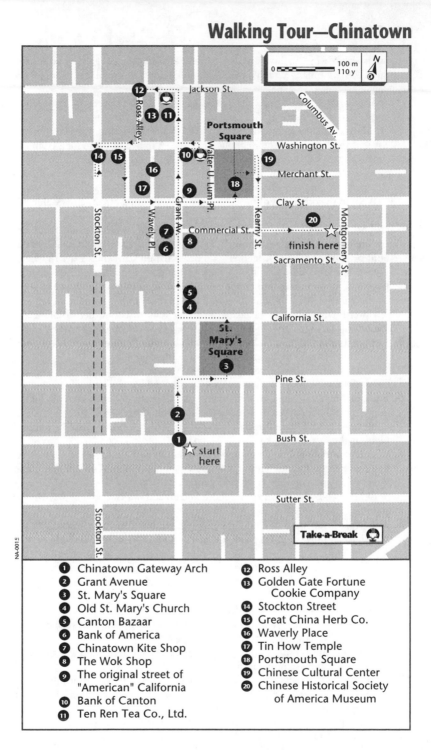

① Chinatown Gateway Arch
② Grant Avenue
③ St. Mary's Square
④ Old St. Mary's Church
⑤ Canton Bazaar
⑥ Bank of America
⑦ Chinatown Kite Shop
⑧ The Wok Shop
⑨ The original street of "American" California
⑩ Bank of Canton
⑪ Ten Ren Tea Co., Ltd.
⑫ Ross Alley
⑬ Golden Gate Fortune Cookie Company
⑭ Stockton Street
⑮ Great China Herb Co.
⑯ Waverly Place
⑰ Tin How Temple
⑱ Portsmouth Square
⑲ Chinese Cultural Center
⑳ Chinese Historical Society of America Museum

interspersed with quality imports, decent restaurants, and grocery stores frequented by Chinese residents ranging from children to the oldest living people you've ever seen.

Tear yourself away from the shops, go right at the corner of Pine Street, crossing to the left side of Pine, and on your left you'll come to:

3. **St. Mary's Square,** where you'll find a huge metal-and-granite statue of Dr. Sun Yat-sen, the founder of the Republic of China. A native of Guandong (Canton) Province, Sun Yat-sen's goal was to overthrow the Qing Dynasty.

   Note also the second monument in the square, which honors Chinese-American victims of both world wars.

   Walk to the other end of the square toward California Street, cross California and you'll be standing in front of:

4. **Old St. Mary's Church.** The first Catholic cathedral in San Francisco and also the site of the Chinese community's first English-language school, St. Mary's was built primarily by Chinese laborers and dedicated on Christmas Day, 1854.

   Step inside to find a written history of the church and turn-of-the-century photos of San Francisco. Stop in on a Tuesday or Thursday at 12:30pm and you'll be privy to the free half-hour classical music performance.

   Upon leaving the church, take a right and walk to the corner of Grant and California, then go right on Grant. Here you'll find a shop called the:

5. **Canton Bazaar,** at 616 Grant Ave. Of the barrage of knickknack and import shops lining Grant Avenue, this is one of the most popular.

   Continue in the same direction on Grant Avenue, cross Sacramento Street and Grant Avenue to arrive at the northwest corner and the doorstep of:

6. **Bank of America,** which is in the traditional Chinese architectural style. Notice dragons subtly portrayed on many parts of the building.

   Heading in the same direction (north) on Grant, a few doors down at 717 Grant is the:

7. **Chinatown Kite Shop.** This store's assortment of flying objects includes attractive fish kites, windsock kites in nylon or cotton, hand-painted Chinese paper kites, wood-and-paper biplanes, and pentagonal kites.

   Other take-home treasures of a more functional kind can be found across the street at:

8. **The Wok Shop** at 804 Grant Ave., where you can purchase just about any utensil, cookbook, or vessel you might need to do Chinese-style cooking in your own kitchen.

   When you come out of the Wok Shop, go right; walk past Commercial Street and you'll arrive at the corner of Grant Avenue and Clay Street; cross Clay and you'll be standing on the:

9. **Original street of "American" California.** Here the first tent was set up by an English seaman named William Richardson in 1835. A plaque between 823 and 837 Grant Ave. commemorates this event.

   Continue north on Grant to Washington Street. Go right, and at 743 Washington you will be standing in front of the:

10. **Bank of Canton,** which boasts the oldest (1909) Asian-style edifice in Chinatown. This three-tiered temple-style building once housed the China Telephone Exchange, known as "China-5" until 1945.

    You're probably getting thirsty by now, so follow Washington a few doors down (east) and on your right-hand side you will come upon:

☕ **TAKE A BREAK**   **Washington Bakery & Restaurant.** No need to actually have a full meal here—the service can be abrupt and the food, mediocre. Do stop in, however, for a little potable adventure: snow red bean with ice cream. The sugary-sweet drink mixed with whole beans and ice cream is not something you're likely to have tried elsewhere and it happens to be quite tasty. Whatever you do, don't fill up—a few sites away some wonderfully fresh dim sum awaits you.

Go back to Grant Avenue, cross Washington and then Grant, and follow the west side of Grant 1 block to no. 949, the location of:

11. Ten Ren Tea Co., Ltd. In this amazing shop you can sample whatever freshly brewed variation they're offering and check out the dozens of drawers and canisters labeled with over 40 varieties of tea.

When departing Ten Ren, take a left, and when you reach Jackson Street, make another left. On the left-hand side at 735 Jackson, through the storefront window you'll notice stacks of steaming wooden baskets manned by a Chinese cook. You've reached your snacking destination.

☕ **TAKE A BREAK**   It's the **House of Dim Sum**—nothing fancy, for sure, but the dumplings are fresh, cheap, and delicious, and the staff is friendly. Order at the counter: pork, chive and shrimp, and shark-fin dumplings; sweet buns; turnip cake; or sweet rice with chicken wrapped in a lotus leaf. Unless they're taken, it's best to sit at one of the two tables to enjoy your feast.

As you leave the House, turn left up the hill and make another left on:

12. Ross Alley. As you walk along the narrow street, it's not difficult to imagine that this block was once rife with gambling dens.

As you follow the alley south, on the left-hand side of the street you'll encounter:

13. Golden Gate Fortune Cookie Company, at 56 Ross St. It's just a tiny place where one woman sits at a conveyer belt, folding messages into warm cookies as the manager calls out to tourists to buy a big bag of the fortune-telling treats.

Over the years as more and more tourists stop by, the company has become less and less gracious: They'll let you watch for about 5 seconds before they pressure you to buy a bag.

As you exit the alley, take a right on Washington and follow it up to:

14. Stockton Street. From Broadway to Sacramento Street, Stockton is where most of the residents of Chinatown do their daily shopping.

A good stop if you're in the market for some jewelry is at Jade Galore (1000 Stockton St. at the corner of Stockton and Washington streets).

You might want to wander up Stockton Street to absorb the atmosphere and street life of this less-tourist-oriented Chinese community before doubling back to Washington Street.

Once back at Stockton and Washington, turn left down Washington and head back toward Grant Avenue. On the right side of the street you will stumble upon the:

15. Great China Herb Co. at 857 Washington (Stockton and Grant). Chinese and holistic Westerners come to shops like this one—full of exotic herbs, roots, and other natural substances—to buy what they believe cures all types of ailments and ensures good health and long life. Thankfully, unlike many similar shops in the area, owners Mr. and Mrs. Ho speak English, so you will not be met with a blank stare as you inquire what exactly is in each box, bag, or jar arranged along dozens of shelves.

Continue back toward Grant Avenue, and take a right on:

16. Waverly Place, or "The Street of Painted Balconies." This is probably Chinatown's most popular side street or alleyway because of its painted balconies and colorful architectural details—a sort of Chinese-style New Orleans street.

Most buildings aren't open to the public, but one temple you can visit (but make sure it's open before you go climbing up the long narrow stairway) is the:

17. Tin How Temple, at 125 Waverly Place. Accessible via a narrow stairway four floors up, this incense-laden sanctuary decorated in traditional black, red, and gold lacquered wood is a house of worship. Chinese Buddhists come here to pray, meditate, and send offerings to their ancestors and to Tin How, the Queen of the Heavens and Goddess of the Seven Seas. When you visit, try to be as unobtrusive as possible. It is customary to give a donation or buy a bundle of incense during your visit.

Once you've finished exploring Waverly Place, walk down Clay Street past Grant Avenue and continue until you come upon the block-wide urban playground that is also the most important site in San Francisco's history:

18. Portsmouth Square. This very spot was the center of the region's first township, which was called Yerba Buena before it was renamed San Francisco in 1847.

Around 1846, before any semblance of a city had taken shape, this plaza was at the foot of the eastern shoreline of the bay. There were less than 50 non-Indian residents, no substantial buildings to speak of, and the few boats that pulled into the cove did so less than a block from where you're standing.

In 1846 when California was claimed as American territory, the marines who landed here named the square after their ship, the USS *Portsmouth.* (Today there's a bronze plaque that marks the spot where they raised the American flag.)

Yerba Buena briefly remained a modest township until the gold rush of 1849. Immediately following the rush the population would grow from under 1,000 to over 19,000 as gold-seekers from around the world made their way here.

When the square became crowded, long wharves were constructed to support new buildings above the bay. Eventually, the entire area would become landfill.

That was almost 150 years ago, but today the square still serves as an important meeting place for neighborhood Chinese—a sort of communal outdoor living room. Some practice tai chi here in the early morning; children play and elderly men gamble over Chinese cards.

It is said that Robert Louis Stevenson also used to love to sit on a bench here and watch life going on all around him. (You'll find a monument to his memory at the northeast corner of the square.)

Exit to the east, at Kearny Street. Directly across the street, at 750 Kearny, is the Holiday Inn. Cross the street, enter the hotel, and take the elevator to the third floor where you'll find the:

19. Chinese Cultural Center, which is oriented toward both the community and tourists, offering lectures, films, and seminars; there are also interesting display cases housing Chinese art and a gallery with rotating exhibits of Asian art and writing.

When you leave the Holiday Inn, take a left on Kearny and go 3 short blocks to Commercial Street. Halfway down this street on the left is the:

20. Chinese Historical Society of America Museum, founded in 1963. Head downstairs to this basement-cum-museum and you'll find a small but fascinating collection that illuminates the role of Chinese immigrants in American history, particularly in San Francisco and the rest of California.

Admission is free, but the museum appreciates any donation you can give. It's open from about noon to 4pm Tuesday to Saturday. The curator sometimes closes early if there are no visitors, so get there well before 4pm if you want to visit.

WALKING TOUR 2
Noshing through North Beach

Start: Intersection of Montgomery Street, Columbus Avenue, and Washington Street.

Public Transportation: 15, 30X, 41 or 42 bus as near as you can get to the intersection of Montgomery Street, Columbus Avenue, and Washington Street.

Finish: Washington Square.

Time: 3 hours, including a stop for lunch.

Best Times: Start the tour Monday to Saturday anytime between 11am and 4pm.

Worst Times: Sunday when shops are closed.

Hills That Could Kill: The Montgomery Street hill that runs from Broadway to Vallejo Street; otherwise, this is a very easy walk.

Along with Chinatown, North Beach is one of the city's oldest neighborhoods. Originally the city's Latin Quarter, it became the city's Italian Quarter when Italian immigrants moved "uphill" in the early 1870s, crossing Broadway from the Jackson Square area and settling in. They quickly set up restaurants, cafes, bakeries, and other businesses familiar to them from their homeland. The "beat generation" helped put North Beach on the map, with the likes of Jack Kerouac and Allen Ginsberg holding court in the area's cafes during the 1950s. Although most of the original beat poets are gone, their spirit lives on in North Beach, which is still a haven for bohemian artists and writers. The neighborhood, thankfully, still retains the Italian village feel, where residents from all walks of life enjoy taking time for conversation over a pastry and a frothy cappuccino.

If there's one landmark you can't miss, it's the familiar looking building on the corner of Montgomery Street and Columbus Avenue, the:

1. TransAmerica Pyramid. Noted for its spire (which rises 212 ft. above the top floor) and its "wings" (which begin at the 29th floor and stop where the spire begins), the pyramid is San Francisco's tallest building and an identifying landmark of the city's skyline. You may wish to take a peek at one of the rotating art exhibits in the lobby, or go around to the right and into the half-acre Redwood Park, which is part of the TransAmerica Center.

The site occupied by the TransAmerica Pyramid, in addition to the rest of the 600 block of Montgomery Street, was once occupied by a historic building called:

2. The Montgomery Block. Originally four stories high, it was the tallest building in the West when it was built in 1853. San Franciscans called it "Halleck's Folly" because it was built on a raft of redwood logs that had been bolted together and floated at the edge of the ocean (which was right at Montgomery Street at that time). The building was demolished in 1959 but is fondly remembered for its historic importance as the power center of the city, whose tenants also included artists and writers of all kinds, among them Jack London, George Sterling, Ambrose Bierce, Bret Harte, and Mark Twain.

From the southeast corner of Montgomery and Washington streets, look across Washington to the corner of Columbus Avenue, and you'll see the:

3. Original TransAmerica Building, across the street at 4 Columbus Ave. (now Sanwa Bank). A beaux arts flat-iron building covered in white terra-cotta, it was also the home of the old Fugazi Bank. Built for the Banco Populare Italiano Operaia Fugazi in 1909, it was originally a two-story building, but a third floor was added in 1916. In 1928, Fugazi merged his bank with the Bank of America, which was started by A. P. Giannini, who also created the TransAmerica Corporation.

Cross Washington Street and continue north on Montgomery Street to no. 730, the:

4. Golden Era Building, erected in about 1852. The building is named after the literary magazine, the *Golden Era,* which was published here. Part of the group of young writers who worked on the magazine were known as the Bohemians, and they included Samuel Clemens (a.k.a. Mark Twain) and Bret Harte (who began as a typesetter here). Backtrack a few dozen feet and stop for a minute to admire the annex, located at no. 722 (marked by a faded black-and-white–striped awning). The Belli Annex, as it is currently known, is registered as a Historic Landmark.

Continue north again and take the first right onto Jackson Street. Now you're in the:

5. 400 block of Jackson Square, where you'll find some of the only commercial buildings to survive the 1906 earthquake and fire. 415 Jackson served as the headquarters for the Ghirardelli chocolate company from 1855 to 1894 and was built around 1853. The Hotaling Building (no. 451) was built in 1866. At no. 472 is another of the buildings that survived the disaster of 1906.

Continue toward the intersection of Columbus Avenue and Jackson Street, turn right on Columbus and look across the street for the small triangular building at the junction of Kearny and Columbus, the:

6. Columbus Tower (a.k.a. Sentinel Building). If you walk up a little farther and then turn around and look back down Columbus, you'll be able to get a better look at this flatiron—a building shaped to a triangular site—beauty erected between 1905 and 1907, which was bought and restored by movie director and producer Francis Ford Coppola in the mid-1970s and is now home to his film production company, American Zoetrope Studios. This is one of the few pre-1906 earthquake buildings in the city center.

Across the street from the Tower on Columbus Avenue is the:

7. Purple Onion, at 140 Columbus Ave. Many famous headliners have played here (often before they were famous), including Phyllis Diller (now so big that she's famous for something as simple as her laugh), who was still struggling when she played a 2-week engagement here in the late 1950s.

Turn right on Pacific Avenue, and just after you cross Montgomery Street you'll be at brick-lined Osgood Place on the left, which is now registered as a Historic Landmark and, as a result, is one of the few quiet—and car-free—little alleyways left in the city. Stroll up Osgood and go left on Broadway to:

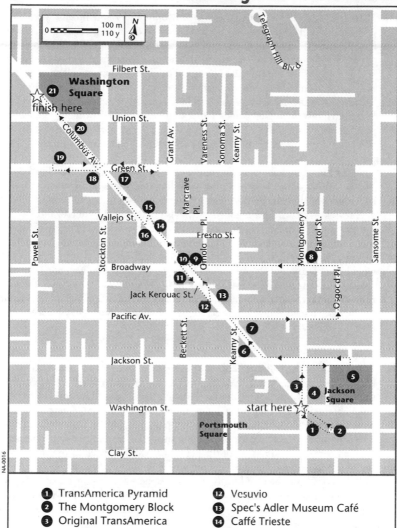

1. TransAmerica Pyramid
2. The Montgomery Block
3. Original TransAmerica Building
4. Golden Era Building
5. 400 block of Jackson Square
6. Columbus Tower
7. Purple Onion
8. 1010 Montgomery Street
9. hungry i
10. Former site of the Condor Club
11. City Lights Bookstore
12. Vesuvio
13. Spec's Adler Museum Café
14. Caffé Trieste
15. Biordi Art Imports
16. Molinari Delicatessen
17. R. Matteucci and Co. four-faced clock
18. North Beach Museum
19. Club Fugazi
20. Mario's Bohemian Cigar Store
21. Washington Square

8. 1010 Montgomery St. (at the corner of Montgomery and Broadway). This is where Allen Ginsberg lived during the time he wrote his legendary poem *Howl*, first performed on October 13, 1955, in a converted auto-repair shop at the corner of Fillmore and Union streets. By the time Ginsberg finished reading he was crying and the audience was going wild. Jack Kerouac proclaimed, "Ginsberg, this poem will make you famous in San Francisco." Continue along Broadway toward Columbus Avenue. This particular stretch of Broadway is San Francisco's answer to New York's Times Square, complete with strip clubs and peep shows. Currently it's among the most sought-after locations in the city as more and more highly profitable restaurants and clubs continue to spring up.

Along the way, on the right side of the street, you'll come to Columbus Books, 540 Broadway, which sells new and used discount books and is worth a quick trip inside for a good, cheap read.

A few dozen yards further up Broadway is the current location of the:

9. hungry i, 546 Broadway. Now a seedy strip club, the original "hungry i" (which was located at 599 Jackson St.) was owned and operated by the vociferous "Big Daddy" Nordstrom. If you had been here while Banducci was in charge, you would have found only a plain room with an exposed brick wall and director's chairs around small tables, but a who's who of nightclub entertainers fortified their careers at the original hungry i, including Lenny Bruce, Billie Holiday (who first sang "Strange Fruit" here), Bill Cosby, Richard Pryor, Woody Allen, and Barbra Streisand.

When you get to the corner of Broadway and Columbus Avenue you will also see the:

10. Former site of the Condor Club, 300 Columbus Ave., where Carol Doda scandalously bared her breasts and danced topless for the first time in 1964 (note the bronze plaque claiming the Condor Club as "Birthplace of the world's first topless & bottomless entertainment"). Go inside what is now the Condor Bistro and have a look at the framed newspaper clippings that hang around the dining room. From the elevated back room you can see Doda's old dressing-room and, on the floor below, an outline of the piano that would descend from the second floor with her atop it (stand on the piano and look up).

When you leave the Condor Bistro, cross to the south side of Broadway. Note the mural of jazz musicians painted on the whole side of the building directly across Columbus. Across Columbus Avenue, diagonally across the intersection from the Condor Bistro, is the:

11. City Lights Bookstore, at 261 Columbus Ave. Owned by one of the first beat poets to arrive in San Francisco, Lawrence Ferlinghetti, City Lights is now a city landmark and literary mecca—one of the last of the Beat-era hangouts in operation. As an active member in the Beat movement, Ferlinghetti established his shop as a meeting place where writers and bibliophiles could (and still do) attend poetry readings and other events. It's still a vibrant part of the literary scene in San Francisco; a well-stocked bookshop prides itself on its collection of art, poetry, and political paperbacks.

Upon exiting the City Lights Bookstore, turn right, cross aptly named Jack Kerouac Street, and stop by the bar named:

12. Vesuvio, 255 Columbus Ave. (at Broadway). Because of its proximity to City Lights Bookstore, Vesuvio became a favorite hangout of the Beats. Originally opened in 1949, Dylan Thomas used to drink here, as did Jack Kerouac, Ferlinghetti, and Ginsberg. Even today, Vesuvio still maintains its original bohemian atmosphere. The building itself dates from 1913, and is an excellent example of pressed-tin architecture.

Facing Vesuvio across Columbus Avenue are two other favorite spots of the Beat Generation:

13. **Spec's Adler Museum Café,** 12 Saroyan Place, is one of the city's funkiest bars, a small, dimly-lit watering hole with ceiling-hung maritime flags and exposed brick walls crammed with a hodgepodge of memorabilia. Within the bar is a minimuseum that consists of a few glass cases filled with mementos brought back and dropped off by various seamen who have frequented the pub.

From here, go up Columbus across Broadway to Grant Avenue, where you should turn right, walking until you come to Vallejo Street. At 606 Vallejo St. (at the corner of Vallejo Street and Grant Avenue) is:

14. **Caffé Trieste,** yet another favorite spot of the Beats that was founded by Gianni Giotta in 1956 and still run by family members. The quintessential San Francisco coffeehouse, Trieste features opera on the jukebox and the real thing, performed by the Giottas, on Saturday afternoons. Any day of the week is a good one to stop in for a cappuccino or espresso, since the beans are roasted right next door.

Go left out of Caffé Trieste onto Vallejo Street, turn right on Columbus Avenue, and bump into the loveliest shop in all of North Beach:

15. **Biordi Art Imports,** at 412 Columbus Ave. The shopkeepers have been importing hand-painted Majolica pottery from the hill towns of central Italy for more than 50 years. Some of the colorful patterns date from the 14th century. Biordi hand-picks its artisans, and in their catalog you'll find biographies of those who are currently represented.

Across Columbus Avenue at the corner of Vallejo is:

16. **Molinari Delicatessen,** 373 Columbus Ave. (☎ **415/421-2337**), which has been selling its pungent, air-dried salamis since 1896. They still make their own ravioli and tortellini in the back of the shop, but it's the mouthwatering selection of cold salads, cheeses, and marinades up front that captures the attention of most folks. The Italian subs are big enough for two hearty appetites.

Continue up Columbus Avenue about half a block, and across the street you'll see the:

17. **R. Matteucci and Co. four-faced clock.** Located directly in front of the R. Matteucci jewelry store at 450 Columbus Avenue, the ornate clock, which dates from 1908, is the only four-faced clock in working order in San Francisco and one of the few fine-quality old street clocks left in the city. It's a spring-wound clock manufactured by Seth Thomas, and the proprietor of the jewelry store, Matteo Ciuffreda, dutifully winds it every Saturday morning. Legend has it that it kept excellent time until its owner, jeweler Rocco Matteuchi, died, after which it stopped for a week of mourning and began again.

Walk back to the lively intersection of Columbus, Green, and Stockton, cross Columbus Avenue, and look for the Eureka Bank at 1435 Stockton St. (between Vallejo and Green). On the second floor of the bank you'll find the:

18. **North Beach Museum,** displaying historical artifacts that tell the story of North Beach, Chinatown, and Fisherman's Wharf. Just before you enter the museum you'll find a framed, handwritten poem by Lawrence Ferlinghetti that captures his impressions of this primarily Italian neighborhood. After you pass through the glass doors you'll find many photographs of some of the first Chinese and Italian immigrants, as well as pictures of San Francisco after the 1906 earthquake. You can visit the museum any time the bank is open (unfortunately, it's closed on weekends), and admission is free.

Now backtrack toward Columbus Avenue and go left on Green Street to:

19. Club Fugazi, at 678 Green St. (between Columbus and Powell Streets). It doesn't look like much from the outside, but Fugazi Hall stages San Francisco's legendary musical revue "Beach Blanket Babylon." The show evolved from Steve Silver's Rent-a-Freak service, which consisted of a group of party-goers who would attend parties dressed as any number of characters in outrageous costumes. The fun caught on, and soon came Beach Blanket Babylon. You'll love this supercharged show, which is definitely worth the price of admission.

On the way back to Columbus Avenue, be sure to stop in at O'Reilly's Irish Pub (622 Green St.) to see the mural of Irish authors that peer out from the back wall (How many can you name?). As you come out of O'Reilly's, turn left, cross Columbus Avenue, and proceed 1 block northwest on Columbus to:

20. Mario's Bohemian Cigar Store. Located across the street from Washington Square at 566 Columbus Ave. is one of North Beach's most popular neighborhood hangouts: Mario's. This historic, tiny, and charmingly threadbare bar has long been a popular meeting place for aged Sicilians and beat poets, though nowadays it attracts all types, including the occasional tourist in search of a cigar (of which none are sold nor welcome in this former cigar store). Oddly enough, they don't serve regular ol' coffee, though the hot focaccia sandwiches are superb.

Our next stop, directly across Union Street, is:

21. Washington Square, one of the oldest parks in the city. This land was designated a public park in 1847 and has undergone many changes since then. Its current landscaping dates from 1955. Even though it's called a "square," this little oasis in the middle of such a bustling neighborhood sort of lost its square status when Columbus Avenue was laid out and one of its four corners was lopped off. Why isn't it named Columbus Square? Because the park was named in the 1850s before Montgomery Avenue was changed to Columbus Avenue.

Shopping 9

Like its population, San Francisco's shopping is worldly and intimate. Every persuasion, style, era, and fetish is represented here, not in a big, tacky shopping mall, but rather in hundreds of quaint and dramatically different boutiques scattered throughout the city. Whether it's Chanel or Chinese herbal medicine you're looking for, San Francisco's got it. Just pick a shopping neighborhood and break out your credit cards—you're sure to end up with at least a few take-home treasures.

1 The Shopping Scene

MAJOR SHOPPING AREAS

San Francisco has many shopping areas, but the following places are where you'll find most of the action:

Union Square and Environs San Francisco's most congested and popular shopping mecca is centered around Union Square and enclosed by Bush, Taylor, Market, and Montgomery streets. Most of the big department stores and many high-end specialty shops are in this area. Be sure to venture to Grant Avenue, Post and Sutter streets, and Maiden Lane.

Chinatown When you pass under the gate to Chinatown on Grant Avenue, say good-bye to the world of fashion and hello to a swarm of cheap tourist shops selling everything from linen and jade to plastic toys and $2 slippers. But that's not all Chinatown has to offer. The real gems here are tucked on side streets or are small, one-person shops selling Chinese herbs, original art, and jewelry. Grant Avenue is the area's main thoroughfare, and side streets between Bush Street and Columbus Avenue are full of restaurants, markets, and eclectic shops. Walking is best, since traffic through this area is slow at best and parking is next to impossible. Most of the stores in Chinatown are open daily from 10am to 10pm. Serviced by bus lines 9X, 15, 30, 41, and 45.

Union Street Union Street, from Fillmore to Van Ness, caters to the upper–middle-class crowd. It's a great place to stroll, window-shop the plethora of boutiques, cafes, and restaurants, and watch the beautiful people parade by. Serviced by bus lines 22, 41, 42, and 45.

Chestnut Street   Parallel to and a few blocks north of Union Street, Chestnut is a younger Union Street, with endless shopping and dining choices, and the ever-tanned, superfit population of postgraduate singles who hang around cafes and scope each other out. Serviced by bus lines 22, 28, 30, 41, 42, 43, and 76.

Fillmore Street   Some of the best shopping in town is packed into 5 blocks of Fillmore Street in Pacific Heights. From Jackson to Sutter streets, Fillmore is the perfect place to grab a bite and peruse the high-priced boutiques, craft shops, and incredible houseware stores. Don't miss Zinc Details and Fillamento. Serviced by bus lines 1, 2, 3, 4, 12, 22, and 24.

Haight Street   Green hair, spiked hair, no hair, or mohair—even the hippies look conservative next to Haight Street's dramatic fashion freaks. The shopping in the 6 blocks of upper Haight Street, between Central Avenue and Stanyan Street, reflects its clientele and offers everything from incense and European and American street styles to furniture and antique clothing. Bus lines 7, 66, 71, and 73 run the length of Haight Street. The Muni metro N line stops at Waller Street and at Cole Street.

SoMa   Though this area isn't suitable for strolling, you'll find almost all the discount shopping in warehouse spaces South of Market. You can pick up a discount-shopping guide at most major hotels. Many bus lines pass through this area.

Hayes Valley   It may not be the prettiest area in town (with some of the shadier housing projects a few blocks away), but while most neighborhoods cater to more conservative or trendy shoppers, lower Hayes Street, between Octavia and Gough, celebrates anything vintage, artistic, or downright funky. Though still in its developmental stage, it's definitely the most interesting new shopping area in town, with furniture and glass stores, thrift shops, trendy shoe stores, and men's and women's clothiers. There are also lots of great antique shops south on Octavia and on nearby Market Street. Bus lines include 16AX, 16BX, and 21.

Fisherman's Wharf & Environs   The tourist-oriented malls run along Jefferson Street and include hundreds of shops, restaurants, and attractions. Ghirardelli Square, Pier 39, the Cannery, and the Anchorage are all outlined under "Shopping Centers & Complexes," below.

HOURS, TAXES & SHIPPING

Store hours are generally Monday to Saturday from 10am to 6pm and Sunday from noon to 5pm. Most department stores stay open later, as do shops around Fisherman's Wharf, the most heavily visited area.

Sales tax in San Francisco is 8.5%, which is added on at the register for all goods and services purchased. If you live out of state and buy an expensive item, you may want to consider having the store ship it home for you. You will escape paying the sales tax, but will have to pay for its transport.

Most of the city's shops can wrap your purchase and ship it anywhere in the world via United Parcel Service (UPS). If they can't, you can send it yourself, either through **UPS** (☎ **800/742-5877**) or through the U.S. mail (see "Fast Facts: San Francisco" in chapter 4).

2 Shopping A to Z

ANTIQUES

Jackson Square, a historic district just north of the Financial District's Embarcadero Center, is the place to go for the top names in fine furniture and fine art. There are also a lot of Asian-art dealers here. More than a dozen dealers on the

2 blocks between Columbus and Sansome streets specialize in European furnishings from the 17th to the 19th centuries. Most shops here are open Monday to Friday from 9am to 5pm and Saturday from 11am to 4pm.

Fumiki Fine Asian Arts. 272 Sutter St. (at Grant Ave.). ☎ **415/922-0573.**

Although this store moved recently, it's new, much bigger space still has one of the largest collections of antique Japanese Imari and Korean and Japanese tansus in the country, as well as an extensive collection of Asian art and antiques, including Japanese baskets and Chinese artifacts and embroidery. Open Monday to Saturday from 10am to 6pm and Sunday from noon to 5pm.

ART

The San Francisco Gallery Guide, a comprehensive, bimonthly publication listing the city's current shows, is available free by mail. Send a self-addressed stamped envelope to San Francisco Bay Area Gallery Guide, 1369 Fulton St., San Francisco, CA 94117 (☎ **415/921-1600**), or pick one up at the San Francisco Visitor Information Center at 900 Market St. Most of the city's major art galleries are clustered downtown in the Union Square area.

Atelier Dore. 771 Bush St. (between Mason and Powell sts.). ☎ **415/391-2423.**

Atelier Dore features American and European paintings from the 19th and 20th centuries, including some WPA art. Open Tuesday to Saturday from 11am to 5pm.

✪ **Catharine Clark Gallery.** 49 Geary St., 2nd floor (between Kearny and Grant sts.). ☎ **415/399-1439.**

Catharine Clark's is a different kind of gallery experience. While many galleries focus on already-established artists and out-of-this world price points, Catharine's exhibits up-and-coming contemporary artists (who are mainly from California) and nurtures beginning collectors by offering an unusual purchasing plan. Almost unheard of in the art business, you can buy a piece here on layaway and take up to a year to pay for it—interest free! Prices here make art a realistic purchase for everyone for a change, but serious collectors still frequent her shows because she has such a keen eye for talent. Shows change frequently. No credit cards are accepted. Open Tuesday to Friday from 10:30am to 5:30pm and Saturday from 11am to 5pm; 1st Thursday of the month from 10:30am to 7:30pm.

Eleonore Austerer. 540 Sutter St. (between Powell and Mason sts.). ☎ **415/986-2244.**

Limited-edition graphics by modern masters like Braque, Matisse, Miró, Picasso, Calder, Chagall, and Hockney, as well as original works by European and American contemporary artists can be found at Eleonore Austerer. The gallery, located in a beautiful old building near Union Square, is open Monday to Saturday from 10am to 6pm.

Fraenkel Gallery. 49 Geary St., 4th floor (between Grant Ave. and Kearny St.). ☎ **415/981-2661.**

This photography gallery features works by contemporary American and European artists. Excellent shows change frequently. Open Tuesday to Friday from 10:30am to 5:30pm and Saturday from 11am to 5pm.

Images of the North. 1782 Union St. (at Octavia St.). ☎ **415/673-1273.**

The highlight here is one of the most extensive collections of Canadian and Alaskan Inuit art in the United States. There's also a fine collection of Native American masks and jewelry. Open Monday to Saturday from 11am to 5:30pm and Sunday from noon to 4pm.

Maxwell Galleries. 559 Sutter St. (between Powell and Mason sts.). ☎ **415/421-5193.**

The specialties at Maxwell Galleries are 19th- and 20th-century European and American sculpture and paintings, including works by Raphael and Butler. Open Monday to Friday from 9:30am to 5:15pm and Saturday from 11am to 5pm.

Meyerovich Gallery. 251 Post St., 4th floor (at Stockton St.). ☎ **415/421-7171.**

Works on paper by modern and contemporary masters here include Chagall, Dine, Haring, Hockney, Lichtenstein, Matisse, Miró, Picasso, Rosenquist, and Stella, as well as sculpture by Bruskin and Chadwick. Open Monday to Friday from 9:30am to 6pm, Saturday from 10am to 5pm, and by appointment.

BOOKS

The Booksmith. 1644 Haight St. (between Clayton and Cole sts.). ☎ **800/493-7323** or 415/863-8688. www.booksmith.com. E-mail: read@booksmith.com.

Haight Street's best selection of new books is housed in this large, well-maintained shop. It carries all the top titles, along with works from smaller presses, and more than 1,000 different magazines. Open Monday to Saturday from 10am to 9pm and Sunday from 10am to 6pm.

✪ **City Lights Booksellers & Publishers.** 261 Columbus Ave. (at Broadway). ☎ **415/362-8193.**

Brooding literary types browse this famous bookstore owned by Lawrence Ferlinghetti, the renowned beat-generation poet. The three-level bookshop prides itself on a comprehensive collection of art, poetry, and political paperbacks, as well as more mainstream books. Open daily from 10am to midnight.

✪ **A Clean, Well-Lighted Place for Books.** 601 Van Ness Ave. (between Turk St. and Golden Gate Ave.). ☎ **415/441-6670.**

Voted best bookstore by the *San Francisco Bay Guardian,* this independent has good new fiction and nonfiction sections and also specializes in music, art, mystery, and cookbooks. The store is very well known for its schedule of author readings and events. For a calendar of events, call the store or check their Web site at **www.bookstore.com**. Open Sunday to Thursday from 10am to 11pm, and Friday and Saturday from 10am to midnight.

✪ **Green Apple Books.** 506 Clement St. (at 6th Ave.). ☎ **415/387-2272.**

The local favorite for used books, Green Apple is crammed with titles—more than 60,000 new and 100,000 used books. Their extended sections in psychology, cooking, art, history; collection of modern first editions; and rare graphic comics are only superseded by the staff's superlative service. Open Sunday to Thursday from 10am to 10:30pm, and Friday and Saturday from 10am to 11:30pm.

CHINA, SILVER & GLASS

The Enchanted Crystal. 1895 Union St. (at Laguna St.). ☎ **415/885-1335.**

This shop has an extensive collection of fine crystal, art glass, jewelry, and one-of-a-kind decorative art, including one of the largest crystal balls in the world (from Madagascar). Open Monday to Saturday from 10am to 6pm and Sunday from noon to 5pm.

✪ **Gump's.** 135 Post St. (between Kearny St. and Grant Ave.). ☎ **415/982-1616.**

Founded over a century ago, Gump's offers gifts and treasures ranging from Asian antiquities to contemporary art glass and exquisite jade and pearl jewelry. Many items are made specifically for the store. Gump's also has one of the most revered window displays each holiday season. Open Monday to Saturday from 10am to 6pm.

CRAFTS

The Canton Bazaar. 616 Grant Ave. (between Sacramento and California sts.). ☎ 415/362-5750.

Amid a wide variety of handicrafts you'll find an excellent selection of rosewood and carved furniture, cloisonné enamelware, rose Canton chinaware, porcelain ware, carved jade, embroideries, jewelry, and antiques from mainland China. Open daily from 10am to 10pm.

The New Unique Company. 838 Grant Ave. (between Clay and Washington sts.). ☎ 415/981-2036.

Primarily a calligraphy- and watercolor-supplies store, the shop also has a good assortment of books relating to these topics. In addition, there is a wide selection of carved stones for use as seals on letters and documents. The store will carve seals to order should you want a special design or group of initials. Open Monday to Saturday from 10:30am to 6pm and Sunday from 11am to 6pm.

Silkroute International. 3119 Fillmore St. (at Filbert St.). ☎ 415/563-4936.

Owned and operated by an Afghan who offers fascinating wares, old and new, from his native country, the shop sells Oriental and tribal rugs, kilims, dhurries, textiles, jewelry, clothing, pillows, arts, and antiques. Open Monday to Friday from 11am to 6:30pm and Saturday from 11am to 6pm.

DEPARTMENT STORES

Macy's. Corner of Stockton and O'Farrell sts., Union Sq. ☎ 415/397-3333.

The seven-story Macy's West features contemporary fashions for women and juniors, including jewelry, fragrances, cosmetics, and accessories. The third floor offers a "hospitality suite" where visitors can leave their coats and packages, grab a cup of coffee, or find out more about the city from the concierge. The top floors contain home furnishings, while the Cellar sells kitchenware and gourmet foods. You'll even find a Boudin Cafe (great sandwiches!) and Wolfgang Puck Cafe on the premises. Across the street, Macy's East has five floors of men's and children's fashions, as well as the recently added largest Men's Polo by Ralph Lauren shop in the country and the Fresh Choice cafe. Macy's most recent acquisition, the old Emporium building at 835 Market (between Fourth and Fifth streets), is now temporarily Macy's Home Store. Open Monday to Saturday from 10am to 8pm and Sunday from 11am to 7pm.

Neiman Marcus. 150 Stockton St., Union Sq. ☎ 415/362-3900.

Some call this unit of the Texas-based chain "Needless Mark-up." But if you've got the cash, the men's and women's clothes, precious gems, and conservative formal wear here are some of the most glamorous in town. The Rotunda Restaurant, on the top floor, is a beautiful, relaxing place for lunch and afternoon tea. Open Monday, Thursday, and Friday from 10am to 6pm, Tuesday, Wednesday, and Saturday from 10am to 7pm, and Sunday from noon to 6pm.

Nordstrom. 865 Market St. (in the San Francisco Shopping Centre). ☎ 415/243-8500.

Renowned for its personalized service, this is the largest member of the Seattle-based fashion department-store chain. Nordstrom occupies the top five floors of the

San Francisco Shopping Centre (see "Shopping Centers & Complexes," below) and is that mall's primary anchor. Equally devoted to women's and men's fashions, the store has one of the best shoe selections in the city, and thousands of suits in stock. The Nordstrom Café, on the fourth floor, has a panoramic view and is an ideal place for an inexpensive lunch or light snack. The fifth floor is occupied by Nordstrom Spa, the perfect place to relax after a hectic day of bargain-hunting. Open Monday to Saturday from 9:30am to 9pm and Sunday from 10am to 7pm.

DISCOUNT SHOPPING

There are many factory-outlet stores in San Francisco, selling overstocked and discontinued fashions at bargain prices. All of the following shops are located south of Market Street, in the city's warehouse district (SoMa).

Esprit Outlet Store. 499 Illinois St. (at 16th St.). ☎ **415/957-2550.**

All the Esprit collections and Susie Tompkins merchandise are available here at 30% or more off regular prices. In addition to clothes, the store sells accessories, shoes, and assorted other items. Open Monday to Friday from 10am to 8pm, Saturday from 10am to 7pm, and Sunday from 11am to 5pm.

✪ **Jeremys.** 2 South Park. (between Bryant and Brannan sts. at Second St.). ☎ **415/882-4929.**

This SoMa boutique offers top designer fashions from shoes to suits at rock-bottom prices. There are no cheap knockoffs here, just good men's and women's clothes and accessories. Jeremy's also has its own stylish clothing line. Open Monday to Saturday 11am to 7pm and Sunday noon to 6pm.

The North Face. 1325 Howard St. (between 9th and 10th sts.). ☎ **415/626-6444.**

Well known for its sporting, camping, and hiking equipment, this off-price outlet carries a limited but high-quality selection of ski wear, boots, sweaters, and goods such as tents, packs, and sleeping bags. The North Face makes heavy use of Gore-Tex, down, and other durable, lightweight materials. Open Monday to Wednesday, Friday, and Saturday from 10am to 6pm, Thursday from 10am to 7pm, and Sunday from 11am to 5pm.

FABRICS

Britex Fabrics. 146 Geary St. (between Stockton and Grant sts.). ☎ **415/392-2910.**

A San Francisco institution since 1952, Britex offers an absurd amount and variety of fabrics, not to mention over 30,000 button selections. Open Monday to Wednesday and Sunday from 9:30am to 6pm, and Friday and Saturday from 9:30am to 7pm. Closed Sunday.

FASHIONS

Grand. 1435 Grant Ave. (between Green and Union sts.). ☎ **415/951-0131.**

Invited to an underground club and forgot your funky rave attire? Grand's North Beach shop features the latest in fashion-forward street wear by local designers. Garb comes both baggy and tight; the style is club, and the price is right. Open daily from noon to 7pm.

Gucci America. 200 Stockton St. (between Geary and Post sts.). ☎ **415/392-2808.**

Donning Gucci's golden Gs is not a cheap endeavor. But if you've got the cash, you'll find all the latest lines of shoes, leather goods, scarves, and pricey accessories, such as a $7,000 handmade crocodile bag. Open Monday to Saturday 10am to 6pm and on Sunday noon to 5pm.

Niketown. 278 Post St. (at Stockton St.). ☎ **415/392-6453.**

Here it's not "I can," but "I can spend." At least that's what the kings of sportswear were banking on when they opened this megastore in 1997. As you'd expect, inside the doors it's Nike's world, offering everything the merchandising team could create. Open Monday to Friday from 10am to 8pm, Saturday from 10am to 7pm, and Sunday from 11am to 6pm.

Three Bags Full. 2181 Union St. (at Fillmore). ☎ **415/567-5753.**

Snuggling up in a cozy sweater can be a fashionable event if you do your shopping at this pricey boutique, which carries the gamut in handmade and one-of-a-kind playful and extravagant knitwear. Open Monday to Saturday from 10:30am to 6pm and on Sunday from noon to 5pm. Other city locations are 500 Sutter St. and 3314 Sacramento St.

✪ **Wilkes Bashford.** 375 Sutter St. (at Stockton). ☎ **415/986-4380.**

Wilkes Bashford is one of the most expensive and well-known clothing stores in the city. In its 31 years in business the boutique has garnered a reputation for stocking only the finest clothes in the world (which can often be seen on Mayor Willie Brown, who does his suit shopping here). Most fashions come from Italy and France and include women's designer sportswear and couture and men's Kiton and Brioni suits (at $3,000 and up, they're considered the most expensive suits in the world). Open Monday to Wednesday and Friday and Saturday from 10am to 6pm, Thursday from 10am to 8pm. Closed Sunday.

MEN'S FASHIONS

All American Boy. 463 Castro St. (between Market and 18th sts.). ☎ **415/861-0444.**

Long known for setting the mainstream style for gay men, All American Boy is the quintessential Castro clothing shop. Open Monday to Saturday from 11am to 6pm and Sunday from 11am to 7pm.

Brooks Brothers. 201 Post St. (at Grant Ave.). ☎ **415/397-4500.**

In San Francisco, this bulwark of tradition is located 1 block east of Union Square. Brooks Brothers introduced the button-down collar and single-handedly changed the standard of the well-dressed businessman. The multilevel shop also sells traditional casual wear, including sportswear, sweaters, and shirts. Open Monday to Friday from 9:30am to 7pm, Saturday from 9:30am to 6pm, and Sunday from 11am to 6pm.

Cable Car Clothiers. 441 Sutter St. (between Grant Ave. and Kearny St.). ☎ **415/ 397-4740.**

Dapper men head to this beautiful landmark building for traditional attire, such as three-button suits with natural shoulders, Aquascutum coats, McGeorge sweaters, and Atkinson ties. Open Monday to Saturday from 9:30am to 5:30pm.

Citizen Clothing. 536 Castro St. (between 18th and 19th sts.). ☎ **415/558-9429.**

The Castro has some of America's best men's casual clothing stores, and this is one of them. Stylish (but not faddish) pants, tops, and accessories are sold here. Open Monday to Saturday from 10am to 8pm and Sunday from 11am to 7pm.

MAC. 5 Claude Lane (off Sutter St. between Grant Ave. and Kearny St.). ☎ **415/837-0615.**

The more-classic-than-corporate man shops here for imported tailored suits in new and intriguing fabrics. Lines include London's Katherine Hamnett, Belgium's SO, Italy's Alberto Biani, New York's John Bartlett, and one of our personal favorites, San Francisco's Lat Naylor. Open Monday to Saturday from 11am to 6pm and Sunday from noon to 5pm. Their women's store is located at 1543 Grant Ave. (between Filbert and Union streets; ☎ **415/837-1604**).

WOMEN'S FASHIONS

Bella Donna. 539 Hayes St. (between Laguna and Octavia sts.). ☎ **415/861-7182.**

Another blessing to the small but growing Hayes Valley alternative shopping mecca is this expensive but quality boutique offering luxurious women's clothing, such as hand-knit sweaters, silky slip dresses, and fashionable knit hats. There's also a wonderful (albeit expensive) collection of vases and other household trinkets, as well as a small selection of remainder fabrics. Upstairs, the wedding and bridal section focuses on the vintage look. Open Tuesday through Saturday from 11am to 7pm and Sunday from 11am to 5pm; bridals by appointment.

The Chanel Boutique. 155 Maiden Lane (between Stockton St. and Grant Ave.). ☎ **415/981-1550.**

Ever fashionable and expensive, Chanel is appropriately located on Maiden Lane, the quaint downtown side street where the most exclusive stores and spas cluster. You'll find what you'd expect from Chanel: clothing, accessories, scents, cosmetics, and jewelry. Open Monday to Saturday from 10am to 6pm and Sunday from 11am to 5pm.

Métier. 355 Sutter St. (between Grant and Stockton sts.). ☎ **415/989-5395.**

The classic, sophisticated, and expensive creations for women found here include European ready-to-wear lines and designers Peter Cohen, Georgina Von Etzdorf, Alberto Biani, and local Lat Naylor, as well as a distinguished collection of antique-style, high-end jewelry from LA's Kathie Waterman. Open Monday to Saturday from 10am to 6pm. Closed Sunday.

Solo Fashion. 1599 Haight St. (at Clayton St.). ☎ **415/621-0342.**

While strolling upper Haight, stop in here for a good selection of upbeat, contemporary, English-style street wear, along with a collection of dresses designed exclusively for this shop. Open daily from 11am to 7pm.

CHILDREN'S FASHIONS

Minis. 2042 Union St. (between Webster and Buchanan sts.). ☎ **415/567-9537.**

Christina Profili, a San Francisco native who used to design for Banana Republic, opened this children's clothing store selling her own creations. Every piece, from shirts to pants and dresses, is made from cotton or organic cotton. Every outfit perfectly coordinates with everything else in the store. Minis also offers educational and creative toys and storybooks with matching dolls, and most recently, maternity wear. Open daily from 10:30am to 6:30pm.

FOOD

Golden Gate Fortune Cookies Co. 56 Ross Alley (between Washington and Jackson sts.). ☎ **415/781-3956.**

This tiny, touristy factory sells fortune cookies hot off the press. You can purchase them in small bags or in bulk, and if your order is large enough, you may even be able to negotiate your own message. Even if you're not buying, stop in to see how these sugary treats are made (although the staff can get pushy for you to buy). Open daily from 10am to 7pm.

✪ **Joseph Schmidt Confections.** 3489 16th St. (at Sanchez St.). ☎ **415/861-8682.**

Chocolate takes the shape of exquisite sculptural masterpieces—such as long-stemmed tulips and heart-shaped boxes—that are so beautiful, you'll be hesitant to bite the head off your adorable chocolate panda bear. But once you do, you'll know why this is the most popular chocolatier in town. Prices are also remarkably reasonable. Open Monday to Saturday from 10am to 6:30pm.

✪ **Ten Ren Tea Company.** 949 Grant Ave. (between Washington and Jackson sts.). ☎ **415/362-0656.**

At the Ten Ren Tea Company you will be offered a steaming cup of roselle tea, made of black tea and hibiscus. In addition to a selection of almost 50 traditional and herbal teas, the company stocks related paraphernalia, such as pots, cups, and infusers. If you can't make up your mind, take home a mail-order form. Open daily from 9am to 9pm.

GIFTS

Art of China. 839–843 Grant Ave. (between Clay and Washington sts.). ☎ **415/981-1602.**

Amid a wide variety of collectibles, this shop features exquisite, hand-carved Chinese figurines. You'll also find a lovely assortment of ivory beads, bracelets, necklaces, and earrings. Pink-quartz dogs, jade figurines, porcelain vases, cache pots, and blue-and-white barrels suitable for use as table bases are just some of the many collectibles on offer. Open daily from 10am to 6pm.

Babushka. 333 Jefferson St. (at Leavenworth St.). ☎ **415/673-6740.**

Located near Fisherman's Wharf, adjacent to the Anchorage Shopping Center, Babushka sells only Russian products, most of which are wooden or papier-mâché nesting dolls. Open daily from 9am to 10pm.

Cost Plus Imports. 2552 Taylor St. (between North Point and Bay sts.). ☎ **415/928-6200.**

At the Fisherman's Wharf cable-car turntable, Cost Plus is a vast warehouse crammed to the rafters with Chinese baskets, Indian camel bells, Malaysian batik scarves, and innumerable other items from Algeria to Zanzibar. More than 20,000 items from 40 nations are purchased directly from their country of origin and packed into this well-priced warehouse. They also have a decent wine shop. Open daily from 9am to 9pm.

✪ **Dandelion.** 55 Potrero Ave. (at Alameda St.). ☎ **415/436-9500.**

Many locals were dismayed when, after almost 20 years in business, Dandelion closed its doors on California Street a few years back. But owners Steve, Del, and Carl weren't finished for good. Their new location is larger and even more packed with the most wonderful collection of gifts, collectibles, and furnishings. There's something for every taste and budget here, ranging from an excellent collection of teapots, decorative dishes, and gourmet foods, to silver, books, cards, and picture frames. Don't miss the Zen-like second floor, with its variety of peaceful furnishings in Indian, Japanese, and Western styles. Open Tuesday through Saturday from 10am to 6pm; closed Sunday and Monday.

Distractions & Euphoria. 1552 Haight St. (between Ashbury and Clayton sts.). ☎ 415/252-8751.

This is the best of the Haight Street shops selling pseudo-sixties memorabilia, street fashion, and rave wear. You'll find retro hippie clothes, pipes, toys, and stickers are liberally intermixed with tie-dyed Grateful Dead paraphernalia and lots of cool stuff to look at. Open Monday to Saturday from 10am to 8pm and Sunday from 10am to 7pm.

Flax. 1699 Market St. (at Valencia and Gough sts.). ☎ **415/552-2355.**

If you're the type of person who goes into an art store for a special pencil and comes out $300 later, don't go near this shop. Flax has everything you can think of in art and design supplies, along with an amazing collection of locals' arts and crafts, blank bound books, children's art supplies, frames, calendars, you name it. There's a gift for every type of person here, especially you. If you can't make it by, call for a mail-order catalog. Open Monday to Saturday from 9:30am to 6pm.

Good Vibrations. 1210 Valencia St. (at 23rd St.). ☎ **800/BUY-VIBE** for mail order, or 415/974-8980.

A laypersons' sex-toy, book, and video emporium, Good Vibrations is specifically designed (but not exclusively) for women. Unlike most sex shops, it's not a back-alley business, but rather a straightforward shop with healthy and open attitudes about human sexuality. They also have a vibrator museum. Open daily from 11am to 7pm. A second location is in Berkeley at 2504 San Pablo Ave.

Quantity Postcards. 1441 Grant St. (at Green St.). ☎ **415/986-8866.**

You'll find the perfect postcard for literally everyone you know here, as well as some depictions of old San Francisco, movie stars, and Day-Glo posters featuring concert-poster artist Frank Kozik. Prices range from 35¢ to $2 per card, and even if you don't need any cards, you'll enjoy browsing the eclectic collection of mail-ables. Open daily from 11am to 11pm.

○ **SFMOMA MuseumStore.** 151 Third St. (2 blocks south of Market St., across from Yerba Buena Gardens). ☎ **415/357-4035.**

With an array of artistic cards, books, jewelry, housewares, knickknacks, and creative tokens of San Francisco, it's virtually impossible not to find something you'll consider a must-have. Aside from being one of the locals' favorite shops, it also offers far more tasteful mementos than most Fisherman's Wharf options. Open Friday to Wednesday from 10:30am to 6:30pm and Thursday from 10:30am to 9:30pm.

Smile. 500 Sutter St. (between Powell and Mason sts.). ☎ **415/362-3436.**

Need a little humor in your life? Smile specializes in whimsical art, furniture, clothing, jewelry, and American crafts guaranteed to make you grin. Open Monday to Saturday from 9:30am to 5:30pm.

HOUSEWARES

○ **Biordi Art Imports.** 412 Columbus Ave. (at Vallejo St.). ☎ **415/392-8096.**

Whether it's your intention to decorate your dinner table, color up your kitchen, or liven the living room, Biordi's Italian Majolica pottery is the most exquisite and unique way to do it. The owner has been importing these hand-painted collectibles for 50 years, and every piece is a show-stopper. Call for a catalog if you like. They'll ship anywhere. Open Monday to Saturday from 9:30am to 6pm. Closed Sunday.

✪ **Fillamento.** 2185 Fillmore St. (at Sacramento St.). ☎ **415/931-2224.**

The best housewares store in the city, Fillamento's three floors are always packed with shoppers searching for the most classic, artistic, and refined housewares. Whether you're looking to set a good table or revamp your bedroom, you'll find it all here. Open daily from 10am to 6pm.

Victorian Interiors. 575 Hayes St. (at Laguna St.). ☎ **415/431-7191.**

Draped with an array of period floral wallpapers, this little store is the perfect place to shop for any Victorian fanatic. Along with traditional Victorian housewares such as wallpapers, moldings, drapery cornices and rods, tiles, fabrics, and carpets, you'll find a great collection of old pipes and knickknacks. Open Tuesday to Saturday from 11am to 6pm and Sunday from noon to 5pm.

The Wok Shop. 718 Grant Ave. (at Clay St.). ☎ **888/780-7171** for mail order, or 415/989-3797.

This shop has every conceivable implement for Chinese cooking, including woks, brushes, cleavers, circular chopping blocks, dishes, oyster knives, bamboo steamers, strainers—you name it. The shop also sells a wide range of kitchen utensils, baskets, handmade linens from China, and aprons. Open Sunday to Friday from 10am to 6pm and Saturday from 10am to 9pm.

✪ **Zinc Details.** 1905 Fillmore St. (between Bush and Pine sts.). ☎ **415/776-2100.**

One of our favorite stores in the city, Zinc Details has received accolades from everyone from Elle Decor Japan to Metropolitan Home for its amazing collection of locally handcrafted glass vases, pendant lights, ceramics, and furniture. Each piece is a true work of art created specifically for the store (except vintage items) and these pieces are in such high demand that the store's wholesale accounts include Barney's New York and The Guggenheim Museum Store. Open daily from 11am to 7pm.

JEWELRY

Dianne's Old & New Estates. 2181A Union St. (at Fillmore St.). ☎ **888/346-7525** for mail order, or 415/346-7525.

Buy yourself a bauble, treat yourself to a trinket at this shop featuring top-of-the-line antique jewelry—pendants, diamond rings, necklaces, bracelets, and natural pearls. For a special gift, check out the collection of platinum wedding and engagement rings and vintage watches. Don't worry if you can't afford it now—this shop offers 1-year interest-free layaway. Open Thursday to Tuesday from noon to 6pm.

Jerusalem Shoppe. 313 Noe St. (at Market St.). ☎ **415/626-7906.**

Known for its extensive collection of silver and gold gemstone jewelry by more than 300 local and international artists, this shop also displays other unique treasures, from clothing and accessories to imported antique Indian quilts. Open Monday to Friday from 11am to 10pm and Sunday from 10:30am to 9pm.

The Magical Trinket. 524 Hayes St. (between Laguna and Octavia sts.). ☎ **415/626-0764.**

Do-it-yourself jewelry makers beware. This store, brimming with beads, baubles, and bangles, will inspire you to make your own knickknacks and kick yourself for the prices you've been paying for costume jewelry in retail stores. If you're overwhelmed by all the bead options, colors, shapes, and styles, owner Eve Blake calmly explains how to create your wearable masterpiece and offers more extensive classes for those who are really bead-dazzled. Open Monday from noon to 6pm, Tuesday to Saturday from 11am to 7pm, and Sunday from noon to 5pm.

Pearl Empire. 127 Geary St. (between Stockton St. and Grant Ave.). ☎ **415/362-0606.**

The Pearl Empire has been importing jewelry from all over the world since 1957. They are specialists in unusual pearls and jade and offer restringing on the premises. Open Monday to Saturday from 9:30am to 5:30pm.

Tiffany & Co. 350 Post St. (at Powell St.). ☎ **415/781-7000.**

Even if you don't have lots of cash to buy an exquisite bauble that comes in Tiffany's famous light-blue box, enjoy this renowned store à la Audrey Hepburn in *Breakfast at Tiffany's.* The designer collection features Paloma Picasso, Jean Schlumberger, and Elsa Peretti in both silver and 18-karat gold, and there's an extensive gift collection in sterling, china, and crystal. Open Monday to Saturday from 10am to 6pm.

Union Street Goldsmith. 1909 Union St. (at Laguna St.). ☎ **415/776-8048.**

A showcase for Bay Area goldsmiths, this exquisite shop sells custom-designed jewelry in all karats. Many pieces emphasize colored stones in their settings. Open Monday to Saturday from 11am to 5:45pm and Sunday from noon to 4:45pm.

MARKETS/PRODUCE

❂ **Farmers Market.** Embarcadero, in front of the Ferry Building. ☎ **510/528-6987.**

Every Tuesday and Saturday from 8:30am to 1:30pm, northern California fruit, vegetable, bread, and dairy vendors join local restaurateurs in selling fresh, delicious edibles. There's no better way to enjoy a bright San Francisco morning than strolling this gourmet street market and snacking your way through breakfast. You can also pick up locally made vinegars and oils—they make wonderful gifts.

RECORDS & CDS

Recycled Records. 1377 Haight St. (between Central and Masonic sts.). ☎ **415/ 626-4075.**

Easily one of the best used-record stores in the city, this loud shop in the Haight has a good selection of promotional CDs and cases of used "classic" rock LPs. Sheet music, tour programs, and old *TV Guides* are sold. Open Monday to Saturday from 10am to 10pm and Sunday from 11am to 7pm.

Streetlight Records. 3979 24th St. (between Noe and Sanchez sts.). ☎ **415/282-3550.**

Overstuffed with used music in all three formats, this place is best known for its records and excellent CD collection. Rock music is cheap here, and a money-back guarantee guards against defects. Their second location is at 2350 Market St., between Castro and Noe streets (☎ **415/282-8000**); call for open hours. Open Monday to Saturday from 10am to 10pm and on Sunday from 10:30am to 8:30pm.

Virgin Megastore. 2 Stockton (at Market St.). ☎ **415/397-4525.**

With thousands of CDs, including an impressive collection of imports, videos, laser discs, a multimedia department, a cafe, and related books, any music-lover could blow his or her entire vacation fund in this enormous Union Square store. Open Monday to Thursday from 9am to 10pm, Friday and Saturday from 9am to midnight, and Sunday from 10am to 10pm.

SHOES

Birkenstock Natural Footwear. 1815 Polk St. (between Washington and Jackson sts.). ☎ **415/776-5225.**

This relaxed store is known for its California-style, form-fitting sandals. Other orthopedically correct shoes are also available, including Finn Comforts and traditional Danish clogs by Dansko. Open daily from 10:30am to 6pm.

Bulo. 437A Hayes St. (at Gough St.). ☎ **415/864-3244.**

If you have a fetish for foot fashions, you must check out Bulo, which carries nothing but imported Italian men's and women's shoes. The selection is small but styles run the gamut, from casual to dressy, reserved to wildly funky. Since new shipments come in every 3 to 4 weeks, their selection is ever-changing, eternally hip, and unfortunately, ever-expensive, with many pairs going for close to $200. Open Monday to Saturday from 11:30am to 6:30pm and Sunday from noon to 6pm.

Kenneth Cole. 865 Market St. (in the San Francisco Shopping Centre). ☎ **415/227-4536.**

High-fashion footwear for men and women is sold at this trendy shop. There is also an innovative collection of handbags and small leather goods and accessories. A second shop is located at 2078 Union St., at Webster Street (☎ **415/346-2161**). Open Monday to Saturday from 11am to 8pm.

SHOPPING CENTERS & COMPLEXES

The Anchorage. 2800 Leavenworth St. (at Beach and Jefferson sts. on Fisherman's Wharf). ☎ **415/775-6000.**

This touristy waterfront mall has close to 55 stores that offer everything from music boxes to home furnishings; street performers entertain during opening hours.

The Cannery. 2801 Leavenworth St. (at Jefferson St.). ☎ **415/771-3112.**

Once a Del Monte fruit-canning plant, this complex is now occupied by a score or two of shops, restaurants, and nightspots, and thankfully only a few chain stores. Shops include **Gourmet Market** (☎ 415/673-0400), selling international foods, coffees, and teas; **The Print Store** (☎ 415/771-3576), offering a well-chosen selection of fine-art prints and local original art; and the **Basic Brown Bear Factory** (☎ 415/931-6670), where you can stuff your own teddy bear. Vendors' stalls and sidewalk cafes are also set up in the courtyard, amid a grove of olive trees. On summer weekends street performers entertain. The **Museum of the City of San Francisco** (☎ 415/928-0289) is on the third floor.

    Cobb's Comedy Club (see chapter 10, "San Francisco After Dark") is also here, along with several restaurants. The Cannery is open Monday to Saturday from 10am to 6pm and Sunday from 11am to 6pm; there are extended hours during the summer and on holidays.

Crocker Galleria. 50 Post St. (at Kearny St.). ☎ **415/393-1505.**

Modeled after Milan's Galleria Vittorio Emanuele, this glass-domed, three-level pavilion, about 3 blocks east of Union Square, features about 40 high-end shops. Fashions include Nicole Miller, Gianni Versace, and Polo/Ralph Lauren. Open Monday to Saturday from 10am to 6pm.

Ghirardelli Square. 900 North Point (between North Point and Beach sts.). ☎ **415/775-5500.**

This former chocolate factory is one of the city's largest malls and most popular landmarks. It dates from 1864 when it served as a factory making Civil War uniforms, but it's best known as the former chocolate-and-spice factory of Domingo Ghirardelli (say "Gear-a-deli"). The whole complex is crowned by a clock tower that is an exact replica of the one at France's Château de Blois. Inside the tower, on the mall's plaza level, is the Ghirardelli soda fountain, where small amounts of chocolate are still made and are available for purchase, but the big draw is the old-fashioned ice-cream parlor. A free map and guide to the mall is available from the information booth, located in the center courtyard.

Many chain stores are located here, including the women's clothier **Ann Taylor** (☎ 415/775-2872), and **The Sharper Image** (☎ 415/776-1443) for unique, upscale electronics and designs.

The complex is open Sunday to Thursday from 10am to 6pm and Friday and Saturday from 10am to 9pm. Main plaza shops' and restaurants' hours vary, with extended hours during the summer. (Incidentally, the Ghirardelli Chocolate Company still makes chocolate, but it's located in a lower-rent district in the East Bay.)

Pier 39. Embarcadero and Beach St. (on the waterfront). ☎ **415/981-8030.**

The automated information voice mail boasts Pier 39 is the "third most visited attraction in the country" and in almost the same breath reminds callers not to forget to bring along their Visa card. To residents, that pretty much wraps up Pier 39—an expensive tourist trap where out-of-towners go to waste money on worthless souvenirs and greasy fast food. For vacationers, though, Pier 39 does have some redeeming qualities—fresh crab (when in season), playful sea lions, phenomenal views, and plenty of fun for the kids. If you want to get to know the real San Francisco, skip the cheesy T-shirt shops and limit your time here to 1 afternoon.

Some of the most interesting stores include **Puppets on the Pier** (☎ 415/781-4435), a store that sells, you guessed it, puppets; and **Kite Flight** (☎ 415/956-3181), where you can buy a fanciful creation to fly in the breezes off the bay.

Open weekdays from 10:30am to 8:30pm; weekends from 10am to 8:30pm; store and restaurant hours vary; extended hours during the summer.

San Francisco Shopping Centre. 865 Market St. (at Fifth St.). ☎ **415/495-5656.**

Opened in 1988, this $140-million complex is one of the few vertical malls in the United States. Its most stunning features are the four-story spiral escalators that circle their way up to Nordstrom (see "Department Stores," above) and the nine-story atrium covered by a retractable skylight. More than 90 specialty shops include Adrienne Vittadini, Ann Taylor, Bebe, Mondi, Benetton, Footlocker, J. Crew, and Victoria's Secret. Open Monday to Saturday from 9:30am to 8pm and on Sunday from 11am to 6pm; holiday hours may vary.

TOYS

The Chinatown Kite Shop. 717 Grant Ave. (between Clay and Sacramento sts.). ☎ 415/391-8217.

This shop's astonishing assortment of flying objects includes attractive fish kites, wind socks in nylon or cotton, hand-painted Chinese paper kites, wood-and-paper biplanes, pentagonal kites, and do-it-yourself kite kits, all of which make great souvenirs or decorations. Computer-designed stunt kites have two or four control lines to manipulate loops and dives. Open daily from 10:30am to 9pm.

The Disney Store. 400 Post St. (at Powell St.). ☎ **415/391-6866.**

Capitalizing on the world's love for The Mouse and his friends, this store offers everything Disney-oriented you could possibly want—from clothes and toys to high-end commissioned art from the Disney gallery. Those looking for a simple token can fork over $3 for a plastic character, while more serious collectors can throw down $9,000 for a Yamagata Disney lithograph. Open in winter Monday to Friday from 10am to 7pm, Saturday from 10am to 6pm, and Sunday from 11am to 5pm. Hours are extended during the summer and holiday season; call for details. Another location is at Pier 39 (☎ **415/391-4119**).

FAO Schwarz. 48 Stockton St. (at O'Farrell St.). ☎ **415/394-8700.**

The world's greatest—and most overpriced—toy store for both children and adults is filled with every imaginable plaything, from hand-carved, custom-painted carousel rocking horses, dolls, and stuffed animals, to gas-powered cars, train sets, and hobby supplies. At the entrance is a singing 22-foot clock tower with 1,000 different moving parts. Open Monday to Friday from 10am to 6pm and on Sunday from 11am to 5pm.

TRAVEL GOODS

On the Road Again. Embarcadero and Beach St. (In Pier 39). ☎ **415/434-0106.**

In addition to lightweight luggage, this smart shop sells toiletry kits, travel bottles, travel-size items, and a good selection of other related goods. Open Sunday to Thursday from 10am to 7pm, and Friday and Saturday from 10am to 8:30pm; hours vary seasonally.

Thomas Bros. Maps & Books. 550 Jackson St. (at Columbus Ave.). ☎ **800/969-3072** for mail order, or 415/981-7520.

The best map shop in the city, Thomas Bros. sells street, topographic, and hiking maps depicting San Francisco, California, and the world, as well as an extensive selection of travel guides and atlases. Open Monday to Friday from 9:30am to 5:30pm.

VINTAGE CLOTHING

Aardvark's. 1501 Haight St. (at Ashbury St.). ☎ **415/621-3141.**

One of San Francisco's largest secondhand clothing dealers, Aardvark's has seemingly endless racks of shirts, pants, dresses, skirts, and hats from the last 30 years. Open daily from 11am to 7pm.

Buffalo Exchange. 1555 Haight St. (between Clayton and Ashbury sts.). ☎ **415/431-7733.**

This large storefront on upper Haight Street is crammed with racks of antique and new fashions from the 1960s, 1970s, and 1990s. It stocks everything from suits and dresses to neckties, hats, handbags, and jewelry. Buffalo Exchange anticipates some of the hottest new street fashions. Open Monday to Saturday from 11am to 7pm and Sunday from noon to 6pm. A second shop is located at 1800 Polk St. (at Washington Street; ☎ **415/346-5741**).

✪ **Good Byes.** 3463 Sacramento St. (between Laurel and Walnut sts.). ☎ **415/346-6388.**

One of our favorite new- and used-clothes stores in San Francisco, Good Byes carries only high-quality clothing and accessories, including an exceptional selection of men's fashions at unbelievably low prices (for example, $350 preowned shoes for $35). Women's wear is in a separate boutique across the street. Open Monday to Wednesday, Friday, and Saturday from 10am to 6pm; Thursday from 10am to 8pm; and Sunday from 11am to 5pm.

La Rosa. 1711 Haight St. (at Cole). ☎ **415/668-3744.**

On a street packed with vintage-clothing shops, this is one of the more upscale options, featuring a selection of high-quality, dry-cleaned secondhand goods. Formal suits and dresses are its specialty, but you'll also find sport coats, slacks, and shoes. You may also want to visit its more moderately priced sister store, Held Over, on Haight near Ashbury. Open daily from 11am to 7pm.

WINE

✪ **Wine Club San Francisco.** 953 Harrison St. (between Fifth and Sixth sts.). ☎ **415/512-9086.**

The Wine Club is a discount warehouse that offers bargain prices on more than 1,200 domestic and foreign wines. Bottles cost between $4 and $1,100. Open Monday to Saturday from 9am to 7pm and Sunday from 11am to 6pm.

San Francisco After Dark 10

For a city with fewer than a million inhabitants, San Francisco's overall artistic enterprise is nothing short of phenomenal. The city's opera is justifiably world renowned, the ballet is well respected, and the theaters are high in both quantity and quality. Dozens of piano bars and top-notch lounges are augmented by one of the best dance-club cultures this side of New York, and skyscraper lounges offer some of the most dazzling city views in the world. In short, there's always something going on in the City, so get off your fanny and get out there.

For up-to-date nightlife information, turn to the *San Francisco Weekly* and the *San Francisco Bay Guardian,* both of which contain comprehensive current listings. They are available free at bars and restaurants, and from street-corner boxes all around the city. *Where,* a free tourist monthly, also has information on programs and performance times; it's available in most of the city's finer hotels. The Sunday edition of the *San Francisco Examiner* and *Chronicle* also features a "Datebook" section, printed on pink paper, with information and listings on the week's upcoming events.

TICKETS

Tix Bay Area (☎ 415/433-7827) sells half-price tickets to theater, dance, and music performances on the day of the show only; tickets for Sunday and Monday events, if available, are sold on Saturday. They also sell advance, full-price tickets for most performance halls, sporting events, concerts, and clubs. A service charge, ranging from $1 to $3, is levied on each ticket. Only cash or traveler's checks are accepted for half-price tickets; Visa and MasterCard are accepted for full-price tickets. Tix is located on Stockton Street, between Post and Geary streets on the east side of Union Square (opposite Maiden Lane). It's open Tuesday to Thursday from 11am to 6pm, and Friday and Saturday from 11am to 7pm.

Tickets to most theater and dance events can also be obtained through **City Box Office,** 153 Kearny St., Suite 402 (☎ 415/392-4400). American Express, MasterCard, and Visa are accepted.

BASS Ticketmaster (☎ 510/762-2277) sells computer-generated tickets to concerts, sporting events, plays, and special events. Downtown BASS Ticketmaster ticketing offices include Tix Bay Area (see above) and at Warehouse stores throughout the city. The most convenient location is at 30 Powell St.

1 The Performing Arts

Special concerts and performances are staged in San Francisco year-round. **San Francisco Performances,** 500 Sutter St., Suite 710 (☎ **415/398-6449**), has been bringing acclaimed artists to the Bay Area for more than 15 years. Shows run the gamut from classical chamber music to dance and jazz. Performances are in several venues, including the city's Performing Arts Center, Herbst Theater, and the Center for the Performing Arts at Yerba Buena Center. The season lasts from late September through May. Tickets cost $12 to $55, and are available through **City Box Office** (☎ **415/392-4400**). There is also a 6pm Thursday after-work concert series at the EC Cabaret, 3 Embarcadero Center, in fall and winter; $6 admission at the door (☎ **415/398-6449** for information).

CLASSICAL MUSIC

In addition to two world-class groups, described below, visitors might also be interested in the **San Francisco Contemporary Music Players** (☎ **415/252-6235**), whose concerts are held at the Center for the Arts at Yerba Buena Gardens; they play modern chamber works by international artists. Tickets, available by phone (☎ **415/978-ARTS**), cost $14 for adults, $10 for seniors, and $6 for students. Another commendable group is the **Women's Philharmonic** (☎ **415/437-0123**). For more than 15 years, this critically acclaimed orchestra has been playing works by historical and contemporary women composers. Most performances, at least for the next season, are held at Herbst Theater. Phone for dates, programs, and ticket prices.

Philharmonia Baroque Orchestra. Performing in the Herbst Theater, 401 Van Ness Ave. ☎ **415/392-4400** (box office). Tickets $29–$39.

Acclaimed by the *New York Times* as "the country's leading early music orchestra," Philharmonia Baroque performs in San Francisco and all around the Bay Area. The season lasts from September through April. The company's administrative offices can be reached at ☎ **415/391-5252.**

San Francisco Symphony. Performing at Davies Symphony Hall, 201 Van Ness Ave. (at Grove St.). ☎ **415/864-6000** (box office). Tickets $11–$73.

Founded in 1911, the internationally respected San Francisco Symphony has long been an important part of this city's cultural life under such legendary conductors as Pierre Monteux and Seiji Ozawa. In 1995, Michael Tilson Thomas took over from Herbert Blomstedt and has already led the orchestra to new heights and crafted an exciting repertoire of classical and modern music. The season runs from September through June. Summer symphony activities include a Composer Festival and a Summer Pops series.

OPERA

In addition to San Francisco's major opera company, you might also check out the amusing **Pocket Opera,** 44 Page St., Suite 404A (☎ **415/575-1100**). From mid-January to mid-June, this comic company stages farcical performances in English of well-known operas accompanied by a chamber orchestra. The staging is intimate and informal, without lavish costumes and sets. The cast ranges from 3 to 16 players, and is supported by a similar-size orchestra. The rich repertoire includes such works as *Don Giovanni* and *The Barber of Seville.* Performances are on Saturday or Sunday. Call for complete information and show times. Tickets cost $10 (students) to $25.

San Francisco Opera. Performing at newly refurbished War Memorial Opera House, 301 Van Ness Ave. (at Grove St.). ☎ **415/864-3330** (box office). Tickets $10–$140.

The San Francisco Opera was the United States's first municipal opera, and is one of the city's cultural icons. Brilliantly balanced casts may feature celebrated stars like Frederica Von Stade and Placido Domingo, along with promising newcomers and the regular members, in productions that range from traditional to avant-garde. All productions have English supertitles. The opera season starts in September and lasts just 14 weeks. Performances are held most evenings, except Monday, with matinees on Sundays. Tickets go on sale as early as June, and the best seats sell out quickly. Unless Pavarotti or Domingo is in town, some less-coveted seats are usually available until curtain time.

THEATER

After 12 successful years, **Climate,** 252 Ninth St., at Folsom Street (☎ **415/978-2345**), is still showcasing avant-garde and experimental works in a casual and intimate atmosphere. **Eureka Theatre Company,** 330 Townsend, Suite 210, at Fourth Street (☎ **415/243-9899**), produces contemporary plays. The season runs from September through June, and performances are usually presented Wednesday to Sunday. Tickets cost $15 to $25, with discounts for students and seniors (call for specific theater location). **Theatre Rhinoceros,** 2926 16th St. (☎ **415/861-5079**), founded in 1977, was America's first (and still the foremost) theater ensemble devoted solely to works addressing gay and lesbian issues. The company presents five main stage shows and a dozen studio productions of new and classic works each year. The theater is located 1 block east of the 16th Street/Mission BART station.

✪ **American Conservatory Theater (A.C.T.).** Performing at the Geary Theater, 415 Geary St. (at Mason St.). ☎ **415/749-2228.** Tickets $14–$51.

American Conservatory Theater (A.C.T.) made its debut in 1967 and quickly established itself as the city's premier resident theater group. The troupe is so venerated that A.C.T. has been compared to the superb British National Theatre, the Berliner Ensemble, and the Comédie Française. The A.C.T. season runs from October through June and features both classical and experimental works.

A.C.T. recently returned to its home, the fabulous **Geary Theater** (1910), a national historic landmark, after the theater sustained severe damage in the 1989 earthquake and was closed for renovations. Now it's fully refurbished and modernized to such an extent that it is regarded as one of America's finest performance spaces.

Lorraine Hansberry Theatre. Performing at 620 Sutter St. ☎ **415/474-8800.**

San Francisco's top African-American theater group performs in a 300-seat theater off the lobby of the Sheehan Hotel, near Mason Street. Special adaptations from literature are performed along with contemporary dramas, classics, and world premieres. Tickets range from $15 to $25. Phone for dates and programs.

The Magic Theatre. Performing at Bldg. D, Fort Mason Center, Marina Blvd. (at Buchanan St.). ☎ **415/441-8822.** Tickets $15–$26. Discounts for students and seniors.

The highly acclaimed Magic Theatre continues to be a major West Coast company dedicated to presenting the works of new playwrights; over the years it has nurtured the talents of such luminaries as Sam Shepard and Jon Robin Baitz. Shepard's Pulitzer prize–winning play *Buried Child* premiered here. More recent productions have included works by Athol Fugard, Claire Chafee, and Nilo Cruz. The season usually runs from September through July; performances are offered Wednesday to Sunday.

DANCE

In addition to the local companies, top traveling troupes like the Joffrey Ballet and the American Ballet Theatre make regular appearances. Primary modern dance spaces include the **Theatre Artaud,** 450 Florida St., at 17th Street (☎ 415/621-7797); the **Cowell Theater,** at Fort Mason Center, Marina Boulevard, at Buchanan Street (☎ 415/441-3400); **Dancer's Group/Footwork,** 3221 22nd St., at Mission Street (☎ 415/824-5044; Web site: www.dancenet.org); and the **New Performance Gallery,** 3153 17th St., at Shotwell in the Mission District (☎ 415/863-9834). Check the local papers for schedules or contact the theater box offices directly.

San Francisco Ballet. Performances at War Memorial Opera House, 301 Van Ness Ave. (at Grove St.). ☎ 415/865-2000. Tickets and information. Tickets $7–$100.

Founded in 1933, the San Francisco Ballet is the oldest professional ballet company in the United States and is regarded as one of the country's finest, performing an eclectic repertoire of full-length, neoclassical, and contemporary ballets. Even the *New York Times* proclaimed, "The San Francisco Ballet under Helgi Tomasson's leadership is one of the spectacular success stories of the arts in America." The 1998/1999 Repertory Season runs from February through June. All performances are accompanied by the San Francisco Ballet Orchestra.

2 Comedy & Cabaret

Bay Area Theatresports (BATS). Bayfront Theater at the Fort Mason Center, Bldg. B, 3rd floor. ☎ 415/474-8935. Tickets $5–$15.

Combining improvisation with competition, Bay Area Theatresports (BATS) operates an improvisational tournament, in which four-actor teams compete against each other, taking on improvisational challenges from the audience. Judges then flash scorecards good-naturedly, or honk a horn for scenes that just aren't working. Shows are staged on Monday only. Phone for reservations.

✪ **Beach Blanket Babylon.** At Club Fugazi, 678 Green St./Beach Blanket Babylon Blvd. (between Powell St. and Columbus Ave.). ☎ 415/421-4222. Tickets $20–$50.

Now a San Francisco tradition, Beach Blanket Babylon evolved from Steve Silver's Rent-a-Freak service—a group of party-givers extraordinaire who hired themselves out as a "cast of characters" to entertain, complete with fabulous costumes and sets, props, and gags. After their act caught on, it was moved into the Savoy-Tivoli, a North Beach bar. By 1974, the audience had grown too large for the facility, and Beach Blanket has been at the 400-seat Club Fugazi ever since.

The show is a comedic musical send-up that is best known for its outrageous costumes and oversized headdresses. It's been playing almost 22 years now, and still almost every performance sells out. The show is updated often enough that locals still attend. Those under 21 are welcome at Sunday matinees at 3pm when no alcohol is served; photo ID is required for evening performances. It's wise to write for tickets at least 3 weeks in advance for weekend-performance tickets, or obtain them through Tix (see above). *Note:* When you purchase tickets, they will be within a specific section depending upon price; however, seating is still first-come/first-seated within that section. Performances are given on Wednesday and Thursday at 8pm, on Friday and Saturday at 7 and 10pm, and on Sunday at 3 and 7pm.

Cobb's Comedy Club. 2801 Beach St. (between Leavenworth and Hyde sts.). ☎ 415/928-4320. Cover $5 Mon–Wed, $10–$13 Fri–Sat, $10 Thurs and Sun (plus a 2-beverage minimum nightly). Validated parking.

Located in the Cannery at Fisherman's Wharf, Cobb's features such national head-liners as George Wallace, Emo Philips, and Jake Johannsen. There is comedy every night, including a 15-comedian All-Pro Monday showcase (a 3-hr. marathon). Cobb's is open to those 18 and over, and occasionally to kids ages 16 and 17 if they are accompanied by a parent or legal guardian (call ahead first). Shows are Monday to Wednesday at 8pm, Thursday and Sunday at 9pm, and Friday and Saturday at 8 and 10pm.

Finocchio's. 506 Broadway (at Kearny St.). ☎ **415/982-9388.** Cover $14.50 (2-drink minimum).

For more than 50 years this family-run cabaret club has showcased the best female impersonators in a funny, kitschy show. Three different revues are presented nightly (usually Thurs to Sat at 8:30, 10, and 11:30pm), and a single cover is good for the entire evening. Parking is available next door at the Flying Dutchman.

Punch Line. 444 Battery St., plaza level (between Washington and Clay sts.). ☎ **415/397-4337** or 415/397-7573 for recorded information. Cover $5 Sun, $8–$15 Tues–Sat (plus a 2-drink minimum nightly).

Adjacent to the Embarcadero One office building, this is the largest comedy night-club in the city. Three-person shows with top national and local talent are featured Tuesday to Saturday. Showcase night is Sunday, when 15 to 20 rising stars take the mike. There's an all-star showcase or a special event on Monday nights. Buy tickets in advance (if you don't want to wait in line) from **BASS** outlets (☎ **510/762-2277**). Shows are Tuesday to Thursday and Sunday at 9pm, and on Friday and Saturday at 9 and 11pm.

3 The Club & Music Scene

The greatest legacy from the 1960s is the city's continued tradition of live enter-tainment and music, which explains the great variety of clubs and music scenes available in a city of this size. The hippest dance places are located South of Market Street (SoMa), in former warehouses, while most popular cafe culture is still cen-tered in North Beach.

Note: The club and music scene is always changing, often outdating recommen-dations before the ink can dry on a page. Most of the venues below are promoted as different clubs on various nights of the week, each with its own look, sound, and style. Discount passes and club announcements are often available at hip clothing stores and other shops along upper Haight Street.

Drink prices at most bars, clubs, and cafes range from about $3.50 to $6, unless otherwise noted.

DIAL-A-SCENE   The local newspapers won't direct you to the city's under-ground club scene, nor will they advise you which of the dozens of clubs are truly hot. To get dialed in, do what the locals do—turn to the **Be-At Line** (☎ **415/626-4087**) for its daily recorded update on the town's most hoppin' hip-hop, acid-jazz, and house clubs. The scene is reported by one of its coolest residents, Mayor Brown's street-suave son, Michael. For the grooviest message and inside scoop on the feel-good, underground party scene, tune in to the **Bug Out Line** (☎ **415/437-6905**). **Housewares Rave** (☎ **415/281-0125**) highlights the heavy techno scene. The **Spot Line** (☎ **415/346-7768**) will tell you where to find their DJ spinning R&B and acid jazz. The far more commercial **Club Line** (☎ **415/979-8686**) offers up-to-date schedules for the city's larger dance venues.

ROCK & BLUES CLUBS

In addition to the following listings, see "Dance Clubs," below, for (usually) live, danceable rock.

Biscuits and Blues. 401 Mason (at Geary St.). ☎ **415/292-2583.**

With a crisp, blow-your-eardrums-out sound system, New Orleans–speakeasy (albeit commercial) appeal, and nightly line-up of live entertainment, there's no better place to muse the blues than at this basement-cum-nightclub. During performances there can be a hefty cover charge (around $10), but entrance is free during happy hour (Mon to Fri from 5 to 7pm) when there's usually recorded music, drink specials, and inexpensive snacks—not to mention the only opportunity to socialize: once the bands get going, it's so loud you can't even hear yourself holler. *Note:* There's a full dinner menu here, but the only *notable* treat is the moist and flaky biscuits.

Blues. 2125 Lombard St. (at Fillmore St.). ☎ **415/771-BLUE.** Cover $3–$6.

This small, dark blues bar is packed most nights with an eclectic ethnic mix of locals. The bands are usually pretty good and easy to dance to. Owner Max Young claims it's "the only real dark, dingy blues club in the city." Gotta love that.

The EndUp. 401 Sixth St. (at Harrison St.). ☎ **415/357-0827.** Cover varies.

For over a decade, this place has thrown some of the most kickin' parties in town. Here it's a different theme every night: Monday is Reggae with Club Dread; Thursday sets swinging singles loose at the Kit Kat Club; Fag Friday is just what it sounds like, plus lots of throw-down dancing; Saturday is the very festive lesbian club The G Spot; and Sunday is ever-popular with the sleepless dance-all-day crowd who come here after the other clubs close (it opens at 5am). Call to confirm nights—venues change from time to time.

The Fillmore. 1805 Geary Blvd. (at Fillmore St.). ☎ **415/346-6000.** Tickets $9–$25.

Reopened after years of neglect, The Fillmore, made famous by promoter Bill Graham in the 1960s, is once again attracting big names. Check the local listings in magazines, or call the theater for information on upcoming events.

Grant & Green. 1371 Grant Ave. (at Green St.). ☎ **415/693-9565.** Cover $1–$4 Fri–Sat.

The atmosphere at this North Beach dive rockery is not that special, but the local bands are pretty good. Look for daytime shows on the weekends.

The Saloon. 1232 Grant Ave. (at Vallejo St.). ☎ **415/989-7666.** Cover $4–$5 Fri–Sat.

An authentic gold rush survivor, this North Beach dive is the oldest extant bar in the city. Popular with both bikers and daytime pinstripers, there's live blues nightly.

Slim's. 333 11th St. (at Folsom St.). ☎ **415/522-0333.** Cover free to $20 (plus a 2-drink minimum when seated at table).

Co-owned by musician Boz Scaggs, who sometimes takes the stage under the name "Presidio Slim." This glitzy restaurant/bar seats 300, serves California cuisine, and specializes in excellent American music—homegrown rock, jazz, blues, and alternative music—almost nightly. Menu items range from $3 to $8.50.

JAZZ & LATIN CLUBS

✪ **Cafe du Nord.** 2170 Market St. (at Sanchez St.) ☎ **415/861-5016.** Nominal cover varies.

Although it's been around since 1907, this basement-cum-jazz-supper club has finally been recognized as a respectable jazz venue. With a younger generation now appreciating the music, the place is often packed from the 40-foot mahogany bar to the back room with a pool table. Du Nord is even putting out its own compilation CDs now, which are definitely worth purchasing.

Jazz at Pearl's. 256 Columbus Ave. (at Broadway). ☎ **415/291-8255.** No cover, but there is a 2-drink minimum. Valet parking $3.

This is one of the best venues for jazz in the city. Ribs and chicken are served with the sounds, too, with prices ranging from $4 to $8.95. The live jams last until 2am nightly.

Rasselas. 2801 California St. (at Divisadero St.). ☎ **415/567-5010.** Cover free to $5.

Large, casual, and comfortable, with couches and small tables, this is a favorite spot for hearing local jazz and R&B combos. The adjacent restaurant serves Ethiopian cuisine under an elegant Bedouin tent. Menu items range from $3 to $10.75.

Up & Down Club. 1151 Folsom St. (between 7th and 8th sts.). ☎ **415/626-2388.** Cover varies.

One of the original homes for SoMa's now-familiar new-jazz scene, the Up & Down jazz supper club attracts a trendy crowd to both its restaurant and dance floor. Dinner's at 8pm (reservations required), the music starts at 9:30pm, and dancing begins at 10pm.

DANCE CLUBS

While a lot of clubs around town allow dancing, at the followings clubs dancing is the number-one priority—these are the places to go if all you want to do is shake your groove thang.

Club 181. 181 Eddy St. (at Taylor St.). ☎ **415/673-8181.** Cover $5–$10.

Twenty-something and looking to gyrate the night away in a dark retro club crammed with glamorous hotties? Since this place is located on probably the absolute shadiest street in San Francisco, we thought that its popularity would die down once the limos stopped double-parking out front, but we were dead wrong. It may be true that the core hip crowd long abandoned this scene for newer and less-known parties, but that doesn't mean the place isn't jumping. With a combination of great ambiance, decent food, and throw-down funk and acid jazz, 181 has made a niche for itself. Early evening there's live entertainment and later a DJ spinning slamming old-school. All night the pool room is packed with both players and voyeurs who recline along terraced banquettes, smoke cigarettes, and look cool. In the front room, if you're not dancing, head to the bar or you're liable to get swept away in the sweaty groove. A decent dinner is served here too, and there's parking next door for $6. Dress code says no tennis shoes, torn Levi's, or baseball caps. Open Tuesday to Saturday from 9pm to 3am.

Club Ten 15. 1015 Folsom St. (at Sixth St.). ☎ **415/431-1200.** Cover $5–$10.

Get decked out and plan for a late-nighter if you're headed to this enormous party warehouse. Three levels and dance floors offer a variety of dancing venues, complete with a 20- and 30-something gyrating mass who live for the DJs' pounding house, disco, and acid-jazz music. Each night is a different club that attracts its own crowd that ranges from yuppie to hip-hop. As this book goes to press, **Nikita** (☎ 415/267-0568) is held on Friday from 10pm to 6am, featuring different sounds: 1970s disco, progressive house, techno, trip-hop, and acid jazz. Saturday is **Release,** a combo of hip-hop and disco, deep house, and acid jazz (☎ 415/281-0823 for schedules). Other nights are hot, too, so call ☎ 415/431-1200 for a complete schedule of events.

Nickie's Bar-be-cue. 460 Haight St. (between Fillmore and Webster sts.). ☎ **415/621-6508.** Cover $3–$5.

Don't show up here for dinner. The only hot thing you'll find here is the small, crowded dance floor. But don't let that stop you from checking it out—Nickie's is a sure thing. Every time we come here, the old-school disco hits are in full-force, casually dressed happy dancers lose all inhibitions, and the crowd is mixed with all types of friendly San Franciscans. This place is perpetually hot, so dress accordingly. And you can always cool down with a pint from the wine-and-beer bar. Keep in mind, lower Haight is on the periphery of some shady housing projects, so don't make your rental car look tempting, and stay alert as you walk through the area.

Paradise Lounge. 1501 Folsom St. (at 11th St.). ☎ **415/861-6906.** Cover $3–$15.

Labyrinthine Paradise features three dance floors simultaneously vibrating to different beats. Smaller, auxiliary spaces include a pool room with a half-dozen tables. Poetry readings are also given.

Sound Factory. 525 Harrison St. (at First St.). ☎ **415/243-9646.** Cover $10 Fri, $15 Sat.

Herb Caen dubbed this disco theme park the "mother of all discos." The maze of rooms and nonstop barrage of house, funk, lounge vibes, and club classics attracts swarms of young urbanites looking to rave it up until sometimes as late as 6am. Management tries to eliminate the riffraff by enforcing a dress code (no sneakers, hooded sweatshirts, or sports caps).

SUPPER CLUBS

If you can eat dinner, listen to live music, and dance (or at least wiggle in your chair) in the same room, it's a supper club—that's our criteria.

Coconut Grove Supper Club. 1415 Van Ness Ave. (between Bush and Pine sts.) ☎ **415/776-1616.** Cover $5 Tues–Thurs, $8 Fri–Sat.

Reopened in 1996 after being shunned for outrageous prices, the new—and far less expensive—Coconut Grove Supper Club is doing a brisk business serving a California/tropical/Cajun menu and live music to a mostly young, hip audience. Dancing and chocolate martinis are the main attraction. The dress code is lax, but vintage is definitely the main attire.

Harry Denton's. 161 Steuart St. (between Mission and Howard sts.). ☎ **415/882-1333.** $10 cover after 10pm Thurs–Sat (free other times).

Early evening it's filled with working "suits" and secretaries on the prowl. But weekend nights reflect the restaurant owner, Harry Denton, who, although now sober, is known for getting himself and his guests intoxicated and dancing on tables and being the all-around wildest party host in town. When the stately restaurant with mahogany bar, red velvet furnishings, and chandeliers clears away dining utensils and turns up the music, a glitzy crowd pulls up to the valet with their boogie shoes on. In the front lounge R&B or jazz performers usually play loud enough to drown out the disco and pop dancing in the back room. But that's where all the action is, so head back there and join the 30- and 40-something yuppie masses flailing to 1970s disco hits. Eat dinner at neighboring Boulevard first—the food here is not memorable.

Harry Denton's Starlight Room. Atop the Sir Francis Drake Hotel, 450 Powell St., 21st floor. ☎ **415/395-8595.** Cover $5 Wed–Thurs after 7pm, $10 Fri–Sat after 8pm.

Come dressed to the nines or in casual attire to this old-fashioned cocktail-lounge-cum-nightclub where tourists and locals sip cocktails at sunset and boogie down to live swing and big-band tunes after dark. The room is classic 1930s San Francisco, with red-velvet banquettes, chandeliers, and fabulous views. But what really attracts flocks of all ages is a night of Harry Denton–style fun, which usually includes plenty of drinking and unrestrained dancing. The full bar stocks a decent collection of single-malt scotches and champagnes, and you can snack from the pricey Starlight appetizer menu. Like Harry's SoMa dance club, early evening is more relaxed, but come the weekend, this place gets loose.

Johnny Love's. 1500 Broadway (at Polk St.). ☎ **415/931-6053.** Cover $10 Fri–Sat, $5 Wed–Thurs. Free before 9pm.

Named after the friendly owner-cum-house-bartender who woos flocks of women with a canned line, boyish grin, and a kiss, Johnny Love's is the city's quintessential singles spot and one of the best bars in town to dance to live music. The crowd here is definitely out for a good time, so the scene is festive (while most bar atmospheres around town are too posed to really get down). This place is mainly a bar and restaurant, so be prepared to bump elbows with your neighbors on the small dance floor. Love's serves food, too, but there are better dining options within a few blocks.

Julie's Supper Club. 1123 Folsom St. (at Seventh St.). ☎ **415/861-0707.** No cover.

Julie's is a longtime standby for cocktailing and late dining. Divided into two rooms, the vibe is very 1950s cartoon, with a space-aged "Jetsons" appeal. Good-looking singles prowl, cocktails in hand, as live music plays by the front door. The food is hit-and-miss, but the atmosphere is definitely a casual and playful winner with a little interesting history; this building is one location where the Symbionese Liberation Army held Patty Hearst hostage back in the 1970s. Menu items range from $7.50 to $16. A smaller, more stylish sister of the Supper Club is **Julie Ring's Heart and Soul,** located in the Russian Hill district at 1695 Polk St. at Clay (☎ **415/673-7100**).

330 Ritch. 330 Ritch (between 3rd and 4th sts. off Townsend). ☎ **415/541-9574** or 415/522-9558 (for recorded band information). Cover $3–$10.

If you can find the place, you must be cool. It's located on a 2-block alley in SoMa, and even locals have a hard time remembering how to get there. But once you do, expect happy-hour cocktails (specials on a few select mixed drinks and draft brews), pool tables, and a hip, young crowd at play. On weekends, the place really livens up when bands take center stage on Fridays, and the Latin lovers salsa all night to the spicy beat. Free swing-dancing lessons (with $5 cover charge) are offered every Wednesday to the Bay Area's best swing bands. A "hearty American" dinner is served Wednesday to Saturday from 6 to 10pm.

RETRO CLUBS

Well, daddyo, I hope you didn't throw out those old duds of yours, because America's halcyon days are back in fashion. So don your fedora and patent leather shoes, cause you don't mean a thing if you can't swing.

Bruno's. 2389 Mission St. (at 20th St.). ☎ **415/550-7455.** Cover $3–$7 after 9:30pm.

Before its recognition as a destination restaurant, Mission District hipsters were already keen on this retro hot spot. There's live music nightly in the back lounge, and the long, 1950s-style full bar is almost always crowded with a mixture of wanna-bes, the cool, and the curious. Appetizers and desserts are served until 1am.

Club Deluxe. 1511 Haight St. (at Ashbury St.). ☎ **415/552-6949.** Cover $4.

Before the recent 1940s trend hit the city, Deluxe and its fedora-wearing clientele had been celebrating the bygone era for years. Fortunately, even with all the retro-hype, the vibe here hasn't changed. Expect an eclectic mix of throw-backs and generic San Franciscans in the intimate, smoky bar and adjoining lounge, and live jazz or blues most nights. Although many regulars dress the part, there's no attitude here, so come as you like.

Hi-Ball Lounge. 473 Broadway (between Kearny and Montgomery sts.). ☎ **415/397-9464.** Cover $3–$7.

Retro-jazz is in full swing in the city, and one of the most popular places to hear it—and dance to it—is at this North Beach joint. Harking back to Broadway at its best, the vibe is full-on 1940s/1950s, from the red banquettes and stage curtains, to the small, dark, and smoky room. Live bands perform nightly to a young, swingin' crowd. There's also a swing-dance class 1 night a week.

4 The Bar Scene

Finding your idea of a comfortable bar has a lot to do with picking a neighborhood filled with your kind of people and investigating that area. There are hundreds of bars throughout San Francisco, and although many are obscurely located and can't be classified by their neighborhood, the following is a general description of what you'll find and where:

- Chestnut and Union Street bars attract a postcollegiate crowd.
- Mission District haunts are frequented by young alternatives.
- Upper Haight caters to eclectic neighborhood cocktailers.
- Lower Haight is skate-/snowboarder grungy.
- Downtown pubs mix tourists with theatergoers and thirsty businesspeople.
- North Beach serves all types.
- Castro caters to gay locals and tourists.
- South of Market (SoMa) offers an eclectic mix.

The following is a list of a few of San Francisco's more interesting bars.

Albion. 3139 16th St. (between Valencia and Guerrero sts.). ☎ **415/552-8558.**

This Mission District club is a grit-and-leather in-crowd place packed with artistic types and various SoMa hipsters. Live music plays Sunday between 5 and 8pm and ranges from ragtime and blues to jazz and swing.

Backflip. 601 Eddy St. (at Larkin St.). ☎ **415/771-FLIP.**

Adjoining the rock 'n' roll Phoenix Hotel, this shimmering aqua-blue cocktail lounge—designed to induce the illusion that you're carousing in the deep end—serves tapas and Caribbean-style appetizers to a mostly young, fashionable crowd, so please don't order a Cosmopolitan. Since this is a new hot spot in town, the scene continues to change. On Thursday the crowd seems to be young and gay/alternative; weekends, wanna-be-cool yuppies tend to pack the place. Regardless, if you're headed here, you can expect the unexpected, kick back with a martini, and enjoy the city's finest eye candy.

Beer Cellar. 685 Sutter (at Taylor St.). ☎ **415/441-5678.** Minimal cover.

This is a good place to get drunk and dance when you can't think of anywhere else to go. Always a scene, with a mostly young, eclectic crowd grooving to guest DJs spinning everything from R&B to funk, techno, seventies, Latin—you name it. It's usually dark, smoky, and funky downstairs, but reliably fun if you're in the mood to dance. Happy hour's from 5 to 7pm, though most don't show up until 10pm.

✪ **Bottom of the Hill.** 1233 17th St. (at Missouri St.). ☎ **415/621-4455.** Cover $3–$7.

Voted one of the best places to hear live rock in the city by the *San Francisco Bay Guardian,* this popular neighborhood club attracts an eclectic crowd ranging from rockers to real-estate salespeople. The main attraction is live music every night of the week, but it also offers pretty good burgers and kebabs, outdoor seating on the back patio, and an awesome $4 all-you-can-eat barbecue on Sunday from 4 to 7pm. There's also happy hour Monday to Friday from 4 to 7pm.

Caribbean Zone. 55 Natoma St. (between 1st and 2nd sts.). ☎ **415/541-9465.** No cover.

Not just another restaurant bar, this is a visual Disneyland, jam-packed with a cluttered, tropical decor that includes a full-size airplane fuselage. It's been around a little too long, but tourists seem to love it. Dinner ranges from $12 to $20.

Chalkers Billiard Club. One Rincon Center, 101 Spear St. (at Mission St.). ☎ **415/512-0450.**

Pool hall meets men's smoking club at this enormous, classy billiards joint. Food and drinks are delivered to the 30 cherry-wood tables, which you can rent by the hour. Happy hour on weekdays from 5 to 7pm offers more beer for your buck.

Edinburgh Castle. 950 Geary St. (between Polk and Larkin sts.). ☎ **415/885-4074.**

Since 1958 this legendary Scottish pub has been known for unusual British ales on tap and the best selection of single-malt scotches in the city. The huge pub, located near Polk Street, is decorated with Royal Air Force mementos, horse brasses, steel helmets, and an authentic Ballantine caber used in the annual Scottish games. On Friday and Saturday nights, live bagpipers pump their bladders. Fish-and-chips and other traditional foods are available until 11pm.

The Great Entertainer. 975 Bryant (at Eighth St.). ☎ **415/861-8833.**

This is a glorified pool hall with 50 pool tables, plus five private billiard suites, snooker, shuffleboard, darts, table tennis, and a video arcade. Drinks, pizza, and other dishes accompany the games. Menu items range $2 to $20.

Li Po Cocktail Lounge. 916 Grant Ave. (between Washington and Jackson sts.). ☎ **415/982-0072.**

A divey Chinese bar, Li Po is made special by a clutter of dusty Asian furnishings and mementos that include an unbelievably huge rice-paper lantern hanging from the ceiling, and a glittery golden shrine to Buddha behind the bar.

Perry's. 1944 Union St. (at Laguna St.). ☎ **415/922-9022.**

If you read *Tales of the City,* you already know that this bar and restaurant has a colorful history as a pickup place for Pacific Heights and Marina singles. Though the times are not as wild, locals still come to casually check out the happenings at the dark mahogany bar. A separate dining room offers breakfast, lunch, dinner, and brunch at candlelit tables. It's a good place for hamburgers, simple fish dishes, and pasta. Menu items range from $5 to $20.

Persian Aub Zam Zam. 1633 Haight St. (at Clayton St.). ☎ **415/861-2545.**

If you make it through the forbidding metal doors you'll feel as if you're in Casablanca, but the catch is that most people don't even get that far. The owner/bartender, Bruno, who has poured here for over 40 years, opens the place when he wants some company and arbitrarily chooses who's allowed to join him at the bar. If you meet his random requirements, play it safe and order a martini—a drink Bruno likes to serve (we've been banned for ordering a Coors Light). Along with the challenge of getting in, locals love Bruno's ne'er-changing rituals: yesteryear's prices, a classic martini, and 50¢ pieces as change. Strategic tips to better your chances at entering and being allowed to stay: Don't come with a large party (he never lets anyone sit at the tables and there are very limited bar seats); don't wear unusual attire (backward baseball hats are definitely out of the question!); drink beer from a glass, not the bottle; and don't order fancy cocktails. Then just sit back and enjoy watching everyone else get kicked out.

Pied Piper Bar. In the Sheraton Palace Hotel, 2 New Montgomery (at Market St.). ☎ **415/512-1111.**

The huge Pied Piper mural by Edwardian illustrator Maxfield Parrish steals the show at this historic mahogany bar, where high stakes were once won and lost on the roll of the dice.

The Red Room. 825 Sutter St. (at Jones St.). ☎ **415/346-7666.**

At one time the hottest cocktail lounge in town (though it's cooled off a bit), this ultramodern, Big Apple–style bar and lounge reflects no other spectrum but ruby red. Really, you gotta see this one.

The Savoy-Tivoli. 1434 Grant Ave. (at Green and Union sts.). ☎ **415/362-7023.**

Euro-trash (and wanna-bes) crowd the few pool tables and indoor and patio seating to smoke cigarettes and look cool at this popular, trendy bar. It's mostly tourists and newcomers who frequent here because posing gets tiring after a while, and there are far cooler bars in town. But a sidewalk-facing table in the heart of North Beach allows for great people-watching and the high-profile clientele does create an entertaining atmosphere. Take heed of the waitresses, who have been known to overcharge for drinks, which are supposed to range from $3.50 to $6.

Shotwell 59. 3349 20th St. (at Shotwell St.). ☎ **415/647-1141.**

Those hankering for an out-of-the-way gritty neighborhood bar featuring "beers, chicks, dogs, and bikes" (says the owner) should seek out Shotwell 59, where the young, attractive Gen-X crowd hangs in the garagelike setting. The scene is oddly complemented by a 1930s wooden bar (allegedly shipped from Germany), popcorn (free), French wine, sake, and happy hour from 5 to 7pm nightly. There's no hard booze, but draft beer comes by the pitcher for $7 (happy hour) and $9 (regularly), and if the locals don't keep you occupied, the two pool tables will.

Spec's. 12 Saroyan Place (off Columbus Ave.). ☎ **415/421-4112.**

Spec's incognito locale on Saroyan Place, a tiny alley at 250 Columbus Ave., makes it less of a walk-in bar and more of a lively locals' hangout. Its funky decor— maritime flags that hang from the ceiling, exposed brick walls lined with posters, photos, and various oddities—gives it character that intrigues every visitor. A "museum," displayed under glass, contains memorabilia and items brought back by seamen who drop in between sails, and the clientele is funky enough to keep you preoccupied while you drink a beer.

Toronado. 547 Haight St. (at Fillmore St.). ☎ **415/863-2276.**

Lower Haight isn't exactly a charming street, but there's plenty of nightlife there catering to an artistic/grungy/skateboarding twentysomething crowd. While Toronado definitely draws in the young 'uns, its 40-plus microbrews on tap and 60 bottled beers also entice a more eclectic clientele who come in search of beer heaven. The brooding atmosphere matches the surroundings: an aluminum bar, a few tall tables, dark lighting, and a back room packed with tables and chairs. A DJ picks up the pace on Friday and Saturday nights.

✪ **Tosca.** 242 Columbus Ave. (between Broadway and Pacific Ave.). ☎ **415/986-9651.**

Open daily from 5pm to 2am, Tosca is a popular watering hole for local politicos, writers, media types, and similar cognoscenti of unassuming classics. Visiting celebrities have been known to drop in as impromptu bartenders, serving martinis in chilled long-stemmed glasses. Equipped with dim lights, red leather booths, and the requisite vintage jukebox spilling out Italian arias, it's everything you'd expect an old North Beach legend to be.

Vesuvio. 255 Columbus Ave. (at Broadway). ☎ **415/362-3370.**

Situated along Jack Kerouac Alley across from the famed City Lights Bookstore is this renowned literary beatnik hangout that's not just riding its historic coattails. The atmosphere is way cool, as are the people who frequent it. Bring a chess board, borrow a game here, or write in a notebook, but whatever you do, make sure you look brooding and intense. Popular with neighborhood writers, artists, songsters, and wanna-bes, Vesuvio is crowded with self-proclaimed philosophers, and everyone else ranging from longshoremen and cab drivers to businesspeople. The convivial space is two stories of cocktail tables, complemented by a changing exhibition of local art and an ongoing slide show. In addition to drinks, Vesuvio features an espresso machine. No credit cards are accepted.

BREW PUBS

GordonBiersch Brewery. 2 Harrison St. (on the Embarcadero). ☎ **415/243-8246.**

GordonBiersch Brewery is San Francisco's largest brew-restaurant, serving decent food and tasty brew. There are always several beers to choose from, ranging from light to dark. Menu items range from $3.50 to $17.50. (See the review in chapter 6, "Dining," for more information.)

San Francisco Brewing Company. 155 Columbus Ave. (at Pacific St.). ☎ **415/434-3344.** www.sfbrewing.com.

Surprisingly low-key for an ale house, this cozy brew pub serves its brew along with burgers, fries, and the like. The bar is one of the city's few remaining old saloons, aglow with stained-glass windows, tile floors, skylit ceiling beveled glass, a mahogany bar, and a massive overhead fan running the full length of the bar—a bizarre contraption crafted from brass and palm fronds. The handmade copper brew kettle is visible from the street. There's music most evenings. Darts, chess, backgammon, cards, and dice are all available. Menu items range from $3.25 to $16. The happy-hour special, a dollar per 10-ounce microbrew beer (or $1.75 a pint), runs daily from 4 to 6pm and midnight to 1am.

Thirsty Bear Brewing Company. 661 Howard St. (1 block east of the Moscone Center). ☎ **415/974-0905.**

Seven superb, handcrafted varieties of brew, ranging from a fruit-flavored Strawberry Ale to a steak-in-a-cup stout, are always on tap at this stylish high-ceilinged

Midnight Mochas

If you happen to be wandering around North Beach past your bedtime and need to satisfy your caffeine fix, these three cafes offer not only excellent espresso, but also a glimpse into what it must have been like back in the days of the beatniks, where nothing was as crucial as a strong cup of coffee, a good smoke, and a stimulating environment.

Doing the North Beach thing is little more than hanging out in a sophisticated but relaxed atmosphere over a well-made cappuccino. You can do it here at **Caffè Greco,** 423 Columbus Ave., between Green and Vallejo streets (☎ 415/397-6261), and grab a bite, too. The affordable cafe fare includes beer, wine, a good selection of coffees, focaccia sandwiches, and desserts (try the gelato or house-made tiramisu).

Caffè Trieste, 601 Vallejo St., at Grant Avenue (☎ 415/392-6739), is one of San Francisco's most beloved cafes—very down-home Italian, with only espresso drinks, pastries, and indoor and outdoor seating. Opera is always on the jukebox, unless its Saturday afternoon, when the family and their friends break out in operatic arias from 2 to 5pm.

Vesuvio, 255 Columbus Ave., at Broadway (☎ 415/362-3370), situated across Jack Kerouac Alley from the famed City Lights Bookstore, is a renowned literary beatnik hangout not merely riding its historic coattails. The atmosphere is way cool, as are the people who frequent it. Bring a chess board, borrow a game here, or write in a notebook, but whatever you do, look brooding and intense. Popular with neighborhood writers, artists, songsters, and wanna-bes, Vesuvio is crowded with self-proclaimed philosophers, and everyone else ranging from longshoremen and cab drivers to businesspeople. The convivial space is two stories of cocktail tables, complemented by a changing exhibition of local art and an ongoing slide show. In addition to drinks, Vesuvio features an espresso machine. No credit cards are accepted.

brick edifice. Excellent Spanish food, too (see chapter 6, "Dining"). Pool tables and dart boards are upstairs, and live music (jazz, flamenco, blues, alternative, and classical) can be heard most nights.

20 Tank Brewery. 316 11th St. (at Folsom St.). ☎ **415/255-9455.**

Right in the heart of SoMa's popular strip, this huge, come-as-you-are bar is known for serving good beer at fair prices. Pizzas, sandwiches, chilies, and assorted appetizers are also available. Menu items range from $1.95 to $12.95. Pub games include darts, shuffleboard, and dice.

COCKTAILS WITH A VIEW

The Carnelian Room. 555 California St., in the Bank of America Building (between Kearny and Montgomery sts.). ☎ **415/433-7500.**

On the 52nd floor of the Bank of America Building, the Carnelian Room offers uninterrupted views of the city. From a window-front table you feel as if you can reach out, pluck up the TransAmerica Pyramid, and stir your martini with it. In addition to cocktails, "Discovery Dinners" are offered for $35 per person. Jackets and ties are required for men. *Note:* The restaurant has the most extensive wine list in the city—1,275 selections to be exact.

Cityscape. Atop Hilton Tower I, 333 O'Farrell St. (at Mason St.), 46th floor. ☎ **415/923-5002.**

When you sit under the glass roof and sip a drink here, it's as if you're sitting out under the stars and enjoying views of the bay. There's nightly dancing to a DJ's picks from 10pm. The mirrored columns and floor-to-ceiling draperies help create an elegant and romantic ambiance.

Crown Room. In the Fairmont Hotel, 950 Mason St., 24th floor. ☎ **415/772-5131.**

Of all the bars listed here, the Crown Room is definitely the plushest. Reached by an external glass elevator, the panoramic view from the top will encourage you to linger. In addition to drinks (steep at $7 to $9), dinner buffets are served for $34.

Equinox. In the Hyatt Regency Hotel, 5 Embarcadero Center. ☎ **415/788-1234.**

The sales "hook" of the Hyatt's rooftop Equinox is a revolving floor that gives each table a 360° panoramic view of the city every 45 minutes. In addition to cocktails, dinner is served daily.

Harry Denton's Starlight Room. Atop the Sir Francis Drake Hotel, 450 Powell St., 21st floor. ☎ **415/395-8595.**

See "Supper Clubs" above for a full review.

✪ **Top of the Mark.** In the Mark Hopkins Intercontinental, 1 Nob Hill (California and Mason sts.). ☎ **415/616-6916.**

This is one of the most famous cocktail lounges in the world and for good reason— the spectacular glass-walled room features an unparalleled view. During World War II, it was considered de rigueur for Pacific-bound servicemen to toast their goodbye to the States here. Live entertainment is offered at 8:30 nightly, but there is a $6 to $10 cover charge these nights, too. There's afternoon tea service from 3 to 5pm Monday to Saturday, and Sunday brunch, which is served from 10am to 2pm, costs $35 without champagne, $45 with. Drinks are also pricey, ranging from $6 to $8.

PIANO BARS

San Francisco is lucky to have several lively piano bars. As in other cities, these specialized lounges are perfectly suited to the grand hotels in which they are usually located.

Nob Hill Terrace. In the Mark Hopkins Intercontinental, 1 Nob Hill (California and Mason sts.). ☎ **415/392-3434.**

Drinks ($5 to $8) are served nightly in a delightfully intimate, skylit room with hand-painted murals. It's located just off the lobby.

The Piazza Lounge. In the Parc Fifty-Five Hotel, 55 Cyril Magnin St. (Market and North Fifth sts.). ☎ **415/392-8000.**

Sink into a handsome velvet chair, gaze out into the three-story atrium, and relax to a mix of old and new melodies played on an ebony grand piano.

The Redwood Room. In the Clift Hotel, 495 Geary St. ☎ **415/775-4700.**

A true art-deco beauty, this ground-floor lounge is one of San Francisco's most comfortable and nostalgic piano bars. Its gorgeous redwood interior was completely built from a single 2,000-year-old tree. It's further enhanced by the large, brilliantly colored Gustav Klimt murals. Drinks go for $6 to $9.

SPORTS BARS

Bayside Sports Bar and Grill. 1787 Union St. (at Octavia St.). ☎ **415/673-1565.**

This is easily one of the largest sports bars in the city, equipped with a state-of-the-art superlarge-screen television, 29 smaller ones, 19 beers on tap, and two pool tables. The crowd is mainly Marina yuppies (lots of baseball caps, sweatshirts, and Lycra shorts), which is made bearable by the fast, friendly food service (mostly burgers, sandwiches, and such) and the myriad of sports channels. Happy hour is Monday to Friday from 4 to 6pm.

Greens Sports Bar. 2239 Polk St. (at Green St.). ☎ **415/775-4287.**

If you think San Francisco sports fans aren't as enthusiastic as those on the East Coast, we dare you to try to get a seat (or even get in) at Green's during a 49ers game. It's a classic old sports bar, with lots of polished dark woods and windows that open out onto Polk Street, but it's loaded with modern appliances, including a large-screen television, 10 smaller ones, 18 beers on tap, and a pool table. They don't serve food here, but you can bring in grub for the game. A late-night happy hour runs Sunday to Wednesday from 10pm to 2am.

WINE BARS

Alain Rondelli. 126 Clement St. (at Second Ave.). ☎ **415/387-0408.**

One of San Francisco's premier French restaurants, Rondelli also offers its entire selection of California and French wines by the glass. A good choice if you're already in the Avenues.

Eos. 101 Carl St. (at Cole St.). ☎ **415/566-3063.**

If you're downtown, London Wine Bar. If you're around the Civic Center, Hayes and Vine. For anything west of these two, your top choice is Eos, a fairly new and highly successful restaurant and wine bar in Cole Valley (near the Haight). Around the corner from the restaurant is this chic, lively wine bar filled mostly with a young Cole Valley clientele who dabble among the 400 vintages from around the world.

Hayes and Vine. 377 Hayes St. (at Gough St.). ☎ **415/626-5301.**

Choose among 350 wines from around the world at this unpretentious wine bar staffed by true cognoscenti of fine wine (which is a good thing, since you'll probably have never heard of 90% of these wines). Be sure to ask about taking a "flight," where you can try several different wines for a fixed price. Cheese, breads, and desserts are also served.

London Wine Bar. 415 Sansome St. (between Sacramento and Clay sts.). ☎ **415/ 788-4811.**

This British-style wine bar and store is a popular after-work hangout among Financial District suits. It's more of a place to drink and chat than to admire fine wines. Usually two to three dozen wines are open at any given time, mostly from California. It's a great venue for sampling local Napa Valley wines before you buy.

5 Gay & Lesbian Bars & Clubs

As with straight establishments, gay and lesbian bars and clubs target varied clienteles. Whether you're into leather or Lycra, business or bondage, there's gay nightlife here just for you.

Check the free weeklies, the *San Francisco Bay Guardian* and *San Francisco Weekly,* for listings of events and happenings. The *Bay Area Reporter* is a gay paper with comprehensive listings, including a weekly community calendar. All the above papers are free and are distributed weekly on Wednesday or Thursday. They can be found stacked at the corner of 18th and Castro streets, and Ninth and Harrison streets, as well as in bars, bookshops, and stores around town. To find out what's up with lesbian events in San Francisco ranging from women's golf to nightlife, call **Girl Spot** (☎ 415/337-4962). There are also a number of gay and lesbian guides to San Francisco. See "For Gay Men & Lesbians," in chapter 2, "Planning a Trip to San Francisco," for further details.

Listed below are some of the city's more established, mainstream gay hangouts.

Alta Plaza. 2301 Fillmore St. (at Clay St.). ☎ **415/922-1444.** www.altaplaza.com. No cover.

Pacific Heights's wealthy gays flock to this classy Fillmore establishment, with both bar and restaurant. Cocktail hour, from 4 to 7pm nightly, offers $2.50 well and call drinks and is especially festive on Friday and Saturday. Later in the evening, the restaurant fills with yuppie diners who come for the northern California cuisine with Pacific Rim and Italian influences or to hang at the bar area and check out the hotties. There's live jazz Sunday to Thursday and a DJ on weekend nights.

Badlands. 4121 18th St. (at Castro St.). ☎ **415/626-9320.** No cover.

This popular hangout is decorated with license plates from practically everywhere, and a bar that stretches the length of the place. A pool table and pinball machine offer entertainment, but so do the Levi's-clad clientele for that matter.

✪ **The Café.** 2367 Market St. (at Castro St.). ☎ **415/861-3846.**

When this place first got jumping, it was the only predominantly lesbian dance club on Saturday nights in the city. But once the guys found out how much fun the girls were having, they joined the party. Today, it's still a very happening mixed gay and lesbian scene with two bars, a steamy, free-spirited dance floor, and a small patio.

Castro Station. 456B Castro St. (between 17th and 18th sts.). ☎ **415/626-7220.** No cover.

A well-known gay hangout in the Castro District, this bar is popular with the leather and Levi's crowd, as well as trendy boys from around the country who come here looking for action. Drinks range from $1.75 to $4, except for during "Beer Bust," when it's $6 for all the suds you can drink.

The Cinch Saloon. 1723 Polk St. (near Washington St.). ☎ **415/776-4162.** No cover.

Among the popular attributes of this cruisey neighborhood bar are the outdoor patio, Sunday barbecue or buffet, and progressive music and videos. Forty-niner fans also gather here for televised games. Decorated in a Southwestern theme ("down home in Arizona"), the bar attracts a mixed crowd of gays, lesbians (now that there are almost no exclusively lesbian bars left in San Francisco), and gay-friendly straight folk. There are "beer busts" or theme drink nights weekly. The nominal charge for barbecues and buffets is donated entirely to various AIDS organizations.

Detour. 2348 Market St. (near Castro St.). ☎ **415/861-6053.** No cover.

Right in the heart of gay San Francisco, this bar attracts a young, often hot crowd of boys, with its low lighting and throbbing house music. Chain-link fences seem to hold in the action, while a live DJ spins a web of popular hits. Special events, including the Saturday go-go dancers, keep this place jumping.

The Eagle. 398 12th St. (at Harrison St.). ☎ **415/626-0880.** www.sfeagle.com.

One of the city's most traditional Levi-leather bars, The Eagle boasts a heated outdoor patio, a happy hour Tuesday to Friday from 4 to 8pm, and a popular Sunday-afternoon beer fest. There's an $8 donation at the beer bust on Sunday, which goes to benefit local AIDS and other organizations.

The EndUp. 401 Sixth St. (at Harrison St.). ☎ **415/357-0827.** Cover varies.

It's a different nightclub every night of the week, but regardless of who's throwing the party, the place is always jumping with the DJ's blasting tunes. There are two pool tables, a flaming fireplace, outdoor patio, and a mob of gyrating souls on the dance floor. Some nights are straight, so call for gay nights.

Giraffe Lounge. 1131 Polk St. (near Sutter St.). ☎ **415/474-1702.** No cover.

Favored by a younger, action-seeking crowd, this video bar, with its 12 ceiling-mounted monitors, is a good place for cruising or shooting pool. It's a friendly neighborhood hangout during the week and livens up on weekends.

Kimo's. 1351 Polk St. (at Pine St.). ☎ **415/885-4535.** Free to nominal cover.

This neighborhood bar located in the seedier gay section of town is a friendly oasis, decorated with plants, pictures, and "gay banners." The bar provides a relaxing venue for chatting, drinking, and quiet cruising, and things occasionally liven up when drag shows preside.

Lonestar. 1354 Harrison St. (between 9th and 10th sts.). ☎ **415/863-9999.** No cover.

Expect dykes and a heavier, furrier motorcycle crowd (both men and women) most every night. The Sunday-afternoon beer bust on the patio is especially popular.

Metro. 3600 16th St. (at Market St.). ☎ **415/703-9750.** No cover.

With modern art on the walls and much use of terra-cotta, the Metro provides the gay community with high-energy dance music and the best view of the Castro District from its large balcony. The bar seems to attract people of all ages who enjoy the friendly bartenders and the highly charged, cruising atmosphere. There's also a Chinese restaurant on the premises if you get hungry.

The Mint. 1942 Market St. (at Laguna St.). ☎ **415/626-4726.** No cover.

Come out of the closet and the shower and into The Mint, where every night you can sing show tunes at this gay and lesbian karaoke bar. Along with song, you'll encounter a mixed 20- to 40-something crowd who like to combine cocktails with do-it-yourself cabaret.

Rawhide II. 280 Seventh St. (at Folsom St.). ☎ **415/621-1197.** Weekend cover charge ($5) includes 1 free drink.

Gay or straight, this is one of the city's top country-western dance bars, patronized by both men and women. Free dance lessons are offered Monday to Friday from 7:30 to 9:30pm.

The Stud. 399 Ninth St. (at Harrison St.). ☎ **415/863-6623.** Cover $2–$6 weekends.

The Stud has been around for 30 years, is one of the most successful gay establishments in town, and is mellow enough for straights as well as gays. The interior has an antique-shop look and a miniature train circling over the bar and dance floor. Music here is a balanced mix of old and new, and nights vary from cabaret and oldies to disco. Call in advance for the evening's venue. Drink prices range from $1.25 to $5.75.

The Swallow. 1750 Polk St. (between Clay and Washington sts.). ☎ **415/775-4152.** No cover.

Some consider this classy piano bar for the middle-age-and-up crowd the best gay bar on Polk.

Twin Peaks Tavern. 401 Castro St. (at 17th and Market sts.). ☎ **415/864-9470.** No cover.

Right at the intersection of Castro, 17th, and Market streets is one of the Castro's most famous gay hangouts, which caters to an older crowd and is considered the first gay bar in America. Because of its relatively small size and desirable location, the place becomes fairly crowded and convivial by 8pm, earlier than many neighboring bars.

6 Film

The **San Francisco International Film Festival,** held in March of each year, is one of America's oldest film festivals. Tickets are relatively inexpensive. Entries include new films by beginning and established directors. For a schedule or information, call ☎ **415/931-FILM.** Tickets can be charged by phone through **BASS Ticketmaster** (☎ **510/762-2277**).

Even if you're not here in time for the festival, don't despair. The classic, independent, and mainstream cinemas in San Francisco are every bit as good as the city's other cultural offerings.

REPERTORY CINEMAS

Castro Theatre. 429 Castro St. (near Market St.). ☎ **415/621-6120.**

Built in 1922, the beautiful Castro Theatre is known for its screenings of classic cinema and for its Wurlitzer organ, which is played before each show. There's a different feature here almost nightly, and more often than not it's a double feature. Bargain matinees are usually offered on Wednesday, Saturday, Sunday, and holidays. Phone for schedules, prices, and show times.

Red Vic. 1727 Haight St. (between Cole and Shrader sts.). ☎ **415/668-3994.**

The worker-owned Red Vic movie collective recently moved from the Victorian building that gave it its name. The theater specializes in independent releases and contemporary cultish hits. Prices are $6 for adults, $3 for seniors and kids 12 and under. Phone for schedules and show times.

Roxie. 3117 16th St. (at Valencia St.). ☎ **415/863-1087.**

The Roxie consistently screens the best new alternative films anywhere. The low-budget contemporary features shown here are largely devoid of Hollywood candy coating; many are West Coast premieres. Films change weekly, sometimes sooner. Phone for schedules, prices, and show times.

11

A Side Trip to the Wine Country

Even if you're having the time of your life in downtown San Francisco, we highly recommend you consider at least a quick jaunt to the valley, which happens to be a mere hour or so north by car. Amidst the mountains dipping into a grapevine-trellised valley, you'll experience an entirely different northern California: fresh country air, hot weather, some of the world's finest wineries, incredible restaurants, green pastures, and virtually nothing to do but overindulge. With eating, drinking, and lounging as the encouraged attractions, there's virtually no better definition of a vacation than a few days here.

To decide which of the Wine Country's two distinct valleys (Napa and Sonoma) you'll prefer to visit, you'll need to consider the differences between them. The most obvious distinction is size—Napa Valley dwarfs Sonoma Valley both in population, number of wineries, and sheer volume of tourism (and traffic). Napa is definitely the more commercial of the two, with many more wineries to visit, spas (at far cheaper rates) to choose from, and a far superior selection of fine restaurants, hotels, and quintessential Wine Country activities like hot-air ballooning. Further, if your goal is to really learn about the wonderful world of wine making, Napa Valley is your choice. World-class wineries such as Sterling and Robert Mondavi offer the most interesting and edifying wine tours in North America, if not the world (though Sonoma's Benziger Winery gives them a run for their money).

If you're planning a more extensive trip to the area, consult *Frommer's Portable California Wine Country.*

1 Napa Valley

55 miles N of San Francisco

Napa and its neighboring towns have an overall tourist and big-business feel to them. You'll still get plenty of rolling hills, flora and fauna, and vast stretches of vineyards, but they come hand-in-hand with large, upscale restaurants; designer discount outlets; rows of hotels; and in summer, plenty of traffic. Even with hordes of visitors year-round, Napa is still pretty sleepy, focusing on daytime attractions (wine, outdoor activities, and spas) and, of course, food. Nightlife is very limited, but after indulging all day, most visitors are ready to turn in early anyway.

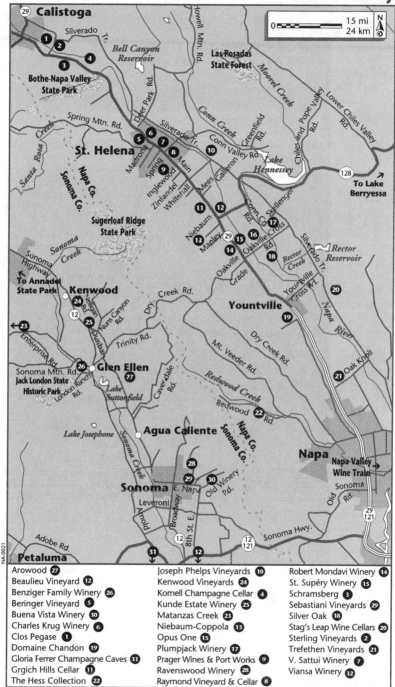

The Wine Country

0 ‖‖‖‖‖ 15 mi
         24 km

Calistoga ㉙

Silverado ❶ ❷
❹
Bothe-Napa Valley ❸
State Park

Bell Canyon
Reservoir

Las Posadas
State Forest

St. Helena
❺ ❻ ❼
❽
❾
⑩

Silverade Tr.

Conn Creek

Lake
Hennessey

⑫⑧

Sugarloaf Ridge
State Park

⑪ ⑫
⑬
⑭ ⑮ ⑯
⑰
⑱

128

To Lake
Berryessa

Rector
Reservoir

To Annadel
State Park

Kenwood
㉔
⑫ ㉕

②③

Yountville
⑲
⑳

Sonoma Mtn. Rd.
Jack London State
Historic Park

㉖
Glen Ellen
㉗

Napa River

Oak Knoll

㉑

Agua Caliente

Redwood Creek

㉒

Napa
Napa Valley
Wine Train

Lake Josephone

Sonoma
㉘
㉙ ㉚
E. Napa
Leveroni

Old Winery Rd.

29
121

Sonoma Hwy.

⑫
121

Petaluma
Adobe Rd.
㉛
㉜

Arowood ㉗	Joseph Phelps Vineyards ⑩	Robert Mondavi Winery ⑭
Beaulieu Vineyard ⑫	Kenwood Vineyards ㉔	St. Supéry Winery ⑮
Benziger Family Winery ㉖	Kornell Champagne Cellar ❹	Schramsberg ❸
Beringer Vineyard ❺	Kunde Estate Winery ㉕	Sebastiani Vineyards ㉙
Buena Vista Winery ㉚	Matanzas Creek ㉓	Silver Oak ⑱
Charles Krug Winery ❻	Niebaum-Coppola ⑬	Stag's Leap Wine Cellars ⑳
Clos Pegase ❶	Opus One ⑯	Sterling Vineyards ❷
Domaine Chandon ⑲	Plumpjack Winery ⑰	Trefethen Vineyards ㉑
Gloria Ferrer Champagne Caves ㉛	Prager Wines & Port Works ❾	V. Sattui Winery ❼
Grgich Hills Cellar ⑪	Ravenswood Winery ㉘	Viansa Winery ㉜
The Hess Collection ㉒	Raymond Vineyard & Cellar ❽	

NA-0021

239

While "Napa Valley" seems ominous on a map, it's actually relatively condensed and only 25 miles long, which means you can venture up from the town of Napa all the way to Calistoga in less than half an hour (traffic permitting).

ESSENTIALS

GETTING THERE   From San Francisco, cross the Golden Gate Bridge and continue north on U.S. 101. Turn east on Calif. 37, then north on Calif. 29, the main road through the wine country.

California Highway 29 runs the length of Napa Valley. You really can't get lost—there's just one north-south road, on which most of the wineries, hotels, shops, and restaurants are located.

VISITOR INFORMATION   Get wine-country maps and brochures from the **Wine Institute** at 425 Market St., Suite 1000, San Francisco, CA 94105 (☎ 415/512-0151). Once in the Napa Valley, stop first at **The Napa Conference & Visitors Bureau,** 1310 Town Center Mall, Napa, CA 94559 (☎ 707/ 226-7459) and pick up the slick *Napa Valley Guide* or call in advance to order their $10 package, which includes the guide plus a bunch of brochures, a map, a *Four Perfect Days in The Wine Country Itinerary,* and hot-air–balloon discount coupons. If you want less to recycle, call **Vintage Publications,** 760 Adobe Dr., Santa Rosa, CA 95404 (☎800/651-8953) to mail-order just the guide ($6, plus $3 for shipping within the U.S.). If you don't want to pay the bucks for the official publications, point your browser to **www.napavalley.com/nvcvb.html,** the NVCVB's official site, which has lots of the same information for free.

TOURING THE VALLEY & WINERIES

Napa Valley claims 34,000 acres of vineyards, making Napa the most densely planted wine-growing region in the United States. It's an easy venture from one end to the other; you can drive it in less than half an hour (although expect it to be closer to 50 min. during high season).

Conveniently, most of the large wineries—as well as most of the hotels, shops, and restaurants—are located along a single road, Calif. 29, which starts at the mouth of the Napa River, near the north end of San Francisco Bay, and continues north to Calistoga and the top of the growing region. All of the Napa Valley coverage in this chapter—every town, winery, hotel, and restaurant—is organized below from south to north, beginning in the village of Napa, and can be reached from this main thoroughfare.

NAPA

55 miles from San Francisco

The village of Napa serves as the commercial center of the Wine Country and the gateway to Napa Valley—hence the high-speed freeway that whips you right past it and on to the "tourist" towns of St. Helena and Calistoga. However, if you do veer off the highway, you'll be surprised to discover a small but burgeoning community of 63,000 residents with the most cosmopolitan (if you can call it that) atmosphere in the county—and some of the most affordable accommodations in the valley. Unfortunately, any charm Napa may exude is all but squelched by the used-car lots and warehouse superstores surrounding the quaint neighborhoods. But head even a few minutes north of the town of Napa and the real Wine Country atmosphere begins instantly with wineries, vineyards, and wide-open country views.

✪ **The Hess Collection.** 441 Redwood Rd., Napa. ☎ 707/255-1144. Daily 10am–4pm. From Calif. 29 north, exit Redwood Rd. west, and follow Redwood Rd. for 6½ miles.

Napa Valley Traffic Tip

Travel the Silverado Trail as often as possible to avoid Highway 29's traffic. Avoid passing through Main Street in St. Helena during high season. While a wintertime cruise from Napa to Calistoga can take 20 minutes, in summer you can expect the trek to take you closer to 50 minutes.

No place in the valley brings together art and wine better than this combination winery/art gallery on the side of Mount Veeder. While others strive to pair wine with food, Swiss art collector Donald Hess went a different route: After acquiring the old Christian Brothers winery in 1978, he continued to produce wine while funding a huge restoration and expansion project that would honor both wine and the fine arts. The result is a working winery interspersed with gloriously lit rooms that exhibit his truly stunning art collection; the free self-guided tour takes you through these galleries as it introduces you to the wine-making process.

For a $3 fee, you can sample the winery's current cabernet and chardonnay as well as one other featured wine. If you want to take some with you, by-the-bottle prices start at $9.95 for the second-label Hess select brand, while most other selections range from $15 to $35.

Stag's Leap Wine Cellars. 5766 Silverado Trail, Napa. ☎ **707/944-2020.** Daily 10am–4pm. Tours by appointment only. From Calif. 29, go east on Trancas St. or Oak Knoll Ave., then north to the cellars.

Founded in 1972, Stag's Leap shocked the oenological world in 1976 when its 1973 cabernet won first place over French wines in a Parisian blind tasting. For $5 per person, you can be the judge of the winery's current releases, or you can fork over another fiver for one of Stag's Leap's best-known wines, Cabernet Sauvignon Cask 23. The 1-hour tour runs through everything from the vineyard to production facilities and ends with a tasting; by the end of 1998, it could also include their new caves, which are currently under construction.

Trefethen Vineyards. 1160 Oak Knoll Ave., P.O. Box 2460, Napa, CA 94558. ☎ **707/255-7700.** Daily 10am–4:30pm; tours by appointment year-round. To reach Trefethen Vineyards from Calif. 29, take Oak Knoll Ave. E.

Listed on the National Register of Historic Places, the vineyard's main building was built in 1886, and remains Napa's only wooden, gravity-powered winery. The bucolic brick courtyard is surrounded with oak and cork trees, and free wine samples are distributed in the brick-floored and wood-beamed tasting room. Although Trefethen is one of the valley's oldest wineries, it did not produce its first chardonnay until 1973—but thank goodness it did. Their whites and reds are both award-winners and a pleasure to the palate. Tours are offered by appointment only.

YOUNTVILLE

70 miles from San Francisco

Yountville (population 3,500) was founded by the first white American to settle in the valley, George Calvert Yount. While it lacks the small-town charm of neighboring St. Helena and Calistoga—primarily because it has no rambunctious main street—it does serve as a good base for exploring the valley, and it's home to a handful of excellent wineries, inns, and restaurants, including James Beard's 1997 top dining spot in the nation, The French Laundry.

Domaine Chandon. 1 California Dr. (at Calif. 29), Yountville. ☎ **707/944-2280.** Nov–Apr Wed–Sun 10am–6pm; May–Oct daily 10am–6pm. Free tours every hour on the hour 11am–5pm; no reservations necessary.

The valley's most renowned sparkling winery was founded in 1973 by French champagne house Möet et Chandon. The grounds suit Domaine Chandon's reputation perfectly—this is the kind of place where the world's wealthy might stroll the beautifully manicured gardens under the shade of a delicate parasol, stop at the outdoor patio for sips of the famous sparkling wine, then glide into the dining room for a world-class luncheon.

If you can pull yourself away from the bubbly (sold by the glass for $3.50 to $6.25 and served with complimentary bread and spread), the comprehensive tour of the facilities is worth the time. In addition to a shop, there's a small gallery housing artifacts from Möet et Chandon depicting the history of champagnes. The Domaine Chandon restaurant is one of the best-known in the valley.

OAKVILLE

68 miles from San Francisco

Driving farther north on the St. Helena Highway (Calif. 29) brings you to Oakville, most easily recognized by Oakville Cross Road and the Oakville Grocery Café (see p. 260).

Robert Mondavi Winery. 7801 St. Helena Hwy. (Calif. 29), Oakville. ☎ **800/MONDAVI** or 707/226-1395. May–Oct daily 9:30am–5:30pm; Nov–Apr daily 9:30am–4:30pm. Reservations recommended for the guided tour (book 1 week in advance, especially for weekend tours).

If you continue on Calif. 29 up to Oakville, you'll arrive at the ultimate high-tech Napa Valley winery, housed in a magnificent mission-style facility. At Mondavi, almost every variable in the wine-making process is controlled by computer—it's absolutely fascinating to watch. After the tour, you can taste the results of all this attention to detail in selected current wines (free of charge). You can also taste without taking the tour, but it will cost you: The Rose Garden (an outdoor tasting area open in summer) offers an etched Reidel glass and three wines for $10; tastings in the ToKalon Room go from $3 for a 3-ounce taste to $15 for a rare library wine.

Fridays feature an "Art of Wine and Food" program, which includes a slide presentation on the history of wine, a tour of the winery, and a three-course luncheon with wine pairing; the cost is around $55 and you must reserve in advance. Though there's no picnicking on the grounds, Mondavi does offer gourmet picnic lunches from time to time. The Vineyard Room usually features an art show, and you'll find some exceptional antiques in the reception hall. In summer, the winery also hosts some great outdoor jazz concerts. Call to learn about upcoming events.

Opus One. 7900 St. Helena Hwy. (Calif. 29), Oakville. ☎ **707/944-9442.** Daily 10:30am–3:30pm. Tours by appointment only (in high season, book 3 weeks in advance).

Unlike most other vineyard experiences, a visit to Opus One is a serious and stately affair that takes after its wine and its owners: Robert Mondavi and Baroness Phillipe de Rothschild, who, after years of discussion, embarked on this state-of-the-art collaboration. Architecture buffs in particular will appreciate the tour, which takes in both the impressive Greco-Roman–meets–20th-century building and the no-holds-barred ultra–high-tech production and aging facilities.

This entire facility caters to one ultrapremium wine, which is offered here for a whopping $15 per 4-ounce taste (and a painful $90 per bottle). But wine-lovers should happily fork over the cash: It's likely to be one of the most memorable reds you'll ever sample. Grab your glass and head to the redwood rooftop deck to enjoy the view.

RUTHERFORD

If you so much as blink after Oakville you're likely to overlook Rutherford, the next small town that borders on St. Helena. Still, each has its share of spectacular wineries, but you won't see most of them while driving along Highway 29.

Silver Oak Wine Cellars. 915 Oakville Cross Rd. (at Money Rd.), Oakville. ☎ **707/ 944-8808.** Tasting room Mon–Sat 9am–4pm. Tours Mon–Thurs at 1:30pm, by appointment only.

Twenty-five years ago, an oil man from Colorado, Ray Duncan, and a former Christian Brothers monk, Justin Meyer, formed a partnership and a mission to create the finest cabernet sauvignon in the world. "We still haven't produced the best bottle of cabernet sauvignon of which Silver Oak is capable," admits Meyer, but this small winery is still the Wine Country's undisputed king of cabernet.

A narrow tree-lined road leads you to the handsome Mediterranean-style winery, where roughly 44,000 cases of 100% varietal cab are produced annually. The elegant tasting room is refreshingly quiet and soothing, adorned with redwood panels stripped from old wine tanks and warmed by a wood fire. Tastings and tours are $5, which include a beautiful German-made burgundy glass. At press time, only two wines were released: a 1993 Alexander Valley and a 1993 Napa Valley. If the $40-per-bottle price tag is a bit much, for half the price you can take home one of the winery's first noncab releases in 25 years—a velvety Meyer Family Port. No picnic facilities are available.

☆ **PlumpJack Winery.** 620 Oakville Cross Rd. (just west of Silverado Trail), Oakville. ☎ **707/945-1220.** Daily 10am–4pm.

If most wineries are like a traditional and refined Brooks Brothers suit, PlumpJack stands out as the Todd Oldham of wine tasting—chic, colorful, a little wild, and popular with a young, hip crowd. Like the franchise's PlumpJack restaurant and wine shop in San Francisco and resort in Tahoe, this playfully medieval winery is a welcome diversion from the same old, same old. But with Getty bucks behind what was once Villa Mount Eden winery, the budget covers far more than just atmosphere: There's some serious wine making going on here, too, and for $5 you can sample the cabernet, petite sirah, Riesling, and chardonnay—each an impressive product from a winery that's only been open to the public since mid-1997. The few vintages for sale currently range from $15 to $30, and average around $20 per bottle. There are no tours or picnic spots, but this refreshingly stylized and friendly facility will make you want to hang out for a while nonetheless.

Cakebread Cellars. 8300 St. Helena Hwy. (Calif. 29), Rutherford. ☎ **800/588-0298** or 707/963-5221. Daily 10am–4:30pm. Tours by appointment only.

This winery's moniker is actually the owners' surname, but it suits the wines produced here, where the focus is on making wine that pairs well with food. They've done such a good job that 85% of their 65,000 annual cases go directly to restaurants, which means only a select few wine drinkers get to take home a bottle. Even if you've found their label in your local wine store, your choice has been limited: Just three varieties are distributed nationally. Here you can sample the sauvignon blanc, chardonnay, cabernet, merlot, zinfandel, pinot noir, the Rubaiyat blend wine, and their dry rose Vin de Porche, which are all made from Napa Valley grapes.

Prices range from an affordable $14 for a bottle of the 1996 sauvignon blanc to a pricey $53 for the 1994 reserve cab, but the average bottle sells for just a little more than $20. In the tasting room, a large barnlike space, the hospitable hosts pour either a $3 or $6 sampling; both include a keepsake wineglass.

St. Supéry Winery. 8440 St. Helena Hwy. (Calif. 29), Rutherford. ☎ **800/942-0809** or 707/963-4507. Daily 9:30am–4:30pm.

The outside may look like a modern corporate office building, but inside you'll find a functional and welcoming winery that encourages first-time wine tasters to learn more about oenology. On the self-guided tour, you can wander through the demonstration vineyard where you'll learn about growing techniques. Inside, kids gravitate toward "SmellaVision," an interactive display that teaches you how to identify different wine ingredients. Adjoining is the Atkinson House, which chronicles more than 100 years of wine-making history. For $3 you'll get lifetime tasting privileges, and though they probably won't be pouring their ever-popular Moscato dessert wine, the sauvignon blanc and chardonnay flow freely. Even the prices make visitors feel at home: Many bottles go for around $8, although their 1994 Meritage cabernet will set you back $40.

Niebaum-Coppola. 1991 St. Helena Hwy. (Calif. 29), Rutherford. ☎ **707/963-9099.** Daily 10am–5pm. Tours offered daily.

In March 1995, Hollywood met Napa Valley when Francis Ford Coppola bought historic Inglenook Vineyards. Although the renowned film director has been dabbling in wine production for years (he's had a home in the valley for almost 25 years), Niebaum-Coppola (pronounced *nee*-bomb *coh*-pa-la) is his biggest endeavor yet. He plunked down millions to renovate the beautiful 1880s ivy-draped stone winery and restore the surrounding property to its historic dimensions, gilding it with the glitz and glamour you'd expect from Tinseltown in the process. On display are Academy Awards and memorabilia from such Coppola films as *The Godfather* and *Bram Stoker's Dracula;* the Centennial Museum chronicles the history of the estate and its wine making as well as Coppola's filmmaking.

In spite of all the Hollywood hullabaloo, wine is not forgotten. Available for tasting are a Rubicon (a blend of estate-grown cabernet, cabernet franc, and merlot, aged for more than 5 years), cabernet franc, merlot, chardonnay, zinfandel, and others, all made from organically grown grapes and ranging from around $10 to more than $50. There's also a wide variety of both expensive and affordable gift items. Speaking of expensive, the steep $7.50-per-person tasting fee might make you wonder whether a movie is included in the price—it's not (but you'll at least get to keep the souvenir glass). And at $20 a pop for the château-and-garden tour, you've gotta wonder whether you're funding his next film. But the grounds are indeed spectacular, and the 1½-hour journey includes private tasting and glass.

Don't let the prices deter you; if nothing else, at least visit the grounds—they're absolutely stunning and it costs nothing to stroll. You can also perk yourself up at the cappuccino bar, where you'll get *Godfather*-like atmosphere with your latte. You're welcome to picnic at any of the designated garden sites.

Beaulieu Vineyard. 1960 S. St. Helena Hwy. (Calif. 29), Rutherford. ☎ **707/963-2411.** Daily 10am–5pm. Tours daily 11am–4pm; in summer, roughly every half hour; call for winter schedule.

Bordeaux native Georges de Latour founded the third-oldest continuously operating winery in Napa Valley in 1900—and, with the help of legendary oenologist

André Tchelistcheff, produced world-class, award-winning wines that have been served by every president of the United States since Franklin D. Roosevelt. The brick-and-redwood tasting room isn't much to look at, but with Beaulieu's (pronounced *bowl*-you) stellar reputation, they have no need to visually impress. They do, however, offer a complimentary glass of chardonnay the minute you walk through the door as well as a variety of bottles under $15. The Private Reserve Tasting Room offers a "flight" of reserve wines to taste for $12.50—but if you want to take a bottle to go, it may cost as much as $50. A free tour explains the wine-making process and the vineyard's history. No reservation is necessary.

Grgich Hills Cellar. 1829 St. Helena Hwy. (Calif. 29, north of Rutherford Cross Rd.), Rutherford. ☎ 707/963-2784. Daily 9:30am–4:30pm. Free tours by appointment only, Mon–Fri 11am and 2pm; Sat–Sun 11am and 1:30pm.

Yugoslavian émigré Miljenko (Mike) Grgich made his presence known to the world when his Château Montelena chardonnay bested the top French white burgundies at the famous 1976 Paris tasting. Since then, this master vintner has teamed up with Austin Hills (of the Hills Brothers coffee fortune) and started this extremely successful and respected winery in Rutherford.

The ivy-covered stucco building isn't much to behold, and the tasting room is even less appealing, but people don't come here for the scenery: As you might expect, Grgich's (pronounced *grr*-gitch) chardonnays are legendary—and priced accordingly. The smart buys, however, are Grgich's outstanding zinfandel and cabernet sauvignon, which are very reasonably priced at around $18 and $25, respectively. The winery also produces a fantastic fumé blanc for as little as $15 a bottle. Before you leave, be sure to poke your head into the barrel aging room and inhale the divine aroma. Tastings cost $3 on weekends, which includes the glass, and are free on weekdays. No picnic facilities are available.

ST. HELENA

73 miles from San Francisco

Located 17 miles north of Napa on Highway 29, this former Seventh Day Adventist village manages to maintain a pseudo Old West feel while simultaneously catering to upscale shoppers with deep pockets—hence the Vanderbilt's, purveyor of fine housewares, at 1429 Main St. It's a quiet, attractive little town hosting a slew of beautiful old homes and first-rate restaurants and accommodations.

Raymond Vineyard & Cellar. 849 Zinfandel Lane (off Calif. 29 or the Silverado Trail), St. Helena. ☎ 800/525-2659 or 707/963-3141. Daily 10am–4pm. Tours by appointment only.

As fourth-generation vintners from Napa Valley and relations of the Beringers, brothers Walter and Roy Raymond have had plenty of time to develop terrific wines—and an excellent wine-tasting experience. The short drive through vineyards to reach Raymond's friendly, unintimidating cellar is case in point: Passing the heavy-hanging grapes makes you feel you're really in the thick of things before you even get in the door. Then comes the spacious, warm room, complete with dining table and chairs—a perfect setting for sampling the four tiers of wines, most of which are free for the tasting and well priced to appeal to all levels of wine drinkers: The Amber Hill label starts at $9 a bottle for the chardonnay and $13 for the cab; the reserves are priced in the midteens, while the "Generations" cab costs $35.

Along with the overall experience, we also liked the great gift selection, which includes barbecue sauces, mustard, a chocolate wine syrup, and a gooey hazelnut merlot fudge sauce. Private reserve tastings cost $2.50. Sorry, there are no picnic facilities.

✪ **V. Sattui Winery.** 1111 White Lane (at Calif. 29), St. Helena. ☎ **707/963-7774.** Winter daily 9am–5pm; summer daily 9am–6pm.

One of our friends has always wanted to write a guidebook on the best places for free food tastings in northern California. If that book ever comes to be, V. Sattui (pronounced vee sa-*too*-ee) will be one of the highlights. At this combination winery-and-enormous-gourmet-deli, you can fill up on wine, pâté, and cheese samples without ever reaching for your pocketbook. The gourmet store stocks more than 200 cheeses, sandwich meats, pâtés, breads, exotic salads, and delicious desserts such as a white-chocolate cheesecake. It would be an easy place to graze were it not for the continuous mob scene at the counter.

The long wine bar in the back offers everything from chardonnay, sauvignon blanc, Riesling, cabernet, and zinfandel to a tasty Madeira and a muscat dessert wine. Their wines aren't distributed, so if you taste something you simply must have, buy it. (If you buy a case, ask to talk with a manager, who'll give you access to the less crowded, more exclusive private tasting room.) Wine prices start around $9, with many in the $13 range; reserves top out at around $75.

V. Sattui's expansive and grassy picnic facilities make this a favorite for families. This is one of the most popular stops along Highway 29, so prepare for an enormous picnic party and you won't be disappointed. *Note:* To use the facilities, food and wine must be purchased here.

✪ **Joseph Phelps Vineyards.** Taplin Rd. (off the Silverado Trail), P.O. Box 1031, St. Helena. ☎ **800/707-5789.** Mon–Sat 9am–5pm; Sun 9am–4pm. Tours and tastings by appointment only.

Visitors interested in intimate, comprehensive tours and looking for a knockout tasting should schedule a tour at this stellar winery. A quick and discreet turn off the Silverado Trail in Spring Valley (there's no sign, so watch for Taplin Road or you'll blast right by it), Joseph Phelps was founded in 1973 and has since become a major player in both the region and the worldwide wine market. Phelps himself is attributed with a long list of valley firsts, including launching the syrah varietal in the valley and extending the 1970s Berkeley food revolution (led by Alice Waters) up to the Wine Country via his store, the Oakville Grocery (see p. 261).

Joseph Phelps is a favorite stop for serious wine-lovers. The modern, state-of-the-art winery and big-city vibe are proof that Phelps's annual 100,000 cases prove fruitful in more ways than one. Once you pass through the wisteria-covered trellis to the entrance of the redwood building, you'll encounter an air of seriousness that hangs heavier than harvest grapes. Fortunately, the mood lightens as the well-educated tour guide explains the details of what you're tasting while pouring samples of five to six wines, which may include Riesling, sauvignon blanc, gewürztraminer, syrah, merlot, zin, and cab. (Unfortunately, some wines are so popular that they sell out quickly; come late in the season and you may not be able to taste or buy them.) The three excellently located picnic tables, on the terrace overlooking the valley, are available by reservation.

✪ **Prager Winery & Port Works.** 1281 Lewelling Lane (just west of Calif. 29, behind Sutter Home), St. Helena. ☎ **800/969-PORT** or 707/963-7678. Daily 10:30am–4:30pm.

If you want a real down-home, off-the-beaten-track experience, Prager's can't be beat. Turn the corner from Sutter Home and roll into the small gravel parking lot;

you're on the right track—but when you pull open the creaky old wooden door to this shack of a wine-tasting room, you'll begin to wonder. By all means, don't turn back! Pass the oak barrels and you'll quickly come upon the clapboard tasting room, made homey with a big Oriental rug, a cat, and, during winter, a small space heater. Most days, your host will be Jim Prager himself, who's undeniably a sort of modern Santa Claus in both looks and demeanor. But you won't have to sit on his lap for your wish to come true: Just fork over $5 (refundable with purchase) and he'll pour you samples of his delicious $25 Madeline dessert wine, a late-harvest Johannisberg Riesling, the recently released 10-year-old port (which costs close to $50 per bottle), and a few other yummy selections like chardonnay and cab, which retail in the mid-$30s. Also available is "Prager Chocolate Drizzle," a chocolate liqueur that tops ice creams and other desserts.

We recommend tasting here even if you can't afford to purchase; if you do want to buy, this is the only place to do it, as Prager doesn't distribute. If you're looking for a special gift, Jim's daughter custom etches bottles for around $100 in the design of your choice, plus the cost of the wine.

Beringer Vineyards. 2000 Main St. (Calif. 29), St. Helena. ☎ **707/963-7115.** Off-season daily 9:30am–5pm (last tour 4pm, last tasting 4:30pm); summer 9:30am–6pm (last tour 5pm, last tasting 5:30pm). Free 45-min. tours offered every hour between 9:30am–4pm; no reservations necessary.

Follow the line of cars just north of St. Helena's business district to Beringer Vineyards, where everyone stops at the remarkable Rhine House to taste wine and view the hand-dug tunnels carved out of the mountainside. Founded in 1876 by brothers Jacob and Frederick, this is the oldest continuously operating winery in the Napa Valley—it was open even during Prohibition, when Beringer kept afloat by making "sacramental" wines. While their white zinfandel is still the winery's most popular nationwide seller, the 1994 chardonnay is the choice for more discerning palates: It won *Wine Spectator*'s 1996 Wine of the Year award. Free tastings of current vintages are conducted in the upstairs gift shop, where there's also a large selection of bottles for less than $20. Reserve wines are available in the Rhine House for a fee of $2 to $6 per taste.

Charles Krug Winery. 2800 St. Helena Hwy. (just north of the tunnel of trees at the northern end of St. Helena), St. Helena. ☎ **707/963-5057.** Daily 10:30am–5:30pm. Tours daily at 11:30am, 1:30, and 3:30pm.

Founded in 1861, Krug was the first winery built in the valley, and is today owned by the family of Peter Mondavi (yes, Robert is his brother). It's worth paying your respects here with a $3 tour, which takes just under an hour and encompasses a walk through the historical redwood Italianate wine cellar, built in 1874, as well as the vineyards, where you'll learn more about grapes and varietals. The tour ends with a tasting in the retail center. But you don't have to tour to taste: Just stop by and fork over $3 to sip current releases, $5 to sample reserves; you'll also get a souvenir glass. On the grounds are picnic facilities with umbrella-shaded tables overlooking vineyards or the historic wine cellar.

CALISTOGA

81 miles from San Francisco

Calistoga, the last tourist town in Napa Valley, was named by Sam Brannan, entrepreneur extraordinaire and California's first millionaire. After making a bundle supplying miners during the gold rush, he went on to take advantage of the natural geothermal springs at the north end of the Napa Valley by building a hotel and spa

The Ins & Outs of Shipping Wine Home

Perhaps the only thing more complex than that $400 case of cabernet you just purchased are the rules and regulations regarding shipping it home. Due to absurd and forever fluctuating "reciprocity laws"—which are supposedly created to protect the business of the country's wine distributors—wine shipping is limited by state regulations that vary in each of the 50 states. Shipping rules also vary from winery to winery—not to mention that, to make matters more confusing, according to at least one shipping company the list of reciprocal states (those that have agreements with Calif. that make it no problem to ship wine there) changes almost daily! Hence, depending on which state you live in, sending even a single bottle of wine can be a truly Kafkaesque experience.

If you happen to live in a reciprocal state and the winery you're buying from offers shipping, you're in luck. You buy, pay the postage, and the winery sends your purchase for you. It's as simple as that. If that winery doesn't ship, they will most likely be able to give you an easy shipping solution.

If you live in a nonreciprocal state, the winery may still have shipping advice for you, so definitely ask! Some refuse to ship at all, while others are more than accommodating ("New York has bigger fish to fry," we've been told). Do be cautious of wineries that tell you they can ship to nonreciprocal states, and make sure you get a firm commitment: When one of our New York–based editors visited Napa, a winery promised her they could, in fact, ship her purchase; but when she got home they reneged, leaving her with no way to get the wine and no potable memories of the trip.

It's possible that you'll face the challenge of finding a shipping company yourself. If that's the case, keep in mind that it's technically illegal to box your own wine and send it to a nonreciprocal state; the shippers could lose their license and you could lose your wine. However, if you do get stuck shipping illegally (not that we're recommending you do that), you might want to head to a post office, UPS, or other shipping company outside of the Wine Country area; it's less obvious that you're shipping wine from Vallejo or San Francisco than from Napa Valley.

Napa Valley Shipping Companies

Aero Packing, 1733 Trancas St. (at Highway 29), Napa (☎ **707/255-8025**), will pack and ship to reciprocal states and insures the first $100 (it's 50¢ extra per hundred beyond the first). Ground shipping of one case to Los Angeles is $19 and Florida is $41. They currently do not ship to a handful of states, including New York and Massachusetts.

The **St. Helena Mailing Center,** 1241 Adams St. (at Highway 29), St. Helena (☎ **707/963-2686**), tells us that they will pack and ship anywhere in the United States, with rates around $17 per case for ground delivery to Los Angeles and $33 to New York. While those who live in reciprocal states insure their package for up to $100 (it costs extra beyond the first $100), the Mailing Center does not insure packages shipped to nonreciprocal states. However, it's no big deal; each bottle is well-packed in Styrofoam and should make it home without a problem.

In Sonoma Valley

Mail Boxes, Etc., 19229 Sonoma Hwy., (at Verano Street), Sonoma (☎ **707/935-3438**), which has a lot of experience with shipping wine, claims it will ship your wine to any state, either via UPS (which as of now only ships to a dozen states) or Federal Express. Prices vary from $14 to LA via UPS to as much as $78 to the East Coast via FedEx.

here in 1859. Flubbing up a speech in which he compared this natural California wonder to New York State's Saratoga Springs resort, he serendipitously coined the name "Calistoga," and it stuck. Today, this small, simple resort town with 4,400 residents and an old-time main street (no building along the 6-block stretch is more than two stories high) is popular with city folk who come here to unwind. Calistoga is a great place to relax and indulge in mineral waters, mud baths, Jacuzzis, massages, and, of course, wine. The vibe is more casual—and a little more groovy—than you'll find in neighboring towns to the south.

✪ **Kornell Champagne Cellars.** 1091 Larkmead Lane (just off the Silverado Trail), Calistoga. ☎ **707/942-0859.** Daily 10am–4:30pm.

You've gotta love this place, which used to be the Larkmead Winery. Kornell's wine dudes—Dennis, Bob, Chris, and Rich—will do practically anything to maintain their self-proclaimed reputation as the "friendliest winery in the valley." They'll serve you all the bubbly you want (four to six varieties: brut, blanc de blanc, blanc de noir, and extra dry reserve, all ranging from $15 to $20 a bottle). They guarantee that you'll never wait more than 10 minutes to take the 20-minute tour of the oldest champagne cellar in the region, and even offer up a great story about Marie Antoinette's champagne-glass design.

Considering that the winery is owned by former Disney president Richard Frank, it's not surprising that, as one employee pointed out, the unpretentious place is a "celebrity stopover." But that's nothing new—it was once the summer home of San Francisco's renowned Lillie Hitchcock Coit (as in Coit Tower), and Marilyn used to hang out here when she was married to DiMaggio.

While the tasting room is so casual you may find yourself kicking back on a case of wine, the stone cellar (listed on the National Register of Historic Places) captures the essence of the Wine Country's history. Be sure to meander into the Back Room, where chardonnay, zinfandel, and cabernet are poured. Kornell makes fewer than 500 cases of still wines a year, which means if you don't try (and buy) 'em here, you may never get another chance; the same goes for their motto T-shirt: "Kiss French, Drink California." Behind the tasting room is a choice picnic area, situated under the oaks and overlooking the vineyards.

✪ **Schramsberg.** 1400 Schramsberg Rd. (off Calif. 29), Calistoga. ☎ **707/942-4558.** Daily 10am–4pm. Tours and tastings by appointment only.

This 200-acre champagne estate, a landmark once frequented by Robert Louis Stevenson, has a wonderful old-world feel and is one of our all-time favorite places to explore. Schramsberg is the label that presidents serve when toasting dignitaries from around the globe, and there's plenty of historic memorabilia in the front room to prove it. But the real mystique begins when you enter the champagne caves, which wind 2½ miles (the longest in North America, they say) and were partly hand-carved by Chinese laborers in the 1800s. The caves have an authentic Tom Sawyer ambiance, complete with dangling cobwebs and seemingly endless passageways; you can't help but feel you're on an adventure. The comprehensive, unintimidating tour ends in a charming tasting room, where you'll sit around a big table and sample several surprisingly varied selections of bubbly. Tasting prices are a bit dear at $7.50 per person, but it's money well spent. Note, however, that tastings are only offered to those who take the free tour, and you must reserve a spot in advance.

✪ **Clos Pegase.** 1060 Dunaweal Lane (off Calif. 29 or the Silverado Trail), Calistoga. ☎ **707/942-4981.** Daily 10:30am–5pm. Tours daily at 11am and 2pm.

What happens when a man falls in love with art and wine making, purchases more than 450 acres of prime growing property, and sponsors a competition commissioned by the San Francisco Museum of Modern Art to create a "temple to wine?" You'll find out when you visit this magnificent winery. Renowned architect Michael Graves designed this incredible oasis, which integrates art, 20,000 square feet of aging caves, and a luxurious hilltop private home. Viewing the art here is as much the point as tasting the wines—which, by the way, don't come cheap: Prices range from $18.50 for the 1995 Mitsuko's chardonnay to as much as $50 for the 1994 Hommage Artist Series Reserve, an extremely limited blend of the winery's finest lots of cabernet sauvignon and merlot. Tasting all the current releases will cost $2.50, and reserves are $2 each. The grounds at Clos Pegase (pronounced *clo* pay-*goss*) feature an impressive sculpture garden as well as scenic picnic spots.

Sterling Vineyards. 1111 Dunaweal Lane (off Calif. 29, just south of Calistoga), Calistoga. ☎ **707/942-3300.** Daily 10:30am–4:30pm.

No, you don't need climbing shoes to reach this dazzling white Mediterranean-style winery, perched 300 feet up on a rocky knoll. Just fork over $6 and you'll arrive via aerial tram, which offers dazzling bucolic views along the way. Once on land, follow the self-guided tour (the most comprehensive in the entire Wine Country) of the entire wine-making process. Currently owned by the Seagram company, the winery produces more than 200,000 cases per year. Samples at the panoramic tasting room are included in the tram fare. Expect to pay anywhere from $8 to $50 for a souvenir bottle ($16 is the average), and if you can find a bottle of their 1995 Napa Valley chardonnay (currently going for about $14), buy it—it's already garnered a septuplet of awards.

BEYOND THE WINERIES: WHAT TO SEE & DO IN NAPA VALLEY

While wine tasting is the area's undisputed main attraction, there are plenty of other things to do in Napa Valley. We've listed a few of our favorites below.

NAPA

If you have time and a penchant for Victorian architecture, the **Napa Valley Conference and Visitors Bureau,** 1310 Napa Town Center Mall, off First Street (☎ 707/226-7459; Web site: www.napavalley.com), offers self-guided walking tours of the town's historic buildings.

Anyone with an appreciation for art absolutely must visit the ✪ **di Rosa Preserve,** which until recently was closed to the public. Rene and Veronica di Rosa, who have been collecting contemporary American art for more than 40 years, converted their 88 acres of prime Wine Country property into a monument to northern California's regional art and nature. Their world-renowned collection features 1,500 works in all media by more than 600 greater Bay Area artists. Their treasures are displayed practically everywhere, from along the shores of their 30-acre lake to each nook and cranny of their 110-year-old winery-turned-residence, adjoining building, two new galleries, and gardens. With hundreds of surrounding acres of rolling hills protected under the Napa County Land Trust, this place is truly a must-see for both art- and nature-lovers. It's located at 5200 Sonoma Hwy. (Highway 121/12)—look for the blue-colored gate. Visits are by appointment only, when a maximum of 25 guests are guided through the preserve. Each tour lasts 2 to 2-½ hours and costs $10 per person. Call ☎ 707/226-5991 to make reservations.

SHOPPING Plan to spend at least an hour if you make a visit to **Red Hen's** co-op collection of antiques. You'll find everything from baseball cards to living-room sets, and prices are remarkably affordable. You can't miss this enormous red barn-style building at 5091 St. Helena Hwy., on Calif. 29 at Oak Knoll Avenue West (☎ 707/257-0822). It's open daily from 10am to 5:30pm.

St. Helena's Main Street is the best place to go if you're suffering serious retail withdrawal. Take, for example, ✪ **Vanderbilt and Company,** 1429 Main St., between Adams and Pine streets (☎ 707/963-1010), which offers the crème de la crème of cookware, hand-painted Italian dishware, and everything else you could possibly convince yourself you need for your gourmet kitchen and dining room. Open daily from 9:30am to 5:30pm.

Shopaholics won't be able to avoid at least one sharp turn off Highway 29 for a stop at the **St. Helena Premium Outlets,** which is located 2 miles north of downtown St. Helena (☎ 707/963-7282). Featured designers include Donna Karan, Coach, Movado, London Fog, and more. The stores are open daily from 10am to 6pm.

One last favorite stop: **Napa Valley Olive Oil Manufacturing Company,** 835 Charter Oak Rd., at the end of the road behind Tra Vigne restaurant (☎ 707/963-4173), a tiny market that presses and bottles its own oils and sells them at a fraction of the price you'll pay elsewhere. In addition, they have an extensive selection of Italian cooking ingredients, imported snacks, and the best deals on exotic mushrooms we've ever seen. You'll also love their age-old method for totaling the bill, which you simply must find out for yourself.

SPA-ING IT If you're sick of pampering your palate, give the rest of your body a treat with a treatment or two from either of the spas listed below. ✪ **White Sulphur Springs Retreat & Spa,** 3100 White Sulphur Springs Rd. (☎ 707/963-4361), offers a spiritual day of cleansing and pampering. Mother Nature takes the credit for the magic here: acres of redwoods, streams, grassy fields, wooded groves, and hiking trails galore. The spa treatments, which include massages, aromatherapy treatments, seaweed or mineral mud wraps, as well as access to a pool and Jacuzzi, only make the experience that much more relaxing. Massages are given in the homey spa building or outside amidst the redwoods ($55 to $65 per hr.). A day of peaceful pampering doesn't come any cheaper, but take note: this is a casual place. Five-star fanatics should stick with Sonoma Mission Inn & Spa (see p. 273) or Health Spa Napa Valley (see below), which covers the other end of the spa spectrum.

If you're a fitness freak, **Health Spa Napa Valley,** 1030 Main St. (Highway 29; ☎ 707/967-8800), is a mandatory stop after a few days of inevitable overindulgence. You can Treadmill or Stairmaster yourself silly or you can work off that second helping of crème brûlée with a spin class, yoga, or a few laps in the outdoor pool. Then reward yourself with spa treatments: a grape-seed mud wrap, a Pancha Karma treatment (two massage therapists get out the knots with synchronized motion), or a facial. Memberships are $15 per day Monday to Thursday, $20 per day Friday to Sunday, and free for guests of the Inn at Southbridge. Spa treatments are an additional cost.

BICYCLING The quieter northern end of the valley is an ideal place to rent a bicycle and ride the Silverado Trail. **St. Helena Cyclery,** 1156 Main St. (☎ 707/963-7736), rents bikes for $7 per hour or $25 a day, including rear rack and picnic bag.

CALISTOGA

NATURAL WONDERS Old Faithful Geyser of California, 1299 Tubbs Lane (☎ 707/942-6463), is one of only three "old faithful" geysers in the world. It's been blowing off steam at regular intervals for as long as anyone can remember. The 350°F water spews out to a height of about 60 feet every 40 minutes, day and night (varying with natural influences such as barometric pressure, the moon, tides, and tectonic stresses). The performance lasts about a minute, and you can watch the show as many times as you wish. Bring along a picnic lunch to munch on between spews. An exhibit hall, gift shop, and snack bar are open daily. Admission is $6 for adults, $5 for seniors, $2 for children 6 to 12, and free for children under 6. Open daily from 9am to 6pm (to 5pm in winter). To get there, follow the signs from downtown Calistoga; it's between Calif. 29 and Calif. 128.

You won't see thousands of trees turned into stone, but you'll still find many interesting petrified specimens at the **Petrified Forest,** 4100 Petrified Forest Rd. (☎ **707/942-6667**). Volcanic ash blanketed this area after the eruption of Mount St. Helena three million years ago. As a result, you'll find redwoods that have turned to rock through the slow infiltration of silicas and other minerals, as well as petrified seashells, clams, and marine life indicating that water covered this area even before the redwood forest. Admission is $4 for adults, $3 for seniors and children 11 to 17, $1 for children 4 to 11, and free for children under 4. Open daily from 10am to 5:30pm (to 4:30pm in winter). Heading north from Calistoga on Calif. 128, turn left onto Petrified Forest Road, just past Lincoln Street.

CYCLING   Cycling enthusiasts can rent bikes from **Getaway Adventures BHK** (Biking, Hiking, and Kayaking), 1117 Lincoln Ave. (☎ **800/499-BIKE** or 707/942-0332; Web site: www.getawayadventures.com). Full-day tours cost $89 and include lunch and a visit to four or five wineries; downhill cruises ($49) are available for people who hate to pedal. On weekdays they'll even deliver bikes to you.

HORSEBACK RIDING   If you like horses and venturing through cool, misty forests, then $40 will seem like a bargain for a 1½-hour ride with a friendly tour guide from **Napa Valley Trail Rides** (☎ **707/996-8566;** Web site: www. thegridnet/trailrides/). After you've been saddled and schooled in the basics of horse handling at the stable, you'll be led on a leisurely stroll (with the occasional trot thrown in for excitement) through beautiful **Bothe–Napa Valley State Park,** located off Highway 29 near Calistoga. Napa Valley Trail Rides also offers a Western Barbecue Ride, Sunset Ride, Full Moon Ride, and Gourmet Boxed Lunch Ride & Winery Tour. We've taken the trip ourselves and loved every minute of it—sore butts and all.

✪ **MUD BATHS**   The one thing you should do while you're in Calistoga is what people have been doing here for the last 150 years: Take a mud bath. The natural baths are composed of local volcanic ash, imported peat, and naturally boiling mineral hot-springs water, all mulled together to produce a thick mud that simmers at a temperature of about 104°F.

Indulge yourself at any of these Calistoga spas: **Dr. Wilkinson's Hot Springs,** 1507 Lincoln Ave. (☎ 707/942-4102); **Lincoln Avenue Spa,** 1339 Lincoln Ave. (☎ 707/942-5296); **Golden Haven Hot Springs Spa,** 1713 Lake St. (☎ 707/942-6793); **Calistoga Spa Hot Springs,** 1006 Washington St. (☎ 707/942-6269); **Calistoga Village Inn & Spa,** 1880 Lincoln Ave. (☎ 707/942-0991); **Eurospa & Inn,** 1202 Pine St. (☎ 707/942-6829); **Indian Springs Resort,** 1712 Lincoln Ave. (☎ 707/942-4913); **Lavender Hill Spa,** 1015 Foothill Blvd. (☎ 800/528-4772); **Mount View Spa,** 1457 Lincoln Ave. (☎ 707/942-5789); **Nance's Hot Springs,** 1614 Lincoln Ave. (☎ 707/942-6211); or the **Roman Spa Motel,** 1300 Washington St. (☎ 707/942-4441).

WHERE TO STAY IN THE NAPA VALLEY

Accommodations here run the gamut—from motels and B&Bs to world-class luxury retreats—and all are easily accessible from the main highway. While we recommend shacking up in the more romantically pastoral areas such as St. Helena, there's no question you're going to find better deals in the towns of Napa or laid-back Calistoga.

We've arranged the listings below first by area and then by price, using the following categories: **Very Expensive,** more than $250 per night; **Expensive,** $200 to $250 per night; **Moderate,** $150 to $200 per night; and **Inexpensive,** less than $150 per night (sorry—the reality is that anything less than $150 a night qualifies as inexpensive 'round these parts).

When planning your trip, keep in mind that during the high season—between June and November—most hotels charge peak rates and sell out completely on weekends; many have a 2-night minimum. If you need help organizing your Wine Country vacation, contact one of the following companies: **Accommodation Referral Bed & Breakfast Exchange** (☎ **800/240-8466,** 800/499-8466 in Calif., or 707/963-8466), which also represents hotels and inns; **Bed & Breakfast Inns of Napa Valley** (☎ **707/944-4444**), an association of 26 Napa Valley B&Bs, provides inn descriptions and makes reservations; or **Napa Valley Reservations Unlimited** (☎ **800/251-NAPA** or 707/252-1985), which is also a source for everything from hot-air-balloon and glider rides to wine-tasting tours by limousine.

NAPA

Moderate

✪ Cedar Gables Inn. 486 Coombs St., Napa, CA 94559. ☎ **800/309-7969** or 707/224-7969. Fax 707/224-4838. www.CedarGablesInn.com. 6 units. $129–$189 double ($10 less in winter). Rates include breakfast. AE, DISC, MC, V. From Calif. 29 north, exit onto First St. and follow signs to downtown; turn right onto Coombs St.; the house is at the corner of Oak St.

Innkeepers Margaret and Craig Snasdell have developed quite a following with their cozy, romantic B&B in Old Town Napa. The Victorian was built in 1892, and rooms reflect the era with rich tapestries and stunning gilded antiques. Four rooms have fireplaces; four have whirlpool tubs; and all feature queen-size brass, wood, or iron beds. Guests meet each evening in front of the roaring fireplace in the family room for complimentary wine and cheese. At other times, it's a perfect place to cuddle up and watch the large-screen TV.

Inexpensive

Chablis Inn. 3360 Solano Ave., Napa, CA 94558. ☎ **707/257-1944.** Fax 707/226-6862. 34 units. A/C TV TEL. Early Nov to Mar $60–$95 double; Apr to early Nov $75–$125 double. AE, DC, DISC, MC, V.

There's no way around it. If you want to sleep cheaply in a town where the average room goes for upward of $200 per night in high season, you're going to have to motel it. But look on the bright side: Since your room is likely to be little more than a crash pad after a day of eating and drinking, a clean bed and a remote control are all you'll really need. But Chablis offers much more than that. Each of the superclean motel-style rooms has a refrigerator and coffeemaker; some even boast kitchenettes and/or whirlpool tubs. Guests have access to an outdoor heated pool and hot tub, plus a basic continental breakfast. Friendly owner Ken Patel is on hand most of the time and is constantly upgrading his tidy highway-side hostelry; his current project is replacing all mattresses in 1998.

Wine Valley Lodge. 200 S. Coombs St. (between First and Imola sts.), Napa, CA 94558.
☎ **707/224-7911.** 53 units. A/C TV TEL. $57–$94 double; $77–$154 suite. AE, DISC, MC, V.

Dollar for dollar, the Wine Valley Lodge offers the most for the least in all of Wine Country. Located at the south end of town in a quiet residential neighborhood, the mission-style motel is extremely well kept and accessible, just a short drive from Calif. 29 and the wineries to the north. Soft pastels dominate the color scheme, featured prominently in the matching quilted bedspreads, furniture, and objets d'art. Its decor is reminiscent of Grandma's house, to be sure, but at these prices, who cares? The clincher on the whole deal is a fetching little oasis in the center courtyard, consisting of a sundeck, barbecue, and pool flanked by a cadre of odd teacup–shaped hedges.

YOUNTVILLE
Moderate
✪ **Maison Fleurie.** 6529 Yount St. (between Finnel Rd. and Humboldt St.), Yountville, CA 94599. ☎ **800/788-0369** or 707/944-2056. 13 units. A/C TV TEL. $110–$230 double. Rates include full breakfast and afternoon hors d'oeuvres. AE, DC, MC, V.

Maison Fleurie is one of the prettiest hotels in the Wine Country, a trio of beautiful 1873 brick-and-fieldstone buildings overlaid with ivy. Seven rooms are located in the main house—a charming Provençal replica complete with thick brick walls, terra-cotta tile, and paned windows—while the remaining rooms are split between the old bakery building and the carriage house. All have private bathrooms, and some feature private balconies, patios, sitting areas, Jacuzzi tubs, and fireplaces. Breakfast is served in the quaint little dining room; afterwards, you're welcome to wander the landscaped grounds, use the pool or outdoor spa, or borrow a mountain bike (free of charge) to ride around town, returning in time for afternoon hors d'oeuvres. It's truly impossible not to enjoy your stay at Maison Fleurie.

✪ **Napa Valley Lodge.** 2230 Madison St., Yountville, CA 94599. ☎ **800/368-2468** or 707/944-2468. Fax 707/944-9362. 55 units. A/C MINIBAR TV TEL. $172–$320 double. Rates include champagne breakfast buffet. MC, V.

Many frequent visitors compare this contemporary hotel to the town's popular Vintage Inn, noting that its even more personable and accommodating. The lodge is just off Highway 29, though they do a good job of disguising it. Facilities include a pool, redwood sauna, and small exercise room; the newly upgraded guest rooms are large, ultraclean, and better appointed than many in the area. Many have vaulted ceilings and 33 have fireplaces. All come with a king- or queen-size beds, wicker furnishings, coffeemakers, robes, and either a private balcony or a patio. In 1997 all the bathrooms were also upgraded to include a vanity area and nice tile work. The cheapest rooms are at ground level; these are smaller and get less sunlight than those on the second floor. Extras include concierge, on-demand video, afternoon tea and cookies in the lobby, Friday-evening wine tasting in the library, and a full champagne breakfast—with all this, it's no wonder AAA gave the Napa Valley Lodge the four-diamond award for excellence. Ask about winter discounts—they can be as much as 30%.

Inexpensive
Napa Valley Railway Inn. 6503 Washington St. (adjacent to the Vintage 1870 shopping complex), Yountville, CA 94599. ☎ **707/944-2000.** 9 units. A/C TV. $75–$130 double. AE, MC, V.

This is one of our favorite places to stay in the Wine Country. Why? Because it's inexpensive and really cute. Looking hokey from the outside, the Railway Inn consists of two rows of sun-bleached cabooses and railcars sitting on a stretch of Yountville's original track and connected by a covered wooden walkway. Things get considerably better, though, as you enter your private caboose or railcar, each sumptuously appointed with comfy love seats, queen-size brass beds, and tiled full bathrooms. The coups de grâce are the bay windows and skylights, which let in plenty of California sunshine. The railcars are all suites, so if you're looking to save your pennies, opt for the cabooses. Adjacent to the inn is Yountville's main shopping complex, which includes wine tastings and some good low-priced restaurants.

OAKVILLE & RUTHERFORD

Very Expensive

✪ Auberge du Soleil. 180 Rutherford Hill Rd., Rutherford, CA 94573. ☎ **707/963-1211.** Fax 707/963-8764. 50 units. A/C MINIBAR TV TEL. $350–$535 double; $700–$900 suite; $2,000 cottage suite. Rates discounted Dec–Mar. AE, DC, DISC, MC, V. From Rutherford, turn right on Calif. 128 and go 3 miles to the Silverado Trail; turn left and head north about 200 yd. to Rutherford Hill Rd.; turn right.

This spectacular Relais & Châteaux member is the kind of place you'd imagine movie stars frequenting for clandestine affairs or weekend retreats. Set high above the Napa Valley in a 33-acre olive grove, it's quiet, indulgent, and luxuriously romantic. The Mediterranean-style rooms are large enough to get lost in—and you might want to once you discover all the amenities. The bathtub alone—an enormous hot tub with a skylight overhead—will entice you to grab a glass of California red and settle in for a while. A wood-burning fireplace is surrounded by oversized, cushy furniture—the ideal place to relax and listen to CDs (the stereo comes with a few selections, and there's also a VCR). Fresh flowers, original art, terra-cotta floors, and natural wood and leather furnishings whisk you out of the Wine Country and into the Southwest. Each sun-washed private deck has views of the valley that are nothing less than spectacular. Those with money to burn should opt for the $2,000-per-night cottage suite; the 1,800-square-foot hideaway's got two fireplaces, two full bathrooms, a den, and a patio Jacuzzi. Now that's living. All guests have access to a celestial swimming pool and a tiny exercise room with one of the grandest views around, plus an array of spa services. All in all, this is one of the best places we've ever stayed.

Dining: Another ethereal experience. See "Where to Dine in the Napa Valley," below.

Amenities: Concierge, newspaper delivery, valet parking, 24-hour room service, twice-daily maid service, laundry/valet, complimentary shoe-shine, outdoor pool with sundeck, massage rooms, three tennis courts, exercise room, beauty salon, a sculpture-lined nature trail with picnic areas that crisscrosses the property.

Moderate

Rancho Caymus. 1140 Rutherford Rd. (P.O. Box 78), Rutherford, CA 94573. ☎ **800/845-1777** or 707/963-1777. Fax 707/963-5387. 26 suites. A/C MINIBAR TV TEL. $145–$175 double; from $245 Master Suite; $295 2-bedroom suite. Rates include continental breakfast. AE, DC, MC, V. From Calif. 29 north, turn right onto Rutherford Rd./Calif. 128 E.; the hotel is ahead on your left.

This Spanish-style hacienda, with two floors opening onto wisteria-covered balconies, was the creation of sculptor Mary Tilden Morton (of Morton Salt). Morton wanted each room in the hacienda to be a work of art, thus she hired the most skilled craftspeople of her day. She designed the adobe fireplaces herself, and wandered through Mexico and South America purchasing artifacts for the property.

Guest rooms are situated around a whimsical garden courtyard with an enormous outdoor fireplace. The mix-and-match interior decor is on the funky side, with overly varnished dark-wood furnishings and braided rugs. The inn is cozy, however, and rooms are decent-sized, split-level suites with queen beds. Other amenities include wet bars, sofa beds in the sitting areas, and small private patios. Most of the suites have fireplaces, and five have kitchenettes and whirlpool tubs. Breakfast, which includes fresh fruit, granola, orange juice, and breads, is served in the inn's dining room. There are plans to open a full-service restaurant by the time this book is published.

ST. HELENA
Very Expensive
The Inn at Southbridge. 1020 Main St., St. Helena, CA 94574. ☎ **800/520-6800** or 707/967-9400. Fax 707/967-9486. MINIBAR TV TEL. Nov–Mar $205–$295 double; Mar to mid-June $235–$325 double; mid-June to Nov $245–$335 double. AE, CB, DC, JCB, MC, V.

Eschewing the lace-and-latticework theme that plagues most Wine Country inns, the Inn at Southbridge takes an unswervingly modern, pragmatic approach to accommodating its guests. Instead of stuffed teddy bears, you'll find terry-cloth robes, fireplaces, bathroom skylights, down comforters, private balconies, and a host of other little luxuries. The decor is upscale Pottery Barn—trendy, and for some a welcome departure from quaintly traditional hotel-style stuff. Functional touches include voice mail and fax modems. One notable bummer—the hotel is located along the highway, so it lacks that reclusive feel many other upscale hotels offer.

Dining: On the premises is Tomatina, owned and run by the owners of Tra Vigne, an Italian restaurant conveniently located next door (see "Where to Dine in the Napa Valley," below).

Amenities: Concierge, limited room service, dry cleaning, laundry, newspaper delivery, in-room massage, twice-daily maid service, baby-sitting, secretarial services, complimentary refreshments in lobby. The spa offers access to an excellent gym (including classes), steam, sauna, outdoor heated pool, Jacuzzi, and spa treatments.

◎ Meadowood Resort. 900 Meadowood Lane, St. Helena, CA 94574. ☎ **800/458-8080** or 707/963-3646. Fax 707/963-3532. 85 units. A/C MINIBAR TV TEL. $320–$465 double; 1-bedroom lodge from $540; 2-bedroom from $850; 3-bedroom from $1,180; 4-bedroom from $1,575. Ask about promotional offers and off-season rates. 2-night minimum on weekends. AE, DISC, DC, MC, V.

Less reclusive than Auberge du Soleil, Meadowood is the wealthy–grown-ups' summer camp. The resort, tucked away on 250 acres of pristine mountainside amidst a forest of madrone and oak trees, is quiet and exclusive enough to make you forget that busy wineries are just 10 minutes away. Rooms, furnished with American country classics, have beamed ceilings, private patios, stone fireplaces, and wilderness views; many are individual suite-lodges that are so far removed from the common areas that you must drive to get to them (lazier folks can opt for more centrally located accommodations). You can spend your days playing golf, tennis, or croquet; lounging around the pools or spa; or hiking the surrounding areas. Those who actually want to leave the property to do some wine tasting can check in with John Thoreen, the hotel's wine tutor, whose sole purpose is to help guests better understand and enjoy Napa Valley wines.

Dining: one of Napa's finer four-course dinners is served at the Restaurant at Meadowood, located within the resort's gazebo-style clubhouse dining room overlooking the golf course. Dishes range from warm quail salad with smoky lentils to crispy skinned salmon trout served with exotic mushrooms and truffle oil. The wine list is excellent, as is the service. As you might expect, prices are steep

Amenities: Concierge, room service, dry cleaning and laundry, full-service spa, newspaper delivery, secretarial service, baby-sitting, 9-hole golf course, croquet lawns, two outdoor pools with sundeck, massage rooms, seven tennis courts, exercise room, hiking trails, an executive conference center.

Moderate

☉ Wine Country Inn. 1152 Lodi Lane, St. Helena, CA 94574. ☎ **707/963-7077.** Fax 707/963-9018. E-mail: romance@winecountryinn.com. 24 units, all with bathroom (12 with shower only). A/C TEL. $130–$258 double. Rates include breakfast. MC, V.

Just off the highway behind Freemark Abbey vineyard, this attractive wood-and-stone inn, complete with a French-style mansard roof and turret, overlooks a pastoral landscape of Napa Valley vineyards. The individually decorated rooms are furnished with iron or brass beds, antique furnishings, and handmade quilts; most have fireplaces and private terraces overlooking the valley, while others have private hot tubs. One of the inn's best features, besides the absence of TVs, is the outdoor pool (heated year-round), which is attractively landscaped into the hillside.

Another favorite is the selection of suites, which come with stereos, plenty of space, and lots of privacy. The family that runs this place puts their personal touches everywhere and makes every guest feel welcome. Wine and plenty of appetizers are served nightly, along with a big dash of hotel-staff hospitality in the inviting living room. A full buffet breakfast is served there, too. *Note:* Half the bathrooms have showers only.

Inexpensive

☉ Deer Run Bed & Breakfast. 3995 Spring Mountain Rd., P.O. Box 311, St. Helena, CA 94574. ☎ **800/843-3408** or 707/963-3794. Fax 707/963-9026. 4 units, all with bathroom (shower only). A/C TV. $130–$165 double. AE, MC, V.

Regardless of your budget, if romantic solitude is a big part of your vacation plan, Deer Run had better be on your itinerary. Situated 4½ miles (10 min. by car) from downtown St. Helena along a winding mountain road, this four-room B&B is the ultimate heavenly hideaway. Each of the wood-paneled rooms looks onto owners Tom and Carol Wilson's 4 acres of forest, and all feature gorgeous antiques, feather beds, a private entrance, deck, decanter of brandy, fridge, coffee and tea, robes, hair dryer, and access to hiking trails. Deer often meander by the Honeymoon Suite (the most secluded), a sweet split-level cottage with a separate bedroom and gas fireplace; its price includes breakfast delivered to your doorstep. The full breakfast served in the main house may include a frittata or apple crepes with chicken apple sausage. Outside you'll find Cody, the resident chocolate Lab, hanging out by the very small pool.

☉ El Bonita Motel. 195 Main St. (at El Bonita Ave.), St. Helena, CA 94574. ☎ **800/541-3284** or 707/963-3216. Fax 707/963-8838. 41 units. A/C MINIBAR TV TEL. Dec–Mar $75–$89 double; Apr–May and Nov $89–$115 double; June–Oct $95–$115 double. AE, CB, DC, DISC, MC, V.

This 1930s art-deco motel was built a bit too close to Calif. 29 for comfort, but the 2½ acres of beautifully landscaped gardens behind the hotel (away from the road) help even the score. The rooms, while small, are spotlessly clean and decorated with new furnishings; all have microwaves and coffeemakers, and some have kitchens or whirlpool bathtubs. Families, attracted to the larger bungalows with kitchenettes, often consider El Bonita one of the best values in Napa Valley—especially considering the heated outdoor pool, Jacuzzi, sauna, and new massage facility.

○ **White Sulphur Springs Retreat & Spa.** 3100 White Sulphur Springs Rd., St. Helena, 94574. ☎ **707/963-8588.** Fax 707/963-2890. 28 units, 9 cottages. Carriage House (shared bathroom) $65–$115 double; The Inn $85–$125 double; small Creekside Cottages $105–$155; large Creekside Cottages $125–$185. Additional person $15 extra. Discounts available during off-season and midweek. Single-night stays accepted in Carriage House rooms, but cottages require a 2-night minimum weekends from Apr–Oct and all holidays. MC, V.

If your idea of the ultimate vacation is a cozy cabin set among 330 acres of creeks, waterfalls, hot springs, hiking trails, and redwood, madrone, and fir trees, paradise is a short winding drive away from downtown St. Helena. Established in 1852, Sulphur Springs claims to be the oldest resort in California. Guests stay at the inn or in small and large creek-side cabins. Each is decorated with simple but homey furnishings; some have fireplaces or wood-burning stoves, and/or kitchenettes. The most upscale are the newly renovated cabins, but the well-worn, wood-paneled ones seem appropriate considering the natural surroundings. From here you can venture off on a hike; take a dip in the natural hot sulphur spring; lounge by the pool; sit under a tree and watch for deer, fox, raccoon, spotted owl, or woodpecker; or schedule a day of massage, aromatherapy, and other spa treatments. *Note:* No RVs are allowed without advance notice.

CALISTOGA
Moderate
○ **Cottage Grove Inn.** 1711 Lincoln Ave., Calistoga, CA 94515. ☎ **800/799-2284** or 707/942-8400. Fax 707/942-2653. 16 cottages. A/C TV TEL. $195 double. Rates include continental breakfast and evening wine and cheese. AE, DC, MC, V.

Standing in two parallel rows at the end of the main strip in Calistoga are the perfect couples retreats—brand-spanking-new cottages that, though located on a residential street, seem well-removed from the action once you've stepped across the threshold. Each compact guest house comes complete with a wood-burning fireplace, homey furnishings (perfect for curling up in front of the fire), cozy quilts, and an enormous bathroom with a skylight and a deep, two-person Jacuzzi tub, plus such niceties as gourmet coffee, a stereo with CD player, VCR (a video library is on site), wet bar, and fridge. Smokers beware—it's not allowed inside, but you can puff all you want on the small front porch. Several major spas are within walking distance. This is our top pick if you want to do the Calistoga spa scene in comfort and style. One cabin is accessible for travelers with disabilities.

Inexpensive
Calistoga Spa Hot Springs. 1006 Washington St. (at Gerrard St.), Calistoga, CA 94515. ☎ **707/942-6269.** 57 units, 1 family unit. A/C TV TEL. Winter $70 double; $95 family unit; $110 suite. Summer $85 double; $110 family unit; $130 suite. MC, V.

Very few hotels in the Wine Country welcome children, which is why we strongly recommend the Calistoga Spa Hot Springs for families. Even if you don't have kids in tow, it's still a great bargain, offering unpretentious yet clean and comfortable rooms with kitchenettes, as well as a plethora of spa facilities ranging from exercise rooms to four naturally heated outdoor mineral pools, aerobic facilities, volcanic ash mud baths, mineral baths, steam baths, blanket wraps, massage sessions, and more. All of Calistoga's best shops and restaurants are within easy walking distance, and you can even whip up your own grub at the barbecues set up near the large pool and patio area.

WHERE TO DINE IN THE NAPA VALLEY

Recently Napa's restaurants have been drawing as much attention to the valley as its award-winning wineries.

Nowhere else in the state are kitchens as deft at mixing fresh seasonal, local, organic produce into edible magic, which means that menus change constantly to reflect the best available ingredients. Add that to a great bottle of wine and stunning Wine Country views and you've got yourself one heck of an eating experience.

To best enjoy Napa's restaurant scene, keep one thing in mind: reserve—especially for a seat in a more renowned room.

The restaurants below are divided first by area, then by price category, using the following guide: **Expensive,** more than $45 per person; **Moderate,** $25 to $45 per person; and **Inexpensive,** less than $25 per person. These categories reflect the price of the majority of dinner menu items and include an appetizer, main course, coffee, dessert, tax, and tip.

NAPA
Moderate

Bistro Don Giovanni. 4110 St. Helena Hwy. (on Calif. 29, just north of Salvador Ave.), Napa. ☎ **707/224-3300.** Reservations recommended Fri–Sat. Main courses $11–$17. AE, DC, MC, V. Mon–Thurs 11:30am–10pm; Fri–Sun 11:30am–11pm. NORTHERN ITALIAN.

Donna and Giovanni Scala—who also run the fantastic Scala's Bistro in San Francisco—serve refined Italian fare prepared with top-quality ingredients and California flair at this large, lively, Mediterranean-style restaurant. The menu features pastas, risottos, pizzas (baked in a wood-burning oven), and a half-dozen other main courses such as braised lamb shank and Niman Schell bistro burgers. Less traditional appetizers include a grilled pear with a frisee-and-arugula salad with bleu cheese, caramelized walnuts, and bacon. Pasta-lovers should go for the farfalle with asparagus, porcini, wild mushrooms, pecorino cheese, and truffle oil. Alfresco dining among the vineyards is available—and highly recommended on a warm, sunny day.

Inexpensive

❂ **Alexis Baking Company.** 1517 Third St. (between Main and Jefferson sts.), Napa. ☎ **707/258-1827.** Main courses: breakfast $3.25–$6.25, lunch $$6–$8, dinner $6.75–$13. No credit cards. Mon–Fri 6:30am–3pm; Sat 7:30am–3pm; Sun 8am–2pm. BAKERY/CAFE.

This bakery/restaurant is so popular, on weekend mornings there's almost always a line out the door. But once you order from the counter and find a seat in the sunny room, you can relax, enjoy the casual coffeehouse atmosphere, and start your day with spectacular pastries, coffee drinks, and breakfast goodies like pumpkin pancakes with sautéed pears. Lunch also bustles with locals who come for the daily specials like fusilli pasta with roasted pumpkin, white beans, ham, and Parmesan in a cream sauce; grilled-chicken Caesar salad; roast lamb sandwich with minted mayo and roasted shallots on rosemary bread; and lentil bulgar orzo salad. Desserts run the gamut and include a moist and magical steamed persimmon pudding during the holiday season. This is a great stopover for vegetarians and sweet tooths.

OAKVILLE & RUTHERFORD
Expensive

Auberge du Soleil. 180 Rutherford Hill Rd., Rutherford. ☎ **707/963-1211.** Reservations recommended. Main courses $25–$30. AE, DISC, MC, V. Daily 7–11am, 11:30am–2:30pm, and 6–9:30pm. WINE COUNTRY CUISINE.

Alfresco dining is taken to an entirely new level here, particularly on warm summer nights when diners are rewarded with a gorgeous sunset view of the mountains.

Inside, a magnificent fireplace, huge wood pillars, and fresh flowers create a warm, rustic ambiance. Chef Andrew Sutton characterizes his cooking as "Wine Country cuisine," a reflection of the region's produce and international influences: Pacific Rim, Southwestern, and Mediterranean styles predominate. Signature dishes include a tasting platter of truffled deviled quail egg, smoked sturgeon, Thai lobster salad, caviar, and more; and a grapevine smoked salmon with walnut-wheat croutons and roasted shallot-caper relish. Regardless of what you order, be sure to arrive before sunset and beg for terrace seating.

Inexpensive

✪ **Oakville Grocery Café.** 7848 St. Helena Hwy. (Hwy. 29, at the Oakville Cross Rd.), Oakville. ☎ **707/944-0111.** Reservations available for parties of 8 or more. Breakfast $4–$7.50; lunch main courses $5.50–$9. AE, MC, V. Daily 7:30am–11am breakfast; 11am–4pm lunch. CALIFORNIA.

This is one of our favorite places to come for delicious, relatively cheap food. The melt-in-your-mouth salmon, watercress, and herb aioli sandwich ($8); soups, such as a hearty vegetable barley; salads (Niçoise, goat cheese with field greens and peach-chardonnay vinaigrette, and hearts of romaine); pizzas, such as wild-mushroom; and lasagna round out the ovation-worthy lunch menu. Breakfast is celebrated with "Small Plates" such as granola ($3.75), toasted breads with house preserves ($2), and a breakfast fruit tart, and "Big Plates" of chicken hash ($7), eggs, omelets, and frittatas. Counter service keeps the prices down, thick windows keep traffic noise out, and an absolutely fab meal and sweet ambiance keep the local constituency coming back for more. Our only complaint: They weren't open for dinner yet. (But as of March 1998, they are open a few nights a week; call for details).

YOUNTVILLE

Expensive

Brix. 7377 St. Helena Hwy. (Calif. 29), Yountville. ☎ **707/944-2749.** Reservations recommended. Main courses $17–$24. AE, DC, DISC, MC, V. Sun–Thurs 11:30am–9:30pm; Fri–Sat 11:30am–10pm. ASIAN FUSION.

Executive Chef Tod Michael Kawachi does a wonderful job integrating Asian flavors with California cuisine, and the result is a rich culinary adventure. While starters—such as a very tasty grilled-portobello-mushroom salad with blue cheese and sherry walnut vinaigrette (ask them not to go too heavy on the dressing!)—are interesting, only the starved should indulge, as portions tend to be large. We tried the Hawaiian ono with a rock-shrimp and shiitake coconut curry ragout, and a Thai pesto smoked rack of lamb with spicy peanut sate and zinfandel glaze. Both were very good, with knockout sauces, but what really impressed us was the Chinese-style whole crispy fish with cilantro black-bean sauce—an absolute must-have.

✪ **The French Laundry.** 6640 Washington St. (at Creek St.), Yountville. ☎ **707/944-2380.** Reservations required. Fixed-price lunch $44; 5-course dinner $65; 9-course dinner $80. AE, MC, V. Fri–Sun 11:30am–1:45pm; daily 5:30–9:30pm. CLASSIC AMERICAN/FRENCH.

If your restaurant has the chutzpah to post neither a sign nor an address, it had better be good. Fortunately, this Yountville institution is that good. Though it's been around since 1978, it wasn't until renowned chef/owner Thomas Keller bought the place a few years back that it caught the attention of epicureans worldwide (including the judges of the James Beard awards, who dubbed him 1997's "Chef of the Nation"). Dinner is an all-night affair; when it's finally over, you'll be ready to sit down and do it all over again—it's truly that wonderful.

Where to Stock Up for a Gourmet Picnic

You could easily plan your whole trip around restaurant reservations. But put together one of the world's best gourmet picnics, and the valley's your oyster.

One of the finest gourmet food stores in the Wine Country, if not all of California, is the **Oakville Grocery Co.,** 7856 St. Helena Hwy. at Oakville Cross Road (☎ **707/944-8802**). Here you can put together the provisions for a memorable picnic, or, if you give them at least 24 hours' notice, the staff can prepare a picnic basket for you. The store, with its small-town vibe and claustrophobia-inducing crowds, can be quite an experience. You'll find shelves crammed with the best breads and the choicest selection of cheeses in the northern Bay Area, as well as pâtés, cold cuts, crackers, top-quality olive oils, fresh foie gras (domestic and French, seasonally), smoked Norwegian salmon, fresh caviar (Beluga, Sevruga, Osetra), and, of course, an exceptional selection of California wines. The Grocery Co., which was launched by Joseph Phelps long before food and wine were mentioned in the same breath, is open daily from 9am to 6pm; it also has an espresso bar tucked in the corner (open daily from 7am to 3pm), offering breakfast and lunch items, house-baked pastries, and 15 wines available by the glass or for tasting.

Another of our favorite places to fill a picnic basket is New York City's version of a swank European marketplace, **Dean & DeLuca,** 607 South Main St. (Highway 29), north of Zinfandel Lane and south of Sulphur Springs Road in St. Helena (☎ **707/967-9980**). The opening of this enormous California outpost in late 1997 offered just one more indication that the Wine Country is becoming the epicenter of palatable perfection. The ultimate gourmet grocery store is more like a world's fair of foods, where everything is beautifully displayed and often painfully pricey. But even if you choose not to buy, this place is definitely worth a browse for the 200 domestic and imported cheeses; shelves of tapenades, pastas, oils, hand-packed dried herbs and spices, chocolates, sauces, and cookware; an espresso bar; one hell of a bakery section; and more. Head to the back where chefs prepare gourmet takeout or grab a bottle of vino with the help of wine master John Hardesty who presides over the 1,200-label collection. Hours are Monday to Saturday from 10am to 7pm (the espresso bar opens at 8am), and Sunday from 10am to 6pm.

Technically, the prix-fixe menu offers a choice of five or nine courses (including a vegetarian menu), but after a slew of cameo appearances from the kitchen, everyone starts to lose count. Signature dishes include Keller's "tongue in cheek" (a marinated and braised round of sliced lamb tongue and tender beef cheeks) and "macaroni and cheese" (sweet butter-poached Maine lobster with creamy lobster broth and orzo with mascarpone cheese). Portions are small, but only because Keller wants his guests to taste as many different things as possible—nobody leaves hungry. The excellent staff is well acquainted with the wide selection of regional wines; the house charges a $20 corkage fee if you choose to bring your own bottle. On warm summer nights, request a table in the flower-filled garden.

Moderate

Mustards Grill. 7399 St. Helena Hwy. (Calif. 29), Yountville. ☎ **707/944-2424.** Reservations recommended. Main courses $11–$17. DC, DISC, MC, V. Apr–Oct daily 11:30am–10pm; Nov–Mar daily 11:30am–9pm. CALIFORNIA.

Mustards is a safe bet for anyone in search of quality, but not overly adventurous, food and casual atmosphere. Housed in a convivial, barn-style space, it offers an 11-page wine list and an ambitious chalkboard list of specials. We started out with a wonderfully light seared ahi tuna that melted in our mouths the way ahi should. Although the Hoisin quail with apricot sauce and bok choy and the lamb shank braised in syrah with fennel and onions were tempting, we opted for a moist, perfectly flavored grilled chicken breast with mashed potatoes and fresh herbs. The menu includes something for everyone, from gourmands and vegetarians to good old burger-lovers.

○ **Piatti.** 6480 Washington St. (between Mission and Oak sts.), Yountville. ☎ **707/944-2070.** Reservations recommended. Main courses $7–$16. AE, DC, MC, V. Mon–Thurs and Sun 11:30am–10pm; Fri–Sat 11:30am–11pm. ITALIAN.

This local favorite—the first (and best) of a swiftly growing northern California chain—is known for serving excellent, reasonably priced food in a rustic Italian-style setting. Chef Peter Hall, a seasoned Napa Valley cook who honed his culinary art at Tra Vigne and Mustards before taking over the helm here, performs to a mostly sold-out crowd nightly. For the perfect meal, start with a salad of morning-cut field greens mixed with white corn and Napa Valley strawberry crostini, accompanied by a bowl of the spaghetti squash and sweet-potato soup. Though Hall offers a wide array of superb pastas and pizzas, it's the wood-oven–roasted duck—basted with a sweet cherry sauce and served over a bed of citrus risotto—that brings back the regulars. There are far fancier and more intimate restaurants in the valley, but we can't think of any that can fill you up on such outstanding fare at these prices. *Note:* Piatti also offers patio dining year-round, weather permitting.

ST. HELENA
Expensive
○ **Pinot Blanc.** 641 Main St., St. Helena. ☎ **707/963-6191.** Most lunch main courses $9–$15; dinner main courses $16–$24. AE, DC, DISC, JCB, MC, V. Tues–Thurs lunch 11:30am–3pm, dinner 5–9pm; Fri–Sun lunch 11:30am–4pm, dinner 4–9pm. Extended summer hours. FRENCH BISTRO.

Reviews were mixed as LA celebrity chef Joachim Splichal's formal new restaurant settled in over the past 2 years. But when we dined here, nothing could be more clear—Pinot Blanc rocks! The dark wood-paneled walls, lushly draped fabrics, and smoking-club atmosphere aren't exactly typical Wine Country, but on the flip side, it's a welcome change of pace. Besides, the room's serious integrity is the appropriate setting for one hell of a good meal prepared by executive chef Sean Knight. Lunch offerings might include a delicate roasted-beet salad with hazelnuts, blood oranges, and a duck prosciutto crouton; carpaccio of yellowtail hamachi; a stellar foie gras with butternut squash, Oregon huckleberries, and shallots; a slew of salads; sandwiches; and pasta (ricotta cheese gnocchi with braised veal cheeks and baby artichokes—wow!). The unique menu features such unusual entrees as oxtail pot pie, squab, and Scottish wood pigeon, plus more common but equally adventurous dishes such as striped bass with celery root and brandade potatoes; grilled meats; salmon with shallots, smoked bacon crust, baby artichokes, white beans, and arugula. Attention is paid to every detail at this restaurant, including the wine list, which features over 200 selections. There is patio seating during the summer.

○ **Terra.** 1345 Railroad Ave. (between Adams and Hunt sts.), St. Helena. ☎ **707/963-8931.** Reservations recommended. Main courses $14–$23. CB, DC, MC, V. Sun–Mon and Wed–Thurs 6–9pm; Fri–Sat 6–10pm. CONTEMPORARY AMERICAN.

St. Helena's restaurant of choice is the creation of Lissa Doumani and her husband, Hiro Sone, a master chef who hails from Japan and once worked with Wolfgang Puck at LA's Spago. Sone makes full use of the region's bounty; he seems to know how to coax every nuance of flavor from his fine local ingredients. The simple dining room is a perfect foil for Sone's extraordinary food. Among the appetizers, the terrine of foie gras with apple, walnut, and endive salad and the home-smoked salmon with beets, potatoes, and frisee are the stars of the show. The main dishes successfully fuse different cooking styles: try the grilled salmon with Thai red-curry sauce or the sake-marinated sea bass with shrimp dumplings in shiso broth. A recommended finale? The chocolate cognac mousse cake with sun-dried cherry ice cream.

✪ **Trilogy.** 1234 Main St. (at Hunt Ave.), St. Helena. ☎ **707/963-5507.** Reservations required. 3-course fixed-price menu $33, with wine pairing $45. MC, V. Dinner Tues–Sat 6–9pm. Wine bar Tues–Fri noon–9pm; Sat 3–9pm. Closed 3 weeks in Dec and 2 weeks in June. CALIFORNIA/FRENCH.

With a wine list that's probably second to none in the valley, this small, low-key restaurant is a favorite among Wine Country moguls. Diane Pariseau and her assistant do virtually everything themselves, turning out exceptionally fresh, well-prepared food. You can sample wines at the wine bar, but the real treat is the $33 three-course fixed-price menu, with each course accompanied by the appropriate glass of superior-quality wine for an extra $12 ("The best deal around," says Pariseau). The menu changes daily, but expect such delectable starters as salmon-potato cakes with chili aioli or seared tuna with Japanese-noodle salad and wasabi dressing. Other selections may include roasted pork tenderloin with shiitake-mushroom sauce (recommended with a hearty Ravenswood 1994 zinfandel) or a sautéed duck breast with sun-dried cherry sauce (best accompanied by a glass of 1992 Hanzell pinot noir).

Moderate

Tra Vigne Restaurant. 1050 Charter Oak Ave., St. Helena. ☎ **707/963-4444.** Reservations recommended. Main courses $12.50–$22; Cantinetta $4–$8. CB, DC, DISC, MC, V. Daily 11:30am–10pm; Cantinetta daily 11:30am–6pm. ITALIAN.

Tra Vigne's combination of good food, high-energy atmosphere, and "reasonable" prices (reasonable being a relative term) makes this restaurant a long-standing favorite among visitors.

The enormous dining room packs 'em in every night—and whether seated on the veranda (heated on cold nights) or in the center of the bustling scene, diners are usually thrilled just to have a seat. Even though the wonderful bread served with house-made flavored olive oils is tempting, save room for the robust California dishes, cooked Italian style, that have made this place everyone's favorite. The menu features about five or so pizzas, including a succulent caramelized onion, thyme, and Gorgonzola version. The dishes of the day might include grilled Sonoma rabbit with teleme-layered potatoes, oven-dried tomatoes, and mustard pan sauce, and a dozen or so antipasti. Equally tempting are the pastas—which include ceppo with sausage, spinach, potatoes, sun-dried tomatoes, and Pecorino—and the delicious desserts. When ordering, plan wisely—most dishes are very rich.

The adjoining Cantinetta offers a small selection of sandwiches, pizzas, and lighter meals (see below).

Wine Spectator Greystone Restaurant. At the Culinary Institute of America at Greystone, 2555 Main St., St. Helena. ☎ **707/967-1010.** Reservations strongly recommended. Tapas $3–$7; main courses $14–$19 (same prices at both lunch and dinner). AE, CB, DC, MC, V.

Daily 11:30am–3pm; Mon–Thurs 5:30–9pm; Fri–Sat 5:30–10pm; 3:30–5:30pm tapas at the bar. MEDITERRANEAN.

This place offers a combination visual and culinary feast that's unparalleled in the area, if not the state. The room itself is an enormous stone-walled former winery, but the festive decor and heavenly aromas warm the space up. Cooking islands— complete with scurrying chefs, steaming pots, and rotating chicken—provide edible entertainment. The tapas menu focuses on Mediterranean-inspired dishes, including an excellent pork kebab and a grilled calamari that contradicts the sea dweller's rubbery reputation with every moist and peppery bite. Tapas portions are small but affordable; pastas and salads are a bit heftier. Main courses, such as a Moroccan spiced roasted lamb with apricot, pearl onion, and pine-nut relish, are well portioned and darn good, but we recommend you opt for a barrage of appetizers for your table to share. You should also order the "Flights of Fancy," where for $14 to $20 you can sample three 3-ounce pours of local wines such as white rhones, pinot, or zinfandel. While the food is serious, the atmosphere is playful—casual enough that you'll feel comfortable in jeans or shorts. If you want to ensure a meal here (which we recommend you do), reserve far in advance.

Inexpensive

✪ **The Cantinetta.** At Tra Vigne Restaurant, 1050 Charter Oak Ave., St. Helena. ☎ **707/963-8888.** Main courses $4–$8. CB, DC, DISC, MC, V. Daily 11:30am–6pm. ITALIAN.

Regardless of where we dine while in the valley, we always make a point of stopping at the Cantinetta for an espresso and a snack. Part cafe, part shop, it's a casual place with a few tables and a counter. The focaccias (we've never had better in our lives!), pasta salads, and pastries are outstanding, and there's also a selection of cookies and other wonderful treats, flavored oils (free tastings), wines, and an array of gourmet items, many of which were created here. You can also get great picnic grub to go.

Tomatina. At The Inn at Southbridge, 1016 Main St., St. Helena. ☎ **707/967-9999.** Pasta $6–$8; pizza $8–$19. DC, DISC, MC, V. Daily 11:30am–10pm. ITALIAN.

When we've had it up to our ears with intense eating extravaganzas, we head Tomatina for a $3.50 chopped salad and other respites from gluttonous excess. Families and locals come here for another reason—though the menu is limited, it's a total winner for anyone looking for freshly prepared, wholesome food at atypically cheap Wine Country prices. A Caesar salad, for example, costs a mere $4.50. "Apizzas"—pizzas folded like a soft taco—are the house specialty, and come filled with such delights as fresh Maine clams and oregano. Pizzas are of the build-your-own variety with gourmet toppings like sautéed mushrooms, fennel sausage, baby spinach, sun-dried tomatoes, and homemade pepperoni. The 26 respectable local wines are served by the glass at a toast-worthy cost of $3.75, or $18 per bottle. As for dessert, at less than $4 a pop for gelato, biscotti, or pound cake, it's an overall sweet deal. Everything is ordered at the counter and brought to the small or family-style tables in the very casual dining area or the outdoor patio. Kids especially like the pool table and big-screen TV.

CALISTOGA
Moderate

All Seasons Café. 1400 Lincoln Ave. (at Washington St.), Calistoga. ☎ **707/942-9111.** Reservations recommended on weekends. Main courses $10.25–$19 at dinner. MC, V. Mon–Tues and Thurs–Fri 11am–3pm; daily 5:30–10pm. Wine shop Thurs–Tues 11am–7pm. CALIFORNIA.

Wine Country devotees often wend their way to the All Seasons Café in downtown Calistoga because of its extensive wine list and knowledgeable staff. The trick here is to buy a bottle of wine from the cafe's wine shop, then bring it to your table; the cafe adds a corkage fee of around $7.50 instead of tripling the price of the bottle (as they do at most restaurants). The diverse menu ranges from pizzas and pastas to such main courses as braised lamb shank "osso buco" in an orange, Madeira, and tomato sauce. Anything with the house-smoked salmon or spiced sausages is also a safe bet. Chef John Coss saves his guests from any major faux pas by matching wines to his dishes on the menu, so you know what's just right for smoked salmon and Crescenza cheese pizza.

✪ **Catahoula.** 1457 Lincoln Ave. (between Washington and Fairway sts.), Calistoga. ☎ **707/942-2275.** Reservations recommended. Main courses $11–$20. MC, V. Breakfast Sat–Sun 8:30–10am in winter, Fri–Sun 8:30–10am in summer; lunch Mon and Wed–Fri noon–2:30pm, Sat–Sun noon–3:30pm; dinner daily 5:30–10:30pm. AMERICAN/SOUTHERN.

The domain of chef Jan Birnbaum, formerly of New York's Quilted Giraffe and San Francisco's Campton Place, this restaurant is the current favorite in town. And for good reason—it's the only place in Napa where you can get a decent rooster gumbo. You'd have to travel all over Louisiana to find another pan-fried jalapeno-pecan catfish like this one. Catahoula's funky and fun, and the food that comes out of the wood-burning oven—like the roast duck with chili cilantro potatoes or the whole roasted fish with lemon broth, orzo, and escarole—is exciting (and usually spicy). Start with the spicy gumbo ya ya with andouille sausage, and finish with what may be a first for many non-Southerners—buttermilk ice cream.

Wappo Bar & Bistro. 1226B Washington St. (off Lincoln Ave.), Calistoga. ☎ **707/942-4712.** Main courses $8.50–$14.50. AE, MC, V. Wed–Mon 11:30am–2:30pm and 6–9:30pm. INTERNATIONAL.

One of the best alfresco dining experiences in the Wine Country is under Wappo's honeysuckle-and-vine–covered arbor, but you'll also be comfortable inside this small bistro at one of the well-spaced, well-polished tables. The menu offers a wide range of choices, from Chilean sea bass with mint chutney to roast rabbit with potato gnocchi. The desserts of choice are the black-bottom coconut cream pie and the strawberry rhubarb pie.

Inexpensive

Smokehouse Café. 1458 Lincoln Ave., Calistoga. ☎ **707/942-6060.** Main courses $8–$21. MC, V. Daily 7:30am–10pm (closed Tues–Wed Jan–Feb). REGIONAL AMERICAN BBQ.

Who would have guessed that some of the best spareribs and house-smoked meats in northern California would come from this little kitchen in Calistoga? Here's the winning game plan: Start with the Sacramento delta crawfish cakes (better than any wimpy crab cakes you'll find in San Francisco) and husk-roasted Cheyenne corn, then move on to the slow pig sandwich, a half slab of ribs, or homemade sausages—all of which take up to a week to prepare (not while you wait, luckily). The clincher, though, is the fluffy all-you-can-eat cornbread dipped in pure cane syrup, which comes with every full-plate dinner. Kids are especially catered to—a rarity in these parts—and patio dining is available during the summer for breakfast, lunch, and dinner.

2 Sonoma County

A pastoral contrast to Napa, Sonoma still manages to maintain a backcountry ambiance thanks to its far-lower density of wineries, restaurants, and hotels. Small, family-owned wineries are Sonoma's mainstay; tastings are low-key, and they come with plenty of friendly banter with the wine makers (who often will be doing the pouring themselves). Basically, this is the valley to visit if your ideal vacation includes visiting a handful of wineries along quiet, gently winding, woodsy roads, avoiding shopping outlets and Napa's high-end glitz, and simply enjoying the laid-back country atmosphere.

Truth is, even though there are far fewer wineries here, Sonoma wines have actually won more awards than any other California wine-growing region for 7 years running (much to the chagrin of Napa vintners, no doubt).

The valley itself is some 17 miles long and 7 miles wide, and is bordered by two mountain ranges: the Mayacamas to the east and Sonoma Mountains to the west. Unlike Napa Valley, you won't find palatial wineries with million-dollar art collections, aerial trams, and Hollywood ego trips (read: Niebaum-Coppola). Rather, the Sonoma Valley offers a refreshing dose of reality, where modestly sized wineries are integrated into the community rather than perched on hilltops like corporate citadels. If the Napa Valley feels more like a fantasyland, where everything exists to service the almighty grape and the visitors it attracts, then the Sonoma Valley is its antithesis, an unpretentious gaggle of ordinary towns, ranches, and wineries that welcome tourists but don't necessarily rely on them. The result, as you wind your way through the valley, is a chance to experience what Napa Valley must have been like long before the Seagrams and Möet et Chandons of the world turned the Wine Country into a major tourist destination.

As in Napa, you can also pick up *Wine Country Review* throughout Sonoma—it will give you the most up-to-date information on wineries and related area events.

ESSENTIALS

GETTING THERE   From San Francisco, cross the Golden Gate Bridge and stay on U.S. 101 north. Exit at Highway 37; after 10 miles, turn north onto Highway 121. After another 10 miles, turn north onto Highway 12 (Broadway), which will take you directly into the town of Sonoma.

VISITOR INFORMATION   While you're in Sonoma, stop by the **Sonoma Valley Visitors Bureau,** 10 E. Spain St. (☎ **707/996-1090;** Web site: www. sonomavalley.com), right on the plaza next to the Sonoma Cheese Factory. It's open daily from 9am to 7pm in summer and from 9am to 5pm in winter. An additional **Visitors Bureau** is located a few miles south of the square at 25200 Arnold Dr. (Highway 121), at the entrance to Viansa Winery (☎ **707/996-5793**); it's open daily from 9am to 5pm.

If you prefer some advance information, the free pocket-size *Sonoma Valley Visitors Guide* offers most every lodging, winery, and restaurant in the valley. Contact the **Sonoma Valley Visitors Bureau,** 10 East Spain St., Sonoma, CA 95476 (☎ **707/996-1090**), to order one, or check out their Web site at www. sonomavalley.com.

TOURING THE VALLEY & WINERIES

Sonoma Valley is currently home to about 35 wineries (including California's first winery, Buena Vista, founded in 1857) and 13,000 acres of vineyards, which produce roughly 25 types of wines totaling more than five million cases a year. Chardonnay is the varietal for which Sonoma is most noted, and it represents almost one-quarter of the valley's vine acreage. Unlike the rigidly structured tours at many of Napa Valley's corporate-owned wineries, tastings and tours on the Sonoma side of the Mayacamas Mountains are usually free and low-key, and come with plenty of friendly banter between the wine makers and their guests.

The towns and wineries covered below are organized geographically from south to north, starting at the intersection of Highway 37 and Highway 121 in the Carneros District and ending in Kenwood. The wineries here tend to be a little more spread out than they are in Napa, but they're easy to find. Still, it's best to decide which wineries you're most interested in and devise a touring strategy before you set out so you don't find yourself doing a lot of backtracking.

We've reviewed our favorite Sonoma Valley wineries here—more than enough to keep you busy tasting wine for a long weekend. If you'd like a complete list of local wineries, be sure to pick up one of the free guides to the valley available at the Sonoma Valley Visitors Bureau (see "Visitor Information" above).

THE CARNEROS DISTRICT

As you approach the Wine Country from the south, you must first pass through the Carneros District, a cool, windswept region that borders the San Pablo Bay and marks the entrance to both Napa and Sonoma valleys. Until the latter part of the 20th century, this mixture of marsh, sloughs, and rolling hills was mainly used as sheep pasture (*carneros* means sheep in Spanish). After experimental plantings yielded slow-growing yet high-quality grapes—particularly chardonnay and pinot noir—several Napa and Sonoma wineries expanded their plantings here, eventually establishing the Carneros District as an American Viticultural Appellation. Though about a dozen wineries are spread throughout the region, there are no major towns or attractions—just plenty of gorgeous scenery as you cruise along Highway 121, the major junction between Napa and Sonoma.

✪ **Viansa Winery and Italian Marketplace.** 25200 Arnold Dr. (Calif. 121), Sonoma. ☎ **800/995-4740** or 707/935-4700. Daily 10am–5pm. Guided tours by appointment only.

The first major winery you'll encounter as you enter Sonoma Valley from the south is Viansa; this sprawling Tuscany-style villa is perched atop a knoll overlooking the entire lower valley. Viansa is the brainchild of Sam and Vicki Sebastiani, who left the family dynasty to create their own temple to food and wine (Viansa being a contraction of Vicki and Sam). While Sam, a third-generation wine maker, runs the winery, Vicki manages the marketplace, a large room crammed with a cornucopia of high-quality preserves, mustards, olive oils, pastas, salads, breads, desserts, Italian tableware, cookbooks, and such (if you're looking for wine-related gifts, this is the place).

The winery, which does an extensive mail-order business through its Tuscany Club (well worth joining if you love getting mail and good wine), has quickly established a favorable reputation for its cabernet, sauvignon blanc, and chardonnay, blended from premium Napa and Sonoma grapes and sold in the sexiest-shaped bottles in Sonoma. Sam is also experimenting with Italian grape varieties such as Muscat canelli, sangiovese, and nebbiolo, most of which are sold exclusively at the winery. Tastings, which are poured at the east end of the marketplace, are free, and the self-guided tour includes a trip through the underground barrel-aging cellar adorned with colorful fresco-style hand-painted murals.

Viansa is also one of the few wineries in Sonoma Valley where you can purchase deli items—the focaccia sandwiches are delicious—and dine alfresco under their grape trellis while you admire the bucolic view.

Gloria Ferrer Champagne Caves. 23555 Carneros Hwy. (Calif. 121), Sonoma. ☎ **707/996-7256.** Daily 10am–5:30pm. Tours hourly from 11am to 4pm.

When you've had it up to here with chardonnays and pinots, it's time to pay a visit to Gloria Ferrer, the grand dame of the Wine Country's sparkling wine producers. Who's Gloria, you ask? She's the wife of José Ferrer, whose family has been making sparkling wine for the past 5 centuries and whose company, Freixenet, is the largest producer of sparkling wine in the world (Cordon Negro being their most popular brand). All of which equals big bucks, and certainly a good chunk of it went into building this palatial estate. Glimmering like Oz high atop a gently sloping hill, it overlooks the verdant Carneros District. On a sunny day, it's impossible not to enjoy a glass of dry Brut while soaking-in the magnificent views of the vineyards and valley below.

If you're unfamiliar with the term *méthode champenoise,* be sure to take the free 30-minute tour of the fermenting tanks, bottling line, and caves brimming with racks of yeast-laden bottles. Afterwards, retire to the elegant tasting room for a flute-full of Brut or Cuvée ($3 to $5.50 a glass, $16 and up per bottle), find an empty chair on the veranda, and say, "Ahhh. This is the life." Yes, there are picnic tables, but it's usually too windy up here for an enjoyable experience—plus, you have to purchase a bottle of their sparkling wine to reserve a table.

SONOMA

At the northern boundary of the Carneros District along Highway 12 is the centerpiece of Sonoma Valley, the midsized town of Sonoma, which owes much of its appeal to Mexican General Mariano Guadalupe Vallejo. It was Vallejo who fashioned this pleasant, slow-paced community after a typical Mexican village—right down to its central plaza, Sonoma's geographical and commercial center. The plaza sits at the top of a T formed by Broadway (Highway 12) and Napa Street. Most of the surrounding streets form a grid pattern around this axis, making Sonoma easy to negotiate. The plaza's Bear Flag Monument marks the spot where the crude Bear Flag was raised in 1846, signaling the end of Mexican rule; the symbol was later adopted by the state of California and placed on its flag. The 8-acre park at the center of the plaza, complete with two ponds populated with ducks and geese, is perfect for an afternoon siesta in the cool shade. Our favorite attraction, however, is the gaggle of brilliantly feathered chickens that roam unfettered through the streets of Sonoma—a sight you'll definitely never see in Napa.

Sebastiani Vineyards Winery. 389 Fourth St. E., Sonoma. ☎ **800/888-5532** or 707/938-5532. Daily 10am–5pm. Tours offered 10:30am–4pm, every half hour in summer, every 45 min. to an hr. in winter; no reservations necessary.

The name Sebastiani is practically synonymous with Sonoma. What started in 1904, when Samuele Sebastiani began producing his first wines, has, in three successive generations, now grown into a small empire and Sonoma County's largest winery, producing some six million cases a year. Oddly enough, the winery occupies neither the most scenic setting nor structures in Sonoma Valley, yet its place in the history and development of the region is unparalleled.

The 25-minute tour is interesting, informative, and well worth the time. You can see the winery's original turn-of-the-century crusher and press as well as the world's largest collection of oak-barrel carvings, crafted by local artist Earle Brown. If you don't want to take the tour, head straight for the charmingly rustic tasting room, where you can sample an extensive selection of wines sans tasting fee. Bottle prices are very reasonable, ranging from $5 for a 1996 white zin to $15 for a 1994 cabernet sauvignon. A picnic area is adjacent to the cellars, though a far more scenic picnic area is located across the parking lot in Sebastiani's Cherryblock Vineyards.

Buena Vista. 18000 Old Winery Rd. (off E. Napa St., slightly northeast of downtown), Sonoma. ☎ **800/926-1266** or 707/938-1266. Daily 10:30am–5pm. Self-guided tours only.

The patriarch of California wineries was founded in 1857 by Count Agoston Haraszthy, the Hungarian émigré who is universally regarded as the father of

---

Touring the Sonoma Valley by Bike

Sonoma and its neighboring towns are so small, close together, and relatively flat that it's not difficult to get around on two wheels. In fact, if you're in no great hurry, there's no better way to tour the Sonoma Valley than via bicycle. You can rent a bike at the **Goodtime Bicycle Company,** 18503 Sonoma Hwy. (Calif. 12), Sonoma (☎ **888/525-0453** or 707/938-0453). They'll happily point you to easy bike trails, or you can take one of their organized excursions to Kenwood-area wineries or to south Sonoma wineries. Not only do they provide a gourmet lunch featuring local Sonoma products, they'll also carry any wine you purchase for you and help with shipping arrangements. Lunch rides start at 10:30am and end at around 3pm. The cost, including food and equipment, is $55 per person (that's a darn good deal). Rentals cost $25 a day or $5 per hour, and include helmets, locks, and everything else you'll need (delivery is a $25 flat day rate). Bikes are also available for rent from **Sonoma Valley Cyclery,** 20093 Broadway, Sonoma (☎ **707/935-3377**), for $20 a day, $6 per hour.

California's wine industry. A close friend of General Vallejo, Haraszthy returned from Europe in 1861 with 100,000 of the finest vine cuttings, which he made available to all winegrowers. Although Buena Vista's wine making now takes place at an ultramodern facility in the Carneros District, the winery still maintains a complimentary tasting room inside the restored 1862 Press House—a beautiful stone-crafted room brimming with wines, wine-related gifts, and accessories (as well as a small art gallery along the inner balcony).

Tastings are free for most wines, $3 for the really good stuff; bottle prices range from as low as $8.50 for a buttery 1996 sauvignon blanc to $26 for the Carneros Grand Reserve cabernet sauvignon (which was so good that we bought three). There's also a self-guided tour that you can follow any time during operating hours, and a "Historical Presentation," offered daily at 2pm, that details the life and times of the Count. After tasting, grab your favorite bottle, a selection of cheeses from the Sonoma Cheese Factory, salami, bread, and pâté (all available in the tasting room), and plant yourself at one of the many picnic tables recessed into the lush, verdant setting.

Ravenswood Winery. 18701 Gehricke Rd. (off Lovall Valley Rd.), Sonoma. ☎ **800/NO-WIMPY** or 707/938-1960. Daily 10am–4:30pm. Tours by reservation only.

Compared to old heavies like Sebastiani and Buena Vista, Ravenswood is a relative newcomer to the Sonoma wine scene, but it has quickly established itself as the sine qua non of zinfandel, the versatile grape that's quickly gaining popular ground on the rapacious cabernet sauvignon. In fact, Ravenswood is the first winery in the United States to focus primarily on zins, which accounts for three quarters of its 150,000-case production. It also produces a merlot, cabernet sauvignon, and a small amount of chardonnay.

The winery is smartly designed—recessed into the Sonoma hillside to protect its treasures from the simmering summers. Tours follow the wine-making process from grape to glass, and include a visit into the aromatic oak-barrel aging rooms. A gourmet "Barbecue Overlooking the Vineyards" is held each weekend (from 11am to 4:40pm, from Memorial Day through the end of September; call for details and reservations), though you're welcome to plop your own picnic basket down at any of their tables. Tastings are free and generous, though you may not find some of the pourers to be as witty as they think they are (ours was a jerk, though we've known people who have had great experiences here). Bottle prices range from $8.50 for a 1996 light and crisp French Colombard to $16 for a 1995 cab, but it's the kick-butt zins—priced well in the low to mid-teens—that you'll want to stock up on.

GLEN ELLEN

About 7 miles north of Sonoma on Highway 12 is the town of Glen Ellen, which, though just a fraction of the size of Sonoma, is home to several of the valley's finest wineries, restaurants, and inns. Aside from the addition of a few new restaurants, this charming Wine Country town hasn't changed much since the days when Jack London settled on his Beauty Ranch, about a mile west. Other than the wineries, you'll find few real signs of commercialism; the shops and restaurants, located along one main winding lane, cater to a small, local clientele—that is, until the summer tourist season, when traffic nearly triples on the weekends. If you're as yet undecided where you want to set up camp during your visit to the Wine Country, we highly recommend this lovable little town.

Arrowood. 14347 Sonoma Hwy. (Calif. 12), Glen Ellen. ☎ **707/938-5170.** Daily 10am–4:30pm. Tours by appointment only, Mon–Fri at 10:30am and 2:30pm.

Richard Arrowood had already established a reputation as a master wine maker at Château St. Jean before he and his wife, Alis Demers Arrowood, set out to build their own winery in 1986. Their utterly picturesque winery is perched on a gently rising hillside lined with perfectly manicured vineyards. Tastings take place in the Hospitality House, the newest of Arrowood's two stately gray-and-white buildings that were fashioned after a New England farmhouse, complete with wraparound porches. Richard's focus is on making world-class wine with minimal intervention, and his results are impressive: four out of his five current releases have scored over 90 points. Mind you, such excellence doesn't come cheaply: Prices start at $24 for a 1996 chardonnay and quickly climb to the mid- to high 30s. Arrowood is only one of the very few wineries in Sonoma that charge for tastings ($3), but if you're curious what near-perfection tastes like, it's well worth it. No picnic facilities are available.

✪ The Benziger Family Winery. 1883 London Ranch Rd. (off Arnold Dr., on the way to Jack London State Historic Park), Glen Ellen. ☎ **800/989-8890** or 707/935-3000. Tasting room daily 10am–5:30pm. Tram tours daily (weather permitting) at 11:30am, 12:30, 2, and 3:30pm.

When Bruno Benziger moved from New York, purchased the plot next to Jack London State Park, and started the Glen Ellen label (see above), he had no idea that he would become the valley's second-largest wine producer. After the Benziger family's fast track to the top, they sold the rights to that label in order to create lower-volume, higher-quality wines under this one.

A visit here confirms that you are indeed visiting a "family" winery; at any given time three generations of Benzigers (pronounced *ben*-zigger) may be running around tending to chores, and you're instantly made to feel as if you're part of the clan. The pastoral property has a spacious tasting room manned by an amiable staff, as well as an art gallery, beautiful gardens, and an exceptional self-guided tour ("The most comprehensive tour in the wine industry," " exclaims *Wine Spectator* magazine). The free 40-minute tram tour, pulled by a beefy tractor, is both informative and fun as it winds through the estate vineyards before making a champagne-tasting pit stop on a scenic bluff. (*Tip:* Tram tickets—a hot item in the summer—are available on a limited first-come, first-served basis, so either arrive early or stop by in the morning to pick up tickets for an afternoon ride.)

Tastings of the standard release wines are free, and bottle prices range from $10 for a 1996 fumé blanc to $18 for a 1995 pinot noir. The best buy, however, is the award-winning 1995 zinfandel (Sonoma County), priced to move at $16 a bottle. You can also purchase a full glass of wine for $5 and tour the estate in style. Additionally, the winery offers several scenic picnic spots.

KENWOOD

A few miles north of Glen Ellen along Highway 12 is the tiny town of Kenwood, the northernmost outpost of the Sonoma Valley. Though Kenwood Vineyards' wines are well known throughout the United States, the town itself consists of little more than a few restaurants, wineries, and modest homes recessed into the wooded hillsides. The nearest lodging, the luxurious Kenwood Inn & Spa, is located about a mile south. Kenwood makes for a pleasant day trip—lunch at Café Citti, a tour of Château St. Jean, dinner at Kenwood Restaurant—before returning to Glen Ellen or Sonoma for the night.

Kunde Estate Winery. 10155 Sonoma Hwy., Kenwood. ☎ **707/833-5501.** Tastings daily 11am–5pm. Cave tours Fri–Sun approximately every half hour from 11am–4pm.

Expect a friendly, unintimidating welcome at this scenic winery, run by four generations of the Kundes since 1904. One of the largest grape suppliers in the area, the Kunde family (pronounced *kun*-dee) has converted 800 acres of their 2,000-acre ranch for growing ultrapremium-quality grapes, which they provide to about 30 Sonoma and Napa wineries. It is this abundance that allows them to make nothing but estate wines (wines made from grapes grown on the Kunde property, as opposed to purchased from other growers).

The tasting room is located in a spiffy new 17,000-square-foot wine-making facility, which features specialized crushing equipment that allows the wine maker to run whole clusters to the press—a real advantage in white-wine production. Tastings of the dozen or so releases are free; bottle prices range from $11 for a 1996 Magnolia Lane sauvignon blanc to $24 for a 1993 Reserve cabernet sauvignon; most labels sell in the mid- to high teens. The tasting room also has a gift shop and large windows overlooking the bottling room and tank room.

The tour of the property's extensive wine caves includes a history of the winery. Private tours are available by appointment, but most folks are happy to just stop by for some vino and to relax at one of the many picnic tables placed around the man-made pond. Animal-lovers will appreciate Kunde's preservation efforts; the property has a rare-duck estuary with more than 50 species (seen by appointment only). *Gossip note:* The Kunde Estate also happens to be where actress Geena Davis and director Renny Harlin tied the knot in 1993.

Kenwood Vineyards. 9592 Sonoma Hwy. (Calif. 12), Kenwood. ☎ **707/833-5891.** Daily 10am–4:30pm. Tours by appointment only.

Kenwood's history dates back to 1906, when the Pagani brothers made their living selling wine straight from the barrel and into the jug. In 1970 the property was bought by the Lee family, who dumped a ton of money into converting the aging winery into a modern, high-production facility (though they have cleverly concealed most of it within the original barnlike buildings). Since then, Kenwood's wines have earned a solid reputation for consistent quality with each of their varietals: cabernet sauvignon, chardonnay, zinfandel, pinot noir, merlot, and their most popular wine, sauvignon blanc—a crisp, light wine with hints of melon.

Though the winery looks rather modest in size, its output is staggering: 275,000 cases of ultrapremium wines fermented in 60 steel tanks and 7,000 French and American oak barrels. Popular with wine collectors is wine maker Michael Lee's Artist Series cabernet sauvignon, a limited production from the winery's best vineyards featuring labels with original artwork by renowned artists. The tasting room, housed in one of the old barns, offers free tastings of most varieties, as well as gift items for sale. Wine prices are moderate, ranging from $7.50 for a bottle of 1995 Vintage Red table wine to $20 for a 1995 Sonoma County merlot; the Artist Series, on the other hand, runs anywhere from $50 to $250.

JUST UP FROM THE VALLEY: SANTA ROSA

✪ **Matanzas Creek.** 6097 Bennett Valley Rd. (off Warm Springs Rd.), Santa Rosa. ☎ **707/528-6464.** Daily 10am–4:30pm. Tours daily by appointment only at 10:30am, 1, and 3pm. From Hwy. 12 in Kenwood or Glen Ellen, take Warm Springs Rd. turnoff to Bennett Valley Rd.; the drive takes 15–20 min.

Okay, so it's not technically in Sonoma Valley—but if there's one winery that's worth the detour, it's Matanzas Creek. After a wonderfully scenic 20-minute drive along Bennett Valley Road you'll arrive at one of the prettiest wineries in California, blanketed by fields of lavender and surrounded by rolling hills of well-tended vineyards.

The winery itself has a rather unorthodox history. In 1978, Sandra and Bill MacIver, neither of whom had any previous experience in the worlds of wine making or business, set out with one goal in mind: to create the finest wines in the country. Actually, they've overshot their mark. With the recent release of their Journey 1990 chardonnay, they've been hailed by critics as the proud parents of the finest chardonnay ever produced in the United States, comparable to the finest white wines in the world.

This state-of-the-art, environmentally conscious winery produces only three varietals—the above-mentioned chardonnay, plus sauvignon blanc and merlot—all of which are available for tasting free of charge. Prices for current releases are, as you would imagine, at the higher end, ranging from $18 for a 1996 sauvignon blanc to a whopping $75 for the 1993 Estate merlot—but it's easily the finest merlot you'll sample in the Wine Country. Also available for purchase is culinary lavender from Matanzas (pronounced mah-*tan*-zas) Creek's own lavender field, the largest outside of Provence and a breathtaking sight when it's in bloom in June (*Tip:* Purchase a glass of wine and bring it outside to savor as you wander through these wonderfully aromatic gardens). Picnic tables hidden under groves of oak have pleasant views of the surrounding vineyards. On the return trip, be sure to take the Sonoma Mountain Road detour for a real backcountry experience.

WHERE TO STAY IN SONOMA COUNTY

We've arranged the hotel listings below first by area and then by price, using the following categories: Very Expensive: more than $250 per night; Expensive: $200 to $250 per night; Moderate: $150 to $200 per night; and Inexpensive: less than $150 per night. Keep in mind that during the peak season and on weekends, most B&Bs and hotels require a minimum 2-night stay. Of course, that's assuming you can even find a vacancy, so be sure to make reservations as far in advance as possible.

If you *are* having trouble finding a vacancy, try calling the **Sonoma Valley Visitors Bureau** at ☎ 707/996-1090. They'll try to refer you to a lodging that has a room to spare, but they won't make reservations for you. Another option is calling the **Bed and Breakfast Association of Sonoma Valley** at ☎ 800/969-4667. They will refer you to a B&B that belongs to their Association and will make reservations for you as well.

SONOMA
Very Expensive

✪ **Sonoma Mission Inn & Spa.** 18140 Sonoma Hwy. (Calif. 12; P.O. Box 1447), Sonoma, CA 94576. ☎ **800/862-4945** or 707/938-9000. Fax 707/935-1205. 198 units. A/C MINIBAR TV TEL. Nov–Apr $170–$255 Historic Inn room; $200–$360 Wine Country room; $285 suite. May–Oct $180–$285 Historic Inn room; $245–$345 Wine Country room; $395 suite. AE, CB, DC, MC, V. From central Sonoma, drive 3 miles north on Calif. 12.

As you drive through Boyes Hot Springs, you may wonder why someone decided to build a multimillion-dollar spa resort in this ordinary little town. There's no view to speak of, and it certainly isn't within walking distance of any wineries or fancy restaurants. So what's the deal? It's the water, of course, the lifeblood of every Wine Country spa—naturally heated artesian mineral water, to be precise, piped from directly underneath the spa and into the temperature-controlled pools and whirlpools. Set on 12 meticulously groomed acres, the Sonoma Mission Inn consists of a massive three-story replica of a Spanish mission (well, aside from the pink paint job), an array of satellite wings housing 30 superluxury suites, and, of course, the spa facilities. It's a popular retreat for the wealthy and the well known, so don't be surprised if you see Barbra Streisand or Harrison Ford strolling around in their skivvies.

The modern rooms are furnished in a modern theme with plantation-style shutters, ceiling fans, down comforters, and such extra amenities as bathroom scales, hair dryers, and oversized bath towels. The Wine Country rooms are in a newer building and feature king-size beds, desks, refrigerators, and huge limestone and marble bathrooms; some offer wood-burning fireplaces, and many have balconies. The older, slightly smaller Historic Inn Rooms are sweetly appointed with homey furnishings, and most have queen-size beds; they are, however, overpriced for what you get and in serious need of renovation. All rooms have video access on command and come with a complimentary bottle of wine. The new Texan owners have plans to expand the resort even further, including a whole new spa menu.

Dining: The Grille, run by chef Jeff Jake, is known for its low-calorie, low-sodium, and low-cholesterol California cuisine as well as its 200 varieties of Napa and Sonoma wines (see "Where to Dine in the Sonoma Valley," below). The casual cafe, serving American cuisine at lunch, is renowned for its bountiful breakfasts.

Amenities: Room service, concierge, laundry, dry cleaning, newspaper delivery, baby-sitting, secretarial services, valet parking, complimentary refreshments. Full spa facilities with a wide range of treatments and nutritional consultation; health club; tennis courts (The tariff for individual spa and salon services ranges from $35 to $134). The use of the spa's bathhouse, which includes a sauna, steam room, whirlpool, outdoor exercise pool, and gym with weight equipment, costs $10 weekdays and $20 weekends, but is complimentary with any spa service.

Moderate

El Dorado Hotel. 405 First St. W., Sonoma, CA 95476. ☎ **800/289-3031** or 707/996-3030. Fax 707/996-3148. 26 units. A/C TV TEL. Summer $130–$160 double; winter $100–$130 double. Rates include continental breakfast and a split of wine. AE, MC, V.

This place may look like a 19th-century Wild West relic from the outside, but inside it's all 20th-century deluxe. Each modern, handsomely appointed guest room—designed by the same folks who put together the ultraexclusive Auberge du Soleil resort in Rutherford (see above)—has French windows and tiny terraces;

The Super Spa

There's no question about it: **Sonoma Mission Inn & Spa,** 18140 Sonoma Hwy. (☎ **800/862-4945** or 707/938-9000), is the most complete—and the most luxurious—spa in the whole Wine Country. At this elegant, pink, Spanish Mission–style palace, you can pamper yourself in myriad ways: Take a soak in mineral baths; get a facial, body wrap, or massage; aerobicize; work out with weights and cardio machines or let go of your tension in a yoga class; relax with a steam or a sauna; play tennis; or just lounge or lunch by the pool. Or you can opt for our (okay, Erika's) personal favorite—the Rejuvinator, a 1-hour-40-minute mega-treatment: First you're wrapped in blankets on a massage table. Then comes an "oil drip" onto your hair and scalp, followed by a scalp massage and a hair mask that smells so much like cookie dough that you'll be tempted to nibble on it. Next comes a face mask and a rinse. Finally, the crowning glory—a stress-relieving back massage.

The Rejuvenator's $174 price tag is steep, but if you can swing it, this package of pampering is well worth the cost—it really does the trick. Be prepared to also fork over the $35 spa fee that all nonhotel guests have to pay (hotel guests pay $10 on weekdays, $20 on weekends to use the facilities). But even if you don't go for any of the spa selections, consider spending the 35 bucks just to hang out here—a perfect poolside day followed by a workout in the exercise room and a sauna, steam, and mineral plunge is one of our favorite ways to unwind in the Wine Country.

some offer lovely views of the plaza, while others overlook the hotel's private courtyard and heated lap pool. Each room has a private bathroom with plush towels and hair dryer. All rooms (except those for the disabled) are on the second floor, and have private bathrooms with plush towels and hair dryers. The two rooms on the ground floor are off the private courtyard, and each has its own partially enclosed patio. Services include a concierge, laundry, in-room massage, bicycle rental, and access to a nearby health club. Breakfast, served either inside or out in the courtyard, includes coffee, fruits, and freshly baked breads and pastries. Within the hotel is Piatti, a popular restaurant serving regional Italian cuisine (see "Where to Dine in the Sonoma Valley," below).

Inexpensive

Victorian Garden Inn. 316 E. Napa St., Sonoma, CA 95476. ☎ **800/543-5339** or 707/996-5339. Fax 707/996-1689. 4 units. $95–$165 double. Rates include breakfast and afternoon wine and sherry. AE, DC, MC, V.

Proprietor Donna Lewis runs what is easily the cutest B&B in Sonoma Valley. A small picket fence and wall of trees enclose an adorable Victorian garden brimming with bowers of violets, roses, camellias, and peonies, all shaded under flowering fruit trees. It's a truly marvelous sight in the springtime. Four guest rooms—three in the century-old water tower and one in the main house, an 1870s Greek Revival farmhouse—are in keeping with the Victorian theme: white wicker furniture, floral prints, padded armchairs, claw-foot tubs. The most popular rooms are the Top o' the Tower, which has it's own entrance and view overlooking the garden, and the Woodcutter's Cottage, which also has its own entrance and garden view, plus a sofa and armchairs set in front of the fireplace. A breakfast of croissants, muffins, gourmet coffee, and fruit picked from the garden is served at the dining table, in the garden, or in your room; evening wine and sherry are served in the parlor. After a hard day's wine tasting, spend the afternoon cooling off in the swimming pool or on the shaded wraparound porch, enjoying a mellow merlot while soaking in the sweet garden smells.

Sonoma Hotel. 110 W. Spain St., Sonoma, CA 95476. ☎ 800/468-6016 or 707/ 996-2996. Fax 707/996-7014. 17 units, 5 with bathroom. Summer $75–$85 double without bathroom, $115–$125 double with bathroom. Winter Sun–Thurs $59 double without bathroom, $90 double with bathroom; Fri–Sat $75 double without bathroom, $115–$125 double with bathroom. Rates include continental breakfast. AE, MC, V.

This cute little historic hotel on Sonoma's tree-lined Town Square retains the same ambiance it had over a century ago. With an emphasis on European-style elegance and comfort, each room is decorated in an early California style, with antique furnishings, fine woods, and floral-print wallpapers. Some of the rooms feature brass beds, and all are blissfully devoid of phones and TVs. Five of the third-floor rooms share immaculate bathrooms (and significantly reduced rates), while rooms with private bathrooms have deep claw-foot tubs with overhead showers. Perks include continental breakfast and a bottle of wine on arrival. Also within the hotel is Le Bistro, a small restaurant serving Mediterranean cuisine for lunch, dinner, and Sunday brunch.

GLEN ELLEN
Moderate
✪ **Gaige House Inn.** 13540 Arnold Dr., Glen Ellen, CA 95442. ☎ 800/935-0237 or 707/935-0237. Fax 707/935-6411. 11 units. A/C TEL. Winter $155–$275 double; summer $170–$325 double. Rates include full breakfast and evening wines. AE, DISC, MC, V.

When you review hotels and B&Bs for a living—and we've reviewed thousands of them—it's hard to be impressed. When we visited the Gaige House Inn, however, we were more than impressed, and didn't want to leave. The inn's new owners, Ken Burnet, Jr., and Greg Nemrow, have managed to turn what was already a fine B&B into the finest in the Wine Country, and they've done it by offering a level of service, amenities, and decor normally associated with outrageously expensive resorts (and without the snobbery). Breakfast is made with herbs from the inn's garden and prepared by a chef who commutes daily from San Francisco. Firm mattresses are graced with wondrously silk-soft linens and premium down comforters, and even the furniture and artwork are of museum quality.

But wait, it gets better. Behind the inn is a 1.5-acre oasis with perfectly manicured lawns, a 40-foot-long swimming pool, and an achingly inviting creek-side hammock shaded by a majestic Heritage Oak. All 11 rooms, each artistically designed in a plantation theme with Asian and Indonesian influences (trust us, they're beautiful), have private bathrooms, direct-dial phones, and king- or queen-size beds; two rooms have Jacuzzi tubs, and several have fireplaces. The Gaige Suite is their finest room, bright and airy with large windows, a private balcony overlooking the lawn, a fireplace, and a Jacuzzi tub so large you could swim in it. Personally, we prefer Garden Room no. 10, exquisitely decorated with mahogany trim and flooring, a corner fireplace, a private deck, a huge glass-walled shower with dual heads, and a Jacuzzi tub for two. On sunny days, breakfast is served at individual tables on the large terrace. Evenings are best spent in the reading parlor sipping premium wines. Future plans include two additional suites in the creek-side house, and an outdoor hot tub.

Inexpensive

Beltane Ranch. 11775 Sonoma Hwy. (Hwy. 12), Glen Ellen, CA 95442. ☎ **707/996-6501.** 5 units. TEL. $110–$145 double. Rates include full breakfast. No credit cards (though checks are accepted).

The word "Ranch" conjures up the impression of a big ol' two-story house in the middle of hundreds of rolling acres, the kind of place where you laze away the day in a hammock watching the grass grow or pitching horseshoes in the garden. Well, friend, you can have all that and more at the Beltane Ranch, a century-old but-tercup-yellow manor that's been everything from a bunkhouse to a brothel to a turkey farm. You simply can't help but feel your tensions ease away as you kick your feet up on the shady wraparound porch overlooking the vineyards, sipping a cool, fruity chardonnay while reading *Lonesome Dove* for the third time. Each of the inn's five rooms is uniquely decorated with American and European antiques; all have private bathrooms, sitting areas, and separate entrances. Innkeeper Deborah Mahoney serves a big country breakfast in the garden or on the porch overlooking the vineyards. For exercise, you can play tennis on their private court or hike the trails meandering through the 1,600-acre estate. *Tip:* Request one of the upstairs rooms, which have the best views.

✪ **Glenelly Inn.** 5131 Warm Springs Rd. (off Arnold Dr.), Glen Ellen, CA 95442. ☎ **707/996-6720.** Fax 707/996-5227. 8 units. $115–$150 double. Rates include full break-fast and afternoon hors d'oeuvres. MC, V.

The Glenelly Inn is one of our favorite places to stay in the Wine Country. First off, the rates are reasonable, particularly when you factor in breakfast and afternoon snacks. But more importantly, this former 1916 railroad inn is positively drenched in serenity. Located well off the main highway on an oak-studded hillside, the peach-and-cream inn comes with everything you would expect from a country retreat—long verandas with comfy wicker chairs and verdant views of the verdant Sonoma hillsides; a hearty country breakfast served beside a large cobblestone fire-place; and bright, immaculate rooms with old-fashioned claw-foot tubs, Scandina-vian down comforters, and ceiling fans. But innkeeper Kristi Hallamore, a native San Franciscan of Norwegian descent (and a darn good cook), also understands that it's the little things that make the difference. Hence, the firm mattresses, good reading lights, and a simmering hot tub well ensconced within a grapevine- and rose-covered arbor. All rooms are decorated with authentic antiques and country furnishings, and come with queen beds, private bathrooms with/showers, terry-cloth robes, and private entrances. Top picks are either the Vallejo or Jack London cottages, both with large private patios, though we also like the rooms on the upper veranda—particularly in the spring when the terraced gardens below are in full bloom.

KENWOOD

Very Expensive

✪ **Kenwood Inn & Spa.** 10400 Sonoma Hwy., Kenwood, CA 95452. ☎ **800/353-6966** or 707/833-1293. Fax 707/833-1247. 12 units. Apr–Oct $255–$395 double (2-night min-imum on weekends). Nov–Mar $225–$365. Rates include gourmet breakfast and bottle of wine. AE, MC, V.

Inspired by the villas of Tuscany, the honey-colored Italian-style buildings, flower-filled flagstone courtyard, and pastoral views of vineyard-covered hills are enough to make any northern Italian homesick. We were immediately impressed with the friendly staff who made us feel right at home. Every spacious room here is lavishly and exquisitely decorated with imported tapestries, velvets, and antiques; each has a fireplace, balcony (unless you're on the ground floor), feather bed, CD player, and down comforter—but no phone or TV, so you can relax. A minor caveat is road noise, which you're unlikely to hear from your room, but can be slightly heard over the tranquil pumped-in music around the courtyard and pool.

An impressive two-course gourmet breakfast is served poolside or in the Mediter-ranean-style dining room; ours consisted of a poached egg accompanied by light, flavorful potatoes, red bell peppers, and other roasted vegetables, all artfully arranged, followed by a delicious homemade scone with fresh berries and a small lemon tart.

Amenities: Available spa treatments from the inn's own full-service spa offers aromatherapy, massage, and various skin and body treatments such as a Mediter-ranean salt scrub of lemon rind, rosemary, and salt.

WHERE TO DINE IN THE SONOMA VALLEY

The restaurants below are divided first by area, then by price, using the following guide: Expensive: more than $45 per person; Moderate: $25 to $45 per person; Inexpensive: less than $25 per person. These categories reflect the price of the majority of dinner menu items and include an appetizer, main course, coffee, dessert, tax, and tip.

SONOMA
Expensive

Babette's Cafe. 464 First St. E. (at the square), Sonoma. ☎ **707/939-8921.** Reservations recommended for both cafe and dining room. Cafe main courses $10.25–$15.95; dining room fixed-price menu $59. MC, V. Cafe daily noon–1pm; dining room Tues–Sat 6–10pm. FRENCH.

After it was voted the "Best Best-Kept Secret" by the *San Francisco Bay Guardian*, Babette's Cafe soon became one of the hottest places to dine in Sonoma. Thank-fully, this quaint little spot across from Sonoma's plaza has managed to maintain its homey atmosphere despite its new-found success. Like most of Sonoma's restau-rants, Babette's is both intimate and casual; its front-room cafe feels like a cozy French bistro, while the main dining room is a smaller, more formal space. But its down-home appeal doesn't extend to the food, which continues to garner rave reviews while remaining affordably priced. Along with soups, salads, and sand-wiches (all less than $8), main courses include cassoulet baked with duck confit, house-made pork sausage, lamb, and white beans; and Moroccan spiced vegetables on couscous. Chef Daniel Patterson (formerly of Domaine Chandon and Mustards Grill) also offers an fantastic five-course fixed-price dinner with tempting selections ranging from a caviar starter to roasted quail with garden cress, quinoa, and blood-orange vinaigrette; roasted monkfish on a sauce of smoked ham hocks, leeks, and red wine; and pan-roasted veal on vegetables and black chanterelles. Be sure to start your feast with the fresh goat cheese on toast (served with an endive-and-herb salad), and end with the warm peach-and-blueberry napoleon. Wines can be paired with each course for an additional $39.

✪ The Grille. At Sonoma Mission Inn, 18140 Sonoma Hwy., Sonoma. ☎ **707/938-9000.** Reservations recommended. Main courses $18–$28. AE, MC, V. Sat 11:30am–2pm; Sun brunch 10am–2pm; daily 6pm–9:30pm. CALIFORNIA/SPA.

The Grille, one of the most well-known restaurants in the Wine Country, has long suffered from a solid reputation for serving high-caliber spa cuisine. The problem, of course, is the word "spa," which conjures up visions of blue-haired ladies eating boiled vegetables and soybean salads. Fortunately, The Grille has found a solution:

Jeffrey Jake, a wondrously talented chef with a reputation for turning no-name restaurants into award-winning success stories. One bite of his corn risotto flavored with wild mushrooms and molten *reggiano parmigiano* cheese and you'll see why: it's one of the best we've ever tasted, and we're risotto addicts. About half of Jake's menu is spa-conscious, with the calorie and cholesterol percentages listed below selected entrees ranging from roasted medaillons of ostrich in apple sauce (11mg cholesterol, 18.1gm fat) to oven-roasted breast of Petaluma chicken in a crimini-mushroom cabernet sauce (105mg cholesterol, 4.6gm fat). He mercifully spares us the cholesterol and fat gram counts, however, for the dishes we *really* want such as the seared Sonoma foie gras with caramelized apples, white truffle oil, and a zin-fandel reduction sauce (yes, it's as good—and as bad for you—as it sounds), or the rack of herb-marinated lamb, roasted in Levain crumbs and pistachios and served with garlic mashed potatoes. Pastry chef Steve Fischer is equally as adept at making more from less, working wonders with low-cal lemon desserts such as the tart lemon chiffon topped with a sweet berry purée. The restaurant's soothing decor features peach-colored walls, bentwood chairs, and just the right amount of elbow room. Service is professional yet friendly, and though jackets are requested, we saw few. The wine list is extensive and expensive.

Moderate

Della Santina's. 133 E. Napa St. (just east of the square), Sonoma. ☎ **707/935-0576.** Reservations recommended. Main courses $8.95–$14.75. DISC, MC, V. Daily 11:30am–9:30pm. ITALIAN.

Those of you who just can't take another expensive, chichi California meal should follow the locals to this friendly, and traditional Italian restaurant. How traditional? Just ask father/son team Dan and Robert: when we last dined here they pointed out Señora Santina's hand-embroidered linen doilies as they proudly told us about her Tuscan recipes. And their pride is merited: Every dish we tried here was refreshingly authentic, in huge portions, and well flavored—without overbearing sauces or one hint of California pretentiousness. Be sure to start with traditional antipasti, especially the sliced mozzarella and tomatoes or the delicious white beans. There are nine pasta dishes that are, again, wonderfully authentic (gnocchi lovers, rejoice!). The spit-roasted meat dishes are a local favorite (though we found them to be a bit overcooked), and for those who can't choose between chicken, pork, turkey, rabbit, or duck, there's a selection that offers a choice of three. Don't worry about breaking your bank on a bottle of wine, as most of the savory choices here go for under $25. Portions are huge, but save room for dessert—they're wonderful, too.

Piatti. 405 First St. W., Sonoma. ☎ **707/996-2351.** Reservations recommended. Main courses $9.95–$18.95. AE, DC, MC, V. Sun–Thurs 11:30am–10pm; Fri–Sat 11:30am–11pm. ITALIAN.

Part of a northern California chain that originated in Napa, Piatti has built a stead-fast and true clientele by consistently serving large portions of good Italian food at a fair price in a fun and festive setting (got all that?). The restaurant occupies the ground floor of the El Dorado Hotel at the northwest corner of Sonoma Plaza (just follow your nose). Good-tasting pizzas and braised meats—such as the superb lamb shank flavored with a rich port-wine sauce and fresh mint—emerge from a wood-burning oven. There's also an array of satisfying pastas, our favorite being the canel-loni stuffed with roasted veal, spinach, porcini mushrooms, and ricotta. Other recommended dishes include a wonderful roast-vegetable appetizer, the teeming pile of fresh mussels in a tomato-and-herb broth, the rotisserie chicken with garlic mashed potatoes, and the veal scaloppine. Granted, there are fancier and more intimate restaurants in the valley, but none that can fill you up with such good food at these prices. And if the sun is out, there's no prettier place in Sonoma to dine alfresco than Piatti's courtyard.

Inexpensive

Basque Boulangerie Cafe. 460 First St. E., Sonoma. ☎ **707/935-7687.** Menu items $3–$7. MC, V. Daily 7am–6pm. BAKERY/DELI.

If you want a big breakfast with eggs, sausage, and the works, head to The Feed Store down the street at 529 First St. But, if you prefer a lighter morning meal and strong coffee, stand in line with the locals at the Basque Boulangerie Cafe, the most popular gathering spot in the Sonoma Valley. Most everything—sourdough Basque breads, pastries, quiche, soups, salads, desserts, sandwiches, cookies—is made in-house, and made well. Daily lunch specials, such as a grilled veggie sandwich with smoked mozzarella cheese ($4.75), are listed on the chalkboard out front. Seating is scarce, and if you can score a sidewalk table on a sunny day, consider yourself one lucky person. A popular option is ordering to go and eating in the shady plaza across the street. The cafe also sells wine by the glass, as well as a wonderful cinnamon bread by the loaf that's ideal for making french toast.

✪ **Lo Spuntino.** 400 First St. E., Sonoma. ☎ **707/935-4743.** Deli items $5–$9. AE, CB, DISC, MC, V. Sun–Thurs 10am–6pm; Fri–Sat 10am–9pm. ITALIAN DELI.

Lo Spuntino, Italian for "snack" or a tiny taste, is the sexiest thing going in Sonoma, a suave deli and wine bar owned by Sam and Vicki Sebastiani, who also run Viansa Winery. It's a visual masterpiece, with shiny black-and-white–checkered flooring, long counters of Italian marble, track lighting, and a center deli and wine bar where a crew of young men slice meats, pour wines, and scoop gelato. Start by sampling the preserves and jams at the entrance, then wander the aisle and choose among the armada of cured meats, cheese, fruit, pastas, salads, and breads lining the deli. Popular choices are the hefty sandwiches on herbed focaccia bread or the herb-marinated rotisserie chickens served by the half with your choice of pasta or salad. Roasted turkey, duck, pork, lamb, and rabbit are also available. Opposite the deli is the wine bar, featuring all of Viansa's current wine releases for both tasting and purchase, as well as a small selection of microbrewed beers on tap. On your way out, stop at the gelateria and treat yourself to some intense Italian ice cream. *Note:* Lo Spuntino also hosts live jazz bands every Friday night from 6 to 9pm.

GLEN ELLEN

✪ **The Girl & The Fig.** 13690 Arnold Dr., Glen Ellen. ☎ **707/938-3634.** Reservations recommended. Main courses $12–$19. AE, MC, V. Daily 5:30–9pm; Sun brunch 10am–2:30pm. COUNTRY FRENCH.

This modern, attractive cafe with mustard-yellow walls, tile floors, and an open kitchen is the creation of Sondra Bernstein (The Girl), who, after spending the past 4 years working at Viansa Winery and Italian Marketplace, left to open her own restaurant in August of 1997. The coup de grâce to her finishing touches was convincing San Francisco chefs/couple Gina Marie Armanini and John Gillis to come work for her. "They make a fantastic team," boasts Bernstein, and if the ever-crowded dining room is any indication, both tourists and locals agree. The cuisine is nouveau-country with French nuances, and yes, figs are sure to be on the menu in one form or another, such as the wonderful winter fig salad made with arugula, pecans, dried figs, Laura Chenel goat cheese, and a fig-and-port vinaigrette. Garden-fresh produce and local meats, poultry, and fish are used whenever possible in dishes such as the braised winter greens that accompany the pan-roasted medaillons of lamb served with braised winter greens, mashed potatoes, and fresh mint sauce (when's the last time you had fresh mint sauce?), or the hearty winter vegetable stew over couscous—a bargain at $11.95. For dessert try the warm-pear galette topped with gingered crème fraîche, a glass of the Quady Essensia Orange Muscat, and a sliver of raclette from the cheese cart. Sondra knows her wines, and will be happy to choose the best accompaniment to your meal. *Note:* Monday nights in Glen Ellen are a whole lot more fun since Sondra introduced Fondue Night.

Glen Ellen Inn Restaurant. 13670 Arnold Dr., Glen Ellen. ☎ **707/996-6409.** Reservations recommended. Main courses $12–$22. AE, MC, V. Off-season Thurs–Tues 5:30pm–closing (depending on reservations); summer nightly 5:30pm–closing. CALIFORNIA.

Christian and Karen Bertrand, a happily married young couple oozing with charm, run this popular Glen Ellen restaurant. The dining room is so small and cozy that you feel as if you're dining in their home, but that's exactly the place's charm. Garden seating is the favored choice on sunny days, but the covered, heated patio is always welcoming. First courses from Christian's open kitchen might include a wild-mushroom–and-sausage "purse" served in a brandy cream sauce and warm goat-cheese croquettes. Main courses change with the seasons, but might range from linguini with artichoke hearts and feta to a stellar late-harvest ravioli, which is stuffed with pumpkin, walnuts, and sun-dried cranberries on a bed of butternut squash. Other favorites include the marinated pork tenderloin on smoked mozzarella polenta, topped with roasted-pepper onion compote; and, of course, the classic filet mignon accompanied by a full-bodied cabernet sauvignon. On our last visit, the Sonoma Valley mixed green salad, seared ahi tuna, and homemade French vanilla ice cream floating in bittersweet caramel sauce made a perfect meal. The wine list offers numerous Sonoma selections, as well as more than a dozen wines by the glass.

KENWOOD

Kenwood Restaurant & Bar. 9900 Sonoma Hwy., Kenwood. ☎ **707/833-6326.** Reservations recommended. Main courses $12.50–$24.50. MC, V. Tues–Sun 11:30am–9pm. CALIFORNIA/CONTINENTAL.

This is what California Wine Country dining should be. From the terrace of the Kenwood Restaurant, you'll enjoy a view of the vineyards set against Sugar Loaf Ridge as they imbibe Sonoma's finest at umbrella-covered tables. On nippy days, you can retreat inside to the Sonoma-style roadhouse, with its shiny wood floors, pine ceiling, vibrant artwork, and cushioned rattan chairs set at white-cloth–covered tables. Chef Max Schacher serves first-rate cuisine, perfectly balanced between tradition and innovation, marked by the heightened, distinctive flavors of California's Wine Country, and complemented by a reasonably priced wine list. Great starters are the Dungeness crab cake with herb mayonnaise; the superfresh sashimi with ginger, soy, and wasabi; and the wonderful Caesar salad. Main-dish choices might include poached salmon in a creamy caper sauce, prawns with saffron Pernod sauce, or braised Sonoma rabbit with grilled polenta. But the Kenwood doesn't take itself too seriously—they also serve sandwiches and burgers.

More Easy Excursions from San Francisco

The Bay City is, without question, captivating, but don't let it ensnare you to the point of ignoring its environs, which contain a multitude of natural spectacles like Mount Tamalpais and Muir Woods; scenic communities like Tiburon and Sausalito; and cities like gritty Oakland and its youth-oriented next-door neighbor, Berkeley. And to the southwest lies Half Moon Bay, an adorable little coastal town perched on a wide expanse of golden beach.

From San Francisco you can reach any of these points in an hour or less by car. Another option is to hitch a ride with **Tower Tours** (☎ **800/587-9484** or 415/434-8687), which runs regularly scheduled tours by micro bus to San Francisco's neighboring towns and countryside. Half- and full-day trips to Muir Woods, Sausalito, Napa, and Sonoma are also available, as are excursions to Yosemite and the Monterey Peninsula. Phone for price and departure information.

1 Berkeley

10 miles NE of San Francisco

Berkeley would be little more than a quaint, sleepy town east of the big city if it weren't for the University of California at Berkeley, which is world-renowned for its first-rate academic standards, 16 Nobel Prize winners, and protests that led to the most renowned student riots in U.S. history. Today, there's still hippie idealism in the air, but the radicals have aged; the sixties are only present in tie-dye and paraphernalia shops, and the students have less angst. Still, it's a charming town teeming with all types of people, a beautiful campus, vast parks, great shopping, and some incredible restaurants.

ESSENTIALS

The Berkeley **BART** station is 2 blocks from the university. The fare from San Francisco is under $3.

If you are coming **by car** from San Francisco, take the Bay Bridge (go during evening commute and you'll think Los Angeles's traffic is a breeze), follow I-80 east to the University Avenue exit, and follow University until you hit the campus. Parking is tight near the campus, so either leave your car at the Sather Gate parking lot on Telegraph and Durant or expect to fight for a spot.

Phone the **Visitor Hot Line** (☎ 510/549-8710) for automated information on events and happenings in Berkeley.

WHAT TO SEE & DO

Hanging out is the preferred Berkeley pastime, and the best place to do it is on Telegraph Avenue, the street that leads to the campus's southern entrance. Most of the action lies between Bancroft Way and Ashby Avenue, where coffeehouses, restaurants, shops, great book and record stores, and craft booths swarm with life. Pretend you're local: Plant yourself at a cafe, sip a latte, and ponder something intellectual or survey the town's unique residents bustling by.

Bibliophiles must stop at **Cody's Books,** at 2454 Telegraph Ave., ☎ 510/845-7852, to peruse their gargantuan selection of titles, independent-press books, and magazines. The avenue is also packed with street vendors selling everything from T-shirts and jewelry to I Ching and tarot-card readings.

UC BERKELEY CAMPUS

The University of California at Berkeley itself is worth a stroll as well. It's a beautiful old campus with plenty of woodsy paths, architecturally noteworthy buildings, and, of course, many of the 31,000 students scurrying to and from classes. Among the architectural highlights of the campus are a number of buildings by Bernard Maybeck, Bakewell and Brown, and John Galen Howard.

Contact the **Visitor Information Center** at 101 University Hall, 2200 University Ave. (at Oxford Street) (☎ 510/642-5215), to join a free, regularly scheduled campus tour (Mon through Sat at 10am, Sun at 1pm; no tours offered from mid-Dec to mid-Jan); or stop by the office and pick up a self-guided walking-tour brochure.

You'll find the university's southern entrance at the northern end of Telegraph, at Bancroft Way. Walk through the main entrance into Sproul Plaza, and when school is in session you'll encounter the gamut of Berkeley's inhabitants here: colorful street people, rambling political zealots, chanting Hare Krishnas, and ambitious students. You'll also find the Student Union, complete with a bookstore, cafes, and an information desk on the second floor where you can pick up a free map of Berkeley, as well as the local student newspaper (also found in dispensers throughout campus).

You might be lucky enough to stumble upon some impromptu musicians or a heated, and sometimes absurd, debate. There's always something going on, so stretch out on the grass for a few minutes and take in the Berkeley vibe.

For viewing more traditional art forms, there are some noteworthy museums here, too. The **Lawrence Hall of Science** (☎ 510/642-5132), offering hands-on science exploration, is open from 10am to 5pm daily and is a wonderful place to watch the sunset. Admission is $6 for adults, $4 for seniors and children 7 to 18, $2 for children 3 to 6, free for kids under 3. The **University Art Museum** (☎ 510/642-0808) is open from 11am to 5pm on Wednesday and Friday through Sunday, and Thursday from 11am to 9pm. Admission is $6 for adults, $4 for seniors and children 12 to 17, and free for kids under 12. This museum includes a substantial collection of Hans Hofmann paintings, a sculpture garden, and the Pacific Film Archive.

If you're interested in notable off-campus buildings, contact the **Berkeley Convention and Visitors Bureau** (☎ 510/549-7040) for an architectural walking tour brochure.

The Bay Area

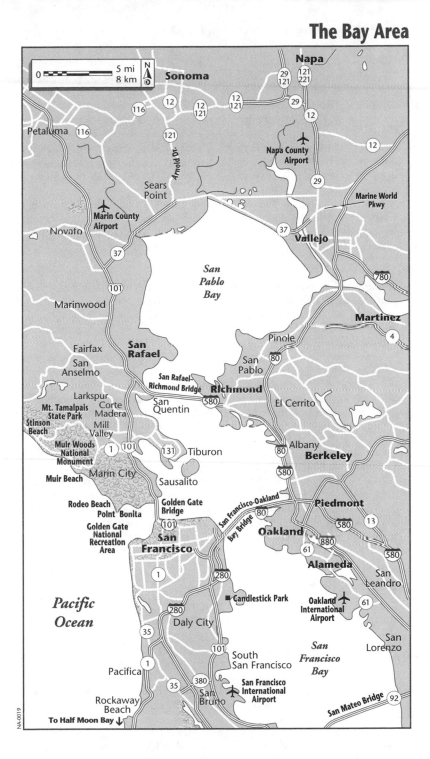

PARKS

Unbeknownst to many travelers, Berkeley has some of the most extensive and beautiful parks around. If you want to wear out the kids or enjoy hiking, swimming, or just getting a breath of California air and sniffing a few roses, jump in your car and make your way to **Tilden Park.** On the way, stop at the colorful terraced Rose Garden, located in north Berkeley on Euclid Avenue between Bay View and Eunice Street. Then head high into the Berkeley hills to Tilden, where you'll find plenty of flora and fauna, hiking trails, an old steam train and merry-go-round, farm and nature area for kids, and a chilly tree-encircled lake (☎ **510/843-2137** for further information).

Another worthy nature excursion is the **University of California Botanical Garden,** which features a vast collection of herbage ranging from cacti to redwoods; it's located in Strawberry Canyon on Centennial Drive (☎ **510/642-3343** for details).

WHERE TO SHOP

If you're itching to exercise your credit cards, head to one of two places. College Avenue from Dwight all the way down to the Oakland border is crammed with eclectic boutiques, antique shops, and restaurants. The other option is Fourth Street, in west Berkeley just 2 blocks north of the University Avenue exit. This 2-block expanse is the perfect place to go on a sunny morning. Grab a cup of java, read the paper at a patio table, and then hit the **Crate and Barrel Outlet** (where prices are 30% to 70% off retail) at 1785 Fourth St., between Hearst and Virginia (☎ **510/528-5500**), which is open Monday to Saturday from 10am to 6pm and Sunday from 11am to 6pm, or any of the small, wonderful stores crammed with imported and locally made housewares. Nearby is **REI,** the Bay Area's favorite outdoor outfitters at 1338 San Pablo Ave., near Gilman Street (☎ **510/527-4140**).

WHERE TO STAY

Bed and Breakfast California, P.O. Box 282910, San Francisco, CA 94128 (☎ **800/872-4500** or 650/696-1690; fax 650/696-1699), accommodates visitors in more than 150 private homes and apartments in the San Francisco–Berkeley area. The cost ranges from a reasonable $65 to $300 per night, and there's a 2-night minimum. The **Berkeley Convention and Visitor's Bureau,** 2015 Center St., Berkeley, CA 94704 (☎ **800/847-4823,** 510/549-7040, or the hot line 510/ 549-8710), is staffed Monday to Friday from 9am to 5pm and can also find accommodations for you, as well as provide free visitor guides, maps, and area literature.

WHERE TO DINE

East Bay dining is a relaxed alternative to the city's gourmet night out—there are plenty of ambitious Berkeley restaurants worth foraging and, unlike San Francisco, plenty of parking.

If you want to do it student-style, eat on campus Monday to Friday. Buy something at any of the sidewalk stands or in the building directly behind the Student Union. The least-expensive food is available downstairs in the **Cafeteria,** on Lower Sproul Plaza. There's also the **Bear's Lair Pub and Coffee House,** the **Deli,** the **Terrace,** and the **Golden Bear Restaurant.** All the university eateries have both indoor and outdoor seating.

Telegraph Avenue has an array of small, ethnic restaurants, cafes, and sandwich shops. Follow the students: if the place is crowded, it's either good, super cheap, or both.

Berkeley

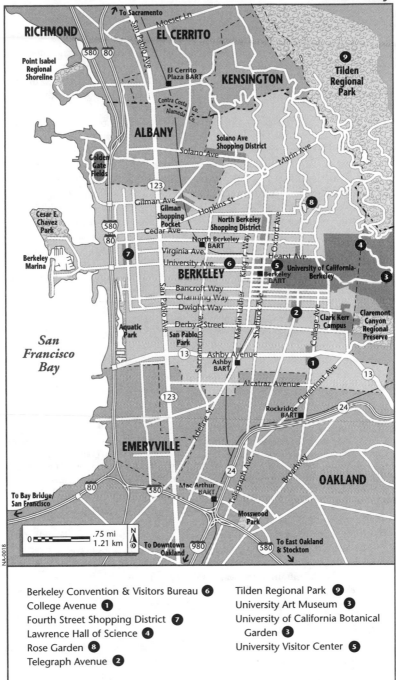

Berkeley Convention & Visitors Bureau **6**
College Avenue **1**
Fourth Street Shopping District **7**
Lawrence Hall of Science **4**
Rose Garden **8**
Telegraph Avenue **2**

Tilden Regional Park **9**
University Art Museum **3**
University of California Botanical Garden **3**
University Visitor Center **5**

People's Park/People's Power

In late 1967, the university demolished an entire block of buildings north of Telegraph Avenue. The destruction, which forced hippies and other "undesirables" from the slum housing that stood there, was done under the guise of university expansion and urban renewal—good liberal causes. But after the lot lay vacant for almost 2 years, a group of Berkeley radicals whose names read like a who's who of 1960s leftists, including Jerry Rubin, Bobby Seale, and Tom Hayden, decided to take the land for "the people."

On April 29, 1969, hundreds of activists invaded the vacant lot with gardening tools and tamed the muddy ground into a park. One month later, Berkeley's Republican mayor sent 250 police officers into the park, and 4,000 demonstrators materialized to challenge them. A riot ensued, the police fired buckshot at the crowd, and one rioter was killed and another blinded. Gov. Ronald Reagan sent in the National Guard, and for the next 17 days the guardsmen repeatedly gassed innocent students, faculty, and passersby. Berkeley was a war zone, and People's Park became the most important symbol of "people power" during the 1960s.

People's Park once again sparked controversy in 1992 when university officials decided to build volleyball courts there. In August of that year, a park activist broke into the campus home of the university's chancellor. When a police officer arrived, the activist lunged at him with a machete and was shot dead. On the victim's body was a note with the message: "We are willing to die for this land. Are you?" On news of the contemporary radical's death, more than 150 of her supporters rioted. Today you can visit the park and watch the volleyballers self-consciously setting, bumping, and spiking.

EXPENSIVE

✪ **Chez Panisse.** 1517 Shattuck Ave. (between Cedar and Vine). ☎ **510/548-5525.** Fax 510/548-0140. Reservations essential for restaurant—accepted a month in advance; for cafe, accepted for lunch at 9am on the day, not accepted for dinner. Main courses $13–$18; fixed-price dinner $38–$68. AE, CB, DC, MC, V. Restaurant dinner seatings Mon–Sat at 6–6:30pm and 8:30–9:15pm. Cafe Mon–Thurs 11:30am–3pm and 5–10:30pm; Fri–Sat 11:30am–4pm and 5–11:30pm. From I-80 north, take the University exit and turn left onto Shattuck Ave. BART: Berkeley. CALIFORNIA.

California cuisine is so much a product of Waters's genius that all other restaurants following in her wake should be dated "AAW" (After Alice Waters). Read the menus posted outside and you'll understand why. Most of the produce and meat comes from local farms and is organically produced, and after all these years, Alice still attends to her restaurant with great integrity and innovation.

Alice's creations are served in a delightful redwood and stucco cottage with a brick terrace filled with flowering potted plants. There are two separate dining areas—the upstairs cafe and the downstairs restaurant, both offering Mediterranean-inspired cuisine.

In the upstairs cafe there are displays of pastries and fruit, and large bouquets of fresh flowers adorning an oak bar. At lunch or dinner, a delicately smoked gravlax or a roasted eggplant soup with pesto, followed by lamb ragout garnished with apricots, onions, and spices served with couscous might be featured. Dinner reservations are not taken for the cafe, so there will be a wait, but it's worth it.

The cozy downstairs restaurant, strewn with blossoming floral bouquets, is an appropriately warm environment to indulge in the fixed-price four-course gourmet dinner, which is served Tuesday to Thursday. Friday and Saturday, it's four courses plus an aperitif, and Monday is bargain night with a three-course dinner for $38.

The menu, which changes daily, is posted outside the restaurant each Saturday for the following week. Meals are complemented by an excellent wine list ($20 to $200).

MODERATE

O Chamé. 1830 Fourth St. (near Hearst). ☎ **510/841-8783.** Reservations necessary Fri–Sat. Main courses $7–$17.50. AE, DC, MC, V. Mon–Sat 11:30am–3pm; Mon–Thurs 5:30–9pm; Fri–Sat 5:30–9:30pm. JAPANESE.

Spare and plain in its decor, with ochre-colored walls marked with etched patterns, this spot has a meditative air to complement the traditional and experimental Japanese-inspired cuisine. The menu, which changes daily, offers meal-in-a bowl dishes (from $7 to $11) that allow a choice of soba or udon noodles in a clear soup with a variety of toppings—from shrimp and wakame seaweed to beef with burdock root and carrot; appetizers and salads, which include a flavorsome melding of grilled shiitake mushrooms and sweet peppers and portobello mushrooms, watercress, and green-onion pancakes; a sashimi of the day; and specials that range in price from $10 to $17.50 and always include a delicious roasted salmon.

✪ Rivoli. 1539 Solano. ☎ **510/526-2542.** Reservations recommended. Main courses $10.25–$15.75. MC, V. Mon–Thurs 5:30–9:30pm; Fri 5:30–10pm; Sat 5–10pm; Sun 5–9pm. CALIFORNIA.

One of the favored dinner destinations in the East Bay, Rivoli's winning combination is top-notch food at amazingly reasonable prices. The owners have done the most with an otherwise uninteresting space by creating a warm, intimate dining environment, which overlooks a sweet little garden with visiting raccoons and possums. Aside from a few house favorites, the menu changes entirely every 3 weeks in order to serve whatever's freshest and in season. While many love it, we weren't thrilled with the portobello-mushroom fritter, which in our mind was a glorified variation on the fried zucchini stick. However, we did have an absolute A+ dish here (very rare): the hearty oven-braised pork ragout with butternut squash and dandelion greens intermingled with tender and crispy semolina gnocchi. Perfection at this price ($13.50 for the ragout) is enough to put most high-end San Francisco restaurants to shame. Finish the evening with the Meyer lemon cheesecake; it's a decadent sour-cream–like affair with a subtle pistachio crust.

INEXPENSIVE

Cambodiana's. 2156 University Ave. (between Shattuck and Oxford). ☎ **510/843-4630.** Reservations recommended, especially Fri–Sat. Main courses $7.50–$13; fixed-price dinner $11.25. AE, CB, DC, JCB, MC, V. Mon–Fri 11:30am–3pm; Mon–Thurs and Sun 5–9:30pm; Fri–Sat 5–10:30pm. CAMBODIAN.

For those who relish the spicy cuisine of Cambodia, this is quite a find. The decor is as colorful as the fare—amidst brilliant blue, yellow, and green walls with Breuer-style chairs set at tables, you can feast on a variety of dishes. Especially tasty is the curry (chicken, beef, and so on) or Naga dishes with a sauce of tamarind, turmeric, lemongrass, shrimp paste, coconut-milk galinga, shallot, lemon leaf, sugar, and green chili. This sauce may smother salmon, prawns, chicken, or steak. Another tempting dish is the chicken chaktomuk prepared with pineapple, red peppers, and zucchini in soy and oyster sauce. There are plenty of vegetarian and low-cal options, and the three-course, fixed-price dinner is an excellent value.

2 Oakland

10 miles E of San Francisco

Though it's less than a dozen miles from San Francisco, the city of Oakland is worlds apart from its sister city across the bay. Originally little more than a cluster of ranches and farms, Oakland's size and stature exploded practically overnight as the last mile of transcontinental railroad track was laid down. Major shipping ports soon followed, and to this day Oakland has retained its hold as one of the busiest industrial ports on the West Coast.

The price for all this economic success, however, is Oakland's lowbrow reputation for being a predominantly working-class city, forever in the shadow of San Francisco's chic spotlight. But with all its shortcomings and bad press, Oakland still manages to offer a few pleasant surprises for the handful of tourists who venture this way. Rent a sailboat on Lake Merritt, stroll along the waterfront, explore the fantastic Oakland Museum: They're all great reasons to hop the bay and spend a fog-free day exploring one of California's largest and most ethnically diversified cities.

ESSENTIALS

Bay Area Rapid Transit (BART) makes the trip from San Francisco to Oakland through one of the longest underwater transit tunnels in the world. Fares range from $1 to $4, depending on your station of origin; children 4 and under ride free. BART trains operate Monday to Friday from 4am to midnight, Saturday from 6am to midnight, and on Sunday from 8am to midnight. Exit at the 12th Street station for downtown Oakland.

By car from San Francisco, take I-80 across the San Francisco–Oakland Bay Bridge and follow the signs to downtown Oakland. Exit at Grand Avenue South for the Lake Merritt area.

Downtown Oakland is bordered by Grand Avenue on the north, I-980 on the west, Inner Harbor on the south, and Lake Merritt on the east. Between these landmarks are three BART stations (12th Street, 19th Street, and Lake Merritt), City Hall, the Oakland Museum, Jack London Square, and several other sights.

WHAT TO SEE & DO

Lake Merritt is Oakland's primary tourist attraction along with Jack London Square (see below). Three and a half miles in circumference, the tidal lagoon was bridged and dammed in the 1860s and is now a wildlife refuge that is home to flocks of migrating ducks, herons, and geese. It's surrounded on three sides by the 122-acre **Lakeside Park,** a popular place to picnic, feed the ducks, and escape the fog. At the **Sailboat House** (☎ 510/444-3807), in Lakeside Park along the north shore, you can rent sailboats, rowboats, pedal boats, or canoes for $6 to $12 per hour.

Another site worth visiting is Oakland's **Paramount Theatre** (☎ 510/893-2300), an outstanding example of art-deco architecture and decor. Built in 1931 and authentically restored in 1973, it now functions as the city's main performing-arts center. Guided tours of the 3,000-seat theater are given the 1st and 3rd Saturday of each month, excluding holidays. No reservations are necessary; just show up at 10am at the box office entrance on 21st Street at Broadway. Cameras are allowed, and admission is $1.

If you take pleasure from strolling sailboat-filled wharves or are a die-hard fan of Jack London, you might actually enjoy a visit to **Jack London Square.** Oakland's only patent tourist area, this low-key version of San Francisco's Fisherman's Wharf shamelessly plays up the fact that Jack London spent most of his youth along this waterfront. The square fronts the harbor, housing a tourist-tacky complex of boutiques and eateries that are about as far away from the "call of the wild" as you can get. Most are open Monday to Saturday from 10am to 9pm (some restaurants stay open later). In the center of the square is a small reconstructed Yukon cabin in which Jack London lived while prospecting in the Klondike during the gold rush of 1897.

In the middle of Jack London Square you'll find a more authentic memorial, **Heinold's First and Last Chance Saloon**—a funky, friendly little bar and historic landmark that's worth a visit. This is where London did some of his writing and most of his drinking; the corner table he used has remained exactly as it was nearly a century ago. Also in the square are the mast and nameplate from the USS *Oakland*, a ship that saw extensive action in the Pacific during World War II, and a wonderful museum filled with interesting London memorabilia.

The square is located at Broadway and Embarcadero. Take I-880 to Broadway, turn south, and go to the end. BART: 12th Street station; then walk south along Broadway (about half a mile) or take bus no. 51a to the foot of Broadway.

Oakland Museum of California. 1000 Oak St. ☎ **510/238-3401** or 510/238-2200 for recorded information. Admission $8 adults, $6 students and seniors, free for children 5 and under; $3 for everyone 1st Sun of every month. Wed–Sat 10am–5pm; Sun noon–7pm. Closed Thanksgiving Day, Christmas Day, New Year's Day, and July 4. From I-880 north, take the Oak St. exit; the museum is 5 blocks east at Oak and 10th sts. Alternatively, take I-580 to I-980 and exit at the Jackson St. ramp. BART: Lake Merritt station (1 block south of the museum).

Located 2 blocks south of the lake, the Oakland Museum of California includes just about everything you'd want to know about the state, its people, history, culture, geology, art, environment, and ecology. Inside a low-swept, modern building set down among sweeping gardens and terraces, it's actually three museums in one: exhibitions of works by California artists from Bierstadt to Diebenkorn; collections of artifacts from California's history, from Pomo Indian basketry to Country Joe McDonald's guitar; and re-creations of California habitats from the coast to the White Mountains. The museum holds major shows of California artists, like the recent exhibit of the work of ceramic sculptor Peter Voulkos, or shows dedicated to major California movements, such as arts and crafts from 1890 to 1930. The museum also frequently shows photography from its huge collections.

There are 45-minute guided tours leaving the gallery information desks on request or by appointment. There is a fine cafe, a **gallery** (☎ 510/834-2329) selling works by California artists, and a book and gift shop. The cafe is open Wednesday to Saturday from 10am to 4pm, and on Sunday from noon to 5pm.

WHERE TO DINE
EXPENSIVE

✪ **Oliveto Restaurant.** Rockridge Market Hall, 5655 College Ave. (off the northeastern end of Broadway at Keith St., across from the Rockridge BART station). ☎ **510/547-5356.** Reservations recommended. Main courses $16–$21. AE, DC, MC, V. Mon–Fri 11:30am–2pm; Mon–Sat 5:30–10pm; Sun 5–9pm. ITALIAN.

Paul Bertolli, former chef at the world-renowned Chez Panisse restaurant, jumped ship to open one of the top Italian restaurants in the Bay Area (certainly the best in

Oakland). During the week it's a madhouse at lunchtime, when BART commuters pile in for the wood-fired pizzas and tapas served at the restaurant's lower level. The main dining room upstairs—suavely bedecked with neo-Florentine decor and partial open kitchen—is slightly more civil, packed nightly with fans of Bertolli's house-made pastas, sausages, and prosciutto. New additions include a wood-burning oven, flame-broiled rotisserie, high-end liquor cabinet (i.e., hard alcohol, but no mixed drinks), and an expanded kitchen. An assortment of pricey grills, braises, and roasts anchor the daily changing menu, but it's the reasonably priced pastas, pizzetas, and awesome salads that offer the most tang for your buck. *Tip:* There's free parking in the lot at the rear of the Market Hall building.

MODERATE

Bay Wolf. 3853 Piedmont Ave. (off Broadway between 40th St. and MacArthur Blvd.). ☎ **510/655-6004.** Reservations accepted. Main courses $15–$18. MC, V. Mon–Fri 11:30am–2pm; daily 6–9pm. CALIFORNIA.

The life span of most Bay Area restaurants is about 1 year; Bay Wolf, one of Oakland's most venerable and revered restaurants, has been going strong for nearly 2 decades. This converted brown Victorian is a comfortably familiar sight for most East Bay diners, who have been coming here for years to let chef/owner Michael Wilds do the cooking. Though Wilds has passed his apron on to chef Lauren Lyle, Bay Wolf's reputation for simple yet sagacious preparations using only fresh ingredients remains. Main courses vary from a flavorful seafood stew seasoned with saffron, and brimful of cracked Dungeness crab, prawns, rockfish, and mussels, to tender braised lamb shanks with white beans, artichokes, and rosemary. Informal service means you can leave the tie at home. New additions include heat lamps on the front deck, allowing for open-air evening dining—a treat San Franciscans rarely experience.

Citron. 5484 College Ave. (off the northeastern end of Broadway between Taft and Lawton sts.) ☎ **510/653-5484.** Reservations accepted. Main courses $12–$18. MC, V. Mon–Tues 5–9pm; Wed–Thurs 5:30–9:30pm; Fri–Sat 5:30–10pm; Sun 5–9pm. FRENCH/MEDITERRANEAN.

This petite, adorable French bistro was an instant smash when it first opened in 1992, and it continues to draw raves for its small yet enticingly eclectic menu. Chef Chris Rossi draws the flavors of France, Italy, and Spain together with fresh California produce for Chez Panisse–like results. Though the menu changes every few weeks, dishes range from grilled Colorado lamb sirloin with wild-mushroom spoon bread and rosemary jus, to osso buco of lamb on a bed of flageolet bean and sun-dried tomato ragout and sprinkled with a pistachio gremolata garnish. The fresh salads and Citron "40 clove" chicken are also superb.

3 Angel Island & Tiburon

8 miles N of San Francisco

A federal and state wildlife refuge, Angel Island is the largest of the San Francisco Bay's three islets (the others being Alcatraz and Yerba Buena). The island has been, at various times, a prison, a quarantine station for immigrants, a missile base, and even a favorite site for duels. Nowadays though, most of the people who visit here are content with picnicking on the large green lawn that fronts the docking area; loaded with the appropriate recreational supplies, they claim a barbecue, plop their fannies down on the lush green grass, and while away an afternoon free of phones,

Marin County

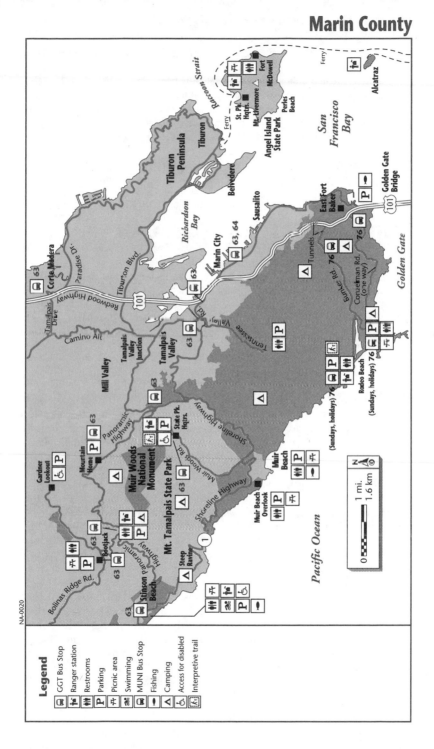

televisions, and traffic. Hiking, mountain biking, and guided tram tours are also popular options.

Tiburon, situated on a peninsula of the same name, looks like a cross between a fishing village and a Hollywood western set—imagine San Francisco reduced to toy dimensions. This seacoast town rambles over a series of green hills and ends up at a spindly, multicolored pier on the waterfront, like a Fisherman's Wharf in miniature. But in reality it's an extremely plush patch of yacht-club suburbia, as you'll see by both the marine craft and the homes of their owners. Main Street is lined with ramshackle, color-splashed old frame houses that shelter chic boutiques, souvenir stores, antique shops, and art galleries. Other roads are narrow, winding, and hilly, and lead up to dramatically situated homes. The view of San Francisco's skyline and the islands in the bay is a good enough reason to pay the precious price to live here.

ESSENTIALS

Ferries of the **Blue & Gold Fleet** (☎ **415/705-5555**) leave from Pier 43½ (Fisherman's Wharf) and travel to both Angel Island and Tiburon. Boats run on a seasonal schedule; phone for departure information. The round-trip fare is $10 to Angel Island, $11 to Tiburon; half price for kids 5 to 11, and free for kids under 5.

By car from San Francisco, take U.S. 101 to the Tiburon/Highway 131 exit, then follow Tiburon Boulevard all the way into downtown, a 40-minute drive from San Francisco. Catch the **ferry** (☎ **415/435-2131** or 415/388-6770) to Angel Island from the dock located at Tiburon Boulevard and Main Street. The 15-minute round-trip, which only runs on weekends, costs $6 for adults, $4 for children 5 to 11, and $1 for bikes.

WHAT TO SEE & DO ON ANGEL ISLAND

Passengers disembark from the ferry at Ayala Cove, a small marina abutting a huge lawn area equipped with tables, benches, barbecue pits, and rest rooms. Also at Ayala Cove is a small store, gift shop, cafe (with surprisingly good grub), and overpriced mountain-bike rental shop (helmets included).

Among the 12 miles of Angel Island's hiking and mountain-bike trails is the **Perimeter Road,** a partly paved path that circles the island and winds its way past disused troop barracks, former gun emplacements, and other military buildings; several turnoffs lead up to the top of Mount Livermore, 776 feet above the bay. Sometimes referred to as the "Ellis Island of the West," from 1910 to 1940 Angel Island was used as a holding area for Chinese immigrants awaiting their citizenship papers. You can still see some faded Chinese characters on the walls of the barracks where the immigrants were held. During the warmer months you can camp at a limited number of sites; reservations are required.

Also offered at Angel Island are guided sea-kayak tours. The all-day trips, which include a catered lunch, combine the thrill of paddling stable one-, two-, or three-person kayaks with an informative, naturalist-led tour that encircles the island (conditions permitting). All equipment is provided, kids are welcome, and no experience is necessary. Rates run about $100 per person. For more information, call **Sea Trek** at ☎ **415/488-1000.**

For recorded information about **Angel Island State Park,** call ☎ **415/435-1915.**

WHAT TO SEE & DO IN TIBURON

The main thing to do in Tiburon is stroll along the waterfront, pop into the stores, and spend an easy $50 on drinks and appetizers before heading back to the city. For a taste of the wine country, stop in at **Windsor Vineyards,** 72 Main St. (☎ **800/214-9463** or 415/435-3113)—their Victorian tasting room dates from 1888. Thirty-five choices are available for a free tasting. Wine accessories and gifts—glasses, cork pullers, gourmet sauces, posters, and maps—are also available. Carry-packs are available (they hold six bottles). Ask about personalized labels for your own selections. The shop is open Sunday to Thursday from 10am to 6pm and Friday to Saturday till 7pm.

WHERE TO DINE IN TIBURON

Guaymas. 5 Main St. ☎ **415/435-6300.** Reservations accepted. Main courses $12–$18. AE, CB, DC, MC, V. Mon–Thurs 11:30am–10pm; Fri–Sat 11:30am–11pm; Sun 10:30am–10pm Ferry: Walk about 10 paces from the landing. From U.S. 101, exit at Tiburon/Hwy. 131; follow Tiburon Blvd. 5 miles and turn right onto Main St. The restaurant is situated directly behind the bakery. MEXICAN.

Guaymas offers authentic Mexican regional cuisine and a spectacular panoramic view of San Francisco and the bay. In good weather, the two outdoor patios are almost always packed with diners soaking in the sun and scene. Inside, beige walls are hung with colorful Mexican artwork, illuminated by modern track lighting. Should you be feeling chilled, to the rear of the dining room is a beehive-shaped adobe fireplace.

Guaymas is named after a fishing village on Mexico's Sea of Cortez, and both the town and the restaurant are famous for their *camarones* (giant shrimp). In addition, the restaurant features ceviche, handmade tamales, and charcoal-grilled beef, seafood, and fowl. Save room for dessert, especially the outrageously scrumptious fritter with "drunken" bananas and ice cream. In addition to a good selection of California wines, the restaurant offers an exceptional variety of tequilas, Mexican beers, and mineral waters flavored with flowers, grains, and fruits.

✪ **Sam's Anchor Café.** 27 Main St. ☎ **415/435-4527.** Main courses $8–$16. AE, MC, V. Mon–Thurs 11am–10pm; Fri 11am–10:30pm; Sat 10am–10:30pm; Sun 9:30am–10pm. Ferry: Walk from the landing. From U.S. 101, exit at Tiburon/Hwy. 131, follow Tiburon Blvd. 4 miles and turn right onto Main St. SEAFOOD.

Summer Sundays are liveliest in Tiburon, when weekend boaters tie up to the docks at waterside restaurants like this one, the kind of place where you and your cronies can take off your shoes and have a fun, relaxed time eating burgers and drinking margaritas outside on the pier. The fare is pretty typical—sandwiches, salads, and seafood such as deep-fried oysters—but the quality and selection of the food is inconsequential: beers, burgers, and a designated driver are all you really need.

4 Sausalito

5 miles N of San Francisco

Just off the northern end of the Golden Gate Bridge is the eclectic little town of Sausalito, a slightly bohemian, nonchalant, and studiedly quaint adjunct to San Francisco. With approximately 7,500 residents, Sausalito feels rather like St. Tropez on the French Riviera—minus the starlets and the social rat race. It has its quota of paper millionaires, but they rub their permanently suntanned shoulders with a good number of hard-up artists, struggling authors, shipyard workers, and fishers. Next to the swank restaurants, plush bars, and antique shops and galleries, you'll see hamburger joints, beer parlors, and secondhand bookstores. Sausalito's main touring strip is Bridgeway, which runs along the water, but those in the know make a quick detour to Caledonia Street 1 block inland; not only is it less congested, there's a far-better selection of cafes and shops.

ESSENTIALS

The **Golden Gate Ferry Service** fleet, Ferry Building (☎ 415/923-2000), operates between the San Francisco Ferry Building, at the foot of Market Street, and downtown Sausalito. Service is frequent, departing at reasonable intervals every day of the year except New Year's Day, Thanksgiving Day, and Christmas Day. Phone for exact schedule. The ride takes a half hour, and one-way fares are $4.25 for adults and $3.20 for kids 6 to 12. Seniors and passengers with disabilities ride for $2.10; children 5 and under ride free. Family rates are also available.

Ferries of the **Blue & Gold Fleet** (☎ 415/705-5555) leave from Pier 43½ (Fisherman's Wharf) and cost $11 round-trip; half price for kids 5 to 11. Boats run on a seasonal schedule; phone for departure information.

By car from San Francisco, take U.S. 101 north, then the first right after the Golden Gate Bridge (Alexander exit). Alexander becomes Bridgeway in Sausalito.

WHAT TO SEE & DO

Above all, Sausalito has scenery and sunshine, for once you cross the Golden Gate Bridge you're out of the San Francisco fog patch and under blue California sky (we hope). The town's steep hills are covered with houses that overlook a forest of masts on the waters below, but almost all the tourist action, which is almost singularly limited to window shopping and eating, takes place at sea level on Bridgeway.

Bay Model Visitors Center. 2100 Bridgeway. ☎ **415/332-3871.** Free admission. Tues–Sat 9am–4pm.

The U.S. Army Corps of Engineers uses this high-tech, 1½-acre model of San Francisco's bay and delta to resolve problems and observe what impact any changes in water flow will have. The model reproduces (in scale) the rise and fall of tides, the flows and currents of water, and the mixing of fresh- and saltwater, and indicates trends in sediment movement. There's a 10-minute film that explains it all and a tour, but the most interesting time to visit is when it's actually being used, so call ahead.

WHERE TO SHOP

Sausalito is a mecca for shoppers seeking handmade, original, and offbeat clothes and footwear, as well as arts and crafts. The town's best shops are found in the alleys, malls, and second-floor boutiques reached by steep, narrow staircases on and off Bridgeway. Additional shops are found on Caledonia Street, which runs parallel to and 1 block inland from Bridgeway.

Village Fair, at 777 Bridgeway, is Sausalito's closest approximation to a mall. It's a complex of 30 shops, souvenir stores, coffee bars, and gardens. Among them, **Quest Gallery** (☎ 415/332-6832) features fine ceramics, functional art, contemporary glass, hand-painted silks, woven clothing, art jewelry, and graphics. The shop specializes in celebrated California artists, many of whom sell exclusively through this store. The complex is open daily from 10am to 6pm; restaurants stay open later.

WHERE TO STAY
VERY EXPENSIVE

✪ **Inn Above the Tide.** 30 El Portal (next to the Sausalito Ferry Landing), Sausalito, CA 94965. ☎ **800/893-8433** or 415/332-9535. Fax 415/332-6714. 30 units. A/C TV TEL.

$195–$425 double (2-night minimum stay on weekends). Rates include continental breakfast. AE, MC, V. Parking $8.

Perched directly over the bay atop well-grounded pilings, this former luxury apartment complex underwent a $4-million transformation into one of Sausalito's—if not the Bay Area's—finest accommodations. It's the view that clinches it: every room comes with an unparalleled panorama of the San Francisco Bay, including a postcard-quality vista of the city glimmering in the distance. Should you manage to tear yourself away from your private deck (we were tempted to drag our mattress outside), you'll find that your sumptuously appointed room sports a romantic little fireplace, a vast sunken tub with Jacuzzi jets, remote-control air-conditioning, and wondrously comfortable queen- or king-size beds. Soothing shades of pale green and blue highlight the decor, which blends in well with the bayscape outside. Be sure to request that your breakfast and newspaper be delivered to your deck, then cancel your early appointments: on sunny mornings, nobody checks out early.

EXPENSIVE

Casa Madrona. 801 Bridgeway, Sausalito, CA 94965. ☎ **800/567-9524** or 415/332-0502. Fax 415/332-2537. 35 units. MINIBAR TEL. $138–$260 double; $448 Madrona Villa suite. Breakfast free from 7:30–9am. 2-night minimum stay on weekends. AE, MC, V. Parking $7. Ferry: Walk across the street from the landing. From U.S. 101 north, take the 1st right after the Golden Gate Bridge (Alexander exit); Alexander becomes Bridgeway in Sausalito.

Sooner or later most visitors to Sausalito look up and wonder at the ornate mansion on the hill. It's part of Casa Madrona, a hideaway by the bay built in 1885 by a wealthy lumber baron. The epitome of luxury in its day, the mansion had slipped into decay when it was saved by Henri Deschamps and converted into a hotel and restaurant. Successive renovations and extensions have added a rambling, New England–style building to the hillside below the main house. Now a certified historic landmark, the hotel offers rooms, suites, and cottages. The 16 newest units are each uniquely decorated by different local designers. The "1,000 Cranes" is Asian in theme, with lots of ash and lacquer. "Artist's Loft" is reminiscent of a rustic Parisian artist's studio. "Summer House" is decked out in white wicker. Other rooms in the mansion are also decorated in a variety of styles; some have Jacuzzis, while others have fireplaces. The newest rooms are located on the water with panoramic views of the San Francisco skyline and bay.

Within the Casa Madrona is **Mikayla Restaurant** (☎ **415/331-5888**), which serves superb American West Coast Cuisine—scallopine of leg of lamb with grilled leeks, caramelized scallops with crispy onion rings—in an unbelievably beautiful setting overlooking the bay and San Francisco skyline (it's decor was orchestrated by renowned local artist/designer Laurel Burch). It's open for dinner nightly from 6 to 10pm and for Sunday brunch from 10am to 2:30pm.

WHERE TO DINE
MODERATE

Guernica. 2009 Bridgeway. ☎ **415/332-1512.** Reservations recommended. Main courses $10–$17. AE, MC, V. Daily 5–10pm. From U.S. 101 north, take the 1st right after the Golden Gate Bridge (Alexander exit); Alexander becomes Bridgeway in Sausalito. FRENCH/BASQUE.

Established in 1976, Guernica is one of those funky old kinds of restaurants that you'd probably pass up for something more chic and modern down the street if you didn't know better. What? You don't know about Guernica's legendary Paella Valenciana? Well now you do, so be sure to call ahead and order it in advance, and bring a partner 'cause it's served for two but will feed three. Begin with an appetizer of artichoke hearts or escargots. Other main courses range from grilled rabbit with a spicy red diablo sauce to a hearty Rack of Lamb Guernica and medaillons of pork loin with baked apples and Calvados. Rich desserts include such in-season specialties as strawberry tart, peach Melba, and Basque-style rice pudding.

Horizons. 558 Bridgeway. ☎ **415/331-3232.** Reservations accepted weekdays only. Main courses $9–$21; salads and sandwiches $6–$11. AE, MC, V. Mon–Fri 11am–11pm; Sat–Sun 10am–11pm. 1-hr. free valet parking. SEAFOOD/AMERICAN.

Eventually, every San Franciscan ends up at Horizons to meet a friend for Sunday Bloody Marys. It's not much to look at from the outside, but it gets better as you head past the funky dark-wood interior toward the waterside terrace. On warm days it's worth the wait for alfresco seating if only to watch dreamy sailboats glide past San Francisco's distant skyline. The food here can't touch the view, but it's well portioned and satisfying enough. Seafood dishes are the main items, including steamed clams and mussels, freshly shucked oysters, and a variety of seafood pastas. In fine Marin tradition, Horizons has an "herb tea and espresso" bar, and is a totally non-smoking restaurant.

PICNIC FARE & WHERE TO EAT IT

Even Sausalito's naysayers have to admit that it's hard not to enjoy eating your way down Bridgeway on a warm, sunny day. If the crowds are too much or the prices too steep at the bay-side restaurants, grab a bite to go for an impromptu picnic in the park fronting the marina.

Caledonia Kitchen. 400 Caledonia St. ☎ **415/331-0220.** No credit cards. Sun–Thurs 8am–8pm; Fri–Sat 8am–9pm.

Caledonia Kitchen is the sort of place you wish were just around the corner from your house—a beautiful little cafe serving a huge assortment of fresh salads, soups, chili, gourmet sandwiches, and inexpensive entrees like herbed roast chicken or vegetarian lasagna for only $4.95. Continental-style breakfast items and good coffee and espresso drinks are also on the menu.

Hamburgers. 737 Bridgeway. ☎ **415/332-9471.** No credit cards. Daily 11am–5pm.

Like the name says, the specialty at this tiny, narrow cafe is juicy flame-broiled hamburgers, arguably Marin County's best. Look for the rotating grill in the window off Bridgeway, then stand in line and salivate with the rest (chicken burgers are a slightly healthier option). Order a side of fries, grab a bunch of napkins, then head over to the park across the street.

5 Muir Woods & Mount Tamalpais

12 miles N of the Golden Gate Bridge

While the rest of Marin County's redwood forests were being devoured to feed the building spree in San Francisco around the turn of the century, the trees of Muir Woods, in a remote ravine on the flanks of Mount Tamalpais, escaped destruction in favor of easier pickings.

MUIR WOODS

Although the magnificent California redwoods have been successfully transplanted to five continents, their homeland is a 500-mile strip along the mountainous coast of southwestern Oregon and northern California. The coast redwood, or *Sequoia sempervirens,* is the tallest tree in the immediate region, and the largest-known specimen towers 367.8 feet. It has an even larger relative, the *Sequoiadendron giganteum* of the California Sierra Nevada, but the coastal variety is stunning enough. Soaring toward the sky like a wooden cathedral, it is unlike any other forest in the world, and an experience you won't soon forget.

Granted, Muir Woods is tiny compared to the Redwood National Forest further north, but you can still get a pretty good idea of what it must have been like when these redwood giants dominated the entire coastal region. What is truly amazing is that they exist a mere 6 miles (as the crow flies) from San Francisco; close enough, unfortunately, that tour buses arrive in droves on the weekends. You can, however, avoid the masses by hiking up the Ocean View Trail and returning via the Fern Creek Trail—a moderate hike that shows off the woods' best sides and leaves the lazy-butts behind.

To reach Muir Woods from San Francisco, cross the Golden Gate Bridge heading north on Highway 101, take the Stinson Beach/Highway 1 exit heading west and follow the signs (and the traffic). The park is open daily from 8am to sunset, and while there is no admission, a donation box is posted out front to prompt your conscience. There's also a small gift shop, educational displays, and docent-led tours that you're welcome to stand in on. For more information, call the **Muir Woods information line** (☎ **415/388-2595**).

If you don't have a car, you can book a bus trip with the **Red & White Fleet,** which takes you straight to Muir Woods via the Golden Gate Bridge, and on the way back makes a short stop in Sausalito. The 3.5-hour tours run several times daily, and costs $30 for adults, $14 for children. Call for more information and specific departure times (☎ **800/229-2784** or 415/447-0597).

MOUNT TAMALPAIS

The birthplace of mountain biking, Mount Tam—as the locals call it—is the Bay Area's favorite outdoor playground and the most dominant mountain in the region. Most every local has his or her secret trail and scenic overlook, as well as an opinion on the dilemma between mountain bikers and hikers (a touchy subject around here). The main trails—mostly fire roads—see a lot of foot and bicycle traffic on the weekends, particularly on clear, sunny days when you can see a hundred miles in all directions, from the foothills of the Sierra to the western horizon. It's a great place to escape from the city for a leisurely hike and to soak in the breathtaking views of the bay.

To get to Mount Tamalpais **by car,** cross the Golden Gate Bridge heading north on Highway 101 and take the Stinson Beach/Highway 1 exit. Follow the shoreline highway about 2½ miles and turn onto the Panoramic Highway heading west. After about 5½ miles, turn onto Pantoll Road and continue for about a mile to Ridgecrest Boulevard. Ridgecrest winds to a parking lot below East Peak. From there, it's a 15-minute hike up to the top.

6 Point Reyes National Seashore

35 miles N of San Francisco

The National Seashore system was created to protect rural and undeveloped stretches of the coast from the pressures brought on by soaring real-estate values and increasing population. Nowhere is the success of the system more evident than at Point Reyes. Residents of the surrounding towns—Inverness, Point Reyes Station, and Olema—have steadfastly resisted runaway development. You won't find any strip malls or fast-food joints here, just a laid-back coastal town with cafes and country inns, where gentle living prevails.

Though the peninsula's people and wildlife live in harmony above the ground, the situation beneath the soil is much more volatile. The infamous San Andreas Fault separates Point Reyes—the northernmost land mass on the Pacific Plate—from the rest of California, which rests on the North American Plate. Point Reyes is making its way toward Alaska at a rate of about 2 inches per year, but there have been times when it has moved much faster. In 1906, Point Reyes jumped north almost 20 feet in an instant, leveling San Francisco and jolting the rest of the state. The half-mile Earthquake Trail, near the Bear Valley Visitor Center, illustrates this geological drama with a loop through an area torn by the slipping fault. Shattered fences, rifts in the ground, and a barn knocked off its foundation by the quake illustrate how alive the earth is here. If that doesn't convince you, a seismograph in the visitor center will.

ESSENTIALS

Point Reyes is only 30 miles northwest of San Francisco, but it takes at least 90 minutes to reach by car (it's all the small towns, not the topography, that slows you down). The easiest route is via Sir Francis Drake Boulevard from Highway 101 south of San Rafael; it takes its bloody time getting to Point Reyes, but does so without any detours. For a much longer but more scenic route, take the Stinson Beach/Highway 1 exit off Highway 101 just south of Sausalito and follow Highway 1 north.

As soon as you arrive at Point Reyes, stop at the **Bear Valley Visitor Center** on Bear Valley Road (look for the small sign posted just north of Olema on Highway 1) and pick up a free Point Reyes trail map. The rangers here are extremely friendly and helpful, and can answer any questions you have about the National Seashore. Be sure to check out the great natural-history and cultural displays as well. It's open weekdays from 9am to 5pm and weekends from 8am to 5pm (☎ **415/663-1092**).

Entrance to the park is free. **Camping** is $10 per site per night, and permits are required (reservations can be made up to 2 months in advance by calling ☎ **415/663-8054** Mon to Fri from 9am to 2pm).

WHAT TO SEE & DO

When headed out to any part of the Point Reyes coast, expect to spend the day surrounded by nature at its finest. But bear in mind that as beautiful as the wilderness can be, it's also untamable. Waters in these areas are not only bone-chilling and home to a vast array of sea life, including sharks, but are also unpredictable and dangerous. There are no lifeguards on duty and waves and riptides make swimming strongly discouraged. Pets are not permitted on any of the area's trails.

By far the most popular—and crowded—attraction at Point Reyes National Seashore is the venerable **Point Reyes Lighthouse,** located at the westernmost tip of Point Reyes (Visitor Center ☎ **415/669-1534**). Even if you plan to forego the 308 steps to the lighthouse, it's still worth the visit to marvel at the dramatic scenery, which includes thousands of common murres and prides of sea lions that bask on the rock far below (binoculars come in real handy).

The lighthouse is also the top spot on the California Coast to observe **gray whales** as they make their southward and northward migration along the coast January through April. The annual round-trip is 10,000 miles—one of the longest mammal migrations known. The whales head south in December and January, and return north in March. *Note:* If you plan to drive out to the lighthouse to whale-watch, arrive early because parking is limited. If possible, come on a weekday. On a weekend or holiday, it's wise to park at the Drake's Beach Visitor Center and take

Johnson's Oyster Farm

If you want to escape the crowds and have some stinky man-made entertainment, head to Johnson's Oyster Farm. Located right on the edge of Drakes Estero (a large saltwater lagoon within the Point Reyes peninsula that produces nearly 20% of California's commercial oyster yield), Johnson's may look and smell like a dump, but those tasty bivalves don't come any fresher or cheaper. Granted, it doesn't look like much—a cluster of trailer homes, shacks, and oyster tanks surrounded by huge piles of oyster shells—but that certainly doesn't detract from the taste of fresh-out-of-the-water oysters dipped in Johnson's special sauce. The popular modus operandi is 1) to buy a couple dozen, 2) head for an empty campsite along the bay, 3) fire up the barbecue pit (don't forget the charcoal), 4) split and 'cue the little guys, 5) slather them in Johnson's special sauce, then 6) slurp 'em down. Johnson's is located off Sir Francis Drake Boulevard, about 6 miles west(ish) of Inverness (☎ **415/669-1149**). Open Tuesday to Sunday from 8am to 4pm.

the free shuttle bus to the lighthouse. Dress warmly—it's often quite cold and windy—and bring binoculars.

Whale watching is far from being the only activity offered at the Point Reyes National Seashore. Rangers conduct many different tours: You can walk along the Bear Valley Trail, spotting the wildlife at the ocean's edge; see the waterfowl at Five-brooks Pond; explore tide pools; view some of North America's most beautiful ducks in the wetlands of Limantour; hike to the promontory overlooking Chimney Rock to see the sea lions, harbor seals, and seabirds; or take a guided walk along the San Andreas Fault to observe the site of the epicenter of the 1906 earthquake and learn about the regional geology. And this is just a sampling. Since tours vary seasonally, you can either call the **Bear Valley Visitors Center** (☎ **415/663-1092**) or request a copy of *Park Paper,* which includes a schedule of activities and other useful information. Many of the tours are suitable for travelers with disabilities.

Some of the park's best—and least crowded—highlights, however, can only be approached on foot, such as **Alamere Falls,** a freshwater stream that cascades down a 40-foot bluff onto Wildcat Beach, or **Tomales Point Trail,** which passes through the Tule Elk Reserve, a protected haven for roaming herds of tule elk that once numbered in the thousands. Hiking most of the trails usually ends up being an all-day outing, however, so it's best to split a 2-day trip within Point Reyes National Seashore into a "by car" day and a "by foot" day.

If you're into bird watching, you'll definitely want to visit the **Point Reyes Bird Observatory** (☎ **415/868-1221**), one of the few full-time ornithological research stations in the United States, located at the southeast end of the park on Mesa Road. This is where ornithologists keep an eye on more than 400 feathered species. Admission to the visitor center and nature trail is free, and visitors are welcome to observe the tricky process of catching and banding the birds. (Open daily 15 min. after sunrise to sunset. Banding hours vary, call for exact times: ☎ **415-868-0655.**

One of our favorite things to do in Point Reyes is paddling through placid Tomales Bay, a haven for migrating birds and marine mammals. Kayak trips, including 3-hour sunset outings, 3½-hour full-moon paddles, yoga tours, day trips, and longer excursions, are organized by **Tomales Bay Kayaking.** Instruction, clinics, and boat delivery are available, and all ages and levels are welcome. Prices start at $45 for tours. Rentals begin at $25 for one person, $35 for two. Don't worry, the kayaks are very stable and there are no waves to contend with. The launching point is located on Highway 1 at the Marshall Boatworks in Marshall, 8 miles north of Point Reyes Station. Open Friday to Sunday from 9am to 6pm, and by appointment (☎ **415/663-1743**).

WHERE TO STAY

Inns of Marin, P.O. Box 547, Point Reyes Station, CA 94956 (☎ **800/887-2880** or 415/663-2000), is a free service that will help you find accommodations ranging from one-room cottages to inns and complete vacation homes. Keep in mind that many places here have a 2-night minimum, though in slow season they may make an exception. They'll also refer you to restaurants, hiking, and attractions in the area.

EXPENSIVE

✪ Manka's Inverness Lodge & Restaurant. P.O. Box 1110, on Argyle St. (off Sir Francis Drake Blvd., 3 blocks north of downtown Inverness), Inverness, CA 94937. ☎ **800/ 58-LODGE** or 415/669-1034. Fax 415/669-1598. 8 units, 2 cabins. $135–$165 double; $185–$295 cabin. MC, V.

If there was ever a reason to pack your bags and leave San Francisco for a day or two, this is it. A former hunting-and-fishing lodge, Manka's Inverness Lodge looks like something out of a Hans Christian Anderson fairy tale, right down to the tree-limb bed stands and cook's roasted venison sausage in front of the hearth. It's all terribly romantic in a Jack London–ish sort of way, and tastefully done as well. The lodge consists of a superb restaurant on the first floor, four rooms upstairs (*Tip:* Rooms 1 and 2 come with large private decks), four rooms in the Redwood Annex, and two spacious one-bedroom cabins located behind the lodge that come with living rooms and kitchenettes. For the ultimate romantic splurge, inquire about their three secluded guest houses: Grizzly Lodge, Boat House, and Chicken Ranch.

The lodge's reputation is built on its restaurant, which dominates the bottom floor. The specialty of the house is game and fish, including oysters from Tomales Bay. Prices range from $18 to $22. The limited menu might feature pheasant with a Madeira jus, mashed potatoes, and a wild-huckleberry jam; black-buck antelope chops with sweet-corn salsa; or everybody's favorite, pan-seared elk tenderloin. It's open for dinner Thursday to Monday with a brunch on Sunday.

MODERATE

Bear Valley Inn. 88 Bear Valley Rd., Olema, CA 94950. ☎ **415/663-1777.** 3 units, all with shared bathroom. $75–$135 double. AE, DISC, MC, V. Rates include breakfast.

Ron and JoAnne Nowell's venerable two-story 1899 Victorian has survived every-thing from a major earthquake to a recent forest fire, which is lucky for you because you'll be hard pressed to find a better B&B for the price in Point Reyes. Granted, the Bear Valley Inn isn't perfect—the rooms lack private bathrooms and the main highway is a tad too close—but it's loaded with Victorian charm, right down to the profusion of flowers and vines outside and comfy chairs fronting a toasty-warm woodstove inside. It's in a great location, too, with three good restaurants only a block away, and the entire National Seashore at your doorstep. Ron, who also runs a mountain-bike rental shop next door, can set you up wheel-wise for about $25 a day and point you in the right direction.

INEXPENSIVE

Motel Inverness. 12718 Sir Francis Drake Blvd., Inverness, CA 94937. ☎ **415/669-1081.** 7 units. TV. $69–$99 double; kids 12 and under stay free in parents' room. AE, DISC, MC, V.

Finding an inexpensive place to stay in Point Reyes is next to impossible, as hoity-toity B&Bs reign supreme. There is, however, one exception—Motel Inverness, a homey, well-maintained lodging fronting Tomales Bay. For the outdoor adventurer who plans on spending as little time indoors as possible, it's the perfect place to hole up, as the entire National Seashore is at your doorstep. Those seeking a little romance out of their vacation, however, should dig a little deeper in their wallets and opt for Manka's (see above). Each guest room—all of which were completely renovated and refurnished in May of 1996—comes with a queen size bed, linoleum floors, rosewood blinds, and a color television; smoking is strictly verboten. Attached to the hotel is a giant rec room, complete with pool table, pinball machine, and big-screen TV to distract the kids (who stay free), while parents can relax on the back lawn overlooking the bay, bird sanctuary, and rolling green hills beyond. No pets and no smoking.

WHERE TO DINE
EXPENSIVE
✪ Manka's Inverness Lodge & Restaurant.

See "Where to Stay," above.

MODERATE
Station House Café. Main St., Point Reyes Station. ☎ **415/663-1515.** Reservations recommended. Breakfast $4.45–$7.50; main courses $9–$17.50. DISC, MC, V. Sun–Thurs 8am–9pm; Fri–Sat 8am–10pm. AMERICAN.

For more than 2 decades the Station House Café has been a favorite pit stop for Bay Areans headed to and from Point Reyes. It's a friendly, low-key establishment with a cozy fireplace, an open kitchen, an outdoor garden dining area (key on sunny days), and live music on weekends. Breakfast dishes range from bread pudding with stewed fruit compote to a frittata with asparagus, goat cheese, and olives. Lunch and dinner specials might include fettuccine with fresh, local mussels steamed in white wine and butter sauce, or two-cheese polenta served with fresh spinach sauté and grilled garlic-buttered tomato—all made from local produce, seafood, and organically raised Niman-Schell Farms beef. The cafe has an extensive list of fine California wines, plus local imported beers.

INEXPENSIVE
The Gray Whale. 12781 Sir Francis Drake Blvd., Inverness. ☎ **415/669-1244.** Main courses $5–$10. MC, V. Daily 11am–8pm. ITALIAN.

For more than a decade, The Gray Whale cafe has been another popular pit stop for Bay Areans heading to the lighthouse at Point Reyes. Why so popular? First off, it's cheap: sandwiches—such as the roasted eggplant with pesto and mozzarella—are only $5, as are most of the salads and pastas. Second, it's pretty good: our personal favorites are the specialty pizzas, such as the Californian (artichoke hearts, fresh basil, and tomatoes) and the Vegetarian (baked eggplant, roasted onions and romas, broccoli, and piles of freshly grated Parmesan cheese). Veteran hikers and mountain bikers stop by for an espresso booster, sipped on the small patio overlooking the block-long town of Inverness.

Taqueria La Quinta. 11285 Hwy. 1 (at Third and Main sts.), Point Reyes Station. ☎ **415/663-8868.** Main courses $4–$6. No credit cards. Wed–Mon 11am–9pm. MEXICAN.

Fresh, good, fast, and cheap: What more could you ask for in a restaurant? Taqueria La Quinta has been one of our favorite lunch stops in downtown Point Reyes for years and years. A huge selection of Mexican-American standards are posted above the counter, but those-in-the-know inquire about the seafood specials. Since it's all self-serve, you can skip the tip, but watch out for the salsa—that sucker's hot.

7 Half Moon Bay

28 miles SW of San Francisco

A mere 45-minute drive from the teeming streets of San Francisco lies a heavenly little seaside hamlet called Half Moon Bay, one of the finest—and friendliest—small towns on the California coast. While other coastal communities like Bolinas take strides to make tourists unwelcome, Half Moon Bay residents are disarmingly amicable, bestowing greetings to anyone and everyone who stops for a visit.

Only in the last decade has Half Moon Bay begun to capitalize on its golden beaches, mild climate, and close proximity to San Francisco, so you won't find the ultratouristy machinations that result in gaudy theme parks and time-share condos. What you will find, however, is a peaceful, unfettered slice of textbook California: pristine beaches, redwood forests, nature preserves, rustic fishing harbors, horse ranches, organic farms, and a host of superb inns and restaurants—everything you need for the perfect weekend getaway.

ESSENTIALS

GETTING THERE   There is no public transportation from San Francisco to Half Moon Bay, so it's either come **by car** or don't come. There are two ways to get here: the fast way and the scenic way. To save time, take Highway 92 West from either Highway 280 or Highway 101 out of San Francisco, which will take you over a small mountain range and drop you directly into Half Moon Bay. A better—and far prettier—route is via Highway 1, which technically starts at the south end of the Golden Gate Bridge and veers southwest to the shoreline a few miles south of Daly City. Both routes to Half Moon Bay are clearly marked with numerous signs, so don't worry about getting lost.

Downtown Half Moon Bay, however, is easy to miss since it is not on Highway 1. Rather, it's a few hundred yards inland, reached by heading 2 blocks up Highway 92 from the Highway 1 intersection, then turning south at the Shell gas station onto Main Street until you cross a small bridge.

VISITOR INFORMATION   For more information call the **Half Moon Bay Coastside Chamber of Commerce** at ☎ **650/726-8380.**

Note: Temperatures rarely venture into the 70s in Half Moon Bay, so be sure to pack for cool (and often wet) weather.

WHAT TO SEE & DO

The best things to do in Half Moon Bay are the same things the locals do. For example, there's a wonderful paved beach trail that winds 3 miles from Half Moon Bay to Pillar Point Harbor. Walking, biking, jogging, and skating are all kosher, and be sure to keep a lookout for dolphins and whales. Bicycles can be rented from the **Bicyclery,** 432 Main St. (☎ **650/726-6000**), in downtown Half Moon Bay. Prices range from $6 an hour to $24 for all day.

Half Moon Bay is also known for its organically grown produce, and the best place to stock up on fruits and vegetables is the **Andreotti Family Farm** (☎ **650/726-9461**). Every Friday, Saturday, and Sunday a member of the Andreotti family slides open the door to their weathered old barn at 10am sharp to reveal a cornucopia of strawberries, artichokes, cucumbers, and the like. It's a horribly charming old-fashioned outfit that's been in business since 1926. The barn is located at 227 Kelly Ave. off Highway 1 (head toward the beach and you'll see it on your right-hand side); it's open till 6pm year-round.

A few miles up Highway 92 is the **Obester Winery,** 12341 San Mateo Rd. (☎ 650/726-9463), a small wood shack filled with award-winning wines that are free for the tasting. It's open daily from 10am to 5pm; and exactly 3 miles up Highway 92 is **Half Moon Bay Nursery,** 11691 San Mateo Rd. (☎ 650/ 726-5392), a wonderful family-owned nursery where all the serious green thumbs in the county go to get their prized perennials. It's open daily from 9am to 5pm.

If you're the adventurous type, you might want to consider a day of deep-sea fishing with **Captain John's Fishing Trips** (☎ 800/391-8787 or 650/726-2913) or **Huck Finn Sportfishing** (☎ 800/572-2934 or 650/726-7133). Either outfit will take you out for a full day's fishing for about $55. You don't need experience, tackle, or even a fishing license; they'll provide everything, as well as clean, fillet, and bag your catch. January through March they also offer whale-watching trips for about $20 per person (reservations recommended). Both charters depart from picturesque Pillar Point Harbor, a full-service harbor that houses over 350 commercial fishing vessels and recreational boats. Whether you plan to go fishing or not, it's worth a gander to watch the trawlers unload their daily catch.

One of the most popular activities in Half Moon Bay is horseback riding along the beach. **Sea Horse Ranch** (a.k.a. Friendly Acres Horse Ranch) offers either guided or unguided (assuming you know how to ride a horse) rides along the beach or on well-worn trails for about $35. It's open daily from 8am to 6pm and located on Highway 1, 1 mile north of Half Moon Bay (☎ 650/726-2362 or 650/ 726-8550). And, of course, there's the requisite golf course, **Half Moon Bay Golf Links** (2000 Fairway Dr., at the south end of Half Moon Bay adjacent to the Half Moon Bay Lodge; ☎ 650/726-6384). Designed by Arnold Palmer, the ocean-side 18-hole course has been rated among the top-100 courses in the country, as well as no. 1 in the Bay Area. It ain't cheap, though, with greens fees ranging from $85 to $115. Make reservations as far in advance as possible.

BEACHES & PRESERVES

The 4-mile arc of golden-colored sand that rings Half Moon Bay is broken up into three state-run beaches (Dunes, Venice, and Francis), all a part of **Half Moon Bay State Beach.** There's a $5 per-vehicle entrance fee for all three beaches, though unless you plan on camping or using the rest room often, you're better off saving your lunch money and accessing the beach farther up north via Mirada Road. Though surfing is allowed, swimming isn't a good idea unless you happen to be cold-blooded.

When the surf is really up, be sure to check out the banzai surfers at **Maverick Beach,** located just south of the radar-tracking station past Pillar Point Harbor. To get here, take Westpoint Road to the West Shoreline Access parking lot and follow the trail to the beach (while you're there, keep a lookout for sea lions basking on the offshore rocks). Also adjacent to the parking lot is tiny **Pillar Point Marsh,** a unique fresh- and saltwater marsh that's home and way station to nearly 20% of all North American bird species—from great blue herons to snowy egrets and red-winged black birds.

A few miles farther north on Highway 1 is the **Fitzgerald Marine Reserve,** a 35-acre tidal reef housing more than 200 species of marine animals, including starfish, snails, urchins, sponges, sea anemones, and hermit and rock crabs. In fact, it's one of the most diverse tidal basins on the West Coast, as well as one of the safest thanks to a wave-buffering rock terrace 50 yards from the beach. Call before coming to find out when it's low tide (everything's hidden at high tide) and about the docent-led tour schedules (usually offered on Sat). No dogs are allowed, and rubber-soled shoes are recommended. It's located at the west end of California Avenue off Highway 1 in Moss Beach (☎ 650/728-3584).

Sixteen miles south of Half Moon Bay on Highway 1 (at the turnoff to Pescadero) is the **Pescadero Marsh Natural Preserve,** one of the few remaining natural marshes left on the central California coast. Part of the Pacific flyway, it's a resting stop for nearly 200 bird species, including great blue herons that nest in the northern row of eucalyptus trees. Passing through the marsh is the mile-long **Sequoia Audubon Trail,** accessible from the parking lot at Pescadero State Beach on Highway 1 (the trail starts below the Pescadero Creek Bridge). Docent-led tours take place every Saturday at 10:30am and every Sunday at 1pm, weather permitting.

Starting in December and continuing through March, the **Año Nuevo State Reserve** is home to one of California's most amazing animal attractions—the hallowed breeding grounds of the **northern elephant seal.** Every winter people reserve tickets months in advance for a chance to witness a fearsome clash between the 2½-ton bulls over mating privileges among the harems of females. Reservations are required for the 2½-hour naturalist-led tours (held rain or shine Dec 15 to Mar 31). For tickets and tour information, call ☎ 800/444-4445. Even if it's not mating season, you can still see the elephant seals lolling around the shore almost year-round, particularly between April and August when they come ashore to molt.

WHERE TO SHOP

Half Moon Bay's Main Street is a shopper's paradise. Dozens of small stores and boutiques—ranging from chic to shit-kickin'—line the half-mile strip; you'll find everything from feed and tack stores (should you be on the lookout for a used saddle) to custom furniture and camping gear. Must-see stores (from north to south) include the **Buffalo Shirt Company,** 315 Main St. (☎ 650/726-3194), which carries a fine selection of casual wear, Indian rugs, and outdoor gear; **Cartwheels,** 330 Main St. (☎ 650/726-6060), a nifty store specializing in rustic wood furniture, rugs, and toys; and **Half Moon Bay Feed & Fuel,** 331 Main St. (☎ 650/726-4814), a great place to pick up a treat for your pet.

Cedanna, 421 Main St. (☎ 650/726-6776), is loaded with colorful glassware, artistic furnishings, and unusual home accessories, but no country boy can survive without **Cunha's Country Store,** 448 Main St. (☎ 650/726-4071), the town's beloved grocery and general store that's a mandatory stop for regular visitors from the Bay Area. And, of course, what would Half Moon Bay be without a good bookstore like **Coastside Books,** 521 Main St. (☎ 650/726-5889), which also carries a fair selection of children's books and postcards.

End your shopping spree with a stop at **Cottage Industries,** 621 Main St. (☎ 650/712-8078), to marvel at the high-quality handcrafted furniture, as well as the western wear, jewelry, and saddlery next door at **Coyote Creek,** 641 Main St. (☎ 650/712-8731).

WHERE TO STAY

Beach House Inn. 4100 N. Cabrillo Hwy. (3 miles north of Half Moon Bay on Hwy. 1), Half Moon Bay, CA 94109. ☎ 800/315-9366 or 650/712-0220. Fax 650/712-0693. 54 units.

MINIBAR TV TEL. $145–$325 double. Rates include complimentary continental breakfast. AE, DC, DISC, MC, V.

It was only a matter of time before big-time developers clued in to the potential of Half Moon Bay, so no one was surprised when ground was broken for the three-story Beach House Inn & Conference Center (though everyone was shocked when someone burned the first version down in retaliation for blocking the neighbors' ocean view). While the facade has a rather unimaginative Cape Cod look, the rooms are surprisingly well-designed and decorated with modern prints, stylish furnishings, soothing yellow tones, and spectacular views of the bay and harbor. Every room comes fully-loaded with a wood-burning fireplace, king-size bed and sleeper sofa, large bathrooms, stereo with CD player, private patios or deck access, two color TVs and VCR, four telephones with data ports and voice mail, and a kitchenette with microwave and refrigerators. *Tip:* Opt for one of the corner rooms, which offers a more expansive view for the same price.

Amenities: Daily maid service, self-service laundry, free parking, free daily newspaper, heated pool, ocean-view whirlpool, fitness room, sauna, conference room.

☉ Cypress Inn on Miramar Beach. 407 Mirada Rd. (go 3 miles north of the junction of Highways 92 and 1, then turn west on Medio to the end), Half Moon Bay, CA 94019. **☎ 800/83-BEACH** or 650/726-6002. Fax 650/712-0380. 12 units. TV TEL (in Beach House rms only). $170–$275 double. Rates include breakfast and afternoon tea/wine/hors d'oeuvres. AE, MC, V.

Easily our favorite place to stay in Half Moon Bay, the Cypress Inn is blissfully free of Victorian charm (nary a lace curtain in this joint). Instead, you have a modern, artistically designed and decorated building infused with colorful native folk art and rustic furniture made of pine and heavy wicker. Each room has a billowy feather bed, private balcony, gas fireplace, private bathroom, and an unobstructed ocean view. Adjacent to the inn are four Beach House rooms equipped with built-in stereo systems and hidden TVs, though they lack the Santa-Fe-meets-California effect that we adore in the main house. The ace in the hole is, however, that it's the only B&B perched right on the beach.

Mill Rose Inn. 615 Mill St. (1 block west of Main St.), Half Moon Bay, CA 94019. **☎ 650/726-9794.** Fax 650/726-3031. 6 units. TV TEL. $205–$285 double. Rates include breakfast and afternoon tea/wine/hors d'oeuvres. AE, DISC, MC, V.

Fashioned after an English country house, the Mill Rose Inn looks like it was pulled from the cover of a Harlequin romance. The elaborate gardens are replete with flowers (literally thousands of them), while the rooms are equally gussied up with a profusion of brass, porcelain, antiques and lace—a textbook antithesis to the Cypress Inn. Six spacious rooms are loaded with comforts such as private entrances and bathrooms, king- or queen-size feather beds, fireplaces (with the exception of the Baroque Rose room), well-stocked refrigerators, televisions with cable and VCRs, and access to a Jacuzzi that's tucked inside a frosted-glass gazebo. It's in a good spot, too, just off Main Street in a quiet neighborhood.

☉ Seal Cove Inn. 221 Cypress Ave., Half Moon Bay, CA 94038. **☎ 650/728-4114.** Fax 650/728-4116. 10 units. MINIBAR TV TEL. $180–$260 double. Rates include breakfast and complimentary wine/sherry. DISC, MC, V. The inn is 6 miles north of Half Moon Bay off Hwy. 1; follow signs to Moss Beach Distillery.

Before Karen Herbert and her husband Rick opened this top-notch B&B, she was the writer and publisher of *Karen Brown's Country Inns Series*, so you can bet that she knows what it takes to create and run a superior bed-and-breakfast. The result is a stately, sophisticated B&B that harmoniously blends California, New England,

and European influences in a spectacular seacoast setting. All rooms have wood-burning fireplaces, country antiques, original watercolors, grandfather clocks, hidden televisions with VCRs, refrigerators stocked with free beverages, and views overlooking the distant cypress trees and a colorful half-acre wildflower garden dotted with birdhouses. In the morning, you'll find coffee and a newspaper outside your door, brandy and sherry by the living-room fireplace in the evening, and at night a plate of chocolates beside your turned-down bed. The ocean is just a short walk away.

The Zaballa House. 324 Main St. (at the north end of town), Half Moon Bay, CA 94019. ☎ **650/726-9123.** Fax 650/726-3921. 12 units. $80–$250 double. Rates include breakfast and afternoon tea/wine/hors d'oeuvres. AE, DISC, MC, V.

The oldest building in Half Moon Bay, this pale-blue Victorian is decidedly pretty and unpretentious. Simon, the British innkeeper, is an immediately likable bloke who has a gift for making you feel like a favored guest. The nine guest rooms in the main house are pleasantly decorated with understated wallpaper and country furniture; some have fireplaces, vaulted ceilings, or Jacuzzi tubs, and all have private bathrooms. Three new minisuites have been added behind the main house, each equipped with a kitchenette, double Jacuzzi, fireplace, TV/VCR, and private deck (our favorite is the Casablanca room, which comes with an eponymous video). None have telephones, but guests are welcome to use the phone in the front parlor. Prices are quite reasonable considered the amenities and central location.

WHERE TO DINE

✪ **Mezza Luna.** 3048 N. Cabrillo Hwy. (Hwy. 1), Half Moon Bay. ☎ **650/712-9223.** Reservations recommended. Main courses $8–$17. DISC, MC, V. Mon–Sat 11:30am–3pm; Sun–Thurs 5:30–10pm; Fri–Sat 5:30–10:30pm. ITALIAN.

Though Pasta Moon serves excellent Italian food, it's not truly authentic Italian. For that, there's Mezza Luna. Run by a gaggle of suave, soft-spoken Italian men, the red-and-green cinder-block building looks rather cheesy from the outside, but things get better as you enter, and all is forgiven when you bite into the antipasto della casa, a large platter of marinated grilled vegetables doused with the perfect blend of extra-virgin olive oil and red-wine vinegar. Among the entrees, the *penne del pastore*—perfectly cooked tube pasta quenched with a tangy tomato sauce, fresh eggplant, and topped with aged ricotta cheese—is delicious. Heck, even the dipping sauce for the warm focaccia bread is fantastic. The wine list and decor could use more work, but as far as the food goes there's little room for improvement.

Moss Beach Distillery. Beach St. (at Ocean St.), Moss Beach (6 miles north of Half Moon Bay off Hwy. 1). ☎ **650/728-5595.** Reservations recommended. Main courses $13–$25. MC, V. Mon–Sat noon–10pm (closing hours vary); Sun brunch 10am–3pm (closing hours vary). CALIFORNIA/CONTINENTAL.

Ever since its Prohibition bootlegging days almost a century ago, this old stucco distillery on a cliff above Moss Beach has been a wildly popular hangout for both locals and city folk passing through. In the 1920s, silent-film stars and San Francisco politicos frequented the distillery for drinks and the bordello next door for . . . other pastimes. Time and weather have aged it considerably, but a recent renovation succeeded in spiffying things up. The food—seared sea bass, grilled pork chops, Dungeness crab cakes, bouillabaisse—has never been the main draw here; rather, it's the phenomenal view of the rugged coast from almost every window. Your best bet is to come at sunset, order off the appetizer menu (the oysters are always fresh), and snuggle with your partner in the cocktail lounge.

Dinner at Duarte's

Always a worthy side trip from Half Moon Bay is a jaunt down the coast to Pescadero, a tiny coastal community whose nightlife centers around the **Duarte's Tavern,** 202 Stage Rd. (☎ **650/879-0464**), still owned and operated by the family that built it in 1894. The town's population literally triples on weekends as folks pile into this unassuming wood-paneled restaurant for a bowl of their legendary artichoke soup. You'll also find steak, prime rib, and plenty of fresh seafood on the menu, as well as fruits and vegetables straight from the Duartes' own gardens behind the restaurant. It's open for breakfast, lunch, and dinner every day, and reservations are recommended for dinner.

Before dinner, you might want to stop at **Phipps Ranch,** 2700 Pescadero Rd. (☎ **650/879-0787**), a sort of Knott's Berry Farm in miniature, located a few miles east of Duarte's Tavern on Pescadero Road. You'll find a huge assortment of fresh, organically grown fruits and vegetables here, as well as an amazing selection of dried beans. Green thumbs will enjoy browsing the nursery and gardens. A popular early-summer pastime is picking your own olallieberries and boysenberries in the adjacent fields. It's open daily from 10am to 7pm (in the winter from 10am to 6pm).

✪ **Pasta Moon.** 315 Main St., Half Moon Bay. ☎ **650/726-5125.** Reservations recommended. Main courses $8–$23. AE, DISC, MC, V. Mon–Fri 11:30am–2:30pm; Sat noon–3pm; Sun–Thurs 5:30–9:30pm; Fri–Sat 5:30–10pm; Sun brunch 11am–2:30pm. ITALIAN.

When visitors ask, "Where is the best place to eat around here?" the inevitable answer is Pasta Moon, a handsome nouveau-Italian restaurant in downtown Half Moon Bay that specializes in making everything from scratch and using only the freshest ingredients. Chef Sean Lynd's pasta dishes, always freshly made and perfectly cooked, earn the highest recommendations, such as the house-made black-pepper fettuccine with spicy calabrese sausage and braised winter greens or hand-cut papperdelle with sweet fennel sausage, tomatoes, and cream. Another favorite is the fresh oak-smoked pork tenderloin braised with savoy cabbage. For dessert try the wonderful tiramisu, with its layers of Marsala-and-espresso–soaked ladyfingers and creamy mascarpone.

✪ **Sushi Main Street.** 696 Mill St., Half Moon Bay. ☎ **650/726-6336.** Main courses $5–$10. MC, V. Mon–Sat 11:30am–2:30pm and 5–9pm; Sun 5–9pm. JAPANESE.

Who woulda thunk that one of the most exquisite Japanese restaurants in California would be in tiny Half Moon Bay? Chef/owner Hirohito Shigeta started out his business 9 years ago in a tiny space on Main Street and kept the old name when he moved into larger digs down the street. His wife Karolynne—an interior designer with impeccable taste—in turn decorated the new space with her vast collection of museum-quality Balinese artifacts, and the result is astoundingly beautiful. But even if it looked like the inside of a trailer home, it would still be worth a visit for the exceptional sushi, tempura, and soba, prepared in part by Andrew, one of the few *gai-jin* (white man) sushi chefs on the West Coast. Adventurous sushi warriors will want to try the New Zealand roll (mussels, radish, sprouts, avocado, and teriyaki), the unagi papaya, and the marinated salmon roll with cream cheese and spinach. For a traditional shoeless Japanese meal, request the knee-high table perched in the corner.

Index

See also separate Accommodations and Restaurant indexes, below.
Page numbers in italics refer to maps.

RESTAURANTS

FROMMER'S® COMPLETE TRAVEL GUIDES

(Comprehensive guides with selections in all price ranges—from deluxe to budget)

Alaska
Amsterdam
Arizona
Atlanta
Australia
Austria
Bahamas
Barcelona, Madrid & Seville
Belgium, Holland &
    Luxembourg
Bermuda
Boston
Budapest & the Best of
    Hungary
California
Canada
Cancún, Cozumel & the
    Yucatán
Cape Cod, Nantucket &
    Martha's Vineyard
Caribbean
Caribbean Cruises &
    Ports of Call
Caribbean Ports of Call
Carolinas & Georgia
Chicago
China
Colorado
Costa Rica
Denver, Boulder &
    Colorado Springs
England
Europe
Florida

France
Germany
Greece
Hawaii
Hong Kong
Honolulu, Waikiki & Oahu
Ireland
Israel
Italy
Jamaica & Barbados
Japan
Las Vegas
London
Los Angeles
Maryland & Delaware
Maui
Mexico
Miami & the Keys
Montana & Wyoming
Montréal & Québec City
Munich & the Bavarian Alps
Nashville & Memphis
Nepal
New England
New Mexico
New Orleans
New York City
Nova Scotia, New
    Brunswick &
    Prince Edward Island
Oregon
Paris
Philadelphia & the Amish
    Country

Portugal
Prague & the Best of the
    Czech Republic
Provence & the Riviera
Puerto Rico
Rome
San Antonio & Austin
San Diego
San Francisco
Santa Fe, Taos &
    Albuquerque
Scandinavia
Scotland
Seattle & Portland
Singapore & Malaysia
South Pacific
Spain
Switzerland
Thailand
Tokyo
Toronto
Tuscany & Umbria
USA
Utah
Vancouver & Victoria
Vermont, New Hampshire &
    Maine
Vienna & the Danube Valley
Virgin Islands
Virginia
Walt Disney World &
    Orlando
Washington, D.C.
Washington State

FROMMER'S® DOLLAR-A-DAY GUIDES

(The ultimate guides to comfortable low-cost travel)

Australia from $50 a Day
California from $60 a Day
Caribbean from $60 a Day
England from $60 a Day
Europe from $50 a Day
Florida from $60 a Day
Greece from $50 a Day
Hawaii from $60 a Day
Ireland from $50 a Day

Israel from $45 a Day
Italy from $50 a Day
London from $70 a Day
New York from $75 a Day
New Zealand from $50 a Day
Paris from $70 a Day
San Francisco from $60 a Day
Washington, D.C., from
    $60 a Day

FROMMER'S® MEMORABLE WALKS

Chicago
London

New York
Paris

San Francisco

FROMMER'S® PORTABLE GUIDES

Acapulco, Ixtapa/
  Zihuatanejo
Bahamas
California Wine
  Country
Charleston & Savannah
Chicago

Dublin
Las Vegas
London
Maine Coast
New Orleans
New York City
Paris

Puerto Vallarta, Manzanillo
  & Guadalajara
San Francisco
Sydney
Tampa Bay & St. Petersburg
Venice
Washington, D.C.

FROMMER'S® NATIONAL PARK GUIDES

Grand Canyon
National Parks of the American West
Yellowstone & Grand Teton

Yosemite & Sequoia/
  Kings Canyon
Zion & Bryce Canyon

THE COMPLETE IDIOT'S TRAVEL GUIDES

(The ultimate user-friendly trip planners)

Cruise Vacations
Planning Your Trip to Europe
Hawaii

Las Vegas
Mexico's Beach Resorts
New Orleans

New York City
San Francisco
Walt Disney World

SPECIAL-INTEREST TITLES

The Civil War Trust's Official Guide to
  the Civil War Discovery Trail
Frommer's Caribbean Hideaways
Israel Past & Present
New York City with Kids
New York Times Weekends
Outside Magazine's Adventure Guide
  to New England
Outside Magazine's Adventure Guide
  to Northern California

Outside Magazine's Adventure Guide
  to the Pacific Northwest
Outside Magazine's Guide to Family Vacations
Places Rated Almanac
Retirement Places Rated
Washington, D.C., with Kids
Wonderful Weekends from Boston
Wonderful Weekends from New York City
Wonderful Weekends from San Francisco
Wonderful Weekends from Los Angeles

THE UNOFFICIAL GUIDES®

(Get the unbiased truth from these candid, value-conscious guides)

Atlanta
Branson, Missouri
Chicago
Cruises
Disneyland

Florida with Kids
The Great Smoky
  & Blue Ridge
  Mountains
Las Vegas

Miami & the Keys
Mini-Mickey
New Orleans
New York City
San Francisco

Skiing in the West
Walt Disney World
Walt Disney World
  Companion
Washington, D.C.

FROMMER'S® IRREVERENT GUIDES

(Wickedly honest guides for sophisticated travelers)

Amsterdam
Boston
Chicago

London
Manhattan

New Orleans
Paris

San Francisco
Walt Disney World
Washington, D.C.

FROMMER'S® DRIVING TOURS

America
Britain
California

Florida
France
Germany

Ireland
Italy
New England

Scotland
Spain
Western Europe

www.frommers.com

rthur Frommer's OUTSPOKEN ENCYCLOPEDIA OF TRAVEL

You've Read our Books, Now Visit our Website...

With more than 6,000 pages of the most up-to-date travel bargains and information from the name you trust the most, Arthur Frommer's Outspoken Encyclopedia of Travel brings you all the information you need to plan your next trip.

Register to Win free tickets, accommodations and more!

Arthur Frommer's Daily Newsletter

Bookmark the daily newsletter to read about the hottest travel news and bargains in the industry or subscribe and receive it daily on your own desktop.

Hot Spot of the Month

Check out the Hot Spot each month to get the best information and hottest deals for your favorite vacation destinations.

200 Foreign & Domestic Destinations

Choose from more than 200 destinations and get the latest information on accommodations, airfare, restaurants, and more.

Frommer's Travel Guides

Shop our online bookstore and choose from more than 200 current Frommer's travel guides. Secure transactions guaranteed!

Bookmark www.frommers.com for the most up-to-date travel bargains and information—updated daily!